DOLL MAKERS & MARKS

A GUIDE TO IDENTIFICATION

BY DAWN HERLOCHER

ANTIQUE TRADER BOOKS
A Division of Landmark Specialty Publications
Norfolk, Virginia

I lovingly dedicate this book to my parents, Pat and Bill Tyson, and my sister, Trina Miller, for their constant support and encouragement.

Inquiries should be addressed to Managing Editor, Landmark Specialty Books, 150 W. Brambleton Ave., Norfolk VA 23510.

ISBN: 1-58221-000-4
Library of Congress Catalog Card Number: 99-61140

Managing Editor: Allan Miller
Editor: Sandra Holcombe
Art Director: Chris Decker
Graphic Designers: Kevin Gilbert and Jeff Hellerman
Printed in the United States of America

To order additional copies of this book, or to obtain a catalog, please contact:

Antique Trader Books
P.O. Box 1050
Dubuque, Iowa 52004
1-800-334-7165

DOLL MAKERS & MARKS

A GUIDE TO IDENTIFICATION

TABLE
OF CONTENTS

ACKNOWLEDGMENTS

After writing *200 Years of Dolls, Identification and Price Guide*, I received letters and phone calls from so many wonderful people asking more about how to identify dolls. It was their interest that prompted me to write *Doll Makers & Marks, a Guide to Identification*.

I wish to thank everyone who communicated with me. Not only did you inspire the writing of another book, but I truly enjoyed, not to mention learned, so much in corresponding with each and every one of you.

There are those, however, who need special recognition. David Cobb of Cobb's Doll Auction was a real inspiration. His immediate and positive response to *200 Years of Dolls* was motivating to say the least. Not only did he encourage me to write a more detailed identification guide, but he also generously provided me with many wonderful photographs. Thank you, David.

In addition to David Cobb, there are others who furnished portraits of their dolls—or the dolls themselves—to be photographed and/or studied. Sheri McMasters, of McMasters Doll Auctions, was always there when I needed an example of a particular doll. I appreciate the assistance given to me by Ellen Schroy, editor of *Warman's Antiques and Their Prices*. Thanks also to Dr. Georgia Kemp Caraway, and Billy Nelson Tyrrell for providing information and photos of unusual dolls. A very special thank you to my dear friends, Mr. and Mrs. Adam Condo, for opening up their beautiful home and wonderful collection to me. And, to Mrs. Gene Patterson (president of the Lock Haven Doll Club) and her husband for sharing their dolls and time. Last, but far from least, I am very grateful for my very best and faithful buddy, Helen Brooke, who is always there for me no matter what.

I must extend a thank you to Rose Ann Wilt, art teacher at Bald Eagle Nittany High School. It was her assurance of being able to reproduce the markings of dolls and labels that gave me the confidence I needed to begin this book.

Merci Beaucoup to John Newcomer for his help with the French terms.

I extend my appreciation to my acquaintance at Rinker Enterprises, Inc. Harry Rinker was unquestionably my very first motivator and confidant in the publishing world. It was Harry who believed, even when I did not, that writing books was a possibility.

Thank you to my colleagues at Antique Trader Books. The degree of professionalism in designing and editing every book they do is phenomenal. It is a joy to work with each and every one of them. A very special thanks to the managing editor, Allan Miller. It is not Allan's encouraging me to start a new project that makes him so special—it is that, in general, he is really a nice person.

I put my wonderful family last, but it goes without saying that they are first in my heart. I am so thankful to be the mother of the three most wonderful children in the world—Jennifer, Maribeth, and Ty. I am so very proud of them.

I also thank my mother and father, Pat and Bill Tyson—who devoted endless hours to graphic artwork and research for this undertaking—my sister Trina Miller, her husband Billy, and their sons Billy Grant and Jordan. How blessed I am to have such a family!

Finally, thank you to my husband and very best friend, Rusty. Always, without fail, he is my most constant supporter. It may very well be a cliché, but nevertheless true: I couldn't have done it without him.

Dawn

INTRODUCTION

Welcome to the adventure of identifying dolls. Once you begin a journey of doll discovery, it is essential to gather all the pieces of information available so that you can reach your destination of a positive identification. Although the appeal of dolls is immediate and universal, their identity can be somewhat ambiguous.

This book, you will notice, makes use of charts and lists to map your course of doll discovery. When speed as well as accuracy is a consideration, I find charts to be irreplaceable. Their effectiveness will become apparent once you begin using them as a source of information. Charts allow for an explanation and comparison of data which is simple and direct. Analogously, a listing of facts provides a straightforward approach, rather than a wordy explanation.

I have tried to assemble as many clues as possible to aid you in your quest—starting with brief histories of doll manufacturers. Although hundreds of companies are listed in the first chapter, it is only a limited inventory at best. I would like to tell you that every doll maker ever known is catalogued in this book, but such is not the case. Volumes would be needed only to list the names, let alone give any information. Therefore, a brief synopsis of the most-likely-to-be-encountered makers are offered. Included are the social influences and technological improvements that have affected the doll making industry over the years. These manufacturers' histories are listed alphabetically by the company or by the maker.

It is a fact that the majority of antique dolls are incised with some kind of marking, though most newer or contemporary dolls are not. Contemporary manufacturers are prone to naming their dolls. It is their practice to use the same doll mold for several differently named dolls. Assigning a new, or different, name to basically an identical doll can result in multiple sales to the same consumer with no need to develop new faces. Case in point: Alexander Doll Company has used the same doll face for hundreds of different characters. A whole collection can be built with only one face appearing. In past generations little girls were rewarded with only one doll at a time. Consequently, manufacturers had no commercial need to name a doll. A mold number was a more practical form of identification.

Chapter two contains over three thousand names that have been assigned to dolls, and the companies with whom those names are associated. The listings cite the dolls' names alphabetically—contrary to the normal practice of arranging lists according to manufacturers' names. It is my experience that often a doll's name is remembered, but the necessary clue, the manufacturer, is unknown. Knowing where to look for the manufacturer's name is the first and most important step in verifying a doll's credentials.

Chapters three and five are numerical listings. Chapter three gives the previously mentioned mold numbers—the numbers incised or stamped on many dolls. When a mold number was incised on a bisque head, it was intended as a manufacturer's internal identification. Whereas names are assigned for marketing to the consumers, mold numbers had a more practical manufacturing purpose. We use these mold numbers to differentiate one doll from another.

Letters and groups of letters found in chapter four can be yet more clues in discovering your doll's identity. The letters may be initials used by a manufacturer, such as Simon & Halbig's *S & H*, or they may be abbreviations, such as Peter Scherf's *P Sch*—or groups of letters forming seemingly strange words, such as Johannes Gotthilf Dietrich's *Jgodi*. Along with these doll manufactures, I have also included the letters used by organizations or associations connected with the manufacturing or collecting of dolls. Most doll collectors are familiar with U. F. D. C., but perhaps not so familiar with the International Doll Makers Association's use of the letters I. D. M. A. as a form of identification.

The numerical listings found in chapter five are presented for comparing a doll's size, using a factory-assigned size number. Size numbers do exactly as the title implies—they indicate the size of the head or finished doll. Also included in this chapter is a sizing chart for hard plastic dolls. While contemporary manufacturers seldom make use of a size numbering system, they do maintain a limited doll size product.

There seems to be, beyond the rational explanation of identifying a doll for its monetary value, an acute desire to know its heritage. Chapter six, devoted to markings, should help you pinpoint a particular manufacturer or distributor. For lack of a more appropriate option, the markings are again listed by manufacturer alphabetically. You will notice while searching for a mark that many seem repetitive in their representation. Further study will reveal that subtle differences often occur. The positioning of a phrase, such as "Made in Germany," or the addition or deletion of a number may be very significant when identifying a manufacturer's marking. Doll markings may be found on the back of the head, on the torso, between the shoulders, the bottom of a foot, or even on the derriere. Of course, many fine dolls will have no markings at all. Other indicators will dictate our path in identifying these dolls that so cautiously guard their lineage.

Chapter seven is a roster of hundreds of pieces of information. The advertising section is designed to be one more tool to use in your exploration. If the only clue you have is the memory of a phrase or advertising byte used to promote a doll, you may find that phrase within this chapter. The following section includes many helpful bits of information—including museum addresses and doll periodical listings, definitions for words such as "autoperipatetikos," and hints on how to distinguish china-head styles. Not only the beginner,

but also the astute collector, can benefit from tips given for doll care and preservation. Our little inanimate treasures will hopefully survive long after this voyage of documentation is filed away. To assist you, the caregivers, many fundamental principles developed over the years of doll collecting have been compiled and catalogued.

The final chapter may appear at first glance to be a montage of information. The purpose in writing this book is to give swift and precise information. Chapter eight gives these "at a glance" clues. Not every doll has, or needs, a clue to identify it. Often the identity of a doll is obvious, but sometimes it is not. This latter group is the focus of the last chapter, which includes a collection of clues to help you with everything from Barbie dolls and G. I. Joe dolls to seventeenth-century wooden dolls.

A doll's story is more than an analytical study of the body construction and the facial sculpturing, it is also the significance of its conception, the background of the creating artisan, as well as the exquisite beauty that keeps the collector eternally enthralled. Looking for clues that may assist us is restricted only by our own limitations of knowledge and/or the time we can invest in the search.

Magnificent Kämmer & Reinhardt Child Standing an Impressive 32 Inches Tall (Photo courtesy of Leah and Gene Patterson.)

Kestner Character, Hilda Baby #245 (Photo courtesy of Cobb's Doll Auction.)

ADVICE
ON COLLECTING

The following are procedures given for your enjoyment and information. Neither the author nor the publisher accepts liability or responsibility in respect to any type of loss or damage caused, or alleged to be caused, directly or indirectly by the information or products contained in this book. We simply intend to share some old tricks and methods that have been used over the years.

Like children, dolls require constant tender loving care. They need to be repaired, restored, handled, displayed, and stored properly. The following tips should help you develop skills to guarantee the well-being of your dolls through the loving treatment they deserve.

When considering restoration of a doll, the best approach is to be a minimalist. Do only what is necessary to restore a doll to the display level, or to halt any further deterioration. Always retain rather than destroy. Period commodities count significantly when considering a doll's value. Plan any repairs in a step-by-step process, evaluating as you go along.

Maintain great care and respect for a doll when cleaning or performing any maintenance task. If you are unsure of how to execute a certain procedure, stop and ask an expert in the field. We have an obligation to future doll collectors to preserve the dolls in our care, and to maintain them in as good or better condition as they were in when we received them.

CARE: Bisque, china, and Parian are all made of clay, feldspar, and flint. The differences between them are subtle. Parian is unglazed and untinted porcelain. China is glazed porcelain. Bisque is unglazed porcelain with a flesh color.

The earliest bisque, china, and Parian dolls were pressed into a mold by hand; later examples, though, were poured.

Cleaning porcelain is fairly simple. The decorations have been fired on; therefore, it is highly unlikely that you will harm them by cleaning. Start with the least abrasive technique, which is usually washing with warm soapy water. If this is not sufficient, try a wet eraser, or a soft toothbrush. As a last resort, very gently clean with a low abrasive cleaner such as Tilex or Soft Scrub. Use extreme caution. Some cleaners contain bleaching agents that are devastating to antique clothing, wigs, or bodies. Avoid direct sunlight when displaying a bisque, china, or Parian doll—as the ultraviolet rays are damaging, especially to clothing and wigs.

If the doll is placed on a doll stand, take measures to assure that it is secure and that the stand is sufficiently weighted to support it.

Wax dolls tend to intimidate many collectors. While it is true that they require special care, it must be remembered that all dolls require some kind of special care. Basic common sense will preserve a wax doll that is in perfect condition. Of course, never place one in direct sunlight nor near any heat source, such as a fireplace mantle.

A long accepted practice for cleaning wax dolls is to start with the safest method and then gradually progress to more drastic methods until a suitable remedy is found. Begin by trying a solution of cool water and Woolite. Saturate a cotton ball or Q-tip with the solution to wash the wax. If this is unsuccessful, try a dab of cold cream on a Q-tip, followed by a wash of the Woolite solution, and then rinse with clean, cool water. As a last resort, clean the wax with denatured alcohol on a cotton ball, followed by washing thoroughly with the Woolite solution, and then rinse with clean, cool water. Never use turpentine, because it can soften the wax.

Celluloid dolls are extremely perishable. They are easily broken, becoming quite brittle over time. Proper care and respect for a celluloid doll will help a perfect example remain in that condition. Heat is celluloid's unrivaled adversary. Keep these dolls in a cool room with good ventilation—remembering never to store celluloid in a sealed case, as it is known for its spontaneous combustion.

Cloth dolls have a special place in every doll collector's heart. Even a well-loved rag doll tugs at your heartstrings. Vintage, and even the not-so-vintage, cloth art dolls are often valued at several thousands of dollars. Therefore, they deserve your best efforts to preserve them and to prevent needless deterioration.

Clean fabric is a prerequisite to preservation. Exposing a doll to any pollutants through storage or display weakens the fabric. Direct sunlight is a deadly enemy to cloth dolls and must be avoided at all times.

Inspect cloth dolls regularly for signs of insect activity. Insecticides designed specially for textiles are available under several brand names. When used according to the manufacturer's instructions, the results are usually excellent.

Should you decide to vacuum your cloth doll, place a nylon screen over the fabric first to protect delicate fibers. Routinely, a protected, thorough vacuuming is enough to restore a doll to display condition. Again, approach this procedure with appropriate caution. If a valuable or historically significant cloth doll is badly soiled, please seek the advice of a professional specializing in textile conservation.

Some stains on cloth dolls can be removed with an eraser. Art gum, tapeten, and reinger and absorene appear to give the best results. Use this technique with careful, gentle application. Some stains, such as ink, may be removed with hair spray. It is essential to test the fabric first on an inconspicuous location to assure that no damage will occur. Apply the hair spray with a clean white cloth; wipe using a light rubbing motion. Change the cloth often so as not to reapply the stain.

Simon & Halbig's Beautifully Dressed Child with Original Mohair Wig (Photo courtesy of Leah and Gene Patterson.)

Lenci once advertised that a Lenci doll could be cleaned by rubbing it with a piece of bread!

To preserve and display cloth dolls, it is best to keep them in protective cases, inspecting them regularly. Moth crystals should be placed near your dolls. Many collectors recommend placing a small cloth pouch filled with moth crystals under a doll's hat, or tied around the waist beneath the clothing.

Composition and papier-mâché dolls are both made from a pulp-based material; therefore, they require similar attention. Composition and papier-mâché are particularly susceptible to damage from temperature and humidity changes. Never store them in a hot or cold attic—or in a damp basement.

Most collectors will accept some signs of aging of composition dolls. Fine craze lines or crackled eyes are now considered part of the normal aging process. Think long and hard before performing irreversible restorations that can compromise a doll's historic and practical value. Remember that a good restoration can later be undone. A temporary cover-up to craze lines will probably be a wiser choice than a permanent application of paint.

There are several popular methods for cleaning composition. Test any method first on an inconspicuous area of the doll. Work quickly! Never allow any substance to remain on the doll's surface for any length of time. Pond's Cold Cream, or Vaseline, and a soft tissue are favorites of many collectors. Another option is paste window cleaner—not an ammonia type, but the old fashioned paste available at most hardware stores.

Wigs on composition dolls are usually mohair, which is difficult to work with. One method proven to work is a light spray of Johnson's and Johnson's No More Tangles, and carefully working out the tangles with a plastic fork. Faded or worn facial features can be touched up with an artist's colored pencils; when moistened, they are quite easy to apply. Crackled eyes are best left alone. The old practice of placing a drop of sewing machine oil in the eyes to clear them is now not recommended. Although it does appear to clear the eyes for a time, the oil eventually dries and leaves the eyes in a more deteriorated condition than they were in before the oil treatment.

Wooden dolls have withstood the test of time quite well, as proven by the sheer number that have survived the years. Chipping paint or gesso is the major problem with wooden dolls. Humidity, mistreatment, and insect infestation are the main culprits. Keep wooden dolls in a dry atmosphere. Expanding and contracting associated with high humidity causes paint to chip. Knocks and bumps can also chip paint; therefore, extreme care should be given when displaying or moving wooden dolls. Check regularly for any signs of insects. Remember that reasonable care and attention will insure a flawless preservation.

Tin dolls often have chipped paint. When the metal becomes very cold, the paint lifts easily from the surface. Store or display metal dolls in an environment with a relatively constant temperature.

Heinrich Handwerck, Kämmer & Reinhardt, and Kestner (Photo courtesy of Cobb's Doll Auction.)

Untinted Bisque Doll with Mohair Wig and Paperweight Eyes (Photo Courtesy of Helen Brooke.)

Rubber dolls will deteriorate no matter what precautions are taken, but you can delay the process. Any form of grease is harmful and accelerates the deterioration. Always wear clean cotton gloves when handling a Magic Skin or rubber doll. The old practice of rubbing cornstarch into the doll twice a year, once every six months, is helpful. Remember to always maintain an even temperature and relative humidity, and by all means, keep the doll out of direct sunlight—and away from any heat source.

Hard plastic dolls are quickly becoming a favorite with collectors. The sharp features and beautiful detailing achieved by using hard plastic as a doll medium explain their sudden rise in popularity.

Hard plastic is very resilient and can be cleaned with almost any soap detergent. Stubborn stains may be removed with cold cream or waterless hand cleaner. Avoid chlorine bleach and ammonia. Facial features are not as durable; therefore, approach painted surfaces with caution, checking paint stability as you proceed. Never use fingernail polish remover or lacquer thinner, which may eat into the plastic.

Satisfactory results have been attained using Oxy-10 to remove stains that are not close to painted surfaces. Moisten a cotton ball and allow it to sit on the stain for several hours. You may need to repeat this process several times. After each cleaning, wash the area thoroughly with mild soap and rinse well.

When displaying or storing hard plastic dolls, avoid direct exposure to ultraviolet light. Though seemingly indestructible, hard plastic can slowly oxidize and change color. Direct heat may also cause warping.

Vinyl dolls are probably the most lifelike in appearance and touch. Special care is needed to keep them looking good. Extreme room temperatures are harmful. Even quality vinyl dolls subjected to heaters or air conditioners can be damaged in just a few months. Direct sunlight is deadly. Vinyl is also sensitive to fluorescent lighting; use indirect non-fluorescent lights for display purposes. Avoid, also, tightly sealed showcases or glass domes, as condensation can form and damage the vinyl.

Victor Hugo, the nineteenth-century French littérateur, wrote, "In the same way a bird makes a nest of anything, children will make a doll of no matter what."

CHAPTER ONE

THE HISTORY OF THE MANUFACTURERS

The history of dolls and doll collecting is a fascinating one. I find the complexities and interwoven lives of the doll manufacturing community intriguing. The following accounts give only a brief exposé of the companies.

To know when and where a firm operates is helpful in identifying a doll. For example, if the doll in question is plastic, knowing that plastic had not been used commercially until after World War II would eliminate any company that had ceased doing business before that time. An English mark found on a doll would eliminate a German-based company.

You will notice that many companies will show a date as being "possible," or only give an approximate date of operation. This is because no more appropriate date can be given. Many times, when researching a manufacturer, the only source of obtaining an operating date is a business directory for that area. In other cases, unfortunately, even less accurate records are available.

Dolls have a distinctive history, albeit at times discreet. Doll making as an occupation has its roots in Germany dating from the middle of the 1600s. These earliest dolls were made from wood. Economically, that is understandable, as wood was the only material that was completely without cost. There was no expense to gather wood and carve it into a doll. Of course, cloth dolls were also popular, but even rags, in that frugal society, had a cost. In our "throw-out" world that notion may seem strange, but such were the circumstances at that time.

Dolls with china and papier-mâché heads, introduced around 1860, were actually the beginning of the doll industry as we know it. Wax dolls also enjoyed a brief time in the limelight. The time and expense involved in their manufacture explains why these beautiful creations were not, at the time, more popular.

Attempting to market a more lifelike and yet affordable doll resulted in tinted or washed bisque with delicate coloring. The appearance of jointed bodies, sleep eyes, and open mouths proved to be yet another financial achievement. Eventually, though, mothers began to demand a more durable doll. Efforts were made to generate a market for tin and metal dolls, but to no avail.

The continuing bid for a preferred type of doll ushered in improvements to composition.

World War I eliminated the European dominance over the doll industry. American doll companies quickly found the product to fill the breach: With the production of composition mama babies and whimsical characters, they captured the hearts of the masses. After 1945, hard plastic proved to be the logical expansion to the industry. The durability and realism that could be achieved was astonishing. Today, the vinyl dolls can talk, laugh, write, roller-skate, and even teach a foreign language. It seems as though we must surely be at the end of the doll evolution. However, as long as children love dolls, new ideas will emerge onto the marketplace and the story will continue.

A

A&H DOLL MANUFACTURING CORP.—U.S.A., 1948-1956. Plastic dolls with decorative costuming, ranging in sizes from 8 to 12 inches, that appealed to adults as well as children. Dolls from A&H were popular, inexpensive display dolls of mediocre quality.

A&M—Bohemia, 1890-1930. Bisque heads most likely on composition bodies. A&M is believed to be Aich Menzel or perhaps Anger & Moehling. This manufacturer's mark is often mistaken for Armand Marseille. Even experienced doll collectors will refer to A&M as "Austria's AM," which can be very misleading. A&M dolls are of mediocre quality.

A. P. B. CO.—U.S.A., 1920-1928. Stoneware heads on bodies of composition including an open mouth dolly face. Although A. P. B. dolls are quite rare, their historic importance far outweighs their beauty or quality.

A. P. D. MANUFACTURING CO.—U.S.A., 1911-1918. Ceramic or stoneware heads on cloth bodies, including dolls with molded hair and painted eyes. A. P. D. dolls are rarely found, and the character dolls are of mediocre quality.

A. T. (A. THUILLIER)—France, 1875-1893. Bisque heads on wood and composition or kid bodies, including open and closed mouth Bébés and Fashion type. At least some of the heads were produced by François Gaultier. A. T. dolls are quite rare and valuable, with beautifully decorated bisque.

ABRAMSON, H. C.—U.S.A., 1918-1919. Composition heads on composition or cloth bodies, character dolls with molded and painted hair and eyes. Abramson dolls, although originally nicely dressed, are generally of lesser quality than other dolls produced during the same time period.

ABT & FRANKE—Prussia, 1865-1922, and possibly as late as 1930. Specialized in well-dressed small dolls and celluloid dolls with kid bodies. Known for their character babies in pillows, baskets, christening gowns—and dolls, complete with trousseaux in suitcases. Abt & Franke dolls are generally above average in their decoration and presentation.

ACME TOY COMPANY—U.S.A., 1908-1930s. Dolls of composition, including a large line of mama dolls and babies. Also supplied doll parts to other companies, and is credited with producing at least some of the Kiddiejoy line for Hitz, Jacobs & Kassler. Acme Toy Company dolls are of a very good quality and were originally dressed in silks, crepe de Chine, and other fine fabrics.

ACORN DOLL CO.—U.S.A., 1919-1921. All composition or composition heads on cloth bodies, including dolls with mohair wigs and sleep eyes, or molded and painted hair and eyes. Acorn dolls, typical of the middle-priced dolls of the time, are of fair quality.

ACTIVE DOLL CORP.—U.S.A., mid-twentieth century. Produced vinyl and plastic teen-type and baby dolls from 8 to 26 inches in height. Active plastic dolls are of good quality.

ADLER FAVOR & NOVELTY CO. (STELLA ADLER)—U.S.A., 1925-1930. Cloth dolls with long floppy arms and legs, including character dolls and babies. Distributed by F. W. Voetsch of New York City. Charming rag dolls of fair quality.

ADLER, J. & CO.—U.S.A., 1850-1890. Papier-mâché, shoulder-head dolls on cloth bodies with leather hands. Molded and painted hair and eyes. Similar in appearance to the Greiner dolls. Although several manufacturers describe this doll as "superior," Adler papier-mâché dolls are of good quality and are an important part of the doll community.

ADMIRATION TOY CO., INC.—U.S.A., mid-twentieth century. Produced several types of vinyl and plastic dolls. Best known for Francie, a 10-inch teen doll. Admiration dolls are becoming very collectible and are of good quality.

ADVANCE—U.S.A., early 1950s. Hard plastic and vinyl dolls. Best known for "Wanda the Walking Wonder." Although little is known about this company, it must be assumed that the dolls were not only well made, but also very popular, made evident by the number of Wanda dolls that are available on the secondary market.

ADVERTISING DOLLS—U.S.A., 1890-present. All types of advertising dolls have been produced to promote a variety of products from food to movies. The earliest examples were made of paper and lithographed cloth to be sewn at home. Later, factory-completed cloth dolls were offered. Moving with the times, dolls of composition, rubber, plastic, and vinyl were included. Advertising dolls enjoy the benefits of cross-over collecting—for example, a Coca-Cola Barbie® would appeal to both Coke collectors and Barbie collectors. Quality is not as important as the product that is being advertised.

AETNA DOLL COMPANY—U.S.A., 1901-1925. Known for composition dolls. Reportedly produced 4,000 doll heads a day for Horsman Doll Company before merging with them in 1925. Aetna Doll Company purchased the American Doll and Toy Company along with their secret process for the famous "Can't Break Em" dolls in 1909. Aetna Doll Company dolls are of very good quality.

AICH, MENZEL & CO.—Austria, 1848-1930. This porcelain factory began producing dolls in 1918. Bisque-head dolls most likely had composition bodies. This manufacturer's mark is often mistaken for Armand Marseille. Even experienced doll collectors will refer to this as "Austria's AM," which can be very misleading. A&M dolls are of mediocre quality.

ALABAMA INDESTRUCTIBLE DOLL—U.S.A., 1920-1925. Handmade cloth dolls with charming facial features of both white and African-American design having various foot designs, from bare toes that are stitched to high-buttoned boots. Alabama Indestructible Dolls, also known as Ella Smith Dolls, are among the most sought-after, Early American art-craft dolls.

ALDIS, FREDERIC—England, 1878-1901. Wax doll heads and limbs on cloth bodies. At least some of the wax heads were produced by Pierotti. Frederic Aldis dolls are of very good quality and are often found with glass eyes and inserted human hair.

ALEXANDER DOLL COMPANY—U.S.A., 1923-present. Often referred to as Madame Alexander Dolls. Produced dolls of cloth, composition, hard plastic, and vinyl. Among the best-known and most popular dolls. Well-known for the attention shown to classic figures. Alexander Doll Company dolls are of the highest quality and are beautifully costumed.

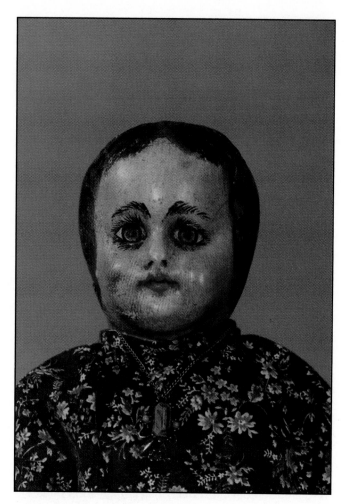

Alabama Indestructible Doll (Photo courtesy of McMasters Doll Auctions.)

ALEXANDRE, HENRI—France, 1889-1891. Bisque doll heads on bodies of wood and composition, including open- and closed-mouth Bébés. Best known for designing and registering the thirty models of the Phenix Bébé. Henri Alexandre produced lovely, high-quality dolls.

ALISTO MANUFACTURING—U.S.A., 1919-1920. A small, short-lived doll manufacturer, that produced 12-inch high dolls with molded clothes. Alisto dolls are of mediocre quality.

ALKID DOLL CO.—U.S.A., 1920-1921. All leather-covered dolls, including a closed-mouth, socket-head dolly-face doll with separate shoulder plate, glass eyes, and mohair wig. Alkid dolls are of good quality, but are all too often found with repainted facial features.

ALL BISQUE—Various countries, 1860-present. All types, including babies, children, adults, and comic characters. Jointed or unjointed, painted or glass eyes, wigs or molded hair, nude or molded clothes. Includes immobile, nodders, Frozen Charlottes and Charlies; bathing dolls, piano babies, and snow babies. All Bisque dolls can be of fine to poor quality.

ALL BRITISH DOLL MANUFACTURING CO.—England, 1915-1919. All composition or composition heads on kid bodies. Along with child and baby dolls, manufactured an exercise doll complete with booklet showing how to exercise by pulling the arms of the doll. The All British Dolls are of fair to good quality.

ALLIANCE TOY CO.—England, 1917-1920. All cloth character dolls, including the popular Golliwoggs. (Note that other manufacturers also produced Golliwoggs.) Alliance Toy dolls are of good quality.

ALLIED-GRAND DOLL MANUFACTURING CO.—U.S.A., 1915-1980. Produced dolls of composition, hard plastic, and vinyl, including early black character dolls and the large bride and fashion dolls so popular during the 1950s. Allied dolls are of good quality.

ALMA—Italy, 1929-1933. Felt dolls had molded faces with painted features, mohair wigs, and folded felt ears along with the unique characteristic of elastic stringing. Beautifully designed felt costumes. Alma dolls are similar in appearance and quality to the famous Lenci dolls.

ALT, BECK & GOTTSCHALCK—Germany, 1854-1941. Bisque or china head dolls on bodies of wood and composition, cloth, or kid. Credited with the beautiful shoulder heads, mold numbers 639-1288, along with their registered child and baby dolls having molded hair or wigs, painted or glass eyes, open or closed mouths. Alt, Beck & Gottschalck dolls are of very good quality.

ALTHOF, BERGMANN & CO.—U.S.A., 1848-1881. Generally accepted as a doll and toy importer, Althof, Bergmann & Co. was also a manufacturer holding the patent for several dolls. Although rarely found, Althof, Bergmann & Co. dolls are of fairly good quality.

AM TORG TRADING CORPORATION—U.S.A., late 1920s. Import house retailed Russian folk art including dolls and Matryoshkas.

AMBERG & HERGERSHAUSEN—Germany, 1924-1925. Produced dolls of rubber and/or composition. Most dolls are found with mohair wigs, sleep or painted eyes, and mama/papa voice boxes. Nicely costumed. Amberg & Hergershausen dolls are of mediocre quality.

AMBERG & SON, LOUIS—U.S.A., 1878-1930. This company made dolls of bisque and composition. They were among the first to manufacture dolls made completely in America, including the famous Charlie Chaplin and the IT doll. Louis Amberg & Son dolls are generally of very good quality.

AMERICAN ART DOLLS—U.S.A., 1916-1917. Cloth character dolls of stockinette or treated canvas, jointed at the shoulders and hips. Resembling the Käthe Kruse dolls, with painted hair and features. Dressed in regional costumes. American Art Dolls are of good quality.

AMERICAN BISQUE DOLL COMPANY—U.S.A., 1919-1921. Dolls of bisque and composition, including babies, mama dolls, Frozen Charlottes, long-limbed ladies, and a soft-bodied toddler. American Bisque Doll Company dolls are of a lesser quality than other dolls produced during this time.

AMERICAN CHARACTER DOLL CO.—U.S.A., 1919-1968. Dolls of composition, hard plastic, and vinyl. Among the hundreds of dolls introduced are the early composition Campbell Kids, in addition to the later Tiny Tears and Betsy McCall. American Character dolls were well made and beautifully costumed.

AMERICAN DOLL—U.S.A., late 1930s. Very little is known about this small doll company that operated in New York City after the Great Depression. A trademark using the name Betsey Ross was registered in 1939.

AMERICAN DOLL CO.—U.S.A., 1916-1926, and possibly earlier. There seems to be some confusion about dolls found with the American Doll Co. marking. It is altogether possible, and even highly likely, that several different companies used this name. Many of the dolls possess similar characteristics, such as composition shoulder heads with painted eyes. They were also well costumed. American Doll Co. dolls are of very good quality.

AMERICAN DOLL & TOY CO.—U.S.A., 1892-1908. Until 1895 operated as the First American Doll Factory, also known as Goldstein & Hoffmann and Hoffmann & Co. The founder, Solomon Hoffmann, a subject of the Czar of Russia, obtained a U.S. patent in 1892 for making Can't Break 'Em composition. After Hoffmann's death, the company and the secret rights to Can't Break 'Em were sold to Aetna. The composition dolls manufactured were usually shoulder heads on cloth bodies with wigs and glass eyes, and may have a marking of "F. A. D. F." Hoffmann composition dolls are of good quality.

AMERICAN GLUELESS DOLL CO.—U.S.A., 1918. A short-lived, little-known company whose claim to fame lies in the fact that their dolls were made completely without glue—and are, therefore, washable and guaranteed not to peel or crack. Limbs were attached with socket joints.

AMERICAN MADE TOY CO.—U.S.A., 1929. Produced cloth character dolls with printed features and removable clothing. American Made Toy dolls, along with the soft stuffed animals and other toys manufactured by this company, tend to be of fair quality.

AMERICAN MERCHANDISE CO.—U.S.A., 1891. A doll distributor, not manufacturer, that supplied dolls of all types for the wholesale market.

AMERICAN MUSLIN HEAD/AMERICAN MUSLIN-LINED HEAD—U.S.A., mid-1870s-1880s. Composition shoulder heads completely lined with muslin which had been saturated with glue, giving the heads great strength. Molded and painted hair and facial features. American Muslin Head dolls are of good quality and are an important link in the American doll manufacturing chain.

AMERICAN OCARINA AND TOY COMPANY—U.S.A., early twentieth century. A little-known doll company that produced rather poor quality novelty-type dolls. They advertised an all-composition doll with no joints and a body molded as an ear of corn with an Indian papoose face, and named Karo—"certain to be the biggest seller of 1920."

AMERICAN PRODUCED STUFFED TOY CO.—U.S.A., 1917-1920. Large dolls with composition heads and hands on cloth bodies. May have wigs or molded and painted hair. Most popular were the Military dolls and the babies. American Produced Stuffed Toy dolls are of only mediocre quality.

AMERICAN STUFFED NOVELTY CO.—U.S.A., 1923-1930. Long-limbed, sateen-covered art and boudoir dolls with hand-painted facial features, along with composition mama and baby dolls. Some in elaborate costumes designed by Morris Polizer. The earlier American Specialty art dolls are quite nice; however, the later composition dolls are of a lesser quality.

AMERICAN TOY & DOLL MANUFACTURING CO.—U.S.A., 1917-1918. This company gave every indication that it would grow to become one of the leaders in the doll industry. However, after a successful first year of producing composition teen and baby dolls, they closed their doors. Dolls from the American Toy & Doll Manufacturing Co. are of good quality.

AMERICAN TOY & NOVELTY CO.—U.S.A., 1917-1930 (merged with the Frank Plotnick Co. in 1930). Produced character, baby, and teen dolls of all composition or composition and cloth. May be found with molded and painted hair and facial features, or sleep eyes with wigs. The American Toy & Novelty Co. dolls are of good quality.

AMERICAN UNBREAKABLE DOLL CORP.—U.S.A., 1923-1927. Produced mama dolls with composition heads and limbs on cloth bodies. Also supplied the composition arms and legs to other doll manufacturers. American Unbreakable Doll Corp. dolls are of a lesser quality than other dolls produced during that time.

AMFELT ART DOLLS—U.S.A., 1928-1930. Taken over in 1930 by Paul Cohen Co. These well-made European dolls were marketed by the American company Louis Amberg & Son to compete with the popular Lenci dolls. Beautifully costumed dolls made of heavy felt and cloth jointed at neck, hips, and shoulders. Amfelt Art Dolls are of the highest quality.

AMMIDON & CO.—U.S.A., 1930. Little is known about this small, short-lived company, except that they registered and manufactured a line of dolls known as Amico Dolls.

ANCHOR TOY CORP.—U.S.A., 1924. Imported German and French dolls and registered the anchor as a trademark. The quality of Anchor dolls is determined by the manufacturer, ranging from very good to poor.

ANDEREGG—Switzerland, early 1900s. Jointed all-wooden dolls with carved and painted hair and facial features. Anderegg dolls show a considerable degree of artistic talent.

ANDRI, FERDINAND—Austria, 1906-present. A recognized wooden doll artist. The lifelike dolls represented peasant life in Europe at the turn of the twentieth century. The early Ferdinand Andri dolls are of the highest quality, as are the wooden dolls produced today carrying the Andri name.

ANEL & FRAISSE—France, 1913-1940s, and possibly later. By 1921 known as Anel & Fils. Produced celluloid dolls of children, babies, and character type. Anel & Fraisse celluloid dolls are of fair to better quality.

ANGERMÜLLER, F.—Germany, 1927-1928. Little is known about this small, short-lived doll manufacturer. At least one name was registered in 1927: Fancora-Wunder Baby.

ANILI—Italy, contemporary. Anili is the daughter of Madame Scavini (a name long associated with Lenci) and the subject of Anili dolls made by Lenci. She started her own doll manufacturing company in the 1950s which continues to produce felt dolls with pressed and hand-painted facial features. The Anili dolls are high quality collectibles.

ANITA NOVELTY CO.—U.S.A., 1929-mid 1930s. Merged with the European Doll Company and adopted that name. H. Altburch, self-proclaimed inventor of the "French Head" or boudoir doll, held a position in the company. Anita Novelty cloth flapper-type and boudoir dolls are of good quality.

ANNALEE MOBILITEE DOLLS—U.S.A., contemporary. Felt dolls representing children, adults, imaginary characters, and animals. Beautifully painted facial features and well costumed. Annalee dolls are of the finest quality and enjoy an active collector following.

ANNIN & CO.—U.S.A., 1925-1926. Made printed lithograph cloth dolls to be stitched at the sides from two-piece patterns. Annin & Co. cloth dolls are among the most popular and desirable of the lithograph type, having good design and color.

APFELBAUM & BATZNER—Bavaria, 1925-1927. Manufactured petite dollhouse dolls of both bisque and celluloid. This company's dolls are of good quality.

ARCY TOY MANUFACTURING CO.—U.S.A., 1912-1930. Produced several types of dolls from numerous materials, including composition, bisque, and celluloid. May be found with molded and painted facial features and hair, or sleep eyes and wigs. Arcy Toy Manufacturing dolls are generally of good quality.

ARENA, FÉLIX—France, 1918-1920. Produced bisque-head dolls with glass eyes and mohair wigs in a 21-inch size. Felix Arena dolls are of mediocre quality.

ARLINGTON TOY CO.—Germany and U.S.A., 1920-at least 1924. Produced and distributed dolls, many through the Bush Terminal.

ARNO, S. & SON—England, 1917-1918. This small, short-lived doll manufacturer produced cloth dolls. Little is known about the company or the dolls.

ARNOLD, J. M.—Germany, 1918-1934 and possibly later. Produced dolls of celluloid and rubber. These play dolls will most likely be found with molded and painted hair and facial features. J. M. Arnold dolls are of a lesser quality.

ARNOLD, MAX OSCAR—Germany and, later, Bavaria, 1877-1931. Produced and manufactured bisque dolls, mostly of the dolly-face type; however, there were also Arnold dolls of wax, leather, and composition. Well-known for the "Arnoldia" phonograph doll. Max Oscar Arnold dolls are of good quality.

ARNOLD PRINT WORKS—U.S.A., 1896-well into the twentieth century. Produced charming cut-out, sew-at-home dolls. The bright color lithographs and popular characters often depicted help explain why Arnold Print Works dolls are among the most desirable of the early cloth dolls.

ARNOLDT DOLL CO.—U.S.A., 1879-1933. Imported, repaired, dressed, and distributed dolls of all types, including, but not limited to, the famous Munich Art Dolls. Apparently the celebrated art pottery master Artus Van Briggle painted at least some of the faces of the bisque and china heads imported by this company. The quality of an Arnoldt Doll Co. doll can be as varied as the type produced.

ARNOULT—France, 1881-1882. This little-known doll manufacturer produced dolls with bisque heads supplied by François Gaultier. Arnoult dolls would be of very good quality, considering the source of their doll heads.

ARRANBEE DOLL CO.—U.S.A., 1922-1959 (Vogue purchased Arranbee in 1959, but continued to use the R & B mark until 1961). Look for dolls of bisque, composition, rubber, hard plastic, and vinyl. In the early years of this well-known company, dolls and doll parts were imported; however, in later years they produced their own. Arranbee Dolls are of exceptionally good quality.

ARRENBERG, ELSE—Germany, 1920-1930. A small doll manufacturer responsible for importing dolls to the United States after World War I.

ARROW DOLL WIG CO.—U.S.A., 1924-1927. Although best known, as their name implies, for manufacturing doll wigs and parts supplied to doll hospitals, they did produce several types of dolls including, but not limited to, mama and boudoir dolls. Arrow Doll Wig Co. dolls are of mediocre quality.

ARROW NOVELTY CO.—U.S.A., 1920-1950s. Manufactured dolls of cloth, composition, hard plastic, and vinyl. Perhaps best known for the Skookum Indian dolls designed by Mary McAboy. Arrow Novelty Co. dolls are of good quality, and at present are enjoying an active secondary market.

ARROW PLASTICS INDUSTRIES—U.S.A., mid-twentieth century. During the late 1940s and into the 1950s, manufactured and sold millions of vinyl dolls, but still is only known as a "knockoff" company. Doll collectors find the arrow within a diamond very familiar. Arrow Plastic dolls were a modestly priced doll, but nevertheless are of good quality.

ART FABRIC MILLS—U.S.A., 1899-at least 1910 and possibly later. Produced charming lithograph dolls with printed hair, facial features, and clothing. Art Fabric Mills dolls are very collectible, due to their good quality.

ART METAL WORKS—U.S.A., 1914-1930. Produced dolls with metal heads, including child and baby dolls. The company was headed by Louis V. Aronson, a name often used in advertising their dolls, along with the doll parts they also manufactured. Art Metal Works dolls are of good quality, but, unfortunately, metal dolls, in general, do not enjoy the prestige other types of dolls seem to have.

ART STATUE CO.—England, 1917-1918. Produced not only their own composition dolls, but supplied heads and parts to other companies. Best known for their baby dolls. Art Statue dolls are of fair quality.

ART TOY MANUFACTURING CO.—England, 1919-1923. Produced cloth-stuffed dolls. Once advertised as, "Manufacturing the prettiest dolls in England." Art Toy dolls are of good to very good quality.

ARTCRAFT TOY PRODUCTS CO.—U.S.A., 1918-1920, and until 1921 as Artcraft Plaything Corp. Produced composition dolly-face and baby dolls with sleep eyes and good quality wigs—sold doll heads and wigs separately. This company's dolls are of fair quality.

ARTEL—Bohemia, early 1900s. Produced all-wooden dolls. Frequently found with painted features and regional clothing. Generally jointed at the arms only, yet occasionally one is found jointed at the neck. Artel dolls, although collectible, are of a lesser quality.

ASHTON-DRAKE GALLERIES—U.S.A., 1985-present. Over thirty-five recognized artists and sculptors design beautiful display dolls, mostly of bisque. A recently formed strategic alliance with Disney, Warner Bros., and McDonald's enables this company to create licensed character dolls. Ashton-Drake dolls are of good quality.

ATLANTIC PLAYTHINGS CO.—U.S.A., 1917-1930. Produced white and black composition mama dolls with either molded and painted facial features or sleep eyes with a good quality wig. At least some of Atlantic Plaything dolls were sold by Joseph Krauss, an indication of the good quality established by this company.

Arranbee's Composition Nancy, Nancy with Wrist Tag, and DebuTeen; Effanbee's Anne Shirley Dolls (Photo courtesy of Cobb's Doll Auction.)

ATLAS DOLL & TOY CO. U.S.A., 1917-1930. Produced metal and composition dolls. Having either molded and painted hair and facial features or sleep eyes with wigs. Also advertised a line of mechanical dolls that jumped through hoops and over ropes. Atlas Dolls tend to be of a better quality than other metal dolls of the time, showing more artistic talent and innovation.

ATLAS MANUFACTURING CO.—England, 1914-1918. Produced mainly cloth dolls, although a few with British Ceramic head and arms in elaborate satin costumes were also introduced. Atlas Manufacturing Co. dolls are of fair quality, but rarely surface.

AU NAIN BLEU—France, 1836-1940s. A famous Paris store that distributed dolls by Roullet & Decamps; Jules Steiner; Lenci, and probably others. Bébés, talking dolls, and Bébé Teteur in swaddling clothes were advertised. One would think from the suppliers listed that Au Nain Blue dolls would be of the highest quality. This, however, is not the case. Although some are extremely beautiful, most will be found of only mediocre quality.

AU PARADIS DES ENFANTS—France, 1864-1925. Assembled and distributed dolls supplied by various manufacturers. Wax over and china heads were among their inventory as were cloth dolls. Au Paradis des Enfants tend to be of fair to good quality.

AU PERROQUET CIE—France, 1924, and possibly other years. Little is known of this small company, other than the registering of the La Négresse Blonde trademark.

AUNT JEMIMA MILLS CO.—U.S.A., 1908-1910 (became the Davis Milling Co. in 1910). Lithograph cloth dolls of "Aunt Jemima" and related rag dolls. Good quality cloth dolls.

AUSTEN & HABEN—England, 1916. Produced character dolls of British Ceramic and cloth. Austen & Haben dolls are of only mediocre quality.

AUX ENFANTS SAGES—France, 1870-1890s. Assembled and distributed dolls. At least some of the bisque heads were supplied by E. Barrois. Although rare, dolls bearing the Aux Enfants Sages mark are of very good quality.

AUX TROIS QUARTIERS—France, 1905-1924. A famous store in Paris that sold dolls bearing its name. These special-order dolls from various manufacturers will be found of bisque and cloth. The Aux Trois Quartiers dolls can vary in quality from very good to only fair, depending on the supplier.

AVERILL MANUFACTURING CO.—U.S.A., 1913-1965. Manufactured bisque, composition, celluloid, hard plastic, and vinyl dolls of all types. The Averill name is also associated with Bing-Wolf, Madame Hendren, Paul Averill Inc., Borgfeldt Brothers, and Georgene Novelty. Averill Manufacturing dolls are above average in both artistic innovation and materials used.

AVERILL, PAUL, INC.—U.S.A., 1920-1924. Produced composition baby dolls known as Wonder Dolls that walked and talked. These dolls are of good quality. (Paul is the husband/partner of Georgene Averill.)

B

B. J. & CIE—France, mid-1800s. Very little is known about this Paris-based manufacturer, other than they exported dolls. At least some had kid bodies and could be purchased dressed or undressed.

BABS MANUFACTURING CORP.—U.S.A., 1917-1921. Produced a line of walking dolls with a mesh torso and wooden limbs, jointed with flexible steel springs. Babs Manufacturing Corporation dolls are of mediocre quality.

BABY PHYLLIS DOLL CO.—U.S.A., 1919-1929. Imported at least some of its bisque dolls from Germany in addition to the composition dolls manufactured in the United States. Baby Phyllis Dolls are charming, desirable, and of good quality.

BACH BROTHERS—U.S.A., 1908-1909. A rather obscure doll company located in New York. Manufactured flat-faced cloth dolls with painted hair and features in both white and black versions, marketed as Bye Bye Kids. Bach Brothers dolls are charming folk art-type dolls.

BAGNARO, G.—France, 1928-1920. A small cottage-type industry using the name La Pompadour. Produced cloth dolls with mask-type faces, and a shoulder head doll. Most Bagnaro dolls were sold through toy fairs.

BÄHR & PRÖSCHILD—Germany, 1871-1919 (then purchased by Bruno Schmidt continuing until the 1930s). Porcelain factory and doll manufacturer, also spelled "Beahr & Proeschild." Made dolls of china, bisque, and celluloid along with doll parts. Supplied bisque heads for Bruno Schmidt, Kley & Hahn, Heinrich Stier, and others. After 1919 their markings included a heart with the initials *BP*. Bähr & Pröschild dolls are of good quality.

BAITZ, LILLI & R—Germany, 1920s. A small cottage-type industry that created folk art character dolls. At least some of the dolls can be found with composition heads and wire armature bodies. Seldom found, but quite collectible due in most part to the charming design and costuming.

BAKER & BENNETT—U.S.A., 1902-1916 and possibly later. A small and little-known manufacturer of composition dolls. Best known for the Spearmint Kid. Baker & Bennett dolls are of mediocre to good quality.

BAMBERGER, L. & CO.—U.S.A., 1892-1930s. Began as a doll distributor operating in New Jersey. In 1927 they registered at least one trademark and in 1930 used "Under the China-berry Tree" for a line of their cloth dolls.

BARROIS, E.—France, 1844-1877. One of the earliest manufacturers of bisque and china doll heads. Look for pale pressed-into-the-mold porcelain with delicate blush, small slightly smiling closed mouth, glass or painted eyes, and good wig or painted hair. E. Barrois dolls are of the finest quality.

BARTENSTEIN, FRITZ—Germany, 1880-1898. A small doll manufacturer that is best known for their two-faced bisque dolls. Many will be found with pull string voice boxes. Bartenstein dolls are of very good quality.

BARTLER TOY—U.S.A., contemporary. Imports dolls to be sold under the Bartler Toy or Out of The Closet Inc. brand name. Sells fringe dolls, such as their best-known doll, Gay Bob. A lifelike fully jointed vinyl doll with flocked hair, painted eyes, and a pierced ear, presented in a box representing his closet. Bartler dolls, although enjoying a select secondary market, are of rather mediocre quality.

BATGER & CO.—England, 1915-1922. Manufactured doll and doll parts. Best known for their dolls with molded and colored wax heads, arms, and legs on cloth bodies. Also produced a line of composition dolls.

BATTLE, MARTHA—U.S.A., 1937. Little is known of this American doll marker, other than the registering of the trademark Evangeline in 1937.

BAUER & RICHTER, INC.—Germany, 1921-1930s. A small manufacturer of porcelain and celluloid babies, mama and child dolls. No established markings are known. Bauer & Richter dolls are of mediocre to good quality.

BAUERSACHS, EMIL—Germany, 1882-late 1920, and possibly beyond. A small, but worthy-of-attention manufacturer of character as well as child dolls. Most of the bisque heads will be found on composition bodies. Best known for the Caprice line of character dolls. Emil Bauersachs dolls are of good quality.

BAUM, FRANK—U.S.A., 1924. Author of the famous series of *Oz* books. Registered a trademark of a *Z* within a circle for character, fancy dolls, and clowns.

BAUMANN, KARL—Germany, mid-1920s. A small, rather obscure doll manufacturer. Most known Karl Baumann dolls are of bisque with composition bodies and are fair to good in quality.

BAWO & DOTTER—Bohemia, 1838-possibly as late as the mid-1920s. A porcelain factory that produced china- and bisque-head dolls, along with doll parts for other manufacturers. Had branches in New York; Limoges, France; and perhaps Waltershausen, Germany. Bawo & Dotter dolls are of very good quality.

BAYERISCHE CELLULOIDWARENFABRIK—Germany, 1897-at least 1927. Founded by Albert Wacker, manufactured celluloid child and character dolls of fair quality.

BAZZONI, ANTHONY—England, 1828-1878. Produced elegantly costumed wax and composition dolls. Reported as having made a speaking doll that was later sent to Germany.

BEAUMONT, IRIS—Berlin, mid-1920s. A small, independent business that manufactured art-type play dolls along with character and novelty dolls made for tea cozies. Iris Beaumont dolls are of fair to good quality.

BEAVER DOLL COMPANY—U.S.A., first quarter of the 1900s. Also had outlets in Canada and London. Best known for wooden dolls. Beaver dolls are interesting additions to any collection and are of good quality.

BÉBÉ BON MARCHÉ—France, 1894-1925. Named for a large popular department store in Paris. The bisque heads on fully jointed composition bodies share some characteristics with the Jumeau dolls, but Bébé Bon Marché are, although quite good, of a somewhat lesser quality than the Jumeau Bébés.

BÉBÉ TOUT EN BOIS—Accepted as French; however, most likely German, 1901-1914. Also known as Bébé Tout Bois. Name used for the all-wood dolls that were sold and distributed through most Paris stores. May be found with or without wigs, painted or glass eyes, and on bent limb baby or child wooden bodies. Original chemise was stamped "Bébé Tout Bois."

BECK & GLASER—Germany, 1892-1941. Porcelain factory using the initials *T. P. K.* Produced dolls as early as 1897, and later was known as "Factory of porcelain, dolls, and stoneware." Also made dollhouse dolls.

BECK MANUFACTURING CO.—U.S.A., 1888-1921. In the early years, they manufactured composition babies and child dolls with glass eyes and wigs. And, later added imported bisque-head dolls to their inventory. Advertised, "the dolls were dressed in dark knit costumes so they would not show soiling."

BECK, RICHARD & CO.—Germany, early 1900s. A small toy company that manufactured dolls of leather, wood, papier-mâché, and porcelain. They also advertised doll parts. Richard Beck & Co. dolls are of fair to good quality.

BEECHER BABY—U.S.A., 1893-1910. Charming cloth dolls made by Julia Jones and the Sewing Circle of the Congregational Church in Elmira, New York. Beecher Babies are also known as Missionary Rag babies, and are a welcomed addition to any collection. Scarcity and charm add greatly to their desirability and value.

BEEHLER ARTS, LTD.—U.S.A., mid-twentieth century. A small little-known company that produced rather poor-quality composition and rigid vinyl dolls.

BELL & FRANCIS— England, 1906-1923. Produced cloth character dolls, many that represented the Allies during the war. Also included in their inventory were dolls of British Ceramic and composition.

BELLAS HESS & CO.—U.S.A., 1914-1920. Sold primarily bisque-head, child-type dolls (in sizes over 16 inches) with wigs, sleep glass eyes, and eyelashes. Also sold bisque-head babies and composition dolls.

BELLE DOLL AND TOY CORP.—U.S.A., mid-twentieth century. Produced several types of vinyl and plastic dolls. Belle dolls tend to be of good quality.

BELLET, HENRI—France, 1919-1920s. Was a member of Chambre Syndicale. Produced dolls—some of cardboard with molded clothing known as "Poupard Art," a name registered in 1919.

BELLEVILLE & CIE—France, 1920s and possibly other years. A little-known company that manufactured bisque dolls and also patented and produced a mechanism for moving eyes. A seldom-found collectible doll.

BELTON—Accepted as French; however, most likely German after 1870—and possibly as late as 1900. To date, no firm evidence has surfaced confirming any one company as the probable source of the lovely bisque-head dolls. One common characteristic is the uncut pate section of the head with 1, 2, or 3 small holes. Belton-type dolls range in quality from extremely fine to only moderately fair.

BERG, ERICH VON—Germany, 1930s. Little is known of the Von Berg doll other than that the company was listed as a doll manufacturer in the early 1930s—and, according to existing records, a trademark was registered.

BERG, HERMANN VON—Germany, 1904-mid 1930s. Originally began as a doll parts manufacturer, they eventually produced dolls of celluloid and bisque with talking and moving mechanisms. Best known for

their later Habeka doll that crawled and talked. Hermann von Berg dolls are of fair to good quality.

BERGFELD, SOL & SON—U.S.A., late 1910s-at least the mid to late 1920s. Manufactured dolls distributed by Borgfeldt, including the famous Storybook Line. No known mark is attributed to Bergfeld dolls. The dolls tend to be of good quality.

BERGMANN, C. M.—Germany, 1888-1931. Manufactured bisque-head child and baby dolls. Best known for their Eleonore and Columbia character child, C. M. Bergmann dolls were distributed in the United States by Louis Wolf and were of good to very good quality.

C.M. Bergmann's Child Doll, and Bähr & Pröschild's Character Baby #585 (Photo courtesy of Cobb's Doll Auction.)

BERGMANN, JOSEF—Germany, 1883-1891. Doll factory that produced dolls with bisque and papier-mâché heads on bodies of kid or composition. At least some of the bisque heads were supplied by Bähr & Pröschild. Also acquired a patent for a "yes/no" doll that was operated by pulling strings going through the head.

BERGMANN JR., S. & CO.—Germany, 1920s. Porcelain factory that is known to have produced bisque doll heads, including a character baby. Although this company reportedly had three hundred employees during the early 1920s, little information is available. The few dolls that have been identified as S. Bergmann Jr. & Co. are of very good quality.

BERGNER, CARL—Germany, 1860-at least 1930. Manufactured bisque-head dolls, many of which were supplied by Simon & Halbig. Best known for the two and three multi-faced dolls so in demand during the early 1920s. Carl Bergner dolls are extremely popular with collectors in large part due to their very good quality.

BERLICH, ROLF—Germany, 1920-at least 1924. Manufactured cloth dolls and other stuffed toys. The dolls had glass side glancing eyes, mohair wigs, and were jointed at the neck, shoulders, and hips. The boy and girl costumes were removable. Most notably marked with a lead seal attached to the hand of the dolls. Rolf Berlich dolls are both charming and well made.

BERLINER, EMILE—Germany, 1890-1894. Produced a phonograph-type doll with at least some of the bisque heads supplied by Kämmer & Reinhardt. When activated, the doll recited prayers or sang children's songs in either French, German, or English. Emile Berliner dolls are of good to very good quality, and very desirable.

BERNER JACQUES—France, 1888. Little is known of this small Paris manufacturer other than that the name Bébé Moujik was registered in 1888 and that boxes have been found with their trademark attached.

BERNHEIM & KAHN—France, early 1900s. A small Paris manufacturer of bisque dolls. Registered the names Etoile Bébé and Bébé Mondain. Bernheim & Kahn dolls tend to be of good quality.

BERNHOLD, JULIUS—France, mid-1910s and possibly later. Manufactured fine composition character dolls. Julius Bernhold dolls are of very good quality.

BERRY & ROSS—U.S.A., 1919. An innovated company for the time. Completely owned and operated by black individuals. Produced black composition dolls and military dolls. Highly collectible not only for their charm and quality, but also for their historical significance to doll manufacturing.

BERTRAND, RENÉ—France, mid-1920s. Little is known of this doll manufacturer, other than the name Gaby was registered in 1923.

BERWICK DOLL CO.—U.S.A., 1918-1925. Manufactured the well-known "Famlee" dolls. Composition doll patented by David Wiener that came boxed as a set. The sets included a basic doll body with a screw-type neck, three to twelve interchangeable heads, and the appropriate costumes to match the heads. Famlee dolls are very collectible and of good quality.

BEST & CO.—U.S.A., 1902-1927. Distributed dolls and registered the trademark Snuggles in 1917 to be used on their dolls of glass, wood, metal, celluloid, cotton, wool, wax, bisque, china, rubber, or composition. There is no evidence that Best produced dolls in all of the mediums, but according to the registration for trademarks, they could have.

BESTER DOLL MANUFACTURING CO.—U.S.A., 1919-1921. A rather short-lived doll manufacturer based in New Jersey. The majority of composition dolls manufactured by Bester were sold under the their trade name, Bloomfield, although there is evidence that at least some were distributed through Morimura Brothers.

BIBERIAN, GREGOIRE—France, 1929-at least 1931. Produced cloth art dolls using M. Manuel as his Paris representative. Registered an elaborate *B* and *G* intertwined as a trademark. Very few examples of Gregoire Biberian dolls have been reported—but they appear to be of good quality.

BIERER, L.—Germany, 1845-1930. Probably did not manufacture dolls until the early 1920s, although this is not definite. At least some of the bisque-head dolls were manufactured by Theodor Recknagel, which would explain why the quality of an L. Bierer doll is only fair.

BIERSCHENK, FRITZ—Germany, 1906-1930s. There has always been confusion about the dates that Fritz Bierschenk manufactured dolls. There is a marked Bierschenk cloth doll in the Sonneberg Museum which has been dated 1890, although records do not indicate any registering until after Fritz Bierschenk purchased the doll factory of E. Escher, Jr. in 1906. There is further evidence that an explosion at his factory in the early 1920s put an end to his doll production, although he continued to register patents until at least 1927. Production included cloth dolls with mask-type faces and bisque-head dolls of the baby or child type.

BIJOU DOLL CO., THE—U.S.A., 1915-1917. Produced cloth-body dolls with composition heads and hands. The smaller (11-inch) dolls had mohair wigs, and the larger (14-inch) had painted hair and eyes. Various costumes were offered, such as sailor boys and girls, baby dress and bonnet, a girl with an Eton jacket or a plaid jumper and a striped blouse. Bijou Dolls are of rather poor quality.

BIMBLICK, W. & CO.—U.S.A., 1926-1930. Manufactured dolls made from a series of wooden beads. The varying shaped beads were painted in waterproof enamels and strung together. Faces were hand painted. In 1930, Cameo Doll Co. won an infringement case filed against Bimblick for copying their Margie doll.

BINDER & CIE—France, 1918 and possibly other years. Also known as Société Binder & Cie. Manufactured cloth dolls. Registered an elaborate script-type trademark with the initials *B. K.*

BING BROTHERS ART DOLL CO.—Germany, 1882-1932. Founded by Gebrüder Bing, also known as Bing Werke and Bing Wolfe Corporation. Best known for the fabric art dolls that closely resemble either Käthe Kruse or Lenci dolls. By 1920, Bing Werke was a large conglomerate consisting of thirty-one subsidiary companies until going bankrupt in 1932. It is interesting to note that it was the only toy factory in Nürnberg that did not close during World War I. Bing art dolls are of very good quality.

BING KUNSTLERPUPPEN UND STOFF-SPIELWARENGESELLSCHAFT—Germany, 1921-1932. Manufactured art dolls and cloth toys. Founded with the purchase of Albert Schlopsnies business and incorporated into the Bing Art Doll conglomerate. The cloth dolls so closely resembled the Käthe Kruse dolls that she claimed they infringed upon her copyrights.

BING, JOHN CO.—U.S.A., early 1900s-1928. Held the exclusive American and Canadian rights for the Bing Art Dolls, and also acted as an agent for Kämmer and Reinhardt, Heinrich Handwerck, and other German manufacturers. Max Bing overtook the operation in 1928 becoming the Bing Wolfe Corp.

BISC NOVELTY MANUFACTURING CO.—U.S.A., c. 1900. Founded by Ernst Reinhardt. Among the first American doll manufacturers to design and produce dolls of bisque. Bisc Novelty dolls are well marked and are an important link in the doll evolution chain. Bisc Novelty dolls are of fair quality.

BLACK DOLLS—Various countries, 1830-present. Black dolls of all mediums have been popular since their introduction. Vintage folk art rag dolls have a special appeal. Black bisque may only be a Caucasian mold painted brown or a specially designed mold with ethnic features. Black dolls are all collectible and can range in quality from the humblest handmade cloth to the finest French bisque.

BLAND-HAWKES, MABEL—England, 1918-1930 and possibly later. Manufactured small cloth and mascot dolls known as Cuddley, along with doll costumes, a life-sized character baby known as Baby Royal, a three-faced doll named Caprice, and a series of elaborately costumed dolls. Mabel Bland-Hawkes dolls are of good quality.

BLECHMAN, S. & SONS—U.S.A., 1922-1927. Little is known about this company, except the registering of the trademark Charm in 1927, although there is evidence that the name was used for composition dolls as early as 1922.

BLEIER BROTHERS—U.S.A., early twentieth century. Produced at least a composition Abe Kabibble doll. Little else is known of this manufacturer, other than registering the Bee Bee Brand trademark.

BLOCK DOLL CORPORATION—U.S.A., mid-1950s. Produced hard plastic dolls for a short time not only for their own company, but also small inexpensive dolls to be marketed under other names. Best known for the Answer Doll, operated by a button through the body. Block dolls are of mediocre quality.

BLOSSOM PRODUCTS CORP.—U.S.A., 1930s. Little is known about this small, short-lived company, other than a trademark of a circle containing five little doll faces and the name Quints was registered in 1936.

BOHNE, ERNST—Germany, 1854-1930. A well-known porcelain factory that produced doll heads. Several markings were registered. The crown and *N* are often confused with Capo di Monte's trademark. Ernst Bohne dolls are of fair to good quality.

BÖHNKE, CLARA & ZIMMERMANN, HELENE—Germany, 1902-1922. Registered the name Henny for the dolls and doll parts, including heads, wigs, and costumes they manufactured.

BOLTON, JAMES A.—U.S.A., 1926-1927. Produced a patented kissing doll. Activated by pressing the doll against a surface. When the doll is removed, air rushes from a chamber within the doll's body, up through a duct, and produces a smacking sound.

BONIN & LEFORT & CIE—France, 1923-1928. Also known as Société Bonin & Lefort. Best known for the nicely costumed cloth dolls. Registered several trademarks for dolls and doll heads, the most common being a circle with a silhouetted boy and girl pulling on a doll. Bonin & Lefort dolls are of good quality.

BONNAL, CLAUDE VALÉRY—France, 1898-1904, and possibly later. According to advertisements, this company was entirely concerned with the manufacture of bébés incassable (indestructible babies).

BONOMI—Italy, mid-twentieth century. Produced chic vinyl dolls with large deep-set eyes. Advertised as "Have you ever seen outfits so smartly styled, so beautifully detailed, so definitely continental in fashion?" Bonomi dolls are of good quality.

BONSER DOLL CO.—U.S.A., 1925-1930. Also known as Bonser Products, Inc., this company was founded by Helen Haldane Wyse. Best known for their washable stockinette cloth dolls with hand-decorated faces. Also distributed, through their firm of Wyse-Bailey, a composition rattle doll and a long-limbed character doll. Bonser dolls, although somewhat charming in their simplicity, are only of mediocre quality.

BORGFELDT, GEORGE & COMPANY—U.S.A., 1881-1950s. Imported and produced dolls, but did not manufacture them. They held the exclusive American and Canadian rights to many of the leading European doll manufacturers, along with several American companies. Responsible for commissioning two of the most successful dolls ever made, namely the Kewpie and Bye Lo dolls. Borgfeldt dolls are of good quality and are highly collectible.

BOROUGH BRITISH DOLLS—England, 1915-1920. Crafted and produced dolls and doll accessories. Best known for their handmade British Ceramic dolls and Borough Baby Dolls, a line of crying babies with an assortment of outfits. Borough British dolls and accessories range in quality from the very fine to poor.

BOSTON POTTERY COMPANY—U.S.A., early 1920s. Although not positively documented, it is assumed that bisque-head dolls incised with "B. P. D. Co." and "Made in Boston, Mass. U.S.A." were manufactured by the Boston Pottery Co.

BOUCHET, ADOLPHE HENRI—France, 1889-1899. An apparently successful doll manufacturer—as made evident by records from both the 1895 and 1899 Expositions, and the gold and silver medals Bouchet won at the Brussels toy fairs. After the formation of S. F. B. J., Bouchet's contributions were of a more practical nature, such as commercial properties, supplying materials, and lending his registered name of Bébé Géant, rather than the production of his earlier bisque-head dolls.

BOUTON, DEWITT C.—U.S.A., 1899 and probably later. Obtained a patent and produced a topsy turvy cloth doll. One end of the doll was white and the other black. The sateen faces were painted as was the hair. The skirt was split to ease in turning the doll. Dolls with this description, and those having a purple patent stamp, are assumed to be Bouton dolls. They are both charming and desirable.

BOUTON, J. & CO.—U.S.A., 1902-1930s and possibly later. Produced and sold several styles and types of dolls, including bisque child and baby dolls, composition mama babies and characters. Best known for the introduction of the musical Baby Phyllis labeled "press me and I will play sweet lullabies."

BOUTON WOOLF CO., INC.—U.S.A., early twentieth century. Manufactured composition dolls in their own factory, and supplied dolls to other dealers. Most dolls appear to be copies of other established characters, for example a Patsy look-alike called Phyllis. Bouton Woolf dolls are of mediocre quality.

BRANDNER, HERMANN & CO.—Germany, 1922-1930. A small company that reportedly produced a large assortment of dolls including child, character babies, toddlers, art dolls, and boudoir dolls. Advertised a jointed mechanical doll with moving arms, head, eyes, and tongue.

BRAXTED DOLL VILLAGE INDUSTRY—England, 1918-1928. Probably a postwar cottage-type industry producing mostly composition baby dolls with cloth bodies, glass eyes, wigs, along with cloth, leather, and hand-carved wooden dolls.

BREVETE GEGE OF FRANCE—France, mid-twentieth century. Produced lovely vinyl and plastic dolls with rooted hair, sleep eyes with real lashes, and a wide selection of costumes. GeGe dolls are of very good quality.

BRISTOL, EMMA L.—U.S.A., 1886-1900. Possibly manufactured her dolls as early as 1860. A 1903 editorial mentions a doll maker in Rhode Island having made dolls (with blue eyes and real hair) for forty years. Emma Bristol was the only doll maker in that area according to records that have thus far been found. If this is Emma Bristol, as is assumed, then she was in the doll making business longer than the doll registries indicate. The known marked Emma Bristol dolls have composition shoulder heads on leather bodies, with human hair wigs, molded and painted blue eyes, and closed mouths. Very good quality early doll.

BRITANNIA TOY CO.—England, 1919-1926. Manufactured cloth dolls that were distributed through Bush Terminal and Cowan, de Groot.

BRITISH DOLL MANUFACTURING CO.—England, 1917. A little-known doll company that produced soft bodied character dolls with British Ceramic heads.

BRITISH PRODUCTS MANUFACTURING CO.—England, 1917-1921. Produced dolls with British Ceramic heads, specializing in dressed and undressed character dolls.

BROOKGLAD CORP.—U.S.A., mid-twentieth century. Produced the famed Poor Pitiful Pearl of vinyl. Later manufactured by Horsman. Brookglad Poor Pitiful Pearl is very collectible and of good quality.

BRU JNE & CIE—France, 1866-1899, when it became a charter member of S. F. B. J. One of the most famous and sought-after antique bisque dolls. Produced three basic types: the Fashion Lady or Poupée de Mode, the Bébé on a kid body with beautifully molded shoulder plate and hands, and the Bru on a wooden and composition body. Bru Jne & Cie dolls are of the highest quality.

Bru Jne's Bébé with Original Dress and Bonnet (Photo courtesy of Cobb's Doll Auction.)

BRUCHLOS, GEORGE FABRIK GEKLEIDETER PUPPEN—Germany, 1883-1930. Produced a wide variety of doll types including doll candy boxes and a doll with a patented parachute. Bruchlos dolls range from the only fair quality small dolls with crude cardboard bodies to better quality, nicely costumed mechanical dolls.

BRUCKMANN, HATTIE BARTHOLOMAY—U.S.A., 1917-at least until after the war years. Cottage-type industry that produced dolls, using a mixture of papier-mâché, cornstarch, and a soft plaster pressed into a facial mold, then covered with chamois skin and given a layer of glaze before hand-painting the facial features and adding a natural hair wig. During World War I, Bruckmann supplied an all-kid doll to Meier & Franke Co. Also lists in their inventory papier-mâché, kid-covered heads with glass eyes; and waxed and cloth dolls. The historic significance far outweighs any artistic appeal these dolls may have.

BRÜCKNER, ALBERT—U.S.A., 1901-1930. In its later years, the company became Albert Brückner's Sons. Manufactured molded face cloth dolls with printed features. Many of his dolls were released through Horsman where they were advertised as having compressed fabric faces. Brückner dolls are a very good quality, highly prized rag doll.

BUCHERER, A. & CIE—Switzerland, 1921-early 1940s. The patented metal ball-jointed body of the numerous characters manufactured makes identification of these dolls rather easy. Composition heads represent comic personalities, celebrities, and everyday civilians such as chauffeurs, policemen, and firemen. Clothing is usually sewn directly onto the doll. Bucherer dolls are of good quality.

BÜHL, H. & SÖHNE—Germany, 1869-1898. Also spelled *Bühle*. Very early porcelain factory founded in 1780. In 1869 Bühl purchased the factory from the Greiner family and soon after began manufacturing porcelain doll heads and eventually bathing dolls. There is a school of thought that connects the Bühl and Limbach porcelain factories, validated by the Greiner name and the trefoil mark that both companies use.

BURGARELLA—Italy, 1929-late 1930 and possibly later. Produced a high-priced, all-composition doll with wigs, molded and painted eyes, and a unique semi-spherical jointed body. Designed with uncommon facial features. The distinguishing appearance and high quality explains the demand for Burgarella dolls.

BUSCHBAUM—Germany, 1859-1928 and possibly later. An export and wholesale doll factory. Produced porcelain dolls, Frozen Charlies and Charlottes, bathing dolls, and dolls in costume. In 1911 the company suffered a devastating fire but rebuilt that same year. Buschbaum dolls are of fair quality.

BUSCHOW, WILHELM—Germany, 1896-at least 1929. A rubber and celluloid factory produced dolls and doll parts and distributed leather bodies, teddy bears, and dollhouse dolls, along with operating a doll hospital. Buschow celluloid dolls are of mediocre quality.

BUSCHOW & BECK—Germany, 1888-mid 1930s. Best known for their unbreakable doll heads of pressed metal. Also produced dolls of celluloid, cloth, and celluloid-coated metal. Supplied doll parts, wigs, shoes, and stockings to other doll manufacturers and to the public. Although not in great demand by today's collectors, Buschow & Beck dolls are of good quality.

BUTLER BROTHERS—U.S.A. and Germany, 1877-the 1930s. It began as a mail-order business by the three brothers—Edward, Charles, and George—and grew to be one of the largest distributors of dolls in America. They sold wax dolls and china dolls, including the Pet Name collection and French bisque from various manufacturers.

BUZZA CO., THE—U.S.A., 1927. A small, short-lived doll manufacturer that produced 9-inch cloth dolls with flat painted faces, felt hair, and simple cotton costumes. More notable than the doll was the box that it came in. The boxes were nicely lithographed with a picture of the doll and a poem that related to the doll. Although Buzza dolls are themselves of poor to mediocre quality, if found in their original box they are quite collectible.

C

CALIFORNIAN BISQUE DOLL CO.—U.S.A., at least 1925 and probably other years. Produced bisque doll heads under the direction of Mrs. H. T. Epperson. A character doll with closed mouth and single stroke brows has a *C. B. D. Co.* marking on it that has been attributed to California Bisque; the quality is fair.

CAMEO DOLL COMPANY—U.S.A., 1922-1970. This Port Allegheny, Pennsylvania, company was founded by Joseph Kallus. Gaining notoriety by modeling the Kewpie doll designed by Rose O'Neill, along with Baby Bo-Kaye and many others in composition, wood, hard plastic, and vinyl. The entire company, including equipment, was acquired by the Strombecker Corporation of Chicago in 1970. Cameo Dolls are among the finest quality American dolls made in the twentieth century.

CANZLER & HOFFMANN—Germany, 1906-1930 later. In the early years the company operated as a wholesale and export business. By 1910, it occupied a factory with a workshop for making doll dresses and outfits. Later, it produced soft stuffed, leather, celluloid, and combination dolls, and adopted the acronym Caho as its trademark.

CAPITAL TOY CO.—U.S.A., 1923-early 1930s. Manufactured the Cee Tee line of mama dolls along with character and baby dolls of composition and cloth. Costumes were well made of percale trimmed with piqué. Capital Toy dolls are of good quality.

CAPO DI MONTE—Italy, 1700s-present. One of the finest and best-known porcelain factories. Famous for the exquisite figurines and other decorative commodities, the crown and *N* trademark found on a porcelain piece must be verified because the Capo Di Monte mark is often forged, not to mention the Ernst Bohne marking that is very similar.

CARL, MAX & CO.—Germany, 1891-1905. Produced dolls having wax, wax over composition, china, and bisque heads on bodies of kid, cloth, or composition. In 1902 obtained a patent for a drinking doll, operated by means of a tube connecting a drinking bottle and a rubber ball hidden in the doll's body.

CARL, ROBERT—Germany, 1895-1929. Produced dolls with bisque heads mainly supplied by Armand Marseille. Best known for a talking doll with the mechanism placed within the head. Also advertised cloth dolls and animals that cried when touched. Robert Carl sold his company in 1911 to Frickmann & Lindner; however, they retained the Carl name for more than a decade after the sale. Robert Carl dolls are of fair to good quality.

CARLÉGLE, CHARLES-EMILE & HELLÉ, ANDRÉ—France, 1918 and beyond. A talented artist. Not only the creator of wooden toy characters, but a gifted humorist, illustrator, painter, and engraver. Printemps sold the cowboys, Indians, sailors, and other figures crafted by Carlégle. Enormously popular in doll collecting, Carlégle wooden figures are of very good quality.

CARLES, JEAN—France, 1926. Very little is known, other than the registering of the Mousmé name.

CARTWRIGHT, A. S.—U.S.A., 1880-1917. Manufactured rubber dolls and doll accessories, such as bottles and a type of comforter. Little is known and no examples of its dolls are recorded.

CARVAILLO, ADRIEN—France, 1923. Very little is known other than the registering of the name La Vénus for a cloth doll.

CASS, N. D. & CO.—U.S.A., 1918-1927. Best known for peg-jointed dolls made of wood. The Funny Face Family, including the parts for Reddy, Whitey, and son Bluey, were interchangeable. Doll trunks bearing the Cass label contain well-made clothing for cloth dolls. Cass dolls and accessories are of good quality.

CASSANET, A. & CIE—France, 1881-1890s. Produced lovely bisque dolls with heads purchased from François Gaultier. Cassanet dolls are of very good quality considering the source of the heads used.

CATTERFELDER PUPPENFABRIK—Germany, 1894-1930s. Kestner provided most of the bisque heads used to produce their child and baby dolls on composition bodies, along with the very rare character mold numbers 207, 219, and 220. Catterfelder dolls are of very good quality.

CAYETTE, E. MADAME—France, early 1900s. Very little information is available for this company, other than the active registering of trademarks, including a five-pointed star, a four-leaf clover, Bébé Prophéte, Bébé Oracle, La Fée au Gui, La Fée au Tréfle, La Fée aux Tréfles, and La Fée Bonheur.

CELLBA CELLULOIDWARENFABRIK—Germany, 1923-1930 and later. Entered the doll business by producing celluloid doll body joints, later expanding to include dolls with glass eyes, black dolls, Café au lait, and a "first class baby." Cellba celluloid dolls are of good quality.

CELLULOID—Various countries, 1869-late 1950s and perhaps beyond. Celluloid became illegal in the United States in the 1940s, because it burned or exploded if placed near high heat. All types of dolls were manufactured, including baby, child, adult, comic characters, and others. Jointed or unjointed, painted or glass eyes, wigs or molded hair, nude or molded clothes. Celluloid dolls can be of very good to very poor quality.

CENTRAL DOLL MANUFACTURING CO.—U.S.A., 1917-1921. Manufactured a variety of composition dolls so in demand during and immediately after World War I. Their inventory consisted of character dolls often dressed as soldiers, sailors and nurses; child and baby dolls; and several types of carnival dolls, some as large as 30 inches.

CENTURY DOLL CO.—U.S.A., 1909-1929. Founded by Max Scheuer and his sons, Bert and Harold. Manufactured a wide variety of composition mama, child, and baby dolls. Best known for the popular bisque infant designed and produced by Kestner to compete with the Bye Lo Babies. After Max retired,

his sons continued the business until it merged with Domec in 1929 and became the Doll Corporation of America. Century dolls are of very good quality.

CHAD VALLEY, LTD.—England, 1917-1940s. Manufactured toys as early as 1897. Began producing dolls as part of England's National Scheme for employment of disabled men in 1917. Various types of cloth dolls were made: the earliest were predominately made with stockinette faces, and later hand-painted felt faces were used on dolls of velvet or velveteen. The quality of Chad Valley dolls varies from mediocre cloth dolls with printed clothes to fine dolls with hand-painted faces, wigs, and glass eyes.

CHAMBON ET BAYE—France, 1899. Little-known company. Produced at least one three-faced cloth doll. A mechanical lever under the doll bonnet operated the movement of the head. Registered a trademark of a beetle within a circle the same year.

CHAMBRE SYNDICALE DES FABRICANTS DE JOUETS ET JEUX ET ENGINS SPORTIF—France, 1886-1928. Trade organization composed of several French toy manufacturers, including: Vichy, Henri Alexandre, Falck-Roussel, Unis France, Lambert,

Century's Baby in Joel Ellis-Type Buggy (Photo courtesy of McMasters Doll Auction.)

Dehais, Pintel Fils, Roullet & Decamps, S. F. B. G., Lefebvre, Geoffroy, Renault & Bon-Dufour, and Bossuat. The diamond mark with Marque and Déposée will most often be followed with the manufacturer's number. Syndicale des Fabricants dolls range in quality from very good to very poor, depending on the manufacturer.

CHANTILLY, CIE—France, 1924-1928. Chantilly had two factory locations in France, indicating that they were successful; however, from the rarity of doll heads, it must be assumed that they produced other articles. They advertised dolls with unbreakable heads made of silica. It appears that the heads must have been made of a heavy ceramic-type material. Chantilly was registered as a trademark in 1925.

CHASE, MARTHA—U.S.A., 1889-1970. The later vinyl dolls have little in common with the early Martha Chase dolls with stockinette fabric stretched over a mask with raised features. Head and limbs were sized with a coating of glue and paste, dried and painted with oils. Features were hand-painted with rough brush stokes providing a realistic texture to the hair. Ears and thumbs were applied separately. The earliest bodies were of pink sateen; later ones were from heavy white cotton. Also known as Hospital dolls, because of their use in nurses' training schools. Early Martha Chase dolls are of very good quality and extremely desirable; the later dolls do not enjoy such credentials.

CHESSLER CO., THE—U.S.A., 1920-late 1930s Manufactured cloth dolls with embroidered features, many representing nursery rhyme characters. Also, a line of Chessler Durable mama babies with composition heads and cloth bodies originally dressed in crepe de Chine and other expensive fabrics. Chessler dolls are of good quality.

CHILDREN'S NOVELTY CO.—U.S.A., 1909-1911. Distributed flat-faced cloth dolls with lithographed features. According to advertisements, they registered a U.S. patent in 1909.

CHINA HEAD DOLLS—Various countries, 1840-present, although the vast number and best-known were produced in Germany from 1840-1928. Identifying china heads according to manufacturer is nearly impossible. Most shoulder heads have painted eyes and hair, full cheeks, and a small closed mouth. Some have glass eyes, pierced ears, a pink luster tint, solid dome head and wig, or a socket head attached to a separate shoulder plate. Identification is achieved by hair style. (See Chapter VII for explanations of types.) Quality can range from very fine to very poor.

CHIQUET, F. & LE MONTRÉER—France, 1865-1885. Manufactured fine bisque-head talking dolls with

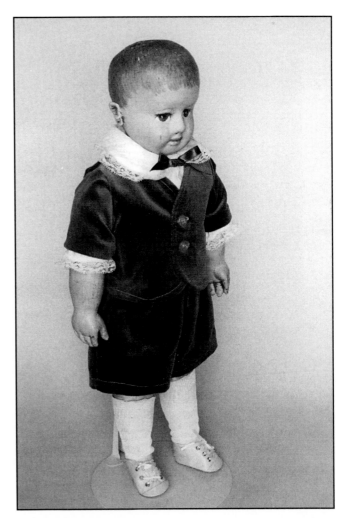

Early Martha Chase Boy

wood and composition bodies. At least some of the heads were supplied by François Gaultier. Apparently, Le Montréer left the company in 1870, several years before Chiquet received Honorable Mention at a Paris Exposition. Chiquet & Le Montréer dolls are of very good quality.

CISSNA, W. A. & CO.—U.S.A., 1897-1898 and, most likely, other years. A mail-order business that sold dolls through their catalog, *The Hustler*. The majority of dolls were bisque shoulder heads on kid bodies with open month and mohair wigs. Cissna was a distributor of a lesser quality doll.

CITRO—U.S.A., mid-twentieth century. Produced vinyl teen-type dolls.

CLAUSEN & CO.—U.S.A., 1922. An American-based company with a branch in Germany that imported dolls made in the cottage industries from the Thüringian region.

CLEAR, EMMA C.—U.S.A., 1888-1950s when Lillian Smith took over the business. Well-known for her Humpty Dumpty Doll Hospital and the reproduction china head dolls she made. Also, designed several dolls sculptured by Martha Oathout Ayers, who often used her children as models. The early reproductions were not marked. Later ones will be found with the year and the name Clear or with *H. D. D. H.* Emma Clear dolls are of good quality and are collectible in their own right.

CLÉMENT, VVE.—France, 1870s. Very likely to be a relative of Pierre Victor Clément who made pressed-leather dolls. Several leather-bodied dolls made during this time have been found with the Widow (Vve. French term) Clément marking.

CLERC, LES FILS DE N.—France, 1908-1927. Was a member of the Chambre Syndicale and manufacturer of composition, wood, and/or cardboard babies in swaddling clothes or with lead strings and a diaper. Also made a Bébé and sold doll parts.

CLOTH DOLLS—U.S.A., earliest pioneering days-the present. The two most popular are the pillow or rag-type and the vintage folk-art dolls. The printed or lithographed rag dolls were designed to cut, sew, and stuff at home. The war years between 1914 and 1918 meant sacrifices for everyone. Dolls were limited to materials not essential to the war effort. Consequently, rag dolls enjoyed a boom. Folk-art dolls handmade by known or unknown crafters have always been popular. The quality of cloth dolls varies from excellent to poor depending on the talent and skill of the maker.

COCHECO MANUFACTURING CO.—U.S.A., 1827-1893. Did not manufacture their printed cut-out dolls until 1889. Celia and Charity Smith, along with Ida Gutsell, contributed the designs used to produce the colorful sew-at-home rag dolls. Cocheco dolls are of good quality.

COCHRAN, DEWEES—U.S.A., 1934-1970s. A gifted artist who designed dolls for Effanbee and independently, including the famous Look Alike, Grow Up Series, and Cindy dolls. The marked Dewees Cochran dolls are made of a rubbery latex number less than 1,000. Dewees Cochran dolls are highly desirable, and show great artistic talent.

COHEN, HERMAN—U.S.A., early twentieth century. Manufactured composition character doll, best known for Puzzy and Sizzy, the Good Habit Kids. Herman Cohen dolls are of good quality and very collectible.

COHEN, L. & SON—U.S.A., 1923-1929. Produced the Elco line of mama dolls with composition heads and limbs on cloth bodies with sleep or painted eyes. Also advertised a singing and talking doll.

COHEN, W. & SON—England, 1924-1930s. Produced various types of dolls including child dolls with heads supplied by Armand Marseille and Ernst Heubach.

COLE, ROXANNA ELIZABETH MCGEE—U.S.A., 1868-1930s. Although Roxanna died in 1907, her daughter-in-law Molly Hunt Cole continued the business until 1930. Early dolls were made of fine muslin with delicate hand-stitched sculptured features that were beautifully hand painted. Later dolls were less delicate with a rounder face. Roxanna Cole dolls are very good quality and represent an important link in the doll evolution chain.

COLLINGBOURNE MILLS—U.S.A., 1920s. This company manufactured cloth, cut-out rag dolls to sew at home, along with their more famous sewing sets to make doll clothing.

COLONIAL TOY MANUFACTURING CO.—U.S.A., 1915-1920. Founded by David Zaiden, who spent years perfecting his recipe for composition used in the manufacturing of his dolls. Advertised as "bisque finish" the heads are often incised with "Zaiden." Dolls were all composition with fully jointed bodies or composition heads on cork-stuffed cloth bodies. Also used Fulper bisque heads.

COLUMBIA DOLL & TOY CO.—U.S.A., 1917-1922. Manufactured all-composition dolls with joints at the neck only. Painted high-button boots, and side glancing eyes. With or without wigs. Original costumes were knitted with feather trimmings. Columbia dolls are of poor quality.

COLUMBIAN DOLL—U.S.A., 1891-about 1910. Emma and Marietta Adams, sisters living in New York, made and dressed cloth dolls in the home. The name comes from the Columbian Exposition at the 1893 Chicago World's Fair where the dolls were exhibited. Hand-painted facial features on a flat face wearing simple cotton dresses. Columbian dolls are of very good quality and actively sought by collectors.

COLUMBUS MERCHANDISE CO.—U.S.A., 1917 and possibly other years. A wholesale distributor for several German and American manufacturers, including, but not limited to, Gebrüder Heubach, Amberg, and Schoenhut.

COMMERCIAL TOY COMPANY—Canada, 1917. A very short-lived doll company only operating for six months. The composition heads are on ball-jointed or kid bodies. Painted eyes and mohair wigs. Marked "Commercial Toy Co."

COMMONWEALTH CORP.—U.S.A., mid-twentieth century. Produced several types of vinyl dolls. Commonwealth dolls are of mediocre quality.

CONFETTI DOLLS, INC.—U.S.A., early twentieth century. Produced an inexpensive copy of the Nancy Ann Story Book dolls. All composition with painted eyes, long lashes, and felt costumes. Confetti dolls are of poor quality.

CONTA & BÖHME—Germany, 1804-1937. Founded by Ernst Conta and Christian Böhme. Specializing in all-bisque Frozen Charlottes and bathing dolls, they also produced doll heads. Additionally known to have made lovely pressed china heads that are glazed on both the inside and out. Registered the trademark of a bent arm holding a dagger inside of a shield. Conta & Böhme porcelain dolls are of very good quality.

CONTINENTAL TOY & NOVELTY CO.—U.S.A., 1929. Manufactured boudoir-type dolls, cloth dolls, and other stuffed toys until merging with Sil-Kov Art Pillow Co.

CONVERSE, MORTON E. & SON—U.S.A., 1925-1926. A rather small, short-lived company whose claim to fame lies in a small wood-jointed doll designed by Mrs. Ripley Hitchcock known as "Flexy."

COOK'S FLAKED RICE CO.—U.S.A., 1900. Manufactured a lithographed doll as a premium. The success of this doll is evident from the vast number that have survived. According to company records, several thousands were delivered.

COOPER, FREDERICK & SON—England, 1915-1920. Manufactured a line of baby and mama dolls with composition or British Ceramic heads on bodies of plush or jointed cloth.

CO-OPERATIVE MANUFACTURING CO.—U.S.A., 1873-1874. Joel Ellis operated this Vermont company and employed about sixty employees, most of them women. Unique mortise and tendon body of rock maple, with pewter hands and feet. The wood for the head was cut into a cube and steamed until softened and compressed in a hydraulic press with steel dies to form the features. Hair and facial features were painted. Joel Ellis dolls are valued not only for their artistic appeal, but also for their historic significance.

COSMAN FRÉRES—France, 1892-1893 and possibly other years. Manufactured bébés with bisque heads and jointed bodies. Also traded under the names of Bébé le Splendide and Bébé Prime.

COSMOPOLITAN TOY & DOLL CORPORATION—U.S.A., mid-twentieth century. One of the larger manufacturer of vinyl and hard plastic dolls. Best known perhaps for the 8-inch Ginger, a competitor to the famous Ginny doll®. Cosmopolitan dolls are of good quality.

COUTERIER, ALICE—France, 1865-1894. Also spelled "Couturier." This early manufacturer also dressed marottes. The bisque heads used for fashion-type dolls and bébés were poured at a fine, but unidentified, porcelain factory. Alice Couterier dolls are rare, and of very good quality.

CRABET SHAPE CO.—England, 1916-1918. Manufactured inexpensive cloth dolls with mask faces and wigs.

CRÄMER & HÉRON—Germany, 1892-1920s. Also spelled Creamer & Heron. Carl Crämer and his son-in-law, Edmond Héron, purchased the Illfelder & Co. toy business and changed the name to Crämer & Héron. In 1908, they founded the Porzellanfabrik Mengersgereuth. It is assumed that at least some of the dolls found with the *P M* marking, including a character baby on a bent limb body, are from Crämer & Heron. They exhibited dolls at the 1892 Chicago Exposition, and were part of the grand prize-winning group that was awarded at the Brussels Exposition.

CREMER & SON—England, 1862-1900. Founded by Henry Cremer, this famous London Toy Shop was later managed by his son William Henry, Jr. Aside from the dolls that were imported and sold in the shop, several dolls were transacted under the Cremer name. At least some of these dolls were imported from France and were more than likely of very good quality.

CRESCENT TOY MANUFACTURING CO.—U.S.A., 1907-1921. Very little information is available for this Brooklyn-based company. Soft stuffed character dolls seem to be the extent of their manufacturing. In 1920 they advertised a Sweater doll.

CROWN DOLL MANUFACTURING CO.—U.S.A., 1927-1929. A small, short-lived doll manufacturer. What is known comes primarily from Voices, Inc., a voice box company. According to their records, "Crown Doll Manufacturing of New York City was licensed to use their mama voices and criers in Crown dolls."

CROWN STAFFORDSHIRE PORCELAIN CO.—England, 1889-1940s and possibly later. Supplied British Ceramic doll heads to several British doll manufacturers.

CROWN TOY MANUFACTURES CO., INC.—U.S.A., early twentieth century. Most famous for the well-made and publicized composition Disney Characters. Crown's Pinocchio is one of the most popular collectibles in today's market, primarily because of the good quality workmanship and materials used in its manufacture.

CURRIE & CO.—England, 1912-1913. Manufactured a wooden doll that was advertised as being made without paint or glue, but was colored with a harmless coloring. The dolls were made of a series of white wooden blocks screwed together. They were constructed with joints at the shoulders, neck, and hips.

D

DALLWIG MANUFACTURING CO.—U.S.A., 1918-1922. Collectors assume that the name for this company was chosen to describe the type of doll manufactured, but that is not the case. The founder and president of the company was Paul Dallwig. It may only be a coincidence that the dolls were made with interchangeable wigs that were included with the doll. The majority of dolls produced were mama types with jointed bodies. The wigs were made of either good quality mohair or human hair, and attached to the doll by way of a patented crown piece that fit into the head.

DAMERVAL FRÈRES & LAFFRANCHY—France, early 1900s-1916. The brothers Jules and Charles Damerval, along with Laffranchy, are credited with the production of fine bisque-head dolls on composition bodies in the 12- to 13-inch height range. Commonly represented men, complete with molded mustaches, and dressed in military costumes or period clothing. Damerval Frères and Laffranchy dolls are of good to very good quality.

DANDY DOLL CO.—U.S.A., 1918-1921. A small, little-known company operating in Brooklyn, New York. According to records, a Toy and Novelty company trading as Dandy produced Dandy Dolls.

DANEL & CIE—France, 1889-1995. Founded by Messieurs Danel, past director of Jumeau, and Guépratte. Produced lovely bisque bébés. Especially noteworthy are the black and mulatto dolls. All bébés are reported with jointed bodies. Well-known for the Eiffel Tower and Paris Bébé marking. A long and tangled association with Jumeau is connected to the Danel firm. It is known that Jumeau sued Danel for copying molds, and perhaps borrowing tools and enticing Jumeau workers to join the Danel company. Obviously Jumeau was successful in their suit, for it appears that by 1896 Jumeau had influence on, if not complete control of, the company. Danel & Cie dolls are of very good quality.

DANVILLE DOLL CO.—U.S.A., 1922-1923. Produced a reported 5,000 dolls a day. A 13-inch spring-jointed composition doll with mohair wig and painted eyes was known as the Dumpie Doll. Many were dressed in crepe paper costumes. Dumpie Dolls are of rather poor quality.

DAVIS, M S. & CO.—U.S.A., 1902-1909. Produced a leather doll patented by Gussie Decker. The unique construction and appearance allows this doll to be easily recognized: The doll is all leather, with a seam down the middle of the face, and a body that is laced up in front. Hair and facial features are hand-painted and the doll is stuffed with cotton. Advertised as "impossible for baby to hurt themselves on" and that "leather is very fine for a baby to chew on when teething." Davis leather dolls have a great historic if not aesthetic quality about them.

DAVIS MILLING CO.—U.S.A., 1910-1930. A member of the textile industry responsible for manufacturing cloth cut-out dolls that were sold by the yard to sew at home. Most famous for Aunt Jemima and her family dolls. In fact, so popular were these lithographed dolls that the company became known as the Aunt Jemima Mills Co. The cloth or pillow dolls by Davis are of good quality and highly collectible.

DAVIS, REES TOY & NOVELTY SHOP—U.S.A., 1920-1927. Named for the founder Rees Davis, a retired actress who pursued a career as a doll maker. Also known as Rees Davis Toy Co. The Rees studio originally produced hand-painted cloth dolls that were distributed primarily through Marshall Field. After being acquired by Pollyanna Co., they added a line of floating cork dolls.

DAVIS & VOETSCH—U.S.A., 1917-late 1930s and possibly after. So successful were Isaac Davis and Fred Voetsch as importers and jobbers that in 1923 the trademark Dee Vee was registered. Though not a manufacturer, the name Dee Vee may still be found on many dolls of fair to good quality.

DE FUISSEAUX—Belgium, prior to World War I. A small, little-known doll manufacturer. Created stunning character-face dolls. Most examples will be shoulder heads with extending plates. Although the sculpturing and painting is outstanding, the bisque can be less than perfect. Collectors prize these dolls, not only for their beauty, but also for their rarity.

DE TOY MANUFACTURING CO.—U.S.A., 1916. Also spelled "Detoy." A short-lived but proficient manufacturer of character cloth dolls that were jointed at neck, shoulder, and hips. Head and limbs were stuffed with cotton and the body with excelsior. Hair and facial features were painted.

DEAN'S RAG BOOK CO.—England, 1903-present. Has produced cloth books, toys, and dolls since its inception. Founder Samuel Dean claimed that he started the company for "children who wear their food and eat their clothes." The three-dimensional molded, pressed, and painted dolls known as Tru To Life dolls were introduced in 1920. Dean's rag dolls are of very good quality.

DEBBIE TOY CO.—U.S.A., mid-twentieth century. Founded by John Landers, Shelley Greenburg, and William Cohen. Landers had been an associate of Valentine Dolls and was responsible for that company's Ballerina doll before becoming a member of the Debbie Doll team. Aside from the vinyl dolls manufactured by Debbie, they offered an extended line of baby items. Debbie dolls are of good quality.

DEE & CEE COMPANY, LTD.—Canada, 1932-at least 1938 and later. During the Great Depression when other companies were closing, the Amusement Supply Company first opened its doors. Later to become Dee & Cee Co. Responsible for manufacturing several types of composition dolls. Frequently they purchased molds or the right to the molds from large American doll companies. Dee & Cee dolls are of good quality.

DEEDLE DUM DOLLS—U.S.A., 1917. An obscure line of handcrafted wooden character dolls made by Richard Humbert and distributed by Baker & Bennett.

DEHLER, KARL—Germany, 1878-1892. Produced bisque doll heads using the initials *W. D.* as a marking. Heads found with three small holes or an open crown.

DEKLINE, MR.—U.S.A., early 1900s. Manufactured composition dolls. According to early accounts this New Jersey-based company was the first to produce wood pulp composition dolls by using the Hot Press method of hot die pressure to form the head.

DELCROIX, HENRI—France, 1865-1887. Also may be found spelled *Delacroix*. Produced fine bisque heads using several type markings that graduate with the size of the head. It is assumed that at least some of the heads were used by Grandjean. Also known for the Pan dolls so highly regarded by collectors. Delcroix dolls are of very good quality.

DELLY PUPPENFABRIK—Germany, mid-1920s. Advertised "softly stuffed art dolls" in three sizes, 12, 15, and 19 inches, with elegant costumes of the best felt.

DELUXE DOLL & TOY CO.—U.S.A., 1918-1921. Produced mama-type dolls with composition shoulder heads and limbs on cloth bodies stuffed with cork. Most were distributed by the Bush Terminal.

DELUXE READING CORP.—U.S.A., 1951-1972. Also may be found spelled DeLuxe. Originally the DeLuxe Premium Co.—and the parent company of Deluxe Toys, Deluxe Topper, Topper Corp., Topper Toys, and Deluxe Toy Creations—was founded by Henry Orenstein. Well-known for the lovely vinyl and plastic fashion dolls, many of which were sold through supermarkets across the country. Good quality dolls.

DEMALCOL—London, 1921-1924. Also spelled Demacol, an acronym for Dennis Malley & Co. of London. Specialized in bisque-head dolls that were produced in Germany and Bavaria. Responsible for Dainty May, Little Sunshine, and May Blossom for which trademarks were registered. The Demalcol mark is found on a variety of dolls from fair to good quality.

DENAMUR, ETIENNE—France, 1857-1899. Produced beautiful bisque doll heads as proven by the gold medal award won at the 1890 London Exhibition. Many of the marked E. D. Bébés that have open or closed mouths are of very good quality—and have been attributed to Denamur.

DENIVELLE, OTTO ERNST—U.S.A., 1910-1917. Otto Denivelle remained in the doll manufacturing community for many years after this date, but apparently as an employee for other companies. He, along with his brother, were true pioneers in the composition doll world. Besides perfecting the cold press glue-type composition, they were responsible for much of the training Joseph Kallus received by working for them while attending school. Ironically, Denivelle eventually worked for Kallus at his famous Cameo doll company. Look for the Deco name to identify the good quality composition Denivelle dolls.

DEP—France/Germany, originated in the 1880s. Do not confuse DEP dolls with dolls commonly found with the addition of the letters DEP or Dep. to a registered mold number. DEP was used in both France (for *depose*) and in Germany (for *deponiert*) as a symbol of registration when used in conjunction with a molded and registered number. DEP dolls, on the other hand, are marked only with the letters DEP and a size number incised on the back of the bisque head. Early closed-mouth DEP dolls have exceptionally fine bisque and delicate decoration; later open-mouth DEP dolls, although generally very good in quality, lack the beauty of the earlier dolls. Long accepted as French, at least the later DEP dolls are now widely considered to be German, and most probably manufactured by Simon & Halbig. Quality would be judged on an individual basis from good to very good.

DEPTFORD TOY MAKING INDUSTRY—England, 1917-1919. Also known as the Deptford Fund Toy Making Industry. Produced baby, cloth character, plush, felt, wooden, and jointed dolls. Ostensibly created to raise money needed by the area and its inhabitants during a war-ravaged Europe.

DIETRICH, JOHANNES GOTTHILF—Germany, 1915-1930. Various companies supplied bisque heads for the dolls bearing the Igodi trademark. Remembering that *I* and *J* are interchangeable in German explains how Igodi is the acronym for this doll producer. Bisque heads were supplied by Ernst Heubach and celluloid from Kohl & Wengenroth. The Igodi heads used were of fair quality.

DISNEY—U.S.A., 1930-present. Walt Disney characters are everyone's favorite. Mickey Mouse has been produced in an endless variety of sizes, materials, and styles, but there is always that certain something that makes him instantly recognizable! Every character created by the Walt Disney Studio has been translated into a doll or puppet. One character after another has obtained celebrity status and the parade continues to grow. Quality and desirability varies from the small plastic figures, easily found at flea markets, to the rare and early Mickeys that are in great demand.

DOLÉAC, L. & CIE—France, 1881-1908. Produced bisque dolls on jointed bodies. At least some of the heads used were purchased from François Gaultier.

DOLL, JOHN SR.—U.S.A., 1837-1879, and with his son, John Doll Jr., 1879-1915. One of the interesting companies associated with the doll industry, and another instance of interwoven lives. It was through the efforts of the senior Doll that arrangements were made for Albert Schoenhut, founder of the world-famous Schoenhut Toy Company of Philadelphia, to come to America. The father and son team of Doll were importers and doll jobbers. They supplied inexpensive dolls to wholesalers across the country. This background in importing and distribution may account for John Jr. starting the famous Wanamaker's Toy Department. Unfortunately, John Jr. was aboard the Lusitania when it was sunk during the war in 1915.

DOLL & STUFFED TOY MANUFACTURERS' ASSOCIATION—U.S.A., 1920s. Group of over fifty principal doll and toy manufacturers under the direction of Louis Amberg. Formed to facilitate industrial advancement and to protect investments against a labor strike.

DOLL BODIES COMPANY—U.S.A., mid-twentieth century. Along with marketing a line of hard plastic and vinyl dolls this company also supplied dolls and doll parts to other knockoff companies. Doll Bodies dolls are of fair quality.

DOLL CORPORATION OF AMERICA—U.S.A., 1928-1930 and later. Formed by the merging of Century and Domec doll companies, with a doll factory in Lancaster, Pennsylvania. Century Doll company is a name long associated with good quality dolls, while Domec produced inexpensive dolls of rather poor quality.

DOLL CRAFT—U.S.A., early twentieth century. Produced several knockoff dolls sold through department stores and mail-order catalogs. These composition dolls are found with painted eyes and usually coarse mohair glued directly over molded hair. Although somewhat charming in their appearance and costuming, the quality of Doll Craft dolls is rather poor.

DOLL MANUFACTURERS—England, 1917-1920. Produced dolls with heads and limbs of British Ceramic on cloth bodies. Also made mask face and black dolls.

DOLL POTTERY CO.—England, 1916-1920. Manufactured and sold dolls of British Ceramic using parts supplied by Crown Staffordshire Porcelain Co. A wide variety of types of dolls were offered, including socket and shoulder heads, molded hair or wearing wigs, painted or glass eyes. Also produced a multi-faced doll with one of the faces representing a black child. Many of the molds used to make their dolls were taken from German dolls' heads. The quality of Doll Pottery dolls ranges from poor to good.

Dollcraft Novelty's the Lone Ranger and Tonto, Atlas' Golliwogg, Art Fabric's Foxy Grandpa, Ideal's Howdy Doody, and *Golliwogg in the African Jungle* by Florence Upton (Photo courtesy of Cobb's Doll Auction.)

DOLLCRAFT COMPANY OF AMERICA—U.S.A., 1918-1919. A little-known company located in Newark, New Jersey. Advertised dolls "with clay heads, sleep eyes, and real hair wigs on rubber jointed wooden bodies." Used the name Gie Wa for their dolls.

DOLPHITCH MANUFACTURING CO.—England, 1915-1918. Founded by D. A. and Mrs. W. Fitch for the purpose of manufacturing dolls and doll clothing. Various types of dolls were produced including composition, British Ceramic, cloth, and wax. The most popular appears to be composition and wax babies with articulated composition bodies.

DOMEC TOY CO.—U.S.A., 1918-1928. Merged with Century Doll Company and formed the Doll Corporation of America. The Domec trademark was used for several years after the 1928 merger. Responsible for a variety of inexpensive composition dolls. Best known for Giggles and Kewty doll. Domec produced a rather poor quality doll.

DOMINION TOY MANUFACTURING CO.—Canada, 1911-1919. Produced several sizes of character dolls of composition with rivet joints at shoulder and hips.

DOOR OF HOPE DOLLS—China, 1901-1949. Named for the Protestant mission founded to rescue destitute children and slave girls in Shanghai. The girls were taught needlework, embroidery, knitting, and other skills needed to costume the wooden dolls that they sold. The clothing representation was so exact that a girl working five days a week could dress only one doll a month. The head, hands, and arms—to the elbows—were carved of pearwood. The finish was so smooth that no paint or varnish was required except for the eyes and mouth. A few rare examples have fancy buns or flowers carved in their hair. Cloth bodies were stuffed with raw cotton and occasionally a doll is found with cloth stub hands. The handmade elaborate costumes were exact copies of clothing worn by the Chinese people and are of excellent quality. Reportedly less than 50,000 Door of Hope Dolls were ever produced, adding greatly to their desirability.

DORST, JULIUS—Germany, 1839-mid 1930s and possibly later. Produced wooden and composition dolls—important in the German doll and toy industry. One of the founders of the Sonneberg Industrial School. The wood-jointed dolls by Dorst won several awards. A 1904 catalog features patented circus dolls that closely resembled the Schoenhut entourage. In 1909, the Crown Prince of Prussia ordered an assortment of Dorst's wooden toys to be made for his children. Although rare, occasionally a Dorst doll will be found.

DREAM WORLD DOLLS—U.S.A., early twentieth century. Manufactured small inexpensive composition shelf dolls by the thousands. Most popular were the international and personality dolls. All composition, jointed at neck, shoulders, and hips with painted side glancing eyes. Dream World Dolls are of surprisingly good quality.

DRESSEL, CUNO & OTTO—Germany, 1700s-1945. The Dressel family operated a toy business in Sonneberg for over two hundred years. It is the oldest toy manufacturer for which there are conclusively accurate business records. The firm passed from one generation of Dressels to the next, and in 1873 became the Cuno & Otto Dressel Factory. The toys they sold were not all original products—they purchased bisque doll heads from Armand Marseille, Simon & Halbig, Ernst Heubach, and Gebrüder Heubach. They also depended on cottage industries to help stock the incredible assortment of 30,000 different toys and dolls in their inventory. The Dressel partnership proved to be very successful. They expanded to three factories: one in Sonneberg for dolls, one in Nürnberg for metal toys, and one in Grunhainichen for wooden toys. It is not surprising that Cuno & Otto Dressel produced several different types of dolls. Bisque, composition, and wax in character babies, child, lady, and portrait styles. Generally the quality of Dressel dolls is quite good.

DRESSEL & KOCH—Germany, 1893-1897. Porcelain factory that produced doll heads among other things. In 1896 they advertised "immediate vacancy for a capable sculptor whose position, at the same time should involve the task of a technical director." The next year the company was dissolved and became Koch & Weithase, until 1902, when the ownership changed again and continued for a time under the Hering & Weithase name.

DRESSEL & PIETSCHMANN—Germany, early to mid-1900s. Advertised a jointed doll. The Puppen und Spielwarenfabrik (factory for dolls and toys) at Coburg obviously produced a variety of toys as their trademark indicates; however, little information is available about this company.

DURA PORCELAIN CO.—England, 1915-1918. Produced doll heads and limbs of British Ceramic. They can be found with shoulder or socket heads, painted hair or a wig, painted or glass eyes. The quality of the known examples is good. It must be remembered that British Ceramic cannot be compared to bisque, as they are manufactured differently.

E

EAST LONDON TOY FACTORY—England, 1915-1928. Also known as the East London Federation of Suffragettes Toy Factory. Produced cloth dolls with molded faces jointed at the neck and shoulders. Also, character babies with British Ceramic or wax heads, and a long-limbed novelty doll.

EATON, T. CO.—Canada, around turn of the twentieth century-1930s and possibly later. Sold various types of dolls under the Eaton name, some of which were supplied by Cuno & Otto Dressel. This information is according to Dressel's records and not Eaton's. Advertised a complete line of dolls including mama, black, rubber, dollhouse, bisque, china, and metal.

ECCLES—England, 1921-1926. Also trading as New Eccles Rubber Works. Manufactured dolls made from rubber with molded costumes.

ECKART & CO.—Germany, 1820-1930s. Also had outlets in England. Sold dolls produced by Bessels, Carl Max, Wittzak, and Ernest Heubach. In 1922 they advertised that their entire inventory was being shipped for immediate sales to their London warehouse.

ECKSTEIN, HERMANN—Germany, 1899-1920. Produced waxed, papier-mâché, and bisque bent-limb character babies and infants, along with long-limbed cloth novelty dolls. At least some of the bisque-head dolls had flirty eyes. Hermann Eckstein dolls are of fair quality.

ECLIPSE DOLL MANUFACTURING CO.—U.S.A., 1919-1921. The early dolls from this New England doll company were all composition, fully jointed child dolls in heights of 15, 19, and 22 inches. Later, composition-head baby dolls were introduced having molded and painted hair, or wearing a wig with painted facial features and cloth bodies.

EDELMANN, EDMUND—Germany, 1921-at least 1933. Produced bisque and celluloid dolls to be exported under the business names of Melitta, Mine, and Mona. Most of the bisque heads used to produce the character babies and child dolls were from Armand Marseille or Schoenau & Hoffmeister. Edmund Edelmann dolls are of fair quality.

EDEN BÉBÉ—France, 1890-1899. The trade name is a more familiar term than the manufacturer, Fleischmann & Bloedel, that produced them. The company was established in 1873, and in 1899 Salomon Fleischmann formed, and became director of, the S. F. B. J., making Fleischmann & Bloedel Doll Factory its first charter member. When World War I erupted in Europe, Fleischmann was unwilling to forfeit his German citizenship, and returned to his native land. He died soon after in Spain. The company changed directors and ownership many times and eventually claimed bankruptcy in the early 1920s. The Eden Bébé was the pride of Fleischmann & Bloedel. Offered in several different versions, including open or closed mouth, white, black, walking, and kissing. Also available in bisque and composition. The bisque and composition heads were supplied by various French and German doll factories. The quality of an Eden Bébé can be very good to mediocre.

EDWARDS & PAMFLETT, MESDAMES—England, 1918-1923. Produced dolls with composition head and limbs on cloth bodies along with fully jointed all-composition dolls. Registered the name Cecily Dolls.

EEGEE DOLL MANUFACTURING CO.—U.S.A., 1917-contemporary. Founded by Mr. and Mrs. E. Goldberger, the trademark EEGEE was adopted in 1923. Eegee is one of the longest running, continuously operating manufacturers of dolls in the United States. Never really achieving the level of fame acquired by many other doll companies, they constantly strove to introduce innovative and appealing quality dolls.

EFFANBEE—U.S.A., 1910-present. An acronym for Fleischaker & Baum, the founders. One of the great pioneers of the American doll industry and responsible for many of the significant innovations and improvements made in the last century, including the realistically proportioned Patsy, the first doll for which companions were created, who had a specially designed

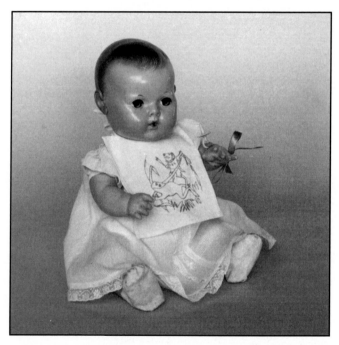

Effanbee Dy-Dee Baby

wardrobe and her own fan club. Also, makers of the contemporary Limited Edition Doll Club Dolls. Effanbee continues its image of being on the edge of innovation. Effanbee dolls can be found in all styles of composition, hard plastic, rubber, and vinyl. A high quality play doll.

EHRICH BROTHERS—U.S.A., 1827-1907. It is possible that they operated in other years besides these that are documented. Advertised dolls with bisque heads on bodies of composition, kid, or cloth. Also a line of china-head, composition, wax, and rubber dolls.

EICHHORN, CHRISTIAN & SÖHNE— Germany, 1909-1930. Porcelain factory founded by Max and Albert Eichhorn at a much earlier date. By 1910 porcelain dolls and doll heads were shown at the Leipzig Toy Fair. Also advertised bisque bathing dolls, marbles, and other glass toys. Christian Eichhorn dolls are of good quality.

EICHHORN, MARTIN—Germany, 1889-late 1930s. The factory and export doll business was founded by Martin and Ida. Produced several types of dolls distributed by Borgfeldt in the United States, and Rees & Co. in England. At least some of the bisque baby heads were supplied by Armand Marseille and used on cloth bodies. A contract was also negotiated between Eichhorn and Berghold, Blechschmidt & Liebermann, owners of a slip mill for the production of "solid doll heads." Martin Eichhorn dolls are of fair quality.

EISEN, LOUIS—U.S.A., 1927-1929. Manufactured and imported cloth dolls. It is assumed that the dolls were from France. Advertisements included, "Exquisite Parisian Beauties at Low Prices." Expect to find felt dolls with pressed mask-type faces, large side glancing eyes, and closed mouth. Appropriately dressed to portray clowns, French peasants, artists, and children. The art dolls offered by Louis Eisen are of good quality.

EISENMANN & CO.—England and Bavaria, 1881-at least until 1940. Also known as Einco. Founded by Gabriel (at Fürth) and Joseph (at London) Eisenmann. (Eisenmann was known as King of the Toy Trade.) Einco produced and distributed dolls for which Gebrüder Heubach supplied the bisque heads. Eisenmann & Co. dolls are of good quality.

EISENSTÄDT, ISIDOR & CO.—Germany, 1895-1903. A small, little-known doll factory that produced walking dolls—including a cloth-bodied walking doll, and a doll that was jointed with the company's patented "interlocking forks."

ELECTROSOLIDS CORPORATION—U.S.A., mid-twentieth century. Also known as Elsco. Produced Ellie Echo, the Famous Tape Recorder Doll.

ELEKTRA TOY & NOVELTY CO.—U.S.A., 1912-1920. Produced an overwhelming number of composition dolls in the relatively short time that they were in business. Both cloth-bodied and all-composition-types are found, most with painted eyes and hair. Some are molded with a hole at the top of the head in which hair was inserted into and left to fall naturally around the face. The earlier Elektra dolls are of good quality; the later dolls, however, lose some of the workmanship that was obvious in the earlier dolls.

ELITE DOLL CO.—England, 1915-1918. Produced several lines of British Ceramic-head dolls. Also produced shoulder-head dolls on cloth bodies with British Ceramic hands or socket heads on jointed composition bodies. The dolls wear wigs and have painted, stationary, or sleep eyes. They range from 10 to 16 inches tall.

ELLIS, JOEL—See Co-Operative Manufacturing Co.

ELLISON, REES & CO.—England, 1920. Founded by Leon Rees, later to be known as L. Rees & Co. Trading with the name Ellarco, Chesham Brand, & Dolleries. Distributed Impy and Union Jack Baby. It is unclear if Impy was a doll molded after a character in a comic strip, or simply shared his name. The Union Jack baby had a fully jointed body and was advertised as the first doll sold in England with sleep eyes.

ELMS & SELLON—U.S.A. At least 1910-1918. Also known as Elms & Co. Produced cut-out sew-at-home dolls by the yard. The lithographed dolls were printed at Art Fabric Mill and Arnold Print Works. The characters that Elms and Sellon sold are among the most collectible of rag dolls, including Punch and Judy and Topsy Turvy.

ELTONA TOY CO.—U.S.A., 1919-1921. Imported dolls from various manufacturers. Advertised quality bisque-head dolls with sleep eyes and human hair wigs. Also sold more moderately priced dolls with cardboard or cloth bodies and painted eyes.

EMPIRE PORCELAIN CO.—England, 1916-1970. A long-running porcelain factory that apparently produced British Ceramic doll heads for a time during World War I. The Empire Porcelain dolls are of good quality, and they are collectible for their comeliness and historic value.

ENGLISH DOLL MANUFACTURING CO.—England, 1916-1917. A short-lived manufacturer that produced dolls with British Ceramic heads on cloth bodies, wigs or molded and painted hair and facial features, or glass sleep eyes. Also offered an inexpensive cloth doll.

ENGLISH RAG DOLLS—England, 1892. A line of cloth dolls with mask-type faces with blown-glass eyes. Well dressed to represent nursery rhyme and story book characters. Advertised as a Marshall Field exclusive.

ENGLISH TOY MANUFACTURING CO.—England, 1914-1915. Another interesting member of the doll world. Established by and for women at the outbreak of World War I. The purpose was to provide employment to women and young girls affected by the war. Reportedly, they manufactured all the doll parts themselves. According to their own accounts, by the end of the first year they were producing 1,000 doll heads and

300 "ready made dolls" per week. They further claimed to develop a process of producing eyes of such good quality as to rival the Germans.

ERHARD, STEPHEN—England, 1887-1930. After 1926, the company became S. Erhard Son. Produced and imported dolls. According to records, celluloid dolls dominated the inventory carried by this company. Also advertised an Indian rubber doll. Registered a diamond with *S. E. S.* as their trademark.

ESCHER, J. G.—Germany, 1790-1928. Also known as J. G. Escher & Sohn. An early toy factory, but no conclusive records of dolls being manufactured until after 1874. Known to have produced wooden dolls and bisque dolls using Armand Marseille's 390 head on fully jointed and straight-legged bodies. Also advertised celluloid-head dolls from their own painting shop. Used the initials *I. G. E. S.*

ETTA INC.—U.S.A., 1927-1930. An innovated and progressive company founded by Miss Etta Kidd, a doll designer. The company was not only founded and owned by a woman, but all the employees were also women. Best known for the boudoir-type dolls, they also produced a complete line of art dolls with hand-painted faces. Etta dolls are well made and of good quality.

EUREKA DOLL CO.—U.S.A., 1923-1930 and beyond. With S. O. Ludwig as their factory agent, this company, also known as Eureka Doll Manufacturing Co., grew from a small company offering a few moderately priced composition mama dolls to selling a large variety of character babies, including their own Baby in a Cradle. The dolls came with molded and painted hair and eyes, or with a wig and sleep eyes; beautifully costumed in silks. Eureka dolls range in quality from fair to good.

EUROPEAN DOLL MANUFACTURING CO.—U.S.A., 1911-1930s. Contrary to the name, this company, using the acronym EDMA, manufactured dolls in their own United States factory. Produced composition mama, baby, and infant dolls—the majority of which were wholesaled to various doll companies. Towards the end of the 1920s, cloth novelty dolls were introduced to meet the demands of the consumer. EDMA dolls are of rather mediocre quality.

EXELOID CO.—U.S.A., perhaps as early as 1915, but surely by 1918-1920. With factories in New Jersey and Pennsylvania to meet the demands for the lightweight, inexpensive celluloid dolls produced by this company. The plastic used was marketed by the name Pyralin and manufactured by Du Pont. By a process where a thin sheet, approximated 5/1000-20/1000 of an inch, is forced by hot air into molds, and was used to produce the novelty dolls made of pink, blue, and white. Exeloid also offered a wooden doll produced at a third factory.

EXPOSITION DOLL & TOY MANUFACTURING CO.—U.S.A., 1921-at least 1934. Manufactured a variety of dolls, including composition mama dolls with Voices, Inc., criers, baby dolls, and character dolls. Some dolls were offered with sleep eyes and mohair wigs. Also licensed by the Gruelle family to produce the famous Raggedy Ann and Andy dolls; however, the legal problems with Molly-'es erupted about the same time, and few Exposition Raggedy Ann or Andys exist today.

F

FABRICIUS TOY & NOVELTY CO.—U.S.A., 1858-1914. Importer and wholesaler to several jobbers in the mid-western parts of the United States. Supplying bisque, composition, and celluloid dolls and doll parts.

FAIR TRADING CO.—U.S.A., 1921-1927. Small and short-lived company which distributed dolls from its New York City office, until they were sued for infringement rights by the American Doll Manufacturers' Association.

FAIRY GIFT CO.—U.S.A., 1925-1926. Produced a sew-at-home doll kit complete with an all-bisque doll jointed at shoulder and hips with painted eyes, closed mouth, and mohair wig. Came boxed with fabric, ribbons, lace, safety scissors, needle, and thimble. Fairy Gift doll sets are highly collectible.

FAIRYLAND DOLL CO.—U.S.A., 1903-1909. Wholesale and retail dealer of dressed cloth dolls with flat hand-painted faces, manufactured at the M. C. W. Foote factory. Could be purchased by mail order.

FALCK & ROUSSEL—France, 1880-1902. Also known as Adolphe Falck. Produced dolls with bisque heads on composition and wood-jointed bodies. Look for molded and painted hair and eyes, and bébés with wigs and glass eyes. At least some of the bisque heads were supplied by François Gaultier. Falck & Roussel bisque-head dolls are of good quality.

FAM DOLL CO.—U.S.A., early twentieth century. Produced an all-composition doll with tin sleep eyes, and an open/closed mouth with molded upper teeth on a fully jointed composition body.

FAMOUS DOLL STUDIO—U.S.A., 1906-1922. Advertised using a bisque-finished composition known as bisquette. Produced character dolls with composition head and arms on cloth bodies with either painted or sleep eyes and wig.

FARNELL, J. K. & CO.—England, 1871-1940 and beyond. Farnell's Alpha Toys began producing dolls made of felt, velvet, stockinette, and fabrics around 1920. The chubby felt dolls featured painted side glancing eyes and smiling mouths. Stockinette bodies have seams at the front, back, and sides of each leg. Hair consists of mohair sewn in a circular pattern onto the head, or a human hair wig. Dolls with velvet faces and bodies were also made. All Farnell dolls are of good quality. Especially collectible is the King Edward VIII Coronation Doll, which was quickly removed from the market following his abdication.

FASHION TYPE DOLLS—France, Germany, and Austria, 1860-1930. Also known as Poupée de Mode. Modeled as lady dolls with bisque heads on bodies of kid, cloth, and/or wood. May have painted or glass eyes and closed mouths. There is ample evidence that this type of doll was intended to be a play doll, but at the same time could be it was used by some merchants as mannequins to display the latest fashions. Quality can range between good and excellent depending on the manufacturer.

FAULTLESS RUBBER CO.—U.S.A., 1916-1923. Manufactured all rubber novelty-type dolls with or without molded costumes. Few rubber dolls withstood the test of time without deteriorating.

FEDERAL DOLL MANUFACTURING CO.—U.S.A., 1917-1926. Originally operating two factories, one for the purpose of manufacturing the composition heads and the other as an assembly plant to make the dolls, they shortly consolidated into one. The majority of dolls were made with composition heads and limbs on cloth bodies, with or without wigs, and with painted or tin sleep eyes.

FIBEROID DOLL PRODUCTS CO.—U.S.A., 1927-1930. Members of the Doll Parts Manufacturing Association. Produced composition dolls and doll parts.

FIEGENBAUM & CO.—U.S.A., 1884. A California-based importer and distributor of better dolls from Europe, including German bisque and French Bébés, china and English wax. Also advertised trousseaux, creeping babies, and swimming dolls. It is assumed that all or at least most of Fiegenbaum dolls are of very good quality.

FIRST AMERICAN DOLL FACTORY—U.S.A., 1892-1908. After 1896, known as the American Doll & Toy Co., and after 1908, absorbed by Benjamin Goldenberg. Manufactured dolls with composition heads and hands on cloth bodies with glass eyes and good wigs. Dolls from First American Factory are of good quality and great historic significance.

FISCHER, NAUMANN & CO.—Germany, 1852-1938 and possibly later. A seemingly successful factory that produced bathing dolls, doll accessories, and leather bodies among other household necessities. One advertisement lists a terra cotta doll. The well-made leather bodies were supplied to other companies, and sold directly to the public.

FISHER PRICE—U.S.A., 1930s-present. A well-known toy manufacturer operating through their New York state distribution offices. The earliest toys were wooden pull toys. After 1949 Fisher Price began using plastic in their manufacturing. Dolls are a rather new addition to the lineup. Fisher Price dolls are a good quality play doll of vinyl and cloth.

FLEISCHMANN, GEBRÜDER—Germany, 1880-1940s. Operated as a doll and toy exporting business, and expanded after purchasing Louis Lindner & Söhne in 1928. Lists leather dolls and dressed dolls as being offered for exportation.

FLEISCHMANN, SALOMON & BLOEDEL, JEAN—France, 1873-1926. This company was established in 1873, and continued until 1899, when Salomon Fleishmann formed and became director of the S. F. B. J., making Fleischmann and Bloedel Doll Factory its first charter member. When World War I erupted in Europe, Fleischmann was unwilling to forfeit his German citizenship, therefore returning to his native land. He died soon after in Spain. The company changed directors and ownership many times and eventually claimed bankruptcy in the early 1920s. The Eden Bébé was the pride of Fleischmann and Bloedel. Offered in several different versions, including open or closed mouth, white, black, walking, and kissing, and available in bisque and composition. The bisque and compo-

Fleischmann & Bloedel's Eden Bébé, and Closed-Mouth Rabery & Delphieu Bébé (Photo courtesy of Cobb's Doll Auction.)

sition heads were supplied by various French and German doll factories. The quality of an Eden Bébé can be very good to mediocre.

FLEISCHMANN, ADOLF & CRÄMER, CARL— Germany, 1844-present. (Also spelled *Craemer*) These two entrepreneurs combined their efforts to become a leading force in the German doll and toy industry. Manufactured and distributed doll heads of papier-mâché, Täufling, and wax on bodies of kid or cloth.

FLEMING DOLL CO.—U.S.A., 1922-1924. A very small and little-known doll manufacturer from Kansas City. Advertised Tum Tum rubber dolls and waterproof oil cloth floating dolls.

FLORA'S FAMOUS DOLLS—U.S.A., 1915-1928. Necessity is the mother of inventions, and there is no substitute for Yankee know-how. These two sayings come immediately to mind when thinking of this doll. When trade was interrupted with Europe during World War I, many attempts were made to fill the gap. Mrs. Grace Wheeler and her daughter Florence made and sold dolls through traveling salesmen. Making molds from an Armand Marseille 390, and a Schoenau & Hoffmeister 1906, they poured a plaster of Paris base and covered it with treated cloth. The unbleached muslin bodies were painted a flesh color with black shoes painted on the feet. Wigs of angora were fitted to the head, and facial features were hand painted. Flora's dolls have a great deal of charm and historic value. The craftsmanship that went into their creation and development is really quite good.

FÖSTER, GUSTAV—Germany, 1922-1930s. This maker and exporter of dolls and toys inventoried a wide variety of play and novelty items such as mama, character, baby, black, Indian, and mascot-type dolls. Also, toys and dolls of felt and papier-mâché, carnival dolls, pull toys, and holiday ornaments.

FOULDS & FREURE—U.S.A., 1911-1913, and possibly later. The original founder, Robert Foulds came to America from Scotland in the early 1800s and started a dry goods business. Later, organized by his nephew Robert, the company began specializing in toys. In 1911, Richard Freure joined them to form the new partnership of Foulds & Freure for the purpose of importing dolls and doll parts, as well as being a doll jobber—supplying bisque, celluloid, and metal heads from Germany and, later, Japan.

FRÈRES, BERTOLI—France, late 1890s, and possibly other years. Little is known or reported about the Marseilles-based company, other than the name Idéal Bébé was registered in 1895.

FREUNDLICH, RALPH A., INC.—1923-at least 1942, and perhaps later. Until 1929, this company operated as the Jeanette Doll Co., and then changed the name to Ralph A. Freundlich. It continued to produce dolls, mostly with composition head and limbs, on light-weight cloth bodies. Also popular for the novelty-type composition dolls, such as Douglas MacArthur and Little Orphan Annie. Most Freundlich dolls are not marked; therefore, accurate identification can be difficult. Research has relied largely on old advertisements and catalogs. The quality of the dolls produced over the years varies form very poor to very good.

FULPER POTTERY CO.—U.S.A., 1918-1921. Of course, Fulper was in operation much longer: Since 1805, the company produced lovely art pottery pieces and household goods. It was between 1918 and 1922 that Fulper was in the doll manufacturing business. Due to import shortages caused by World War I, the company began producing bisque dolls and doll heads—using German molds, as well as doll molds from American companies, such as Amberg and Horsman. It is not unusual to find a doll marked with the Fulper name alongside the specific company for which the heads were produced. The quality of Fulper dolls ranges from very poor to very good. The historic value is as noteworthy to collectors as their aesthetic value.

FURGA, LUIGI & CO.—Italy, 1872-present. By way of a history for this Italian doll manufacturer, *Pupeide* once published an article explaining, "In the 1870s Luigi Furga, an Italian nobleman, who owned property in Canneto, decided to begin making dolls with the help of Ceresa, who had acquired the art of making papier-mâché masks in Germany . . . ." The first dolls from the Furga factory were of papier-mâché and wax. Later, bisque heads were imported from Germany to be used on Furga dolls. When doll production was interrupted by World War I, they built their own porcelain factory for their bisque heads and small all-bisque dolls. By 1929, *Playthings* reported that Furga bisque heads rivaled the German bisque that was being produced at the time. They also produced a limited number of pressed felt dolls along with composition, vinyl, and hard plastic. In the span of over one hundred years, they have examined, experimented, and applied all possible techniques to the doll industry. The early dolls were only exported to England, Brazil, and other South American countries, which explains why so few Furga bisque dolls are found on the American secondary market. The fantastically dressed ladies, sweet babies, and charming child dolls of Furga are all collectible and of good quality.

G

GABRIEL, SAMUEL, SONS & CO.—U.S.A., 1916-1928. Produced and sold dolls. Advertised fifty-six character dolls in their Mother Goose series. This company's dolls are small, all composition; jointed at neck, shoulders, and hips; with large side-glancing painted eyes. They also produced a Sew and Dress Doll—a cardboard paper doll-type that was so popular then.

GALLAIS, P. J. & CIE—France, 1917-1925. Although best known as a book wholesaler and distributor, they nevertheless were responsible for Yerri and Gretel dolls (based on the drawings of Hansi). These very collectible Alsatian character dolls with their exaggerated features were made entirely of Prialytine with molded hair and features. Yerri and Gretel are of good quality.

GALLUBA & HOFMANN—Germany, 1888-1926. A well-known and respected porcelain factory, it produced dolls and doll heads, and employed up to five hundred workers at its peak in 1897. Responsible for Vienna-style fashion dolls, bathing beauties in suits of silk net, pincushion dolls, and tea cozy shoulder heads. Sadly, in 1911, Galluba, who had spent years perfecting the porcelain business and improving the conditions of the industry, suffered a seizure and was left partially paralyzed and so physically challenged that he was forced to give up his civic and business activities.

GANS, OTTO—Germany, 1901-1930s. Otto Gans was involved in the doll industry, having registered a patent for eye movement in 1901. Between 1908 and 1922, he was in partnership with Heller & Seyfarth forming the Gans & Seyfarth Puppenfabrik. After the 1922 division of Gans & Seyfarth, Otto once again opened his own company. It advertised, "bisque doll heads of our own fabrication, porcelain bathing dolls marked My Dearie." Later, it is assumed that celluloid dolls were also offered. Otto Gans dolls are of fair quality.

GANS & SEYFARTH—Germany, 1908-1922. A relatively small and short-lived doll manufacturer operating during some of the most difficult years for the German doll industry. The exact relationship and regulating procedures relating to their doll design and manufacturing are difficult to discern. At least some of the bisque heads were supplied by Armand Marseille.

GAULTIER, FRANÇOIS—France, 1860-1899, and until 1916 as part of S. F. B. J. (also spelled *Gauthier* before 1875). An interesting side note: In 1875, François Gauthier was arrested and brought to court, but the charges were dropped because of mistaken identity. Gauthier was understandably upset, and trying to prove his case was hindered by a fire that had destroyed the town records in 1871. To avoid further embarrassment he changed the spelling of his name to Gaultier. Along with Jumeau, Bru, and Steiner, Gaultier earned a reputation for refined and exquisitely crafted bisque dolls—resulting in their producing heads for Gesland, Jullien, Rabery & Delphieu, Thiuller, and others. He also manufactured bisque-head Poupée de Mode with glass or painted eyes, and Block or Scroll mark Bébés with open or closed mouth. Subtle pale complexion, delicately blushed eyelids, large wide-set lustrous paperweight eyes, plump cheeks, and full, slightly outlined, parted lips help to distinguish these high-quality dolls.

GEM TOY CO.—U.S.A., 1913-at least 1931. Adopted the name Gem Doll Corp. in the late 1920s. Produced dolls of all composition or composition head and limbs with cloth bodies. Wearing wigs or molded and painted hair, sleep or painted eyes.

GEORGENE NOVELTIES—U.S.A., 1920-1950s. A name long associated with the doll industry, with affiliations to Averill by way of marriage. The Georgene Doll title was used to register several character dolls. Raggedy Ann and Andy and Maude Tousey Fangel are among the most popular. Georgene Novelties dolls are highly collectible and of good quality.

GERLING TOY CO.—U.S.A., 1912-1930s and possibly later. Produced a large variety of dolls including at least one bisque-head infant characterized by pierced nostrils with softly painted hair, painted or glass eyes, and closed mouth on cloth body with composition limbs. Also produced character, mama, and boudoir dolls from composition, a line of cloth art dolls, and voice boxes to be used in dolls. Registered Black Bottom Doll as a trademark in 1927.

GESLAND, E.—France, 1860-1928. Produced, exported, distributed, and repaired bisque dolls. Advertised that from his Paris factory he could "repair in ten minutes bébés and dolls of all makes and replace broken heads." Most, but not all, of the bisque heads used by Gesland were supplied by Gaultier. Early dolls show outstanding body features, with a frame of steel covered with tin. Joints were riveted to facilitate movement. The framework was wrapped in kapok, or cotton, to give it a natural shape, and then covered with stockinette or fine lambskin, with hands and feet of bisque or painted wood. These early dolls could be posed in a variety of lifelike positions. Gesland bisque dolls of the Poupée de Mode or Bébé type are of good to very good quality.

GIEBELER-FALK DOLL CORP.—U.S.A., 1918-1921. A rather unfamiliar name to many collectors, they produced dolls with aluminum heads on very well-made wooden bodies, some having rubber joints. Primadonna, their phonograph doll, gained a certain degree of popularity. Not only did she have an appealing face, she had an interesting mechanical mechanism. The clockworks were located in the torso. A crank handle in the neck rotated the turntable which was positioned in the head. The head held the record, played by a needle. Access to the turntable to change the records was through the top of the head. Having the mechanism within the head allows the voice to come out through the mouth. Giebeler-Falk dolls are of good quality.

GIROUX, ALPHONSE & CIE—France, about 1860-1880. An obscure manufacturer that apparently made a papier-mâché shoulder head doll with a kid body (according to records), also advertised a doll that "cries mama" and stated that "original articles of the firm's own invention can be obtained nowhere else."

GODEY LADY DOLLS—U.S.A., 1940s. Also known as Ruth Gibbs' Godey's Little Lady Dolls. Small china-head dolls designed by Herbert Johnson and made by Ruth Gibbs of pink or white slip with cloth bodies and crude china limbs. Lightly molded and painted hair (although occasionally one will be found wearing a wig), painted facial features with very little detail. Godey Lady Dolls was a name also used by Charlotte Eldridge for her handcrafted papier-mâché dolls which were made with great attention to detail, especially in costuming and physical characteristics.

GOEBEL, WILLIAM—Germany, 1876-present. Also known as F. & W. Goebel. Founded by the father-son team of Franz Detleff and William Goebel to produce porcelain and earthenware ornamental objects. William, the son, became sole owner of the factory in 1892, changing the company name to William Goebel. Responsible for the manufacturing of fine bisque dolls of all kinds, including all-bisque, shoulder heads on bodies of kid, and socket head on composition bodies, also beautifully sculptured half dolls, bathing dolls and delicate ballerina figurines along with practical and decorative porcelain objects. Goebel dolls are of good quality.

GOLDBERGER, EUGENE—U.S.A., 1917-contemporary. Founded by Mr. & Mrs. E. Goldberger; however, better known as Eegee, a trademark that was adopted in 1923. One of the longest-running continuously operating manufacturers of dolls in the United States. Although the company never achieved the level of fame acquired by many other doll companies, Eegee constantly strove to introduce innovative and appealing quality dolls.

GOLDMAN, MOLLY—U.S.A., 1929-1970. Founder of the International Doll Company, known as Molly-'es. There are several controversies and misunderstandings concerning agreements and licensing with Molly-'es. She was unhappy with her circumstances at several of the companies that she designed for, feeling that she was taken advantage of financially. She also was named in a court case involving copyrights to the Raggedy Ann and Andy dolls that she produced. The Gruelle family was victorious and Molly had to discontinue producing the cloth dolls bearing the Raggedy name. Also see International Doll Company.

GOLDSMITH, PHILIP—U.S.A., 1870-1894. Better known for the patented body construction than for the completed dolls they produced. Founded by Philip Goldsmith and his wife. Goldsmith doll bodies are recognizable by the corset that was often part of the body with braid or rickrack trim. The corset and the footwear were most often of the same color. Patented corset included a separate lacing system up the front, allowing the strings to be drawn up tightly to control the appearance of the body. Some of the Goldsmith bodies did not have the corset incorporated into the body itself, but are still easily detected by their leather hands made with small wooden splinters sewn into the fingers, the high curved-top leather or died cotton boots with tan string tassel, and a band of contrasting colored material encircling the stocking to look like a garter. A patent number, size number, or the name My Dolly may be found stamped on the body. The heads, purchased elsewhere, were of papier-mâché, china, bisque, or composition. Goldsmith dolls are of good quality and great historic value.

GOODWYN, LADY—U.S.A., 1926-1927. Produced handcrafted, often life-sized dolls on a custom order basis. The dolls were made of silk with hand-painted facial features and human hair wigs. Elaborate costumes were also made of silk. According to an early trade article, Goodwyn dolls cost up to $3,000, a considerable sum for the mid-1920s.

GOOGLY-EYED DOLL—Various countries, 1912-1938. Most of the early twentieth-century doll manufacturers produced these charming characters. The name Googly Eyed probably comes from the German *Guck Augen* meaning eyes ogling to one side. The mere mention of a Googly Eyes doll can easily bring any doll collector to their knees. The small comedians demonstrate their youthful exuberance with their snub noses, rounded faces, wide alert eyes, and small smiling mouths. Made from all types of materials.

GÖTZ—Germany, contemporary. Owned and operated by Hans Götz and Ana Kalinke. Manufacturer of soft vinyl dolls with sleep eyes and rooted hair—or, in rare cases, a wig. Nicely costumed. A high quality play doll.

GORHAM COMPANY—U.S.A., contemporary. Produced a large line of collector dolls, nicely costumed. Many contain music boxes. A good quality collectible doll.

GOVE MANUFACTURING CO—U.S.A., 1928-1929. Founded by Helen N. Gove. A small, little-known central Pennsylvania doll manufacturing company, registering the trademark UNEKE for their dolls.

GRÄFENTHAL PORZELLANFABRIK—Germany, 1861-1886. Founded by Unger, Schneider, and Hutschenreuther by the Duke's concession, and named for its location in the region of Thuringia, Germany. Produced, among their practical and ornamental objects, china shoulder heads that were supplied to other doll manufacturers.

GRAND DOLL MANUFACTURING CO.—U.S.A., 1923. A short-lived, little-known doll manufacturer from Brooklyn, New York.

GRANDJEAN—France, 1887-1890. Produced pressed bisque-head dolls on jointed composition and wooden bodies. At least some of the bisque heads were supplied by Delcroix. Reported to have made over two million of their Bébé Bijou dolls in the short time they were in operation. Grandjean dolls are of very good quality.

GRANT PLASTICS, INC.—U.S.A., 1950s-contemporary. One of the many knockoff companies that supplied dress-me type dolls to wholesalers or other profit organizations. Grant hard plastic and vinyl dolls are of fair quality.

GRAY, JANE, CO.—U.S.A., 1915-1929. Also spelled Grey. Designed and produced dolls with cloth bodies including Kuddles, and her most famous Margaret Vale's Celebrity Creation, a collection of famous performers.

GRAY & DUDLEY CO.—U.S.A., 1918. Advertised selling over thirty styles of composition dolls with cloth bodies. Either wearing a mohair wig or molded and painted hair.

GREIF PUPPENKUNST—Germany, 1927-1928. Owned and operated by Erich Reiser. *Puppenkunst* is German for "art dolls." It advertised felt and plush dolls, and the firm's slogan was: "Genuine race, the really softly stuffed extra class, among others also animal art." Produced the soft-bodied dolls with heads of celluloid, bisque, and composition. The bisque heads were supplied by Ernst Heubach.

GREINER, LUDWIG—U.S.A., 1840-1874, and 1874-1883, operated as Ludwig Sons; 1883-1890 as Greiner Brothers; and 1890-1900 as Francis S. Knell AKA Knell Brothers. Although records show Ludwig Greiner was a toy maker in Philadelphia, Pennsylvania, in 1840-1858 marks the years that the first-known patent for a papier-mâché doll's head was granted to him. Papier-mâché heads were reinforced from within by lining with strips of linen or silk, and given molded and painted wavy hair styled to give the appearance of a high forehead and rather broad face. A snub nose and unsmiling closed mouth give a sober expression. Cloth bodies with kid arms. Labeled with either a '58 or an Ext. '72 date. Ludwig Greiner dolls are of good quality, with historical importance.

GREINER & CO.—Germany, 1860-1938 and possibly later. Founded by Christoph Zitzmann and F. C. Greiner. The name remained the same even after Greiner left the company in 1890. Originally a trading company, they began producing leather bodies and doll parts, along with bisque shoulder-head dolls on leather bodies. In later years, also sold a line of oil treated or waxed cloth bodies. Bisque heads were supplied by Armand Marseille, Christian Eichhorn, and Ernst Heubach. Greiner & Co. dolls are of mediocre quality.

GRE-POIR, INC.—U.S.A., 1927-early 1930s. Produced a line of felt and cloth dolls under the supervision of Alvin Grey. Advertised as being designed by Eugenie Poir of Paris; however, the directories do not list Eugenie Poir as a doll designer. Gre-Poir dolls are well made with either a pressed-felt or a mask-type face, with mohair wigs, painted facial features with side glancing eyes, and real hair upper eyelashes. On cloth bodies jointed at the neck, shoulders, and hips. Gre-Poir dolls are of good quality.

GRUELLE, JOHN B.—U.S.A., 1915-1938 and beyond (under various copyright agreements). This company registered the trademark for, and patented, the Raggedy Anne doll. The original Raggedy Ann dolls produced by the Gruelle family are handcrafted and undoubtedly very rare and infrequently found. Made from white cotton, stuffed and loosely jointed, the doll had a long face with hand-painted features, brown yarn hair, and a candy heart was placed within the body. Some found with a rubber stamped date on tummy or back. Although not showing great artistic talent, the uniqueness and emotional attachment connected with these early Gruelle family Raggedy Ann and Andy dolls rank them among the most actively sought-after treasures in the collecting community.

GUND MANUFACTURING CO.—U.S.A., 1898-present. Manufactured a wide and varied selection of toys, dolls, and plush animals over the years. Early advertisements list composition dolls with cloth bodies and even a creeping mechanical doll.

GUTSELL, IDA ANZOLOTTA—U.S.A., 1893. Produced charming handcrafted dolls from a cottage-type industry. Offered in white and black versions with hand-painted facial features with heavy oil paints.

GUTTMANN & SCHIFFNIE—Germany, 1897-1924 and possibly as late as the 1930s. Conducted business under the same trade name as Gebrüder Süssenguth. The direct or indirect relationship is not clear. According to records, Guttmann & Schiffnie exported a significant number of dolls to France.

H

H MOLD—France, 1880 (assumed). The famous H Mold doll is attributed to Halopeau of Paris, around 1880. This is only an assumed manufacturer and assumed production date, as this is one of the elusive mystery doll molds. It was for a time believed to have been produced to celebrate the opening of a major store in Paris, but that theory has long been abandoned. What is known for sure, is that the H doll is exceptionally beautiful, with sumptuous, fine, pale bisque which has been pressed into the mold, gorgeous paperweight eyes, and a closed mouth. Many H dolls have been found on jointed Jumeau bodies. Although long accepted as French, I would suggest that a German manufacturer not be totally disallowed. Case in point: The brow line reflects a Germany influence, as do the shorter lashes with a break at the lid line. The lip color is with a hint of orange, a decidedly German preference. On the other hand, the Jumeau body, the long cheek look, and the paperweight eyes all point to a French origin. Another fascinating mystery to ponder. All H mold dolls are of the very finest quality.

HACHMEISTER, HERMANN—Germany, 1872-1930s and possibly later. Manufactured and exported a variety of dolls including art and mama dolls with composition and wax-over heads, along with accessories, such as wigs and shoes. An interesting note: They also were granted a patent in 1882 for a cardboard box with a cellophane show window inserted in the cover. This is the first patent or registering found for this now popular type of doll presentation.

HALLMARK—U.S.A., 1970-present. Hallmark has a history associated with greeting cards and stationery dating long before the given 1970 date. It was not until the early 1970s, however, that this company began to release dolls and Christmas ornaments that have a special attraction to doll collectors. Several terry cloth character dolls along with vinyl Betsy Clark dolls were introduced, but it was the 1976 Bicentennial Commemorative portrait dolls that started a collecting trend of Hallmark cloth dolls that continued until 1980. The cloth portrait dolls sold between 1976 and 1979, and were packaged in a uniquely designed house-type box, representing either the home or building most associated with a particular character. For example, Betsy Ross is presented in a box fashioned after her home, whereas Babe Ruth is featured in a box designed as the Baseball Hall of Fame. Hallmark dolls and ornaments are of good quality, and enjoy a highly collectible status.

HALPERN, J. CO. –U.S.A. 1951. It is possible that Halpern manufactured dolls in other years; however, no records could be located to confirm this. In 1951 they advertised in the trade papers and published a 12-page order catalog featuring several hard plastic and magic skin dolls. The beautiful facial molding and costuming of the dolls give no clue as to why the company apparently had such a short industrial life. Halpern dolls are of good quality.

HAMBURGER & CO.—U.S.A., 1889-1909. Founded in New York City as an importer of dolls and toys from Germany. Later, opened offices in Berlin and Nuremberg. Although responsible for many well-known and highly collectible German bisque dolls that were imported into the United States during the early part of the twentieth century, the Hamburger name is not often associated with them. (Notably Dolly Dimple and Santa dolls.) Hamburger dolls are of good quality.

HAMLEY BROTHERS—England, 1760-present. Manufactured, imported, exported, and distributed dolls both wholesale and retail. Over the more than two hundred years that the Hamley family owned and operated this company, every conceivable type of doll has been represented, including British Ceramic, wax, porcelain, china, celluloid, composition, cloth, plastic, and vinyl.

HAMMOND MANUFACTURING CO.—England, 1916-1919. Manufactured composition and cloth character and girl dolls. According to records, they purchased the doll heads and made the wigs, clothing, and cloth bodies, which were stuffed with wood, wool, and pine chips.

HANCOCK S. & SON—England, 1857-1937. Also known as Gordon Works, Corona Pottery. Manufactured dolls and doll parts from British Ceramic, and produced stationery and sleep eyes for their own dolls and supplied them to other manufacturers. Created original designed heads by Hilda Cowham, along with reproducing sculptures supplied by other companies. Also held exclusive rights to Fumsup.

HANDWERCK, HEINRICH—Germany, 1876-1932. Heinrich and his wife, Minna, started producing dolls amidst humble beginnings. When Heinrich died in 1902, the factory was purchased by Franz Reinhardt of Kämmer & Reinhardt of Waltershausen, Germany, fol-

Heinrich Handwerck's Child Doll in Original Pristine Condition (Photo courtesy of Mr. & Mrs. Adam Condo.)

lowing the guidelines set and left by Heinrich. This acquisition made Kämmer & Reinhardt world famous, and afforded them the opportunity to obtain a business contract with the prestigious porcelain factory of Simon & Halbig. The new owners continued using the old name, but added oHG to many of the markings. Early on, Heinrich Handwerck developed a working relationship with Simon & Halbig which supplied them with bisque doll heads of Handwerck's own designs. The pretty dolly-faced child dolls and babies became Handwerck's forte. They also offered a limited number of celluloid dolls. The popular character dolls were apparently not included in their repertoire. Heinrich Handwerck dolls are of very good quality.

HANDWERCK, MAX—Germany, 1899-1930. Founded by Heinrich Wortmann and Max Handwerck. Apparently, in 1902, Wortmann left the company and Handwerck died, leaving his widow, Anna, the sole owner of the business. This company sculptured its own facial molds, many of which were produced as bisque doll heads by William Goebel. Max Handwerck dolls are of good quality.

HANSEN, LAURIE & CO.—England, 1915-1921. Manufactured and exported dolls of composition, wax, and British Ceramic, some of which were designed by Hilda Cowham, on cloth or composition-jointed bodies.

HARMUS, CARL, JR.—Germany, 1873-1930 and possibly later. In 1896 Carl Harmus died and the company was taken over by Georg Neugebauer, but retained the Harmus name. Manufactured bisque head dolls, some of which were supplied by the Porzellanfabrik Mengersgereuth and Gebrüder Ohlhaver. Also advertised a baby that drank from a bottle, dolls with felt faces, art dolls, and crying babies. Carl Harmus dolls are of fair quality.

HARTLAND INDUSTRIES—U.S.A., mid-twentieth century. Produced hard plastic cowboy figures on horseback. The Hartland sets are of good quality and are highly collectible.

HARTMANN, CARL—Germany, 1889-1930. Founded by Carl Hartmann for the purpose of exporting small size (usually 5-9 inches) bisque and celluloid dolls. Many of the bisque heads were supplied by Kämmer & Reinhardt. Advertised that he could supply and export "dolls without the brand mark and without any hint of the producer," which may help to explain the origin of some of the many unmarked smaller dolls found. Carl Hartmann dolls are of fair to very good quality.

HARTMANN, KARL—Germany, 1911-1926. Manufactured bisque dolls on jointed composition bodies. Karl Hartmann dolls have a sophisticated worldly look, just a step beyond the delicate, wholesome expression often found on the dolly-faced dolls. This cosmo-politan look may be the reason for their popularity with collectors. Karl Hartmann dolls are of good quality.

HARWIN & CO.—England, 1915-1921. Produced a felt doll designed by Dorothy Harwin similar to the Steiff dolls. Harwin could, by law, copy the popular Steiff doll during the World War I years, because nations were not required to recognize their enemy's patents or copyrights.

HASBRO—U.S.A., 1923-present. Originally known as Hassenfeld Brothers, this company was founded by Henry and Hiller Hassenfeld in Pawtucket, Rhode Island. The family-owned and operated toy business adopted the familiar Hasbro name following a division in the company. One branch went into the pencil box business, the other into the toy business. Dolls were not part of the toy line until later years. G. I. Joe firmly planted Hasbro in the doll producing community along with other character-type dolls. Hasbro dolls are of good quality.

HEINE, GÜNTHER—Germany, 1920-1922. Manufactured art-type dolls with jointed bodies made entirely of composition. Very similar in appearance to the Käthe Kruse dolls, with painted hair and facial features. Marked on the sole of the foot.

HEINE & SCHNEIDER—Germany, 1920-1922. Manufactured art-type dolls with jointed bodies of cardboard covered in muslin. A pressed cloth head with painted hair and facial features. The coloring of the face paint is not the least bit subtle.

HEINRICH GESCHWISTER—Germany, 1925-1931. Produced art dolls, including a felt doll very similar in appearance and costuming to the Lenci dolls.

HEINZ, RUDOLPH & CO.—Germany, 1858-1922 and later under new management. Also known as Aelteste Volkstedter Porzellanfabrik. A porcelain factory that produced doll heads and parts.

HELLER, ADOLF—Germany, 1909-1925. Manufactured dolls at his doll factory after leaving the partnership of Heller & Seyfarth. Advertised character babies with flirting eyes and moving tongues, infants, mama, child, lady, and small dolls.

HELLER, ALFRED—Germany, 1901-1910. A Metallpuppenköpfe, German for "metal doll head." Produced the Diana metal shoulder doll heads either alone or on kid or cloth bodies. Distinguishing characteristics are the rather large ears that are attached separately to the head.

HELVETIC, I. & M., CORP.—U.S.A., 1927-1928. Also known as H. & M. Corp. Produced musical mechanical dolls operated by a squeeze-type bellows within the cloth bodies. Many dolls were presented atop a horse.

HENDERSON GLOVE CO.—U.S.A., 1927-1930s. Manufactured lithographed cloth American Indian dolls. Also sold a cut-out, sew-at-home Indian doll representing a Chief named Buck and an Indian maiden named Squaw.

HERMSDORFER CELLULOIDWARENFABRIK—Germany, 1925-1927. Manufactured celluloid baby and child dolls, along with doll heads. Also advertised a baby that drinks from a bottle and a jointed doll that drinks. Hermsdorfer Celluloid dolls are of good quality.

HERMANN, CARL—Germany, 1914-1926. Manufactured composition dolls and doll parts.

HERTEL, SCHWAB & CO.—Germany, 1910-1930 and probably later. Also known as Stutzhauser Porzellanfabrik. This porcelain factory was founded by sculptors August Hertel and Heinrich Schwab, who designed the dolls, and porcelain painter Hugo Rosenbush, who was a minor partner in the company. Several of the bisque heads were made exclusively for the American market, including Bye Lo Baby for Borgfeldt, Our Baby, and Our Fairy of Louis Wolf and Jubilee Dolls for Strobel & Wilken. Produced bisque heads for other German Manufacturers also including, but not limited to, Wolf, Kley & Hahn, and Koenig & Wernicke. Dolls made by Hertel Schwab & Co. are of good quality.

HERTWIG & CO.—Germany, 1864-at least as late as 1941. Produced porcelain or bisque snow babies and Nanking dolls at their porcelain factory in the Thüringia region of Germany. Nanking dolls have bisque heads and limbs and cloth bodies stuffed with cotton (nanking). This company also made Pet Name china heads exclusively for the American market. Many of the all-bisque dolls have molded clothing and are either unmarked or marked only Germany. Often the first acquisition made by doll collectors, they are relatively easy to find, and their charming vintage appearance makes them a logical first step in the antique doll collecting journey. Hertwig Dolls are of fair quality.

HESS, THEODORE & CO.—U.S.A., 1918-1920. Produced dolls of all composition with socket heads, and dolls with jointed all-celluloid or composition shoulder heads and hands on cloth bodies. Wearing wigs or molded and painted hair, sleep or painted eyes.

HEUBACH, ERNST—Germany, 1887-at least 1932 and probably later. Manufactured bisque dolls in his porcelain factory at Köppelsdorf. The structure of the European doll industry at the end of the nineteenth century was shaped by the traditions of an earlier day, when businesses were bound by strong family ties and intricate interconnections. This company is a classic example. Undoubtedly related to the Heubach porcelain factory in Thüringia, Ernst Jr. added to the complexity by marrying Beatrice Marseilles, daughter of Armand Marseilles, who was unquestionably one of the leading doll manufacturers of the time. A sculptor for Heubach's, Hans Homberger, was brother to the head sculptor of Marseilles. These family connections help to explain the similarities found in bisque character dolls and dolly-face dolls made by the German manufacturers. In 1919, Ernst Heubach and Armand Marseilles merged to become Vereinigte Köppelsdorfer Porzellanfabrik Vorm, Armand Marseilles und Ernst Heubach (The United Porcelain Factory of Köppelsdorf). The new company split into two separate entities, once again, in 1932. Understanding this change makes clear the use of "Köppelsdorf" in the marking that is included only after 1919. Along with the bisque dolly-face babies and characters they manufactured for their own dolls, they produced bisque doll heads for several other companies. Ernst Heubach dolls are of good quality.

HEUBACH, GEBRÜDER—Germany, 1843-1938. The year 1938 was when Gebrüder Heubach filed for bankruptcy. The founding date is a bit more obscure. In 1804 permission was granted to dig for clay. In 1822 a porcelain factory was approved, and the brothers Christoph and Philipp Heubach purchased the business in 1843. There is no mention, though, of doll production until 1910. With the introduction of character dolls, the doll makers in both America and Europe seized upon this new interest to create dolls that would satisfy a growing taste for the exotic. Rarely could other manufacturers compete with the skill and attention to detail used to produce the amusing and extraordinary Gebrüder Heubach character dolls. One secret to their success was the location of an art school for sculptors located near the factory. The school turned out especially skilled artists and sculptors responsible for creating beautiful porcelain figurines and dolls. Gebrüder Heubach manufactured such an enormous quantity and range of character doll heads that positive identification is difficult. Due to their constant use, the molds became worn, causing mold numbers to become unreadable. Consequently, identification of some molds has caused considerable misunderstandings. Adding to the confusion, many heads never had mold numbers but were simply marked S or Q. No logical system has been deciphered, impeding attempts to precisely identify many dolls. Records indicate that more than ten thousand molds were offered. The bisque heads were either socket or shoulder heads with molded and delicately painted hair or wig, the famous intaglio eyes or sleep eyes. Many other German doll manufacturers purchased their bisque heads. Gebrüder Heubach dolls are of good to very good quality.

HEUMANN, CARL—Germany, 1918-1930. Manufactured dolls, mostly of bisque, on composition bodies representing babies, children, and ladies with wigs and sleep eyes. Also advertised a celluloid baby that drank from a bottle, and a suck-a-thumb baby.

44

HEWITT & LEADBEATER—England, 1914-1920. Also known as Willow Pottery and Hewitt Brothers. With the outbreak of World War I, Hewitt was reportedly the first company to supply British Ceramic dolls and doll parts to satisfy a demand for replacement of the German bisque no longer imported. So successful were they that a second factory was purchased solely for the production of the British Ceramic socket and shoulder heads with molded and painted hair or wearing wigs. Painted or sleep eyes. They also offered a small, all-ceramic type doll.

HIBERNIAN NOVELTY CO.—Ireland, 1916-1917. A short-lived, little-known, cloth doll manufacturer. Made dolls with silk faces and painted facial features, or composition heads and limbs on cloth bodies. Also produced a line of doll clothing.

HIGH-GRADE TOY MANUFACTURING CO.—U.S.A., 1916-1921. A small, short-lived doll manufacturer advertising composition dolls with painted or sleep eyes on cloth bodies.

HITZ, JACOBS & KASSLER—U.S.A., 1918-1930s. Responsible for importing several lines of dolls from Europe and also distributing American-made dolls. Best known for their Kiddiejoy line. Dolls were made of bisque on composition and kid bodies, all composition, composition heads and limbs on cloth bodies, with wig or molded and painted hair, and painted or sleep eyes; also hand-painted wooden dolls. Registered Bisqueloid as a material used in doll manufacturing.

HOEST & HENDERSON—U.S.A., 1926-1930s. Also known as Hoest & Co. Founded by Arthur Hoest and George Henderson. Manufactured baby and mama dolls of composition on cloth bodies.

HOFFMEISTER, CARL—Germany, 1892-1925. Lederpuppen-Fabrik (German for "factory for leather dolls"). Named for its founder, Carl Hoffmeister, they produced leather and imitation leather doll bodies and purchased heads from various companies to complete the dolls for export to the United States. Celluloid heads from Rheinische Gummi, metal heads from Buschow & Beck, composition and occasionally bisques from Heubach and Schoenau & Hoffmeister. Carl was the Hoffmeister of the later company, forming that partnership in 1901 with Arthur Schoenau. Dolls on Carl Hoffmeister bodies are of mediocre quality.

HOLLAND, JOHN—U.S.A., 1796-1843. An employee of the Moravian Pottery of North Carolina where he produced at least two types of pottery dolls. Four doll types are mentioned in inventory records; however, physical evidence of only two have been verified: a Frozen Charlotte-type doll with molded clothing, and a socket-head with a cylindrical neck.

HOLLYWOOD DOLL MANUFACTURING CO.—U.S.A., 1941-1956. Founded by Domenick Ippolite. Best known for the small shelf dolls so popular at the time. Usually well-marked dolls of bisque, composition, or hard plastic. Within the span of their fifteen years of business, Hollywood Doll Co. supplied more dolls to the public than any other doll manufacturer. Characters are identified by costumes. Hollywood Dolls are of mediocre quality, but nevertheless a favorite with many collectors.

HOLZER & CIE—Brazil, 1920s-1940s and possibly later years. Produced cloth souvenir, or tourist type dolls as well as large-size cloth dolls. The skin tone is a dark flesh color and the costuming is elaborate and colorful. Many Holzer & Cie dolls were imported into the United States, and they are often found with a Kimport label.

HORN, CARL—Germany, 1906-1930s. Manufactured small bisque and painted bisque dolls. Most jointed at shoulder and hips with mohair wigs or molded and painted hair and eyes. Often dressed in regional costumes or dollhouse family members and household staff. Measuring 1-1/4 to 3-1/2 inches. Carl Horn tiny dolls are of good quality.

HORSMAN, EDWARD IMESON—U.S.A., 1865-present. Also known as E. I. Horsman Co., and for a brief time after merging with Aetna traded as E. I. Horsman & Aetna Co. Starting his career as an office boy earning two dollars a week, Ed Horsman opened a toy company that was to become a leader in the doll industry. By the late 1800s Horsman produced a variety of popular composition dolls. They were produced wearing wigs, with molded and painted hair and eyes, or sleep eyes. About this same time Solomon Hoffmann, a Russian emigrant, was using his formula to make unbreakable composition dolls. Others showed little interest in Hoffmann's formula, overlooking one of the important discoveries within the doll manufacturing community. To his credit, Horsman saw the advantages of using composition, gave it a catchy trade name of "Can't Break 'Em," produced the Billiken doll, and the Horsman Company was off to a tremendous start. He went on to offer dolls of bisque, composition, hard plastic, and vinyl. Horsman dolls are of good quality.

HOYER, MARY DOLL MANUFACTURING CO.—U.S.A., 1925-1970s. Mary Hoyer owned and operated a yarn shop and wanted a doll to use as a model for her knitted and crocheted clothing designs. Thus, the idea of a doll that was sold along with a pattern book of instructions for making her wardrobe. The early dolls were all composition, jointed at neck, shoulders, and hips with mohair wigs, sleep eyes, and real lashes. Later dolls were of hard plastic having the same characteristics as the earlier dolls, except synthetic wigs were used. Mary Hoyer dolls are of good quality.

HUFFMAN, PEGGY ORIGINAL—U.S.A., mid-twentieth century. Produced the inexpensive hard plastic, nicely costumed shelf dolls that were so popular at the time. Peggy Huffman dolls are of fair quality.

HÜLSS, ADOLF—Germany, 1913-1930s and possibly later. Manufactured dolls with bisque child and character baby heads on composition-jointed bodies. It is generally accepted that the bisque heads were supplied by Simon & Halbig. When observing a Hülss marking remember that often in old German Gothic script a double s is shown as a *B*; therefore, the marking may look like this: HülB.

HURET, MAISON—France, 1812 at least the 1930s. Huret was already an established toy company when, in the 1850s under the creative force of Mlle. Calixte Huret, it emerged as a doll manufacturer. Well-known for their beautifully made, gusseted kid and articulated wooden bodies. Huret pioneered numerous patented innovations including the important 1861 socket swivel neck. Reportedly produced about 1,500 dolls a year, a rather modest figure when compared to other doll makers. Made with a full, youthful face of bisque or china, with glass or painted eyes, and wigs of either fur or mohair. Bodies are composition, Gutta-perch, kid, or wood with hands of bisque, china, composition, or metal. Can often be dated by their markings. Those made in the 1850s bear the address 2 Boulevard des Italienos. From the mid to late 1860s dolls were marked 22 Boulevard Montmartre. After 1870, look for 68 Rue de la Boetie. Maison Huret are of excellent quality.

I

IBBETSTON, LEONARD—England, 1917-1920. Also known as Colonial Works. Manufactured composition shoulder heads on imitation kid bodies and jointed cloth, hair-stuffed dolls. Additionally offered doll parts, wigs, dresses, and shoes.

IDEAL NOVELTY & TOY CO.—1906-present. Founded by Morris Mitchom and A. Cohn for the express purpose of producing Mitchom's teddy bears. Inspired by seeing the cartoon of President Theodore Roosevelt's 1903 hunting trip, Mitchom's wife made a pair of handcrafted stuffed bears for a window display at their small stationery store. Mitchom sent President Roosevelt a sample of his "Teddy" bear and asked permission to name his stuffed bear after him. The President answered in a handwritten note, "I doubt if my name will mean much in the bear business, but you may use it if you wish." The rest is Teddy Bear history. The 1930s were prime years for Ideal with the issuance of Shirley Temple, Judy Garland, and Deanna Durbin dolls. One of the few companies which made its own composition and were so proficient at it that in addition to meeting their own needs, they could supply other manufacturers with dolls. Ideal began experi-

Ideal's Shirley Temple with Original Box (Photo courtesy of McMasters Doll Auctions.)

menting with hard plastic in 1936. Although interrupted by World War II, they were still the first in the industry to market a hard plastic doll. Along with composition and hard plastic, Ideal also manufactured cloth, rubber, wood, magic skin, and vinyl dolls. Ideal dolls are of very good quality.

ILLFELDER, LEOPOLD & CO.—Germany, 1874-1901. Father of Max Illfelder. Registered, according to early records, as a doll factory and exporter of dolls and toys. Dolls of bisque on jointed composition bodies and wax on cloth or kid bodies.

ILLFELDER SPIELWAREN—Germany, 1862-1920s. Operating as an export trading company with an office in New York, Max Illfelder distributed dolls in the United States, including wax and bisque. By 1918, this company had stopped using the better German doll heads, and began obtaining Japanese bisque. Although associated with Leopold Illfelder & Co. Max Illfelder Spielwaren ran as an independent business.

IMPERIAL DOLL CO.—U.S.A., mid-twentieth century. This company produced inexpensive hard plastic dolls of mediocre quality.

IMPERIAL TOY CO.—England, 1915-1919. Also known as Toyland Works. Produced cloth character dolls with long limbs, and plush dolls advertised as Eskimo dolls.

INDESTRUCTO SPECIALTIES CO.—U.S.A., 1915-1916. Sold and distributed dolls with sleep or flirty eyes on composition bodies. Best known for the Fairy Tale dolls, which were offered as a boxed set of the principal characters in a story—for example, Red Riding Hood, the Wolf, and Grandma.

INDIA RUBBER COMB CO.—U.S.A., 1851-at least 1863 and possibly later. Produced dolls and doll heads made of hard rubber.

INSAM & PRINOTH—Bavaria, 1820-at least the 1930s. Verlegers responsible for millions of wooden and peg wooden dolls being distributed to the market-place. Reported to have had thirty store rooms filled with painted and unpainted hand-carved wooden dolls, supplied by cottage industry-type workers. An inventory of just the 1-1/2-inch-long peg wooden dolls for one year shows that 30,000 dolls every week were bought, totaling 1,500,000 one and half inch peg wooden dolls in that year alone!

INTERNATIONAL DOLL CO.—U.S.A., 1929-1970. Also known as The Molly Goldman Company. Created cloth and composition dolls and doll costumes, using the Molly-'es trademark. There are several controversies and misunderstandings concerning agreements and licensing with Molly-'es. Goldman was unhappy with her circumstances at several of the companies that she designed for, feeling that she was taken advantage of financially. She also was named in a court case involving copyrights to the Raggedy Ann and Andy dolls that she produced. The Gruelle family was victorious and Molly had to discontinue producing the cloth dolls bearing the Raggedy Ann and Andy name.

INTERNATIONAL DOLL MANUFACTURING CO.—U.S.A., 1920-1921. Sold dolls with composition hands and heads with wigs and painted or sleep eyes on cork-stuffed cloth bodies.

INTERNATIONAL TOY CO.—England and U.S.A., 1926-1929. Produced a line of wooden dolls with some association with Ted Toys.

INTERNATIONAL WALKING DOLL CO.—U.S.A., 1917-1921. A small, little-known doll company. Acknowledged as the distributor for Babs the walking doll made by Babs Manufacturing Corp. Made with a metal mesh torso and wooden limbs jointed by flexible steel springs.

IRWIN & CO.—U.S.A., 1926-contemporary. The early dolls were of cloth, followed by celluloid. One of the earliest companies to change into the production of hard plastic dolls. Favorites were the babies used by crochet enthusiasts as models. All dolls made by Irwin were moderately priced dolls and of rather poor quality.

J

JAPANESE DOLLS—Japan, 1400s-present.
The art of doll making is a tradition that has been handed down from one generation to the next. Dolls were created to be more than just child's playthings. There are more than three hundred different types of Japanese dolls, some of which were commercially produced as early as the 1500s, although, most dolls originally had a ritual significance with religious associations and were made for decorative purposes. For example, the Boys' Day and Girls' Day Festivals are part of the Japanese cult of chivalry, and symbolized bravery and loyalty to country and emperor. The Girls' Day Festival (*Hina Matsuri*), celebrated as early as the 1400s, was intended to instill the virtues of patriotism and domesticity in young girls and to honor the Imperial family. The holiday is still celebrated in Japan on March 3, at the peak of the peach blossom season. Several days before the festival, mothers and daughters take their dolls out of storage and display them on steps (*Hina Dan*) covered with red silk. A set of these dolls traditionally consists of fifteen figures. The Emperor and Empress are placed on the top step with the court musician, ladies in waiting, guard and dancers on the lower steps. The Boys' Day Festival (*Tanono Sekka*) is celebrated on May 5, and was called the Feast of Flags. On this day banners in the shape of carp, the fish signifying fortitude, are flown outside the homes of young boys. Inside, an array of fierce-looking dolls symbolizing strength, valor, and adventure are displayed on cloth-covered tiered stands. The dolls represent warriors such as Monotaro, Yoshitsumen, and Kato Kiyomasa, as well as commanders, generals, and wrestlers. Each year the collection is added to, reminding the boy of the vestiges of Japanese chivalry and the Samurai. The antique Festival Dolls are treasured family heirlooms. Children's play dolls (*Ichimatsu*) and child dolls (*Yamato Ningyo*) are also exceptionally beautiful unmarked dolls with perfect white faces. Their porcelain-like finish is made from polished Gofun, a fine white paste composed of pulverized oyster shells and glue. It is not unusual for a doll's head to have twenty to thirty coats of Gofun. Gorgeously costumed in non-removable clothing made from materials specially woven in miniature patterns. May be equipped with armor and weapons. The traditional glass-eyed Japanese dolls portray three distinct classes: the Royal group, the Samurai, and the peasants. In the early years of the twentieth century, many dolls with Oriental-type faces and clothing were made in Europe and the United States. These dolls should not be confused with the Japanese dolls that were made in Japan. Later Yamato Ningyo and Sakura Ningyo (Cherry Dolls, Traditional Lady Statue Dolls) of lesser quality were made of silk and composition. The labor-intensive workmanship

needed to achieve the look of the early Gofun, combined with the intricate costuming, allows easy distinction between early dolls and the later, less artistic, dolls.

JEANETTE DOLL CO.—U.S.A., 1919-1928. Manufactured dolls with composition shoulder heads and limbs on cloth bodies. With wigs or molded and painted hair. Sleep or painted eyes. Also advertised a line of Nursery Rhyme dolls and leatherette Fairyland dolls. Registered the trademark Jedco.

JENNY LIND DOLL CO.—U.S.A., 1916. A small, little-known doll company that produced a phonograph doll that was advertised as Jenny Lind wearing a chemise and hair ribbons.

JOLLY TOYS—U.S.A., mid-twentieth century. Produced hard plastic dolls of mediocre quality.

JOY DOLL CORP.—U.S.A., 1920-1922. Produced a line of composition dolls, doll heads, and parts. Offered with mohair wigs or molded and painted hair.

JULLIEN—France, 1863-1904 The research concerning the beautiful Jullien Bébé is inconclusive. There appears to have been more than one factory which operated under the name Jullien. They were more than likely interconnected; perhaps one was the porcelain factory, another decorated the heads, and yet another assembled the dolls. It is also unclear exactly when Jullien began to produce bisque doll heads, although it is assumed that Jullien was one of the early French doll makers. Records confirm that Jullien purchased at least some bisque heads from François Gaultier. Marked Jullien dolls are of good to very good quality.

JUMEAU—France, 1842-1899 then became member of S. F. B. J. and continued operating until 1958. Pierre Jumeau began manufacturing dolls in France in a partnership called Belton & Jumeau. Although the death of Belton brought the partnership to an end, Jumeau continued to create some of the most exquisite bisque Bébés in the world. George, the eldest son of Pierre Jumeau, died suddenly, and the second son Emile took charge of the business when his father retired in 1878. Emile had studied to be an architect, but when forced into the family business, he was resolved to make France the world leader in the doll industry. What Emile was not able to accomplish in quantity, he certainly succeed in quality. Jumeau dolls are perfect examples of treasured works of art. After the 1899 membership to S. F. B. J., Jumeau dolls, as other French dolls, lost much of their prestige. The early bisque Poupée de Modes, Portraits, Deposes, Long Face Triste, E. J. Bébés, and Tete Jumeau Bébés have lovely bisque heads, paperweight eyes, cork pates, and closed mouths on wood and composition bodies (except the Fashion type that is found on kid bodies). The later S. F. B. J. bisque heads with glass eyes and open or closed mouths, are on composition bodies. Jumeau dolls are from good to excellent quality.

JURO NOVELTY CO., INC.—U.S.A., mid-twentieth century, being most popular in the 1955-1965 production years. Produced hard plastic celebrity and personality dolls along with a line of ventriloquist dummies. Juro dolls are of mediocre quality.

K

K & K TOY CO.—U.S.A., 1915-1930s. Like may other doll makers of the time, this company imported its bisque heads from Germany. They also supplied cloth and composition bodies to several doll manufacturers, including George Borgfeldt. Composition bodies were often marked "Bisquette" or "Fiberoid." Along with the established connections with Borgfeldt, many K & K dolls were distributed through Butler Brothers. Bisque or composition heads with wigs and sleep eyes on cloth or kid bodies with composition or bisque limbs.

K&K Character Child. (Photo courtesy of Helen Brooke.)

KAGO DOLL CO.—U.S.A., 1921. A small, short-lived doll manufacturer of composition Kewpie-like dolls, some with mohair wigs.

KALBITZ, CARL—Germany, 1866-1930, and possibly later. Also spelled Karl. Produced composition dolls with cloth bodies and art dolls. Registered Kalutu as a trademark in 1929.

KAMKINS—U.S.A., 1919-1928. Also known as "The Louise R. Kampes Studio." Located on the Boardwalk in Atlantic City, New Jersey. Patented in 1920, these charming art dolls were made of heavy cloth treated with rubber, a combination which made the face appear similar to composition. The production of Kamkins was conducted as a cottage-type industry. The studio supplied patterns and materials to home sewers. Also designed a line of doll clothing that could be purchased separately. The most common characteristic shared by all Kamkins is the heavily molded mask-type face. Most are painted a deep healthy color, seldom have eyelashes, and have flange necks. The stuffed cloth bodies usually have seams down the front of the legs and are jointed at shoulders and hips. Kamkins dolls are very good quality art-type dolls.

KÄMMER & REINHARDT—Germany, 1885-1932, and possibly to 1933. Founded by Ernst Kämmer, a sculptor, and Franz Reinhardt, a merchant. When Ernst Kämmer died in 1901 Karl Krausser took over his position as designer and sculptor. About this same time Heinrich Handwerck also passed away. Shortly thereafter, K & R bought the Handwerck factory. Kämmer & Reinhardt designed doll heads, but did not actually make them. Simon & Halbig made most of the bisque heads and was part of the company by 1920. Kämmer & Reinhardt has long been credited with popularizing character dolls, though the company was undoubtedly influenced by Marion Kaulitz, the instigator of the 1908 "Puppen Reform." Along with the lovely bisque child, baby, and wonderful character doll heads on composition bodies, Kämmer & Reinhardt also made several composition-head babies such as mold 926 and the charming Puz. Later cloth dolls with wire cloth-covered armature bodies and hand-painted facial features were introduced. Authentically costumed to represent various professions and stations in life. All Kämmer & Reinhardt dolls are of very good quality.

KÄMPFE & HEUBACH—Germany, 1897-1930. Also known as Wallendorf Porzellanfabrik. This was a well-known porcelain factory that produced dolls, some of which were exhibited at the 1908 Munich Toy Show. Care should be given, however, not to confuse their marking with Meissen, Königliche Porzellan Manufaktur, and Nymphenburg.

KARL, AUGUST FRIEDRICH—Germany, 1926-1927. A small, short-lived doll manufacturer responsible for cloth, mama, and baby dolls with fully jointed bodies. Advertised: "with first-class dresses."

KATAGINI BROTHERS—U.S.A., 1930. Manufactured celluloid dolls.

KAT-A-KORNER KOMPANY—U.S.A., 1925-1941. Manufactured cloth and oilcloth dolls.

KAULITZ , MARION BERTHA—Bavaria, 1901-1920. In 1909 registered the trademark Münchner Künstler Kaulitz-Puppen, German for "Kaulitz Art Dolls of Munich." Marion was one of the artists in charge of exhibits at the Munich Fair. An editorial in *Studio Talk* when reporting on the 1908 Puppen Reforms stated, "When the artistic conscience began to invade the doll industry, it fell to some artists of Dresden and Munich to introduce a change." The well-known composition Munich Art dolls, made by Marion Kaulitz, influenced the doll industry for the next quarter of a century.

KAYBEE DOLL & TOY CO.—U.S.A., 1917-1919. Manufactured composition doll socket heads wearing human hair wigs with sleep eyes and separate shoulder plates on cloth bodies.

KEATS & CO.—England, 1916. Records indicate that the dolls were made with British Ceramic heads dipped in wax, a process patented by Doris Sylvia Bailey and Sarah Baxter, and attached to cloth bodies.

KEEN & CO.—England, 1916-1933 and possibly later. Founded by Julius Kohnstamm, a naturalized British subject from Germany. Established a doll factory in London while maintaining close ties with his German family. It is assumed that the dolls manufactured by Keen were of bisque heads from Germany on composition or kid bodies.

KENNER PARKER TOYS, INC.—U.S.A., contemporary. In 1985 Kenner became an independent company with two divisions: Parker Brothers and Kenner Products. Kenner was once a subsidiary of General Mills. They produced many hard plastic, cloth and vinyl dolls as well as popular action figures. The Kenner *Star Wars* and Strawberry Shortcake characters are among their most popular.

KESTNER, J. D., JR.—Germany, 1805-1938. Johann Daniel Kestner, the charismatic founder of this empire, started in business by trading with the soldiers of the Napoleonic wars necessary items in exchange for the wastes from their slaughtered cattle, such as fat, kid, horn, and bones. So successful was he, that before long he opened a factory to produce papier-mâché items and buttons. Needing a lathe to produce the buttons, it only seemed natural to him that he could also make wooden jointed dolls. By 1820 Kestner was manufacturing a complete line of toys and dolls made from both wood and papier-mâché. In 1840 Kestner participated in the Leipzig Fair as the first toy maker of Waltershausen, Germany, an impressive feat considering the toy capital that area was to become. The doll industry was of the utmost importance in Germany, and J. D. Kestner was the head of this industry, thus he was bestowed the nickname "King Kestner." Kestner's influence was so great and far reaching that he received permission from the Ducal Government to practice polygamy, and kept two wives at his home. His obituary gives credibility to this story by stating, "His two women continue the business." Kestner bisque heads were produced after the 1860 acquisition of the Steudinger, Müller & Co. porcelain factory with three kilns and thirty employees. They were also able to supply bisque heads to several other manufacturers. Kestner produced bisque, composition, wax, wood, papier-mâché, celluloid, china, and porcelain doll heads with wigs or molded hair, painted or glass eyes. On bodies of cloth, kid, wood, and composition with a variety of limbs and joints. All Kestner dolls are of very good quality.

KEWPIE®—U.S.A. and Germany, 1909-present. These sweet little elfin-like creatures made their debut in the December 1909 issue of *Ladies Home Journal*. Famous illustrator Rose O'Neill designed the Kewpies and held the design patents for them until her death in 1944. According to O'Neill, Kewpies first danced across her bed and shared their name with her while she was napping in her art studio—The Bird Café. O'Neill maintained that she did not invent Kewpies, only introduced them. George Borgfeldt held the manufacturing rights for many years, eventually passing them to Joseph Kallus, who retained them until 1984 when Jesco took possession of the trademark and copyright Kewpie. Over the years there have been many legal battles fought over the manufacturing of Kewpies without consent of the copyright. Magazine illustrations of Kewpies were so popular that it was inevitable that a Kewpie doll would be marketed. The first was designed by Joseph Kallus, a friend of Miss O'Neill. Early Kewpies were made of bisque and came from Germany. It is reported that at the peak of the Kewpie craze, thirty German factories were producing Kewpies in order to meet the demand.

Composition, plastic and vinyl Kewpies were manufactured by Cameo Doll Co. and by special licensing, Effanbee, Strombecker, Knickerbocker, and Amsco. To maintain quality control, Joseph Kallus required each licensed company to affix a Cameo label, in addition to its own markings on all their Kewpie dolls. Rose O'Neill passed away more than a half century ago, but she and her immortal Kewpies are by no means forgotten. Kewpie characteristics include blue-tipped wings, star-shaped hands, side-glancing eyes and a top peaked hair style.

KIMPORT DOLLS—U.S.A., 1920s-late 1950s, and possibly other years. No book on dolls would be complete without listing the Kimport Dolls. The young collectors probably have never heard of this Independence, Missouri-based import business, but it is a name well-known to seasoned doll lovers. Although not famous for their high quality dolls, they were nonetheless an important bridge for collectors interested in dolls from foreign lands. They actively sought the less popular doll companies and preferred to concentrate on the cottage industry or souvenir-type dolls. I, like many collectors, was a long time subscriber to the *Kimport Newsletters* (at the subscription rate of $1.00 for two years!!) During an era when doll collecting had few avenues for information, we anxiously awaited the bi-monthly publication, *Doll Talk*, filled with dolls offered for sale, and articles about dolls and doll makers, along with the personal lives of the staff. On a whim I called information for a phone number for Kimport Dolls, but none was listed. I really didn't expect there to be, but I was hopeful. Doll collecting has perhaps become too sophisticated for the charming Kimport dolls, but for us old-time collectors the name Kimport brings fond memories of doll collecting.

KLETZIN, JOHANN HEINRICH & SONS—Germany, 1922-1926. A well-organized and self-contained manufacturer of dolls. The factory that employed three hundred workers was a converted feudal castle. The dolls, which were molded and hot-air dried, were made of clay mined on the grounds. With wigs, glass sleep eyes, real hair lashes, and jointed composition bodies. Costumes were supplied by cottage industry. All dolls manufactured were exported to wholesalers, with the majority going to England.

KLEY & HAHN—Germany, 1902-1924. After Kley died in 1922, Hahn, the sole owner, sold the business to Sigismund Markmann of Berlin, who continued to produce dolls until around 1932. Albert Kley and Paul Hahn started their business with only fifteen employees. They devoted most of their efforts to capitalizing on the character doll boom in the American market. Most doll historians agree that several different porcelain factories contributed to the Kley & Hahn inventory. The bisque doll heads in the 200 series, 680, and the Walküre were made by Kestner. The 100-series characters were produced by Hertel, Schwab & Co. Bähr & Pröschild was responsible for the 500-series characters. In addition to bisque heads on composition and kid bodies, Kley & Hahn also advertised composition and "cellulit... a material not more expensive than our bisque and cheaper than celluloid." Kley & Hahn dolls are of good quality.

KLING, C. F. & CO.—Germany, 1836-1941. Well-known porcelain factory that produced dolls and doll heads and other porcelain doll parts. Also snow babies, pink-tint china heads with painted hair and eyes, all-bisque dolls and bisque heads with sleep eyes, open mouth, and wearing wigs, Nankeen dolls with porcelain heads and limbs on cloth bodies, dollhouse dolls and pincushion and tea cozy doll busts. Kling dolls are of good to very good quality.

KLOSTER VEILSDORF PORZELLAN FABRIK CO.—
Germany, 1765-1930. Manufactured bisque, Parian, and china dolls with molded and painted hair and eyes. Many found with a size number and "Germany" incised on the back shoulder plate. Kloster also advertised jointed all-porcelain dolls and Nankeen dolls, Frozen Charlottes.

KNOCH, GEBRÜDER—Germany, 1877-1919. Founded by the Knoch brothers—Ernst, the doll maker, and Christian, the merchant. Gebrüder (which means brothers) Knoch produced unmarked bisque heads, until being purchased by Max Oscar Arnold in 1919. For many years it was assumed that this company made the doll heads that we now know were made by Gebrüder Kuhnlenz. Along with the bisque dolly-faced dolls Gebrüder Knoch also made character dolls, and although charming, they do not possess the fine detailing and subtle decoration of some German competitors. Brows are often stenciled or have only a single stroke. Of course there are always exceptions, and a well-painted and artistically executed doll may be found.

KNICKERBOCKER DOLL & TOY CO.—U.S.A., 1925-contemporary. Leo L. Weiss was the president and A. S. Ferguson was the company's representative when they first opened their doors for business in New York City in 1925. Disney characters are among the premium products of the well-known American firm, as are the familiar Holly Hobby and the Raggedy Ann and Andy they manufactured for over twenty years. Knickerbocker dolls are a good quality play doll.

KOHL & WENGENROTH—Germany, 1902-1926. Manufactured various types of celluloid dolls and doll parts.

KOHNSTAMM, M. & CO.—Germany, 1867-1935. Founded by Moses Kohnstamm, who adopted the trademark MOKO from his name. The Kohnstamm family was connected to the Keen company in England and continued a close working relationship. Made dolls with bisque heads with sleep eyes and open mouth on composition and kid bodies. Also advertised an all-wood doll.

KÖNIG & WERNICKE—Germany, 1911-possibly as late as 1935. Also spelled Koenig & Wernicke. There are several points of disagreement concerning this company. Uncertainty exists regarding the identities of the founder and owners. Originally known as Koenig & Rudolph of Waltershausen, this team was made up of Max Koenig (König) and Max and August Rudolph. One year later, in 1912, Max and August Rudolph left the company, and their share was taken over by Rudolf Wernicke. Some reports state that Max and August Rudolph retired; however, their names surfaced intermittently in the doll industry over the next ten years. König & Wernicke bisque doll heads were supplied by several good porcelain factories.

Coincidentally, several mold numbers registered by König & Wernicke are identical to Simon & Halbig mold numbers. There is no known relationship between the two companies. König & Wernicke dolls are of good quality.

KÖNIGLICHE PORZELLANMANUFAKTUR—
Germany, 1710- contemporary. This was the first porcelain manufacturer after Friedrich Wilhelm Bottger invented the method of firing clay to produce objects. The first doll heads were manufactured from 1836. The early examples are marked under the shoulder plates. Beautiful porcelain heads with molded and painted hair and features.

KRÖHL, ADOLPH—Germany, 1830-1898. Manufactured and exported dolls of wax, bisque, papier-mâché, wood, leather, metal, and china. Also sold Täuflinge, doll parts, wigs, shoes, stocking, jewelry, and other doll accessories.

KRUEGER, RICHARD G., INC.—U.S.A., 1920s-1930s. Krueger and King Innovations established and maintained close connections, the sole licensed manufacturer of soft-stuffed Kewpie dolls. This license was granted by Rose O'Neill and was fully protected by copyrights, trademarks, and United States patents. Krueger produced a wide variety of cloth dolls, including stuffed animals and rag dolls. Oilcloth was frequently used for the bodies and/or costumes. Krueger cloth dolls are of good quality.

KRUSE, KÄTHE—Germany, 1910-present. Founded by artist Käthe Kruse, this doll manufacturing business was continued by Kruse's daughter Hannah after her mother's death in 1968. Legend tells us that her husband was not in favor of his children playing with toys purchased at stores. To amuse her daughters, Käthe tied a towel to resemble a doll. The girls were happy until the towel came undone. She experimented and continued to improve her dolls, a task which ultimately developed into a successful business. Käthe Kruse dolls are made of waterproof treated muslin, cotton wool, and stockinette—soft likelike cloth hand-painted dolls. A few were produced with wigs, but most have painted hair. Many are weighted with sand to feel like a real baby. Later, celluloid and hard plastic dolls were also produced. Käthe Kruse dolls are of excellent quality.

KUHNLENZ, GEBRÜDER—Germany, 1884-1935. Founded by the Kuhnlenz brothers Julius, Cuno, and Bruno. The dolls from this factory were long thought to be from Gebrüder Knoch or Gebrüder Krauss. Thanks to the extensive research by Jürgen and Marianne Cieslik, we now know about Gebrüder Kuhnlenz and their wonderful dolls. Kuhnlenz once advertised their bisque dolls as "doll heads with strange features." Strange may not be the correct term to describe a doll that is not easily forgotten. Kuhnlenz dolls are lovely with pale bisque brows that are usually heavy and feathered close together, and often with good quality paperweight eyes and black outlining of the eye socket with long lashes. The bisque-head dolls were produced with kid, composition, or tiny papier-mâché bodies. Kuhnlenz dolls are of good to very good quality.

KULPE—Spain, 1930-1970. Popular souvenir dolls. Mask-type faces on cloth-covered wire armature bodies. Dressed in regional costumes. Kulpe dolls are charming display dolls.

L

LAFAYETTE, O. J., & CO.—U.S.A., 1930s. Manufactured washable character dolls and portrait cloth dolls with hand-painted facial features. This company used the name "Hollywood Babes" for their portrait dolls representing performers.

LAFITTE & DÉSIRAT, MMES.—France, 1900-1920. These two sisters created wax dolls costumed in the latest Paris fashions and entered into exhibits. The dolls were never intended to be playthings—they were museum-quality display dolls.

LAKENMACKER CO.—U.S.A., 1921-1924. This company imported and sold small all-bisque, jointed, and novelty-type dolls.

LAMBERT & SAMHAMMER—Germany, 1872-1884. Doll and toy factory founded by Mathias Lambert and Philipp Samhammer. Manufactured bisque head dolls, until the partnership was terminated and Armand Marseille purchased the business. Samhammer went on to start a new business, independent of Lambert, to produce composition and wax over dolls on cloth or kid bodies.

LANG, ÉMILE—France, 1915-1924. Produced cloth dolls with molded and painted faces with articulated bodies. Many of the dolls were designed by Albert Guillaume and Jean Ray. There are records to indicate that Lang maintained an association with S. F. B. J., but he apparently operated from his own independent workshop. Another interesting connection between Land and S. F. B. J. is the relationship of designer Jean Ray, who is listed by both companies as a lead designer. Émile Lang dolls are of very good quality.

LANGE, ERBEN G.—Germany, mid-1800s. Very little is known of this doll crafter, other than he made wooden dolls of such caliber that he won a bronze medal at the 1853 New York International Exhibition.

LANGFELDER, HOMMA & HAYWARD—U.S.A., 1921-probably close to World War II. Took over the import business of Morimura Brothers. Responsible for importing thousands of German and Japanese all-bisque and celluloid, along with wholesaling American rubber and composition dolls.

LANGROCK BROTHERS CO.—U.S.A., 1916-1923. Manufactured composition character dolls dressed in felts to represent regional costumes and American period dolls. Also advertised a composition baby doll on a cloth body and a Hawaiian child named Houla-Houla.

LANTERNIER, A., ET CIE—France, 1915-1924. Although this company was in operation since about 1855, it was not until 1915 that it began producing bisque doll heads. Many of the heads have interesting and dramatic faces, with distinctive modeling; others are less appealing. Considering this porcelain factory was located in Limoges, France, a city known worldwide for its porcelain products, the vast difference in the quality of the bisque is startling, ranging from very good to coarse and grainy.

LARKIN CO.—U.S.A., 1875-1930. Advertised bisque, composition, and wooden dolls on jointed and cloth bodies, along with other toys.

LATEXTURE PRODUCTS—U.S.A., mid-twentieth century. Produced a papier-mâché mannequin-type doll that was packaged with patterns for different doll costumes. Advertised as a teaching tool for little girls to learn to sew.

LAUBSCHER'S PUPPEN FABRIK—South Africa, 1915-1927. Founded by Miss Anna Laubscher. Produced cloth dolls. The early dolls had flat hand-painted faces and were stuffed with sawdust, and jointed at the hips and shoulders. Improvements were made with molding to the face, and cork for stuffing. The hand-painted cloth dolls were popular in South Africa, but few were exported from the area. At the peak of production, 250 dolls a week were crafted. Laubscher dolls are of good quality.

LAUER, D. F.—U.S.A., 1824-1888. Sold all types of dolls, imported and domestic. Included in their inventory of wholesale merchandise were dolls of bisque, china, composition, Parian, rubber, and wax—along with doll parts and accessories.

LAUMONT, BARONESS DE—France, 1914-1921. Also known as Mme. J. Ferrant. Founded the Ligue du Jouet Francais (The League of the French Toy) in 1916. Dressed bisque- or composition-head dolls with composition or wire armatures, covered with cotton, bodies. Many of the heads were supplied by Lanternier. It is apparent that the type of doll used and the material needed for their costuming was dictated by whatever way available.

LAUREL DOLLS, INC.—U.S.A., mid-twentieth century. Produced hard plastic dolls of fair to mediocre quality.

LAZARSKI, MME. THABÉE—Poland, 1913, and France, 1914-1930. Founded the La Groupe Polonaise. A group of Polish refugees established workshops under the direction of Mme. Lazarski. They produced art dolls of cloth, felt, leather, and wax. After the war years, composition and less art-type dolls were produced.

LEE, H. D.—U.S.A., 1920-1962. Also known as Buddy Lee Dolls. Produced composition and hard plastic dolls with painted side-glancing eyes and closed mouths dressed in costumes depicting various occupations. Buddy Lee dolls are of only fair quality, but nevertheless enjoy an active collector following.

LEFEBVRE, ALEXANDRE, ET CIE—France, 1860-1926. A member of the Chambre Syndicale and by 1922 a member of S. F. B. J. Produced bisque and composition-head dolls on jointed bodies. Also advertised character dolls and clowns. Lefebvre dolls range in quality from good to very good.

LEHMANN, ERNST PAUL—Germany, 1881-1902. Manufactured mechanical walking dolls with celluloid heads supplied by Buschow & Beck.

LEIBE & HOFMANN—Germany, 1772-1888. The early years of this porcelain factory were probably not devoted to the production of doll heads. By 1882 Leibe & Hofmann were the owners, and doll heads with open mouths bearing their mark have been found. In 1888, the factory was sold and, according to records, no longer produced doll heads.

LENCI®—Italy, 1918-present. The Lenci doll history is well documented and quite interesting. Young Elena König Scavini was left alone when her husband, Enrico, went off to war in 1918. Elena and her brother Bubine König made the first felt doll in the Scavini's apartment. Bubine steam-pressed the faces and Elena did the artistic work. This was the beginning of the world-famous Lenci doll. There are at least two versions of the origin of the name Lenci. The more romantic is that Lenci was a nickname given to Elena by her husband before he went off to war. This may be true, as there is evidence of Elena having been known by this name as early as 1915, when a gift of a bronze likeness was given to her with "Lenci" engraved on it. However, the Lenci company itself gives an entirely different explanation. According to their records, the Lenci trademark was registered in 1919 as a child's spinning top with the words, "Ludus Est Nobis Constanter Industria" (taken from the Latin motto which freely translates as "To play is our constant work"). The first letters from the motto spelled out LENCI. Achieving worldwide recognition for their artistic beauty, this was the first company to use a pressed-felt method to give the faces dimensional character. Beautifully costumed and made of all felt with wide side-glancing eyes, Lenci dolls are of excellent quality.

LENOX INC.—U.S.A., 1914-1920. Operating as a pottery company for years other then those given, it is between these years that Lenox supplied bisque doll heads to American doll manufacturers. Marked Lenox doll heads are of good quality.

LESCHHORN, RUDOLF—Germany, 1925-1930s. Before founding his own doll company, Leschhorn had been involved with the doll industry for several years. Manufactured bisque head dolls on soft-stuffed bodies. At least some of the heads were supplied by Armand Marseille and Ernst Heubach.

LEVEN, H. JOSEPH—Germany, 1912-1938. Although Joseph Herbert Leven passed away in 1931, the business continued operating under the ownership of Friedrich Engel, but kept the Leven name. Exported bisque baby and child dolls on kid or imitation kid bodies, dressed or undressed, along with character Eskimo and dollhouse dolls. Joseph Leven's company manufactured both very inexpensive and moderately priced dolls.

LEVEN & SPRENGER—Germany, 1891-1912. Founded by Joseph Herbert Leven and Theodor Sprenger for the express purpose of exporting dolls and toys. This is the same Leven that went on to form his own company after Leven & Sprenger dissolved. Advertised three faced dolls, leather dolls, and "dolls with pulling eyes." It is assumed that the bisque heads were supplied by one of the porcelain factories from the Sonneberg area such as Armand Marseille and/or Ernst Heubach.

LEVERD ET CIE—France, 1869. A very small, short-lived, little-known doll manufacturer. Leverd did register his marking, and occasionally an example of a bisque-head doll bearing that mark does surface with a bisque swivel head with a separate shoulder plate on a jointed kid body.

LEVIE, J.—Germany, 1925-1926. Advertised composition mama dolls with cloth bodies, bisque-head child dolls on jointed composition bodies, and novelty dolls.

LIBBY DOLL & NOVELTY CO.—U.S.A., 1930s. Manufactured composition and cloth dolls.

LIEBERMANN, ERNST—Germany, 1894-1930, and later under the name Eli. Founded by Ernst Liebermann, but in 1925 this company fell under the ownership of Franz Albert Liebermann, at which time the factory was converted to a mass-production system for the exclusive exportation of dolls. Ernst had spent several years in the doll community before starting his own company. He had been an apprentice for Löffler & Dill as a Täufling maker, and an employee of both Cuno & Otto Dressel and Max Oscar Arnold. This company advertised bisque head dolls on jointed bodies and celluloid heads. At least some of the bisque heads were supplied by Schoenau & Hoffmeister.

LIGUE DU JOUET FRANÇAIS (League of the French Toy)—France, 1914-1916. Founded by Mme. La Baroness de Laumont with the intent to employ women to produce toys for children. This company dressed bisque or composition head dolls, which had composition or wire armatures covered by cloth bodies. Many of the heads were supplied by Lanternier. It is apparent that the type of doll, and the materials used to dress them, was whatever was available.

LILLI—Germany, 1950s. Also known as Bild Lilli of Germany. One of the most sought-after, and hardest to find of the hard plastic collectible dolls. Most doll students credit Lilli with the creation of Mattel's Barbie®. Few could dispute the resemblance. Found standing 11-1/2 inches tall with a ponytail, heavily lined black and white eyes, and a curvaceous body wearing the latest fashions. Also offered in a smaller, 7-1/2-inch version with identical characteristics. Molded after a German newspaper's cartoon character Lilli, and is of the highest quality.

LIMBACH PORZELLANFABRIK—Germany, 1772-1927. Founded by Gotthelf Greiner in Limbach, near Alsbach. The Limbach porcelain factory was an early doll manufacturing pioneer. The museum at Sonneberg has identified them with the production of an 1850 china-head doll currently in the doll exhibition. The most beautiful bisque, china, and porcelain dolls were made from 1893 to 1899, when doll production was halted for a period of twenty years. In the years between 1899 and 1919 they continued to produce and export all bisque, small jointed bisque babies, bathing dolls, and figurines. The early heads, both socket and shoulder heads, are marked with only a clover leaf and a size number. Dolls made after 1919 include the trade names Norma, Rita, or Wally, along with the clover leaf and crown mark.

LINDNER, EDMUND—Germany, 1829-1902 (but it is 1851 that is significant to the German doll industry). In 1851, Edmund visited the London Exhibition. While there, he stopped by a toy shop and saw a doll that was new to him: a baby or Täufling with a composition head, shoulder, mid-hip section, hands and feet with wooden lower arms and legs, connected with cloth floating joints. The doll's facial features appeared to be oriental, with almond-shaped black blown glass eyes and a closed mouth. Upon his return to Germany, Edmund reproduced the doll he had seen from wood and cloth, and thus produced the first commercial German Täufling.

LINDNER, LOUIS & SÖHNE—Germany, 1830-1928. A true Sonneberg Verleger. Never manufacturing anything of their own, they purchased, accumulated, distributed, wholesaled, and exported all types of dolls and doll-related items. Verlegers were an important part of the German economy. Had it not been for companies like Lindner, the home works and cottage industries of the region would have had no outlet for the crafts. A few bisque heads were produced for Lindner, and at least some of those heads were manufactured by Simon & Halbig.

LININGTON, C. M.—U.S.A., 1866-late 1890s. Imported and distributed, from their Chicago warehouse, wax-over, composition, china, French, and German bisque on jointed bodies and all-bisque dolls.

LIVE LONG TOYS—U.S.A., 1923-1940s and possibly later. Manufactured oilcloth dolls often depicting cartoon characters, designed by Eileen Benoliel. Later dolls were made with snaps sewn into their hands so that they could be snapped together.

LLOYD MANUFACTURING CO.—U.S.A., 1917-1929. A name often found associated with several doll manufacturers. Lloyd Manufacturing produced the voice boxes found in many dolls, especially the mama-doll type.

LÖFFLER & DILL—Germany, 1887-1932, when merged with Eduard Schmidt. Manufactured and exported several types of dolls. Used the trademark Sico and Sicora, also referred to their dolls as *Wunderpuppen* (Wonder dolls). Advertised composition mama dolls with molded and painted hair and eyes or with a wig and sleep eyes, open mouth with teeth on a pink cloth body with wooden or composition lower arms.

LONA ART DOLLS—Germany, 1927, and probably other years. There is very little research material on this high-quality celluloid doll. This company is known from its Lona Dolls advertisement in the February 1927 issue of *Plaything*. Several wrist tags printed "Lona D. R. P." have surfaced. The celluloid heads appear to have been made by Rheinische Gummi und Celluloid Fabrik on cloth bodies made by August Schmidt. Lona Art celluloid dolls are of very good quality.

LOVE DOLL CO.—U.S.A., late 1920s. Manufactured clowns with composition heads with hand-painted features, and hands on soft, stuffed-cloth bodies.

LOVELY DOLL CO.—U.S.A., mid-twentieth century. Produced small, character hard plastic dolls often dubbed as shelf dolls by collectors. Contrary to the name, Lovely dolls are only of mediocre quality.

LUTHARDT, ERNST, EG. M.—Germany, 1868-1938. The German registers list E. Luthardt as a *Lederpuppenfabrik und Export* which is German for "Factory and exporter of leather dolls." Along with the leather, imitation leather, leather cloth, leather and felt, and leather and celluloid—all types of leather bodies that Luthardt advertised—this company also exported composition, celluloid, bisque, and china doll heads for its leather bodies. In 1929, the name "Luta" appears on their leather bodies.

LYNN & CO.—U.S.A., 1903. A small, but interesting, company that manufactured very small all-bisque dolls that were silver plated. The dolls were used as favors baked into cakes, or placed in a lady's tea cup to absorb the heat and prevent the cup from cracking, and even carried in a lady's hand to keep it cool, should she need to give a gentleman her hand.

M

MAAR, E. & SOHN—Germany, 1917-1928 (when Ernst, the founder, died, his son Ernst Karl became sole owner, continuing the business at least for several years). Manufactured bisque dolly-faced and character babies on jointed composition bodies, and composition dolls with molded and painted hair on cloth or kid bodies. E. Maar dolls are of fair quality.

MAASER, ROBERT—Germany (Dates concerning this German Puppenfabrik are conflicting; some records give 1904, and others 1911, as the founding year. There is no conclusive evidence as to its closing, but around 1930 is a safe assumption.). Manufactured bisque, composition, and celluloid heads on jointed and unjointed bodies. Best known for the character baby with the patented moveable jaw. The bisque baby head appears as any other head from the outside, but within the head the teeth are attached to a hinged jaw-like device that allows the lower teeth to move up and down. Robert Maaser dolls are of good quality, and the moveable jaw doll is especially collectible.

MADAME HENDREN—U.S.A., 1915-1965. A part or branch of the Averill Manufacturing Co. Produced a tremendous number of composition dolls, along with the other types made by Averill. Madame Hendren dolls are of good quality.

MADE IN AMERICA MANUFACTURING CO.—U.S.A., 1915-1918. A small, short-lived manufacturer of composition dolls with molded and painted hair and eyes, cloth bodies, and composition hands.

MAGYAR ASSZONYOK NEMZETI SZÖVETSÉG (Hungarian for "National League of Hungarian Women")—Hungary, 1909-1926. Operated as a cottage-type industry in and around Budapest, produced dolls in authentic Hungarian costumes.

MAGYAR BABAVILAG (Hungarian for "Hungarian Dolldom")—Hungary, 1920 and possibly later. Produced and exported handcrafted cloth dolls dressed in regional or historical costumes, or as character dolls.

MAIDEN TOY CO.—U.S.A., 1915-1919. Also known as Maiden America. Manufactured all-composition dolls jointed at the shoulders with molded and painted hair and eyes, or with mohair wigs.

MAIENTHAU & WOLFF—Germany, 1927-1930s. Manufactured art and baby dolls both dressed and undressed.

MAIL—France, 1927-1930s. Sold decorative accessories and dolls made with pincushion doll heads with molded and painted hair and facial features.

MANHATTAN DOLL CO.—U.S.A., 1890-1922. Sold both imported and domestic dolls. Advertised a composition and wood doll that, with no mechanism, walked when led by the hand.

MARCOUX, CHARLES—France, 1920-1923. Manufactured porcelain doll heads.

MARCUS, DAY & CO.—England, 1916-1922. According to some records, Marcus is also spelled "Marcuse." Made cloth and felt character dolls, some with British Ceramic heads, with or without sleep eyes.

MARGAINE LACROIX, HOUSE OF—France, 1873-1918. Margaine Lacroix was a couturier, and using different types of bisque head dolls, she created wonderfully accurate and authentic costumes depicting French and Russian regional and historical personages. Forty of these fantastic dolls are on exhibit at the Carnegie Museum in Pittsburgh.

MARGUERITE DOLLS—U.S.A., 1901. Tinted or untinted bisque shoulder-head dolls on cloth bodies with china lower arms. Molded decorations on the head and front of the bodice, including a four leaf clover, morning glory, flower, and a butterfly. The quality ranges from very good to very poor.

MARIENFELD PORZELLANFABRIK—Germany, 1892-1900 (When the company reorganized and became the Karl Voigt & Albin Müller Co. in 1903, they went bankrupt and were purchased by Hertwig & Co.) The original porcelain factory was founded by Adalbert Voigt. Manufactured bisque and porcelain doll heads and limbs, including legs molded with fancy stockings and a garter.

MARKMANN, SIGISMUND—Germany, 1902-1930 and beyond. Manufactured dolls and other toys. Maintained a close collaboration with Kley & Hahn, enabling both companies to have a greater inventory. Advertised a wide assortment of doll accessories, such as dresses, hats, shoes, stockings, muffs, and stoles. Also, cardboard Easter eggs containing small dolls, and other decorative dolls.

MARKS BROTHERS—U.S.A., 1918-1930s. Affiliated with New England Toy Co., Marks Brothers manufactured and imported celluloid dolls and composition dolls on cloth bodies.

MARQUE, ALBERT—France, 1910-1916. A sculptor and designer of the model for the A. Marque doll. Albert Marque was first known as an Art Nouveau sculptor, and was recognized for his work in bronze, marble, terra cotta, and plaster. The Carnegie Museum, in 1916, purchased five A. Marque dolls and thirty-five S. F. B. J. dolls from Margaine Lacroix. The forty dolls, purchased at $35 each, arrived in the same type of custom-made boxes covered with French wallpaper. This event contributed greatly to the theory that suggested S. F. B. J. could have made the A. Marque dolls, using the model designed by Albert Marque. I have never subscribed to this theory. If correct, there is no explanation for the absence of the usual S. F. B. J. marking. I believe, as do many others, that the A. Marque dolls were made by the artist himself. To date there are only about fifty authentic A. Marque dolls which have been located. The bisque head is a masterpiece of molding, made with five sections so as to avoid any undercuts, very good paperweight eyes, feathered brows, and a deep-creased eye lid. The closed mouth is deep pompadour red (close to the color used by Gaultier), but the eye corner dots and the nostrils are a lighter red color. The jointed composition body has exquisitely molded bisque forearms with graceful hands and fingers. Always 22 inches tall. A. Marque dolls are of excellent quality, extremely desirable, and very costly.

MARSEILLE, ARMAND—Germany, 1885-mid-1950s. After World War I, the doll industry began to decline in Germany; however, until that time, it was one of the largest and best-known doll manufactures in the world. Along with producing their own bisque heads, Marseille also supplied them to Amberg; Arranbee; Bergmann; Borgfeldt; Bouton; Butler; Cohen & Son; Cuno & Otto Dressel; Eckart; Edelman; Foulds & Freure; Otto Gans; Goldberger; Hitz; Jacobs & Kassler; Illfelder; Maar; Montgomery Ward; Müller; Pfeiffer; Quaker Dolls; Roth; Samhammer; Peter Scherf; Sears; Seyfarth & Reinhardt; Seigel Cooper; E. U. Steiner; Wagner & Zetzsche; Wanamaker; Wiegand; Wislizenus and Louis Wolf. Along with the bisque child, baby, and character dolls, they also offered painted bisque and composition dolls. Armand Marseille dolls range in quality from the very poorest to the very finest.

MARSH—England, 1865-1914. Charles Marsh made fine wax dolls and claimed that he was responsible for the Royal Model Dolls, representing the children of Queen Victoria. Other makers of wax dolls have also claimed that distinction. Mary Ann Marsh operated a very successful doll hospital.

MARUEI-OKI DOLL CO.—Japan, 1925-1930. Records only indicate that they made dolls. No further explanation or description is available.

MARX—U.S.A., mid-twentieth century. Produced inexpensive hard plastic dolls of mediocre quality.

Armand Marseille's Character Baby #990, Unmarked Piano Baby, Dalmation with Glass Eyes, and Antique Marionette Cat (Photo courtesy of Cobb's Doll Auction.)

MASCOTTE—France, 1882-1901. Bébés bearing the Mascotte label were the creation of May Freres, Cie. Records indicate that Jules Steiner purchased May Freres and advertised Bébé Mascotte after 1897, as did Jules Mettais, Steiner's successor. Beautiful bisque socket heads with large paperweight eyes, heavy feathered brows, pierced ears, and closed mouths, on jointed wood and composition bodies.

MASON, JOHN—U.S.A., 1765-1785. Imported dolls into America, and was one of the earliest doll dealers in America. Manifesto from the ship Warwick records a "large assortment of toys from Bristol England to John Mason Philadelphia" in 1771. A 1773 manifesto from the ship Catherine lists "a very large and neat assortment of toys such as drest dolls and naked dolls." (Note the spelling for "dressed.") The Independent Gazetteer reported in 1785, "John Mason-Toys, a curious assortment for sale at John Mason's Upholster's Store between Chestnut and Walnut Street, viz. Drest dolls, Naked ditto, Lilliputian dolls and wigs for dolls."

MASTERCRAFT DOLL CO.—U.S.A., 1921-1924. Manufactured cloth dolls.

METAL DOLL CO.—U.S.A., 1902-1903. This short-lived doll company was founded by Vincent Lake and Isaac Risley. The fully jointed dolls were made of thin sheets of steel, jointed and constructed to stand alone. Wigs were attached by snaps, and the eyes were either painted or made of glass. Although well made, the Metal Doll Co. dolls, unfortunately, are not a favorite with collectors.

MATLOCK PATENT WASHABLE DOLL—U.S.A., 1899-1914. With distribution through Butler Brothers, this company produced a composition-head doll with either a wig or molded and painted hair, sleep eyes, and a cloth body with composition limbs.

MATTEL—U.S.A., 1945-present. The company, founded by Harold Matson and Elliot Handler, derived its name from a combination of the letters from the two partners' names. Mattel, the world's largest toy manufacturer, is probably best known for its Barbie doll and her friends and family. Initially a producer of dollhouse furniture, Mattel's toy line was expanded to include music boxes, guns, and a host of other famous dolls such as Chatty Cathy, Sister Bell, and Talking Mrs. Beasley. Because of the innovative dolls created at Mattel, it is understandable why security is one of their top priorities. Only a very few employees have access to the research department. Mattel dolls have attained col-lectible status faster than dolls produced by any other company. Their high quality and imaginative concepts have no doubt contributed to this phenomena. Often action oriented, in addition to the walker and talkers, there are singers, a bike rider, and a doll which plays with puppets, another that juggles, and even one that moves her lips as she tells a secret. Mattel dolls are of very good quality.

MAUS, EDITH—Germany, 1925-1928. Also known as Edith Westphal. Advertised unbreakable child, baby, small, and toddler dolls with wigs on washable rubber bodies.

MAUTNER, EMIL—Austria, 1912-1925. Manufactured composition dolls and doll heads.

MAXINE DOLL CO.—1926-late 1930s. Manufactured moderately priced composition dolls, often copying dolls that had proven to be commercially successful. They followed the trends, producing mama and baby dolls. Best known for their popular Baby Gloria, which was also made in bisque and rubber, as well as in composition. Maxine Doll Co. made a doll called Mitzi that was very similar in appearance to Effanbee's Patsy. Effanbee sued them for infringement rights and obtained an injunction; Maxine, in turn, sued Effanbee for filing a frivolous suit, and won the case in the New York Supreme Court. Effanbee appealed, and the appellate court reversed the decision, awarding Effanbee the rights to a doll having the features, characteristics, and general appearance of the Patsy doll, as well as the trade name.

MAYER & SHERRATT—England, 1915-1920. Manufactured doll heads and limbs of British Ceramic. Produced molded and painted hair and facial features, or with wigs and sleep eyes.

MCEWEN, MARY—U.S.A., 1910-1930s. Produced white and black dolls with wax-over composition heads with glass eyes on cloth bodies.

MEECH, HERBERT JOHN—England, 1865-1917. Made and repaired wax dolls, both poured and wax-over. The poured-wax dolls often have inserted human hair and glass eyes set in wonderfully detailed molded eyelids. Meech poured-wax dolls are of very good quality.

MEGO—U.S.A., marketed dolls during the 1970s and 1980s until going bankrupt in 1983. Mego is most famous for its well-made and appropriately costumed solid vinyl action figures and accessories, particularly the Super Heroes adapted from the popular D. C. Comics and the personality stars of the day. Neal Adams, the renowned comic book artist, was responsible for much of Mego's packaging and toy artwork. Mego dolls are of good quality.

Mattel's Baby Cries for You

MEISSEN (the location of Königliche Porzellanmanufaktur)—Germany, 1710-contemporary. This was the first porcelain manufacturer after Friedrich Wilhelm Bottger invented the method of firing clay to produce objects. The first doll heads were manufactured from 1836. The early examples are marked under the shoulder plates. Beautiful porcelain heads with molded and painted hair and features. Meissen porcelain doll heads are of excellent quality.

MELLIN'S FOOD DOLL—U.S.A., 1920s. This doll was manufactured by Horsman for the Mellin company. A composition head with molded and painted hair and eyes on a bent-limb cloth body.

MERMAID DOLL & TOY CO.—U.S.A., 1921-1927. Manufactured composition mama dolls and were licensed by Voices, Inc. to use their criers in the Mermaid dolls.

MERRYTHOUGHT, LTD.—England, 1930s-present. Manufactured cloth dolls.

METAL DEVICES CORP.—U.S.A., 1926. Manufactured a phonograph doll that sang and recited nursery rhymes by way of a cylinder-type composition record placed inside the body. Not only did the special type of record eliminate the need to change needles, the mechanism was so precise that a single turn of the crank activated the record player and allowed the doll to talk.

METROPOLITAN DOLL CO.—U.S.A., 1924-1929. Members of the Doll Parts Manufacturing Association. In addition to the doll parts, Metropolitan also manufactured composition dolls of various types, including dolls designed by Ernesto Peruggi. Advertised a doll with a molded loop for hair ribbons, infant, mama, and crying dolls with wigs and painted or sleep eyes. Licensed by Voices, Inc. to use the criers in their dolls.

METROPOLITAN TOY & DOLL CO.—England, 1914-1915. This company advertised cloth and Eskimo dolls, along with doll clothing.

METZLER, GEBRÜDER & ORTLOFF—Germany, 1875-1903. This company operated beyond these years, but produced dolls only within these years. Bisque and porcelain doll heads were produced at the porcelain factory, but the painting and assembling of the dolls were accomplished by cottage-type industries. The heads were taken to the homes to be painted, and the finished dolls were returned to the factory.

METZLER, RICHARD—Germany, 1884-1928. Advertised a wide variety of dolls, including wood, papier-mâché, music-squeezing, clapping, wax, mama, papa, dressed, and undressed dolls.

MEYER, CARL—Germany, 1899-1921. Made character and baby dolls, of either bisque or celluloid.

MEYER, HERMANN—Germany, 1926-1930. Advertised celluloid dolls, celluloid heads with or without wigs, and celluloid babies. According to some records, they also made rubber dolls.

MEYER & LORANG—U.S.A., 1929-1930s. Produced felt art dolls advertised as having natural hair and washable faces. One interesting characteristic is the position of the eyes. Contrary to most painted felt dolls of the time with the eyes glancing to the side, these dolls had the eyes looking straight ahead.

MICHAELIS, AMANDUS & CO.—Germany, 1870-into the 1930s. Founded by Amandus Michaelis and later owned by Albert and Hugo Michaelis. Maintained ties and connections with Herman and Alfred Pensky. Advertised Täufling, jointed dressed and undressed, leather, wax, and papier-mâché dolls. Also made a mourning doll for the English trade after the death of King Edward VII.

MICHAELIS, HUGO—Germany, 1887-1892, when the factory was completely destroyed by fire. Reopened as the Porzellanfabrik Rauenstein. Hugo Michaelis founded a porcelain factory and became incorporated into the commercial register for the production of porcelain dolls. In 1890 Messrs. Kellner and Sinnhold became partners and the name of the company changed to Hugo Michaelis & Co. Some of the bisque dolls' heads include the name Alice or Dora.

MIDWESTERN MANUFACTURING CO.—U.S.A., mid-twentieth century. Produced inexpensive hard plastic dolls of mediocre quality.

MILLER, J. P., & CO.—England, 1916-1919. Produced, in their own factory, composition dolls including bent-limbed character babies. Registered the English trademarks Compolene and Compolite for their unbreakable composition used to make their dolls.

MILLION, ISABEL—U.S.A., 1911-1919. Handcrafted dolls made from dried apples.

MILLS, O.—U.S.A., 1851-1856. A toy store that included in their inventory a papier-mâché head doll on a cloth body, with their own label attached to the doll.

MILTON BRADLEY CO.—U.S.A., 1927-contemporary. Along with puzzles, games, and books manufactured by Milton Bradley, they also produced, for a short time, composition dolls that they claimed were painted with celluloid paint so that they could be cleaned with a damp cloth. Also advertised, "Kindergarten doll made to teach sewing, care of the hair, dressing and so on."

MITTELLAND GUMMIWERKE—Germany, 1924-1927. Manufactured rubber dolls, advertised that they were made without seams or joints, yet were movable and washable.

MIYAKO BOEKI GOSHI KAISHA—Japan, 1921-1928. Manufactured dolls.

MIZPAH TOY & NOVELTY CO.—U.S.A., 1930s. Created unique long-limbed art dolls made from rayon and silk in varying shades of pink, green, and violet. Made so the hair, shoes, and stockings matched. Very art-deco in design and application.

MODEL DOLL CO.—U.S.A., 1920-1921. A small, short-lived doll manufacturer of composition dolls with molded and painted hair, or with mohair wigs. Model dolls are of rather poor quality.

MODEL PATENT WASHABLE DOLLS—U.S.A., 1899-1907. Dolls with composition heads and arms on cloth bodies distributed through Butler Brothers.

MODERN DOLL CO.—U.S.A., 1926-1927. Founded by Irving Kaufman to produce composition mama dolls with sleep eyes on cloth bodies. Licensed by Voices, Inc., to use their criers in Modern dolls.

MODERN TOY CO.—U.S.A., 1914-1926. Founded by the partnership of Max Roth and Julius Jacobson. Produced a general line of composition dolls, including mama dolls on cloth bodies, all composition character dolls, some with mohair wigs, bent-limb babies with wigs and sleep eyes, and a line of Hug Me Dollies.

MOEHLING, M. J.—Austria, 1870-1930. Located in the region of Aich, it eventually became Anger & Moehling (also known for a short time as Ludwig Engel & Son). The Aich Porzellanfabrik poured the bisque heads for Anger & Moehling. The Porzellanfabrik of Aich was operated by Menzel & Co. (Menzel & Co. was a partnership of Joseph Menzel, Leo Höhnel and Eduard Wolf) The Porzellanfabrik used *A e M* as its marking for Anger & Moehling's bisque doll heads. It is necessary to understand these relationships, in order to see why there is some confusion in the markings for this company. *A e M* is believed by some to stand for Anger & Moehling. Others, though, are of the opinion that it is for Aich & Menzel. Either of these explanations are reasonable. What is not acceptable, however, is the mistaken identity theory that it is an Armand Marseille marking. *A e M* Austria bisque socket heads with open mouth and sleep eyes are of mediocre quality.

MOGRIDGE, W. H. & CO.—England, 1918. A short-lived cottage industry responsible for the production of cloth dolls with cardboard-lined shoulder heads with glass eyes or as recorded, "printed on paper and stuck in the socket."

MÖLLER, AUGUST & SOHN—Germany 1915-1928. Advertised replacement child and baby porcelain, bisque and celluloid heads, with human or mohair wigs. In later years, also offered dolly-faced bisque dolls on jointed composition bodies, and operated a doll hospital.

MÖLLER & DIPPE—Germany, 1879-1913. A porcelain factory that produced doll heads and arms, pincushion dolls, and figurines.

MONICA STUDIOS—U.S.A., 1942-1947. Hansi Share created beautiful composition dolls with the unique characteristic of inserted human hair into the heads forming a widow's peak in the center of the forehead. The modeling of the face and body is outstanding. Monica dolls are of the highest quality.

MONTANARI, MME. AUGUSTA—England, 1851-1884. Created beautiful, poured-wax dolls. She claimed to have crafted the famous Royal Model Dolls, the portrait dolls of Queen Victoria's children, but almost every wax doll maker in England made the same claim. I personally credit Montanari with the Royal Dolls, as her artistry can not be denied. The modeling and attention to detail is fantastic. The setting and sculpturing of the eyes, hair inserted into the scalp, and eyebrows and eyelashes give a realism to the dolls with cloth bodies and wax lower arms and legs.

MONTGOMERY WARD & CO.—U.S.A., 1872-present. Purchased and sold dolls of all types. Several times over the years, this company commissioned special dolls to be sold only through their outlets.

MOORE & GIBSON CORP.—U.S.A., 1917-1930s. Manufactured oilcloth and terry cloth dolls.

MOO-V-DOLL MANUFACTURING CO.—U.S.A., 1919-1920. Manufactured dolls with composition head and limbs on pink cloth bodies. Patented mechanism that allowed the expression of the doll to change by pushing the nose. Face was either smiling or frowning, the eyes would revolve to be one of the following: both eyes open; both eyes closed; left eye closed, right eye open; right eye closed, left eye open.

MORGENTHALER, SASHA—Switzerland, 1924-contemporary. Sasha dolls are once again being manufactured. Morgenthaler was an artist who, in 1924, began to make cloth dolls for her children. She organized others in a cottage-type industry to produce handmade dolls. She went on to create beautifully realistic art dolls, and eventually sold the rights to the famous Sasha dolls.

MORIMURA BROTHERS—U.S.A., 1915-1926. A Japanese import house operating from the early 1870s to 1941, but only produced dolls within the years 1915-1926. When World War I began, the flow of bisque dolls from Europe had virtually ceased. Morimura Brothers stepped in to supply Japanese-made bisque-head dolls to American customers. They unabashedly set out to imitate the German bisque dolls, and did achieve some success—by projecting a certain amount of charm; however, the company demonstrated a lack of technical knowledge and experience needed to produce fine bisque dolls. Although, occasionally, a fine example of Morimura Brothers dolls are found, the majority are of poor quality.

MORIN, L.—France, 1921-1928. Manufactured composition character dolls.

MORODER—Germany, 1800s. Wooden doll Verlegers for several generations.

MORRIS, MISS CLAIRE—U.S.A., 1926-1927. Immortalized friends and family members by creating long-limbed cloth character dolls resembling them. Complete with bright fingernail polish, gold or silver shoes, and costumes made of the finest silks and satins.

MORSE, LEO—U.S.A., 1920-1923. Crafted turned-wood dolls in several styles that were distributed through Rite Specialty Co.

MOSS, LEO—U.S.A., late 1800s into the 1900s. Created beautifully poignant papier-mâché black dolls. The heads were individually molded and, according to legend, were portraits of his family or neighbors. Moss' dolls show great emotions with expressions of pain and toil. Often they were crafted with a tear on their cheeks. Moss dolls are of excellent quality and are highly collectible for their artistic presentation.

MOTHEREAU, ALEXANDRE—France, 1880-1895. Alexandre Célestin Triburee was the founder of the rather obscure French doll firm. They produced a very rare and lovely bisque Bébé with paperweight eyes; blush, or tinting on the lids; thin feathered brows; pierced ears; closed mouths; and cork pates. For all their loveliness, they have rather poorly proportioned wood and composition bodies. The upper arms and legs are of turned wood. The lower arms and legs have rounded joints with a metal bracket for attaching it to the elastic string. The torso was very long and quite thin. The hands and feet are extremely small. Bébé Mothereau are of very good to excellent quality.

MOTSCHMANN, CHRISTOPH—Germany, 1857-1859. For many years, collectors referred to the Motschmann Baby as a type of wax-over papier-mâché doll. However, it is now widely accepted as fact that Christoph Motschmann received the first patent for a talking mechanism, or voice box, that could be mass-produced fairly inexpensively and placed inside a doll's body. The dolls found with the Motschmann stamp, and that used his voice box, are early dolls probably produced with the operative patent years of 1857-1859. There is no evidence that Motschmann ever produced the dolls in which the mechanism was used. Of course, many collectors will still use the title of Motschmann Baby—old habits die hard!

MOTSCHMANN & HÜFNER—Germany, 1874-1902. Also spelled "Hüffner." Advertised Täufling dolls and "jointed and non-jointed dolls. The changeable doll with its trousseau," which was based on an 1895 patent for dolls with exchangeable dresses and wigs to be affixed by adjusting pivot.

MÜLLER, CARL—Germany, 1883-1926. There were three Carl Müllers associated with the doll industry in Germany operating about the same time. Carl #1 near Coburg in 1926 advertised jointed and non-jointed dolls along with dancing dolls, bent-limb baby, newborn, and mama dolls. Carl #2 from Köppelsdorf in 1897 advertised a talking doll. Carl #3 founded a porcelain factory in 1883 and produced bisque dolls there until 1913. The factory continued operating after the 1913 date given, but not as a doll maker.

MÜLLER, FRIEDRICH—Germany, around the turn of the nineteenth century. Manufactured papier-mâché dolls and doll parts. A talented sculptor who had been taught by the French how to make papier-mâché, Müller later developed an efficient method to mass produce papier-mâché dolls and other items.

MÜLLER, KARL & CO.—Germany 1900-1929. There were three Karl Müllers associated with the doll industry in Germany operating about the same time. Karl #1 in Dresden in 1919 advertised "Drivable Dolls." Karl #2 near Coburg from 1900-1926 operated a doll factory and advertised "Newborn babies with sleeping eyes, indistinguishable from living babies 8-12 inches long." Karl #3 near Sonneberg advertised in 1923 that they made their own good quality dolls and babies. In 1924, they added cloth character dolls to their inventory, and used the name Elie for their dolls.

MÜLLER W. G.—Germany, 1900-1930s. Exported to United States dolls with bisque, celluloid, and composition heads. At least some of the bisque and composition heads were supplied by Armand Marseille and the celluloid heads by Schildkröt.

MUNICH ART DOLL—Germany, 1908-1920. Marion Kaulitz was the undisputed originator of the Munich Art Doll. At an awards ceremony in 1910, Kaulitz was credited with leading the Puppen Reform, a movement in Bavaria towards the creation of realism in dolls. The heads were designed by Marie Marc-Schnür, Paul Vogelsanger, and Josef Wackerle. The faces were hand painted by Marion Kaulitz, and costumed by Lillian Frobenius and Alice Hagemann. The dolls were made with composition heads with painted facial features on ball-jointed composition bodies, dressed to resemble French and German children. Munich Art dolls are extremely collectible, not only for their avant-garde naturalism, but also for their historic importance in the chronology of doll making.

MUTH, ERNA—Germany, 1919-1920. Created and crafted interesting art-deco-style dolls and statuettes from silk and crêpe paper-covered wire armatures with hand-painted facial features, dressed in imaginative costumes made of crêpe paper.

MUTUAL DOLL CO.—U.S.A., 1919-1926. Offered bisque or composition dolls with or without wigs and painted or sleep eyes.

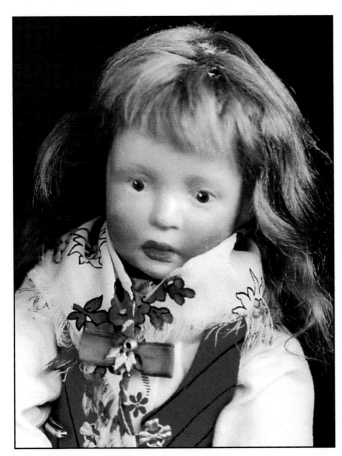

Munich Art Doll (Photo courtesy of Pat Vaillancourt.)

MUTUAL NOVELTY CORP.—U.S.A., 1925-1929. Sold cloth art and novelty dolls along with composition mama and baby dolls.

N

N. A. T. I.—Spain, 1930s-1950s, and possibly other years. Manufactured both art and souvenir tourist-type dolls of cloth, hard plastic, vinyl, and celluloid. The most collectible of the Novedad Arte Tomalidad Ingenio dolls are the cloth dolls with stiffened and molded, large-weave muslin faces. N. A. T. I. dolls, although long overlooked by collectors, have recently enjoyed an appreciation of their charm.

NABER KIDS—U.S.A., 1970s-1994. Founder Harold Naber started by carving wooden Eskimo dolls while piloting in Alaska, and sold them in his Anchorage general store, The Fur Traders. In 1984 these wonderfully happy wooden dolls were put into worldwide production with the introduction of three character dolls. The list of characters continued to grow with the demand for these beautifully carved, high quality art dolls.

NAGAI & CO.—U.S.A., 1917-1918. A short-lived doll company that offered Japanese bisque-head baby dolls on bent-limb composition bodies.

NAKAYAMA, SHOZABURO—Japan, 1929-1940s. Manufactured dolls.

NAKAZAWA, TOTARO—Japan, 1929-1940s. Manufactured dolls.

NANCY ANN STORYBOOK DOLL CO.—U.S.A., 1936-1964. Founded by Nancy Ann Abbott and her partner, A. L. Rowland. Their popular little dolls were first made of painted bisque and, later, hard plastic. Abbott first bought dolls from overseas, but because of their poor quality, they often required a repainting in the United States. By 1938 Nancy Ann began making its own dolls from clay imported from England. In 1960, at the peak of production, over eight thousand dolls a day were produced. The death of Abbott in 1964 marked the end of a very successful doll company. Nancy Ann StoryBook dolls are highly collectible and of fair to good quality.

NANIKAWA, CHUJIRO—Japan, 1930-1940s. Manufactured dolls.

NASCO—U.S.A., mid-twentieth century. Produced hard plastic personality dolls of fair quality.

Nancy Ann StoryBook Doll

NATHAN, FERNAND ET CIE—France, 1925-1929. Manufactured lithographed cut-out dolls to sew at home. Each doll came with a miniature version so that the doll could have a doll.

NATIONAL DOLL CO.—U.S.A., 1923-1940s. Manufactured composition mama and baby dolls with cloth bodies. Their trade name "Just Like" explains the attraction of some of their dolls. They simply made inexpensive dolls copied from successful competitors.

NATURAL DOLL CO.—U.S.A., 1914-1966. Member of the American Doll Manufacturers' Association. Manufactured dolls and doll parts of composition, rubber, hard plastic, and vinyl.

NEAR EAST INDUSTRIES—Greece, 1920-1930s. The Near East Foundation in Athens sponsored Greek refugees to make cloth dolls which were dressed in regional costumes.

NELKE CORP.—U.S.A., 1917-1930. An early manufacturer of undergarments, the Nelke doll was originally made for charity from scrap material. The success of these dolls resulted in their commercial-quantity production with worldwide distribution. The dolls were made of all cloth, and had hand-painted faces. No two were exactly alike.

NELLFOY & CO.—England, 1916-1921. Also spelled "Nell Foy." Made original designed wax-over composition dolls on jointed, cloth, or kid bodies.

NEW ENGLAND TOY CO.—U.S.A., 1918. Manufactured composition dolls with cloth or imitation leather bodies. Maintained an affiliation with Marks Brothers.

NEW ERA NOVELTY CO.—U.S.A., 1914-1916. Also known as Nenco. Advertised their dolls as "guaranteed unbreakable, unburnable and waterproof as well." Offered composition heads on cloth bodies with bent composition limbs, or all composition dolls jointed at neck, shoulders, and hips.

NEW TOY MANUFACTURING CO.—U.S.A., 1912-1921. Produced composition character dolls, a Kewpie-type jointed at the shoulders, all composition dolls with sleep eyes, dolls with composition heads on cloth bodies, and a "New Bisc" doll with special steel spring joints including at the wrists and ankles. Also advertised British Ceramic-head dolls.

NEW YORK DOLL CO.—U.S.A., 1921-1930. Best known for composition novelty dolls.

NEW YORK RUBBER CO.—U.S.A., 1851-1923. Advertised dressed and undressed rubber dolls. The dressed dolls had molded clothing.

NEW YORK STUFFED TOY CO.—U.S.A., 1924-1929. As the name implies, they made stuffed dolls.

NIBUR NOVELTY CO.—U.S.A., 1914-1929. Manufactured composition doll heads and other parts.

NIRESK INDUSTRIES, INC.—U.S.A., mid-twentieth century. Manufactured several hard plastic and vinyl look-alike dolls, copying such well-known and established names as Ginny, Alexander's Ballerina, Saucy Walker, and Miss Revlon. They advertised their moderately priced dolls mostly in hobby and "pulp" magazines. Niresk dolls, although lacking in originality and innovation, are nevertheless of good quality.

NISBET, PEGGY DOLLS—England, 1950s-present. Also known as House of Nisbet Ltd. Manufacturing a complete line of hard plastic and solid vinyl character and personality dolls with wonderful costuming and realistic facial features. Nisbet dolls are of good quality.

NÖCKLER & TITTEL—Germany, 1849-1930s. A successful doll factory that has gained little recognition over the years. Interestingly, on November 27, 1924, Emma Günther, the manager of the company, celebrated her 50th anniversary with the firm. This company advertised all types of dolls—including, cloth, bisque child, baby, and character dolls, rubber, wood, composition, Täufling, and the googly-eyed-type dolls. Also offered a wide assortment of accessories such as wigs, bodies, shoes, and stockings.

NOTTINGHAM TOY INDUSTRY—England, 1914-1920. Founded by Miss Wallis who originally made cloth dolls with mask-type composition faces. Eventually British Ceramic heads designed by Helen Fraser Rock were used on bodies of Compolite. These dolls were called Rock China Dolls. Also made all-composition and cloth dolls.

NOVELTY DOLL MANUFACTURING CO.—U.S.A., 1923-1930. Member of the Doll Parts Manufacturing Association. Made composition dolls and parts.

NOVELTY MANUFACTURING CO.—U.S.A., 1922. Advertised Eskimo dolls dressed in sheepskin.

NUGENT, B., & BROTHERS—U.S.A., 1900-1910. Advertised a "St. Louis Girl" with a German bisque head on a jointed-composition body—with wig and sleep eyes.

NUNN & SMEED—England, 1915-1927. Founded by George L. Nunn and John J. Smeed, who advertised that they were the first company in Britain to make an entire fully jointed composition doll. Dolls can be found with pink bisque or British Ceramic covered in wax.

NYMPHENBURG—Germany, 1761 but only produced dolls between 1890-1930. Also known as Königliche Bayerische Porzellan Manufaktur or The Royal Porcelain Manufactory of Bavaria. Made porcelain dolls' heads reportedly designed by Wackerle.

O

O. K. TOY MANUFACTURING CO.—U.S.A., 1920-1921. A small, little-known manufacturer of composition-head dolls with molded and painted hair or mohair wigs and painted eyes on composition bodies.

OAKHURST STUDIOS—U.S.A., 1925. Manufactured cloth or cloth-bodied dolls, best known for the Cuddlekins line.

OATES WAX STUDIO—U.S.A., 1927-1928. Produced wax figurines and composition dolls.

OBERENDER, NIKOLAUS—Germany, 1908-1927. Originally founded by Nikolaus Oberender and Johann Walther, but by 1910 the partnership came to an end, and Oberender obtained a new partner, Wilhelmine Oberender. Produced bisque doll heads.

OBLETTER—Germany, 1825-1859. This company was a wooden doll Verleger.

OHLHAVER, GEBRÜDER—Germany (Dates concerning the opening and closing of this company conflict. By some accounts 1897—and others 1912—was the founding date, and the company remained in operation until at least 1928.) All sources agree that in 1913 Ohlhaver was advertising bisque-head dolls with jointed bodies. The Ohlhaver brothers forever immortalized their names with the famous "Revalo" trademark, derived from the owner's name being phonetically spelled backwards. The bisque character and child used by Ohlhaver were supplied by several porcelain factories, including Ernst Heubach, Gebrüder Heubach, and Mengersgereuth. Mengersgereuth heads are identified by an X within a circle incised with the markings. Revalo dolls are of good to very good quality.

OLD COTTAGE TOYS—England, late 1940s-contemporary. Starting as a cottage-type industry that crafted handmade cloth-bodied dolls with painted composition, hard plastic, or molded felt faces, and growing to be a true leader in the English doll community. Nicely costumed, often with buttons or other ornamentation added. Originally designed by Greta Fleischmann, and her daughter Susi, they were later joined by many talented craftsmen. Their production could never keep pace with the demand of these charming character dolls; therefore, the dolls always carried a rather high price tag. Old Cottage dolls are of good quality.

ORBEN, KNABE & CO.—Germany, around 1909. Manufactured glazed porcelain shoulder heads often with the initials O K incised on them.

ORIGINAL DOLL CO.—U.S.A., 1925-1929. Manufactured composition mama, baby, and infant dolls on cloth bodies with sleep eyes. Licensed by Voices, Inc., to use their criers in Original dolls.

ORIGINAL TOY CO.—U.S.A., 1915-1924. Made composition character dolls.

ORSINI, JEANNE I.—U.S.A., 1916-1930, and probably later. Designed and manufactured small (5-7 inches) all-bisque dolls including child, baby, and infant dolls. Many were made with glass eyes and mohair wigs and had names as familiar as Mimi and Vivi.

ORSZÁGOS MAGYAR HÁZIIPARI SZÖVETSÉG ("National Hungarian House Industry")—Hungary, 1926. Made dolls in authentic Hungarian regional costumes.

OTTO DOLL SUPPLY CO.—U.S.A., 1917-1918. Manufactured composition dolls and doll parts.

OURINE, G.—France, 1925-1930s. Manufactured a line of dolls known as Poupée Royale. Also advertised art dolls, decorative dolls, and pincushion dolls.

OUVRÉ, MME. VERA—France, 1915-1918. Made cloth dolls.

OWEENEE NOVELTY CO.—U.S.A., 1921-1923. Manufactured terry cloth and flannel. Also advertised dolls with composition heads on cloth bodies.

OZ DOLL & TOY MANUFACTURING CO.—U.S.A., 1924-26. Manufactured cloth Wizard Of Oz character dolls.

OZZERAN MANUFACTURING CO.—U.S.A., 1920. Also has been spelled "Ozzerman." Handmade dolls.

P

P. & M. DOLL CO.—U.S.A., 1918-contemporary. Member of the American Doll Manufacturers' Association. Manufactured dolls, doll heads, and other doll parts of composition and hard plastic.

PAAR, KATARINA—Austria, about 1914-1927. Katarina and Elizabeth Neumayer created cloth art dolls of museum quality. Originally sold at craft shows and bazaars to help benefit the War effort. The artistically executed dolls with their long thin limbs and wonderfully detailed costumes were enthusiastically received by casual observer and art critics alike.

PADEREWSKI, MME. HELENA—France, 1915-1918. Supervised the creation of dolls that were crafted in the workshop of Mme. Lazarski in Paris. Madame Paderewski arranged for a consignment to be sent to the Polish Victims Relief Fund in New York City. They were well received not only for their intrinsic appeal, but for their historic value. Made entirely by hand of heavy cloth stuffed with cork and hand painted.

PALITOY CASCELLOID—England, 1919-1968. Made composition, hard plastic, and celluloid dolls of mediocre quality.

PANDORA—France, 1915-1918. Name of the workshop in Paris where dolls of the same name were manufactured with bisque heads with painted eyes and wigs.

PAPPE, MORITZ—Germany, 1903-1928. Manufactured felt art dolls, celluloid dolls with cloth bodies, character dolls in swimming and skiing costumes, and Eskimo dolls.

PAQUES-NOEL, ESTABLISSEMENTS—France, 1928-1929. A small, short-lived doll manufacturer. Made dolls and doll parts of composition and cardboard. Also advertised small, all-bisque dolls with blown glass eyes and doll accessories.

PARAMOUNT DOLL CO.—U.S.A., 1926-1930. In 1930 became Kaufman, Levenson & Co. Manufactured composition mama and baby dolls on cloth bodies with composition limbs. Licensed by Voices, Inc., to use their criers in Paramount dolls.

PARIS DOLL CO.—U.S.A., mid-twentieth century. Produced hard plastic walker dolls of fair quality.

PARSON-JACKSON CO.—U.S.A., 1910-1919. A fire once destroyed the factory where the white and black celluloid baby dolls were manufactured. Advertised that the dolls, which had smiling or crying expressions, were modeled from real babies.

PATENT NOVELTY CO.—U.S.A., 1929. A short-lived, little-known manufacturer of brightly painted, segmented wood dolls.

PATENT WASHABLE DOLLS—Germany, 1880-1910. A name used to identify a particular type of composition doll made by various German manufacturers. Seldom found in good condition, with the area around the eyes extremely susceptible to damage. Rarely is a Patent Washable doll found with fine-quality material or artistic decoration. Characterized by the composition shoulder head, thin cloth body, long cloth limbs with composition forearms, and lower legs often with molded boots. Mohair or skin wig, bulging glass eyes, and a closed mouth.

PATUREL, J. ET CIE.—France, 1925-1928 and probably other years. A sales advertising catalog lists bisque-head dolls with jointed composition bodies, cloth, rubber, and all-composition dolls, in addition to white and black celluloid child and baby dolls.

PAUFLER, EMIL & CO.—Germany, 1896-1905. Advertised as the oldest doll head manufacturer in Saxony. This company's inventory included papier-mâché, wax, and porcelain dolls—along with Täufling and dollhouse dolls.

PAYNE, W., & SON—England, 1772-1927. Also had an outlet in Paris. A famous department store that sold many types of dolls including celluloid, character, and baby dolls, and bisque dolls with jointed composition bodies. After World War I, they manufactured their own dolls along with importing dolls from France and Germany. Advertised that, "Made to Paynes' own specification and dressed on the premises."

PEACOCK—England, 1862-1889. Autoperipatetikos marked "July 15, 1862. J. Peacock, Doll Maker, The Rocking Horse, New Oxford St., London" has been reported with a china head molded with exposed ears and leather arms.

PECK, MRS. LUCY—England, 1891-1930. Made and repaired wax dolls. Used beeswax and pink wax in her doll productions, inserting hair and eyes, some with a wire mechanism that controls the open/close of the eyes. When repairing a wax doll, Mrs. Peck often stamped her name upon the bodies of the dolls; therefore, it is not always possible to identify a Peck doll. Mrs. Peck, as most other English wax doll makers, has at one time been credited with the Royal Children wax portrait dolls. In later years, Mrs. Peck devoted her talents to sculpturing clay models and making plaster of Paris molds for dolls.

PEDDLER DOLLS—England, and later other countries, 1700s-present. Peddler dolls were an important decorating accent and conversation piece in the most fashionable parlors during the nineteenth century, usually were displayed under glass in a prominent location. Although itinerant traders wandered over Europe and the United States, Peddler dolls seem to be an English phenomenon. The early eighteenth-century dolls were costumed in the ragged clothing as worn by common street merchants. They had crude wooden faces and stump-like bodies. During the Regency and Victorian periods, however, the English Peddler dolls were made to resemble the peddlers and vendors who brought not only the necessities, but decorative items to the remote country towns. It is not unheard of to find a doll carrying as many as one hundred fifty tiny items. Although frequently the creation of the lady of the house, at least some were advertised by commercial doll manufacturers, such as C. H. White of Portsmouth, England. Made of cloth, kid, wood, papier-mâché, wax, or even apples. A careful study of a doll's wares may assist you in dating a Peddler doll. However, bear in mind that it was a common practice for miniatures to be added over time by several different custodians of these amusing treasures. Authentic vintage Peddler dolls are very rare and quite costly. There are many modern examples, from the original artist creations to those of vinyl by well-known doll manufacturers, which are also beguiling and delightful additions to a collection.

PEDIGREE COMPANY SOFT TOYS LIMITED— England, 1942-late 1960s. Manufactured an impressive assortment of hard plastic, magic skin, and vinyl black and white dolls. So successful were their marketing effort that by the mid-1950s, Pedigree had expanded to include factories in Northern Ireland, ten factories in Canada, South Africa, and New Zealand. They also produced a line of accessory doll toys, buggies, tricycles, and toy trains. Pedigree dolls are of good quality.

PELLER-HOFFMANN, MRS. JOHANNA—Austria, 1907, and possibly other years. Made turned-wood dolls. Many with intricately carved and painted details. Assembled with a wooden base to accommodate the carved feet. Peller-Hoffmann dolls are very rare and of good quality.

PENN STUFFED TOY CO.—U.S.A., 1924-1930. Was a member of the American Doll Manufacturers' Association. Manufactured composition and cloth mama and baby dolls of fair quality.

PENNEY, J. C. & CO.—U.S.A., 1872-present. Purchased and sold dolls of all types. Have several times over the years commissioned special dolls to be sold only through their outlets.

PENSKY, ALFRED—Bavaria, 1919-1930s. Founder of the Alfred Pensky Kleinpuppenfabrik (German term for "a factory for miniature dolls"). Also maintained a connection with the Amandus Michaelis & Co. doll factory, with whom he often advertised his petite, pincushion, baby, and dollhouse dolls of bisque, celluloid, or china.

PENSKY, HERMANN—Germany, and later Bavaria, 1911-1930s. Founder of the Hermann Pensky Fabrik Gekleideter Puppen (German term for "factory for dressed dolls"), and partner with Albin Michaelis as owners of the Amandus Michaelis & Co., he also maintained close ties with Alfred Pensky. Advertised mama, baby, and "artistic" dolls.

PEREYRA, MANUELA—Venezuela, 1900-1930, and possibly later. Handcrafted cloth dolls representing the Venezuelan people.

PERFECT TOY MANUFACTURING CO.—U.S.A., 1919-1930s. A member of the American Doll Manufacturers' Association and licensed to use Voices, Inc., patented voice boxes in their composition dolls.

PERFECTION DOLL CO.—U.S.A., 1916-1923. Manufactured all-composition or cloth-bodied composition dolls.

PERFORMO TOY CO.—U.S.A., 1926. Little is known of this small, short-lived doll manufacturer, save the registering of the name Mickey for their dolls that represented acrobats. It is suggested by their advertising of "lacquer enamel finish" that the character dolls were made of wood or composition.

PERLS, CHARLES, MANUFACTURING CO.— England, 1916-1922. Manufactured all-composition, or composition and celluloid, dolls.

PERMOLIN PRODUCTS—U.S.A., 1918. A small, short-lived doll manufacturer of 14- and 15-inch all composition dolls jointed at neck, shoulder, and hips.

PERONNE, MLLE.—France, 1864-1884. Also known as Lavallée-Peronne. Manufactured bisque Poupée de Mode and bébés.

PERRAULT, MME. MARIE—France, 1916. This company handcrafted cloth character dolls, whose costuming was imaginative.

PERRIMOND, GASTON—France, 1924-1930s, and perhaps later. Handcrafted cloth art dolls known as Nicette or La Poupée Nicette.

PERRIN, MME.—France, 1916-1918. Handcrafted cloth dolls using the initials *L. P. A.* for La Poupée des Allies (French term for "Dolls of the Allies").

PETERSON, FRANK W., CO.—U.S.A., 1907-1930. Manufactured segmented wooden dolls with painted features and clothing, under the trademark Petson.

PETIT, JACOB—France, 1790-1865. A porcelain factory that advertised "talking Marottes" and an "Indian Juggler" doll.

PETIT & DUMONTIER—France, 1878-1890. Founded by Frederic Petit and André Dumontier for the production of bisque dolls. At least some of the heads were supplied by François Gaultier indicating that Petit & Dumontier manufactured a very good quality doll.

PETIT & MARDOCHÉE—France, 1843-1860. Manufactured porcelain head dolls.

PETITCOLLIN—France, 1860-1930s. Manufactured celluloid doll heads that were called L'Intrepide Bébé celöid, and supplied them to Le Minor.

PETITES MAINS PARISIENNES—France, 1916. French term for "Little Hands of Paris," the name of the workshop founded by M. and Mme. Et. Bricon where art dolls of cloth, composition, or porcelain were made. Most of the dolls were designed by M. Gardet, a well-known artist.

PETRI & BLUM—U.S.A., 1915-1916. A small, short-lived composition doll manufacturer.

PETRI-LEWIS MANUFACTURING CO.—U.S.A., 1923-1929. Made segmented wooden character dolls.

PETZOLD, DORA, DR.—Germany, 1919-1930s. Dr. Dora Petzold's composition character child dolls are mysterious, but highly sought-after dolls. Little information is available about either Dr. Petzold or her dolls. One fact agreed on, though, is that her dolls are rare. The heads have been variously reported as being silk, layers of paper, composition, and pressed cardboard, and in fact, all of these may be correct. The bodies are stockinette with rather short torsos, jointed at the shoulder and hips. Hands have separate freeform thumbs, with the other fingers only being stitched. The legs have shaped calves. A 1919 German magazine, *Die Post*, reported ". . . These are dolls for the high society, for the elegant world, for the boudoir, for the lady. Worked of velvet and silk...to decorate a room by placing them before an embroidered pillow or having them swing on the handrail of an armchair . . ." It is obvious from her writing that the author deemed Petzold dolls as extraordinary, an opinion shared by many collectors today. Later that same year, Dr. Petzold described her dolls in an interview as, "All Petzold dolls are produced in my workshops under my personal directorship and after my personal designs and models. The body of the dolls consists of high quality knit wear and is stuffed so that all doll joints can be bent to imitate every human movement. The heads are of unbreakable, non-flammable material and painted with non-toxic colors which makes my dolls washable. The outfits for the dolls are fashioned after the best children's outfits and produced of the first class material. All these characteristics make a practical, and at the same time, very nice toy of my doll." Petzold dolls are of good quality.

PFEFFER, FRITZ—Germany, 1873-1925 and after, at least until 1930, as Emil Pfeiffer & Sons, and then later as Fritz Weber & Max Pfeffer. Manufactured porcelain doll heads, Frozen Charlottes, and jointed all-bisque dolls.

PFEIFFER, GEBRÜDER—Germany, 1894-1930s, and possibly later. This company produced bisque dolls with at least some of the heads supplied by Armand Marseille, along with composition mama and baby dolls, and felt art-type dolls.

PFOHL, MAGGIE AND BESSIE—U.S.A., 1900, and probably other years. Handcrafted cloth dolls with flat hand-painted facial features.

PHILADELPHIA BABY—U.S.A., about 1900. Also known as the Sheppard Baby, it is a life-sized cloth doll with head, shoulder, forearms, and legs painted in flesh-colored oil paints. The facial features are molded with large deep eyes having well-defined, heavy eyelids, and a "cupid's bow" closed mouth with a deep indentation in the center of the lower lip. The chin is quite pronounced, as are the nicely molded, applied ears. The entire face has a slightly flattened appearance. Painted hair with matching eyebrows. Jointed at shoulder, hips, and knees. The Philadelphia Babies were sold at the J. B. Sheppard Linen Store on Chestnut Street in Philadelphia, hence the name. The designer, maker, and dates of origin are uncertain. The doll is generally accepted as having been made around the turn of the century. One theory is that it was designed by Elizabeth Washington, a student/artist at the Philadelphia School of Design. Supposedly, J. B. Sheppard's Linen Store held a contest for the best-designed doll which could be used as a model for their baby clothes and could also be offered for sale. Washington's doll won the contest and the rights were purchased by the Sheppard Store. There is no documentation to either support or discredit this story. However, we can thank U. F. D. C. member Frances Walker for offering this legend through her writings in the 1980s.

PHILIPS, MARGARET B.—U.S.A., 1916. Little is known of this western Pennsylvania doll company, except that the name Polly Preparedness Patriotic Person was registered in 1916.

PHOENIX—Germany, 1856-1925. Made character dolls of all rubber with molded and painted features and clothing.

PHOENIX DOLL CO.—U.S.A., 1921-1924. Manufactured composition character and mama dolls.

PIEROTTI—England, 1770-possibly as late as 1942, the date of death of the last Pierotti family doll maker, although it is also reported that the mid-1930s (the date of death of Anne Roache Pierotti) saw the end to the Pierotti doll empire. Following a tradition, the Pierotti family of skilled artists crafted beautifully detailed and realistic poured wax dolls. The dolls often have blown glass eyes with detailed eyelids and inserted lashes and brows. Hair also is inserted into slits in the wax. Bodies are of cloth. Pierotti claimed to have made the Royal Model Doll, the wax portrait dolls of Queen Victoria, but it must be noted that so has every other wax doll artist. However, there is evidence that supports the use of Pierotti wax dolls by the Royal Family, even in the decoration of wedding cakes. Pierotti wax dolls are of very good quality.

PIETSCH, KARL—Germany, 1921-1930. Manufactured and exported jointed and baby dolls.

PILORGÉ, ALEXANDRE SILVAIN—France, 1865. A brother-in-law of François Guiltier. Produced porcelain or bisque doll heads.

PINNER, ERNA—Germany, about 1913-1923. A gifted artist and writer whose work reflects the loathing and contempt of postwar Europe. The cloth art dolls created by Erna Pinner have hand-painted faces, with a cavalier expression, elaborately costumed, long-limbed cloth bodies. Although executed with a great deal of artistic merit and highly prized by collectors, the overall appearance of her dolls is one of total indifference.

PINTEL & GODCHAUX—France, 1887-1899, and after as a member of S. F. B. J. Founded by Henri Pintel and Ernest Godchaux. Registered the name "Bébé Charmant" in 1892 and used it for their doll heads of both bisque and rubber. The bisque doll heads are usually found with good quality paperweight eyes and nicely feathered brows, and may have an open or closed mouth. Pintel & Godchaux dolls are of good quality.

PINTEL, M.—France, 1913-1923. Made cloth and felt dolls. Member of the Chambre Syndicale.

PIRAMOVICZ—France, 1915-1917. Also known as Piramonie. According to the registers, Piramovicz was a maker of cloth dolls, operating in Paris from 1915-1917 and possibly 1918, although records are vague.

PIRCHAN, EMIL—Austria, 1907. Created turned-wood character dolls with painted features and clothing. Dolls were either tall and thin, or short and stout.

PLANO TOY CO.—U.S.A., 1920-1924, when acquired by the Pollyanna Co. Manufactured a composition walking doll made with rollers on its feet.

PLASS & ROESNER—Bohemia, 1907-1930. Austrian registration records, although somewhat lacking in detail, indicate that Josef Plass and Paul Roesner produced bisque doll heads at their own porcelain factory in Buchau, Bohemia. It is assumed that heads found with the "ROMA Austria" or "P & R Austria" mark are in fact Plass & Roesner dolls. It must be remembered that Bohemia was, at the time, part of the Austro-Hungarian empire, explaining the location of origin as Austria in their markings.

PLASTIC MOLDED ARTS—U.S.A., 1949-1955. A very prolific doll parts manufacturer. This company supplied parts and entire dolls to several different knockoff companies.

PLAYHOUSE DOLLS—U.S.A., mid-twentieth century. Produced inexpensive hard plastic shelf dolls.

PLEASANT CO.—U.S.A., 1986-present. Also known as "The American Girls Collection." A leading contemporary doll company, founded by Pleasant Rowland, that has set an elevated standard for others in the industry. The American Girls Collection, including Felicity Merriman, Kristen Larson, Abby Walker, Samantha Parkington, and Molly McIntire are manufactured by Götz of Germany. The dolls have historically accurate clothing and accessories. Each character appears in her own fiction book of tales displaying courage and knowledge gained through her adventures, allowing the reader to view experiences from different points in American history. American Girl Collection dolls are of the finest quality.

PLOTNICK, FRANK, CO.—U.S.A., 1926-1930, when they acquired the American Toy & Novelty Corp. and continued for sometime thereafter. Manufactured cloth, stockinette, plush, and tassel dolls.

PODHAJSKA, FRÄULEIN MINKA—Austria, 1903-1910. A talented artist, tutored at the Art School for Females by Professor Böhme. Crafted turned-wood dolls with jointed limbs.

POGLIANI O.—Italy, 1916. A small, short-lived manufacturer of papier-mâché and wooden dolls.

POLITZER TOY MANUFACTURING CO.—U.S.A., 1914-1930, and possibly other years. The Politzer name has long been associated with the doll and toy industry. The names Morris and Max have, over the years, been linked to several different companies, such as American Stuffed Novelty, New Toy Co., Tip Top Toy Co., and New Era Novelty Co. Often records list only an "M. Politzer," and it is impossible to determine who is responsible for certain designs and manufacturing concepts. Politzer Toy Co. produced composition dolls and cloth dolls of fair to good quality.

POLLACK & HOFFMANN—Bohemia, 1902-1907. Produced porcelain doll heads. Apparently Pollack & Hoffmann had connections with Plass & Roesner; however, Pollack & Hoffmann closed their manufacturing doors about the same time that Plass & Roesner were opening theirs.

POLLYANNA CO.—U.S.A., 1920-1940s. An aggressively run company that was in the practice of acquiring smaller companies to form a larger one. This conglomerate consisted of at least Jessie M. Raleigh Co., Rees Davis, Nelson Young Manufacturing, and Plano Toy Co., and possibly other less significant companies. Although Pollyanna produced mama, baby, novelty, and character dolls of composition or cloth, it is the sew kits, known as "You Sew It," that were responsible for their greatest claim to fame. The You Sew It kits were so appealing and complete with doll, material, sewing notions, patterns, and instructions, that they were embraced by most schools for sewing classes. Pollyanna dolls range in quality from very good to fair.

PORTHEIM & SOHN—Bohemia, about 1840-1860. Credited with the production of porcelain doll heads found with the *P & S* marking, at least some of which were decorated with morning glories.

PORZELLANFABRIK GÜNTHERSFELD—Germany, 1881-1890s. This porcelain factory operated in years before and beyond those given, but it is within this time span that bisque or porcelain doll heads were produced.

PORZELLANFABRIK MENGERSGEREUTH—Germany, 1908-1930. Founded by Carl Craemer and his son-in-law François Héron. Co-partners appear to have been Hans and Kurt Craemer. In 1913, Robert Carl and Gustav Liebermann established ownership, and in 1925 Robert Carl became sole owner. For many years the bisque doll heads made by Robert Carl and marked *P. M.* were incorrectly identified as Otto Reinecke. Other marks including Trebor (Robert spelled backwards), Grete, or Herzi may be found. Mengersgereuth supplied bisque heads to other manufacturers, and evidence exists to show that Ohlhaver and Carl Harmus were both patrons, among others. Porzellan-fabrik Mengersgereuth dolls are of mediocre to good quality.

Porzellanfabrik Mengersgereuth's Character Baby #914, Kestner's Solid Dome Character Baby, and the 1895 *Brownie Year Book*, by Palmer Cox (Photo courtesy of Cobb's Doll Auction.)

PORZELLANFABRIK RAUENSTEIN—Germany, 1880-1930s. Founded in 1783 they did not begin producing porcelain and bisque doll heads and Nanking dolls until 1880.

PORZELLANFABRIK THURINGIA—Germany, 1913 and probably other years, although no records exist to verify that fact. This company advertised bathing dolls, dolls, and knickknacks.

POTTERIES TOY CO.—England, 1914-1918. Also known as British Toy Co. and Potteries Doll Co. Manufactured dolls with ceramic heads supplied by W. H. Goss. Also, baby, cloth, and character dolls representing the Allies.

POULBOT, M. & MME. FRANCISQUE—France, 1908-1929. Well-known and respected artists responsible not only for creating their own cloth character dolls, but for designing models for others, including the eminent mold 239 for S. F. B. J. There are doll scholars today who believe that Madame Poulbot and Francisque Poulbot are one in the same person. It must be noted that two separate people did in fact exist, but it is believed that only one was responsible for the development of dolls. Others are equally indoctrinated in the theory that two artists created the dolls. Poulbot dolls are of very good quality and highly prized for their marvelous artistic interpretation of the children from the streets of Paris.

PRE-GREINER—U.S.A., about 1850. The term Pre-Greiner is used to define the dolls with papier-mâché shoulder heads on cloth or kid bodies with wood, cloth, or leather hands and legs, occasionally with bands of green or red paper covering the junctions between limbs and body. The name is really not very accurate, and in fact, can be misleading, but nevertheless is the title given and used by collectors. Characterized by round, broad plain faces with molded and painted common period hair style, black pupil-less glass eyes, closed mouths with the slightest hint of a smile, and is unmarked. Pre-Greiner dolls are of good quality, but are even more highly prized for their aesthetic and historic value.

PRESBYTERIAN DOLL—U.S.A. 1880s (revived again during the late 1950s, and into the 1960s). Cloth dolls with hand-painted faces, nicely costumed to represent little boys and girls. Crafted by the sewing circle of the First Presbyterian Church in Bucyrus, Ohio, as a fund raiser for the Church and Sunday School. Presbyterian dolls are of good quality and are loved for their charm and historical notability.

PRESSMAN, J. & CO.—U.S.A., 1929-1930. A short-lived manufacturer of "Jerry" dolls with composition heads on cloth bodies with wooden limbs.

PRESSMAN, M. & CO.—U.S.A., 1919-1930s. Imported, exported, and manufactured costumed dolls.

PRESSMAN TOY CORP.—U.S.A., mid-twentieth century. Made inexpensive hard plastic novelty-type dolls.

PREUSSER & CO.—Germany, 1909-1930. Although registration and listing show that Preusser was a factory for the manufacturing of dolls' underclothing and dresses, advertisements from the 1920s indicate that they were also manufacturing dressed dolls.

PRICE, LENORA—U.S.A., 1917-1918. Crafted cloth dolls with unique contoured facial construction.

PRIEUR—France, 1840-1928, when acquired by L. Solomon. A family name long associated with the manufacturing of dolls and doll accessories. At least some of the bisque heads were supplied by François Gaultier of France and Carl Heinz of Germany. The Prieur business survived tumultuous times, including the filing of bankruptcy; however, they were able to recover and continue to produce bisque and china dolls along with offering wigs, shoes, umbrellas, hats, clothing, and doll parts for sale.

PRIMROSE DOLL CO.—U. S. A., 1927-1930. Manufactured composition mama and baby dolls with cloth bodies. Licensed by Voices, Inc., to use their criers. Primrose dolls are of mediocre quality.

PRINCESS ANNA DOLL CO., INC.—U.S.A., mid-twentieth century. Manufactured a nice quality hard plastic doll with inferior quality clothing.

PRINTEMPS—France, 1878-1940s and possibly other years. Paris department store that purchased and sold dolls of all types. Have several times over the years commissioned special dolls to be sold only through their outlets.

PRITZEL, LOTTE—Germany, 1908-late 1920s. Pritzel was a talented artist who used her gifts to create wonderful wax-head art dolls. These dolls had long, slender wire armature skeletons that allowed a pliability of the limbs. Extraordinarily sophisticated and appearing somewhat aloof, Pritzel dolls are of the finest quality and aesthetic splendor.

PROGRESSIVE TOY CO.—U.S.A., 1917-1924. Manufactured composition baby and character dolls along with advertising a line of bisque head dolls. Among the most notable doll offered by Progressive was a mechanical Hula-Hula Dancer Islander doll.

PRÖSCHOLD, A. H.—Germany, 1897-early 1900s. This German porcelain factory (*Porzellanfabrik*) advertised all-bisque and all-china dolls.

PROUZA, WENZEL—Bohemia, 1908-1920, and possibly other years. Produced bisque and porcelain dolls and Frozen Charlottes. Records indicate that at least some of the bisque doll heads found with the *A. P.* marking may be Wenzel Prouza dolls.

PULLMAN DOLL CO.—U.S.A., 1916-1917. Also spelled "Pullmann." A short-lived doll manufacturer that obviously did not fulfill their advertised "several thousand dolls a day" claim. Pullman composition dolls are found with cloth bodies and riveted composition limbs.

PULVERMACHER, ALBERT—Germany, 1890-1892. This company manufactured bisque-head dolls on jointed composition bodies. Pulvermacher sold his business to Carl Hoffmeister, which later became Schoenau & Hoffmeister.

PULVERMACHER & WESTRAM—Germany, 1864-1930. Exported dolls and advertised a doll with "noiseless movements" and another with "changeable heads with a screwdriver." It appears, from the registration drawing (D R P 55484) that the "noiseless movement" jointed doll was connected with springs, rather than the common practice of using elastic. It is curious to think that metal springs would be more quiet than cloth-covered elastic—nevertheless, that is their assertion.

PUPPENFABRIK HERZLIEB—Germany, 1928-1930s. Doll factory managed by H. B. Müller.

Q

Q. B. TOY & NOVELTY MANUFACTURING CO.—U.S.A., before 1915 when amalgamated by National Toy Manufacturing Co. Best known for the "Build Me Up" wooden character dolls with interchangeable parts. Q. B. Toy dolls are of mediocre quality.

QUADDY PLAYTHINGS MANUFACTURING CO.—U.S.A., 1916-1917. New York City-based company that made animal character dolls with composition heads and cloth bodies.

QUAKER DOLL CO.—U.S.A., 1915-possibly as late the 1940s. Imported and distributed composition dolls and doll parts, using the Quaker Quality name.

QUALITOY CO.—U.S.A., 1929-1920. Regardless of the clever play on the company name, Qualitoy was a rather short-lived doll manufacturer of composition mama dolls with cloth bodies and sleep or painted eyes.

QUEHL, CARL—Germany, 1851-1922. A Nürnberg toy store that participated in a limited number of toy fairs, including the 1890 Nürnberg Toy Exhibition, where Quehl dolls and toys were listed. Later records indicate that bisque socket head dolls on jointed wood and composition bodies were manufactured under the Quehl name.

QUIM—France, 1927-1930. Assumed to also be known as Quinn. Listed as a doll manufacturer, located in Paris.

QUINT, A.—Austria, 1907-1908. A small, rather short-lived, manufacturer of dolls and doll parts.

R

R. F. NOVELTY CO.—U.S.A., 1919-1920. Best known for the small, jointed Happy Family Dolls, sold as a set consisting of Mother, Father, Little Sister and Brother, Baby Love, the maid, and a nanny.

RABERY & DELPHIEU—France, 1856-1899, when they joined S. F. B. J. (Société Française de Fabrication de Bébés & Jouets). Named for founders, Alexander Rabery and Jean Delphieu. The company's initial interest was the production of doll bodies, but by 1887 they were offering dressed and undressed dolls at the Paris Exhibition. During the 1880s, François Gaultier supplied Rabery & Delphieu with bisque heads and arms for their bébés. The dolls manufactured during the late nineteenth century are made of very pale creamy bisque; uniquely shaped square facial construction; large, dark, almond-shaped paperweight eyes with black eyeliner; and widely arched, long feathered brows. The delicately colored, outlined, accented, and shaped lips have a high cupid's bow. The later Rabery & Delphieu examples have a somewhat coarse bisque with less delicately applied decoration and rather exaggerated lashes, brows, and mouths. Rabery & Delphieu bébés range in quality from the very finest to mediocre.

RÄDER, MAX—Germany, 1910-1913. Manufactured bisque-head, dolly-faced dolls on both composition jointed or kid bodies. Blown glass eyes and good wigs. Also advertised "Chondrogen" (a special composition) and character dolls. Although not a great number of Räder dolls were produced, the quality is good, and the sculpturing is very pleasing.

RADIANA—France, 1927. A little-known manufacturer of decorative, including automobile, dolls.

RADIGUET & CORDONNIER—France, late 1800s. In 1880, R & C was registered as a trademark, and two patents were obtained for a unique body construction that allowed for metal posts to extend through the feet and insert into a wooden base, facilitating a standing position for their bisque-head dolls. This type of doll has been christened a Poupée Statuettes (the French term for doll statues). Records indicate that George Cordonnier enjoyed a close business arrangement with Emile Jumeau. To date it is believed that all Radiguet & Cordonnier dolls are 17 inches tall. Radiguet & Cordonnier dolls are of good quality.

RAINWATER, WILLIAM—U.S.A., 1928. Manufactured composition dolls.

RAKUEL, GANGUE KABUSHIKI KAISHA—Japan, 1921-1927. Also spelled Rakuse, Gangu Kabushika. Manufactured dolls.

RALEIGH, JESSIE MCCUTCHEON—U.S.A., 1916-1920 (when the company merged with Pollyanna Co.). Named for the founder, artist Jessie McCutcheon Raleigh. Jessie was determined to manufacture dolls after the introduction of her critically acclaimed statuette "Good Fairy." She first obtained the services of the research departments at several large universities, enlisting their aid in perfecting composition to be used in the manufacturing of her dolls. Eventually Dr. W. P. Dun Lany developed a superior material that satisfied the high standards set by Jessie. Next she employed talented sculptors, such as Emory Seidel to design the realistic character faces. Her goal was to produce lightweight composition dolls, having either molded hair or wearing a wig, sleep or painted eyes. The hand-painted faces were often decorated by Chicago Art Institute students. The dolls were jointed with metal springs connected to hardwood plugs inserted into the composition. Often the fingers are curved so that the doll could hold an object. Raleigh dolls are unmarked; however, careful inspection and comparison to the characteristics listed can help give positive identity to a Raleigh doll. Jessie McCutcheon Raleigh dolls are of very good quality.

RALPH, H. S.—England, 1924. A short-lived, little-known manufacturer and distributor of dolls and doll parts.

RÄPPOLD & CO.—Germany, 1921. Advertised a bisque-head "Dloppär" doll, derived from the owners' name being spelled backwards.

RAUSER, KATHERINE A., INC.—U.S.A., 1919-1920, and possibly later. Although best known for creating wonderful doll costumes for other manufacturers, Kitty Rauser advertised her own large size composition doll, named Mlle. Babette. The dolls were lavishly costumed—complete with bonnet and matching shoes—were offered with wigs and sleep eyes, and were beautifully boxed for gift giving. Rauser dolls, if in original condition, are of very good quality and are highly collectible.

RAVCA, DOLLS—France and U.S.A., 1924-1947, and possibly later. Also known as the "Real People Dolls," these dolls were created by Bernard Ravca. After Bernard won first prize at the Paris Fair with two life-size figures of a Norman peasant and his wife, the French government sent him to the United States. Fate intervened when, in 1939, Bernard arrived to exhibit his famous dolls in the French Pavilion at the New York World's Fair. While representing his country in the United States, France fell under the German invasion, leaving Bernard an exile. He spent the next several years raising money for the Free France War Relief, and doing what he could for orphans of the resistance movement. Tragically, during Hitler's occupation of France, Ravca's entire family was lost, his studio pillaged, and his bank accounts seized. Bernard Ravca began life anew, and in 1947 became a United States citizen. The sadness that was so much a part of his life is reflected in his dolls: the peasants with gnarled hands and weathered faces from a life of toil; the aloof expression on persons of royalty, far removed from ordinary life; and corrupt political figures ridden with greed and ruthlessness. All facets of human nature can be seen in Ravca's lifelike soft sculptures made from silk stockinette stretched over sculpted cotton, with painted facial features. These dolls have wire armatures and cloth-covered bodies. Occasionally, a compound made of bread crumbs and glue was used as a sculpturing base, or for various body parts, such as hands or feet. Some Ravca dolls may be found marked with a hang tag or label sewn into their perfectly accurate costumes, but others will have no signs of identification. Many doll makers, influenced by Ravca's creations, have imitated his work with varying degrees of success; therefore, it may be difficult to distinguish an original Ravca doll from a copy. There is no sure-fire way to positively identify an unmarked Ravca, so seek out and examine as many authentic ones as possible—in order to learn to evaluate these exquisitely detailed dolls. It is now believed, though, that at least some of the dolls attributed to Bernard Ravca may, in fact, be the creations of his wife, Frances Eleanor (also spelled Elinor) Ravca. While Ravca dolls normally portray a realistic view of life, several of the dolls seem to have a more idealized presence, and it is this later group that is attributed to Frances. Bernard saw life how it truly was; Frances saw life how she wished it were, and it is shown in their art. Ravca dolls are of very good quality.

RAYBURN TOWNSEND & CO.—England, 1924-1925. A small, little-known manufacturer of cloth dolls. Advertised as being washable with soap and water "once removed from the frame."

RAYNAL, POUPEÉS LES—France, 1922-contemporary. Founded in Paris by Eduard Raynal. Its dolls were made of both cloth and/or felt, and occasionally celluloid. Resembling Lenci dolls, but with less child-like features, Raynal dolls were characterized by painted side-glancing eyes, with eyebrows very wide on the forehead, two painted highlights on the lower lip, and pink cotton bodies with leg seams up the back only. The hands are often the squared-off mitt-type or made of celluloid. Look to the soles of the shoes for markings, or labels sewn into the clothing. The celluloid used in Raynal dolls was called rhodoid and was manufactured by Rhone-Poulenc. Raynal dolls are of good quality.

REBER, LOUIS—Germany, 1910-at least 1930, and possibly later. Produced leather and rubber dolls, ball-jointed dolls and character dolls, and also advertised doll parts.

RECKNAGEL, PHIL. & CO.—Germany, 1881-1891. Advertised and exported toys, marbles, and inexpensive dressed and undressed jointed dolls.

RECKNAGEL, THEODOR—Germany, 1886-1930, and possibly later, although 1930 is listed as the date of the death of Theodor Recknagel. Named for its founder, the Recknagel's porcelain factory shows no evidence of producing bisque dolls before 1893, when he registered two Mulatto doll heads, which were tinted rather than painted. Many mold numbers begin with 19—which is generally assumed to be the registration date of a particular mold; however, this is not the case. For example, mold number 1907 was registered in 1910. Frequently, in addition to (or in place of) a mold number, you may find an *R A* or reverse *A R*—for Recknagel/Alexandrienthal (the location of the porcelain factory). Also, the initials *J K, N G,* or *N K* are frequently used to denote styles. The quality of Recknagel dolls varies from the finest—with extremely artistic application of decoration—to very coarse bisque, with facial features rather haphazardly applied.

REED, C. A.—U.S.A., 1924. This Williamsport, Pennsylvania-based company produced all-celluloid bride and groom dolls with wonderfully detailed crêpe paper clothing.

REES, L. & CO.—England, 1920-1940s, and possibly later. A lifelong member of the doll community, Leon Rees moved to London from Bavaria, married Maud Eisenmann, and became a partner in Eisenmann & Co. After leaving that doll company, he helped form Ellison, Rees & Co. around 1915, but by 1920 it became L. Rees & Co. Leon remained associated with the manufacturing of dolls until his death in 1963.

REGAL DOLL MANUFACTURING CO.—U.S.A., 1918-at least until 1939, and perhaps later. Member of the American Doll Manufacturers' Association. Best known for its composition mama and child dolls. Also advertised rubber dolls. Regal dolls are of fair quality.

REICH, GOLDMANN & CO.—Germany, 1890-1927. Manufactured celluloid child and baby dolls with bent-limb bodies.

REICHE-KIND, WALTER—Germany, 1921. Advertised clown dolls with movable joints.

REICHENAUER, ANTON—Austria, 1853. Listed in registers as a doll maker. No other information could be found.

REIDELER, A.—Germany, 1880-1927. Manufactured small bisque and china dolls, most with cloth bodies.

REINER MANUFACTURING CO.—U.S.A., 1927-1929. A short-lived manufacturer of composition-faced cloth dolls.

REINHARDT, CHRISTIAN—Germany, 1898. Listed as a doll maker.

Dolls by Kämmer & Reinhardt, Kley & Hahn, Kestner (turned head), and Bähr & Pröschild (Photo courtesy of Cobb's Doll Auction.)

REINHARDT, ERNST—Germany, and later U.S.A., 1890s-1930. According to a 1917 article that appeared in the trade papers, Ernst Reinhardt opened a plant which produced bisque-head dolls—which means that Reinhardt started his commercial manufacturing of bisque dolls in the United States two years before Fulper's attempts to fulfill the demands caused by World War I. Also offered composition dolls.

REINHARDT, MORITZ—Germany, 1898. Listed as a doll maker.

REINICK, W.—Germany, 1926. Advertised bisque- and celluloid-head dolls.

REISENWEBER, ADOLF—Germany, 1914-1924, and possibly later. Advertised dressed and undressed character dolls and other toys.

REISENWEBER, CHRISTOPH—Germany, 1861-1930s (There are conflicting dates—depending upon which records are referred to—and although 1861 is the most often accepted date, 1864 and later dates are given.) Advertised dressed stiff-jointed dolls, those of papier-mâché and bisque, along with art dolls.

REISMAN, BARRON & CO.—U.S.A., 1914-at least 1930. Member of the American Doll Manufacturers' Association. Manufactured composition mama dolls with cloth bodies, and advertised that the composition would not peel. Dolls were made with molded, painted hair and eyes, or with mohair wigs and sleep eyes. This company also listed musical, two-faced characters, and bed and baby dolls.

REISSMANN, ALBERT—Germany, and later Bavaria, 1881-1930s. Listed as a doll maker.

RELIABLE DOLL & TOY MANUFACTURING CO.—U.S.A., 1923-1924. A rather short-lived composition doll manufacturer.

RELIABLE TOY COMPANY LIMITED—Canada, 1920-contemporary. This Canadian toy company was originally known as the Canadian Statuary & Novelty Co. It has enjoyed a long and prosperous history of manufacturing excellent quality dolls. In the beginning, Reliable followed the example of so many other doll companies: They assembled parts. The heads were imported, mostly from Germany, and the body parts from the United States. However, by 1922, they began to produce their own composition dolls. So successful were their efforts that they soon outgrew their location, and in 1927 they moved to a larger factory, incorporating many new and innovative methods into their manufacturing. With their high standards of workmanship, it is understandable why they soon became a leading supplier of composition dolls to all parts of the world. Although best known for their typically Canadian dolls—Indians and Mounties, for example—they also purchased well-known doll molds, such as Shirley Temple, and produced their own version, usually with the stipulation that none would be imported into the United States. As the demand for dolls of modern materials began to grow, Reliable kept pace with the bid for hard plastic and vinyl dolls, which also became widely known for their good quality.

RELIANCE NOVELTY CO.—U.S.A., 1913-1918. Advertised composition dolls with mohair wigs.

REMCO INDUSTRIES, INC.—U.S.A., early 1960-1974 (when Azrak-Hamway International bought the Remco and Remco associate names, creating the Remco Industries, Inc., a Division of Azrak-Hamway International, Inc.) Founded by Sol Robbins, this innovative manufacturer of vinyl and hard plastic character dolls never seemed to exhaust their ability to create charming design and modeling ideals for their dolls. Most famous for the Littlechap Family dolls, it is important not to overlook the other character dolls, such as entertainment personalities. Remco dolls are of good quality and are enjoying a surge in popularity with contemporary collectors.

REMDEO—Belgium, 1914-1916, and possibly other years. Doll factory founded by Countess de Mérode, who employed people who were wounded and/or affected by the war.

REMIGNARD, FRÉDÉRIC—France, 1844-1899. Made bisque-head dolls and used the initials *F. F. R.*

RENAULT & BON-DUFOUR—France, 1906-1930, and probably later. Member of the Chambre Syndicale. Although they manufactured bébés, clowns, mignonnettes, and character dolls, they were best known for large composition dolls fashioned with molded and painted hair, eyes, and costumes with jointed shoulders. Renault & Bon-Dufour dolls are of mediocre quality.

RENWAL COMPANY—U.S.A., mid-twentieth century. Manufactured a complete line of well-made, functional dollhouse furniture and highly collectible hard plastic miniature jointed dolls with molded clothing.

REPUBLIC DOLL & TOY CORP.—U.S.A., 1919-1921. Founded by Charles and Samuel Reich for the manufacturing of composition child and baby dolls with molded and painted hair or mohair wig. Republic dolls are of poor to mediocre quality

RESEK, MORITZ—Austria, and later Czechoslovakia, 1889-1927, also spelled Rezek. Made bisque-head, jointed dolls. Registered as a supplier of doll parts, as well as a doll maker.

RESTALL MANUFACTURING CO.—U.S.A., 1918 and probably other years. A small California doll manufacturer of cloth character dolls.

RHEINISCHE GUMMI UND CELLULOID FABRIK CO.—Bavaria, 1873-contemporary. Originally founded as a manufacturer of rubber products, Rheinische Gummi became the leading German celluloid doll producer. The famous turtle mark was registered in 1889, although the first dolls were not produced until 1896. They also supplied finished and unfinished dolls and doll parts to several other manufacturers including, but not limited to, Buschow & Beck, Carl Hoffmeister, Kämmer & Reinhardt, Kestner, König & Wernicke, Bruno Schmidt, and Wagner & Zetzsche. This helps to explain the turtle marking being found with a number of different company names. The fact that unfinished celluloid heads were often sold to the different doll factories explains why a single doll can appear with such varied characteristics. Once a manufacturer received the unfinished head (called a *rawling*), they could decorate it, insert their own eyes, and/or attach wigs allowing the celluloid doll to adopt the styles that are associated with a particular company. In addition to the complete line of celluloid dolls produced, they also advertised rubber dolls. In 1926, the trademark Miblu was registered to denote a new celluloid with a translucent, wax-like appearance. It is interesting to note that a registered design patent, or a G M, can at times help to date a doll; however, the G M number, which can appear with the turtle mark, must be matched with the particular doll on which it is present, because many of the mold numbers were used for more than one doll. By way of example, G M 12 was registered in 1907 as a clown, in 1910 as a boy, in 1912 as a dolly-faced child, and in 1924 as the character doll Putzi. It was long believed within the doll collecting community that a turtle mark could help to date a doll—that the diamond shape around the turtle could be used as a 1900 bench mark—but this was an incorrect hypothesis, as the turtle within a diamond border and the turtle mark alone were used simultaneously. It is, therefore, impossible to determine the date by only considering the addition or absence of a diamond border or rhombus. Rheinische Gummi celluloid dolls are generally of very good quality.

RIBIERE, LEGER HENRI—France, 1929. A small company that little is known of, except the registering of the name Poupée Musette.

RICHWOOD TOYS—U.S.A., mid-twentieth century. Manufactured hard plastic dolls, the most popular being Sandra Sue. This walking doll with stationary head was molded with both flat and high-heeled feet. The eyebrows and lashes below the sleep eyes are an unusual dark orange color that can help identify this charming 8-inch doll. Also offered an extensive line of Sandra Sue clothing, including street, formal, and sportswear. Richwood dolls are of excellent quality.

RIDLEY E. & SONS—U.S.A., 1884-1898. Distributed bisque, china, composition, rubber, and wax dolls and doll parts.

RIEDLER, AUGUST—Germany, 1872-at least as late as 1938. Manufactured all-bisque and china dolls along with dolls of bisque head and limbs with cloth bodies.

RIGOT, MLLE. MARIE GEORGETTE—France, 1927-1930s. Made cloth dolls and registered the trademark L'Idéale in 1928.

RISCHEL, A. & CO.—Germany, 1893-1900. Manufactured, advertised, distributed, and exported dressed dolls, embroidery boxes with doll and extra clothing, and separate doll costumes.

RITE LEE—U.S.A., mid-twentieth century. Manufactured soft vinyl dolls.

RITE SPECIALTY CO.—U.S.A., 1916-1920. Manufactured dolls of hand-painted "Ivorite," a composition of clay-like material.

RIVAILLON, FR. & CAROLINE—France, 1900-1910. An interesting, yet perplexing, couple that made dolls at their factory at Montreuil-sous-Bois, yet Caroline is registered as making dolls at Argenteuil, France. It must be noted that two factories are never mentioned, however. Although Caroline registered the name Bébé Modéle in 1900, the next year Jules Mettais (Jules Steiner's successor) registered the same name. In 1910, Fr. Ch. Rivaillon called his doll Bébé le Vrai Modéle, a name often found stamped on dolls made by Jumeau. Rivaillon dolls are of good quality.

ROBBINS, JOHN D—U.S.A., mid-nineteenth century. Imported, distributed, and sold china, composition, papier-mâché, peg-wooden, rubber, and wax dolls and doll parts.

ROBERTA DOLL COMPANY—U.S.A., mid-twentieth century. The hard plastic and vinyl dolls produced by this knockoff company varies greatly. The most famous LuAnn Simms doll is of excellent quality; however, other lesser known dolls are merely mass copies of popular dolls exhibiting very poor quality.

ROBERTS BROTHERS—England, 1888. This company incorporated into the Chad Valley Co. Made cloth dolls of stockinette.

ROBINS, JOSEPH—England, 1826-1901. Joseph and several members of his family made composition dolls at different locations, all distributed under the name Joseph Robins.

ROCHARD, ED—France, 1860s-1870s. Patented a special arrangement of see-through crystals embedded into the bisque shoulder plates of dolls with French scenes depicted when viewed from the back. Various styles of necklace and doll types have been recorded.

Rochard dolls are of the finest quality and highly sought after by collectors, not only for their beauty, but also for their uniqueness and rarity.

ROCK CHINA DOLLS—England, 1915-1919. Made of British Ceramic heads, modeled by Helen Rock, on cloth or composition bodies.

ROCK & GRANER—Germany, 1813-1911 (or until World War I). Over the years several owners of this company used many different names. It is the R & G N trademark, however, that is most familiar to collectors. The N is for Nachfolger, the German term for "successor." This company advertised many types of dolls, including swaddling cloth babies, papier-mâché, molded hair, and dollhouse dolls. In later years, Rack & Graner specialized in tin toys.

ROCKENDORFER, ADAM—Austria, 1809-1814. Made wooden dolls.

ROCKWELL, GRACE CORRY—U.S.A., around 1920. Although Grace Corry Rockwell designed dolls for several manufacturers, her best-known bisque character doll is simply marked "Copr. By Grace C. Rockwell Germany." It is assumed that Kestner produced this doll for Century Doll Company. The fineness of the bisque and nice application of decoration, coupled with the close association of Rockwell, makes Century Doll Co. and Kestner rather safe assumptions. Grace Corry Rockwell character dolls are of very good quality.

RODDY—England, mid-twentieth century. This company manufactured hard plastic and vinyl dolls of mediocre quality.

ROGNER, HERMANN—Germany, 1924-1926, and maybe as late as the 1930s. According to advertisements, they produced all-felt character and toddler dolls.

ROHMER, MME.—France, 1857-1880. Marie Antoinette Leonine Rohmer operated her doll business in Paris. She produced elegant Parisian fashion ladies, Poupée de Mode, of both china and bisque. During the early years of production, Mme. Rohmer obtained several patents for improvements to doll bodies. The first was the articulated joints on kid bodies, followed by a patent for Gutta Percha, or rubber arms, for kid bodies. The final patent was for a new type of doll head having a cord go through the head, into the body, and coming out through riveted holes in the front of the torso. This facilitated the turning of the head in any direction, and also secured the head onto the body. Examples of bodies utilizing the first and last patents are occasionally found. However, bodies with Gutta Percha arms are seldom seen. One explanation for the absence of these arms may be that they deteriorated and were replaced with bisque. Almost fifty years after Mme. Rohmer registered her patent for articulated joints, Charles Fausel received a patent for a very similar universal joint in the United States. The doll industry of the nineteenth century made great strides in manufacturing, thanks to leaders such as Mme. Rohmer, who continually sought to improve the appearance and movement of her Poupée de Modes. During a time when most companies were directed by men, Mme. Rohmer was apparently quite successful. The bisque or china heads can be found with either painted or glass eyes. All are noted for their sensuous and somewhat dreamy expressions. Rohmer dolls are of very good quality.

ROLFO, LUIGI—Italy, 1928-1920. Registered as a doll maker. Little else is known about this company.

ROLLER, MARIANNE—Austria, 1906-1908. Made turned-wood art dolls with carved and painted costumes and jointed shoulders.

ROLLINSON DOLLS—U.S.A., 1916-1929. Designed and created by Gertrude Rollinson of Holyoke, Massachusetts. Her first dolls were handmade for crippled children confined to hospitals. These first attempts had flat, painted faces. However, she was unhappy with the effect and continually experimented with several sculptured techniques until finally achieving three dimensional features on a stockinette doll. So successful were her efforts that, before long, there was a great demand for her dolls. In 1916, Mrs. Rollinson commercialized her doll-making talents. A large scale manufacturer was needed. Utley Company fulfilled that demand by producing thirty-five styles on a royalty basis. Some are found with mohair wigs and others with painted brush-stroke hair. Painted eyes and closed or open/closed mouths. Occasionally a doll will be found with pierced nostrils. During the production, twenty coats of paint were applied to each head. Between each application, the head would be dried in the sun and smoothed by sandpapering, resulting in a hard, durable, beautifully polished washable surface. Rollinson dolls are of good quality and highly prized not only for their charm, but also for their historic value.

RONCORONE—England, the early 1800s. Made dolls from beeswax.

ROOKWOOD POTTERY—U.S.A., 1880-contemporary. This well-known pottery company made bisque doll heads to help fill the gap created by the absence of German dolls during World War I.

RÖSTRAND PORCELAIN FACTORY—Sweden, 1726-1925. It is unlikely that dolls were produced for the entire time. Beautifully detailed china heads with fine molding and application of decoration were made during the mid- to late 1800s. There is evidence that at least a few bisque doll heads were also produced. Röstrand china head dolls are of very good quality.

ROSE, W. A. & CO.—England, 1921. A short-lived distributor of dolls using the initials W. A. R.

ROSEBUD—U.S.A., mid-twentieth century until taken over by Mattel in 1967. Manufactured hard plastic and vinyl dolls of good quality.

ROSS & ROSS—U.S.A., 1918-1930s. Family-owned and operated manufacturer of cloth dolls.

ROSS PRODUCTS, INC.—U.S.A., mid-twentieth century. Manufactured hard plastic and vinyl dolls. Most famous for the highly collectible Tina Cassini, named for the designer Oleg Cassini and the Yogi Berra dolls. The costumes for Tina Cassini, sold separately, are outstanding examples of the excellence that was a hallmark of this company. Ross dolls are of very good to excellent quality.

ROSSIGNOL, CHARLES—France, around 1878-1900. Produced mechanical dolls; won a Silver Medal at the Paris Exposition of 1878.

ROSTAL, HENRI—France, 1914. Although Rostal may have produced bisque-head dolls in other years, all records and registrations carry the 1914 date. This twentieth-century French doll maker is known for his trademark "Mon Trésor" dolls and "Bébé Mon Trésor" dolls with beautiful paperweight eyes, feathered brows, and open mouths. Occasionally, the initials *H R* were included in the markings. Henri Rostal's dolls are of good quality.

ROTH, JOSEPH MANUFACTURING CO.—U.S.A., 1915-1922. Member of the American Doll Manufacturers' Association, and licensed by Voices, Inc. to use their criers in the dolls. Manufactured pressed-composition mama and character dolls. Also advertised rubber and German bisque-head dolls.

ROTHSCHILD, SIGMUND I.—U.S.A. 1919. A small, little-known doll manufacturer, save the registering of a trademark in 1919.

ROULLET & DECAMPS—France, 1865-1930. Members of the Chambre Syndicale. Produced fantastic automated dolls and characters with intricate movements. The dolls were often supplied by the finest doll makers and can be found with a number of different markings; however, the keys, used to wind the mechanism, usually have the initials *R D*, indicating the Roullet & Decamps family business. Roullet & Decamps mechanical dolls are of very good quality.

ROXY DOLL & TOY CO.—U.S.A., 1929. Member of Doll Parts Manufacturing Association. Produced composition dolls and doll parts.

ROXY FACTORY—England, 1915-1920. Founded by Thomas Dodd for the production of British Ceramic-head dolls.

ROY, JULES—France, 1835-1857. Listed in the Paris directories as a doll maker.

ROYAL COPENHAGEN MANUFACTORY—
Denmark, 1772-contemporary. This company produced lovely porcelain and china-head dolls. Royal Copenhagen dolls are of very good quality.

ROYAL TOY MANUFACTURING CO.—U.S.A., 1914-contemporary. Member of the American Doll Manufacturers' Association. Produced and imported the Royal Dolls of composition or with cloth bodies, composition heads and limbs, with painted or sleep eyes, dressed or undressed, and with human hair wigs. Later, hard plastic and vinyl were added to this line of well-priced quality dolls.

ROZMANN, MLLE.—France, 1915-1916. This company made cloth dolls.

RUDOLPH, AUGUST—Germany, 1928. Listed in business directory as a manufacturer of baby dolls.

RUDOLPH, J. DOLL, CO.—U.S.A., 1924-1929. Licensed by Voices, Inc., to their criers in Rudolph composition mama dolls.

RUDOLPH, MAX—Germany, 1908-late 1930s. Although best known for their production of doll wigs, Max Rudolph advertised a soft stuffed baby; a bent-limb baby with wig and sleep eyes; and separate bisque, celluloid, or composition doll heads—along with other doll parts—well into the late 1930s.

RUF, JOSEPH—U.S.A., 1927. This company was licensed by Voices, Inc., to use their criers in the Joseph Ruf composition mama dolls.

RUFFLES CO.—U.S.A., 1930 and beyond. A flat-faced cloth doll with yarn hair, button eyes, and embroidered facial features. Marked "Ruffles Trade Mark Reg. Design Patent 82656. The Ruffles Company, Kansas City, Missouri." Created by Camille C. Blair.

RUNGGALDIER, JOHANN ANTON—Austria, early to late 1800s. A family of Verleger for the collection and distribution of wooden dolls. Records indicate that in later years they also purchased bisque-head dolls, with at least some being supplied by François Gaultier.

RUSHTON COMPANY—U.S.A., 1920s-1930s. Manufactured cloth dolls designed and created by Mary Waterman Phillips using the acronym "Mawaphil." These art dolls came in several different styles of child and animal characters with hand-painted facial features.

S

S. I. M. A. R. S. A.—Italy, 1928. Manufactured dolls.

S. I R. E.—Italy, 1929. Manufactured dolls.

S. K. NOVELTY CO.—U.S.A., 1917-1927. Also known as S. Kirsch & Co. and the S. K. Doll Manufacturing Co. Made and distributed composition and bisque dolls of various types to jobbers and retailers. Licensed by Voices, Inc., to use their criers in S. K. dolls.

S. & CO.—Germany, 1854-1927. Swaine & Company was a porcelain factory in Hüttensteinach, Germany, founded in the early 1800s, but is not believed to have produced dolls until about 1910. Owned by William Swaine, the factory produced quality dolls for only a brief time. Made from high-grade bisque, the dolls were beautifully sculptured with fine molding, and exhibited extraordinary talent in the application of decoration. Faces were delicate, sweet, and uniquely Swaine. Many collectors believe Swaine produced only one doll, Lori, with several expressions. Her different expressions have been signified by the letters D I; D I I; D I P and so on. Other collectors contend that the character dolls produced by Swaine & Company are entirely different character dolls, each with their own particular characteristics. Whichever school of thought subscribed to, all agree that Swain character dolls are charming, delightful additions to a collection. Authentic Swaine creations have a green ink stamp reading, "Geschützt Germany S & Co." on the back of the bisque heads, in addition to the incised markings. Swain & Co. character dolls are generally of very good quality.

S. & H. NOVELTY CO.—U.S.A., 1925-1930s. Manufactured composition dolls with cloth bodies.

S. & L. MANUFACTURING CO.—England, 1926. This was a rather short-lived manufacturer of velveteen and stockinette dolls.

S. & S. DOLL CO.—U.S.A., 1927-1930s. Manufactured and distributed composition head dolls to jobbers and retailers. Licensed by Voices, Inc., to use their criers in S. & S. mama dolls.

SAALFIELD PUBLISHING CO.—U.S.A., 1907-contemporary. Manufactured printed lithographed cut-out cloth dolls.

SAFONOFF, E. F.—Russia, around the year 1840. Crafted handmade papier-mâché dolls.

SALTER, THOMAS, LTD.—England, 1915-1930. Records indicate that Salter also distributed dolls in France. Produced India rubber dolls.

SAMHAMMER, PHILIPP—Germany, 1872-1915. An early union of Philipp Samhammer and Mathias Lambert resulted in the Lambert & Samhammer Doll Co. After the partnership dissolved, Samhammer went into business for himself. Besides the production of bisque-head dolls, Philipp is credited with being a brilliant business leader and instrumental in founding the Sonneberg Trade Museum, along with being a member of the States assembly and the Parliament.

SAMSTAG & HILDER BROTHERS—Germany, 1894-1920. There is evidence of a close business relationship between Samstag & Hilder and Eisenmann. Produced doll bodies, and dressed dolls. Records also show that facial decorations were applied onto bisque heads made by other doll manufacturers.

SAMUEL & SÖHNE—Bohemia and, later, Czechoslovakia, 1907-1929. Very little information could be amassed concerning this company, except for the advertising of jointed dolls.

SAMULON, J.—Germany, 1892-1930. Manufactured dollhouse dolls.

SAN WASH TOY CO.—U.S.A., 1930 and beyond. Manufactured cloth dolls.

SANONER—Germany, early 1800s-1930s and possibly later. Also spelled *Senoner* or *Sononer*. A prominent family of Verlegers.

SARDEAU, MISS HÉLÈNE—U.S.A., 1920-1924. Hélène and her sister Mathilde Kane made portrait dolls described in a trade journal as "being modeled in plasterine with canvas or stockinette stretched over it and painted in flesh colors." Another article includes this description: "having faces of clay painted with oils, hair of colored wool or cord and long thin bodies." Mathilde is credited with designing the lavish silk and satin costumes.

SASHA DOLLS—Germany and England, 1964-present. Vinyl dolls designed by Sasha Morgenthaler, an extremely gifted artist. Turning her talents to the creation of dolls, she operated a somewhat limited commercial enterprise, finally able to have her dolls mass-produced, according to her artistic specification and high standards of quality. The first Sasha Dolls were produced by Götz of Germany. Production problems occurred, prompting Ms. Morgenthaler to grant the licensing rights to Trenton Toys, Ltd. of England, which continued producing them until the company closed their doors in 1986. All Sasha Dolls are similar in appearance, with wistful serious expressions and a slightly darkened skin tone. The Götz dolls are marked "Sasha Series" within a circle. Also, the upper eyelids of the Götz dolls are painted with a curved line, resulting in a somewhat unnatural appearance. Other Sasha eyelids are painted with a straighter eyelid line. All Sasha Dolls have realistic body construction, which allows for a greater range of movement. Later Sasha Dolls are unmarked, except for a wrist tag. Götz is once again producing Sasha Dolls. The newly introduced Sasha Dolls, although very similar in appearance to the earlier dolls, are easily recognized by the marking: an incised circular logo between the shoulders. The neck is also engraved with the name *Götz*. Sasha Dolls are very collectible and are of very good quality.

SAUER, AUGUST—Germany, 1907-1929. Produced, advertised, and exported bisque-head dolls with jointed bodies. A 1928 advertisement offers a "doll head with voice pulled by pacifier."

SAUERTEIG, JOHANNES—Germany, 1865-1824. Although founded in 1865 Sauerteig was not incorporated into the commercial register until 1883. Advertised a wide and varied collection of dolls, including novel color painting, dolls with animal heads, dolls with a cuckoo voice in the body, and dolls that are stuffed with leaves.

SAUERZAPF, GEORG ANDREAS—Austria, 1834-1851. Manufactured papier-mâché and mechanical dolls.

SAXON NOVELTY CO.—U.S.A., 1927-1929. Member of the American Doll Manufacturing Association and the Doll Parts Manufacturing Association. Produced composition dolls and doll parts.

SCHÄFER & VATER—Germany, 1890-at least until 1941. Porcelain Factory founded by Gustav Schäfer and Günther Vater. Records indicate that doll heads and knickknacks were the principal production output.

SCHANZER, HENRY, CO.—U.S.A., 1927. Advertised small, all-celluloid dolls and all-composition dolls in knitted costumes.

SCHAVOIR RUBBER CO.—U.S.A., 1926-1930s. Manufactured white and red rubber dolls.

SCHEFFLER, KARL—Germany, 1926-1930s. Also spelled "Carl." Produced celluloid dolls with cloth bodies along with all-celluloid child and baby dolls. Also advertised doll clothing.

SCHEIDIG, CARL—Germany, 1896-at least until 1941. There are conflicting records concerning the founding date, as some records list 1906 as the correct year. All records and registers agree that by 1916 the Scheidig Porcelain Factory was producing bathing dolls, and continued to do so for at least the next thirty-five years.

SCHELHORN, MAX FRIEDRICH—Germany, 1907-1925. Over the years Max Schelhorn registered several trade names "for dolls and their components," such as "Fluffy Ruffles," "Peter Pan Playtoys," "Muffles," "Little Snookums," "The Newlywed's Baby," and "The Base Ball Fan." Manufactured numerous styles of bisque-head dolls including multi-faced and other character dolls.

SCHELLHORN, AUGUST—Germany, 1897-at least until 1932 (when records indicate the death of the owner, Hermann Grempel, and the assignment of the new owner, Harry Grempel). Manufactured and advertised bent-limb baby, new born baby, child and mama dolls, along with novelty felt dolls and marottes.

SCHELLHORN, HEINRICH—Germany 1901-1935 (when he fled to England and continued in the doll business). Manufactured celluloid and porcelain head dolls, along with mama and musical dolls with the sound of a xylophone, in addition to doll accessories, such as wigs and bodies.

SCHELHORN, M. A.—Austria, 1853 and possibly other years. Registered as a doll and toy maker.

SCHERF, PETER—Germany, 1879-1929. Founded by Peter Scherf, and located in Sonneberg, the famous "Town of Toys." Following Scherf's death in 1887, the business was divided among various family members; however, bisque dolls continued to be exported to the American market bearing the Peter Scherf mark or the trade name "The Fairy Kid." Most, if not all, of the bisque heads were produced at Armand Marseille's porcelain factory. Peter Scherf dolls are of good quality.

SCHERZER & FISCHER—Germany, 1887-1930. Also known as Richard Scherzer. Manufactured dressed and undressed, mama, and bent-limb baby dolls.

SCHEYER, O. & CO.—Germany, 1920-1929. Manufactured double-jointed dolls, felt and plush characters, along with soft stuffed dolls.

SCHILLING—Germany, 1871-1928. During the early years, Schilling made papier-mâché, wax, or rubber Täuflinge and doll heads. Later, it is probable that they exported composition head dolls with cloth bodies and wax-over composition shoulder head dolls through their connections with Borgfeldt. Over the years, the familiar winged-angle trademark, registered in 1879, has appeared on many different types of dolls, and even doll accessories, such as shoes and wigs.

SCHINDHELM & KNAUER—Germany, 1919-1930 and possibly later. Founded by Oskar Schindhelm and Rudolf Knauer. This company manufactured dressed dolls, miniature dolls, character dolls, and trousseaus and layettes in baskets.

SCHLAGGENWALD—Bohemia, 1793-1930. Owned by Lipfert & Haas until 1876, when it became Haas & Czijzek. Manufactured various styles of china-head dolls—many with wigs—and marked "S." Schlaggenwald china head dolls are of good quality.

SCHLESINGER, LEO—U.S.A., 1874-1927. Also known as Schlesinger Brothers. Manufactured dolls.

SCHLESISCHE SPIELWAREN FABRIK—Silesia (region of central Europe, chiefly in SW Poland and N Czechoslovakia), 1926-1930. Manufactured dolls under the management of Carl Sorneck.

SCHLIEFF & CO.—England, 1922-1924. Also known as Paul S. Schlieff & Co. Manufactured dolls.

SCHLOSSER, ANTON—Austria, 1853 and possibly other years. Registered as a doll maker.

SCHMEISER, ADOLF—Austria, 1907, and possibly other years. Listed in directory for dolls and doll parts, including heads.

SCHMETZER, LOUIS—U.S.A., 1875-1876. Although registered as an American doll manufacturer, there is every indication the Louis Schmetzer resided in Rothenburg, Bavaria.

SCHMEY, GUSTAV—Germany, 1853-1930, and possibly later. Manufactured and exported many different types of bisque, celluloid, cloth, metal, and wood dolls, along with a wide assortment of toys and other accessories. In 1900, Gustav Schmey won the Grand Prix award at the World Exhibition in Paris. Advertisements and promotions displayed a level of high quality dolls and toys.

SCHMIDT, AUGUST—Germany, 1894-1927. Produced celluloid dolls and doll parts.

SCHMIDT, BRUNO—Germany, 1898-1930s. Prior to 1900, Schmidt was in partnership with Hugo Geisler. When Geisler left the business, Schmidt changed the name from H. Geisler & Co. to Bruno Schmidt. Schmidt character dolls are among the most desired dolls in the collecting community. Two of the best-known characters are Tommy Tucker (mold 2048) and his companion Wendy (mold 2033), which is decidedly more rare. Records indicate that the bisque heads were purchased exclusively from Bähr & Pröschild, a company that Schmidt eventually was to take over. Bisque doll heads often bear both firm's trademarks, namely the heart and crossed swords, as well as two sets of mold numbers. The three-digit number was a Bähr & Pröschild, and the four-digit number beginning with a 2 belonged to Bruno Schmidt. In addition to the bisque-head dolls, Bruno Schmidt also advertised lovely celluloid dolls, and through the Bähr & Pröschild factory, tea-cozy and pincushion dolls. Bruno Schmidt dolls are of very good quality.

SCHMIDT, CARL—Germany, 1901-1926. Manufactured bisque character and baby dolls, doll parts and accessories, and items made from papier-mâché.

SCHMIDT, FRANZ CO.—Germany, 1890-1937. The bisque-head dolls from the Franz Schmidt doll factory are well-known for their charming modeling and consistently fine quality. They also provided many innovations to the doll industry, including improved wooden body joints (1899), pierced nostrils (1912), movable tongue (1913), universal joints (1914), and eye bar and voice box (1928). Simon & Halbig porcelain factory supplied the bisque heads, according to the designs and specifications of the Schmidt Company. Two of Schmidt's most famous sculptors were Traugott Schmidt and Albin Scheler. When studying the markings of Franz Schmidt you may note that a *z* often is present; it is assumed that this is an abbreviation of *zentimeter* (German for "centimeter"). Also, they appear to have marked earlier bisque heads "S & Co.," and later heads "FS & C." Franz Schmidt dolls are of very good quality.

SCHMIDT, GEBRÜDER—Germany, 1930. Manufactured character dolls.

SCHMIDT, MINNA MOSCHERSCH—U.S.A., 1923-1930s. Designed and created wax portrait and historical dolls. Later authored a book about her dolls.

SCHMIDT, PAUL—Germany, 1922-1927. Manufactured dolls with voice boxes and mechanically moving heads.

SCHMITT ET FILS—France, 1854-1891. Maurice and Charles Schmitt, of Schmitt & Sons, manufactured Bébés with pressed, rather than poured, bisque. The facial modeling consists of either a full round face, or a long-cheeked oval shape. Lamb's wool wigs are not uncommon. Almond-shaped paperweight eyes possess great depth and richness of color. The eyeliner is black, and the eye shadow matches the delicate cheek color, as well as the matching blushed pierced ears. The mouth is closed, with a slender space between the lips and carefully painted outlines and shading. These enchanting facial features help explain why Schmitt Bébés are numbered among the finest and costliest in today's doll market. Dolls may also be found with the neck ending in a dome shape that fits up into the neck socket, eliminating the line at the base of the neck. Collectors refer to this arrangement as a "cup and saucer" neck. Schmitt et Fils Bébés are of the finest quality.

SCHMUCKLER, HEINRICH—Silesia (region of central Europe, chiefly in SW Poland and N Czechoslovakia), 1891-1928. Also known as Erst Schlesische Puppenfabrik. Listed as Silesia's first doll factory. Manufactured wooden, celluloid, and cloth dolls.

SCHNEIDER, JOHANNES GEORG—Germany, 1895. Believed by many doll experts to have made the bisque doll heads marked "J. S."

SCHNEIDER, OTTO—Germany 1913-1924. Advertised miniature, stiff, and ball-jointed dolls.

SCHNEIDER, RUDOLF—Germany, 1912-1925, and possibly later. Manufactured wooden and papier-mâché dolls. Frequently, the "Bébé Tout en Bois" label is found on a Schneider wooden doll. For many years, it was assumed that this was a French-made doll; however, records have verified the origin as Sonneberg.

SCHNEPF, ALBERT—Germany, 1903-1913. Manufactured composition or papier-mâché dolls with cloth bodies. Also, this company advertised doll costumes and accessories.

SCHÖBERL & BECKER—Germany, 1923-1930 and later. Also known as Cellba Celluloidwarenfabrik. Entered the doll business by producing celluloid doll body joints, later expanding to include dolls with glass eyes, black, Café au lait, and a "first class baby." Look for a mermaid within a shield or the name Cellba as a marking on these celluloid dolls of good quality.

SCHOEN & YONDORF CO.—U.S.A., 1907-1960s, and possibly beyond. Members of the American Doll Manufacturers' Association. The Sayco trademark is more familiar to doll collectors than the company name of Schoen & Yondorf. Over the years, this company has manufactured dolls of varied materials—including composition, cloth, wood, latex, vinyl, and hard plastic—and in 1927, was licensed by Voices, Inc., to use its criers in the Sayco mama dolls. Although Sayco is not a name necessarily associated with high quality dolls, it is, nevertheless, a high prolific company. Selling through mail-order, wholesaled to jobbers, and offered as premiums has helped to make them a well-known and recognized contributor to the doll collection community. Schoen & Yondorf dolls are of fair quality.

SCHOENAU & HOFFMEISTER—Germany, 1901-1953. Arthur Schoenau and Carl Hoffmeister founded this porcelain factory. By 1907, several disagreements erupted between the partners, the worst concerning the merits of socket versus shoulder heads. Although it seems a trivial thing, Carl Hoffmeister insisted upon producing bisque shoulder head dolls, while Arthur Schoenau was equally determined to produce socket-head types. Unable to resolve their differences, the partnership was dissolved. Carl Hoffmeister left the firm, and Arthur Schoenau became sole owner. In 1909, a new partner was added, Magnus Leube. When Arthur Schoenau died in 1911, his son Hans took over as director of the company. Eventually, the directorship passed to Arthur's widow, Caroline, and to Curt Schoenau. Curt supplied Cäsar Schneider, the sculptor of Schoenau & Hoffmeister, with a photo of Princess Elizabeth. This was used as a model for the famous Princess Elizabeth doll. Their enviable record of design includes child, dolly face, ethnic, and a fine line of portrait bisque dolls. Schoenau & Hoffmeister dolls are of fair to very good quality.

SCHOENHUT, A. & CO.—U.S.A., 1872-contemporary. Albert Schoenhut, founder of the company, continued a family tradition of toy makers. Grandfather Anton had carved wooden toys at his home in Germany; his son, Frederick, followed in his footsteps. Albert was destined to become a toy maker! After venturing to the United States at the age of seventeen, Albert worked at different jobs. But, by age twenty-two, he established his own toy factory. His first commodity was a piano. The famous Humpty Dumpty Circus, introduced in 1903, probably included his first attempt at doll making. The ringmaster, lion tamer, acrobats, lady, and gentleman are identified solely by their characteristic painting and costuming. At about this same time, Schoenhut introduced Chinaman,

Hobo, Negro Dude, Farmer, Milkmaid, Max, and Moritz. Rolly-Polly were parented in 1908, as was Teddy Roosevelt and his Teddy Adventures in Africa. In 1909, Albert Schoenhut filed a patent application for his wooden swivel, spring-jointed dolls, but the patent was not granted until 1911. The metal joints had springs that compressed, rather than stretched, when pulled. This added to the durability of the Schoenhut wooden art dolls. In addition to the unique spring joints, the dolls were painted entirely with oil colors. Their solid wood heads came either with mohair wigs or molded hair. The hard wood feet have two holes drilled into the soles to enable the doll to be placed on its stand and pose in an endless array of positions. The early dolls had intaglio eyes, followed by rounded eyes, and finally, sleep eyes. Schoenhut dolls are highly collectible and of good quality.

SCHOTT, HERMANN—Germany, 1922-1927. Possibly other years as well; however, 1922 is recorded as the year in which Hermann Schott incorporated into the commercial register, and in 1927 he is again listed as a doll manufacturer.

S.F.B.J.'s Character Child #227 with Solid Dome and Jewel Eyes (Photo Courtesy of Mr. & Mrs. Adam Condo.)

SCHRAMM, FRANZ—Germany, 1921-1930. Made cloth-bodied dolls and character babies.

SCHREYER & CO—Germany, 1912-1950s. Also known as Schuco. Manufactured bisque, china, celluloid, composition, and metal-head dolls on kid or cloth bodies. At least some of the composition dolls resemble Käthe Kruse dolls. Schreyer dolls are of good quality.

SCHROEDER, ALFRED—Germany, 1921-1926 and possibly later. Advertised "mechanically moving jointed dolls" and other papier-mâché merchandise.

SCHUBERT, FRANZ—Austria, 1925, and possibly other years. Listed in register as a doll supplier.

SCHUBERT, HERMANN—Germany, 1885-1928. Advertised dressed dolls and doll accessories.

SCHUDZE, MAX—France, 1864-1878. Produced and exported mechanical dolls and bébés.

SCHUETZMEISTER & QUENDT—Germany, 1889-1930 and later. Also spelled Schützmeister & Quendt. Wilhelm Quendt and Philipp Schuetzmeister founded this porcelain factory for the "manufacture of doll heads, porcelain toys and luxury articles of bisque" according the commercial register. In 1908, Wilhelm Quendt, left making Schuetzmeister the sole owner. Following the company's acquisition by the Bing conglomerate of Nürnberg in 1918, Schuetzmeister & Quendt limited its production to bisque doll heads for Welsch & Company and Kämmer & Reinhardt. Those companies were members, along with Schuetzmeister & Quendt, of the holding company known as Concentra. The firm's intertwined S & Q trademark can be found with any one of several registered mold numbers. Interestingly, mold numbers 79, 80, and 81—all registered in 1891—have not yet been found. No known examples have surfaced. According to their registration, they are child dolls. Collectors are constantly on the lookout for these dolls. If found, they would solve one of the many mysteries in the doll world. Schuetzmeister & Quendt dolls are of good quality.

SCHUFINSKY, PROF. VICTOR—Austria, 1909-1910. Along with creating turned-wood dolls, the Professor taught others the craft. The dolls are often fashioned in such a manner that the clothing helps to support a standing position. Others are fitted with a round wooden base carved to accommodate the doll's feet.

SCHULTZ, ADOLPHE—France, 1893. Listed in the directory as a doll maker.

SCHWARTZ, SIG. CO.—U.S.A., 1917-1926. Manufactured cloth dolls.

SCHWARZ, JOSEF.—Austria, 1899-1910. Made dolls and doll heads.

SCHWARZKOPF & FRÖBER—Germany, 1882-1927. This was a doll factory for the production of jointed, dressed Täufling dolls.

SCHWEIGLÄNDER, ALBAN LEIMGRUBE—Austria, around 1816. Crafted wooden dolls.

SCHWERDT BROTHERS—U.S.A., 1925-1926. A small little-known manufacturer of cloth-bodied dolls.

SCHWERDT MANUFACTURING CO.—U.S.A., 1910-1930s. Manufactured small soft stuffed dolls with flat faces and side-glancing painted eyes.

SCHWERDTFEGER & CO.—Germany, 1904-1930. Manufactured felt dolls, some with a celluloid covering of the head.

SCHWIMMER & RAKOVSKY—Austria, 1925-1930. Registered as a doll maker.

SCOTT, J. FRED & CO.—England, 1915-1917. Manufactured wax and cloth dolls. Many had a mask-type, hand-painted face pressed from layers of cardboard covered with sateen.

SEAMLESS TOY CORP.—U.S.A., 1918-1929, and possibly later. Manufactured composition dolls.

SEAR, ROEBUCK & CO.—U.S.A., 1888-present. Purchased and sold dolls of all types. Have several times over the years commissioned special dolls to be sold only through their outlets.

SEELEMANN, PAUL—Germany, 1892-1927. Advertised mama, newborn, and soft stuffed dolls, some with criers.

SEHM, FRAU MATHILDE—Germany, 1869-1930. Advertised fairy tale, dollhouse, celluloid, baby, and character dolls—and doll clothing and accessories.

SEIFERT, ERICH—Germany, 1921-1930. Advertised dressed dolls.

SEIFERT, MAX—Germany, 1920-1930s. Manufactured dress dolls and mignonettes.

SELCHOW & RIGHTER—U.S.A., 1864-1930. Elisha Selchow was a toy dealer as early as 1864, and later formed a partnership with John Righter to import and distribute dolls and toys to the wholesale market. In the later years, they expanded their business to include doll parts, wigs, shoes, and other accessories.

SELF SELL DOLL CO.—U.S.A., 1924-1928. Manufactured composition mama, baby, and character dolls.

SELIGMANN & MAYER—Germany, 1925-1930. Advertised dolls, stuffed animals, and wooden toys.

SÈVRES—France, 1738- (apparently produced dolls only in the first quarter of the twentieth century). Best known for the exquisite porcelain objects of art, Sèvres did produce a limited number of beautifully modeled china doll heads. Sèvres dolls are of very good quality.

SEYFARTH & REINHARDT—Germany, 1922-1930. In 1922, Hugo Seyfarth abandoned the partnership of Gans & Seyfarth and joined Hugo Reinhardt to form Seyfarth & Reinhardt. The factory manufactured bisque-head jointed dolls, bent-limb babies, and separate doll parts. As their marking indicates, at least some of the bisque heads used by Seyfarth & Reinhardt were supplied by Ernst Heubach. Seyfarth & Reinhardt dolls are of fair quality.

SHACKMAN, B. & CO.—U.S.A., 1898-contemporary. Founded by Bertha Shackman, a name familiar to all seasoned collectors. Responsible for importing and distributing every conceivable type of doll. Particularly fond of small dolls in ethnic costumes, and warehouse finds. Advertised "old stock" dolls and accessories. Very few doll collections do not contain at least one Shackman doll of mediocre quality.

SHANKLIN TOY INDUSTRY, LTD.—England, 1915-1920. Founded by E. E. Houghton, it later became Nottingham (known as British Toys), under the ownership of Roberts Brothers. Manufactured composition and cloth dolls with mask-type faces.

SHEPPARD, J. B. & CO.—U.S.A., about 1900. This company produced a life-size cloth doll—known as the Philadelphia Baby—with head, shoulder, forearms, and legs painted in flesh-colored oil paints. The facial features are molded, with large deep eyes having well-defined, heavy eyelids and a "cupid's bow" closed mouth, with a deep indentation in the center of the lower lip. The chin is quite pronounced, as are the nicely molded, applied ears. The entire face has a slightly flattened appearance. The hair is painted; the eyebrows match the hair. Jointed at shoulder, hips, and knees. The Philadelphia Babies were sold at the J. B. Sheppard Linen Store on Chestnut Street in Philadelphia, hence the name. The designer, maker, and dates of origin are uncertain. The doll is generally accepted as having been made around the turn of the century. One theory is that it was designed by Elizabeth Washington, a student/artist at the Philadelphia School of Design. Supposedly, J. B. Sheppard's Linen Store held a contest for the best-designed doll which could be used as a model for their baby clothes and could also be offered for sale. Elizabeth Washington's doll won the contest and the rights were purchased by the Sheppard Store. There is no documentation to either support or discredit this story. However, we can thank U. F. D. C. member Frances Walker for offering this legend through her writings in the 1980s. Sheppard dolls are of good quality, and are highly collectible.

SHIKISHIMA SHOKAI —Japan, 1929-1930s. Manufactured dolls.

SHILLMAN, M. & S.—U.S.A., 1925-1930. Although best known for supplying doll clothing and accessories to jobbers, Shillman did advertise dolls with trunks containing clothing—complete with hat, coat, petticoats, pillow, and blanket.

SHIMIZU KATSUZO—Japan, 1900-1930. Manufactured dolls.

SHINDANA TOYS—U.S.A., 1968-contemporary. Shindana (Swahili for "complete") is a black community-owned toy company in the Watts section of Los Angeles. Devoted to producing truly black dolls with beautiful ethnic characteristics in cloth, plastic, and vinyl. Dolls by Shindana, a member of Operation Bootstraps, are of interest to collectors and children alike, in part due to their charm, but also because of the high quality materials used to make the dolls and their costumes.

SHROPSHIRE TOY INDUSTRY—England, 1917. Manufactured dolls with heads of British Ceramic and bodies of cloth.

SKOOKUM INDIAN DOLLS—U.S.A., 1913-contemporary. Designed by Mary McAboy and produced by several companies using the "Bully Good" trademark. The earliest dolls were made from dried apples, followed by composition, clay, plastic, and vinyl.

SIBYL FORTUNE TELLING DOLL CO.—U.S.A., 1925-1930 and later. Composition character face dolls with cloth bodies. The unique characteristics of the Fortune Telling doll include the costume and the old-woman modeling of the face. Multicolored paper leaves, folded in such a manner that a skirt is fashioned, are printed with questions and answers, so that when unfolded the Gypsy gives a "reading." The base of the doll is equipped with a chart giving the days, months, and zodiac signs. Fortune Telling Dolls are highly collectible.

SIBLEY, LINDSAY & CURR CO.—U.S.A., 1913-1914. Imported and distributed bisque-head dolls.

SIEDAR, JOHANN—Austria, 1907-1908. Listed as a doll maker, records indicate that walking dolls were manufactured.

SIEGFRIED—Germany, around 1910. A mystery doll. No records have been verified as to the manufacturer of this bisque-head character baby on a bent-limb body. The quality is good, and the decoration is nicely applied.

SILVER DOLL & TOY MANUFACTURING CO.—U.S.A., 1923-1924. A short-lived manufacturer of composition head and limbs. These dolls had painted or sleep eyes with a cloth body.

SIMMONDS, MR.—England, around 1917. Registered as a doll maker.

SIMON & HALBIG—Germany, 1869-1939 and possibly later. Early documentation for Carl Halbig and Wilhelm Simon is quite elusive. The company's tinted and untinted bisque shoulder heads with molded hair and delicate decoration are typical of the prodigious output of fine quality dolls produced by this German manufacturer. Kid-bodied shoulder heads, originally made in the 1880s, followed closely in the French tradition with large, often paperweight eyes, pierced ears, and heavy brows. A number of swivel heads on kid-lined shoulder plates were made completely in the French manner. Practically all combinations of bisque heads and features have been found with the Simon & Halbig mark, including solid dome and Belton type; molded hair or wigs; and painted, stationary, sleep, or flirty eyes. Mouths can be open, closed, or open/closed. Ears may be pierced. Often a single mold number will be found with a variety of characteristics. Simon & Halbig registered several new ideas. These included eyes operated by a lever, movable eyelids, the use of threads for eyelashes, and glazing the neck of a socket head doll to reduce friction between the neck and the body socket. They not only produced a multitude of dolls from their own molds, but also produced dolls for several other German manufacturers, including C. M. Bergmann, Carl Berger, Hamburger, Handwerck, Hülss, Kämmer & Reinhardt, and Schmidt. If this were not impressive enough, many French firms also relied upon Simon & Halbig for their bisque heads, including Fleischmann & Bloedel, Jumeau, Roullet & Decamp, and S. F. B. J. It is widely accepted that heads marked "DEP" were intended for the French market. While many of these manufacturers were supplied heads from several different porcelain factories, Kämmer & Reinhardt depended entirely upon Simon & Halbig, a dependency that no doubt led to Kämmer & Reinhardt's acquisition of Simon & Halbig in 1920. Most Simon & Halbig dolls are fully marked. The ampersand was added to the markings in 1905. Consequently, it is assumed that doll marks without the ampersand were produced before 1905. Simon & Halbig dolls are of very good quality.

SIMONNE, F.—France, 1842-1881. Produced lovely bisque-head Poupée de Mode and Bébés apparently with heads supplied by Jules Steiner or François Gaultier. Simonne dolls are of fine quality.

SIMPSON, FAWCETT & CO.—England, 1915-1919. Manufactured cloth-bodied dolls.

SIMPSON-CRAWFORD CO.—U.S.A., 1904-1906. Advertised dressed and undressed dolls, Cymbalier, doll parts, and accessories—including parasols, shoes, jewelry, and wigs.

SINDACATO ITALIANO D'IMPORTAZIONE E. D'ESPORTAZIONE—Italy, 1919-1920. Manufactured dolls for export, and also imported dolls.

SINDALL, FREDERICK—England, 1895-1923. Manufactured cloth dolls.

SLOAN & CO.—England, 1915-1918. Manufactured composition and British Ceramic-head dolls.

SMITH, CELIA & CHARITY—U.S.A., 1889-1911. Created and designed printed, lithographed, cut-out cloth dolls.

SMITH, ELLA, DOLL CO.—U.S.A., 1904-1924. Also known as Alabama Indestructible Dolls. According to legend, a neighbor girl brought Ella Smith a broken bisque doll to be repaired. When Ella saw how bad the little girl felt, she was determined to make a doll that couldn't be broken. She obviously succeeded. At one point, so the story goes, a truck ran over one of the dolls and didn't even crack the paint. Each beautifully handcrafted cloth doll was stitched and painted by Mrs. Smith or one of her assistants. It has be reported that at the peak of production 6,000 dolls a year were made. The dolls have heavily painted cloth bodies which are jointed at the hips and shoulders. The hair is usually painted, but occasionally a doll is found with a wig. The faces are molded cloth and painted with ears added. Many have bare feet with stitch toes, but dolls with painted-on button slippers or low boots are more commonly found. The dolls were made to represent white or black children and babies. Stuffed through the top of the head, Alabama Indestructible dolls are easily recognized by a stitched circular crown. Ella Smith dolls are highly collectible, especially the early dolls with applied, rather than molded, ears. All, however, are of very good quality.

SMITH, MRS. PUTNAM DAVID—U.S.A., 1913-1922. Mrs. P. D. (Mabel) Smith, an artist, and her daughter Margaret, modeled the charming faces for their original composition-head dolls with cloth bodies. Occasionally, though, a recycled ball-jointed, German composition body was used. Most often found with glass eyes. The early marked dolls show great artistry and are well made. Later dolls, unfortunately, are of a lesser quality both in the materials used to make the dolls, and in the application of decoration.

SMITH, W. H. & SON—England, 1916-1918. Also known as Toyland. Although originally a book dealer, during World War I they produced dolls with British Ceramic heads and cloth bodies.

SMITH & HOYLE—England, 1916-1917. Also known as Clarendon Works. During World War I they produced dolls with British Ceramic heads and cloth bodies.

SOCIÉTÉ AU BÉBÉ ROSE—France, 1910. A short-lived, little-known company, save the registering of their trademark.

SOCIÉTÉ DES YEUX EXPRESSION ET POUPÉE MYSTÉRE—France, 1926. Listed as a doll manufacturer.

SOCIÉTÉ DU CAOUTCHOUC MANUFACTURÉ—France, 1920s. Member of the Chambre Syndicale. Advertised dressed and undressed rubber dolls.

SOCIÉTÉ ETNA—France, 1926. Manufactured dolls.

SOCIÉTÉ FRANÇAISE DE FABRICATION DE BÉBÉS & JOUETS—France, 1899-1950. This is the French name for the Manufacturing of Dolls and Toys. More commonly referred to as the S. F. B. J. In 1899, the society signed an agreement for locations in Paris and Montreui-sous-Bois, France. French doll manufacturers had struggled against the German competition for many years, finally being forced to economize in an effort to compete. Most of the premier French firms were absorbed by the S. F. B. J. syndicate. Many companies continued to manufacture the same dolls under S. F. B. J. that they had previously produced as individual companies. Dolls produced under the amalgamation rarely met the high standards set by the original firms. Vast differences in quality of bisque, eyes, wigs, costuming, and application of decoration are probably more obvious with S. F. B. J. than with any other doll manufacturer. Good examples are very good, and poor examples are very poor. If you keep in mind that the S. F. B. J. heads were made in several different porcelain factories, with different molds which belonged to different companies, the spectrum of differences seems more logical. Two types of dolls were produced under the S. F. B. J. marking. First, they continued to manufacture the familiar Bébés, similar in concept, if not in quality, to the earlier Bébés. The second thrust was the modeling and production of charming, imaginative character dolls. Character dolls are modeled in the likeness of real children with portrait-like details, as opposed to the idealized "dolly-face" bébés. Characters may be pouting, laughing, screaming, or smiling, as they portray babies, adolescents, or even adults. After viewing these fascinating characters, it becomes obvious why they enjoy a large audience of collectors, and demand such generous prices. Along with bisque dolls, S. F. B. J. also produced composition, hard plastic, and vinyl dolls of various types. S. F. B. J. range in quality from the very poor to the very good.

SOCIÉTÉ INDUSTRIELLE DE CELLULOID—France, 1902-1927. Manufactured celluloid dolls, except for a time during World War I when the factory was used to produce explosives. The trade names Sicoid and Sicoine may be found on their dolls, as might the initials S. I. C. or S. I. M. P.

SOCIÉTÉ INDUSTRIELLE DE FERBLANTERIE—France, 1918. Manufactured dressed and undressed rubber dolls.

SOCIÉTÉ NOBEL FRANÇAISE—France, 1927-1939, and possibly later. The successor of Société Industrielle de Celluloid. Along with inheriting the trade names Sicoid and Sicoine, they also registered and used the initials S. N. F.

SOCIÉTÉ NOUVELLE DES BÉBÉS RÉCLAMES—France, 1929-1930s, and perhaps later. Manufactured dressed and undressed composition head dolls.

SOLOMON, MANNIE & CO.—U.S.A., 1923. Crafted miniature wooden dolls.

SOMMER, KARL—Austria, 1907-1910. Registered as a supplier of dolls and doll heads.

SOMMERS, E. L. & CO.—U.S.A., 1921-1930. Advertised squeaking rubber dolls, and dolls that removed their hats or crawled. The dolls were activated by squeezing a rubber ball attached to the doll by a rubber tube.

SON BROTHERS & CO.—U.S.A., 1917-1919. Imported bisque dolls from Japan.

SOUTHERN CALIFORNIA STATUARY CO.—U.S.A., 1927-1928. Manufactured carnival-type chalk ware or plaster dolls.

SOUTHERN DOLL & CANDY MANUFACTURING CO.—U.S.A., 1930s. Manufactured inexpensive dolls.

SOVIET UNION DOLLS—Soviet Union (Russia), 1940-1991. Made by various and unknown craftsmen. These charming cloth dolls have gained in popularity and value recently due to the demise of the Soviet Union. The evolution of Russian dolls is often linked to the country's changing political climate. Wars and depressions were responsible for so many changes in, not only the materials, but also in the type of dolls produced. Another type of Russian doll is the Trihedrals, the all-wooden three-sided dolls with no joints and carved clothing. Although sentiments play a leading role in doll collecting, handcrafted Soviet Union dolls are of fair to good quality.

SPAGGIARI, MME. YVONNE—France, 1927-1938. Created soft-sculptured cloth dolls dressed in authentic regional costumes, closely resembling dolls made by Ravca.

SPATZ, ULMER—Germany, 1927. Advertised cloth art-type dolls and doll clothing.

SPECIALTY TOY & DOLL CO.—England, 1919-1920. A short-lived manufacturer of British Ceramic-head and cloth dolls.

SPEIER, EMIL—Germany, 1888-1902. Advertised dressed dolls and Täuflinge along with a wide variety of doll accessories, such as shoes, wigs, jewelry, hats, clothing, stockings, and so forth.

SPEIGHTS, LTD.—England, 1900-1924 and probably later. Also known as Classic Works. Initially this company made wigs for dolls, but by 1915, it expanded to make doll bodies—and, eventually, the complete doll using heads of British Ceramic.

SPENCER & CO.—Wales, 1916-1919, and possibly later. This company manufactured dressed and undressed composition-head dolls with glass eyes and cloth bodies.

SPERRHAKE, ARNO—Germany, 1891-1930. Manufactured dressed and undressed dolls, and bisque or celluloid dollhouse dolls.

SPICER, GILBERT H.—England, 1916-1917. Advertised composition, wax, or British Ceramic baby, child, dollhouse, and mascot dolls, along with doll parts and molds.

SPORLIN, MICHAEL & RAHN, HEINRICH—Austria, 1835-1841. Also known as Sporlin & Heinrich Zimmerman. Made molded hair papier-mâché-head dolls.

SQUIER TWINS TOY CO.—U.S.A., 1920-1930s. Manufactured leatherette, cloth, or yarn dolls.

STADLER, JOHANN—Austria, 1809-1816. Made wooden dolls.

STANDARD TOY CO.—U.S.A., 1920. A short-lived manufacturer of composition head dolls.

STANDFUSS, KARL—Germany, 1898-1930 and beyond. Manufactured at his "Metall und Celluloid Puppenfabrik," metal and celluloid dolls. The metal-head dolls often had a coating of celluloid and were furnished with glass sleep eyes. Advertised cloth dolls, dollhouse dolls, and other small dolls and doll parts.

STAR DOLL & TOY CO.—U.S.A., 1915-1960s. Member of the American Doll Manufacturers' Association. Supplied composition head mama and baby dolls to jobbers. Licensed by Voices, Inc., to use criers in their Star dolls. Continued to produce inexpensive character dolls well into the mid-twentieth century.

STAR MANUFACTURING CO.—England, 1887-1929. Manufactured composition and British Ceramic-head dolls with cloth bodies. Also advertised cloth character dolls.

STAR TOY & NOVELTY CO.—U.S.A., 1914-1921. Manufactured composition and wooden dolls.

STARR—U.S.A., mid-twentieth century. Made small hard plastic and vinyl dolls with closed mouth and sleep eyes. Most are unmarked; however, occasionally a "7/3" is found on the head or back.

STEEVAN'S MANUFACTURING CO.—England, 1917. Advertised a walking doll activated without springs or clockwork mechanism.

STEIFF, FRÄULEIN MARGARETE—Germany, 1877-present. The German town of Gienger an der Brenz, the home of Margarete Steiff, dates back to the time of cobblestone streets and gingerbread houses. Born in 1847, Margarete contracted polio at the age of two, which weakened her legs and right hand. This did not, however, dampen her spirits, for she was determined to learn to sew in order to support herself. As a young woman, she became an accomplished seamstress, having her own workshop where she made women's and children's clothing of wool felt. In 1880, a flash of inspiration changed her life forever. Margarete designed and created a small felt elephant pincushion. She is quoted as writing in her diary, " . . . I quite casually came across a picture representing an elephant. Felt is quite the kind of material suitable for making small pattern animals, so I set to work, choosing for the purpose the best wool felt I could lay my hands on. The little elephant will make a lovely pincushion." This little elephant was very popular among the children of the neighborhood, who approached Miss Steiff requesting copies of the little elephant to use as a plaything. It was then that she began commercially producing small stuffed animals. In 1897 Richard, a nephew of Margarete, joined the family business. Richard had studied art in Germany and England. It was while he was in Stuttgart, Germany, that the seeds of the most popular toy of all times were planted. Richard developed a passion for sketching the antics of the brown bears housed at the Nills Animal Show. He was so amused with the playful bears that he filled whole sketchbooks with his drawings. These sketchbooks proved invaluable in 1902, when he designed a small toy bear made of mohair with movable joints. This toy made its debut at the 1903 Leipzig Toy Fair, held each Easter. It was a small bear, very similar to Steiff's premiere bear that President Theodore Roosevelt used in 1906 at his daughter's White House wedding reception: The decorations for the tables were Steiff bears dressed and equipped as hunters and fishermen, a theme chosen because of the President's love of the outdoors. This unusual wedding reception theme created an unparalleled endorsement for a toy. During the next year, one million Steiff bears were sold, a record that still stands. Leadership of the Steiff company was passed to nephews of Miss Steiff following her death in 1909. The making of toys at the Steiff factory continues to this day in much the same way as was done some one hundred years ago. Until very recently, the tradition was that of a cottage industry, with women picking up the raw materials at the factory and returning with the finished products. The marking for Steiff toys has changed over the years. In 1892, a camel was used, but never registered. In 1898, the elephant with his trunk forming the letter S was used, but again, without being registered. The Teddy Bear, was never registered, explaining why so many competing firms were able to manufacture "Teddy Bears." Perhaps the failure to reg-ister trade names and marks in the past prompted Margarete to make an application in December 1904 for the "Button in the ear for toys of felt and similar material." She even wrote to her customers to inform them, " . . . from November 1, 1904 on, each of my products, without exception, shall have as my trademark a small nickel button in the left ear." Although best known for its animals, Steiff also produced, and continues to produce dolls—once advertised "Jovial lads with buxom maidens." Painstaking attention is paid to details—of both structure and dress. Their large feet offer a good foundation. Felt pressed heads characterized by a seam down the middle of the face, mohair wigs, and glass eyes express an individuality which continues to endear these dolls in the hearts of collectors. In 1988, the new line of hard vinyl Steiff dolls became available in the United States. Found with hard vinyl heads, cloth bodies with vinyl arms, and human hair wigs. Steiff dolls are of very good quality.

STEINBERG—Germany, 1927. Manufactured rubber dolls.

STEINER, EDMUND ULRICH—Germany, 1864-1916. Edmund came from a family whose roots were planted deeply in the doll industry. His father produced a high grade doll which was one of the first prominent lines to be marketed in the United States. His brother, Albert, was also a well-known personality in the doll business. Edmund came to America as a young man from his home in Sonneberg, Germany, and reportedly crossed the Atlantic eighty-four times in his career. He maintained a close association with the doll community in both his native country and the United States. Over the years he registered several designs for bisque-head dolls. Edmund Steiner dolly-faced bisque doll heads were supplied by several companies—among them was Armand Marseille. Edmund Ulrich Steiner dolls are of mediocre quality.

STEINER, HEINRICH—Germany, 1895-1912. Advertised dressed and undressed dolls. Records indicate that wax dolls were exported under the Heinrich Steiner name.

STEINER, HERMANN—Germany, 1911-1930 and beyond. Records indicate that the manufacturing of dolls began in 1920. This explains why the majority of dolls found with the Hermann Steiner mark are the character babies which were so popular that they dominated the market at that time. Hermann Steiner had poor timing regarding the manufacturing of bisque dolls, by entering the market at the end of the era. Nevertheless, Hermann Steiner composition and bisque-head dolls—with glass or painted eyes and molded hair, or with a wig, on either cloth, kid, or composition bodies—are of fair to mediocre quality.

STEINER, JULES—France, 1855-1891, succeeded by Amédée La Fosse from 1892-1893 and following his death, by his widow, who ran the business until 1899. From 1899 to 1901, Jules Mettais headed the company.

He, in turn, was succeeded by Edmond Daspres from 1904 to 1908. Often you will find "Bourgoin" marked on a Steiner doll. Bourgoin was a Paris merchant dealing in porcelains and associated with Jules Steiner during the 1880s. Sometime after 1897, the Société Steiner purchased May Freres Cie., the company responsible for the manufacture of Bébé Mascotte. It was long believed that Steiner dolls were produced in Germany, a misconception possibly resulting from the Germanic name, or from distorted recollections. These beliefs have long since been abandoned. It is now generally accepted in the doll community that these exquisite creations are unquestionably French. From the early bisque dolls with their round faces and two rows of tiny pointed teeth, to the later, captivatingly beautiful Bébés, the Société Steiner produced some of the most distinctively high quality bisque dolls of the nineteenth century, while under the leadership and creativity of its founder Jules Nicholas Steiner. There is evidence that Steiner pressed its bisque doll heads even after other French manufacturers were routinely using the poured bisque method. Along with the pressed bisque heads, look for good quality paperweight eyes and nicely applied delicate decorations. Steiner Bébés have been found with a variety of markings, including some that may seem strange. It is important to understand a few basic abbreviations when deciphering these markings. For example:

FI, Fire, or Figure	Face or countenance
Bté	registered
Ste	Steiner
SUCCe	Successor
S. G. D. G.	registered but without government guarantee

Markings usually include one of four letters: *A, B, C* or *D. A* is the most commonly found. The size number is also incorporated into the marking (See Size Charts). Jules Steiner Bébés are of very good quality.

STEINER, NICOL—Germany, 1911-1920. Advertised jointed dolls.

STEINER, PORZELLANFABRIK—Bavaria, 1920-1926. Supplied several doll manufacturers with bisque doll heads and all-bisque dolls.

STEINER, VIKTOR—Germany, 1903-1928. Manufactured dolls and other toys with criers, or voice boxes.

STEINER, WILLI—Bavaria, 1925-1929. This company made cloth dolls.

STEINER & CO. MESSRS.—England, 1915. Advertised mama dolls made entirely by American and British workers.

STELLMACHER, J.—Germany, 1909-1920. Made cloth dolls.

STEPHAN, KARL—Austria, 1907-1910. Listed as a supplier of dolls and doll heads. This company also repaired dolls.

STERLING TOYS—U.S.A., around 1900. Made painted wooden dolls.

STERN BROTHERS—U.S.A., 1883-present. Purchased and sold dolls of all types. Have several times over the years commissioned special dolls to be sold only through their outlets.

STIER, HEINRICH—Germany, 1830s-1880s. Made wax-over composition dolls.

STOLL & EDWARDS CO.—U.S.A., 1925-1930. Made composition cloth-bodied dolls.

STRASSER—Germany, 1920s. Designed and created art dolls.

STRASSERPUPPEN WERKSTÄTTEN—Germany, 1924-1930. Produced rubber head portrait art dolls.

STRAT MANUFACTURING CO.—U.S.A., 1915-1916. A short-lived, and little-known, manufacturer of cloth dolls.

STRATTON, JOHN F., CO.—U.S.A., 1880s. Advertised china-head, all-china, wax, and cloth dolls.

STRAUSS, ADOLPH & CO.—U.S.A., 1857-at least until 1937 and possibly later. Records indicate that they did not import dolls until as late as 1912, at which time the trade name Asco and the slogan "The House of Service" were registered. These were renewed in 1937 under a new name: Strauss-Eckhardt Company.

STRAWBRIDGE & CLOTHIER—U.S.A., 1868-contemporary. Purchased and sold dolls of all types. Have several times over the years commissioned special dolls to be sold only through their outlets.

STROBEL & WILKEN CO.—U.S.A., 1864-1930 and later. Purchased and sold dolls of all types. Have several times over the years commissioned special dolls to be sold only through their outlets and under their name. There is some controversy over the registering of the *W* and *S* markings. Although accepted by many to be the mark for Strobel & Wilken, an equal number feel that the mark is in fact that of Walther & Sohn. At this time no conclusive evidence is known.

STROME & CO.—England, 1892-1930s. Distributed celluloid dolls.

STRUNZ WILHELM—Bavaria, 1909-1911. Made cloth dolls.

SUN ENAMEL WORKS—U.S.A., 1929. Made turned-wood segmented dolls.

SUN RUBBER CO.—U.S.A., 1930-contemporary. Manufactured rubber dolls and other toys.

SUNLIGHT, SIEVE & CO.—England, 1915-1920. This company made cloth, British Ceramic, composition, and celluloid dolls.

SUNNY-TWIN DOLLY CO.—U.S.A., 1919-1920. Made celluloid dolls.

SUPREME DOLL & TOY CO.—U.S.A., 1919. A short-lived manufacturer of all-composition dolls.

SURPRISE SHOP—U.S.A., 1925-1930. This company made cloth dolls.

SÜSSENGUTH, GEBRÜDER—Germany, 1894-1930. Founded by the brothers Christian and Franz for the production of lightweight dolls intended for exportation to the United States.

SUSSFELD & CIE—France, 1863-1930. Distributed and exported bisque-head dolls, along with celluloid and soft cloth dolls and toys.

SUTHERLAND DOLL CO.—England, 1918. Manufactured dolls with British Ceramic heads.

SUTTER, PROFESSOR CONRAD—Germany, 1914. Designed and created wooden dolls at his workshop called Hessische Spielwaren Manufaktur.

Strobel & Wilken's Googly Character Doll

SWAINE & CO.—Germany, 1854-1927. Swaine & Company was a porcelain factory in Hüttensteinach, Germany, founded in the early 1800s, but is not believed to have produced dolls until about 1910. Owned by William Swaine, the factory produced quality dolls for only a brief time. Made from high-grade bisque, the dolls were beautifully sculptured with fine molding, and exhibited extraordinary talent in the application of decoration. Faces were delicate, sweet, and uniquely Swaine. Many collectors believe Swaine produced only one doll, Lori, with several expressions. Her different expressions have been signified by the letters D I; D I I; D I P and so on. Other collectors contend that the character dolls produced by Swaine & Company are entirely different character dolls, each with their own particular characteristics. Whichever school of thought subscribed to, all agree that Swain character dolls are charming, delightful additions to any collection. Authentic Swaine creations have a green ink stamp reading, "Geschützt Germany S & Co." on the back of the bisque heads, in addition to the incised markings. Swain & Co. character dolls are generally of very good quality.

SWEENEY LITHOGRAPHING CO.—U.S.A., 1930s. Manufactured cloth dolls.

SWIECKA, MLLE.—Russia, 1915-1918. Created cloth or leather dolls.

SYLVER, JANE—France, 1927-1930. Listed in the directory as a doll maker.

SZERELEMHEGYI MARGA—Hungary, 1920s-1930s. Made composition or felt dolls with cotton bodies.

T

T. A. F.—Spain, 1930s. Talleres de Arte Fusté manufactured beautifully costumed cloth dolls with painted facial features.

T. W. TOY & NOVELTY CO.—U.S.A., 1922-1923. A short-lived, little-known doll manufacturer.

TAFT, JAMES SCHOLLY—U.S.A., about 1913-1917. Manufactured bisque doll heads.

TAH TOYS LTD.—England, 1917-1918. Made cloth dolls.

TAILLANDIER, E. H.—France, 1925-1927. Made decorative dolls.

TAIYO TRADING CO.—U.S.A. and Canada, early twentieth century. The result of two Japanese import firms' merger—Tajimi & Takito, Ogawa, joined forces and imported bisque-head dolls.

TAKADA KINOSUKEE—Japan, 1930s and later. Manufactured dolls.

TALKING DOLL & NOVELTY CO.—U.S.A., 1913 and possibly beyond. Manufactured talking dolls.

TAMBON CO.—U.S.A., 1913. Manufactured cloth lithograph character cut-out dolls.

TAMMEN CO., H. H.—U.S.A., 1886-1930. Produced leather, composition, cloth, and ceramic dolls, often representing American Indians. At least some of the dolls were supplied by cottage industry-type workers. Records indicate that Mary McAboy, who was well-known for the Skookum Indian dolls, trained and instructed the workers.

TEBBETS, MARIAN CURRY & TEBBETS, MISS—U.S.A., 1921-1930. Made soft-sculptured cloth dolls.

TED TOY-LERS—U.S.A., 1924-1928, when they merged with International Toy Corp. Founded by E. V. Babbitt, an engineer who designed and made segmented wooden toys and dolls to amuse his children. Others, after seeing his creations, requested his toys, thus launching a successful business. Within a few years of opening his production-line factory to produce the toys and dolls, the output was in excess of 5,000 wooden objects a day.

TELMA MANUFACTURING CO.—England, 1917-1918. Advertised dressed and undressed dolls with composition, or British Ceramic heads, along with wooden dolls with removable clothing.

TERRI LEE—U.S.A., 1946-1958. Founded by Mrs. Violet Gradwohl. Starting with ten employees in one room in Lincoln, Nebraska, Mrs. Gradwohl ventured into the doll making business. Concerned with the quality of dolls being offered to children, she wanted to produce a doll that could withstand the loving a child could inflict. Her first challenge was in finding a suitable plastic—one that was both lifelike and durable. The head was molded with a closed mouth, and eyes could be painted, thus eliminating eyes that were easily broken. She also wanted a wig that could be shampooed, combed, curled, and styled. Eventually, Violet received a patent for the process used to create artificial hair wigs woven from Celanese yarn. Once construction details of the Terri Lee Doll were settled upon, the only remaining area of concern was costuming. Mrs. Gradwohl decided that Terri Lee should have a beautiful wardrobe, with all types of outfits made from the finest fabrics. The clothing was designed by Mrs. Gradwohl and her daughter, Terry Lee, for whom the dolls were named. Every little girl needs companionship, and the Terri Lee Doll was no exception. By using the same body with a lamb's wool wig replacement, brother Jerri Lee was created. Friends Bonnie Lu, Patty Jo, Benjie, and Nanooh, an Eskimo child, were also introduced. It is interesting to note that all these dolls used the same doll mold, the only difference being either wig type or painting. Also joining the family was 11-inch Baby Linda. She was soon followed by 10-inch Tiny Terri Lee and Tiny Jerri Lee. An entirely new doll, Connie Lynn, entered the scene. Reportedly, a birth certificate with fingerprints, footprints, and a lifetime guarantee were also issued with each doll. For a small fee (labor costs only), the company would restore a "sick" or "injured" doll. The Terri Lee Doll Company, though, despite its success, was troubled with tragedy. The factory in Lincoln burned to the ground, prompting its relocation to Apple Valley, California. There seems to be some mystery about the closing of this plant, but for whatever reason, they closed their doors in 1958. One interesting article stated that "...the Terri Lee Doll Company was plagued with misfortune.. some printable and others unprintable. Many rumors still abound." It is known that Mrs. Gradwohl died in Virginia in 1972.

TERRY, WILLIAM, J.—England, 1890-1915. Also known as Welbury Works. Manufactured cloth character dolls.

TERSCH, M. FIRM—Germany, 1920-possibly as late as 1930. Listed in registry as a Kunstwerkstätten, the German term for "workshop for arts and crafts." Manufactured dolls, doll heads, toys, and tea and coffee cozies.

TESMINE—France, 1927. Listed in directory as a doll maker.

THÉROUDE, ALEXANDRE NICHOLAS—France, 1837-1895. An early pioneer in the French automaton industry. Théroude produced walking and talking bébés, along with kid bodies child dolls.

THIELE, MAX—Germany, early twentieth century. Designed and created historical and fictional character dolls.

THOMAS, MME. AMBROISE—France, 1915-1916. Designed and created character cloth dolls.

THOMPSON, THOMAS R.—U.S.A., 1919 and perhaps other years. Made wooden dolls called Tots Toie.

THOMSON, MLLE. VALENTINE—France, 1914-1918. Designed and created bisque-head bébés.

THORNE BROTHERS—England, 1915-1918. Advertised wooden head character dolls with cloth bodies and criers.

THREE ARTS TOY INDUSTRY—England, 1920-1927. Manufactured soft, cuddly plush, velvet or felt dolls.

THREE ARTS WOMEN'S EMPLOYMENT FUND—England, 1915-1920. Designed and created dressed and undressed cloth dolls.

THUILLIER, A.—France, 1975-1893. Often referred to as A. T., these lovely bisque-head dolls were made with jointed wood, composition, or kid bodies. At least some of the heads were supplied by François Gaultier. An inventory list from the Gaultier factory shows an outstanding balance for heads produced for A. T. Another interesting note is a label found on a Poupée de Mode kid body. It reads: "A. De La Thuilerie Grand Magasin de Jouet Rue St. Honore' 366 Paris, English Spoken." All known A. Thuillier dolls are marked with *A. T.* and a size number.

THÜRINGER PUPPEN-INDUSTRIE—Germany, 1912-1924. Advertised bisque-head character doll with wig and open mouth on composition toddler body, also dressed dolls of better quality, babies, doll heads, and other accessories.

TILLICUM TOY MANUFACTURING CO.—U.S.A., 1926-1930. Founded by Harriet Robinson to produce small dolls and other toys to be used as educational tools in the classroom. Inventory records show that turned-wood dolls and toys were made from kindling wood purchased for $4.50, netting a return of $72.50!

TINY TOWN DOLLS—U.S.A., 1949-contemporary. Alma LeBlane creates charming small dolls with molded felt faces and painted eyes and mouths. Bodies are made of wire armatures covered with cloth.

TIP TOP TOY CO.—U.S.A., 1912-1921. Advertised composition head dolls with sleep eyes, human hair wigs, and kid bodies with wooden ball joints at shoulders, elbows, and knees. Also produced all-composition character dolls with painted side-glancing eyes.

TISSIER & CIE—France, before and during the 1920s. Advertised dressed and undressed dolls of celluloid.

TODHUNTER, M. E.—England, 1926-1928. Obtained a patent for dolls made with a copper skeleton, oil-painted leather over molded clay head. The body was covered with cotton batting and wrapped with calico. The well-shaped leather hands were molded so as to be able to hold small objects.

TOY PRODUCTS MANUFACTURING CO.—U.S.A., 1925-1930. Member of Doll Parts Manufacturing Association. Manufactured all-composition dolls and composition heads with molded hair, painted eyes, and doll parts. Supplied jobbers with composition dolls and doll parts. Also retailed composition dolls with their own markings.

TOY SHOP, THE—U.S.A., 1922-1929. Member of the American Doll Manufacturers' Association. Manufactured composition mama dolls and supplied jobbers with quality dolls.

TOY TINKERS, THE—U.S.A., 1923-contemporary. Manufactured segmented wooden dolls under the trade name Tinker Toys.

TRANSOGRAM CO.—U.S.A., 1915-1930s. Advertised walking dolls and doll costumes.

TRAUTMANN, CARL—Germany, 1884-1906. Manufactured bisque-head dolls on jointed composition and wood bodies. The heads were supplied exclusively by Simon & Halbig.

TRAVERTINE ART CO.—U.S.A., 1927-1928. Manufactured art dolls.

TREGO DOLL MANUFACTURING CO.—U.S.A., 1918-1921. Manufactured dolls with composition or imported bisque heads on composition bodies. Also advertised character dolls, and all-composition dolls with a matte finish.

TREIDLER, FRIEDRICH & JOSEF—Austria, 1853. Listed in records as doll makers.

TRION TOY CO.—U.S.A., 1911-1921. Skillfully managed by Adolph Cohen, who had over thirty years experience in the doll industry in United States, Germany, and France. Manufactured quality composition dolls, beautifully costumed.

TURNBULL, CHARLES EDWARD & CO.—England, 1895-1925. Advertised wax, china, and bisque dolls and accessories.

TURNER, H. FRANCIS & CO.—England, 1894-1924. Imported and sold celluloid dolls made in Japan.

TURTON, W. S.—England, 1915-1918. Made cloth dolls—the Rainbow doll series.

TWINJOY DOLL CO.—U.S.A., 1925-1929. Manufactured topsy-turvy-type dolls with two dolls in one, most adapted from nursery rhymes. Also made Flower dolls, with costumes made of petals, to represent various flowers, and felt art dolls with hand-painted facial features.

TWISTUM TOY FACTORY—U.S.A., 1921-1919. Made composition and wood-segmented dolls.

TYNESIDE TOYS—England, 1918-1919. Produced dolls with British Ceramic or composition heads on plush bodies.

U

U. S. DOLL COMPANY—U.S.A., 1923-1926. Manufactured dolls.

ÜBLER & BECK—Germany, 1922-1924. Manufactured dolls.

ULHENHUTH, HENRY & CIE—France, 1876-1919. Manufactured bisque dolls, and probably joined S. F. B.

J. ULLMANN, ALOIS—Czechoslovakia, 1914-1923. Listed as a manufacturer of wool and stuffed dolls with celluloid heads.

UNEEDA DOLL CO.—U.S.A., 1917-present. One of the oldest doll manufacturers in the United States. Founded in New York in 1917, it was also known as the Tony Toy Company of Hong Kong. Since its inception, Uneeda has produced thousands of popularly priced dolls made from cloth, composition, hard plastic, and vinyl. The company's success in the doll industry was due to its production of good quality dolls at competitive prices. They also supplied jobbers, mail-order houses, and department stores with a complete line of well-made dolls. Surely most every little girl owned at least one Uneeda Doll. By the 1930s, Uneeda was advertising over 400 different doll models ranging in size from 14 to 28 inches. Dollikins, by Uneeda, was probably the best fully-jointed doll ever made. She featured a unique body construction with joints at the neck, shoulders, upper arms, elbows, wrists, waist, hips, knees, and ankles. The joints were hidden, and allowed the doll to be gracefully posed in almost any position. Uneeda also advertised a "Magic Muscle" doll which walked by means of a weighted screw-type apparatus in its torso. Born from the need for American-made dolls during World War I, Uneeda has proven that high quality and a fair price will be rewarded with success. Over the years they have provided the world with many highly collectible dolls, including personality dolls, babies, toddlers, mamas, boys, and glamorous lady dolls. Uneeda dolls are of good quality.

UNGARISCHE GUMMIWAREN-FABRIK—Hungary 1894-1930. Made celluloid and rubber dolls and doll heads.

UNGER, ROBERT—Germany, 1909-1929. Manufactured dolls that were advertised as "similar to a monkey."

UNGER DOLL & TOY CO.—U.S.A., 1929-1930. A short-lived, little-known manufacturer of character dolls, probably made of celluloid.

UNICA—Belgium, 1921-1971. Manufactured beautiful and innovative hard plastic and vinyl dolls.

UNIQUE NOVELTY DOLL CO.—U.S.A., 1925-1930s. Manufactured bed, or boudoir, dolls with wigs made of silk.

UNIS—France, 1916-contemporary. Unis represents a mark used by S. F. B. J. and found on various bisque and composition French dolls. The letters *U N I S* were used as an acronym for Union National Inter Syndicale.

These initials are often found in a circle or football-shaped mark, and accompanied by numbers: The number to the left of the Unis mark represents the syndicate number (i.e., 71 was the number assigned to Chambre Syndicale); the number to the right of the Unis mark represents the manufacturer (i.e., 149 was the number assigned to the S. F. B. J.); the number beneath the Unis mark represents the mold number (i.e., 60 or 301, the two most frequently found mold numbers). Unis dolls tend to be of a lesser quality bisque and decoration with lesser quality decoration, than earlier S. F. B. J. dolls. Best known for the bisque Bleuette doll and book which was published twice a year. It advertised the commercially made costumes available for the Bleuette doll, and continued to be published until 1960. Unis dolls are of mediocre to poor quality.

UNITED STATES RUBBER CO.—U.S.A., 1918-1920. Advertised rubber dolls with whistles.

UTLEY—U.S.A., 1914-1922. In 1919, they became a subsidiary of the American Tissue Mills, and the name was changed to New England Doll Co. Sold dolls under the name N E D C O. Produced cloth and papier-mâché dolls. Best known for the Rollinson cloth dolls created by Gertrude Rollinson.

V

VALE OF CLWYD TOYMAKERS—Wales, 1917. Manufactured cloth dolls with hand-painted faces.

VALENTINE DOLLS, INC.—U.S.A., mid-twentieth century. Manufactured hard plastic and vinyl dolls.

VAN HOLLEBEKE—Belgium, mid-1800s. Made dolls, doll heads, and automatons.

VAN ROZEN J.—France, early 1912-1914. A Belgian refugee, Van Rozen designed character doll heads in Paris during World War I. He created faces which are known to be extremely realistic in expression. Even the profiles of these dolls are unique, with a distinct nose and cheek line. The heads are made of a bisque-like ceramic material. There is a haunting similarity between Van Rozen character dolls and dolls produced by the De Fuisseaux factory in Belgium just prior to World War I. It is possible, however, that Van Rozen and De Fuisseaux were associates in Belgium before the war. Highly prized by collectors, not only for their creativity, but also for their rarity. Van Rozen dolls are artistically pleasing.

VAN TUSSENBROEK, HARRY—Netherlands, 1929. Designed and created art dolls.

VANNIER, MME. HIPPOLYTE—France, 1864-1865. Registered as a maker of dressed dolls.

VARALE, A. & CO.—Italy, 1927-1930. Manufactured cloth art dolls.

VARGAS, ANTONIO—U.S.A., 1915-1930. Family of wax doll artists.

VASSILIEF, MARIE—Russia and France, about 1910-1926. Also spelled *Vasilyeff*. By any account, Marie Vassilief was a fascinating woman. She, along with friends such as the revolutionist Leon Trotsky, started an art school. The school seemed to be a favorite meeting place for political dissidents of the day. So suspect were Marie's friends and activities, that she spent a year in jail. Her artistic talents lent themselves to the creation of cloth art dolls. Believed by many to be the inspiration for the Madame Paderewski dolls.

VEELO MANUFACTURING CO.—U.S.A., 1928-1930. Made character cloth dolls.

VERITA, MLLE. GABRIELLE—France, 1915-1918. Designed and created cloth child, toddler, and baby character dolls.

VERLINGUE J.—France, 1915-1920s. Manufactured bisque-head dolls during a period of time when the quality of dolls coming from France was questionable. Along with child dolls, Verlingue also made all-bisque bathing dolls that were so very popular at that time. Verlingue dolls are of fair quality.

VICHY, G.—France, 1862-1900 and probably sometime later. Although best known for their wonderful mechanical dolls, many of which were also musical, Vichy and his sons also advertised bisque bébés and "Artistic shoulder heads." Vichy dolls are of the highest quality, as proven by the vast number of awards the dolls were given. A bronze medal in 1880; silver medals in 1878 and 1879; gold medals in 1884, 1888, and 1889; along with the Grand Prize at the Paris Exposition in 1900. At least some of the bisque heads used by Vichy were supplied by François Gaultier.

VICKERS, LTD.—England, 1920. Made cloth dolls.

VILLARD & WEILL—France, 1834-1928. Made bisque-head dolls that won several awards.

VIOLA DOLL CO.—U.S.A., 1917-1926. Manufactured composition dolls.

VIRGA DOLL COMPANY—U.S.A., mid-twentieth century. A subsidiary of Beehler Arts Company. Manufactured hard plastic and vinyl knockoff dolls.

VITALE DOLL CO.—U.S.A., 1927. Listed as a member of the American Doll Manufacturers' Association.

VOGEL, MAX—Germany, 1930. Produced celluloid dolls.

VOGUE—U.S.A., 1922-contemporary. Founded by Jennie H. Graves. Mrs. Graves never dreamed that her modest doll costuming business would grow to be, at one time, the largest doll-only manufacturer in the world. Originally intent on supplementing the family income, Jennie set out to design and make doll clothing. After convincing several department stores to purchase her merchandise, she and her neighbors started designing and sewing doll clothing. The business' sole enterprise remained the production of doll clothing until the mid 1930s. Mrs. Graves then decided to buy undressed quality bisque dolls from German manufacturers such as Kämmer & Reinhardt, design clothing for them, and then sell her creations at shops across the country. Her specially costumed dolls often retailed for $75.00 or more, an excessive price for a doll at that time. The political climate in Europe during the late 1930s forced Jennie to look to the United States for her doll supply. In 1948 the famous Ginny-type doll was born. The original miniature doll was an instant success, proving to be one of the most enduring little dolls of all time. First introduced as a composition doll, it was known as "Toddles." Vogue, over the years, diversified by introducing many new hard plastic and vinyl dolls. Vogue dolls are of very good quality.

VOICES, INC.—U.S.A., 1923-1930. A conglomerate of three principal manufacturers of voice boxes, or criers, made for mama dolls. Records indicate that over fifty doll companies used Voices, Inc., criers in their dolls.

VOIGHT, FRIEDRICH—Germany, 1879-1930s. Manufactured and exported celluloid, wood, and bisque-head dolls. The bisque doll heads were supplied by Schoenau & Hoffmeister.

VOIGT, GEBRÜDER—Germany, 1850-1911. Records indicate that bisque dolls were produced only in the years between 1886-1900. Dolls have been found with a #, very similar to the marking found on the tinted heads attributed to Alt, Beck & Gottschalck. If a connection exists between these two companies, it has not been found.

VÖLKER, CARL—Germany, 1888-1930. Advertised character dolls, and all-bisque, celluloid, and bisque/celluloid head dolls with composition bodies.

VOLLAND, P. F., CO.—U.S.A., early twentieth century. A publishing house best known for the Raggedy Ann and Andy books. It produced cloth dolls in conjunction with the stories.

VON DER WEHD, ADOLF—Germany, 1925-1926. Manufactured dolls.

VON UCHATIUS, FRÄULEIN—Austria, 1900-1906. Created interesting wooden dolls. The form and modeling was achieved by gluing, or cementing, small pieces of wood together. After the pieces were assembled, they were finished and painted. This process, known as Brettle of Brettlein, is believed to have been first used by Fräulein Von Uchatius.

Vogue's International Bride Dolls

VUAQUELIN, M.—France, 1925-1927. Made dolls.

W

W & F MANUFACTURING CO.—U.S.A., 1930s. Manufactured dolls.

W. P. A.—U.S.A., 1930s. Under Franklin D. Roosevelt's New Deal, the Works Progress Administration (W. P. A.) allowed the United States government to become a doll manufacturer. They provided work for artists and seamstresses struggling during the Great Depression. The objective of the project was to create cloth dolls representing characters from fairy tales, and folklore and historical figures from both the United States and various foreign countries. With the exception of Japan, most countries of the world were included in the project. Japan's omission was undoubtedly due to our strained relations during that period of history. Completed dolls were loaned to major department stores for display, and to elementary schools to be used as visual aids. Most of the dolls were approximately 12 inches tall and had cotton-stuffed bodies. Each torso was made from four pieces of material. Three of the seams ran the entire length of the body, and the front seam stopped at the neck. The separate arms were hand-sewn to the body, but the legs were typically part of the body. The wigs were made from yarn, or the hair was painted—as were the facial features. Because each doll was handcrafted, variations did occur. W. P. A. dolls are highly prized by collectors, more for their historic importance than for their beauty.

WACHUDA, FRANZ—Czechoslovakia, 1910. Listed as doll and doll head supplier.

WACKER, ALBERT—Germany, 1904-1930s, and possibly later. This company manufactured celluloid dolls, doll parts, and accessories.

WAGNER & ZETZSCHE—Germany, 1875-1938. Also spelled *Zetsche*. Founded by Richard Wagner and Richard Zetzsche, both of whom had worked for Naumann Fischer before starting their own business on the first day of 1875. Of the two, Zetzsche was the artist, responsible for designing and sculpting the dolls. Wagner was the practical one with the business sense. Four of Zetzsche's grandchildren, Harald, Hansi, Inge, and Barbele, were used as models for their dolls. The bodies of their dolls were made of cloth, leather, papier-mâché, and imitation leather. Numerous doll accessories, including more than 400 different designs of shoes, stockings, and wigs were also made. Many of the marked Wagner & Zetzsche kid bodies are found with fine quality bisque or china heads supplied by Alt, Beck & Gottschalck; Buschow & Beck; Gebrüder Heubach; and others. Around 1916, they acquired the patent for a composition material and process called "Haralit." The material is often described as both a celluloid and composition-like material. In truth, it is more characteristic of composition. Wagner & Zetzsche dolls are of good quality.

WAHN, PROFESSOR—Silesia (region of central Europe, chiefly in SW Poland and N Czechoslovakia) 1902-1907. Made flat wooden, painted dolls.

WALKER, IZANNAH—U.S.A., late 1800s. Izannah Walker made American primitive sculpture dolls in Central Falls, Rhode Island. The dolls have heavily oil-painted features or lightly sculptured faces. They bear an uncanny resemblance to children in American folk art paintings. They are typically unmarked, or marked "Patented Nov. 4th 1873." Collectors have long agreed that Izannah Walker dolls are wonderful, but they cannot agree on when they were made. In June 1873, Walker applied for a patent for her "Rag dolls." According to patent law, it was illegal for her to have made dolls for more that two years prior to her application date. Despite this, other possible dates abound. Mrs. Sheldon of the Chase Doll Company reported in *Doll Collectors of America*, that the first Walker doll was made in 1855. In *Your Dolls and Mine*, Janel Johl, Izannah Walker's great-niece, states that the first Walker dolls were made in 1840, 1845, 1848, and 1855! One solid bit of evidence does exist. The 1865 Census of Rhode Island lists "Walker, Izannah F., from American parentage in Bristol, Rhode Island, living in the village of Central Falls in the town of Smithfield with the occupation of 'Doll Maker'." One special lady, Mrs. Monica Bessette, has devoted years of research to answer these mysteries. We wish her luck, for her sake as well as ours. An interesting story about Walker dolls tells us that Izannah struggled to perfect her doll. One problem, in particular, was how to create a surface resistant to cracking and peeling. One night, coming out of a deep sleep, she sat up in bed and heard a voice say, "USE PASTE." It was after this vision that she obtained a patent for dolls. Izannah Walker dolls are not only charming, they are of great historic value.

WALLACH—Bavaria, 1914. Produced composition head dolls with pink cloth bodies and celluloid arms.

WALTER, GEBRÜDER—Germany, 1923-1926. Advertised stuffed dolls with sleep eyes.

WALTERSHÄUSER PUPPENFABRIK—Germany, 1902-1930, and possibly later. The name given to Heinrich Handwerck's factory after his death. A subsidiary of Kämmer & Reinhardt and later to become part of the Bing conglomerate. Waltershäuser is the probable explanation for the *W* often found on the forehead of many Heinrich Handwerck and Kämmer & Reinhardt dolls.

WALTHER, JOHANN—Germany, 1900-at least 1930. Initially advertised dressed dolls, but in 1908 he became a full partner in a porcelain factory, and from that point on produced bisque doll heads and all-bisque dolls. In 1921, the firm was registered as Walther & Sohn. It is now believed by many collectors and doll historians that the intertwined *S W*—which was long associated with Strobel & Wilken—may, in fact, be the markings of Walther & Sohn.

WANAMAKER, JOHN—U.S.A., 1880-present. Purchased and sold dolls of all types. Have several times over the years commissioned special dolls to be sold only through their outlets.

WANGENHEIM, N.—Germany, 1925-1926. Manufactured dolls.

WATFORD TOY MANUFACTURERS—England, 1915. Produced dressed dolls and undressed cloth-bodied dolls.

WEBSTER, STELLA N.—U.S.A., 1930-sometime before her death in 1941. Designed and created dolls of a plaster-type composition, along with costuming small imported bisque dolls.

WEIERSMÜLLER, WILLY—Germany, 1925-1930. Made cloth dolls.

WEIGNEROVA, H.—Czechoslovakia, 1929-1930. Manufactured dolls.

WEILL, ARMAND—Paris, 1927-1929. Made cloth dolls.

WEINSCHENKER, J. & CO.—U.S.A., 1923-1924. Manufactured composition mama dolls, and also designed dolls on a custom-order basis.

WEISS, KÜHNERT CO.—Germany, 1891-1930. Porcelain factory that produced bisque doll heads.

WELL MADE DOLL CO.—U.S.A., 1911-1930s and later. Member of the American Doll Manufacturers' Association. Made composition mama and character dolls.

WELLINGS, NORAH—England, 1926-1960. Norah Wellings was the chief designer at Chad Valley for several years until she and her brother, Leonard, started their own factory for manufacturing cloth dolls. The company was known as the Victoria Toy Works and was located in Arleston, England. Hundreds of different types of dolls were made representing both children and adults, fantasy characters, and ethnic groups. Made of excellent quality velvet, velveteen, plush, and felt, these detailed dolls ranged in size from 6 to 36 inches. Most of Norah Wellings' dolls are marked with a cloth label sewn to the bottom of the foot. Following the death of her brother in 1960, Norah closed the business and retired.

WELLINGTON, MARTHA L.—U.S.A., 1883 and possibly other years. Designed and created cloth baby dolls with pressed facial features.

WELMAID TOYS—England, 1920. It is known that this company manufactured dolls.

WELSCH, FRIEDERIKE—Silesia (region of central Europe, chiefly in SW Poland and N Czechoslovakia), 1925-1930. Made dolls.

WELSCH & CO.—Germany, 1911-1928. Founded by Ferdinand Welsch and Otto Mühlhäuser, and later to become a member of the Bing Conglomerate. They continued as an independent company. Manufactured bisque-head dolls. At least some of the heads were supplied by Schützmeister & Quendt and Simon & Halbig. Welsch & Co. dolls are of good quality.

WELSH TOY INDUSTRIES—Wales, 1919. Manufactured dolls with British Ceramic or composition heads on cloth bodies.

WENDENBURG, KATHARINE—Austria, 1910. Listed in directories for dolls and doll heads.

WESTERN ART LEATHER CO.—U.S.A., 1917. Advertised stuffed leather dolls.

WESTERN NEWS CO.—U.S.A., 1904, and most likely other years. Advertised "all-bisque dolls with painted facial features and hair; all-bisque dolls with glass eyes and wigs; bisque-head dolls with kid bodies; bisque-head dolls with jointed bodies; baby dolls; all-china dolls; leather dolls and separate bisque, china, and metal heads."

WEYDE, GISELLA—Czechoslovakia, 1920-1922. A well-known artist who also made cloth dolls.

WEYH, KURT—Germany, 1930. Made art dolls.

WEYH, MAX—Germany, 1911-1918. Manufactured character and googly-eyed dolls.

WHEELHOUSE, JAMES—England, 1908-1923. Made dolls.

WHITE, C. & H.—England, early 1800s. Made dolls with leather heads.

WHOLESALE TOY CO.—England, 1915-1921. Made composition character and baby dolls with soft stuffed, cloth bodies.

WIEFEL & CO.—Germany, 1912-1930. The porcelain factory that produced bisque doll heads and used the letters *E st. P.*

WIEGAND, CARL—U.S.A., 1876-1883. Made papier-mâché doll heads.

WIEGAND, HUGO—Germany, 1911-1930. Manufactured and advertised bent-limb character babies and Toddles dolls.

WIENER, AUGUST—Germany, 1903-1930. Produced bisque doll heads that were advertised as with or without wigs.

WIESENTHAL, SCHINDEL & KALLENBERG—Germany, 1858-1926. Although this company specialized in wax dolls, several bisque doll heads have been found marked "Simon & Halbig/W S K." *W S K*, of course, is the registered marking for Wiesenthal, Schindel & Kallenberg.

WIGWAM CO.—U.S.A., 1917-1918. A small, little-known manufacturer of composition dolls with sleep or painted eyes, with wigs or molded and painted hair.

WILSON NOVELTY CO.—U.S.A., 1930s-1951. Founded by John Wilson in Watsontown, Pennsylvania. The devastating effects of the Great Depression left this small central Pennsylvania town in desperate need. The old adage, "necessity is the mother of invention" was especially true in the creation of the little Wilson Walkies—also known as the "Watsontown Walkers." The dolls had a tremendous responsibility placed upon their sloping shoulders: to save the small town—and that is exactly what they did! The first Walkies were rather crude in design and appearance. They had cardboard cone bodies, pipe cleaner arms, and hand-painted faces on round wooden heads. They were dressed in scraps of fabric and paper, but were balanced in such a way that their wooden legs, moving inside the cone body, allowed them to walk along, in a distinctive Watsontown Walkies' gait. Early Walkies were stamped, "Made in U.S.A.," a marking that was used until 1938. Although the early Walkies were a bit short on quality, they were long on appeal. The company continued to grow and, in the process, refined the appearance of the walking dolls. Later Wilson Walkies could boast of nicely applied decal faces and wooden arms, while retaining their cone bodies and wooden legs. The company produced at least twenty-five different characters, ranging in height from 3-inch animals with four legs to the rare 10-inch characters. Thanks in part to F. W. Woolworth's five-and-dime store marketing, the Wilson Novelty Company, at one point, manufactured 13,000 Walkies a day. In 1949, just one year after the death of its founder, Wilson Novelty Co. was sold to a Canadian business, and by 1951 the production of the Walkies had come to an end. Wilson Walkies enjoy a collector following, despite their lack of high quality.

WILTSHAW & ROBINSON—England, 1915-1923. Made dolls with British Ceramic heads and cloth bodies, and dolls made exclusively of British Ceramic.

WINKLER, ERNST, FIRM—Germany, 1908-1929, when it became the Julius Rothschild Firm. Manufactured and exported dolls and doll parts.

WISCONSIN DELUXE DOLL & DRESS CO.—U.S.A., 1927-1930. Manufactured dolls.

WISLIZENUS, ADOLF—Germany, 1851-1931. In 1851 a doll and toy factory was founded by Gottlob Schafft in Waltershausen, Germany. In 1870, Adolf Wislizenus became a partner, and shortly thereafter, took over the company. By all accounts, Wislizenus was sole owner by 1878. In 1894, the company again changed ownership, with W. Heincke as the new proprietor. Records indicate that in 1909, A. Wislizenus was owned by Hans Heincke, who retained ownership until the doll factory went into bankruptcy in 1931. The bankrupt estate was acquired by König & Wernicke. A. Wis-lizenus, through all owners, was a doll factory, not a porcelain factory; therefore, it was necessary to purchase its bisque doll heads elsewhere. Bähr & Pröschild, Simon & Halbig, and, after 1910, Ernst Heubach all supplied bisque heads for Wislizenus dolls. A. Wis-lizenus dolls are of good quality.

WITTHAUER, CHRISTOPHER—Germany, 1899-1903. According to the corporate records, the doll heads were made of "card board or papier-mâché covered with cloth." Also advertised knock-about dolls.

WITTZAK, EMIL—Germany, 1862-1921. Advertised wool character dolls, babies, cloth dolls, and dolls made of celluloid.

Wilson Novelty Co.'s Watsontown Walkers (Photo courtesy of Helen Brooke.)

WOLF, LOUIS & CO.—Germany, 1870-1928, when they merged with Bing to help form the Bing Conglomerate. Best known for bisque-head character dolls with the L. W. & Co. marking.

WOLF DOLL CO.—U.S.A., 1905-1927. Member of the American Doll Manufacturers' Association. Manufactured composition mama and baby dolls. Licensed by Voices, Inc., to use their criers in their dolls.

WOLFF, GEBRÜDER—Germany, 1912-1930. Manufactured celluloid dolls and doll parts.

WOLSTAN DOLL CO.—England, 1918-1928. Made British Ceramic shoulder head and socket head dolls. Also advertised doll wigs, clothing, and other accessories.

WOMEN'S EMERGENCY CORPS WORKSHOP—England, 1914-1917. Made bisque-like composition head portrait dolls, and character and baby dolls.

WONDERCRAFT—U.S.A., early to mid-twentieth century. Manufactured composition dolls, such as Sammy Kaye and Bobbi Mae. All composition, hollow body mounted on a stick fastened to top of leg and attached to the body with metal rod or post. When the doll is touched, it sways. Named after the famous 1930s band leader whose radio show started with the slogan, "It's time to swing and sway with Sammy Kaye."

WONDERLAND TOYMAKING CO.—England, 1921-1923. Produced dolls.

WOOD TOY CO.—U.S.A., 1917-1923. This company was known for the Dolly Walker, which had a wooden body with springs and hinges to facilitate movement. Later advertised that the springs and the hinges had been eliminated.

WOODARD, W. R. & CO.—U.S.A., 1929-1930. Advertised the Hollywood Imps and other cloth dolls with hand-painted faces.

WOODE, R., TOY CO.—England, 1917. Manufactured composition head dolls.

WOODFLOUR NOVELTY CO.—U.S.A., 1927. A member of the American Doll Manufacturers' Association. Made dolls using a type of composition.

WOODS, MRS. MARY FRANCES—U.S.A., 1904-1920. Designed and created American Indian character dolls made from molded and treated crêpe paper. Distributed through Konstructor Co.

WOODS, ROBIN—U.S.A., late 1980s-1992 when she became the creative designer for the Alexander Doll Company. Produced beautifully costumed high-quality vinyl dolls.

WOOLNOUGH—U.S.A., 1927. Designed and created cloth dolls that had embroidered facial features and plush bodies.

WOOLWORTH, F. W. & CO.—Europe and U.S.A., 1879-present. Was the world's largest import house. Purchased and sold dolls of all types. This company, several times over the years, commissioned special dolls to be sold only through its outlets.

WORTHITT & CO.—England, 1916-1917. Made cloth or cloth-bodied dolls.

WRIGHT, JOHN—U.S.A., contemporary doll artist. This company designs and creates wonderful character cloth dolls with fantastic attention to detail in decoration and costuming.

WUNDERLICH, ERNST—Germany, 1913-1918. Manufactured dolls, and advertised a doll that could sit.

WÜRTTEMBERGISCHE SPIELWAREN PUPPEN WERKSTÄTTEN—Germany, 1924-1927. A toy factory and doll workshop. Advertised soft stuffed toys of all kinds. Also produced celluloid character dolls.

WURZBURG, F. A. & SON—U.S.A., 1916. Designed and created cloth dolls with faces to be completed at home by embroidering.

WYWELECKA, APPOLLONIE—Austria, 1907. Listed in that year's directory under "dolls and doll heads."

X

Y

YAGODA BROTHERS—U.S.A., 1925-1930. Manufactured composition head dolls with cloth bodies. Also advertised separate composition doll heads. Licensed by Voices, Inc., to use their criers in their dolls.

Z

ZAIDEN, TOY WORKS—U.S.A., 1906-1930s. Manufactured composition head dolls. The David Zaiden Mechanical Doll, by 1923, was advertised by Overland Products Co.

ZAKUCKA-HARLFINGER, FANNY—Austria, 1903-1907. Made turned-wood dolls with brightly painted clothing. The dolls were jointed with concealed strings.

ZAST, P. R.—Poland, 1920s. Made lovely celluloid dolls, some of which had glass eyes and human hair wigs, and were beautifully costumed.

ZEHNER, BERNHARD—Germany, 1898-1930. Manufactured dolls and toys of papier-mâché. Also advertised dressed dolls, mama dolls, mechanical dolls, and those with roller skates.

ZEHNER, EDMUND CARL—Germany, 1925-1926. Listed in the corporate records as a factory for dressed dolls, toys, and dummies.

ZEUCH & LAUSMANN—Germany, 1888-1925. There is no evidence that dolls were manufactured before 1894. Advertised jointed dolls, Täuflinge, musical dolls, as well as doll heads of bisque, wood, or molded wax.

ZIEROW, PAUL RICHARD—Germany, 1882-1932, and possibly later. Produced wax dolls. Also advertised dolls with celluloid joints. It should be noted that Paul Zierow invented a composition pouring method that he shared with his friends Wagner & Zetsche; they, in turn, used it to produce their "Haralit" dolls.

ZINNER, ADOLF—Germany, 1898-1929. Advertised jointed, movable dolls. It is assumed, from the patents applied for, that the dolls operated by means of a clockwork mechanism.

ZINNER, GOTTLIEB & SÖHNE—Germany, 1845-1926. Manufactured bisque, papier-mâché, wood, and wax-over composition-head dolls, along with a wide and varied inventory of other toys, including musical and mechanical dolls. Although it is widely accepted that France was the authority in automated dolls, Zinner & Söhne was, at that time, the world leader.

ZITZMANN, EMIL—Germany, 1911-1930, and possibly later. Manufactured leather and imitation leather-bodied dolls. Also advertised a walking doll that turns her head when her legs are moved.

ZÖLLNER, GEORG—Germany, 1927-1930. Advertised dressed and undressed dolls, also cloth dolls, doll parts, molds, and matryoshkas.

ZOO SOFT TOY CO.—England, 1928. Made cloth dolls of plush.

ZWANGER, HEINRICH—Germany, 1928-1930s. Manufactured cloth art dolls, some with composition heads and provincial costumes.

Above: Armand Marseille's Character Indian (Photo courtesy of Helen Brooke.)

Above left: Rare Simon & Halbig #989 Closed-Mouth Child (Photo courtesy of Helen Brooke.)

Left: Beautiful Tete Jumeau Preserved in Her Original Box (Photo courtesy of Mr. & Mrs. Adam Condo.)

CHAPTER TWO

TRADEMARKS AND NAMES

In the following pages you will find over three thousand names given to dolls—and the companies with which those names have been associated.

A rather broad allowance has been taken in preparing this listing. In over two hundred years of doll manufacturing many extenuating circumstances have arisen. Several countries have contributed to the production of dolls, but faulty translation and interpretation of records can compromise the accuracy of those records. It should be noted, too, that records were not always kept during economic depression, and that during times of war or natural disaster, documents were often destroyed. That records my be incomplete should not be surprising, but that we have any records at all is astonishing.

Dr. Oscar Arendt gave the following explanation in the March 1926 issue of *The Toy Trader* (according to the *Coleman Encyclopedia*, Volume II): "Trademarks are registered in the name of the applicant by the 'Reichs-patentamt' for the unlimited time, first however, for a period of 10 years, after due examination." The *American College Heritage Dictionary* defines "trade name" as: "A distinctive sign or name by which a person or thing comes to be known." In *Doll Makers & Marks* the definition is: "The accepted name assigned to a doll even if its validity cannot be verified." This does not mean that a flippant attitude has been taken with this task, but that often a legal and binding record has not been found.

Many names accepted and adopted by various companies, stores, businesses, and even individuals are characterized as being in the public domain. For example, several companies market a Red Riding Hood doll, which is perfectly legal inasmuch as the name Red Riding Hood is so common it belongs to the public. This is not to say that all names are so easily assigned. Many companies have gone to court to protect their copyright names.

A 1 Dolls . . . . Amberg, Dean
A Breezy Girl and Arch to
  Worship Me Through March . . . . Nancy Ann StoryBook Dolls
A Dillar A Dollar, a Ten o'clock Scholar . . . . Nancy Ann StoryBook Dolls
A Diller A Dollar . . . . Grace Drayton
A February Fairy Girl for Ice and Snow . . . . Nancy Ann StoryBook Dolls
A Flowergirl for May . . . . Nancy Ann StoryBook Dolls
A Girl for August When It's Warm . . . . Nancy Ann StoryBook Dolls
A January Merry Maid for New Year . . . . Nancy Ann StoryBook Dolls
A l'Ancre . . . . A. Hugonnard
A la Clinique des Poupées . . . . Fernand Paullin Olivier
A la Tentatin . . . . Maison Guyot (Pintel & Godchaux)
A mon Mignon . . . . Fleischmann & Bloedel
A November Lass to Cheer . . . . Nancy Ann StoryBook Dolls
A Rosebud Girl to Love Me
  Through the June Days . . . . Nancy Ann StoryBook Dolls
A Shower Girl for April . . . . Nancy Ann StoryBook Dolls
A Sweet October Maiden Rather Shy . . . . Nancy Ann StoryBook Dolls
A Very Independent Lady for July . . . . Nancy Ann StoryBook Dolls
Abby Walker . . . . Pleasant Co.
ABC Doll . . . . Butler Brothers
Abe Kabibble . . . . Bleier Brothers
Abigail Adams . . . . Alexander Doll Co., Peggy Nesbit
Ace from Kiss . . . . Mego
ACEEDEECEE . . . . American Character
Acrobats (Lady and Gent) . . . . Schoenhut
Action Big Jack . . . . Mattel, Inc.
Action Jackson . . . . Mego
Ada May . . . . Jane Gray's Celebrity Doll (originated by Margaret Vale)
Adalene . . . . Ernst Liebermann, Montgomery Ward
Adlon . . . . O. Schamberger
Admiral Dewey . . . . Cuno & Otto Dressel
Admiral Dot . . . . Ideal
Admiral George Dewey . . . . Cuno & Otto Dressel
Admiral Jellicoe . . . . Hamley Brothers
Admiral William Thomas Sampson . . . . Cuno & Otto Dressel
Admiral Winfield Scott Schley . . . . Cuno & Otto Dressel
Admiration . . . . Progressive Toy Co.
Adora-Belle . . . . Reisman, Barron & Co.
Adorable . . . . Eegee Doll Manufacturing Co., Sayco Doll Corp.
Adorable Cindy . . . . Uneeda Doll Co.
Adrienne . . . . Mattel, Inc. for Annette Himstedt
Aerolite . . . . Chad Valley
African . . . . Alexander Doll Co.
Afternoon Tea . . . . Alexander Doll Co.
Agatha . . . . Alexander Doll Co.
Age of Aquarius . . . . Alexander Doll Co.
Agnes . . . . Alexander Doll Co., Butler Brothers, Käthe Kruse
Ah Sid . . . . Saalfield
Aha Puppe . . . . Andreas Hofmann
Ahabe . . . . Amberg & Hergershausen
AI AI . . . . Arno Lützelberger
Aicha . . . . Fernand Nathan
Aimee . . . . Hasbro, Inc.
Aimée . . . . Amy M. Eshleman
Airman . . . . Dean
Aja . . . . Hasbro, Inc.

Akro . . . . Steiff
Al (Alfons/Alphons) . . . . Steiff
Alabama Indestructible Doll . . . . Ella Smith Doll Co.
Alah . . . . Anni Lonz
Alan Verdono . . . . Mego
Alb . . . . Steiff
Albania . . . . Alexander Doll Co.
Albego . . . . Alt, Beck & Gottschalck
Albert . . . . Steiff
Albrita Dolls . . . . Metropolitan Toy & Doll Co.
Alexander Rag Time . . . . Alexander Doll Co.
Alexander-kins . . . . Alexander Doll Co.
Alfalfa . . . . Mego
Alfred . . . . Steiff
Algeria . . . . Alexander Doll Co.
Alice . . . . Alexander Doll Co., Effanbee, F. Kaempff,
Porzellanfabrik Rauenstein
Alice and Her Book . . . . A & H
Alice in Her Party Kit . . . . Alexander Doll Co.
Alice In Wonderland . . . . Alexander Doll Co., Martha Chase, Duchess Doll Corp.,
Horsman & Co., Peggy Nesbit
Alice Lee . . . . Effanbee
Alice Thru the Looking Glass . . . . Nancy Ann StoryBook Dolls
Alice, Sweet Alice . . . . Nancy Ann StoryBook Dolls
Alida . . . . Steiff
Alix . . . . Käthe Kruse
Alkali Ike . . . . Amberg
Alkico . . . . A. Kiesewetter
All Nation Comical . . . . Cuno & Otto Dressel
Allan . . . . Mattel, Inc.
Allen . . . . Mattel, Inc.
Allison . . . . Alexander Doll Co.
Alma . . . . Armand Marseille, Käthe Kruse
Almut . . . . Käthe Kruse
Alpha . . . . Farnell
Alphabet Man . . . . Twinzy Toy Co.
Alphons (Alfons) . . . . Steiff
Alpine . . . . Confetti Dolls
Aluminia . . . . Strobel & Wilken
Alyssa . . . . Effanbee
Amanda . . . . Alexander Doll Co.
Amanda, by Yolanda Bello . . . . Ashton Drake
Ambisc . . . . Amberg
Ameli . . . . Kämmer & Reinhardt
American Pet . . . . Schillings
American Babies . . . . Alexander Doll Co.
American Beauty . . . . American Bisque Doll Co., American Character, American
Ocarina & Toy Corp., Empire Art Co., Robert Carl,
Seamless Toy Co., Strobel & Wilken
American Character . . . . Alexander Doll Co.
American Countess . . . . Butler Brothers
American Doll . . . . Alisto Manufacturing
American Fashion . . . . Strobel & Wilken
American Girl . . . . Alexander Doll Co., Butler Brothers, B. Illfelder & Co., Saalfield
American Heartland Dolls . . . . Mattel, Inc. for Annette Himstedt
American Indian . . . . Alexander Doll Co.
American Kids in Toyland . . . . Horsman & Co.

DOLL NAME	COMPANY NAME
American Lady	Montgomery Ward
American Maid	Horsman & Co., Montgomery Ward; Sears, Roebuck & Co.
American Maid Dolls	Brückner,
American Pet	Schilling
American Queen	Otto Morgenroth
American Rose Bud	Sophia E. Delavan
American Tots	Alexander Doll Co.
American Trooper	Peggy Nesbit
American Women's Volunteer Service	Alexander Doll Co.
American Wonder Baby	American Character Doll Co.
Amfelt	Amberg
Amfelt Art Dolls	Amberg
Amico Dolls	Ammidon & Co.
Amish Boy	Alexander Doll Co., Effanbee
Amish Father	Effanbee
Amish Girl	Alexander Doll Co., Effanbee
Amish Mother	Effanbee
Amkid	Amberg
Amor	Lenci
Amos N' Andy (Amos N' Andy Check N' Double Check)	Unsuccessfully attempted by the Amos N' Andy Doll Co., Averill Manufacturing Co., S & H Novelty Co.
Amosandra	Sun Rubber Co.
Amour Bébé	Louis Guillet
Amazon	Lauer
Amuso	August Möller & Son
Amy	Alexander Doll Co., Elektra Toy & Novelty Co.
Anabelle	Mattel, Inc.
Anabelle Autodiddle	Mattel, Inc.
Anastasia	Alexander Doll Co.
Andrew	Mme. Paderewski/Mme. Lazarski
Andy	Eegee Doll Manufacturing Co.
Andy Gump	Marshall Field
Angel	Alexander Doll Co., Jeanette Doll Co., Vogue Dolls
Angel Appleseed	Dewees Cochran
Angel Baby	Arranbee Doll Co., Vogue Dolls
Angel Bride	Arranbee Doll Co.
Angel Face	Arranbee Doll Co.
Angela	Handwerck
Angela Appleseed	Dewees Cochran
Angela Cartwright Doll	Natural Doll Co.
Angelica Van Buren	Alexander Doll Co.
Angie	Deluxe Reading/Topper Toy Group
Angie Dickenson, Police Woman	Horsman & Co.
Angeline	Arranbee
Anielka	Mme. Paderewski/Mme. Lazarski
Anili	Lenci, Anili Dolls
Ann Boleyn	*Ladies Home Journal* (Sew at Home Craft Doll)
Ann of Green Gables	Alexander Doll Co., Peggy Nisbet Dolls
Anna	Lenci, Schwarzkopf & Frober
Anna Ballerina	Alexander Doll Co.
Annabelle	Alexander Doll Co., Farnell, Royal Toy Manufacturing Co.
Annchen	Käthe Kruse; Mattel, Inc. for Annette Himstedt
Anne Hathaway	Peggy Nesbit
Anne of Green Gables	Alexander Doll Co., Effanbee
Anne Shirley	Effanbee
Anneliese	Rheinische Gummi und Celluloid Fabrik, Käthe Kruse

Annemirl	Käthe Kruse
Annette	Eegee Doll Manufacturing Co., Horsman & Co.
Annie	Knickerbocker
Annie at the Garden Party	Nancy Ann StoryBook Dolls
Annie Laurie	Alexander Doll Co., Butler Brothers
Annie Oakley	American Character
Annie Rooney	Borgfeldt
Anniversary Baby	Amberg
Anotolia	Alexander Doll Co.
Answer Doll	Block Doll Co., Horsman & Co.
Antebellum Southern Belle Anniversary	Uneeda Doll Co.
Anthony (Anton)	Steiff
Anthony Eden	Alexander Doll Co.
Antoinette	Alexander Doll Co.
Antoinette Lady in Waiting	Nancy Ann StoryBook Dolls
Apache	Louis Eisen
Apple Annie	Alexander Doll Co.
Apriko	Steiff
April	Alexander Doll Co.
April Showers	Arranbee Doll Co., Ideal
Aquaman	Mego
Arab Sheik	Harwin
Arabesque	Strobel & Wilken
Arcadian Babs	Sutherland Doll Co.
Archie Bunker's Joey Stivic	Ideal
Archie Pagliacci	Twistum Toy Factory
Arctic Baby	Ideal
Arcturian	Mego
Argentine	Louis Eisen
Argentine Boy	Alexander Doll Co.
Argentine Girl	Alexander Doll Co.
ARI	A. Riedeler
Arlene Dahl	Alexander Doll Co.
Arlette	Bon Marché, Mme. Elisa Rassant
Armed Forces Doll	Alexander Doll Co.
Armenia	Alexander Doll Co.
Armring	Steiff
Army Nurse	Horsman & Co.
Arnola	Max Oscar Arnold
Arnoldia	Max Oscar Arnold, Sigmund Sprechpuppen
Arrenberg	Arrenberg, Else
Art Character Dolls	Ideal (McDonald Brothers)
Art Doll	Horsman & Co.
Art Felt Dolls	Amberg
Art of the Mariko Collection	Mattel, Inc.
Art Quality	Joseph Kallus, D.B.A., Cameo Doll Co.
Artie	Alexander Doll Co.
Artil	Steiff
As You Like	Buschow & Beck
Asador	Bauer & Richter Inc.
Ashley	Alexander Doll Co.
Asta	Arthur Schoenau
Astor	Alexander Doll Co.
Astrological Dolls	Alexander Doll Co.
Astronaut	Mego
Athlete	Horsman & Co., Sears
August	Steiff

Doll Name	Company Name
Augusta	Ernst Reinhardt
Augustus	Farnell
Aunt Agatha	Alexander Doll Co.
Aunt Betsy	Alexander Doll Co.
Aunt Carolie	Severn & Long (Rag Shoppe Dolls)
Aunt Dinah	Effanbee, Nugenta, Saalfield (Tiny Travelers)
Aunt Jemima	American Specialty Doll Co., American Stuffed Novelty Co., Aunt Jemima Mills, Butler Brothers, Davis Milling Co., Louis Wolf, The Toy Shop
Aunt Jenny Doll	Jeanette Doll Co.
Aunt Kate	Allied Grand Doll Manufacturing
Aunt Pitty Pat	Alexander Doll Co.
Aunt Sally	Butler Brothers
Auntie Blossom	Marshall Field, Shackman
Auntie Jo's Own Rag Babies	Miss Josephine L. Malone
Aurora	Friedrich Richter
Austrian	Alexander Doll Co.
Auto Puppen	Otto Fans, Heho Art Dolls, Bernhard Hermann, Mme. Lazarski, Lenci, Carl Möckel, Karl Völker
Autoliebchen (Auto Sweetheart)	Schoenau & Hoffmeister
Automobile Dolls	Horsman & Co., Moritz Pappe, W. Payne, Shackman
Automobile Girl	Horsman & Co.
Autumno (l'Automne)	Lenci
Aviator	Twinzy Toy Co.
Aviator Skippy	Effanbee
Aviators (Aviatrixes)	(not a registered trade name) The following companies sold aviator-dressed dolls: KarlStadinger, Dean, Roberts Brothers, Julius Petri, J. Block, W. Payne & Son, American Character Doll Co., Bleuette, Kämmer & Reinhardt, S & H Novelty, Louis Eisen, Regal, Squier Twins Toy Co., Butler Brothers, Woodward & Lothrop, and Ungariscke Gummi.
Aviatrix	Louis Eisen
Baba	Mme. Poulbot
Babbie	Alexander Doll Co.
Babbit Boy	Butler Brothers
Babbitt	B. T. Babbitt
Babble Bath Baby	Sayco Doll Corp.
Bäbchen	Käthe Kruse
Babe Ruth	Effanbee
Babee	Fair Amusement Co.
Babee Bee	Sun Rubber Co.
Babes in The Woods	Sol Bergfeld & Son
Babes in Toyland	Uneeda Doll Co.
Babes On Broadway	Ideal
Babet	Mlle. Cécile Lambert
Babette	Alexander Doll Co., Century Doll Co.
Babie Bouquet	Quaker Doll Co., K & K
Babies First Doll	Blumberg
Babies Grumpy	Effanbee
Babies in The Wood	East London Toy Factory
Babs	Alexander Doll Co.; Averill Manufacturing Co.; Babs Manufacturing (International Walking Doll Co.); Chad Valley; Fab-Lu Limited; Horsman & Co.; Mattel, Inc.; Trion
Babs Baby	Trion
Babs Skater	Alexander Doll Co.
Babs Walking Doll	Babs Manufacturing (International Walking Doll Co.)

Doll Name	Company Name
Babsie Baby	Alexander Doll Co.
Babsie Skater	Alexander Doll Co.
Babu	Käthe Kruse
Baby	Art Fabric Mills, Collingbourne Mills, Horsman & Co., Hermann Kröning, Kämmer & Reinhardt, Lorrie, Rheinische Gummi und Celluloik Fabrik Co., Steiff, Sun Rubber Co. (AKA Do)
Baby Adele	Cameo
Baby Aire	Averill Manufacturing Co.
Baby Angel	Alexander Doll Co.
Baby Ann	Shanklin
Baby Barry	Baby Berry Toys
Baby Bauernkind	Horsman & Co.
Baby Bauz	Kämmer & Reinhardt
Baby Beans	Mattel, Inc.
Baby Beautiful	Amberg, Horsman & Co., Ideal
Baby Beauty	Horsman & Co.
Baby Bell	Bawo & Dotter
Baby Belle	C. M Bergmann
Baby Belly Button	Ideal
Baby Betty	Alexander Doll Co., Armand Marseille, Chicago Mail Order House for Joseph Goldstein
Baby Bibs	Live Long Toys
Baby Biddle	Mattel, Inc.
Baby Big Eyes	Ideal
Baby Blanche	Effanbee
Baby Blossom	Horsman & Co., Cameo (Borgfeldt)
Baby Blue Eyes	Saalfield, Averill Manufacturing Co.
Baby Bo Kaye	Joseph L. Kallus (Borgfeldt)
Baby Bobby	European Doll Manufacturing Co., Horsman & Co.
Baby Boo	Deluxe Reading/Topper Toy Group
Baby Booful	Averill Manufacturing Co.
Baby Boy	Amberg, Saalfield
Baby Bright	Averill Manufacturing Co., Eaton
Baby Bright Eyes	Amberg, Effanbee
Baby Brite	Averill Manufacturing Co., Deluxe Reading/Topper Toy Group
Baby Brother	Alexander Doll Co.
Baby Bud	Butler Brothers, Effanbee
Baby Bumpkins	Uneeda Doll Co.
Baby Bumps	Horsman & Co.
Baby Bundie (Bundy)	Joseph L. Kallus
Baby Bundie Doll	Mutual Doll Co.
Baby Bunny	Deluxe Reading/Topper Toy Group
Baby Bunting	Butler Bros., Century, Louis Lindner & Söhne, Meakin & Ridgeway, Needlecraft (premium), Rees Davis
Baby Buster	Horsman & Co.
Baby Butter Ball	Horsman & Co.
Baby Butterball	Effanbee
Baby Buttercup	Butler Brothers, Horsman & Co.
Baby Butterfly	Horsman
Baby Button Nose	Effanbee
Baby Bye Bye	Mattel, Inc.
Baby Catch a Ball	Deluxe Reading/Topper Toy Group
Baby Catherine	Effanbee for Butler Brothers and Sears
Baby Charming	Hitz, Jacobs & Kassler
Baby Chatter	Mattel, Inc.
Baby Cheryl	Mattel, Inc.

DOLL NAME	COMPANY NAME
Baby Clown	Alexander Doll Co.
Baby Colleen	Mattel, Inc.
Baby Coos	Ideal
Baby Crawlalong	Remco
Baby Crissy	Ideal
Baby Cuddles	Effanbee
Baby Cut	Heinrich Handwerck
Baby Dahna	Hoest & Henderson for Baker & Bennett and A. S. Ferguson
Baby Dainty	Effanbee
Baby Dancerina	Mattel, Inc.
Baby Darling	Averill Manufacturing Co., Bing Corp., Horsman & Co., Morimura Brothers
Baby Darling	Horsman & Co., Minerva Doll
Baby Dear	Vogue
Baby Debbi	Super Doll Inc.
Baby Dimples	American Character, Horsman & Co. for J. C. Penney
Baby Dimples	Horsman & Co.
Baby Dingle	Averill Manufacturing Co.
Baby Doll	American Character, Chad Valley, Horsman & Co.
Baby Doll Precision	Alexander Doll Co.
Baby Doll Tinker	Tinker Toys
Baby Dollikins	Uneeda Doll Co.
Baby Doo	Arrow Plastics
Baby Dorothy	C. M. Bergmann
Baby Dressed in Gaucho Clothes	Argentina
Baby Edith	Strawbridge & Clothier
Baby Ella	Eaton, Morimura Brothers
Baby Ellen	Alexander Doll Co.
Baby Face	Effanbee
Baby First Step	Mattel, Inc.
Baby First Tooth	Horsman & Co.
Baby Fleur	Montgomery Ward
Baby Florence	Armand Marseille
Baby Fussy	Deluxe Reading/Topper Toy Group
Baby Genius	Alexander Doll Co.
Baby Georgene	Averill Manufacturing Co.
Baby Giggles	Domec, Ideal
Baby Girl	Ideal, Saalfield
Baby Glee	Louis Amberg & Son
Baby Gloria	Armand Marseille; Made in America Doll Co.; Maxine; Roth, Baitz & Lipstiz; Quaker Doll Co.
Baby Go Bye Bye	Mattel, Inc.
Baby Go Walk	Mattel, Inc.
Baby Greenaway	Petit St. Thomas
Baby Grow a Tooth	Remco
Baby Grow Up	Horsman & Co.
Baby Grumpy	Effanbee
Baby Gurgles	Ideal
Baby Hanie	Shindana
Baby Heart Beat	Effanbee Doll Co.
Baby Helen	Strawbridge & Clothier
Baby Hendren	Averill Manufacturing Co.
Baby Horsman	Horsman & Co.
Baby Huggins	Effanbee
Baby Jane	Alexander Doll Co.
Baby Jeanette	Jeanette Doll Co.
Baby Jeans	Ideal

Baby Jo Anne	Ideal
Baby Joan	Ernst Liebermann, Reliable Toy
Baby Joy	Royal Toy Manufacturing Co.
Baby June	Carl Kalbitz, Ideal
Baby K	American Character
Baby Land Rag (Babyland) Doll	Horsman & Co.
Baby Laugh A Lot	Remco
Baby Linda	Terri Lee
Baby Lindner	Louis Lindner
Baby Love	Adler Stella (Adler Favor and Novelty)
Baby Love Light	Mattel, Inc.
Baby Lovey Dovey	Alexander Doll Co.
Baby Lu	American Character, Ideal
Baby Lynn	Alexander Doll Co.
Baby Mae	Ideal
Baby Magic	Deluxe Reading/Topper Toy Group
Baby Marcia	Averill Manufacturing Co.
Baby Marguerite	Strawbridge & Clothier
Baby Marie	American Character
Baby Marlborough	R. H. Macy
Baby McGuffey	Alexander Doll Co.
Baby Mine	Cameo, C. R. Lauer, Ideal, Montgomery Ward
Baby Nod	Amberg
Baby Olie Ke Wod	Elsie Shaver and later obtained by Alexander Doll Co.
Baby Party	Deluxe Reading/Topper Toy Group
Baby Pat A Burp	Mattel, Inc.
Baby Pataburp	Mattel, Inc.
Baby Patsy	Bing
Baby Pattaburp	Mattel, Inc.
Baby Patty Cake	Horsman & Co.
Baby Peek N Play	Deluxe Reading/Topper Toy Group
Baby Peggy	Amberg, Dean
Baby Peke Wu	Farnell
Baby Peterkin	Horsman & Co.
Baby Petite	American Character, Jesse M. Raleigh
Baby Phyllis	Armand Marseille, Baby Phyllis Doll Co.
Baby Pierrot	Gamage
Baby Play A Lot	Mattel, Inc.
Baby Precious	Alexander Doll Co., Horsman & Co.
Baby Pretty Pout	Mattel, Inc.
Baby Princess	P & M Sales
Baby Puck	Dean
Baby Rose	German, possibly F. Welsch
Baby Rosebud	Horsman & Co.
Baby Royal	Mabel Bland-Hawkes
Baby Ruth	Effanbee; Crämer & Héron; Curtiss Candy Co.; Hasbro, Inc.; Ideal; Armand Marseille
Baby Sad and Glad	Remco
Baby Sandy	Ralph A. Freundlich, Inc.
Baby Say 'n See	Mattel, Inc.
Baby Secret	Mattel, Inc.
Baby Shirley	Century Doll Co.
Baby Sing A Song	Mattel, Inc.
Baby Sister	K & K, Jessie M. Raleigh
Baby Sleep Amber	Uneeda Doll Co.
Baby Smiles	Borgfeldt, Ideal
Baby Sniffles	Eegee Doll Manufacturing Co.

Doll Name	Company Name
Baby Snooks	Ideal
Baby Snoozie	Ideal
Baby Snowball	Effanbee
Baby Softina	Eegee Doll Manufacturing Co.
Baby Sox	Ideal
Baby Step	Mattel, Inc.
Baby Stroll A Long	Remco
Baby Stuart	Jessie M. Raleigh
Baby Suck-A-Thumb	Carl Heumann
Baby Sue	American Character
Baby Sunshine	Sears, Roebuck & Co.
Baby Surprise	American Composition
Baby Surprize	American Composition
Baby Susan	Eegee Doll Manufacturing Co.
Baby Sweetie Pie	Effanbee Doll Co.
Baby Sweetums	Uneeda Doll Co.
Baby Talks	Uneeda Doll Co.
Baby Tears	American Character
Baby Teenie Talk	Mattel, Inc.
Baby Tenderlove	Mattel, Inc.
Baby Tickle Tears	Deluxe Reading/Topper Toy Group
Baby Tinyette as a Dutch Boy	Effanbee
Baby Toddler	American Bisque Dolls
Baby Toodles	Marshall Field
Baby Trix	Uneeda Doll Co.
Baby Tufums	Amberg
Baby Tunes	Louis Wolf
Baby Tweaks	Horsman & Co.
Baby Twinkie	Effanbee
Baby Violet	Abraham & Straus
Baby Virginia	Averill Manufacturing Co.
Baby Walk N Play	Mattel, Inc.
Baby Walker	Block Doll Corp./Deluxe Reading/Topper Toy Group
Baby Walks	Mattel, Inc.
Baby Weepsy Wee Walker	Uneeda Doll Co.
Baby Wendy	Cameo
Baby Wise	Horsman & Co.
Baby Wobbles	Paramount
Baby Wonder Doll	Amberg
Baby's Hungry	Mattel, Inc.
Baby's Joy	American Character
Baby's Pal	American Character
Baby's Playmate	American Character
Babyette	Effanbee
Babykin	Effanbee
Babykins	Borgfeldt, Effanbee
Babyland Beauty	Horsman & Co.
Babyland Doll (Baby Land Rag)	Horsman & Co.
Backfischpuppen	Cuno & Otto Dressel
Bad Little Girl	Alexander Doll Co.
Baigneur habille	Wilhelm Simon & Co.
Ballerina	Alexander Doll Co., Valentine Doll Co.
Ballerina Belle	Belle Doll Corp.
Balletina	Uneeda Doll Co.
Bam Bam	Ideal
Bambetta	Chad Valley
Bambina	Chad Valley, Cuno & Otto Dressel

Doll Name	Company Name
Bambino	Société Française de Fabrication de Bébés & Jouets, Shanklin
Bamboula	Société Française de Fabrication de Bébés & Jouets
Banker's Daughter	Butler Brothers
Banner Kid Dolls	Butler Brothers
Bannister Baby	Sun Rubber Co.
Barbara	Century Doll Co.
Barbara Ann Scott	Reliable Toy
Barbara Jane	Alexander Doll Co.
Barbara-Lee	Effanbee
Barbarino	Mattel, Inc.
Barbary Coast	Alexander Doll Co.
Barbel	Käthe Kruse
Bärbel-Puppe	Bärbel Wichmann
Barbele	Wagner & Zetzche
Barbie	Mattel, Inc.
Barclay Baby Belle	Bawo & Dotter
Bare Bottom Baby	Uneeda Doll Co.
Bare Kid	The Dolly Co.
Barefoot Boy	Ideal
Barefoot Children	Mattel, Inc. for Annette Himstedt
Barney Google	Schoenhut
Baseb (Baseball Player)	Steiff
Baseball Boy	Amberg
Bashful	Knickerbocker
Bashful Boy	Irwin
Bashful Girl	Irwin
Bat Girl	Mego
Bathrobe Baby	Ideal
Bathtub Baby	Uneeda Doll Co.
Bathtub Doll	Alder Favor and Novelty
Batman	Mego
Bauz	Käthe Kruse
Bayaniman	Alexander Doll Co.
Beach Baby	Effanbee
Beach Boy	Amberg
Beach Girl	Amberg
Beach Knut	Chad Valley
Beanie the Clown	William P Beers
Beany	Mattel, Inc.
Beat A Diddle	Mattel, Inc.
Beate	Käthe Kruse
Beatles	Seltael, Inc. NEMS
Beatrice	Butler Brothers
Beatrix	Ideal
Beatrix Potter Collection	Peggy Nesbit
Beau	Uneeda Doll Co.
Beau Brummel	Alexander Doll Co.
Beautee Skin Babies	Effanbee
Beauty	Armand Marseille, Horsman & Co.
Beauty Baby	Bing
Beauty from Beauty and the Beast	Nancy Ann StoryBook Dolls
Beauty Queen	Alexander Doll Co.
Beaver	Aerolite by Chad Valley
Bébé a la Mode	La Place Clichy
Bébé Arc en Ciel	L'Hotel de Ville
Bébé Articule	Emil Pfeiffer
Bébé Articulé	Friedrich Winkler

Bébé B H V	L'Hotel de Ville
Bébé Baptême	Aux Trois Quartiers
Bébé Blanche	Simon & Halbig
Bébé Breveté	Bru
Bébé Bru	Bru
Bébé Camerose	Kämmer & Reinhardt
Bébé Caprice	Petit Saint Thomas
Bébé Carmencita	Arthur Schoenau
Bébé Charmant	Presles Fréres, S. F. B. J.
Bébé Chiffon	Aux Trois Quartiers
Bebe Coiffeure	Gutmann & Schniffnie
Bébé Colosse	A. Benoit Gobert by S. F. B. J.
Bébé Cosmopolite	Heinrich Handwerck
Bébé Criant	Printemps
Bébé Culotte	Aux Trois Quartiers
Bébé de Paris	Rabery & Delphieu
Bébé de Réclame	Heinrich Handwerck
Bébé Diamant	Karl Dehler
Bébé Directoire	Petit St. Thomas
Bébé Dormeur	Bouchet
Bébé Drapeau	L'Hotel de Ville
Bébé Elite	Max Handwerck
Bébé Francais	Danel & Cie
Bébé Fruits	L' Hotel de Ville
Bébé Géant	Bouchet, S. F. B. J.
Bébé Gesland	Gesland
Bébé Gigoteur	Jules Steiner
Bébé Gourmand	Lafayette
Bébé Habillé	La Ville de Paris
Bébé Jumeau	Jumeau
Bebe Kochniss	Carl Kochniss
Bébé l'Avenir	Gebrüder Süssenguth, Gutmann & Schniffnie
Bébé la Georgienne	Lanternier
Bébé la Parisienne	La Place Clichy
Bébé Lafayette	Lafayette Store
Bébé le Vrai Modéle	R. Ch. Rivaillon
Bébé Lefebvre	Alexandre Lefebvre
Bébé Leger	Widow Chalory
Bébé ler Age	Lafayette
Bébé Loulou	Wannez et Rayer
Bébé Madeleine	Aux Trois Quartiers
Bébé Magenta	Magenta Stores
Bébé Maillot	Aux Trois Quartiers
Bébé Maison Dorée	Maison Dorée Store
Bébé Marcheurs	Mme. Lazarski
Bébé Mascotte	May Fréres Cie
Bébé Ménagére	Nouvelle Galeries a la Ménagére
Bébé Merveille	S. F. B. J.
Bébé Merveilleux	Aux Trois Quartiers, Ulhenhuth
Bébé Mignon	Aux Trois Quartiers, Félix Arena
Bébé Miracle	Louvre
Bébé Modéle	Mme. Caroline Rivaillon
Bébé Moncey	La Place Clichy
Bébé Mothereau	Alexandre Célestin Triburee Mothereau
Bébé Moujik	Jacques Berner
Bébé Neva	Aux Trois Quartiers
Bébé Ninon	Bonin & Befort

Bébé Nurse . . . . Louvre
Bébé Olga . . . . Ernst Ballu, Gerbaulet Fréres
Bébé Oracle . . . . Madame E. Cayette
Bébé Palais Nouveauté . . . . Dufayel
Bébé Parisette . . . . Aux Trois Quartiers
Bébé Parisien . . . . Decoster
Bébé Pauvre Jacques . . . . Pauvre Jacques Stores
Bébé Phenix . . . . Henri Alexandre, Pauvre Jacques Stores, Jules Steiner
Bébé Pole Sud . . . . Printemps
Bébé Premier . . . . Horsman & Co.
Bébé Premier Age . . . . Samaritaine Store
Bébé Premier Elan . . . . Paul Girard of Bru
Bebe Princess . . . . Gebrüder Ohlhaver
Bébé Printemp . . . . Printemps
Bébé Prodige . . . . Jumeau, S. F. B. J.
Bébé Promenette . . . . Aux Trois Quartiers
Bébé Prophéte . . . . Madame E. Cayette
Bébé Radieux . . . . Bon Marché
Bébé Ravissant . . . . Pauvre Jacques
Bebe Reclame . . . . Heinrich Handwerck
Bébé Réclame . . . . Société Industrielle de Jouets Francais
Bébé Réclames . . . . Société Nouvelle des Bébé Réclames
Bébé Regence . . . . Magenta Stores
Bébé Réservé . . . . LíHotel de Ville
Bébé Rieur . . . . Bon Marché
Bébé Rivoli . . . . LíHotel de Ville
Bébé Samaritaine . . . . Juneau
Bébé Select . . . . Bonin & Lefort
Bébé Soleil . . . . S. F. B. J.
Bébé Steiner . . . . Jules Steiner
Bébé Success . . . . Petit St. Thomas
Bebe Superior . . . . Heinrich Handwerck
Bébé Systême . . . . Roullet & Decamps
Bébé Teteur . . . . Au Nain Bleu
Bébé Téteur . . . . Bru, S. F. B. J.
Bébé tout en bois . . . . Rudolf Schneider (*Bébé tout en bois* was a term used by several manufacturers, both known and unknown.)
Bébé Triomphe . . . . Fleischmann & Bloedel
Bébé Trois Quartiers . . . . Aux Trois Quartiers
Bébé Unique . . . . Ménagére
Bébé Ville de St. Denis . . . . Ville de St. Denis
Bébé Vrai Modéle . . . . S. F. B. J.
Becky . . . . Mattel, Inc.
Beefeater . . . . Peggy Nesbit
Beha . . . . Berthold Helk
Belgium . . . . Alexander Doll Co.
Belinda . . . . P & M Sales
Belinda Bunyan . . . . Dewees Cochran
Bella . . . . Leo Nordschild
Bellamit . . . . Jochachimsczyk
Belle Brummel . . . . Alexander Doll Co.
Belle Lee . . . . Belle Doll Corp.
Belle Of The Ball . . . . Alexander Doll Co.
Belle Telle . . . . Effanbee
Belle Telle and Her Talking Telephone . . . . Effanbee
Belles in Bells . . . . A & H
Bellows Anne . . . . Alexander Doll Co.

Belly Good Cook	Art Fabric Mills
Ben Cartwright	American Character
Benjamin Franklin	Peggy Nesbit
Benjamin Rabbit	Peggy Nesbit
Benjie	Terry Lee
Bepi Puppen	Bergische Puppenindustrie
Bertha	Butler Brothers
Bess Truman	Alexander Doll Co.
Bessy Bell	Alexander Doll Co.
Bessy Brooks	Alexander Doll Co.
Best Man	Alexander Doll Co.
Beth	Alexander Doll Co.
Betsy Ross	American Doll Co.
Betsy	Alexander Doll Co., Borgfeldt
Betsy Baby	Ideal
Betsy McCall	American Character, Eegee Doll Manufacturing Co., Ideal, Uneeda Doll Co.
Betsey Ross	Alexander Doll Co.
Betsy Wetsy	Ideal
Bette	Kestner
Bettina	Effanbee, Käthe Kruse
Betty	Alexander Doll Co., Averill Manufacturing Co., Horsman & Co., Madame Georgene Inc.
Betty Ann	Averill Manufacturing Co., Horsman & Co.
Betty Bag	Alexander Doll Co.
Betty Ballerina	Remco
Betty Big Girl	Ideal
Betty Blue	Alexander Doll Co.
Betty Bonser	Bonser Doll Co.
Betty Bows	Sun Rubber Co.
Betty Jane	Ideal
Betty Jo	Horsman & Co.
Betty Taylor Bliss	Alexander Doll Co.
Betty the Beautiful Bride	Deluxe Reading/Topper Toy Group
Betty The Beauty	American Character
Bi Ba Bo	Julius Jeidel, Weise & Co.
Bi Lo Baby	Horsman & Co.
Biball	Käthe Kruse
Bible Characters	Alexander Doll Co.
Bicentennial George and Martha Washington	Effanbee
Biddy Baby	Kohnstamm & Co.
Big Ears	Deluxe Reading/Topper Toy Group
Big Girl	Vanity Doll Co.
Big Huggums	Alexander Doll Co.
Big Jack	Mattel, Inc.
Bikey	Deluxe Reading/Topper Toy Group
Bill	Alexander Doll Co.
Billie (Billy)	Alexander Doll Co., Madame Georgene Inc.
Billiken	Horsman & Co.
Billy	Alexander Doll Co., Art Fabric Mills
Billy Boy	Averill Manufacturing Co., Horsman & Co.
Billy Joe	Sayco Doll Corp.
Billydoll	Steiff
Binnie	Alexander Doll Co.
Binnie Walker	Alexander Doll Co.
Binny	Alexander Doll Co.
Birthday Dolls	Alexander Doll Co., Averill Manufacturing Co.

Doll Name	Company Name
Birthstone Bells	A & H
Bisculoid	Hertwig & Co.
Biskuit Imitation	Adolf Zeh
Bisquitfacon	Barbara Schilling
Bit of Heaven	Ideal
Bitsey	Alexander Doll Co.
Bitsy	Effanbee
Bitsy and Butch	Effanbee
Bitsy Bathtub Baby	Uneeda Doll Co.
Blabby	Uneeda Doll Co.
Black Bottom Doll	Gerling Toy Co.
Black Boy Sam	Berwick Doll Co.
Black Forest	Alexander Doll Co.
Black Forest Barbel	Schmider Trachten
Black Grumpykins	Effanbee
Black Knight	Mego
Black Rufus	Averill Manufacturing Co.
Blackbeard	Mego
Blessed Event	Ideal
Bleuette Flapper	S. F. B. J.
Blonde Impco	Imperial Crown Toys
Blue Boy	Alexander Doll Co.
Blue Danube	Alexander Doll Co.
Blue Eyes	Century Doll Co.
Blue Fairy	Uneeda Doll Co.
Blue Ribbon Classic	Fortune Doll Co.
Blue Ribbon Dolls	American Character
Bluebird Doll	Horsman & Co.
Bo Peep	Alexander Doll Co.
Bob	Uneeda Doll Co.
Bob Hope	Peggy Nesbit
Boba Fett	Kenner
Bobbi Mae	Wondercraft
Bobby	Amberg, Averill Manufacturing Co., Eegee Doll Manufacturing Co.
Bobby Black	Amberg
Bobby Blake Bridegroom	Ideal
Bobby Bonser	Bonser Doll Co.
Bobby Doll	Alder Favor and Novelty
Bobby Q	Alexander Doll Co.
Bobby Sox	Ideal
Bobo	Käthe Kruse
Body Twist	Horsman & Co.
Bolivia	Alexander Doll Co.
Bomburst	Mattel, Inc.
Bonanza Characters	American Character
Bonnie	Alexander Doll Co.
Bonnie and Johnny	Ideal
Bonnie Baby	Borgfeldt Brothers (Georgene Averill)
Bonnie Blue	Alexander Doll Co.
Bonnie Blue Bell	Hollywood Doll Manufacturing Co.
Bonnie Braids	Ideal
Bonnie Bride	Allied Grand Doll Manufacturing, Deluxe Reading/Topper Toy Group
Bonnie Fashion	Deluxe Reading/Topper Toy Group
Bonnie Lu	Terry Lee
Bonnie Prince Charlie	Peggy Nesbit

Bonny Braids	Ideal
Bonton	Borgfeldt
Boo	Alder Favor and Novelty
Boo Hoo	Effanbee
Boopsie	Ideal
Bootsie	Horsman & Co.
Bottle Baby	Remco
Bottletot	American Character
Bottom	Peggy Nesbit
Boudoir Doll	Effanbee
Bouncy Baby	Mattel, Inc.
Bouquet	Princess Anna Doll Co.
Boy	Horsman & Co.
Boy Bauernkind	Horsman & Co.
Boy Scout	Horsman & Co.
Boy Scouts	Gutmann & Schniffnie
Boy With a Cap	Amberg
Bozo The Clown	Peggy Nesbit
Brad	Mattel, Inc.
Brandi	Ideal
Brazilian	Alexander Doll Co.
Breezy Bridget	Mattel, Inc.
Brenda Brush	Deluxe Reading/Topper Toy Group
Brenda Starr	Alexander Doll Co.
Brian Swim Doll	Brian Swim Dolls
Briar Rose	Alexander Doll Co.
Brickett	Vogue
Bridal Trousseau	Alexander Doll Co.
Bride	American Character, Confetti Dolls, Deluxe Reading/Topper Toy Group, Nancy Ann StoryBook Dolls, Plastic Molded Arts Co.
Bride in Pink	Alexander Doll Co.
Bridesmaid	Alexander Doll Co., Nancy Ann StoryBook Dolls
Bridget	Art Fabric Mills
Bridgette	Käthe Kruse
Brigetta	Alexander Doll Co.
Bright Eyes	Amberg, Effanbee, Cissna
Brigitta	Alexander Doll Co.
Brikette	Vogue
Bri-tee	Averill Manufacturing Co.
British Traditional Range (at least 86)	Peggy Nesbit
Brooke	Alexander Doll Co.
Brother	Amberg
Brother Coos	Ideal
Brother Ritzie	Natural Doll Co.
Brown Bean	Harrison Manufacturing Co.
Brown Skin Dolls	Century Doll Co.
Brownie	Thorne Brothers
Brüderschen	Friedrichsrodaer Puppenfabrik
Bubbles	Effanbee
Bubikopf	Plaut
Buck Rabbit	Alexander Doll Co.
Buckwheat	Mego
Bud, Alyssa's Boy Friend	Effanbee
Buddy Bonser	Bonser Doll Co.
Buddy Boy	Averill Manufacturing Co.
Buddy Lee	H. D. Lee Co.
Buffalo Bill Cody	Mego

Buffie . . . . Mattel, Inc.
Buffy . . . . Mattel, Inc.
Buffy & Mrs. Beasley . . . . Mattel, Inc.
Bufli . . . . Resi Brandl
Bugle Ben . . . . Deluxe Reading/Topper Toy Group
Bullock's Wilshire . . . . Alexander Doll Co.
Bunchy . . . . Averill Manufacturing Co.
Bundie (Baby Bundie) . . . . Joseph L. Kallus
Bundle of Joy . . . . Eegee Doll Manufacturing Co.
Bundle of Love . . . . Uneeda Doll Co.
Bunnie Bunyan . . . . Dewees Cochran
Bunny . . . . Alexander Doll Co.
Bunny Hug . . . . Vogue
Bunson Burnie . . . . Mattel, Inc.
Bunting Baby . . . . Uneeda Doll Co.
Buporit . . . . Bähr & Pröschild
Burma . . . . Alexander Doll Co.
Bussi . . . . Willi Steiner
Buster Boy . . . . Amberg
Buster Brown . . . . Horsman & Co., Ideal
Busy Ken . . . . Mattel, Inc.
Butch . . . . Alexander Doll Co., Effanbee
Butch McGuffey . . . . Alexander Doll Co.
Butler . . . . registered by an unidentified German doll manufacturer
Butterball . . . . American Character
Buttercup . . . . Borgfeldt, Horsman & Co., Modern Toy Co.
Button Nose . . . . Effanbee
Button Nose Dutch Boy . . . . Effanbee
Button Nose Dutch Girl . . . . Effanbee
Butzi . . . . J. Cyreck
By Precious Baby . . . . Effanbee
Bye Bye Baby . . . . Arrow Plastics, Effanbee
Bye Bye Kids . . . . Bach Brothers
Bye Lo . . . . Grace Storey Putman
Bye Lo Baby . . . . Borgfeldt
C3PO . . . . Kenner
Caho . . . . Canzler & Hofmann
Calamity Jiddle Kiddle . . . . Mattel, Inc.
Caleb . . . . Trendon Toys
Cama . . . . Armand Marseille
Camille . . . . Alexander Doll Co.
Camp Fire Girl . . . . Horsman & Co.
Campbell Kid Baby . . . . Horsman & Co.
Campbell Kid Boy . . . . Horsman & Co.
Campbell Kid Girl . . . . Horsman & Co.
Campbell Kid Mascot Boy . . . . Horsman & Co.
Campbell Kid Mascot Girl . . . . Horsman & Co.
Campbell Kids . . . . American Character, Cee & Dee, Josef Süsskind,
　　　　　　　　　　　　　　　　　　　　　　　Horsman & Co., Ideal
Campbell Puppen . . . . Otto Sauerteig
Canadian . . . . Alexander Doll Co.
Canadian Pioneer Miss . . . . Peggy Nesbit
Candy . . . . Arrow Plastics
Candy Ann . . . . Effanbee
Candy Fashion . . . . Deluxe Reading/Topper Toy Group
Candy Kid . . . . Effanbee, Horsman & Co.
Candy Kid Twins . . . . Effanbee

DOLL NAME	COMPANY NAME
Cane Fait Kien	William Webb
Caprice	Emily Bauersachs
Captain	Knickerbocker
Captain Action	Ideal
Captain America	Mego
Captain Cook	Peggy Nesbit
Captain from Captain and Tenille	Mego
Captain Hook	Plastic Molded Arts Co.
Captain Kangaroo	Baby Berry
Captain Kidd	Averill Manufacturing Co.
Captain Kirk	Mego
Captain Laser	Mattel, Inc.
Captain Patch	Mego
Caractacus Potts	Mattel, Inc.
Caresse	Chad Valley
Carina	Chad Valley
Carl	Kämmer & Reinhardt
Carmen	Alexander Doll Co., Duchess Doll Corp., Mattel, Inc., Uneeda Doll Co.
Carmen Miranda Look a Like	Dream World Dolls
Carmencita	Arthur Schoenau
Carnival Baby	Horsman & Co.
Carnival In Rio	Alexander Doll Co.
Carnival In Venice	Alexander Doll Co.
Carol Ann Berry	American Character
Carol Ann Berry	American Character
Carol Channing	Nasco
Carol the Walking Doll	Ideal
Carolee of Covered Wagon Set	Effanbee
Caroline	Alexander Doll Co.
Caroline Harrison	Alexander Doll Co.
Caroline Kennedy Look-alike	American Character
Carren	Alexander Doll Co.
Carrot Top	Alexander Doll Co.
Casadora	Huttinger & Buschor
Casey	Mattel, Inc.
Casper	Mattel, Inc.
Casper The Ghost	Mattel, Inc.
Cassandra of the Classic Beauty	Mattel, Inc.
Cassock	Alexander Doll Co.
Cat Women	Mego
Catherine	Ideal, Kay Sam Corp.
Catherine de Medici	Alexander Doll Co.
Catherine of the Classic Beauty	Mattel, Inc.
Cavalcade of Hits	Alexander Doll Co.
Cebaso	Carl Beck & Alfred Schulze
Cecelia of the Classic Beauty	Mattel, Inc.
Cecille	Martin Eichhorn
Ceetee	Capital Toy Co.
Cefer	C. F. Reinhardt
Cellulite	Kley & Hahn
Cellulobrin	Franz Schmidt
Cellunova	Kley & Hahn
Century Doll	Kestner
Century of Fashions	Alexander Doll Co.
Cereta	American Cereal Co. (advertising doll)
Certa	Adolf Wislizenus

Doll Name	Company Name
Champ	Cameo
Channel Swimmer	England Rosebud Doll Co.
Chantecler Doll	Borgfeldt, Gehren, Henze & Steinhäuser, Leven & Sprenger
Charakterpuppe	Kämmer & Reinhardt
Charity	Alexander Doll Co.
Charlee	Effanbee
Charley McCarthy	Effanbee
Charlie Brown Skediddle	Mattel, Inc.
Charlie Carrot	Borgfeldt
Charlie Chaplin	Amberg, Peggy Nesbit
Charlie McCarthy	Juro Novelty
Charlie McCarthy	Ideal
Charlie's Angels	Mattel, Inc.
Charlotte	Käthe Kruse
Charlotte Doll	Sol Bergfeld & Son
Charmaine Lady in Waiting	Nancy Ann StoryBook Dolls
Charmin' Chatty	Mattel, Inc.
Chatterbox	Alexander Doll Co.; Mattel, Inc.
Chatty Baby	Mattel, Inc.
Chatty Cathy	Mattel, Inc.
Chatty Cheryl	Mattel, Inc.
Chatty Patter	Mattel, Inc.
Chatty Telle	Mattel, Inc.
Cecily Dolls	Edwards & Pamflett
Cheerful Tearful	Mattel, Inc.
Cheerio Doll, The	Jeanne Brumback
Cheerleader	Alexander Doll Co.
Cher	Mego
Cheri	Alexander Doll Co.
Cherie	Alexander Doll Co.
Cherrie	Arranbee Doll Co.
Cherry Twins	Alexander Doll Co.
Cherub	Alexander Doll Co.
Cherub Babies	Alexander Doll Co.
Cheryl Ladd	Mattel, Inc.
Chewbacca	Kenner
Chicago Tribune	Alexander Doll Co.
Chickie	Averill Manufacturing Co.
Childhood Character	Gund
China	Alexander Doll Co.
Chinese	Alexander Doll Co.
Chinese Doll	Dream World Dolls
Ching Ching Chinaman	Berwick Doll Co.
Chinkie	Horsman & Co.
Chipper	Effanbee
Chiquita	Elite Creations
Chitty Chitty Bang Bang	Mattel, Inc.
Chocolate Drop	Averill Manufacturing Co.
Choir Boys	Alexander Doll Co.
Chondrogen	Max Räder
Chris	Mattel, Inc.
Christening Baby	Alexander Doll Co., Effanbee, Miller Rubber Products Co.
Christincen	Käthe Kruse
Christkind	Käthe Kruse
Christopher Robin	Horsman & Co., Bendy of England
Christopher Robin and Pooh	Peggy Nesbit
Christy	Mattel, Inc.

Doll Name	Company Name
Chubby	Louis Wolf & Co.
Chubby Baby	Horsman & Co.
Chubby Kid	Gem
Chubby Kids	Columbia Doll & Toy Co.
Chubby Tiny Tears	American Character
Chuckles	American Character
Chunky	Sun Rubber Co.
Cinderella	Alexander Doll Co.; Cissna; Duchess Doll Corp.; Horsman & Co.; Mattel, Inc.; Nancy Ann StoryBook Dolls; Peggy Nesbit
Cinderella Baby	C. M. Bergmann
Cindy	Arrow Plastics, Horsman & Co., Roddy Doll Co.
Cindy, Original	Dewees Cochran
Cindy Kay	Horsman & Co.
Cindy Strutter	Horsman & Co.
Cinnamon	Ideal
Circus on Ice	Alexander Doll Co.
Cissette	Alexander Doll Co.
Cissy	Alexander Doll Co.
Cissy Royal Tour	Alexander Doll Co.
Cissy Takes a Trip	Alexander Doll Co.
Civil War	Alexander Doll Co.
Clara Barton	Alexander Doll Co.
Clarabell Clown	Alexander Doll Co.
Clarabelle	Alexander Doll Co.
Clark Gable	Peggy Nesbit
Claudette	Alexander Doll Co.; Clodrey; Nabco Doll, Inc.
Cleaning Day Doll	Confetti Dolls
Cleo	Bayerische Celluloidwarenfabrik; Mattel, Inc.
Cleopatra	Alexander Doll Co.
Clippo	Virginia Stowe Austin
Clippo Clown	Effanbee
Clover Kid	Alexander Doll Co.
Clown	Alexander Doll Co., Gund
Clownie	Amberg
Club Limited Bubbles	Effanbee
Club Limited China Head	Effanbee
Club Limited Crowning Glory	Effanbee
Club Limited Dewees Cochran	Effanbee
Club Limited Girl with Water Can	Effanbee
Club Limited Patsy	Effanbee
Club Limited Precious Baby	Effanbee
Club Limited Princess Diana	Effanbee
Club Limited Red Boy	Effanbee
Club Limited Sherlock Holmes	Effanbee
Club Limited Skippy	Effanbee
Club Limited Susan B. Anthony	Effanbee
Coast Guard	Carlson Dolls
Coca-Cola Santa Claus	Rushon Con.
Cochise	Mego
Coco	Alexander Doll Co.
Co-Ed	American Character
Co-Ed Flapper	American Specialty Doll Co., American Stuffed Novelty Co.
Col. Harland Sanders	Ron Startling Plastics of Canada
Cole Porter	Alexander Doll Co.
Colleen	Alexander Doll Co.
College Kids	Amberg
Collegiate Flapper	American Specialty Doll Co.

Colonial . . . . Alexander Doll Co.
Colonial Dame . . . . Nancy Ann StoryBook Dolls
Colonial Family . . . . Art Fabric Mills
Color & Curl Barbie . . . . Mattel, Inc.
Color Magic Barbie . . . . Mattel, Inc.
Color Me . . . . Eppy
Columbia . . . . Armand Marseille, Borgfeldt, C. M. Bergmann,
      Carl Hartmann, Cissna
Columbian Sailor Boy . . . . Arnold Print Works (patented by Ida Gutsell)
Com A Long . . . . Borgfeldt
Combat Kid . . . . Deluxe Reading/Topper Toy Group
Commencement Girl . . . . Nancy Ann StoryBook Dolls
Conan the Barbarian . . . . Mego
Conductress . . . . Alliance Toy Co.
Confederate Office . . . . Alexander Doll Co.
Connie Lynn . . . . Terry Lee
Conrad . . . . Käthe Kruse
Continental . . . . Ideal
Cookie . . . . Alexander Doll Co., Effanbee
Cool Cat . . . . Deluxe Reading/Topper Toy Group
Coquette . . . . Effanbee, Gebrüder Heubach, Uneeda Doll Co.
Cora . . . . Trendon Toys
Cornelia . . . . Alexander Doll Co.
Cornelius from Plant of the Apes . . . . Mego
Cornoulioud Doll . . . . Max Handwerck
Coronation Doll . . . . Doll Bodies, Duchess Doll Corp.
Coronation Walking Guardsman . . . . Awin Trading Co.
Cotillion . . . . American Character
Cotton Joe . . . . Horsman & Co.
Coty . . . . Arranbee
Coty Girl Doll . . . . Arranbee
Country Cousin . . . . Alexander Doll Co.
Country Girl . . . . Uneeda Doll Co.
Country Picnic . . . . Alexander Doll Co.
Cousin Grace . . . . Alexander Doll Co.
Cousin Karen . . . . Alexander Doll Co.
Cousin Marie . . . . Alexander Doll Co.
Cousin Mary . . . . Alexander Doll Co.
Couturier Dolls . . . . Horsman & Co.
Couturier's Lady . . . . Horsman & Co.
Couturier's Renee Ballerina . . . . Horsman & Co.
Cover Girl . . . . Kenner
Covered Wagon . . . . Effanbee
Cow Belle . . . . Mattel, Inc.
Cowardly Lion . . . . Mego
Cowboy . . . . Alexander Doll Co., Averill Manufacturing Co.,
      Hollywood Doll Manufacturing Co.
Cowgirl . . . . Alexander Doll Co., Hollywood Doll Manufacturing Co.
Cream Puff . . . . Ideal
Creeple People . . . . Mattel, Inc.
Crete . . . . Alexander Doll Co.
Cri Dol . . . . Averill Manufacturing Co.
Cricket . . . . American Character, Ideal
Crissy . . . . Ideal
Crissy, Beautiful Crissy . . . . Ideal
Crusader . . . . Plastic Molded Arts Co.
Cry Baby . . . . Art Fabric Mills

DOLL NAME	COMPANY NAME
Cry Baby Bunting	Amberg
Cry Dolly	Alexander Doll Co.
Cuddle Up	Effanbee
Cuddlekins	Eegee Doll Manufacturing Co.
Cuddles	Ideal
Cuddles a Life Size Baby Doll	Ideal
Cuddles Baby	Horsman & Co.
Cuddley	Mabel Bland Hawkes
Cuddly	Alexander Doll Co.
Cuddly Baby	Uneeda Doll Co.
Cuddly Beans	Mattel, Inc.
Cuddly Cathy	Deluxe Reading/Topper Toy Group
Cuddly Infant	Lorrie
Cuddly Kissy	Ideal
Cupid	Alisto Manufacturing, Kohnstamm & Co.
Cupido	Karl Standfuss
Curley	Famous Plaything
Curly Locks	Alexander Doll Co., Amberg, Nancy Ann StoryBook Dolls
Curly Top	Ideal
Cutie	Jolly Toys
Cutie Pie	Jolly Toys
Cy	Horsman & Co.
Cynthia	Alexander Doll Co.; Mattel, Inc.
Cynthia of the Classic Beauty	Mattel, Inc.
Czechoslovakia	Alexander Doll Co.
Da Da Babies	Atlantic Playthings Co.
Da Da Da	Art Fabric Mills
Dad	Ideal
DADA	Hermsdorfer Celluloidwarenfabrik
Daddy Warbucks	Knickerbocker
Daddy's Girl	Ideal
Daffi-Dill	Uneeda Doll Co.
Daffy Down Dilley	Alexander Doll Co.
Daffy Down Dilly	Nancy Ann StoryBook Dolls
Daffydils	Amberg
Daheim	Carl Hartmann
Dainty Deer Animiddle	Mattel, Inc.
Dainty Dolly	A & H
Dainty Dolly Pink and Blue	Nancy Ann StoryBook Dolls
Dainty May	Demalcol
Daisy	Alexander Doll Co., Borgfeldt, Edmond Princess Anna Doll Co., Ulrich Steiner
Daisy Belle, Daisy Belle	Nancy Ann StoryBook Dolls
Daisy Dalin'	Eegee Doll Manufacturing Co.
Daisy Dimple	Horsman & Co.
DALABA	Arthur Schoenau
Dale Evans	Duchess Doll Corp.
Dan	Averill Manufacturing Co.
Dana Cover Girl	Kenner
Dancerina	Mattel, Inc.
Dancing Dollies	Gerling Toy Co.
Dancing Partner	Etone Co.
Dandy	American Character; Mattel, Inc.
Danielle	Ashton Drake
Danish	Alexander Doll Co.
Danny Kaye	Peggy Nesbit
Danny the Groom	Duchess Doll Corp.

DOLL NAME	COMPANY NAME
Daralene, Lady in Waiting	Nancy Ann StoryBook Dolls
Darci Cover Girl	Kenner
Dardanella Bridal Couple	Home Novelty Co.
Darky Doll	Century Doll Co.
Darla from Our Gang	Mego
Darlin' Dollface	American Character
Darling	Strobel & Wilken
Darling Little Women	Molly-'es
Darth Vader	Kenner
Das Deutsche Kind	Käthe Kruse
Das Kriechende Baby	Kley & Hahn
Das Lachende Baby	Arthur Schoenau
Das Lebende Baby	Julius Henschel
Das Neugeborenes	Gustav Schmey
Das Strampelnde Baby	Kley & Hahn
Das Süsse Trudelchen	Käthe Kruse
Daumenlutscher	Richard Scherzer, Carl Heumann
David	Alexander Doll Co., Averill Manufacturing Co.
David From The Bible	Bible Doll Co. of America
David & Harp	Alexander Doll Co.
David Copperfield	Alexander Doll Co.
David Quack-a-field	Alexander Doll Co.
Davy Crockett	Alexander Doll Co., Mego
Dawk	Transogram Co.
Dawn	Deluxe Reading/Topper Toy Group
Day of the Week Dolls	Alexander Doll Co.
Deanna Durbin	Ideal
Deanna Durbin as Gulliver	Ideal
Dearest	Alexander Doll Co., Arranbee
Dearest One	Vogue
Debbie	Nancy Ann
Debbie Boone	Mattel, Inc.
Debteen	Uneeda Doll Co.
Debteen Toddler	Uneeda Doll Co.
Debu teen	Arranbee
Debutant	Alexander Doll Co.
December	Alexander Doll Co.
Dee and Cee Soup Kid	Dee and Cee Company
Dee Dee	Dee Cee Doll Co. of Canada; Mattel, Inc.
Deena Dollface	American Character
Degas	Alexander Doll Co.
Degas Girl	Alexander Doll Co.
DEKAWE	Carl Hermann
Del Rio	Virga
Delightful	Lorrie
Delly	Delly Puppenfabrik
Delphine Lady in Waiting	Nancy Ann StoryBook Dolls
Denmark	Alexander Doll Co.
Denny Dimwit	Toycraft
Der Bösewicht	Koenig & Wernicke
Der Deutsche Michel	Oscar Kirchner
Der Heitere Fridolin	Fleischmann & Bloedel
Der Kleine Mensch	Mittelland Gummiwerke
Der Kleine Spatz	Bayerische Celluloidwarenfabrik
Der Maxel	Käthe Kruse
Der Rosige Liebling	Kämmer & Reinhardt
Der Schelm	Kämmer & Reinhardt

Doll Name	Company Name
Der Unart	Kämmer & Reinhardt
Dew Drop	Ideal, Uneeda Doll Co.
Diana	Alexander Doll Co., Alfred Heller, Art Fabric Mills, Aunt Jemima Mills Co.
Diana Jemima	Aunt Jemima Mills Co., Davis Milling Co.
Diana Ross	Ideal, Mego
Dianna Ross	Ideal
Diaphanie Lady in Waiting	Nancy Ann StoryBook Dolls
Dick Van Dyke	Mattel, Inc.
Dickie	Amberg
Dicksie & Ducksie	Alexander Doll Co.
Didi	Alt, Beck & Gottschalck; Borgfeldt
Die Kleine Hansi	Wagner & Zetsche
Die Kleine Range	Koenig & Wernicke
Die Kokette	Kämmer & Reinhardt
Die Potsdamer Soldaten	Käthe Kruse
Dill	Peggy Nesbit
Dilly Dally Sally	Alexander Doll Co.
Dimmie	Averill Manufacturing Co.
Dina	Ideal
Dinah	Horsman & Co.
Dinah-mite	Mego
Ding Dong Dell	Alexander Doll Co.
Dinner At Eight	Alexander Doll Co.
Dionne Quints	Alexander Doll Co.
Dixie Mascot	Amberg
Dixie The Pixie	American Character
Doctor Defoe	Alexander Doll Co.
Doctor Doolittle	Mattel, Inc.
Dodi	Ideal
Doll	Edward Remington Ames
Doll House Mother	Hasbro, Inc.
Doll in a Pink Dress	Horsman & Co.
Dollar Store Doll	Albert J. Clark
Dollarprinzessin	Dora Petzold
Dolletta	Alliance Toy Co.
Dollikins	Uneeda Doll Co.
Dolls of Destiny	A & H
Dolls of Far Away Lands	Doll Bodies
Dolls Of The Month	Alexander Doll Co.
Dolly	Alexander Doll Co., Amberg, Imperial Crown
Dolly Ann	Natural Doll Co.
Dolly Darling	Hasbro, Inc.
Dolly Dimple	Art Fabric Mills, Butler Brothers, Hamburger & Co
Dolly Dingle	Averill Manufacturing Co.
Dolly Dollykins	The Dolly Co.
Dolly Drake	Amberg
Dolly Dreamland	Horsman & Co.
Dolly Dress Ups	Uneeda Doll Co.
Dolly Dryper	Alexander Doll Co.
Dolly Ge Ge	Brevete
Dolly Jump Rope	Atlas Doll & Toy Co.
Dolly Madison	Alexander Doll Co.
Dolly Mine	Gans & Seyfarth
Dolly Parton	Eegee
Dolly Pat Travels	Richard Scherzer
Dolly Pep	Uneeda Doll Co.

Doll Name	Company Name
Dolly Record	Averill Manufacturing Co.
Dolly Rekord	Averill Manufacturing Co.
Dolly Varden	Butler Brothers, Cuno & Otto Dressel
Dolly Walker	Baby Manufacturing, Uneeda Doll Co.
Dominican Republic	Alexander Doll Co.
Dona Elvira	Peggy Nesbit
Donald Duck	Gund Manufacturing
Donna Dolls by Marcie	A & H
Donny Osmond	Mattel, Inc.
Doodle Dear	Alder Favor and Novelty
Dopey	Alexander Doll Co., Crown
Dora	Käthe Kruse, Porzellanfabrik Rauenstein
Dorchen	Käthe Kruse
Doris Keane	Alexander Doll Co.
Dorothy	Alexander Doll Co., Butler Brothers, Horsman & Co.
Dorothy Dainty	Amberg
Dorothy Deer	Amberg
Dorothy from Oz	Mego
Dorothy Hamill	Ideal
Dorothy of Wizard of Oz	Ideal
Dottie Dumbunnie	Alexander Doll Co.
Dotty	Borgfeldt
Doug Davis Spaceman	Mattel, Inc.
Douglas MacArthur	Ralph A. Freundlich, Inc.
Dr. "Bones" McCoy	Mego
Dr. John Littlechap	Remco
Dr. Zaius	Mego
Dracula	Mego
Draft Dodger	Horsman & Co.
Drama of the Mariko Collection	Mattel, Inc.
Dream Baby	Arranbee
Dream Bride	Arranbee
Dream Doll	Ideal
Dream Girl	Duchess Doll Corp.
Dreso-Puppe	Fritz Dressel
Dress Me Doll	Commonwealth Doll & Toy, Grant Plastics
Dress Yourself	Plastic Molded Arts Co.
Dressed For Opera	Alexander Doll Co.
Dressy	Mattel, Inc.
Drink 'n Baby	Arranbee
Drinkie Tot	Horsman & Co.
Drinkie Walker	Horsman & Co.
Drowsy	Mattel, Inc.
Drowsy Dick	Horsman & Co.
Drum Majorette	Alexander Doll Co.
Dry Climate	Borgfeldt
Dryper Pantie Baby	Alexander Doll Co.
Duchess	Armand Marseille, Borgfeldt
Ducky	Ideal
Dude Ranch	Alexander Doll Co.
Dumplin' Baby	Alexander Doll Co.
Durabel	Kley & Hahn
Dusty	Kenner
Dutch	Alexander Doll Co.
Dutch Boy	Alexander Doll Co., Amberg
Dutch Child	Averill Manufacturing Co.
Dutch Girl	Amberg

Doll Name	Company Name
Dutch Girl in a Bell	A & H
Dutch Twins	Arranbee
Dwarfs	Knickerbocker
Dy Dee Baby	Effanbee
Dy Dee Darlin	Effanbee
Dy Dee Educational Baby	Effanbee
Dy Dee Ellen	Effanbee
Dy Dee Jane	Effanbee
Dy Dee Kins	Effanbee
Dy Dee Louise	Effanbee
Dy Dee Lu	Effanbee
Dy Deette	Effanbee
DyDee	Effanbee
Dyp a Babe	Cameo
Easter Bonnet Toddler	S & E
Easter Doll	Alexander Doll Co.
Easter Sunshine	Peggy Huffman Originals
Eaton's Beauty Doll	Dominion Toy Co.
EBASO	Emil Bauersachs
ECCO	Eckstein & Co.
Eclaireur	Gutmann & Schniffnie
Ecuador	Alexander Doll Co.
Edelkind	Hugo Wiegand
Eden Bebe	Fleischmann & Bloedel
Edith	Butler Brothers
Edith Roosevelt	Alexander Doll Co.
Edith The Lonely Doll	Alexander Doll Co.
Edith the Nurse	Doll Craft
Edith Wilson	Alexander Doll Co.
Edith With Golden Hair	Alexander Doll Co.
Educational Doll	Amberg
Edwardian	Alexander Doll Co.
Edwina	Amberg
Egypt	Alexander Doll Co.
Egyptian	Alexander Doll Co.
Einco	Eisenmann
Elaine	Alexander Doll Co.
Eleanor Roosevelt	Alexander Doll Co., Effanbee, Peggy Nesbit
Eleonore	C. M. Bergmann, Simon & Halbig
Elfe	Gans & Seyfarth
Elfenhaut	Amberg, Hergershausen
Elfen-Puppe	Koenig & Wernicke
Elfriede	Käthe Kruse
Elfy	Uneeda Doll Co.
Eli	Ernst Liebermann
Elie	Karl Müller
Elise	Alexander Doll Co., Borgfeldt
Elise on Tour	Alexander Doll Co.
Elise on Vacation	Alexander Doll Co.
Elise Takes a Trip	Alexander Doll Co.
Elite	Max Handwerck
Elizabeth Monroe	Alexander Doll Co.
Elizabeth Taylor	Peggy Nesbit
Elizabeth Truman	Peggy Nesbit
Elizabethan Gent	Peggy Nesbit
Elizabethan Lady	Peggy Nesbit
Elke	Mattel, Inc., for Annette Himstedt

Ellar	Armand Marseille
Ellen	Mattel, Inc. for Annette Himstedt
Ellen Wilson	Alexander Doll Co.
Ellie May Clampett	Unique Doll
Elmer Fudd	Dakin & Co.
Eloise	American Character
Elsa	unidentified German doll manufacturer
Elschen	Käthe Kruse
Elsie Marley	Nancy Ann StoryBook Dolls
Elsie Marley Grown so Fine	Nancy Ann StoryBook Dolls
EMASO	Maar
Emerald the Enchanting Witch	Girl's World
Emily	Alexander Doll Co., Cosmopolitan Toy & Doll
Emily by Yolanda Bello	Ashton Drake
Emily Ann	Effanbee
Emily Dickinson	Alexander Doll Co.
Emine of Turkey	Doll Craft
Emmett Kelly	Baby Berry Toys
Emmy	Käthe Kruse
Enchanted Doll	Alexander Doll Co.
English Guard	Alexander Doll Co.
Epstein	Mattel, Inc.
Erfordia	Otto Reipert
Erica Cover Girl	Kenner
Erika	Carl Hartmann, Käthe Kruse, Simon & Halbig
Erna	Käthe Kruse
Esco	Sommer
Escora	Eduard Schmidt
Eskimo	Atlas Manufacturing Co., Peggy Nesbit
Eskimo Pie Boy	Chase Bag Co.
Ester Starring	Western Doll Co.
Esther	Alisto Manufacturing, Butler Brothers, Käthe Kruse
Estonia	Alexander Doll Co.
Esy	Suchetzsky
Ethel	Butler Brothers
Eugenia Marie Lady in Waiting	Nancy Ann StoryBook Dolls
Eulalie Lady in Waiting	Nancy Ann StoryBook Dolls
Eva	Nancy Ann StoryBook Dolls
Eva Lovelace	Alexander Doll Co.
Evangeline	Alexander Doll Co., Martha Battle
Evchen	Käthe Kruse
Excelsior	Louis Wolf
Eyeore	Peggy Nesbit
Fahn	Reupke
Fair Baby	Effanbee
Fair Skin Doll	Horsman & Co.
Fairie Princess	Amberg
Fairy	Horsman & Co., Kim Dolls
Fairy Godmother	Alexander Doll Co.; Vogue
Fairy Moonbeam	Lauer
Fairy Princess	Alexander Doll Co.
Fairy Queen	Alexander Doll Co.
Fairy Tales	Alexander Doll Co.
Faith	Alexander Doll Co.
Falstaff	Peggy Nesbit
Famlee	Berwick Doll Co.
Famlee Doll	European Doll Mfg.

Fancora-Wunder-Baby	Franz Angermüller
Fancora-Wunderbaby	Franz Angermüller
Fannie Brice Flexy	Ideal
Fanny	Armand Marseille, Horsman & Co., Käthe Kruse
Fanny Brice	Ideal
Fanny The Flapper	American Character
Fany	Armand Marseille
Farmer Boy	Horsman & Co.
Farrah Fawcett	Mego
Fashion Award	Alexander Doll Co.
Fashion Flatsy Dale	Ideal
Fashion Miss Revlon	Ideal
Fashion Queen	Mattel, Inc.
Fashion Queen Barbie	Mattel, Inc.
Fat Baby	Kestner
Father Knickerbocker	Averill Manufacturing Co.
Fatou	Mattel, Inc. for Annette Himstedt
Faun	Amberg
Faunalie	Lauer
Favorite Saxonia	Nöckler & Tittel
Featherweight	Borgfeldt
Feldgrauen	Käthe Kruse, Kley & Hahn, Steiff
Felicia	Nancy Ann StoryBook Dolls
Felicity Merriman	Pleasant Co.
Felix	Käthe Kruse
Fema	Beck
Fiene	Mattel, Inc. for Annette Himstedt
Fifi	Käthe Kruse
Fifth Ave. Doll	Cuno & Otto Dressel
Fighting Batman	Mego
Fighting Joker	Mego
Fighting Riddler	Mego
Fighting Robin	Mego
Fine Baby	Amberg
Fingles	Mattel, Inc.
Fingy Legs The Tiny Tot	Borgfeldt
Finland	Alexander Doll Co.
Finnish	Alexander Doll Co.
Finucke	Käthe Kruse
First Ladies	Alexander Doll Co.
First Born Baby	Uneeda Doll Co.
First Communion	Alexander Doll Co.
First Date	Dakin & Co.
First New Mickey	Effanbee
First Steps	Amberg
First Wives	Alexander Doll Co.
Fischer Quints	Alexander Doll Co.
Fishing Boy	Amberg
Five In One Doll	Gem Toy Co.
Five Little Peppers	Alexander Doll Co.
Flags of All Nations	Cuno & Otto Dressel
Flapper	Alexander Doll Co., American Stuffed Novelty Co.
Flatsy	Ideal
Flexy	Morton E. Converse & Son
Flexy Soldier	Ideal
Flip the Football Doll	Columbia Toy Products
Flip Wilson—Geraldine	Shindana

Flippety Flop Kids	Gund
Flirtatious Flowergirl	Princess Ann Dolls
Flirty Sue	Horsman & Co.
Flopsie	Horsman & Co.
Flora	Eisfelder Puppenfabrik
Flora McFlimsey	Alexander Doll Co.
Floradora	Armand Marseille, Borgfeldt
Florence	Butler Brothers
Florence Harding	Alexander Doll Co.
Florence Niddle	Mattel, Inc.
Florence Nightingale	Alexander Doll Co.
Floresta	Scheyer
Florigotto	Florig & Otto
Florosora	Armand Marseille
Florosora Sextet	Amberg
Flossie Came from Dublin Town	Nancy Ann StoryBook Dolls
Flossie Fischer's Own Doll	Borgfeldt
Flossie Flirt	Ideal
Flower People	Uneeda Doll Co.
Flower Girl	Alexander Doll Co., Plastic Molded Arts Co.
Flowerkin-Rosie Red	Eegee Doll Manufacturing Co.
Fluff	Mattel, Inc.
Fluffy	Vogue
Fluffy Official Campfire Bluebird Doll	Effanbee
Fluffy Ruffles	Max Schelhorn
Fluffy Series	Effanbee
Fly Lo	Borgfeldt
Flying Nun	Hasbro, Inc.; Horsman & Co.
Flying Trapeze	Alexander Doll Co.
Fly-Lo	Borgfeldt
Folk Dancers Collection (at least 12)	Peggy Nesbit
Follies Girl	American Specialty Doll Co.
Fonzie	Mego
Foppi Doll	Alder Favor and Novelty
For December Just a Dear	Nancy Ann Storybook Dolls
Formal Elise	Alexander Doll Co.
Foxy Gentleman	Peggy Nesbit
Foxy Grandpa	Art Fabric Mills
Frances Cleveland	Alexander Doll Co.
Francie	Mattel, Inc.
Francie with Growing Hair	Mattel, Inc.
Francine	Arranbee
Frankenstein	Mego
Franklin D. Roosevelt	Effanbee
Franklin Roosevelt	Peggy Nesbit
Freckles	American Character, Uneeda Doll Co.
Freddy	Käthe Kruse
Frederich	Alexander Doll Co.
Frederick	Alexander Doll Co.
Frederike	Mattel, Inc. for Annette Himstedt
Freedom Doll	Alexander Doll Co.
Freedom Train	Alexander Doll Co.
Freezy Sliddle	Mattel, Inc.
Freidrich	Alexander Doll Co.
French	Alexander Doll Co.
French Flowergirl	Alexander Doll Co.
French Girl	Averill Manufacturing Co.

French Provincial Lady	S. F. B. J.
French Provincial Man	S. F. B. J.
French World War I Nurse	International Composition Dolls
Freshie	Louis Amberg & Son
Friar Tuck	Alexander Doll Co., Mego
Friday's Child Must Work for a Living	Nancy Ann StoryBook Dolls
Fridolin	Fleischmann & Bloedel
Friedebald	Käthe Kruse
Friedel	Käthe Kruse, Matthes
Friedericke	Käthe Kruse
Fritz	Pfeiffer, Käthe Kruse
Frivona	Voigt
Frizzi	John Hess
Frou-Frou	Alexander Doll Co.
Frühsahrsamantel	Käthe Kruse
Fumsup	Hamley Brothers
Funny	Alexander Doll Co., Dakin & Co.
Funny Face Clown	Berwick Doll Co.
Funny Face Family	N. D. Cass & Co.
G. I. Joe	Hasbro, Inc.
Gabby Baby	Laurel Dolls
Gabby Jane	Laurel Dolls
Gabby Linda	Laurel Dolls
Gaby	René Kaspa
Gainsbourgh	Alexander Doll Co.
Galen	Mego
Gangy Daglies	Mattel, Inc.
Gänseliessel	Käthe Kruse
Garden Party	Alexander Doll Co.
Gardening	Alexander Doll Co.
Gaucho	Argentina
Gaye of the Unity of Nations Established Set	Effanbee
Ge Ge	G. Giroux Cie
Gee Gee Dolly	Horsman & Co.
Gehrenia	Henze & Steinhäuser
Gemette	Eegee Doll Manufacturing Co.
Gemettes	Eegee Doll Manufacturing Co.
Gene Autry	Terry Lee
Gene Car Kids	Horsman & Co.
Gene from Kiss	Mego
Gene Tierney	Alexander Doll Co.
Gene, Premiere	Ashton Drake
General Ursus	Mego
Geo	Gebrüder Eckardt
George Washington Bicentennial Doll	American Character
George Washington Doll	Toy Products
Georgi	Eleonore Georgi
Georgian Gent	Peggy Nesbit
Georgian Lady	Peggy Nesbit
Geranium	Alexander Doll Co.
Gerber Baby	Gerber Baby Products, Sun Rubber Co.
Gerda	Nancy Ann StoryBook Dolls
German	Alexander Doll Co.
GESUE	Gebrüder Süssenguth
GETE-puppe	Gustav Thiele
Gibson Girl	Alexander Doll Co., Kestner, Steiff
Gidget	Alexander Doll Co.

Doll Name	Company Name
Gie Wa	Dollcraft Co. of America
Giggles	Cameo, Ideal
Gigi	A&H, Alexander Doll Co., Effanbee, Mary Hoyer Doll Manufacturing Co.
Gigi in a Bell	A & H
Gigi Perreaux	Eegee Doll Manufacturing Co.
Ginger	Cosmopolitan Toy & Doll, Ideal
Ginger Rogers	Alexander Doll Co.
Ginnette	Vogue
Ginny	Vogue
Ginny Baby	Vogue
Ginny Tui	Jack Built Toys
Girl	Horsman & Co.
Girl Bauernkind	Horsman & Co.
Girl Davy Crockett	Alexander Doll Co.
Girl from the Southern Series	American Character
Girl from U. N. E. E. D. A.	Uneeda Doll Co.
Girl in A Green Dress	Circle X
Girl in A Pink Dress	Eugenia Doll Co.
Girl in Long Blue Dress	Effanbee
Girl in Patriotic Dress	Horsman & Co.
Girl in Raincoat	Effanbee
Girl in The Blue Dress	Jolly Toys, Inc.
Girl of The Golden West	Doll Craft
Girl On Flying Trapeze	Alexander Doll Co.
Girl Scout	Alexander Doll Co.
Girl With a Curl	Amberg
Give Me A Lassie as Sweet as She's Fair	Nancy Ann StoryBook Dolls
Gladdie	Borgfeldt
Glamour Dolls	Molly-'es
Glamour Girl Bride	Sayco Doll Corp.
Glamour Girls	Alexander Doll Co.
Glamour Misty	Ideal
Glinda "The Good Witch"	Mego
Globe Babies	Carl Hartmann
Glori	Deluxe Reading/Topper Toy Group
Glori Glamour	Deluxe Reading/Topper Toy Group
Gloria	Cosmopolitan Toy & Doll
Gloria Ann of the American Children	Effanbee
Gloria Jean	Horsman & Co.
Gloriosa	Kestner
Go Cart Dolly	Amberg
Godey Groom	Alexander Doll Co.
Godey Lady	Alexander Doll Co.
Godey Man	Alexander Doll Co.
Going To See Grandma	Alexander Doll Co.
Gold Medal Baby	Averill Manufacturing Co., Horsman & Co.
Gold Medal Big Jack	Mattel, Inc.
Gold Medal Doll	Horsman & Co.
Gold Rush	Alexander Doll Co.
Golden Anniversary Doll	Uneeda Doll Co.
Goldey Locks	Sol Bergfeld & Son
Goldherz	Bruno Schmidt
Goldie	Columbus Merchandise Co.
Goldilocks	Alexander Doll Co.; Mattel, Inc.; Nancy Ann StoryBook Dolls
Goldilocks and Three Bears	Hasbro, Inc.
Goldstern	Adolf Hülss

Golf Boy	Horsman & Co.
Golf Girl	Horsman & Co.
Golliwogs	Atlas Manufacturing Co.
Gone With The Wind	Alexander Doll Co.
Goo Goo Eva	Ralph A. Freundlich, Inc.
Good Little Girl	Alexander Doll Co.
Goody Goody	Amberg, L. & A. L. Goodman
Goody Two Shoes	Ideal
Goose Girl	Nancy Ann StoryBook Dolls
Gorgeous	Ideal
Gorgeous Creatures	Mattel, Inc.
Goya	Alexander Doll Co.
Grace	Eegee Doll Manufacturing Co.
Graduate	Plastic Molded Arts Co.
Graduation	Alexander Doll Co.
Gramma	Amsco
Gramma Jane	Alexander Doll Co.
Grandfather	Peggy Nesbit
Grandma Walton	Mego
Grandmother	Peggy Nesbit
Grandpa Walton	Mego
Granitol	Carl Hoffmeister
Graziella Puppen	Max Sachs
Great Britain	Alexander Doll Co.
Grecon Puppe	Grete Cohn
Greek Boy	Alexander Doll Co.
Greek Girl	Alexander Doll Co.
Green Arrow	Mego
Green Goblin	Mego
Greenbrier Maid	Plastic Molded Arts Co.
Gregor	Trendon Toys
Greta Garbo	Peggy Nesbit
Greta Griddle	Mattel, Inc.
Gretchen	Adolf Wislizenus, Averill Manufacturing Co., Geo Gesch, Horsman & Co.
Grete	Horsman & Co., Kämmer & Reinhardt
Gretel	Alexander Doll Co., Nancy Ann StoryBook Dolls
Gretchen	Käthe Kruse
Gretel	Alexander Doll Co.
Grizzly Adams	Mattel, Inc.
Grok	Mego
Groom	Alexander Doll Co.
Groucho Marx	Effanbee
Grow Hair Doll	Eegee Doll Manufacturing Co.
Growing Hair Cricket	American Character
Grown Up Miss	Horsman & Co.
Grumpykins	Effanbee
Guardian Angel	Alexander Doll Co.
Guardian Goddesses	Mattel, Inc.
Guardsman	Peggy Nesbit
Gumdrop	Effanbee
Gummoid	Nöckler & Tittel
Gura	TrachtenPuppen SpielPuppen
Guschi	Gutmann & Schniffnie
Gymnastik Doll	Albin Hess
Gypsy Magic	Alexander Doll Co.
Gypsy Queen	Averill Manufacturing Co.

Doll Name	Company Name
Ha Ha	Effanbee
Habeka	Hermann von Berg
Hafraco Puppe	Schöffl
Hail Columbia	Amberg
Haleloke	Roberta Dolls
Half Pint	Effanbee
Haliso	Heinrich Liebermann
Halloween Dolls	Averill Manufacturing Co.
Halo Angel	Noma Electric
Hamlet	Peggy Nesbit
Han Solo	Kenner
Hanco	Hahn
Handora	Ohrdrufer
Hanka	Gebrüder Pfeiffer
Hanna	Arthur Schoenau
Hannah	Hedwig (Marguerite de Angeli)
Hannelore	Hermann Pensky
Hannerle	Käthe Kruse
Hans	Averill Manufacturing Co., Horsman & Co., Kämmer & Reinhardt, Käthe Kruse, Knickerbocker
Hansa	Carl Hartmann
Hansa-Puppe	W. Reinick
Hansel	Alexander Doll Co., Knickerbocker, Nancy Ann StoryBook Dolls
Hansel & Gretel	Moritz Pappe
Hansi	Wagner & Zetsche
Happifat	Borgfeldt
Happiness	Sears, Roebuck & Co.
Happinus Doll	Amberg
Happy	Alexander Doll Co.
Happy Boy	Effanbee
Happy Cry	Averill Manufacturing Co.
Happy Doll Collection (at least 108)	Peggy Nesbit
Happy Family	Effanbee
Happy Hiram	Horsman & Co.
Happy Hooligan	Borgfeldt, Ideal
Happy Kappy	Sun Rubber
Happy Me	Mattel, Inc.
Happy Pee Wee	Uneeda Doll Co.
Happy Tots	American Character
Hapusa	Hermann Hachmeister
Harald	Wagner & Zetsche
Haralit	Wagner & Zetsche
Hardy Boys	Kenner
Harem Skirt Doll	Amberg
Hariet	Mattel, Inc.
Harmonica Joe	Effanbee
Harriet Hubbard Ayer	Ideal
Harriet Lane	Alexander Doll Co.
Harry Haenigsen	Alexander Doll Co.
Harry S. Truman	Peggy Nesbit
Hawadit	Hammer Munitionswerk
Hawaii	Alexander Doll Co.
Hawaiian	Alexander Doll Co.
He Loves Me, He Loves Me Not	Nancy Ann StoryBook Dolls
Head of Baby	Amberg
Head of Little Girl	Amberg

DOLL NAME	COMPANY NAME
Heart Beat Doll	Ideal Toy Co.
Heart Pin Kiddle	Mattel, Inc.
Heather	Alexander Doll Co.
Heather, by Yolanda Bello	Ashton Drake
HEbee	Horsman & Co.
Hedda-Get-Betta	American Character
Heddi Stroller	Belle Dolls
Hedi	Schwerin
Hedy LaMarr	Alexander Doll Co.
Heico	M. Heider
Heidi	Alexander Doll Co., Remco
Heidi That Grows Up	Remco
Heinerle	Helene Haeusler
Heio-Beio	Schwerin
Heiterer Fridolin	Fleischmann & Bloedel
Helen	Butler Brothers, unidentified
Helen of Troy	Peggy Nesbit
Helen Taft	Alexander Doll Co.
Helgünith	Günthel
Hello Baby	Alexander Doll Co.
Hello Dolly Doll	Nasco
He-Nik	Uneeda Doll Co.
Henny	Böhnke & Zimmermann
Henny Puppe	Loetel
Henriette	Käthe Kruse
Henza	Henze & Steinhäuser
Herald-Tribune	Alexander Doll Co.
Here Am I Little Joan	Nancy Ann StoryBook Dolls
Herka	Köllner
Herkules	Deuerlein
Herman Muster	Mattel, Inc.
Hermann	Käthe Kruse
Herz	Bruno Schmidt
Herzi	Porzellanfabrik Mengersgereuth
Herzkäferchen	Bauer & Richter Inc.
Herzlieb	Hugo Wiegand, Scherzer & Fischer
Herzpuppen	Herzpuppen-Fabrik
Hesli	Heinrich Schmuckler
Hewika	Hertwig & Co.
Hexe	unidentified
Hi Dottie	Mattel, Inc.
Hiawatha	Alexander Doll Co., Amberg, Reliable Toy
Highland Fling	Alexander Doll Co.
Hilda	Alexander Doll Co., Averill Manufacturing Co., Kestner
Hilde	Käthe Kruse
Historical Characters Collection (at least 164)	Peggy Nesbit
Historical Copies	Effanbee
Historical Dolls	Effanbee
Historical Portrait Dolls	Arranbee
Hi-Way Henry	Borgfeldt
Ho Ho	Cameo
Hochtourist	Mathilde Sehm
Holi Diddle	Mattel, Inc.
Holland	Alexander Doll Co.
Holly	Alexander Doll Co., Holiday Fair Inc.
Holly Hobby	Knickerbocker
Hollywood Imps	W. R. Woodard & Co.

DOLL NAME	COMPANY NAME
Holzmasse	Cuno & Otto Dressel, Julius Dorst
Honey	Acme Toy Co., Effanbee
Honey Ballerina	Effanbee
Honey Boy	Amberg
Honey Bun	Effanbee
Honey Bunch	Ideal
Honey Child	American Doll Co.
Honey Formal	Effanbee
Honey Girl	Effanbee
Honey Ice Skater	Effanbee
Honey in outfits by Schiaparelli	Effanbee
Honey Walker	Effanbee
Honey Walkers	Effanbee
Honeyball	Ideal
Honeybea	Alexander Doll Co.
Honeybun	Alexander Doll Co.
Honeyette Baby	Alexander Doll Co.
Honeyfoam	Ideal
Honeykins	Effanbee
Honeymoon	Ideal
Honeysuckle Babies	Ideal
Honeysuckle Line	Ideal
Hopalong Cassidy	Ideal
Horshack	Mattel, Inc.
Hoss Cartwright	American Character
Hot Canary	Deluxe Reading/Topper Toy Group
How the West Was Won	Mattel, Inc.
Howard Biff Boodle	Mattel, Inc.
Howard Buff Boodle	Mattel, Inc.
Howdy Doodie	Effanbee
Howdy Doody	Alexander Doll Co., Effanbee, Ideal

French Bebes by Bru and A. Thiuller. (Photo courtesy of Christie's East)

Huberta	Emil Pfeiffer
Hubsy-Puppen	Emil Pfeiffer
Huckleberry Finn	Alexander Doll Co.
Hug Me Kiddies	Samstag & Hilder Brothers
Huggles	Fun World
Huggums	Alexander Doll Co.
Hula Dancer Baby Bud	Effanbee
Hula-Nik	Uneeda Doll Co.
Human Torch	Mego
Hungarian	Alexander Doll Co.
Hyacinth	Alexander Doll Co.
I G E S	Escher & Son
I G O D I	Kohl & Wengenroth
I Love Lucy Baby Doll	American Character
I Walk I Talk I Sleep	Amberg
I We Em	Ines Wetzel
I'm Going a Milking	Nancy Ann StoryBook Dolls
Ibiza	Alexander Doll Co.
Ice Capades	Alexander Doll Co.
Ice Flirt Boy and Girl	Western Doll Co.
Ice Skater	Alexander Doll Co.
Iceland	Alexander Doll Co.
Ida McKinley	Alexander Doll Co.
Idéal Bébé	Bertoli Frères
IG88	Kenner
Igodi	Amberg
Ilia from *Star Trek*	Mego
Illco	Carl Illing
Illya Kuryakin	Ideal
Imperial	Hamburger & Co.
Impish Elfy	Uneeda Doll Co.
Impish Kewpie	Cameo
In A Minute Thumbelina	Ideal
Incredible Hulk	Mego
Indestructible Heads	Cuno & Otto Dressel
India	Alexander Doll Co.
Indian	Alexander Doll Co.
Indian Child	Averill Manufacturing Co.
Indian Maid	Averill Manufacturing Co.
Indian Splendor	Alexander Doll Co.
Indian Squaw	Reliable Toy
Indian Troll	Scanda House
Indonesia	Alexander Doll Co.
Infant Jumper	Uneeda Doll Co.
Infant of Prague	Alexander Doll Co.
Inge	Käthe Kruse, Wagner & Zetsche
Ingres	Alexander Doll Co.
Ink U Bator Baby	American Character
Inspector	Knickerbocker
Invincible Iron Man	Mego
Invisible Girl	Mego
Iris	Alexander Doll Co., Iris Beaumont
Irish	Alexander Doll Co.
Irish Girl	Peggy Nesbit
Irvington	Borgfeldt
Isolde	Alexander Doll Co.
Israeli	Alexander Doll Co.

Doll Name	Company Name
It	Amberg
IT	Arranbee
Italy	Alexander Doll Co.
Itsy Bitsy	Ideal
Itzebumsack	Käthe Kruse
Ivanhoe	Mego
Jack	Nancy Ann StoryBook Dolls
Jack & Jill	Alexander Doll Co., Sol Bergfeld & Son
Jack Robinson	Horsman & Co.
Jack Tar	Amberg, Horsman & Co.
Jackie	Alexander Doll Co., Horsman & Co.
Jackie Coogan	Borgfeldt, Harburger Gummiwaren Fabrik, Fleischmann & Bloedel, Gustav Förster
Jackie Doll	Ideal
Jackie Robinson	Allied Grand Doll Manufacturing, Horsman & Co.
Jacky	Käthe Kruse
Jaclyn Smith	Mego
Jacobean Lady	Peggy Nesbit
Jacqueline	Alexander Doll Co.
Jacqueline in Riding Habit	Alexander Doll Co.
Jacqueline Kennedy	Alexander Doll Co., Peggy Nesbit
Jaköble	Käthe Kruse
Jama Baby	Vogue
Jamaica	Alexander Doll Co.
Jambo	Effanbee
James Bond	Ideal
James Bond 007	Ideal
James Cagney	Effanbee
Jamie	Reliable Doll Co. of Canada, Roddy Doll Co.
Jamie West	Marx
Jan	Horsman & Co.; Remco; Vogue
Jane	Horsman & Co., Averill Manufacturing Co.
Jane Avril	Alexander Doll Co.
Jane Findlay	Alexander Doll Co.
Jane Pierce	Alexander Doll Co.
Jane Withers	Alexander Doll Co.
Janet	Mattel, Inc.
Janie	Alexander Doll Co., Averill Manufacturing Co., Eegee Doll Manufacturing Co., Uneeda Doll Co.
Janka	Mattel, Inc. for Annette Himstedt
Jap Rose Boy	Horsman & Co.
Jap Rose Girl	Horsman & Co.
Jap Rose Kid	Horsman & Co.
Japan	Alexander Doll Co.
Japanese Baby	Kohnstamm
Jasmine	Alexander Doll Co.
Jason	Ashton Drake
Jawa	Kenner
JDEN	Josef Deuerlein
Jean	Atlas Manufacturing Co.
Jean Harlow	Peggy Nesbit
Jean Lafitte	Mego
Jeanette	Mattel, Inc.; Vogue
Jeannie Walker	Alexander Doll Co.
Jeff	Vogue
Jeff Jones	Dewees Cochran
Jefferson Jones	Dewees Cochran

DOLL NAME	COMPANY NAME
Jem	Hasbro, Inc.
Jemima Puddleduck	Peggy Nesbit
Jennie Set the Table	Nancy Ann StoryBook Dolls
Jennifer, by Yolanda Bellow	Ashton Drake
Jennifer Fashion Doll	Uneeda Doll Co.
Jennifer's Trunk Set	Alexander Doll Co.
Jenny Lind	Alexander Doll Co.
Jenny Lind & Cat	Alexander Doll Co.
Jerri Lee	Terri Lee
Jessica	Alexander Doll Co., Deluxe Reading/Topper Toy Group
Jessica, by Yolanda Bellow	Ashton Drake
Jesus	Peggy Nesbit
Jet Coder	Mattel, Inc.
Jill	Nancy Ann StoryBook Dolls; Vogue
Jim Dandy	Amberg
Jim-in-ee	Elizabeth G. Adrian
Jiminy Cricket	Gund Manufacturing, Ideal, Marx Toys
Jimmie	Averill Manufacturing Co.
Jimmy	Blumberg
Jimmy Osmond	Mattel, Inc.
Jing-Go-Ring Doll	Fritz Lutz
Jo	Alexander Doll Co.
Jo Ann	P & M Sales
Jo Anne	Horsman & Co.
Jo Jo	Horsman & Co.
Joan of Arc	Peggy Nesbit
Joan Palooka	Ideal
Joan Polooka	Ideal
Joanie	Plastic Molded Arts
Joanie Nurse	Alexander Doll Co.
Joe Namath	Mego
Joey Stivic	Ideal
John Adams	Peggy Nesbit
John Boy Walton	Mego
John Bunny Doll	Amberg
John Kennedy	Peggy Nesbit
John Powers Models	Alexander Doll Co.
John Wayne	Effanbee
Johnny Jones	Amberg
Jointed Doll	Adolf Wislizenus, C. M. Bergmann, Gans & Seyfarth
Joker	Mego
Joli Bébé Damerval	Bonin & Lefort
Jolly	Jolly Toys
Jolly Jester	Borgfeldt
Jon of C.H.I.P.S.	Mego
Jordi 2	Käthe Kruse
Jose	Johannes Sauerteig
Josephine	Alexander Doll Co.
Joy	Alexander Doll Co., Cameo, Royal Doll Co.
Jr. Miss Bride	Effanbee
Jubilee Doll	Strobel & Wilken
Judy	Alexander Doll Co., Arranbee, Jolly Toys
Judy (and Punch)	Art Fabric Mills
Judy Doll	Effanbee Doll Co.
Judy Garland	Ideal, Peggy Nesbit
Judy Garland from the Legend Series	Effanbee
Judy Littlechap	Remco

DOLL NAME	COMPANY NAME
Judy Splinter	Ideal
Jugo-Slav	Alexander Doll Co.
Julia	Mattel, Inc.
Julia Grant	Alexander Doll Co.
Julia Tyler	Alexander Doll Co.
Julie	Mattel, Inc.
Juliet	Alexander Doll Co., Peggy Nesbit
Jumpsy	Remco
June Bride	Alexander Doll Co.
June Wedding	Alexander Doll Co.
Junior Miss	American Character, Effanbee
Juno	Karl Standfuss
Just Me	Armand Marseille, Borgfeldt
Jutta	Cuno & Otto Dressel
K O-K O	Borgfeldt
Kai	Mattel, Inc. for Annette Himstedt
Kampy Kiddle	Mattel, Inc.
Kanga	Peggy Nesbit
Karen	Alexander Doll Co.
Karen Ballerina	Alexander Doll Co.
Karlchen	Käthe Kruse
Karo Princess	American Ocarina and Toy Co.
Kasimir	Mattel, Inc. for Annette Himstedt
Kate Greenaway	Alexander Doll Co.
Kate Jackson	Mattel, Inc.
Kathe	Mattel, Inc. for Annette Himstedt
Kathel	Käthe Kruse
Kathleen	Alexander Doll Co.
Kathy	Alexander Doll Co.
Kathy Cry Dolly	Alexander Doll Co.
Kathy Tears	Alexander Doll Co.
Katie	Alexander Doll Co., Effanbee
Katrinchen	Käthe Kruse
Katzenjammer Kids	Knickerbocker
Kay	Eegee Doll Manufacturing Co., Nancy Ann StoryBook Dolls
Keep Smiling	Elise Israel
Kelly	Alexander Doll Co.
Ken	Mattel, Inc.
Ken Murray's Glamour Cowboy	A & H
Ken Murray's TV Cowboy	A & H
Kerry	Ideal
Kewpie	Borgfeldt, Cameo, Carl Völker, Hermann Voigt, Karl Standfuss, Kestner, Steiff
Kewpie Gal	Cameo
Kewty	Domec Toy Co.
Kickapoo	Horsman & Co.
Kid Doll	Carl Hoffmeister
Kiddie Karakters	Averill Manufacturing Co.
Kiddie Pal Dolly	Regal Doll Co.
Kiddie Pay Dolly	Regal Doll Co.
Kiddiejoy	Armand Marseille
Kiddle Kolognes	Mattel, Inc.
Kiddles	Mattel, Inc.
Kidlyne Doll	Carl Hoffmeister
Kidolin	Carl Hoffmeister
Killiblues	Baker & Bennett Co.
Kilroy	Effanbee

Doll Name	Company Name
Kim	Uneeda Doll Co.
Kima	Mattel, Inc. for Annette Himstedt
Kimber	Hasbro, Inc.
Kindergarten Kathy	Horsman & Co.
Kindertraum	Otto Gans
King	Alexander Doll Co.
King Arthur	Mego
King Little	Ideal
King's Jester	American Stuffed Novelty Co.
KISS	Mego
Kiss Me	Ideal
Kissie	Cuno & Otto Dressel
Kissin Kuzzins	Mattel, Inc.
Kissin' Thumbelina	Ideal
Kissy	Ideal
Kitten	Alexander Doll Co.
Kitten Kries	Alexander Doll Co.
Kitty Baby	Alexander Doll Co.
Klärchen	Käthe Kruse
Klaus	Käthe Kruse
Klein Datti	Käthe Kruse
Klein Mammy	Kämmer & Reinhardt
Klingon	Mego
Klondike Kate	Alexander Doll Co.
Knopf in Ohr	Steiff
Know Your Colours	Peggy Nesbit
Know Your Numbers	Peggy Nesbit
Koaster Kid	Amberg
Kola Kiddles	Mattel, Inc.
Kolundro	Josef Deuerlein, Kohler & Rosenwald, Martin Winterbauer
Königskinder	Koenig & Wernicke
Korea	Alexander Doll Co.
Kowenko	Kohl & Wengenroth
Kretor and Zark	Mattel, Inc.
Kretor and Zark the Shark	Mattel, Inc.
Kristen Larson	Pleasant Co.
Kronen Puppe	Kestner
Kuddle Kiddies	Century Doll Co.
Künstlerkopf	Schoenau & Hoffmeister
Kurly Head	Arranbee
Kurt	Käthe Kruse
Kutie Kid	Seamless Toy Corp.
L'Intrepide Bébé	Roullet & Decamps
La Belle	Heinrich Handwerck
La Bonita	Heinrich Handwerck
La Cheri Collection	Mattel, Inc.
La Fée au Tréfle	Madame E. Cayette
La Fée aux Tréfles	Madame E. Cayette
La Fée Bonheur	Madame E. Cayette
La Négresse Blonde	Au Perroquet Cie
La Petite Bretonne	Aux Trois Quartiers
La Superba	Max Oscar Arnold
La Vénus	Adrien Carvaillo
Lady	Horsman & Co.
Lady Bird Johnson	Alexander Doll Co.
Lady Churchill	Alexander Doll Co.

Doll Name	Company Name
Lady Elise Trousseau	Alexander Doll Co.
Lady Fitzherbert	Peggy Nesbit
Lady Hamilton	Alexander Doll Co.
Lady Hampshire	Plastic Molded Arts Co.
Lady In Red	Alexander Doll Co.
Lady In Waiting	Alexander Doll Co.
Lady Lee	Alexander Doll Co.
Lady MacBeth	Peggy Nesbit
Lady Mouse	Peggy Nesbit
Lady Ravencroft	Plastic Molded Arts Co.
Lady Visitor	Peggy Nesbit
Lady Windermere	Alexander Doll Co.
Laffy	Mattel, Inc.
Lambie Pie	Mattel, Inc.
Laos	Alexander Doll Co.
Large Baby Mickey	Effanbee
Latin American	Alexander Doll Co.
Latvia	Alexander Doll Co.
Laughing Allerga	Alexander Doll Co.
Laughing Boy	Amberg
Launa Locket	Mattel, Inc.
Laura Ingalls	Alexander Doll Co.
Laura Partridge	Remco
Laurie	Alexander Doll Co., Elektra Toy & Novelty Co.
Laverna Locket	Mattel, Inc.
Laverne from *Laverne and Shirley*	Mego
Lazy Bones	Ideal
Lazy Dazy	Ideal
Lazy Mary	Alexander Doll Co.
Le Fée au Gui	Madame E. Cayette
Legend of Frozen Time	Alexander Doll Co.
Leggy Jill	Hasbro, Inc.
LeGracieux	Aux Trois Quartiers
Lehowa	Lehowa
Lemons Stiddle	Mattel, Inc.
Lenny from *Laverne and Shirley*	Mego
Lenore Locket	Mattel, Inc.
Leopold	Käthe Kruse
Les Poupées de Mitou	Anne Marguerite Bruent
Leslie	Alexander Doll Co.
Leslie Uggums	Alexander Doll Co.
Letty Bridesmaid	Alexander Doll Co.
Li'l Soul	Shindana
Libby Littlechap	Remco
Liberace	Effanbee
Liberty	Alexander Doll Co.
Liberty Belle	Annin & Co.
Liberty Boy	Ideal
Liddle Biddle Peep	Mattel, Inc.
Liddle Middle	Mattel, Inc.
Liddle Middle Muffet	Mattel, Inc.
Lieb Edelkind	Hugo Wiegand
Liebling Lernt Laufer	Kämmer & Reinhardt
Lieselotte	Käthe Kruse
Liesel	Alexander Doll Co.
Life Like	American Specialty Doll Co., Averill Manufacturing Co.
Life Like Baby Doll	Averill Manufacturing Co.

DOLL NAME	COMPANY NAME
Life Like Line	American Stuffed Novelty Co.
Life Size Doll	Art Fabric Mills
Lifeguard	Peggy Nesbit
Lil Cuddly Dear	Vogue
Lil Darlin'	Effanbee
Lil Happy Fella	Horsman & Co.
Lil Imp	Vogue
Lil Lil	Jolly Toys
Lil Miss Fussy	Deluxe Reading/Topper Toy Group
Lil Sis	Toy Products
Lil Softer	Horsman & Co.
Lil Sweetie	Effanbee
Lila Bridesmaid	Alexander Doll Co.
Lilac Locket	Mattel, Inc.
Lil-Bet	Alexander Doll Co.
Liliput	Geyer, E. U. Steiner
Lilli	Käthe Kruse
Lilli, Bild Lilli of Germany	Lilli of Germany
Lilly	Armand Marseille
Lily Langtry	Peggy Nesbit
Limited Edition Models Collection (at least 48)	Peggy Nesbit
Linda	Ideal, Käthe Kruse, Jolly Toys
Linda Baby	Terry Lee
Linda Lee	Remco
Linda Williams	General Foods (General Foods also advertised this doll as a Natural Doll Co. doll.)
Lingerie Lou	Doll Bodies
Linon	Hermann Landshut, Isidor Eisenstaedt
Lion Tamer	Alexander Doll Co.
Lisa	Elise Israel
Lisa of the Barefoot Children	Mattel, Inc. for Annette Himstedt
Lisa Littlechap	Remco
Lisebill	Käthe Kruse
Lisel	Käthe Kruse
Lissy	Alexander Doll Co.
Lithoid	Nöckler & Tittel
Little Amby	Amberg
Little Angel	Arranbee
Little Annie Rooney	Borgfeldt, Cameo
Little Audrey	Alexander Doll Co.
Little Baby Dear	Vogue
Little Baby Marie	American Character
Little Betty	Alexander Doll Co., Horsman & Co.
Little Betty Blue	Nancy Ann StoryBook Dolls
Little Bitsey	Alexander Doll Co.
Little Bo Peep	Alexander Doll Co.; Amberg; Averill Manufacturing Co.; Horsman & Co.; Ideal; Nancy Ann StoryBook Dolls; Mattel, Inc.; Sol Bergfeld & Son
Little Boy Blue	Alexander Doll Co., Amberg, Averill Manufacturing Co., Brückner
Little Bright Eyes	Borgfeldt
Little Brother	Amberg, Averill Manufacturing Co.
Little Butch	Alexander Doll Co.
Little Cherub	Alexander Doll Co., Amberg, Averill Manufacturing Co.
Little Colonel	Alexander Doll Co.
Little Coquette	Uneeda Doll Co.
Little Debbi Eve	Super Doll Inc.

Little Debutante	Eegee Doll Manufacturing Co.
Little Dorrit	Alexander Doll Co.
Little Edwardian	Alexander Doll Co.
Little Emily	Alexander Doll Co., Horsman & Co.
Little Fairy	Amberg
Little Fellow	Amberg
Little Genius	Alexander Doll Co.
Little Godey	Alexander Doll Co.
Little Granny	Alexander Doll Co.
Little Gumdrop	Effanbee
Little House on the Prairie Child	Knickerbocker
Little Huggums	Alexander Doll Co.
Little Ice Queen	Alexander Doll Co.
Little Jack Horner	Alexander Doll Co.
Little Joan	Nancy Ann StoryBook Dolls
Little Joe Cartwright	American Character
Little John	Mego
Little Jumping Joan	Alexander Doll Co.
Little Kiddles	Mattel, Inc.
Little Lady	Alexander Doll Co., Effanbee
Little Lady Doll	Alexander Doll Co.
Little Lady Line	Effanbee
Little Linda	Lorrie
Little Lord Fauntleroy	Alexander Doll Co., Amberg
Little Lost Baby	Ideal
Little Love	American Character
Little Lulu	Averill Manufacturing Co.
Little Luv	Effanbee
Little Madaline	Alexander Doll Co.
Little Maid	Alexander Doll Co.
Little Mary Mix Up	Horsman & Co.
Little Melanie	Alexander Doll Co.
Little Men	Alexander Doll Co.
Little Minister	Alexander Doll Co.
Little Miss	Alexander Doll Co., Eegee Doll Manufacturing Co.
Little Miss America	Ideal
Little Miss Charming	Goldberger (Eegee Doll Manufacturing Co.)
Little Miss Donnet, She Wore a Big Bonnet	Nancy Ann StoryBook Dolls
Little Miss Echo	American Character
Little Miss Fashion	Deluxe Reading/Topper Toy Group
Little Miss Gadabout	Artisan Novelty Co.
Little Miss Ginger	Cosmopolitan Toy & Doll
Little Miss Ginny	Vogue
Little Miss Joanie	Plastic Molded Arts
Little Miss Marie	American Character
Little Miss Mischief	Ideal
Little Miss Muffet	Hollywood Doll Manufacturing Co., Nancy Ann StoryBook Dolls
Little Miss No Name	Hasbro, Inc.
Little Miss Revlon	Ideal
Little Miss Sweet Miss	Nancy Ann StoryBook Dolls
Little Nannie Etticoat	Alexander Doll Co.
Little Nell	Alexander Doll Co.
Little Nemo	Horsman & Co.
Little One	Hollywood Doll Manufacturing Co.
Little Orphan Annie and Sandy	Ralph A. Freundlich, Inc.
Little Orphan Annie Kiss N Hug Me	Remco

Little Polly Flinders	Nancy Ann StoryBook Dolls
Little Red Riding Hood	Alexander Doll Co., Amberg, Arnold Print Works, Brückner, Nancy Ann StoryBook Dolls, Sol Bergfeld & Son
Little Red Riding Hiddle	Mattel, Inc.
Little Rickey	American Character
Little Ricky	American Character
Little Shaver	Alexander Doll Co.
Little Sister	Averill Manufacturing Co., Borgfeldt, Horsman & Co., Ideal, Amberg
Little Snookums	Max Schellhorn
Little Sophisticates	Uneeda Doll Co.
Little Southern Boy	Alexander Doll Co.
Little Southern Girl	Alexander Doll Co.
Little Stranger	Amberg
Little Sunshine	Catterfelder Puppenfabrik, Demalcol
Little Susan	Eegee Doll Manufacturing Co.
Little Sweet Face	Berwick Doll Co.
Little Sweetheart	Amberg, Max Illfelder
Little Victoria	Alexander Doll Co.
Little Victorian	Alexander Doll Co.
Little Women	Alexander Doll Co.
Littlechaps	Remco
Littlest Angel	Alexander Doll Co.; Arranbee; Vogue
Littlest Kitten	Alexander Doll Co.
Lively Huggums	Alexander Doll Co.
Lively Kitten	Alexander Doll Co.
Lively Pussy Cat	Alexander Doll Co.
Lively Sugar Darlin'	Alexander Doll Co.
Living Baby Tenderlove	Mattel, Inc.
Living Barbie	Mattel, Inc.
Living Fluff	Mattel, Inc.
Living Skipper	Mattel, Inc.
Liz Locket	Mattel, Inc.
Liza	Camay
Lizzie	Horsman & Co.
Lola Bridesmaid	Alexander Doll Co.
Lola Liddle	Mattel, Inc.
Lola Locket	Mattel, Inc.
Lollapalooza	Ideal
Lolli Lemon	Mattel, Inc.
Lollie Baby	Alexander Doll Co.
Lollie Bridesmaid	Alexander Doll Co.
Lolly	Ideal
Lolly Pop Walking	Virga
Lona	Mattel, Inc. for Annette Himstedt
Lona Künstlerpuppe	A. Schmidt
Lone Wolf	Mattel, Inc.
Lonely Lisa	Royal Doll Co.
Lonely Liza	Royal Doll Co.
Long John Silver	Plastic Molded Arts, Mego
Loo Locket Kiddle	Mattel, Inc.
Looby Loo	Alexander Doll Co.
Look N' Say	Mattel, Inc.
Lopto	Thüringer Puppen und Spielwaren Export
Lord Fauntleroy	Alexander Doll Co.
Lord Nelson	Alexander Doll Co.
Lorelie Bracelet Kiddle	Mattel, Inc.

Loretta Locket	Mattel, Inc.
Lori	Swaine & Co.
Lori Ann	Nancy Ann StoryBook Dolls
Lori Martin	Ideal
Lorna Locket	Mattel, Inc.
Lorrie	Lorrie
Lotte	Cuno & Otto Dressel, Victor Steiner
Lotti	Heinrich Handwerck
Lou Hoover	Alexander Doll Co.
Lou Locket	Mattel, Inc.
Louis Amberg & Son's Walking Doll	Amberg
Louis Armstrong	Effanbee
Louisa	Alexander Doll Co., Horsman & Co.
Louisa Adams	Alexander Doll Co.
Louisa May Alcott	Alexander Doll Co.
Louise	Käthe Kruse, Lorrie
Lov You	Artisan Novelty Co.
Lovable Baby	Eegee Doll Manufacturing Co.
Lovable Lynn	Uneeda Doll Co.
Lovable Skin Doll	Eegee Doll Manufacturing Co.
Love Me	Alisto Manufacturing, Imco
Love Me Baby	Horsman & Co.
Love Me Doll	Horsman & Co.
Love Me Linda	Vogue
Love N Touch Real Sisters	Mattel, Inc.
Lovely Coos	Ideal
Lovey	Acme
Lovey Dove	Alexander Doll Co.
Lovey Dovey	Alexander Doll Co.
Lovums	Effanbee
Lovums Heartbeat Baby	Effanbee
Low Locket	Mattel, Inc.
Lt. Uhura	Mego
Lu	Käthe Kruse
Lu Ann Simms	Belle Dolls
Lucille	Martin Eichhorn
Lucille Ball	Effanbee
Lucinda	Alexander Doll Co.
Lucky Aviation Kid	American Character
Lucky Bill	Amberg
Lucky Lindy	Uneeda Doll Co.
Lucky Locket	Mattel, Inc.
Lucky Rastus	Averill Manufacturing Co.
Lucretia Garfield	Alexander Doll Co.
Lucy	Alexander Doll Co., Virga
Lucy Bride	Alexander Doll Co.
Lucy Hayes	Alexander Doll Co.
Lucy Locket	Alexander Doll Co., Nancy Ann StoryBook Dolls
Luke Skywalker	Kenner
Lullabye	Averill Manufacturing Co.
Lullabye Baby	Averill Manufacturing Co., Martin Eichhorn, Horsman & Co.
Luta	Luthardt
Lutt Martin	Käthe Kruse
Luv-able Skin	Eegee Doll Manufacturing Co.
Luv-able Skin Doll	Eegee Doll Manufacturing Co.
Lyf-Lyk	Averill Manufacturing Co.
Lyro	Franz Volpert, Rolfer & Co.

M O A	Max Oscar Arnold
M Ü K A	Müller & Kaltwasser
Maba Künstlerpuppe	Max Barnikol
Mabel	Armand Marseille, Butler Brothers
Mabel Lucie Attwell	Chad Valley
MacBeth	Peggy Nesbit
Machine Gun Mike	Deluxe Reading/Topper Toy Group
Madalaine De Baines	Alexander Doll Co.
Madalaine DuBain	Alexander Doll Co.
Madaline	Alexander Doll Co.
Madame	Alexander Doll Co.
Madame Butterfly	Active Beau Art Co., Max Handwerck
Madame Doll	Alexander Doll Co.
Madame Hendren	Averill Manufacturing Co.
Madame Pompadour	Alexander Doll Co.
Maddie Mod	Mego
Madelaine	Alexander Doll Co.
Madeline	Alexander Doll Co.
Mae Starr	Effanbee
Mae West	Effanbee
Mafuka	Otto Scheyer
Maggie	Alexander Doll Co.
Maggie Mix-up	Alexander Doll Co.
Maggie Mixup Angel	Alexander Doll Co.
Maggie Teenager	Alexander Doll Co.
Maggie Walker	Alexander Doll Co.
Maggie Walker Trousseau	Alexander Doll Co.
Magic Baby	Horsman & Co.
Magic Bottle Baby	Uneeda Doll Co.
Magic Fair Princess	Uneeda Doll Co.
Magic Lips	Ideal
Magic Skin Baby	Ideal
Magic Skin Doll	Ideal
Magic Squeezums	Ideal
Magnetic Dolls	Effanbee
Magnolia	Alexander Doll Co.
Mah-Jong Doll	Averill Manufacturing Co.
Maid Marion	Alexander Doll Co.
Maid Of Honor	Alexander Doll Co.
Maidservant	Peggy Nesbit
Majestic	Ernst Ulrich Steiner, Kämmer & Reinhardt, Kley & Hahn
Major Mason	Mattel, Inc.
Majorette	Alexander Doll Co.
Majorette	Effanbee
Mak-A-Doll	Madame Georgene Inc.
Make up Doll	Vogue
Makimura	Mattel, Inc. for Annette Himstedt
Malibu Barbie	Mattel, Inc.
Malibu Skipper	Mattel, Inc.
Malin	Mattel, Inc. for Annette Himstedt
Mama	Knickerbocker
Mama Doll	Averill Manufacturing Co.
Mama I'm Awake Baby	Amberg
Mama Kitten	Alexander Doll Co.
Mama Walton	Mego
Mamas Herzensschatz	Friedrichsrodaer Puppenfabrik
Mamie Eisenhower	Alexander Doll Co.

Doll Name	Company Name
Mammy	Alexander Doll Co., Kämmer & Reinhardt
Man From Laser	Mattel, Inc.
Manet	Alexander Doll Co.
Mannequin	Transogram Co.
Männe	Käthe Kruse
Mapleleaf Girl	Reliable
Maquette	Pulvermacher & Westram, Wilhelm Simon
Marcella Doll	Alexander Doll Co.
March Hatter	Alexander Doll Co.
Marcie Doll	A & H
Mardi Gras	American Character
Mareile	Käthe Kruse
Margaret O'Brien	Alexander Doll Co.
Margaret Thatcher	Peggy Nesbit
Margaretchen	Käthe Kruse
Margie	Cameo
Margie Make Up	American Character
Margot	Alexander Doll Co.
Margot Ballerina	Alexander Doll Co.
Margret	Armand Marseille, Cuno & Otto Dressel
Maria	Alexander Doll Co., Strasserpuppen Werkstätten
Mariana	Averill Manufacturing Co.
Mariann	England Rosebud Doll Co.
Marie	Kämmer & Reinhardt
Marie Ange, a Doll From France	Petitcollin
Marie Antoinette	Alexander Doll Co.
Marie Doll	Amberg
Marie Osmond	Mattel, Inc.
Mariko	Mattel, Inc.
Marilee	Effanbee
Marilyn	Acme
Marilyn	Acme Toy
Marina	Rotraut Schrott
Marine	Alexander Doll Co.
Mario Lanza	Alexander Doll Co.
Marion	Butler Brothers, Monica
Marjorie	Horsman & Co.
Mark Antony	Alexander Doll Co.
Mark Twain	Effanbee
Marlo Thomas	Alexander Doll Co.
Marm Liza	Alexander Doll Co.
Marme	Alexander Doll Co.
Marsha	Lorrie
Marshmellow Baby	American Character
Marta	Alexander Doll Co., Carl Hartmann
Martha Johnson Patterson	Alexander Doll Co.
Martha Randolph	Alexander Doll Co.
Martha Washington	Alexander Doll Co., Duchess Doll Corp.
Marvel	Butler Brothers, Kestner
Marvel Doll	Averill Manufacturing Co.
Marvel Mama Doll	Century Doll Co.
Mary	Peggy Nesbit
Mary and Her Garden	Sol Bergfeld & Son
Mary and Her Little Lamb	Sol Bergfeld & Son
Mary Ann	Alexander Doll Co., Borgfeldt, Effanbee
Mary Cassatt Baby	Alexander Doll Co.
Mary Ellen	Alexander Doll Co.

Doll Name	Company Name
Mary Ellen Playmate	Alexander Doll Co.
Mary Ellen Walton	Mego
Mary Gray	Alexander Doll Co.
Mary Had a Little Lamb	Averill Manufacturing Co., Nancy Ann StoryBook Dolls
Mary Hartline	Ideal
Mary Hoyer	Mary Hoyer Doll Manufacturing
Mary Jane	Aunt Mary, Borgfeldt, Effanbee
Mary Lee	Effanbee
Mary Louise	Alexander Doll Co.
Mary Lu	Doll Bodies
Mary Maiden	Cissna
Mary Make Up	American Character
Mary Martin	Alexander Doll Co.
Mary McElroy	Alexander Doll Co.
Mary McKee	Alexander Doll Co.
Mary Mine	Alexander Doll Co.
Mary Muslin	Alexander Doll Co.
Mary Poppins	Horsman & Co.
Mary Queen Of Scots	Alexander Doll Co., Peggy Nesbit
Mary Rose Bride	Alexander Doll Co.
Mary Sunshine	Alexander Doll Co.
Mary Todd Lincoln	Alexander Doll Co.
Mary, Mary	Alexander Doll Co.
Marybel	Alexander Doll Co.
MaryBel	Alexander Doll Co.
Masquerade	Hollywood Doll Manufacturing Co.
Master & His Frog	Arrow Rubber Co.
Master Bubbles	Madame Georgene Inc.
Master of House	Peggy Nesbit
Mastercraft Babies	Century Doll Co.
Matinee	Alexander Doll Co.
Matten	Käthe Kruse
Matthew	Ashton Drake
Mattie	Mattel, Inc.
Mattie Mattel, Inc.	Mattel, Inc.
Mausi	Robert Carl
Maver-Nik	Uneeda Doll Co.
Max	Käthe Kruse
Max & Moritz	Kämmer & Reinhardt, Kestner, Kilian Cramer, Kley & Hahn, Mathilde Sehm, Steiff, Theodor Recknagel
Maxi	Max Beuster
May	Duchess Doll Corp., Hollywood Doll Manufacturing Co.
May Blossom	Alfred Lange, Demalcol
Maya	Geschwister Heinrich
Maypole	Alexander Doll Co.
McGuffey Ana	Alexander Doll Co.
McKinley	Cuno & Otto Dressel
Me & My Shadow	Alexander Doll Co.
Meg	Alexander Doll Co.
Mein Augenstern	Paul Zierow
Mein Dicker Kleiner Liebling	Kämmer & Reinhardt
Mein Einziger	Kley & Hahn
Mein Glückskind	Adolf Wislizenus
Mein Goldherz	Bruno Schmidt
Mein Goldstern	Adolf Hülss, C. M. Bergmann
Mein Herz'l	Catterfelder Puppenfabrik
Mein Herzenskind	Wilhelm Buschow

Mein Kleiner Liebling	Kämmer & Reinhardt
Mein Kleiner Schlinger	Bauer & Richter Inc.
Mein Kleines	Kämmer & Reinhardt
Mein Liebes Kind	Alfred Heller
Mein Liebling	Kämmer & Reinhardt
Mein Lieblingsbaby	Kämmer & Reinhardt
Mein Nesthäckchen	Adolf Hülss
Mein Neuer Liebling	Kämmer & Reinhardt
Mein Rosiger Liebling	Kämmer & Reinhardt
Mein Sonnenschein	Catterfelder Puppenfabrik
Mein Stern	Henriette Dunker
Mein Stolz	Koenig & Wernicke
Mein Süsser Liebling	Kämmer & Reinhardt
Mein Süsser Schlingel	Rodaer Puppenfabrik Bauer
Mein Wunschkind	Arthur Schoenau
Mein Ziergold	Elisabeth Schwarz
Meine Einzige	Kley & Hahn
Meine Goldperle	Alfred Heller
Meine Goldsternchen	Bruno Schmidt
Melanie	Alexander Doll Co.
Melinda	Alexander Doll Co.
Melitta	Edmund Edelmann
Melodie	Effanbee
Melody Baby Debbi	Super Doll Inc.
Melvin	Mattel, Inc. for Annette Himstedt
Mendy	American Character
Merrie Marie	Art Fabric Mills
Merry Little Maid	Nancy Ann StoryBook Dolls
Merry Stroller	Eegee Doll Manufacturing Co.
Merry Widow	Max Illfelder
Mew Puss	J. Heinrich Kletzin & Co.
Mexican Boy and Girl	Tipica Munica Mexicana
Mexican Lady	Ideal
Mexico	Alexander Doll Co.
Mi Encanto	Seligmann & Mayer
Mi-Baby	Averill Manufacturing Co.
Mia	M. Hecht, Ideal
Miblu	Kämmer & Reinhardt, Koenig & Wernicke, Rheinische Gummi und Celluloid Fabrik
Mibs	Amberg
Michael	Alexander Doll Co., Horsman & Co.
Michael, by Yolanda Bello	Ashton Drake
Michel	A. Michaelis, Käthe Kruse
Michell	Clodrey
Michiko	Mattel, Inc. for Annette Himstedt
Michu	Fleischmann & Bloedel
Mickey	Effanbee, Mego
Mickey Baby	Effanbee
Middy Boy	Amberg
Middy Girl	Amberg
Midge	Mattel, Inc.
Midnight	Alexander Doll Co.
Midolly	New Toy Manufacturing
Miffy	Peggy Nesbit
Mighty Thor	Mego
Mignon	Félix Arena
Mignonne	Borgfeldt

Doll Name	Company Name
Mike	Deluxe Reading/Topper Toy Group
Mike and Lizzie	Horsman & Co.
Mildred	Amberg
Mildred Mine	Amberg
Miles	Cuno & Otto Dressel
Mill Debteen	Uneeda Doll Co.
Milli Middle	Mattel, Inc.
Milly	Alexander Doll Co.
Mime of the Mariko Collection	Mattel, Inc.
Mimerle	Käthe Kruse
Mimi	Alexander Doll Co.; Alt, Beck & Gottschalck; Borgfeldt; Käthe Kruse
Mimosa	Mimosa
Mimsy	American Character
Mindy	Mattel, Inc.
Mine	Edmund Edelmann
Minka	Käthe Kruse
Minnehaha	Amberg
Minnie Spinach	Borgfeldt
Minnie The Parlor Maid	Peggy Nesbit
Minute Man	Peggy Nesbit
Minute Man's Wife	Peggy Nesbit
Minerva	Buschow & Beck
Mirror Maid	Jeanette Doll Co.
Miss 1953	Plastic Molded Arts Co.
Miss America	Alexander Doll Co., Plastic Molded Arts Co.
Miss America Doll	Sayco Doll Corp.
Miss American Pageant Doll	Sayco Doll Corp.
Miss Anniversary	Natural Doll Co.
Miss B	Belle Doll Corp.
Miss Barbie	Mattel, Inc.
Miss Bonnie	Allied Grand Doll Manufacturing
Miss Brittany France	Virga
Miss Broadway	Amberg
Miss Campbell	Horsman & Co.
Miss Charming	Eegee Doll Manufacturing Co.
Miss Chickadee	American Character
Miss Chips	Effanbee
Miss Chips Bride	Effanbee
Miss Clairol	Ideal
Miss Clairol Glamour Miss	Ideal
Miss Curity	Ideal
Miss Deb	Ideal
Miss Debutante	Uneeda Doll Co.
Miss Ducky Deluxe	Uneeda Doll Co.
Miss Elisabeth	Zum Puppenheim
Miss Fashion	American Character
Miss Flaked Rice (advertising cloth doll)	Am Rice Food Mfg. Co.
Miss Flexie	Eegee Doll Manufacturing Co.
Miss Flora McFlimsey	Alexander Doll Co.
Miss Francie	Admiration Toy Co., Inc.
Miss From Holland	Berwick Doll Co.
Miss Ginny	Vogue
Miss Glamour Girl	Effanbee
Miss Hollywood	Duchess Doll Corp.
Miss Ideal	Ideal
Miss Janet	Horsman & Co.

Miss Joan	Plastic Molded Arts
Miss Judy Grand Tour	Alexander Doll Co.
Miss Leigh	Alexander Doll Co.
Miss Malto-Rice (advertising cloth doll)	Am Rice Food Mfg. Co.
Miss Marie	American Character
Miss Merry Heart	Lauer
Miss Millionaire	Butler Brothers
Miss Mischief	Horsman & Co.
Miss Modern	Uneeda Doll Co.
Miss Muffet	Alexander Doll Co.
Miss Najo	National Joint Limb Doll Co.
Miss Nancy Ann	Nancy Ann StoryBook Dolls
Miss North American	Duchess Doll Corp.
Miss Peep	Cameo
Miss Priscilla	Horsman & Co.
Miss Priscilla Alden	Plastic Molded Arts Co.
Miss Revlon	Ideal
Miss Royal	Zum Puppenheim
Miss Seventeen, a Beauty Queen	Marx
Miss Simplicity	Amberg
Miss Smith	Norah Wellings
Miss Sweet	Kay Sam Corp.
Miss Tastee Freez-America's Sweetheart	Duchess Doll Corp.
Miss Toddler	Marx
Miss Twist	Uneeda Doll Co.
Miss U. S. A.	Alexander Doll Co., Averill Manufacturing Co.
Miss Valentine	Peggy Huffman Originals
Miss Valentine Lady	Plastic Molded Arts Co.
Miss Valentine of 1951	Duchess Doll Corp.
Miss Vermont	Alexander Doll Co.
Miss Victory	Alexander Doll Co.
Misska	Art Toy Manufacturing
Mistress Bubbles	Madame Georgene Inc.
Mistress Mary	Nancy Ann StoryBook Dolls
Mistress of House	Peggy Nesbit
Misty	Ideal
Mit dem Goldreif	Ilse Müller
Mitzi	Ideal
Mlle. Babette	Katherine Rauser
Mobi	Hermann Schiemer
Modern Teen	Molly-'es
Moko	M. Kohnstamm & Co.
Molly	Alexander Doll Co., Molly Goldberg
Molly Cottontail	Alexander Doll Co.
Molly McIntire	Pleasant Co.
Molly Pitcher	A & H
Mom	Ideal
Mombo	Alexander Doll Co.
Mommie & Me	Alexander Doll Co.
Mommie's Pet	Alexander Doll Co.
Mommy's Baby	Effanbee
Mommy's Baby	Sayco Doll Corp.
Mommy's Darling	Horsman & Co.
Mommy's Pet	Alexander Doll Co.
Mommy's Baby	Effanbee
Mon Petit Coeur	Bruno Schmidt
Mon Trésor	Henri Rostal

Mona	Edmund Edelmann
Mona Lisa	Gutmann & Schniffnie
Monday's Child is Fair of Face	Nancy Ann StoryBook Dolls
Monet	Alexander Doll Co.
Monica	Monica Studios
Monkey Man	Atlantic Playthings Co.
Monte-Carlo-Genre	Galluba & Hofmann
Monty	J. Süsskind
Moonbeams	American Character
Moonmaid	Uneeda Doll Co.
Morisot	Alexander Doll Co.
Moritz	Käthe Kruse
Mork	Mattel, Inc.
Morocco	Alexander Doll Co.
Mortimer Snerd	Ideal
Mosca	Max Mocsardini & Co.
Most Happy Family	Effanbee
Mother	Effanbee
Mother & Me	Alexander Doll Co.
Mother Goose	Alexander Doll Co., Averill Manufacturing Co., Nancy Ann StoryBook Dolls
Mother Hubbard	Alexander Doll Co.
Mother of the Bride	Allied Grand Doll Manufacturing
Mousketeer	Walt Disney Productions
Mousmé	Jean Carles
Mr. "Scottie" Scott	Mego
Mr. Ed	Mattel, Inc.
Mr. Fantastic	Mego
Mr. Kotter	Mattel, Inc.
Mr. Mxyzptlk	Mego
Mr. Pogle	Peggy Nesbit
Mr. Spock	Mego
Mrs. Beasley	Mattel, Inc.
Mrs. Buck Rabbit	Alexander Doll Co.
Mrs. March Hare	Alexander Doll Co.
Mrs. Pogle	Peggy Nesbit
Mrs. Quack-a-field	Alexander Doll Co.
Mrs. Snoopie	Alexander Doll Co.
Mrs. Tiggywinkle	Peggy Nesbit
Ms. Giddie Yup	Mattel, Inc.
Ms. Heavenly Hippo	Mattel, Inc.
Muche	Käthe Kruse
Muff Doll	Stuart
Muffie	Nancy Ann StoryBook Dolls
Muffin	Alexander Doll Co.
Muing	Goebel
Muk	Elise Israel
Multi Face Doll	Knickerbocker
Mummy	Mego
Muncy Kid	Mermaid Doll and Toy Co.
Muschi	Martha Lehmann
Music of the Mariko Collection	Mattel, Inc.
Musical Baby	Eegee Doll Manufacturing Co.
Musical Girl	Effanbee Doll Co.
Mutzipuppe	Kirchoff
My Angel	Arranbee
My Annemarie	Wilhelm Follender

My Baby	Horsman & Co., Lorrie
My Best Friend	Amberg
My Cherub	Arthur Schoenau
My Companion	Armand Marseille, Louis Wolf & Co.
My Darling	Kämmer & Reinhardt
My Dearie	Borgfeldt, Otto Gans, Schindel & Kallenberg
My Dream Baby	Armand Marseille, Arranbee
My Fair Baby	Effanbee
My Fair Lady	Alexander Doll Co., Eegee Doll Manufacturing Co.
My Fair Lady	Eegee Doll Manufacturing Co.
My Fairy	Seyfarth & Reinhardt
My Friend	Arrow Rubber Co.
My Girlie	Borgfeldt
My Honey	Edward Römhild
My Honey Doll	Nordicus Colonda Werke
My Little Darling	Hermann Kröning
My Pearl	Hermann Steiner
My Pet	Buschow & Beck
My Playmate	Armand Marseille, Borgfeldt, Koenig & Wernicke
My Playmates	Borgfeldt
My Precious Baby	Effanbee
My Queen Doll	Ohlhaver
My Ruthie	Horsman & Co.
My Sweetheart	Adolf Wislizenus, Illfelder & Co.
Mystére	Belleville & Cie
Mysterious Yokum	Ideal
Naiad	Lauer
Nan McDare	Alexander Doll Co.
Nana Governess	Alexander Doll Co.
Nancy	Arranbee, Averill Manufacturing Co., Ideal
Nancy Ann	Alexander Doll Co., Nancy Ann StoryBook Dolls
Nancy Dawson	Alexander Doll Co.
Nancy Drew	Alexander Doll Co.
Nancy Jean	Alexander Doll Co.
Nancy Lee	Arranbee, Horsman & Co.
Nancy Nurse	Deluxe Reading/Topper Toy Group
Nanette	Alexander Doll Co., Arranbee, Kohnstamm & Co.
Napoleon	Alexander Doll Co.
Nat	Alexander Doll Co.
Natasha	Alexander Doll Co.
National Range Collection (at least 90)	Peggy Nesbit
Natura	P. Hunaeus
Nature Children	Amberg
Naughty	Kämmer & Reinhardt
Naughty Marietta	Ideal
Naughty Sue Whatsit Doll	Horsman & Co.
Nedda Toddles	Uneeda Doll Co.
Needa Toddles	Uneeda Doll Co.
Nellie	Käthe Kruse
Nellie Bird, Nellie Bird	Nancy Ann StoryBook Dolls
Nelly	Plated Moulds Inc.
Neprunain	Mego
Nesthäkchen	Adolf Hülss
Netherland Boy	Alexander Doll Co.
Netherland Girl	Alexander Doll Co.
Neutrality Jim	Averill Manufacturing Co.
New Baby	Plated Moulds Inc.

New Baby Dear	Vogue
New Baby Trix	Uneeda Doll Co.
New Barbie	Mattel, Inc.
New Betsy McCall	Uneeda Doll Co.
New Born	Amberg
New Born Babe	Amber
New Born Baby	American Character
New Born Miss Peep	Cameo
New Born Yummy	Uneeda Doll Co.
New Chatty Cathy	Mattel, Inc.
New Dy Dee	Effanbee
New England Girl	Mattel, Inc.
New Gerber Baby	Uneeda Doll Co.
New Happytime Baby	Sayco Doll Corp.
New Happytot	Arranbee
New Sweet Sue	American Character
New Tiny Tears	American Character
New Tressy	American Character
New Tressy Fashion Doll	American Character
Newborn Baby Tenderlove	Mattel, Inc.
Newborn Thumbelina	Ideal
Newly Wed Kids	Art Fabric Mills
Nibsie	Amberg
Nicole	Alexander Doll Co.
Niddy Impekoven	Selma von Hasberg
Nifty	Borgfeldt
Nikki	Jolly Toys
Nina Ballerina	Alexander Doll Co.
Ninetta	Fortune Doll Co.
Nini Kaspa	Julius Barnhold
Nisbet Victorian Birthday Dolls	Peggy Nesbit
Nobbikid	Armand Marseille, Borgfeldt
Nobrake	Schmidt & Goerke, Vereinigte Spielwarenfabriken
Nollipolli	Kämmer & Reinhardt
Nora	Nora Puppenfabrik
Norah Sue	Norah Wellings
Noris	Carl Debes & Son
Nöris	Bayerische Celluloidwarenfabrik
Norma	Porzellanfabrik Limbach
Norma Talker	Effanbee
Normandy	Alexander Doll Co.
Norway	Alexander Doll Co.
Norwegian	Alexander Doll Co.
Nosy Rosy	Jean L. Friedman
Nuborn	Louis Amberg & Son
Nun	Plastic Molded Arts Co.
Nun Doll	D & D Manufacturing
Nun Nurse	Midwestern Manufacture
Nurse	Alexander Doll Co.
Nurse & Baby	Alexander Doll Co.
Nurse Jane	Averill Manufacturing Co.
Nurse Jane, G. I.	Hasbro, Inc.
Nurse Ruth	Horsman & Co.
Nurse Troll	Scanda House
Nursing Bottle Baby	Arranbee
Oberon	Peggy Nesbit
Obi Wan Kenobi	Kenner

Doll Name	Company Name
Oco	Offenbach & Co.
Off On Shopping Spree	Alexander Doll Co.
Off To School	Alexander Doll Co.
Oga	Otto Gans
Oh My	My Toy Co.
Old Fashioned Girl	Alexander Doll Co.
Old Glory	Adolf Wislizenus
Old Mother Hubbard	Nancy Ann StoryBook Dolls
Old Mrs. Rabbit	Peggy Nesbit
Olga	Käthe Kruse
Olive	Ideal
Oliver Hardy	Peggy Nesbit
Oliver Twist	Alexander Doll Co., Amberg, Horsman & Co.
Olivia	Mattel, Inc.
Olympia	unidentified
One-Two, Button My Shoe	Nancy Ann StoryBook Dolls
Oo-Gug-Luc	Amberg
Open Mouth Baby Dear	Vogue
Opening Night	Alexander Doll Co.
Ophelia	Peggy Nesbit
Orange Ice Cone Kiddle	Mattel, Inc.
Orchard Princess	Alexander Doll Co.
Orm	Mego
Ormond	D. H. Wagner & Son
Orphan Annie	Alexander Doll Co.
Orsini	Alt, Beck & Gottschalck
Oskar	Käthe Kruse
Otto	Käthe Kruse
Our Adele	Cissna
Our Baby	Horsman & Co., Louis Wolf & Co.
Our Beauty	Cissna
Our Bell	Cissna
Our Cadet	Cissna
Our Crescent	Cissna
Our Fairy	Louis Wolf & Co.
Our Favorite	Cissna
Our Halma	Cissna
Our Lindy	Regal Doll Co.
Our Little Girl	Ideal
Our Pet	Armand Marseille, Eckardt
Our Soldier Boys	Arnold Print Works
Our Solitaire	Cissna
Our Steinway	Cissna
Over the Hills to Grandma's House	Nancy Ann StoryBook Dolls
P I G O	Thüringer Puppenindustrie
Pa Walton	Mego
Paddy Potato	Borgfeldt
Pajama Bag Talker	Mattel, Inc.
Paladin Babies	Carl Hartmann, Kämmer & Reinhardt
Palmer Cox Brownies	Arnold Print Works
Pam	Cosmopolitan Toy & Doll, Eugene Dolls, Fortune Doll Co.
Pam Ballerina	Fortune Doll Co.
PAMA Stimmen	G. Herold
Pamela	Ava Milano Art Doll
Pan American	Alexander Doll Co.
Panama	Alexander Doll Co.
Panchita	Mattel, Inc. for Annette Himstedt

Doll Name	Company Name
Pancho	Mattel, Inc. for Annette Himstedt
Pansy	Borgfeldt
Panta	Kämmer & Reinhardt
Papa-Mama Doll	Amberg
Papoose	Averill Manufacturing Co.
Papp Head	Simon Junghans
Paris Bébé	Aux Trois Quartiers
Parisian Precision	Alexander Doll Co.
Parisienne Belle	American Specialty Doll Co.
Parker Stevenson	Kenner
Parlour Maid	Alexander Doll Co.
Parsley	Peggy Nesbit
Party Time	Deluxe Reading/Topper Toy Group
Pastel Miss	Lorrie
Pat a cake	Luge & Co.
Pat O Pat	Effanbee
Patchity Pam & Pepper	Alexander Doll Co.
Patent Head	Fritz Vogel
Patent Lederbebe	Wagner & Zetsche (assumed)
Patentmasse	Kämmer & Reinhardt, L.R. Hörchner & Co.
Patootie	Mattel, Inc.
Patricia	Effanbee
Patricia as Ann Shirley	Effanbee
Patricia Walker	Effanbee Doll Co.
Patriotic Boy and Girl	Elektra Toy and Novelty
Patsy	Effanbee
Patsy Ann	Effanbee
Patsy Ann with Molded Hair	Effanbee
Patsy Baby	Effanbee
Patsy Babyette	Effanbee
Patsy Joan	Effanbee
Patsy Jr.	Effanbee
Patsy Lou	Effanbee
Patsy Mae	Effanbee
Patsy Ruth	Effanbee
Patsyette	Effanbee
Patsyette Hawaiian Twins	Effanbee
Patsykins	Effanbee
Patti	Ideal
Patti Playpal	Ideal
Pattie Duke	Horsman & Co.
Pattie Pattie	Averill Manufacturing Co.
Pattie Prays	Ideal
Patty	Alexander Doll Co.
Patty Duck	Ideal
Patty Jo	Terry Lee
Patty Kix	Uneeda Doll Co.
Patty Pigtails	Alexander Doll Co.
Patty Playful	Ideal
Patty Ruth	Arranbee Doll Co.
Patty-Cake	Amberg
Paul from Kiss	Mego
Paul and Virginia	Tip Top Toy Co.
Paula	Mattel, Inc. for Annette Himstedt
Paula Mae	Deluxe Reading/Topper Toy Group
Paula Marie	Deluxe Reading/Topper Toy Group
Paulette	Alexander Doll Co.
Pauline	Borgfeldt, Butler Brothers, Käthe Kruse

153

Peace	Hasbro, Inc.
Peaches	Effanbee
Peachy	Arranbee
Peachy and Her Puppets	Mattel, Inc.
Peanut	Cameo
Pearly Queen	Peggy Nesbit
Peasant	Alexander Doll Co.
Pebbles	Ideal
Pee Wee	Uneeda Doll Co.
Peek A Boo Toodles	American Character
Peek-A-Boo	Acme
Peg O'My Heart	Amberg
Peggy	Averill Manufacturing Co., Horsman & Co.
Peggy Ann	Averill Manufacturing Co., Horsman & Co.
Peggy Bride	Alexander Doll Co.
Peggy Pen Pal	Horsman & Co.
Peha	P. Hunaeus
Pehaco	Hermann Pensky
Penelope Little Sophisticate	Uneeda Doll Co.
Penguin	Mego
Penny	Alexander Doll Co., American Character, Ideal
Penny Brite	Deluxe Reading/Topper Toy Group
Penny Playpal	Ideal
Penny the Fashion Doll	Laurel Dolls
Penny Walker	Togs and Dolls
Pepi	Käthe Kruse
Pepita Queen of the Beech	Hilda Loose
Pepita Queen of the Ice	Hilda Loose
Pepper	Ideal
Perfect Beauty	American Character
Perfect Patient	Valentine Dolls
Perfectolid	Arthur Schoenau
Perky	Molly-'es, M. G. M.
Perky Bright	Blumberg
Perky Joan Trousseau	Alexander Doll Co.
Perlico Perlaco	Fleischmann & Bloedel
Persia	Alexander Doll Co.
Personality Pla-mate	Eugenia
Personality Playmate	Eugenia
Pert Pierrette	Princess Ann Dolls
Perthy	Horsman & Co.
Peruvian Boy	Alexander Doll Co.
PESO	Paul Schmidt
Pet Mane	Butler Brothers
Pete	Ideal
Pete & Repete	Ideal
Peter	Kämmer & Reinhardt, Käthe Kruse
Peter Burke	Mego
Peter from Kiss	Mego
Peter Pan	Alexander Doll Co., Amberg, Duchess Doll Corp., Ideal, Peggy Nesbit
Peter Pan Playtoys	Schellhorn
Peter Pandiddle	Mattel, Inc.
Peter Playpal	Ideal
Peter Ponsett	Dewees Cochran
Peter Rabbit	Peggy Nesbit
Peterkins	Horsman & Co.

Doll Name	Company Name
Petite	American Character
Petite W. A. V. E.	American Character
Petsy Pliddle	Mattel, Inc.
Pfiffikus	Franz Kiesewetter, Koenig & Wernicke
Pharaoh	Averill Manufacturing Co.
Phenix Bébé	Henri Alexandre, Jules Steiner
Philippines	Alexander Doll Co.
Phoenix	Harburger Gummiwaren Fabrik
Phyllis	Baby Phyllis Doll Co.
Phyllis The Musical Doll	Bouton Woolf Co.
Phyllis Doll	Schmidt & Nüchter
Phyllis May Doll	Amberg
Pickaninny	Arnold Print Works
Picnic Day	Alexander Doll Co.
Picture Girl	Vogue
Piddles	Uneeda Doll Co.
Pierre	Alexander Doll Co.
Pierrette	American Stuffed Novelty Co.
Pierrot	American Stuffed Novelty Co.
Pierrot Clown	Alexander Doll Co.
Piglet	Peggy Nesbit
Pilgrim	Alexander Doll Co.
Pilgrim John Alden	Vogue
Pillow Baby	Uneeda Doll Co.
Pimbo	Effanbee
Pin Up Girl	Ideal
Pinafore Doll	Ideal
Piney Niddle	Mattel, Inc.
Pinkie	Alexander Doll Co.
Pinky	Alexander Doll Co.
Pinocchio	Crown, Ideal
Pioneer	Carl Hartmann
Pioneer Daughter	Mattel, Inc.
Pioneering American Spirit	Effanbee
Pip	Alexander Doll Co.
Pipa	Wagner & Son
Piper	Peggy Nesbit
Piper Laurie	Alexander Doll Co.
Pippin	Peggy Nesbit
Pirate	American Character
Pirola	Wagner & Son
Pirouette	Wagner & Son
Pitter Patty	Horsman & Co.
Pitti Bum	Bing Art Dolls
Pitti-Sing	Arnold Print Works
Pitty Pat	Alexander Doll Co.
Pix I Posie	Eegee Doll Manufacturing Co.
Pixie	Ideal
Pixie Haircut Baby	Uneeda Doll Co.
Pizazz	Hasbro, Inc.
Plassie	Ideal
Plassie	Ideal
Play N Jane	Ideal
Playful	Arrow Plastics
Playmate	Alexander Doll Co., Emil Bauersachs
Playpen Doll	Jolly Toys
Plaything Toys	Atlantic Playthings Co.

Doll Name	Company Name
Plombe in der Hand	Rudolf Säuberlich
Plum	Cameo
Plum Pees	Uneeda Doll Co.
Plush Baby	Elka Toy
Pluto	Gund Manufacturing
Plymouth Colony	Effanbee
Pocahontas	Alexander Doll Co., Horsman & Co.
Pokey	Uneeda Doll Co.
Pola Puppen	Thüringer Puppenindustrie
Polait	Polack
Police Woman	Horsman & Co.
Policeman	Peggy Nesbit
Polichinelle	Aux Trois Quartiers
Polish	Alexander Doll Co.
Polish Girl	Plastic Molded Arts Co., Princess Ann Dolls
Politik-Nik	Uneeda Doll Co.
Polka Dottie	Effanbee
Pollera	Alexander Doll Co.
Polly	Alexander Doll Co., Averill Manufacturing Co.
Polly Anna	American Bisque Dolls
Polly Flinders	Alexander Doll Co.
Polly On Tour	Alexander Doll Co.
Polly Pigtails	Alexander Doll Co.
Polly Pond's	Citro
Polly Prue	Horsman & Co.
Polly Put Kettle On	Alexander Doll Co.
Polly Put The Kettle On	Nancy Ann StoryBook Dolls
Pollyanna	Alexander Doll Co., Amberg, Uneeda Doll Co.
Ponch of *C.H.I.P.S.*	Mego
Poodle	Alexander Doll Co.
Poodle-oodle	Hasbro, Inc.
Poodles	Alexander Doll Co.
Pooksie	Wiltshaw & Robinson
Poor Cinderella	Alexander Doll Co.
Poor Pitiful Pearl	Brookglad, Horsman & Co.
Pooty Tat	Horsman & Co.
Pope John XXIII	Peggy Nesbit
Popeye Puppet	King Features
Popi	American Character
Popo	Sun Rubber
Poppa-Momma	Ideal
Poppin Fresh	Pillsbury
Poppy	Alexander Doll Co.
Poppy Dolls	Cuno & Otto Dressel
Porky	Mego
Portrait	Alexander Doll Co.
Portrait Character Range Collection (at least 167)	Peggy Nesbit
Portrait Doll	Effanbee
Portrait Series	Effanbee
Portugal	Alexander Doll Co.
Porzellanit	Kämmer & Reinhardt
Posable Baby Trix	Uneeda Doll Co.
Posey Elfy	Uneeda Doll Co.
Posey Pat	Alexander Doll Co.
Posey Pet	Alexander Doll Co.
Posi Playmate	Eegee Doll Manufacturing Co.

Posie . . . . Ideal
Posie Pixie . . . . Vogue
Posie the Walking Doll of a
   Hundred Life Like Poses . . . . Ideal
Posing Flopsie . . . . Horsman & Co.
Pos'n Pepper . . . . Ideal
Pos'n Salty . . . . Ideal
Pos'n Tammy . . . . Ideal
Potsdamer Soldaten . . . . Käthe Kruse
Potsy from *Happy Days* . . . . Mego
Poupard Art . . . . Henri Bellet
Poupée Toddler . . . . Bella France Orenete
Poupées Salon . . . . Lenci
Pouting Tots . . . . Amberg
Pouty . . . . Arrow Plastics
Powerful Katrinka . . . . Borgfeldt
Pram Baby . . . . Horsman & Co.
Pre Teen Tressy . . . . American Character
Precious . . . . Alexander Doll Co., Famous Plaything, Ideal
Precious New Born . . . . Effanbee
Precision . . . . Alexander Doll Co.
Preparedness Kids . . . . Averill Manufacturing Co.
Presidents' Ladies . . . . Alexander Doll Co.
Presidents' Wives . . . . Alexander Doll Co.
Preteen Grow Hair . . . . American Character
Pretty As a Picture . . . . Nancy Ann StoryBook Dolls
Pretty Baby . . . . American Character, Eegee Doll Manufacturing Co.,
   Horsman & Co.
Pretty Boy . . . . Deluxe Reading/Topper Toy Group
Pretty Girl . . . . Jolly Toys

Molly-'es Raggedy Ann Baby

Doll Name	Company Name
Pretty Kitty	Hollywood Doll Manufacturing Co.
Pretty Lady	Arrow Plastics
Pretty Maid Where Have You Been	Nancy Ann StoryBook Dolls
Pretty Penny	American Character
Pretty Polly	Seamless Toy Corp.
Pretty Portrait	Uneeda Doll Co.
Pride of The South	Effanbee
Primadonna	Giebeler-Faulk
Primitive Indian	Effanbee
Primrose	Waltershäuser Puppenfabrik
Primula	Thüringer Puppen & Spielwaren Export
Prince Charles	Alexander Doll Co.
Prince Charming	Alexander Doll Co.; Effanbee; Hasbro, Inc.
Prince Charming for Honey	Effanbee
Prince Phillip	Alexander Doll Co.
Prince Souci	Nancy Ann StoryBook Dolls
Princes Miñon Minette	Nancy Ann StoryBook Dolls
Princess	American Unbreakable Doll Corp., Armand Marseille, Borgfeldt, Horsman & Co., Kley & Hahn, Uneeda Doll Co.
Princess Alexandria	Alexander Doll Co.
Princess Angeline	Averill Manufacturing Co.
Princess Ann	Alexander Doll Co., Princess Ann Dolls
Princess Betty Rose	Arranbee
Princess Bride	Uneeda Doll Co.
Princess Doll	Alexander Doll Co., Uneeda Doll Co.
Princess Elizabeth	Alexander Doll Co., Arthur Schoenau, Christian Hopf
Princess Elizabeth Trousseau	Alexander Doll Co.
Princess Flavia	Alexander Doll Co.
Princess Leia	Kenner
Princess Margaret Rose	Alexander Doll Co.
Princess Mary	Ideal
Princess Mary Line	Ideal
Princess Peggy	Horsman & Co.
Princess Pig	Mattel, Inc.
Princess Rosanie	Nancy Ann StoryBook Dolls
Princess Rosetta	Alexander Doll Co.
Princess Sonja	Ideal
Prinzess Bett	Kohnstamm & Co.
Prinzess Sibylla	Hermann Eckstein
Prinzess Wunderhold	Arthur Schoenau
Priscilla	A & H, Alexander Doll Co., American Toy & Novelty Co., Cissna
Pri-thilla	Uneeda Doll Co.
Private Ida	Deluxe Reading/Topper Toy Group
Prize Baby	Averill Manufacturing Co., Borgfeldt
Prom Queen	Arranbee
Pryangtisvasti	Peggy Huffman Originals
Puck	Florig & Otto
Puddin'	Alexander Doll Co., Mattel, Inc.
Pudgie	Amberg
Puggy	American Character
Pugie	Horsman & Co.
Pumkin	Effanbee
Pumpernella	Käthe Kruse
Pumpkin	Alexander Doll Co., Kay Sam Corp.
Punch (and Judy)	Art Fabric Mills
Puppe der Zukunft	Süssenguth

DOLL NAME	COMPANY NAME
Puppet	Alexander Doll Co.
Puppetrina	Eegee Doll Manufacturing Co.
Puppy Pippin	Horsman & Co.
Purdy	Uneeda Doll Co.
Purina Scarecrow	Ralston Purina Co.
Puspi	Wordtmann
Pussy Cat	Alexander Doll Co.
Puzzy	Cohen
Quaker Maid	Nancy Ann StoryBook Dolls
Quality Bilt	Century Doll Co.
Queen	Alexander Doll Co.
Queen Ann	Peggy Nesbit
Queen Cissette Travel Tour	Alexander Doll Co.
Queen Elizabeth	Alexander Doll Co., Peggy Nesbit
Queen For A Day	Hollywood Doll Manufacturing Co.
Queen Isabella of Spain	Peggy Huffman Originals
Queen Louise	Armand Marseille
Queen Mother	Alexander Doll Co.
Queen of Hearts	Nancy Ann StoryBook Dolls
Queen Quality	Adolf Wislizenus
Quintette of Baby Dolls	American Ocarina and Toy Co.
Quints	Alexander Doll Co.
Quintuplets	Alexander Doll Co.
Quiz-kins	Alexander Doll Co.
R2D2	Kenner
Racker	Gans & Seyfarth
Rag	Borgfeldt
Rag Shoppe Dolls	Severn & Long
Raggedy Ann and Andy	Gruelle Family; Volland; Exposition Dolls; Molly-'es; Georgene Novelty; Knickerbocker; Hasbro, Inc./Playskool; Applause
Rags to Riches Doll	Juro Novelty
Ragsy	Cameo
Rain Rain Go Away	Nancy Ann StoryBook Dolls
Rainbow Dolls	Amberg
Ralph	Käthe Kruse
Randy	Mattel, Inc.; De Soto
Randy Reader	Mattel, Inc.
Randy The Teen Age Girl Doll	Fab-Lu Limited
Rapunzel	Alexander Doll Co.
Raving Beauty	Artisan Novelty Co.
Rebecca	Alexander Doll Co.
Red Boy	Alexander Doll Co.
Red Cross Nurse	Alexander Doll Co.
Red Riding Hood	Alexander Doll Co., Hollywood Doll Manufacturing Co., Horsman & Co., Princess Ann Dolls
Red Riding Hood Set	Ralph A. Freundlich, Inc.
Redcoat	Peggy Nesbit
Reflections	Alexander Doll Co.
Reflextions of Youth	Mattel, Inc. for Annette Himstedt
Reformpuppe	George Becker
Reg'lar Fellars	Borgfeldt
Regal Sleepers	Amberg
Regina Lady in Waiting	Nancy Ann StoryBook Dolls
Renoir	Alexander Doll Co.
Renoir Child	Alexander Doll Co.
Renoir Girl	Alexander Doll Co.
Renoir Girl with Watering Can	Alexander Doll Co.

Renoir Mother . . . . Alexander Doll Co.
Reso . . . . Schilling & Zitzmann
Revalo . . . . Carl Harmus, Ernst Heubach, Ohlhaver
Revlon Miss . . . . Ideal
Rhett . . . . Alexander Doll Co.
Richie from *Happy Days* . . . . Mego
Rickey . . . . Mattel, Inc.
Rickey Jr. . . . . American Character
Ricky . . . . Mattel, Inc.
Ricky Jr. . . . . American Character
Ridding Habit . . . . Alexander Doll Co.
Riddler . . . . Mego
Riley's Little Annie . . . . Alexander Doll Co.
Rinaldo . . . . Berthold Helk
Ring Around a Rosy, Pocket Full a Posy . . . . Nancy Ann StoryBook Dolls
Ringbearer . . . . Alexander Doll Co.
Rio . . . . Hasbro, Inc.
Rita . . . . Porzellanfabrik Limbach
Rite-a . . . . Writing Toys Inc.
Rita Hayworth . . . . Uneeda Doll Co.
Robbie Reefer . . . . Horsman & Co.
Robert . . . . Eegee Doll Manufacturing Co., Käthe Kruse
Roberta . . . . Doll Bodies
Robertson's Golly . . . . Peggy Nesbit
Robin, Batman Companion . . . . Mego
Robin . . . . Royal Doll Co.
Robin Hood . . . . Alexander Doll Co., Mego
Rock a Bye Baby . . . . Averill Manufacturing Co., Blumberg, Cuno & Otto Dressel, Hollywood Doll Manufacturing Co.
Rock Me Baby . . . . Arranbee
Roddy . . . . Roddy Doll Co.
Rodeo . . . . Alexander Doll Co.
Roil Cellowachs . . . . Kämmer & Reinhardt
Roller Skater . . . . Alexander Doll Co.
Rollschuhläufer . . . . Bernhard Zehner
Rolly I Tot . . . . Borgfeldt
Rolly Twiddle . . . . Mattel, Inc.
Roma . . . . Plass & Roessner
Romance . . . . Alexander Doll Co.
Romeo . . . . Alexander Doll Co., Peggy Nesbit
Romper Baby . . . . American Bisque Doll Co., Averill Manufacturing Co.
Rompy . . . . Sun Rubber
Ronson . . . . Art Metal Works
Rooh . . . . Peggy Nesbit
Rootie Kazootie . . . . Effanbee
Rosa . . . . Dakin & Co.
Rosamund Bridesmaid . . . . Alexander Doll Co.
Roscamp Puppen Fantasien . . . . Katarina Roscamp
Roschco . . . . Robert Schneider
Röschen . . . . Käthe Kruse
Roscoe . . . . Mattel, Inc.
Rose Fairy . . . . Alexander Doll Co.
Rose of 1963 . . . . England Rosebud Doll Co.
Rose Puppe . . . . F. Welsch
Rosebud . . . . Alexander Doll Co.; Amberg; Armand Marseille; Illfelder & Co.; Mattel, Inc.
Rosemary Roadster . . . . Mattel, Inc.

Doll Name	Company Name
Rosemund	Clodrey
Roses Are Red, Violets Are Blue	Nancy Ann StoryBook Dolls
Rosette	England Rosebud Doll Co.
Rosey Posey	Alexander Doll Co.
Rosi	Kämmer & Reinhardt
Rosie the Waac-ette	Vogue
Rosy Posy	Borgfeldt, Elektra Toy and Novelty
Rotkappchen	Käthe Kruse
Rotkäppchen	Ludwig, Rotkäppchen
Roxy	Hasbro, Inc.
Royal	Cissna, Kestner
Royal Bébé	Aux Trois Quartiers
Royal Canadian Mounted Police	Ron Startling Plastics of Canada, Reliable Toy
Royal Evening	Alexander Doll Co.
Royal Family Members	Peggy Nesbit
Royal Princess	P & M Sales
Royal Wedding	Alexander Doll Co.
Royal Wedding Groom	Alexander Doll Co.
Rozy	Alexander Doll Co.
Rube	Alder Favor and Novelty
Ruckus	Ideal
Rudi	Käthe Kruse
Ruffles Clown	Alexander Doll Co.
Rufus	Averill Manufacturing Co.
Rumania	Alexander Doll Co.
Rumbero	Elite Creations
Rumbero & Rumbera	Alexander Doll Co.
Rumpelstiltskin	Hasbro, Inc.
Rumpumpel	Käthe Kruse
Russian	Alexander Doll Co.
Rusty	Alexander Doll Co., Brookglad, Effanbee
Ruth	Butler Brothers, Cissna, Käthe Kruse, Ideal
Ruthea Puppen	Grete Ruhl
Ruthie	Horsman & Co.
Ruthie's Baby	Horsman & Co.
Ruthie's Sister	Horsman & Co.
Sad Eyes	Chadwick
Sadie	Mattel, Inc.
Sag' Schnucki zu Mir	Wally Fischel
Sage	Peggy Nesbit
Sailor	Alexander Doll Co., Peggy Nesbit
Sailorette	Alexander Doll Co.
Sal	Alder Favor and Novelty
Sally	American Character, Arranbee
Sally Bride	Alexander Doll Co.
Sally Joe	American Character
Sally Joy	American Character
Sally Puppet	Hazelle
Sally Says	American Character
Sally Starr	Natural Doll Co.
Sally The Holiday Girl	Peggy Nesbit
Sallykins	Ideal
Sallykins is Growing up	Ideal
Salome	Alexander Doll Co.
Salty	Ideal
Salvation Army Lad and Lass	A & H
Sam Boy	Kohnstamm & Co.

DOLL NAME	COMPANY NAME
Samantha	Alexander Doll Co.
Samantha Parkington	Pleasant Co.
Samantha The Witch	Ideal
Sampson	Cuno & Otto Dressel
Samson	Amberg
Samuel Whiskers	Peggy Nesbit
Sandi	Eegee Doll Manufacturing Co.
Sandra	Alexander Doll Co., Eugenia
Sandra Sue	Richwood Toys
Sandy McCall	American Character
Sandy McHare	Alexander Doll Co.
Santa	Hamburger & Co., Simon & Halbig
Santa's Helper	Lovely Doll
Sara Ann	Ideal
Sarah, by Yolanda Bello	Ashton Drake
Sarah Bernhardt	Alexander Doll Co.
Sarah Jackson	Alexander Doll Co.
Sarah Polk	Alexander Doll Co.
Saralee	Ideal
Sardinia	Alexander Doll Co.
Sargent	Alexander Doll Co.
Sargent's Girl	Alexander Doll Co.
Sasha	Trendon Toys
Sassy Sue	Amberg
Sasy Cute	Deluxe Reading/Topper Toy Group
Sasy Homemaker	Deluxe Reading/Topper Toy Group
Saturday	Eugenia
Saucy	Mattel, Inc.
Saucy Scottles	Cameo
Saucy Walker	Ideal
Scarecrow	Mego
Scarlet	Duchess Doll Corp., Doll Craft
Scarlett	Alexander Doll Co.
Scarlett O'Hara	Alexander Doll Co.
Scassi Gown	Alexander Doll Co.
Schalk	Gans & Seyfarth
Schelmaugen	Kämmer & Reinhardt
Schiaparelli	Virga
Schiaparelli Go Go	Virga
Schieler	A. F. Carl
Schlenkerchen	Käthe Kruse
Schneeflöckchen	Nöckler & Tittel
Schneewittchen	Kley & Hahn
School Boy	Amberg, Horsman & Co.
School Boy With a Cap	Amberg
School Days	Nancy Ann StoryBook Dolls
School Girl	Alexander Doll Co., Amberg, Horsman & Co.
Schwesterchen	Friedrichsrodaer Puppenfabrik
Scooba Doo	Mattel, Inc.
Scootles	Cameo
Scotch Groom	Plastic Molded Arts Co.
Scotch Miss	Duchess Doll Corp.
Scotland	Alexander Doll Co.
Scots Boy	Peggy Nesbit
Scots Girl	Peggy Nesbit
Scottish Costume	Effanbee
Scottish Piper	Peggy Nesbit

Doll Name	Company Name
Sea Flower	Ozzerman Mfg. Co.
Seasons	Alexander Doll Co.
Seasons Autumn	Nancy Ann StoryBook Dolls
Seasons Spring	Nancy Ann StoryBook Dolls
Seasons Summer	Nancy Ann StoryBook Dolls
Seasons Winter	Nancy Ann StoryBook Dolls
Seco	Strauss-Eckardt Co., G. Eckardt
Secret Sue	Uneeda Doll Co.
See Saw Marjorie Daw	Nancy Ann StoryBook Dolls
Sekiguchi of Japan	Mattel, Inc.
Semper	Käthe Kruse
Sentimental Journey	Alexander Doll Co.
September	Alexander Doll Co.
September's Girl is Like a Storm	Nancy Ann StoryBook Dolls
Seven Dwarfs	Alexander Doll Co.
Sgt. Storm	Mattel, Inc.
Shadow Wave Baby	Horsman & Co.
Sharie Lewis	Alexander Doll Co.
Shaun	Mattel, Inc.
Shaun Cassidy	Kenner
Shazam	Mego
Shea Elf	Alexander Doll Co.
SHEbee	Horsman & Co.
Sheila Friddle	Mattel, Inc.
Shelley	Eegee Doll Manufacturing Co.
She-Nik	Uneeda Doll Co.
Sherily Kiddle	Mattel, Inc.
Sherri	Cey
Sherry	Effanbee
Shirley	Horsman & Co.
Shirley from *Laverne and Shirley*	Mego
Shirley Temple	Armand Marseille, Ideal
Shirley Temple Baby Doll	Ideal
Shirley Temple Texas Ranger	Ideal
Shoppin' Sherri	Mattel, Inc.
Shopping Sheryl	Mattel, Inc.
Show Biz Babies	Hasbro, Inc.
Show Boat	Alexander Doll Co.
Shrinking Violet	Mattel, Inc.
Sicily	Alexander Doll Co.
Sico	Edward Schmidt, Löffler & Dill
Sicora	Edward Schmidt, Löffler & Dill
Siegfried	Kestner
Siha	Simon Hahn
Silk Flapper	American Specialty Doll Co.
Silks and Satins	Nancy Ann StoryBook Dolls
Silly	Sun Rubber
Silly Safari	Deluxe Reading/Topper Toy Group
Simon	Alexander Doll Co.
Simone	Alexander Doll Co.
Sindy	Pedigree
Sing A Song	Mattel, Inc.
Singin' Chatty	Mattel, Inc.
Sir Frances F. Drake	Peggy Nesbit
Sir Galahad	Mego
Sir Lancelot	Mego
Sir Lapin Hare	Alexander Doll Co.

Sir Robert Menzies . . . . Peggy Nesbit
Sir Winston Churchill . . . . Alexander Doll Co., Effanbee
Sis . . . . Averill Manufacturing Co.
Sis Hopkins . . . . Amberg
Sissy . . . . F. D. Co.
Sister . . . . Effanbee, Amberg
Sister & Brother . . . . Effanbee
Sister Belle . . . . Mattel, Inc.
Sister Billiken . . . . Horsman & Co.
Sister Coos . . . . Ideal
Sister Of Bride . . . . Alexander Doll Co.
Sister Small Talk . . . . Mattel, Inc.
Sister Small Walk . . . . Mattel, Inc.
Sitting Bull . . . . Mego
Sitting Pretty . . . . Alexander Doll Co.
Sizzly Friddle . . . . Mattel, Inc.
Sizzy . . . . Cohen
Skaters Waltz . . . . Alexander Doll Co.
Skediddles . . . . Mattel, Inc.
Skididdles . . . . Mattel, Inc.
Skipper . . . . Mattel, Inc.
Skippy . . . . Effanbee
Skookum . . . . Amber, Arrow Novelty Co.
Skookum Apple Indian Doll . . . . Arrow
Skooter . . . . Mattel, Inc.
Skye . . . . Kenner
Sleep Time Twins . . . . Ideal
Sleep Weepy . . . . American Character
Sleeping Baby . . . . Effanbee
Sleeping Babyette . . . . Effanbee
Sleeping Beauty . . . . Alexander Doll Co.; Hasbro, Inc.; Mattel, Inc.
Sleeping Biddle . . . . Mattel, Inc.
Sleepy . . . . Eegee Doll Manufacturing Co., Horsman & Co.
Sleepy Baby . . . . Horsman & Co.
Sleepyhead . . . . Bantam US Toys
Slick Chick . . . . Deluxe Reading/Topper Toy Group
Slipsy Sliddle . . . . Mattel, Inc.
Slugger-Nik . . . . Uneeda Doll Co.
Sluggo . . . . Averill Manufacturing Co.
Slumbermante . . . . Alexander Doll Co.
Small Shots Twins . . . . Mattel, Inc.
Small Talk . . . . Mattel, Inc.
Small Talk Cinderella . . . . Mattel, Inc.
Smarty . . . . Alexander Doll Co.
Smarty Pants . . . . Deluxe Reading/Topper Toy Group
Smiggle Talk . . . . Mattel, Inc.
Smiley . . . . Alexander Doll Co.
Smiling Face . . . . Arranbee
Smokey Tail . . . . Alexander Doll Co.
Smoochie . . . . Ideal
Snip N Tuck . . . . American Character
Snooks . . . . Averill Manufacturing Co.
Snookums . . . . Averill Manufacturing Co., Max Friedrich Schellhorn
Snoozie . . . . Ideal
Snow White . . . . Alexander Doll Co.; Horsman & Co.; Ideal; Knickerbocker; Mattel, Inc.; Peggy Nesbit; Sayco Doll Corp.
Snow White and The Seven Dwarfs . . . . Hasbro, Inc.

Snowbaby	Eegee Doll Manufacturing Co.
Snuggle Doll	Arranbee
Snuggle Muff	Arranbee
Snugglebun	Remco
So Big	Alexander Doll Co., Amberg
So Lite Baby	Alexander Doll Co.
So Lite Toddler	Alexander Doll Co.
So Wee	Sun Rubber Co.
Soapy Siddle	Mattel, Inc.
Soapy Siddle	Mattel, Inc.
Sofie	Käthe Kruse
Softanlite dolls	Averill Manufacturing Co.
Softee	Ideal
Softie	Horsman & Co.
Softie Baby	Horsman & Co.
Softina	Eegee Doll Manufacturing Co.
Softskin	Horsman & Co.
Soldier	Alexander Doll Co.
Soldier Ape	Mego
Soldier Boy	Amberg, Averill Manufacturing Co.
Soldiers	Käthe Kruse
Songster	Horsman & Co.
Sonja Henie	Alexander Doll Co., Arranbee
Sonja Skater	Arranbee
Sonja The Skating Girl	Peggy Nesbit
Sonnenpuppe	Welsch & Co.
Sonny	Averill Manufacturing Co.
Sonny Boy	Hugo Wiegand
Sonny from Sonny and Cher	Mego
Soozie Smiles	Ideal
Sophisticated Bride	American Character
Sound Of Music	Alexander Doll Co.
Soupee	Bella France Orenete
Soupee Bella	Bella France Orenete
Soupy Sales	Knickerbocker
South America	Alexander Doll Co.
South Sea Baby	A. Luge & Co.
Southern Belle	Alexander Doll Co., Nancy Ann StoryBook Dolls
Southern Girl	Alexander Doll Co.
Span	Amberg
Spanish	Alexander Doll Co.
Spanish Boy	Alexander Doll Co.
Spanish Doll	Dream World Dolls
Spanish Girl	Alexander Doll Co.
Spanky	Mego
Spark Plug	Schoenhut
Sparkle Plenty	Ideal
Spearmint Kiddo	Amberg
Special	Adolf Wislizenus, Kley & Hahn
Special Girl	Alexander Doll Co.
Special Q E II Sailor of Conrad Line	Peggy Nesbit
Spezial	C. M. Bergmann, Kuhles
Spic	Amberg
Spider Man	Mego
Splendide Bébé	Aux Trois Quartiers
Sports Girl	Atlas Manufacturing Co.
Spring Beauty	Horsman & Co.

Squiggy from *Laverne and Shirley*	Mego
St. Pat's Day	S & E
St. Patrick	Averill Manufacturing Co.
Stabil	Emil Heyer & Co., Robert Richter
Stacy	Mattel, Inc.
Stan Laurel	Peggy Nesbit
Star	H. Eckstein
Star Brite	Vogue
Star Spangled Dolls	Mattel, Inc.
Star Wars	Kenner
Starlight Starbright	Nancy Ann
Stella	J. Stellmacher
Stephie Sunshine	Mattel, Inc.
Stepping Stepper	Plastic Molded Arts
Steve Sunshine	Mattel, Inc.
Storch	Schwäbische Celluloidwarenfabrik
Stormer	Hasbro, Inc.
Stormie Stormalong	Dewees Cochran
Stormtrooper	Kenner
Story Princess	Alexander Doll Co.
StoryBook Kiddles	Mattel, Inc.
Strampelchen	Edith Maus
Strandfee	O. Eberwein & Co.
Strawman	Ideal
Strike Up The Band	Alexander Doll Co., Ideal
Stuffy	Alexander Doll Co.
Style Show Dolls	Nancy Ann
Suba	Molly-'es
Suck a Thumb	Horsman & Co., Ideal
Suck Thumb Baby	Carl Heumann
Südsee Baby	A. Luge & Co.
Sue	Amberg
Suellen	Alexander Doll Co.
Sugar and Spice and Everything Nice	Nancy Ann StoryBook Dolls
Sugar Baby	Effanbee
Sugar Darlin'	Alexander Doll Co.
Sugar Plum	Effanbee, Borgfeldt
Sugar Tears	Alexander Doll Co.
Suitcase Dolly	Amberg
Suki Skediddle	Mattel, Inc.
Suki Skididdle	Mattel, Inc.
Sulky Sue	Alexander Doll Co.
Sultan	Molly-'es
Summer Girl	Atlas Manufacturing Co.
SUN	Sigmund Ullmann
Sunbaby	Sun Rubber
Sunbeam	Alexander Doll Co.
Sunbonnet Sal	Horsman & Co.
Sunbonnet Sue	Alexander Doll Co., Horsman & Co., Ideal
Sunday	Hasbro, Inc.
Sunday Best	American Character
Sunday's Child	Nancy Ann StoryBook Dolls
Sunflower Clown	Alexander Doll Co.
Sunny Boy	American Character, Averill Manufacturing Co.
Sunny Face	Uneeda Doll Co.
Sunny Girl	Averill Manufacturing Co.
Sunny Jim	Amberg

Doll Name	Company Name
Sunny Orange Blossom	Amberg
Sunshine	Horsman & Co.
Sunshine Girl	Bing Art Dolls
Sunshine Kid	Bing Art Dolls
Super Girl	Mego
Super Walker	Ideal
Superba	unidentified
Superior	Cuno & Otto Dressel, Fleischmann & Co., Georg Lutz, Heinrich Handwerck, Müller & Strasburger
Superior Quints	Alexander Doll Co.
Superman	Mego
SUR	Seyfarth & Reinhardt
Surprise Doll	Uneeda Doll Co.
Susan Stormalong	Dewees Cochran
Susan Stroller	Eegee Doll Manufacturing Co.
Susannchen	Käthe Kruse
Susan's Crochet Doll Kit	G. A. Doherty
Susi Künstlerpuppen	Susi Künstlerpuppen
Susie	Atlas Manufacturing Co., Cuno & Otto Dressel
Susie Q	Alexander Doll Co.
Susie Sunshine	Effanbee
Susie's Sister	American Art Dolls
Suzanne	Effanbee
Suzanne Nurse	Effanbee
Suzanne Somers	Mego
Suzette	Effanbee, Uneeda Doll Co.
Suzette Martha and George Washington	Effanbee
Suzie Sunshine	Effanbee
Suzy	Alexander Doll Co.
Swat Mulligan	Amberg
Sweden	Alexander Doll Co.
Swedish	Alexander Doll Co.
Sweepsy Skiddle	Mattel, Inc.
Sweet Alice	American Character
Sweet April	Remco
Sweet Cookie	Hasbro, Inc.
Sweet Janice	Hollywood Doll Manufacturing Co.
Sweet Nell	Alt, Beck & Gottschalck; Hugo Wiegand
Sweet Pea	Arranbee, King Features
Sweet Rosemary	Deluxe Reading/Topper Toy Group
Sweet Sue	American Character
Sweet Sue American Beauty	American Character
Sweet Sue Godey Load	American Character
Sweet Sue Sophisticate	American Character
Sweet Sue Walker	American Character
Sweet Suzanne	American Character
Sweet Tears	Alexander Doll Co.
Sweet Violet	Alexander Doll Co.
Sweetheart	Amberg
Sweetheart	Horsman & Co.
Sweetheart Jan	Vogue
Sweetie Baby	Alexander Doll Co.
Sweetie Lue	Arranbee
Sweetie Pie	Effanbee
Sweetie Sweetness	Progressive Toy Co.
Sweetie Walker	Alexander Doll Co.
Sweets	Averill Manufacturing Co.

Sweets Sunshine	Mattel, Inc.
Sweetums	Century Doll Co., Uneeda Doll Co.
Swing and Sway with Sammy Kaye	Wondercraft
Swingy	Mattel, Inc.
Swingy Swiddle	Mattel, Inc.
Swiss	Alexander Doll Co.
Swiss Girl	Alexander Doll Co.
Switzerland	Alexander Doll Co.
Syco	Sieder & Co.
Sylvester	Warner Brothers
Sylvia Locket	Mattel, Inc.
Tabatha	Ideal
Taffy	Arranbee
Taft	unidentified
Tag	Borgfeldt
Tago	P. Bühl & Tannewitz
Tak Uki	Norah Wellings
Taki	Mattel, Inc. for Annette Himstedt
Talk A Little	Mattel, Inc.
Talking Baby First Step	Mattel, Inc.
Talking Baby Tenderlove	Mattel, Inc.
Talking Barbie	Mattel, Inc.
Talking Cynthia	Mattel, Inc.
Talking Marie	American Character
Talking Miss Beasley	Mattel, Inc.
Talking P J	Mattel, Inc.
Talking Spanish Barbie	Mattel, Inc.
Talking Terri Lee	Terri Lee
Talking Twin Kip	Mattel, Inc.
Talking Twins	Mattel, Inc.
Talkytot	Ideal
Tammy	Ideal
Tamu	Shindana
Tandy Talks	Eegee Doll Manufacturing Co.
Tango Tots	Amberg
Tara	Mattel, Inc. for Annette Himstedt
Tarzan	Mego
Tastee Freez Sweetheart	Lovely Doll
Tatters	Mattel, Inc.
Tausendschönchen	Franz Schmidt & Co.
T-Bone	Mattel, Inc.
Teach Keen	Mattel, Inc.
Teachy Keen	Mattel, Inc.
Tearful Cheerful	Mattel, Inc.
Tearful Tenderlove	Mattel, Inc.
Tearful Thumbelina	Ideal
Tearie	Ideal
Teaseme	Duckme Doll Co.
Tebu	Theodor Buschbaum
Ted	Ideal
Ted	Ideal
Teddy	Made in America Manufacturing Co.
Teenie Weenie	American Character, Amberg, Borgfeldt
Teens in Bells	A & H
Teensie Baby	Horsman & Co.
Teeny Betsy McCall	American Character
Teeny Tiny Tears	American Character

DOLL NAME	COMPANY NAME
Teeny Twinkle	Alexander Doll Co.
Teeny Weeny Tiny Tears	American Character
Tella	Käthe Kruse
Telly Viddle	Mattel, Inc.
Telly Viddle Kiddle	Mattel, Inc.
Tenille from Captain and Tenille	Mego
Tennis	Alexander Doll Co.
Terry Lee	Terry Lee
Tessie	American Toy & Novelty Co., M. Kohnstamm & Co.
Tex	Deluxe Reading/Topper Toy Group
Thai	Alexander Doll Co.
That Girl	Alexander Doll Co.
That Kid	Hasbro, Inc.
The Amphibious Clown	Giftoy Co.
The Base Ball Fan	Max Friedrich Schellhorn
The Century Doll	Century Doll Co.
The Cheron	Mego
The Child that Was Born on the Sabbath Day is Bonny and Blythe and Good and Gay	Nancy Ann StoryBook Dolls
The Dollar Princess	Kley & Hahn
The Duchess Dressed Doll	M. Kohnstamm & Co..
The Fairy Kid	Peter Scherf
The Falcon	Mego
The Favorite Doll	F. A. O. Schwarz, Kämmer & Reinhardt
The Flirt	Kämmer & Reinhardt
The Go Go's	Deluxe Reading/Topper Toy Group
The Gorn	Mego
The Handwercks Celebrated Doll	Max Handwerck
The Hart Throb Doll	Fortune Doll Co.
The Hollywood Twosome Doll	American Character
The International Doll	Borgfeldt
The Jolly Jester	Borgfeldt
The Keeper	Mego
The Kuinks	Ideal
The Littlest Rebel	Ideal
The Lizard	Mego
The Magic Make Up Face	American Character
The National Doll	Maiden Toy Co.
The Skipper	Borgfeldt
The Snow Queen	Nancy Ann StoryBook Dolls
The Sonny Boy	M. Kohnstamm & Co.
The Spearmint Kid	Baker & Bennett Co.
The Swinger	Deluxe Reading/Topper Toy Group
The Thing	Mego
The Wonder Book and Doll	A&H
The World of Love	Hasbro, Inc.
The Worlds Fairest	Uneeda Doll Co.
There Was A Maiden Bright and Gay	Nancy Ann StoryBook Dolls
Theressa Lady in Waiting	Nancy Ann StoryBook Dolls
Thief of Baghdad Series	Molly-'es
Thirstie Baby	Horsman & Co.
Thomas	Käthe Kruse
Three Little Pigs & Wolf	Alexander Doll Co.
Thumbelina	Ideal
Thumbs Up Victory Doll	Margit Nilsen Studios
Thumkin	Effanbee
Thuringia	A. Luge & Co., Carl Hartmann, Porzellanfabrik Thüringia

Thursday's Child Has Far to Go	Nancy Ann StoryBook Dolls
Tickles	Deluxe Reading/Topper Toy Group
Tickletoes	Ideal
Tickletoes the Wonder Doll	Ideal
Tiddle Diddle	Mattel, Inc.
Tiff	Mattel, Inc.
Tim	Camay
Timey Tell	Mattel, Inc.
Timi and Toni	Mattel, Inc. for Annette Himstedt
Timmie Toddler	Alexander Doll Co.
Timmy	Blumberg, Jolly Toys
Timmy Toddler	Alexander Doll Co.
Tin Woodsman	Mego
Tina	Eegee Doll Manufacturing Co.
Tina Cassini	Ross Products
Tina Marie	American Character
Tinker Bell	Duchess Doll Corp., Sayco Doll Corp.
Tinkerbell	Alexander Doll Co.
Tintair Doll	Effanbee
Tintair Honey	Effanbee
Tiny Baby Kissy	Ideal
Tiny Betsy McCall	American Character
Tiny Betty	Alexander Doll Co.
Tiny Brother	Mattel, Inc.
Tiny Bubbles	Imperial Crown
Tiny Chatty Baby	Mattel, Inc.
Tiny Girl	Ideal
Tiny Jerri Lee	Terri Lee
Tiny Kissy	Ideal
Tiny Pinkie	Alexander Doll Co.
Tiny Swingy	Mattel, Inc.
Tiny Tads	Amberg
Tiny Tearful Cheerful	Mattel, Inc.
Tiny Tears	American Character
Tiny Teens	Uneeda Doll Co.
Tiny Terri Lee	Terri Lee
Tiny Thumbelina	Ideal
Tiny Tim	Alexander Doll Co., Art Fabric Mills
Tiny Toddles	Uneeda Doll Co.
Tiny Tot	Amberg
Tiny Tots	Amberg, Borgfeldt
Tiny Town Dolls	Alma LeBlane
Tiny Travelers	Saalfield
Tiny Trix	Uneeda Doll Co.
Tiny Tubber	Effanbee
Tiny Whimsies	American Character
Tinyteen	Uneeda Doll Co.
Tinyteen Bob	Uneeda Doll Co.
Tinyteen Suzette	Uneeda Doll Co.
Tippee Toes	Mattel, Inc.
Tipperary Tom	Atlas Manufacturing Co.
Tippi	Alexander Doll Co.
Tipple Topple	Emil Pfeiffer
Tippy Toe	Alexander Doll Co.
Tippy Toes	Mattel, Inc.
Tippy Toes	Mattel, Inc.
Tippy Tumbles	Remco

DOLL NAME	COMPANY NAME
Titania	Peggy Nesbit
To Market, To Market	Nancy Ann StoryBook Dolls
Toby	Alexander Doll Co.
Tod L Dee	Sun Rubber Co.
Tod L Tee	Sun Rubber Co.
Tod L Tim	Sun Rubber Co.
Todd	Mattel, Inc.
Toddle Tot	American Character, Effanbee
Toddler	American Bisque Dolls
Toddler Betty	Horsman & Co.
Toddles Brother and Sister	Vogue
Toddles Victory Gardeners	Vogue
Toe Dancing Ballerina	Valentine Doll Co.
Tog	Peggy Nesbit
Tom and the Pig	Sol Bergfeld & Son
Tom from Tom and Jerry	Goldwyn Meyers
Tom Kitten	Peggy Nesbit
Tommy	Alexander Doll Co.
Tommy Bans	Alexander Doll Co.
Tommy Snooks	Alexander Doll Co.
Tommy Tittlemouse	Alexander Doll Co.
Tommy Tucker	Effanbee, Horsman & Co.
Tommy Turnip	Borgfeldt
Toni	American Character, Ideal
Toni and Timi	Mattel, Inc. for Annette Himstedt
Toni Doll	Ideal
Toni Walker	Ideal
Too Dear	Vogue
Toodle-Loo	American Character
Toodles	American Bisque Dolls, Horsman & Co.
Toodles Action Baby	American Character
Toodles Potty Baby	American Character
Toodles Toddles	American Character
Toodles with Peek a Boo Eyes	American Character
Toonga	Effanbee
Toothums	Uneeda Doll Co.
Tootsie	American Art Dolls, Borgfeldt
Topsy	Arnold Print Works, Art Fabric Mills, Brückner, Gem Doll, Horsman & Co., Nancy Ann StoryBook Dolls
Topsy Baby	Bruckner, Horsman & Co.
Topsy Turvy	Alexander Doll Co., Horsman & Co.
Torino	Berthold Helk
Toto from Oz	Mego
Toto the Clown	Averill Manufacturing Co.
Toulouse Lautrec	Alexander Doll Co.
Tout Bois	F. M. Schilling
Tower Treasures "Dumpies" Collection (at least 10)	Peggy Nesbit
Tower Treasures "K" Range Collection (at least 27)	Peggy Nesbit
Tracy	Mattel, Inc.
Trag	Mego
Trapeze Artist	Alexander Doll Co.
Treat 'Em Rough Kiddie	Art Metal Works
Trebor	Porzellanfabrik Mengersgereuth, probably by Crämer & Héron
Treena Ballerina	Alexander Doll Co.
Trego Girl	Trego Doll Manufacturing

Tressy	American Character, Ideal
Tribly	Ideal
Trikey Triddle	Mattel, Inc.
Trilby	American Stuffed Novelty Co.
Trinkets	Elite Creations
Triumph Bebe	Max Handwerck
Trolls	Dam Things
Trousseau Baby	Horsman & Co.
Trudel	Käthe Kruse
Trudila	Käthe Kruse
Trudy	Jolly Toys
Trudy The Three Faced Doll	Three In One Doll Corp.
Truest-to-Like	Amberg
Truly Scrumptous	Mattel, Inc.
Trutzi	Johannes Rejall
Tubbsy	Ideal
Tuesday's Child is Full of Grace	Nancy Ann StoryBook Dolls
Tuffie	Horsman & Co.
Tuftex	Art Statue Co.
Tumbelina	Ideal
Tumbling Tomboy	Remco
Tummy	Ideal
Tunisia	Alexander Doll Co.
Turkey	Alexander Doll Co.
Turn and Learn	American Character
Turtle Brand	Averill Manufacturing Co.
Tutti	Mattel, Inc.
Tweedie	Horsman & Co.
Tweedledee	Greta Fleishmann
Tweedledum	Greta Fleishmann
Tweedledum & Tweedledee	Alexander Doll Co.
Twiggy	Mattel, Inc.
Twiggy London Model	Mattel, Inc.
Twilite Baby	Amberg
Twinkie	Marx
Twinkle Eyes	Ideal
Twinkle Twins	Amberg
Twins	Uneeda Doll Co.
Twins & Quads	Effanbee
Twist & Turn Barbie	Mattel, Inc.
Twist & Turn Julie Nurse	Mattel, Inc.
Twistail	Alexander Doll Co.
Twistee	Jolly Toys
Twistie	Horsman & Co.
Twixie the Twisting Pixie	Belle Dolls
Tynie	Horsman & Co.
Tynie Baby	Horsman & Co.
Tynie Toddler	Horsman & Co.
Tyrolean Girl	Alexander Doll Co.
Tyroler Boy	Horsman & Co.
Tyroler Girl	Horsman & Co.
U.S. Air Corps.	Lovely Doll
U.S. Army	Lovely Doll
U.S. Marine	Lovely Doll
Ugh Nik	Uneeda Doll Co.
Ulla Puppe	Arthur Gotthelf
Ullrich	Käthe Kruse

DOLL NAME	COMPANY NAME
Unbreakable	Lambert & Samhammer
Uncle	Art Fabric Mills
Uncle Mose	Aunt Jemima Mills Co.
Uncle Sam	Averill Manufacturing Co., Cuno & Otto Dressel
Uncle Wiggily	Averill Manufacturing Co.
Under The China Berry Tree	Bamberger
Undergraduate Boy	Peggy Nesbit
Undergraduate Girl	Peggy Nesbit
Undressed Boudoir Dolls for Home Costuming	Gerling Toy Co.
Unerreicht	Adolph Harras
Union Officer	Alexander Doll Co.
United States	Alexander Doll Co.
Unity of Nation Established	Effanbee
Universal Puppe	Carl Bergner
Unsere goldigen Drei	Gebrüder Heubach
Unsere Kleine Mammy	Kämmer & Reinhardt
Unsere Süssen Mädel	Gebrüder Heubach
Ursel	Käthe Kruse
Ursula	E. W. Matthes
U-Shab-Ti	Averill Manufacturing Co.
Uwanta	Borgfeldt
Vacation Gal	Horsman & Co.
Val-encia	Averill Manufacturing Co.
Valentine	Nancy Ann StoryBook Dolls
Valentine Bonnet Toddler	S & C
Valerie	Mattel, Inc.
Vanta Baby	Amberg
Velvet	Ideal
Vermont Maid®	Uneeda
Vicki	Elite Creations
Victoria	Alexander Doll Co.
Victoria Jointed Doll	W. F. Schönhut
Victorian	Alexander Doll Co.
Victorian Land In Bustles	Peggy Nesbit
Victorian Miss	Peggy Nesbit
Victory Doll	Amberg
Vietnam	Alexander Doll Co.
Viktoria	Cuno & Otto Dressel, Julius Hering, Heinrich Schmuckler
Viktoria Luise	Car Hartmann
Viktoriababies	G. Gebert
Viola	Hamburger & Co., Schoenau & Hoffmeister
Violet	Alexander Doll Co., Ernst Liebermann, Käthe Kruse
Violet Kiddle Kologne	Mattel, Inc.
Violetta	Alexander Doll Co., Fortune Doll Co.
Virga Girl Doll	Beehler Art Co.
Virginia Dare	Alexander Doll Co., Averill Manufacturing Co., Dolls By Jerri
Virginia, Ginny for Short	Borgfeldt
Vivi	A. Gorrigenes, Borgfeldt
Vivien Leigh	Peggy Nesbit
Vöglein	Emma Vogel
W E E G E M	W. G. Müller
W. A. A. C.	Alexander Doll Co., American Character, Ralph A. Freundlich, Inc.
W. A. A. F.	Alexander Doll Co.
W. A. V. E.	Alexander Doll Co.; Ralph A. Freundlich, Inc.
W. C. Fields	Effanbee, Peggy Nesbit
Wade Davis	Aunt Jemima Mills Co.

DOLL NAME	COMPANY NAME
Waldkind	Vereinigung Finsterberger Pauppenmacher
Walker Ruth	Horsman & Co.
Walking Bride	Sayco Doll Corp.
Walking Little Colonel	Madame Alexander
Walking Mama Doll	Ideal
Walküre	Kley & Hahn
Wall Eye Dolls	New Toy Manufacturing Co.
Wall Eye Twins	New Toy Manufacturing Co.
Wally	Porzellanfabrik Limbach
Walpu	Waltershäuser Puppenfabrik
Walter	Kämmer & Reinhardt
Waltzing	Alexander Doll Co.
Wanda The Walking Wonder	Advance Doll & Toy Co.
Waschecht	Cuno & Otto Dressel, F. M. Schilling, Kämmer & Reinhardt
Washable Doll	Cuno & Otto Dressel, F. M. Schilling, Kämmer & Reinhardt
Washington	Mattel, Inc.
Weatherbird	American Doll Co.
Wedding Party	Alexander Doll Co.
Wednesday's Child is Full of Woe	Nancy Ann StoryBook Dolls
Wee Bonnie Baby	Horsman & Co.
Wee Imp	Vogue
Wee Nik	Uneeda Doll Co.
Wee Patsy Durable Doll	Effanbee
Wee Patsy Twins	Effanbee
Wee Three	Uneeda Doll Co.
Wee Willie Winkle	Vogue
Weepsy Wiggles	Uneeda Doll Co.
Weimarpüppchen	Thüringer Stoffpuppen Fabrik
Weinende	Albert Schachne; Hertel, Schwab & Co.
Welcome Back Kotter	Mattel, Inc.
Welsh Girl	Peggy Nesbit
Wendy	Alexander Doll Co.
Wendy Angel	Alexander Doll Co.
Wendy Ann	Alexander Doll Co.
Wendy Ballerina Trousseau	Alexander Doll Co.
Wendy Bride	Alexander Doll Co.
Wendy Travel Trunk	Alexander Doll Co.
Wendy Trousseau	Alexander Doll Co.
Wendy Wardrobe	Alexander Doll Co.
Wendy-kins	Alexander Doll Co.
Wera	Käthe Kruse
Western Mill	Nancy Ann StoryBook Dolls
Whatsit Doll	Horsman & Co.
When She Was Good She Was Very Very Good	Nancy Ann StoryBook Dolls
Whimsies	American Character
Whistler	Remco
Whistling Cowboy	Averill Manufacturing Co.
Whistling Jim	Gebrüder Heubach
Whistling Rufus	Averill Manufacturing Co.
Whistling Willie	Amberg
White Rabbit	Alexander Doll Co.
Wicked Witch from Oz	Mego
Wide Awake	Butler Brothers
Wiggles	Uneeda Doll Co.
Wiggy Wags	Sun Rubber Co.
Wild Bill Hickok	Mego
Wildfang	Wagner & Zetsche

Doll Name	Company Name
Wilhelmina	Horsman & Co.
Wilhelminchen	Käthe Kruse
Will Rogers	Peggy Nesbit
Will Scarlet	Mego
Willem	Horsman & Co.
Willi	Käthe Kruse
William Shakespeare	Peggy Nesbit
Wimpern	Heinrich Handwerck, Simon & Halbig
Windy Friddle	Mattel, Inc.
Winkin	F. D. Co.
Winnie	Ideal
Winnie the Pooh	Horsman & Co.
Winnie the Unaided Walking Doll	Advance
Winnie the Wonder Doll	Advance
Winnie Walker	Alexander Doll Co.
Winnie Walker Trousseau	Alexander Doll Co.
Winsome Winnie Walker	Alexander Doll Co.
Wipsy Walker	Uneeda Doll Co.
Wishmaker	Uneeda Doll Co.
Wish-Nics	Uneeda Doll Co.
Wolfman	Mego
Woman and Man Dressed In 18th Century Clothes	Burgarella
Women of The 1860s	Alexander Doll Co.
Wonder	Madame Georgene exclusively for George Borgfeldt
Wonder Baby	Amberg
Wonder Dolls	Averill Manufacturing Co.
Wonder Mama Doll	Madame Georgene Inc.
Wonder Woman	Mego
Wooden "Peg Tops" Collection (at least 20)	Peggy Nesbit
Woody Woodpecker	Mattel, Inc.
World Children, The	Mattel, Inc. for Annette Himstedt
World War I Soldier	Horsman & Co.
Wunderkind	Kestner
Wyatt Earp	Mego
Xtra	Borgfeldt
Yama Doll	American Specialty Doll Co.
Yankee Doodle	Amberg
Yankee Doodle Kids	Averill Manufacturing Co.
Yardley of London	Alexander Doll Co.
Yawning Baby	Averill Manufacturing Co.
Years Ago	Uneeda Doll Co.
Yoda	Kenner
Yogi Bear	Knickerbocker
Yolanda	Alexander Doll Co.
Yugoslavia	Alexander Doll Co.
Yugoslavian	Alexander Doll Co.
Yummy	Uneeda Doll Co.
Zaiden	Baker & Bennett Co.
Zaiden Doll	Colonial Doll Co.
ZaZa	Alexander Doll Co.
Zeb McCahan	Mattel, Inc.
Zira	Mego
Zon from 1 Million B. C.	Mego
Zorina Ballerina	Alexander Doll Co.
Zu Zu Kid	Ideal

CHAPTER THREE

MOLD NUMBERS

Mold numbers are the most frequently used credentials to identify an antique doll. Before World War I the overwhelming majority of dolls sold in the United States were manufactured in Europe. Germany was clearly the dominant influence in the doll market. France created beautiful expensive dolls, but could not effectively compete with the German industry. In 1899, the principal manufacturers of Paris formed a cartel known as the Société de Fabrication de Bébés and Jouets (S. F. B. J.) in an attempt to rival the German authority. Despite their efforts, S. F. B. J. could not alter the commerce of dolls, and Germany maintained its eminent position. Other countries such as Austria, Britain, Russia, and Italy also contributed to the growing demand by Americans for more and more dolls. At the turn of the twentieth century, the United States imported thousands of dolls every day.

Germany assigned mold numbers to most of their dolls. At times the numbering system was a practical designation of numerals for internal identification. For example, Kämmer and Reinhardt used the third number from the right to identify the type of head:

Number 1   Bisque character socket head
Number 2   Shoulder head of various materials, or socket head of a black or mulatto baby
Number 3   Bisque socket head, or celluloid shoulder head
Number 4   Head having eyelashes
Number 5   Black head, or Googly, or white bust and arms for pincushion
Number 6   Mulatto head
Number 7   Celluloid head, or bisque head for walking dolls
Number 8   Rubber head
Number 9   Composition head

Many companies simply used a numerical sequence to assign a mold number. Others routinely adopted the year in which a mold was registered as the marker. Avoid the temptation to use this mold number to date a doll. It is likely that a mold was manufactured for several years after it was registered.

The French doll manufacturers were not as diligent as their German counterparts in assigning mold numbers. It was not unusual for a fine French doll to be marked only with a size number. (See chapter five for size charts.) After the formation of S. F. B. J., mold numbers are more prevalent.

Dolls that were manufactured in the United States are more likely to be named than numbered. Occasionally, a patent or size number will be found.

This chapter notes the mold numbers that were registered by a particular manufacturer. It is important to remember that not all doll companies made their own doll heads. A registered manufacturer can differ from a distributor. For example: Mold number 1296 is a marked Franz Schmidt character doll head. Franz Schmidt was not a porcelain factory, though, and, therefore, could not produce its own heads. Simon & Halbig made and registered mold number 1296 for Franz Schmidt.

Also included in this listing are the digits assigned by contemporary manufacturers. Frequently a digit and a letter appear together, such as Ideal's P-90. These letter/digits included within this listing appear numerically.

MOLD NUMBER	COMPANY NAME
1	Amberg, G. Vichy
2	Amberg
2 H	Eegee
2 S	Uneeda Doll Co.
3	Uneeda Doll Co., Richwood Toys
4	Amberg, Uneeda Doll Co.
5	Henri Alexandre
5 N F	Uneeda Doll Co.
5 S G	Deluxe Reading/Topper Toy Group (assumed)
6	Deluxe Reading/Topper Toy Group
7/3	Starr
8	Effanbee, Uneeda Doll Co.
9	Ideal Tiny Tot
10	Effanbee, Ideal, Vogue
10 1/2	Ideal
11 V W	Valentine
12	Amberg, Ideal, Valentine
12/5	Eegee
13	Falck-Roussel, Gebrüder Kühnlenz, Uneeda, Vogue
14	Arrow, De Soto, Roberta, Star, Valentine
14R	Eegee
14 R 1	Eegee
15	Vogue
15 B A L H H	Belle
15 P	Eegee
15 N	Ideal
16	Arranbee
16 V W	Valentine
P 16	Belle
17	Ideal
17B	Nancy Ann StoryBook Dolls
U P 17	Ideal
17 V W	Valentine
18B	Nancy Ann StoryBook Dolls
18 V W	Valentine
19	Ideal
20	Uneeda Doll Co. Dolls, Vogue
20 H H	Belle
21	Arrow, Gebrüder Kühnlenz
21 H H K 74	Deluxe Reading/Topper Toy Group
22	Crämer & Héron, Recknagel
23	Mary Hoyer, Recknagel
23 A R V	Arranbee
V P 23	Ideal
24	Recknagel
25	Recknagel, Horsman, Uneeda, Vermont Maid
25 H 7	Deluxe Reading/Topper Toy Group
26	Recknagel
27	Recknagel
28	Recknagel
29	Gebrüder Kühnlenz, Recknagel
30	Goebel, Recknagel
31 A E	Horsman & Co.
31	Recknagel, unidentified
32	Gebrüder Kühnlenz, Ideal, Recknagel
33	Recknagel
34	Goebel, Recknagel

35	Recknagel
37	Recknagel
39	Recknagel
40	Max Räder
41	Recknagel
43	Recknagel
44	Gebrüder Kühnlenz, Recknagel
45	Recknagel
46	Goebel
47	Max Räder, Recknagel
48	Recknagel
49	Horsman & Co., Recknagel
49 R & B	Arranbee
50	Goebel, Ideal, Max Räder, Recknagel
52	Arrow
53	Recknagel
54	Max Oscar Arnold, Goebel, Recknagel
55	Recknagel
56	Gebrüder Kühnlenz, Recknagel
58	Recknagel
60	Goebel, S. F. B. J., Unis France
63	American Character
65 R & B	Arranbee
67	Miss Echo
68	Gebrüder Kühnlenz
69	Heinrich Handwerck
71	Gebrüder Kühnlenz, Unis France, Vogue
72	Gebrüder Kühnlenz
73	Goebel, Recknagel
74	Arrow
75	Gebrüder Kühnlenz
76	Gebrüder Kühnlenz
77	Goebel, Gebrüder Kühnlenz, Seyfarth & Reinhardt
79	All Bisque, Heinrich Handwerck, Schützmeister & Quendt
80	Goebel, Schützmeister & Quendt
81	Schützmeister & Quendt
82	Goebel, Horsman & Co.
83	All Bisque, Goebel, Horsman & Co.
84	Goebel
85	Goebel, L. Lambert
86	Deluxe Reading/Topper Toy Group, Goebel
87	Goebel
88	Goebel, Horsman & Co.
89	Goebel
90	Ideal
P 90	Ideal
P 90 W	Ideal
91	Goebel, Ideal
P 91	Ideal
V 91	Ideal
92	Goebel, Ideal
P 92	Ideal
93	Armand Marseille, Ideal
P 93	Ideal
94	Ideal
P 94	Ideal
98	Hertel, Schwab

Mold Number	Company Name
99	Heinrich Handwerck; Hertel, Schwab
100	All Bisque, Arno Frank, Belton type, Kämmer & Reinhardt, A. Möller & Son, Peter Scherf, unidentified
101	B. Illfelder, Kämmer & Reinhardt, Recknagel, Peter Scherf, Schützmeister & Quendt
102	All Bisque, Goebel, Kämmer & Reinhardt, Peter Scherf, Schützmeister & Quendt
103	Kämmer & Reinhardt, Peter Scherf, unidentified
104	Hertwig, Kämmer & Reinhardt, Recknagel, unidentified
105	All Bisque, Kämmer & Reinhardt, Recknagel
106	Dehais, Goebel, Kämmer & Reinhardt
107	Amberg, Goebel, Kämmer & Reinhardt
108	Kämmer & Reinhardt
109	Heinrich Handwerck, Kämmer & Reinhardt
110	Goebel, Kämmer & Reinhardt, unidentified
111	Goebel, Kämmer & Reinhardt, unidentified
112	Kämmer & Reinhardt
114	Goebel, Kämmer & Reinhardt, Porzellanfabrik Rauenstein
115/115A	Kämmer & Reinhardt
116	Belton type
116/116A	Kämmer & Reinhardt, Kling
117	Belton type
117/117A/117n/117X	Kämmer & Reinhardt
118/118A	Kämmer & Reinhardt
118	unidentified
119	Heinrich Handwerck, Kämmer & Reinhardt, Kling
120	All Bisque, Belton type, Goebel, Kämmer & Reinhardt, Kestner, Max Schelhorn
121	Goebel, Kämmer & Reinhardt, Kestner, Recknagel, Max Schelhorn, unidentified (2)
122	Goebel, Kämmer & Reinhardt, Kestner, Kling, Max Schelhorn, unidentified
123	Goebel, Kämmer & Reinhardt, Kestner, Kling, Max Schelhorn
124	Goebel, Kämmer & Reinhardt, Kestner, Kling, unidentified
125	All Bisque, Goebel, Kämmer & Reinhardt, Kestner, Nikolaus Oberender, unidentified (2)
126	Eisenmann; Goebel; Hertel, Schwab; Kämmer & Reinhardt; Kestner; Recknagel; Walther & Son
127	Belton type; Hertel, Schwab; Kämmer & Reinhardt; Kestner; Recknagel
128	Kämmer & Reinhardt, Kestner, Kling, Recknagel, Hermann Steiner, Valentine
129	Belton Type; Hertel, Schwab; Kestner; Kling; Recknagel; Sonneberger Porzellanfabrik
130	Max Oscar Arnold; Hertel, Schwab; Kestner; Kling; Wiesenthal, Schindel & Kallenberg
131	Hertel, Schwab; Kämmer & Reinhardt; Kestner; Kling; M. Pintel Fils; Recknagel
132	All Bisque; Hertel, Schwab; Kämmer & Reinhardt; Kestner; Recknagel
133	Hertel, Schwab; Kämmer & Reinhardt; Kestner; Kling; Hugo Wiegand; Hermann Steiner
134	Hertel, Schwab; Kestner; Recknagel; Roullet & Decamps; Hermann Steiner; Keramisches Werk
135	Hertel, Schwab; Kämmer & Reinhardt; Kestner; Kling; Recknagel
136	Hertel, Schwab; Keramisches Werk; Kestner; Recknagel
137	All Bisque, Belton type, Kestner, Recknagel

Mold Number	Company Name
138	Hertel, Schwab; Kestner; Recknagel
139	Heinrich Handwerck, Kestner
140	Hertel, Schwab; Kestner; Kling; unidentified
141	Hertel, Schwab; Kestner; Kling
142	Borgfeldt; Hertel, Schwab; Kämmer & Reinhardt; Kestner; Kling
143	Hertel, Schwab; Kestner
144	Kämmer & Reinhardt, Kestner
145	Kestner
146	Kestner
147	Hertel, Schwab; Kestner
148	Hertel, Schwab; Kestner; Kling
149	Hertel, Schwab; Kestner; Unis France
149	S. F. B. J.
150	All Bisque; Max Oscar Arnold; Hertel, Schwab; Hertwig; Kestner; Ohlhaver; Simon & Halbig
151	Deluxe Reading/Topper Toy Group; Hertel, Schwab; Kestner; Kling; Ohlhaver; Simon & Halbig
152	Hertel, Schwab; Kestner; Simon & Halbig
153	Kestner, Simon & Halbig
154	Belton type; Hertel, Schwab; Kestner
155	All Bisque, Kestner
156	All Bisque, Kestner, Kling, Simon & Halbig
157	Hertel, Schwab; Simon & Halbig; unidentified
158	Hertel, Schwab
159	Hertel, Schwab; Kestner; Simon & Halbig
160	Hertel, Schwab; Horsman; Kestner; Kling; Simon & Halbig
161	Alexandre Lefebvre; Hertel, Schwab; Kestner
162	Effanbee; Hertel, Schwab; Kestner
163	Hertel, Schwab; Kestner; unidentified
164	Kestner, Simon & Halbig
165	Hertel, Schwab; Kestner; Gebrüder Kühnlenz
166	Effanbee; Hertel, Schwab; Kestner
167	Hertel, Schwab; Kestner; Kling
168	Kestner
169	Hertel, Schwab; Kestner; Porzellanfabrik Burggrub
170	Belle Doll Co.; Borgfeldt; Hertel, Schwab; Horsman & Co.; Kämmer & Reinhardt; Kestner; Porzellanfabrik Burggrub; Simon & Halbig
171	Kämmer & Reinhardt, Kestner, Simon & Halbig
172	Effanbee; Hertel, Schwab; Kestner; Kling; Simon & Halbig
173	Hertel, Schwab; Kämmer & Reinhardt; Kestner; Simon & Halbig
174	Effanbee, Kestner, Simon & Halbig, unidentified
175	Hertel, Schwab; Hertwig; Kämmer & Reinhardt; Simon & Halbig
176	Effanbee; Hertel, Schwab; Karl Beck & Alfred Schulze; Kling; Simon & Halbig
177	unidentified
178	Hertel, Schwab; Kestner; Kling
179	Hertel, Schwab; Kestner; Knoch; A. Luge; unidentified
180	Hertel, Schwab; Horsman & Co.; Kestner; Roberta
181	Hertel, Schwab; Kestner; Knoch; unidentified
182	Kestner, Kling
183	Belton type, Kestner, unidentified
184	Kestner
185	Belton type, Goebel, Kestner, Kling, Knoch
R 185	Valentine
186	Kestner, Kling
187	Kestner

Mold Number	Company Name
188	Kling
189	Heinrich Handwerck, Kestner, Kling, Knoch
190	Belton type, Deluxe Reading/Topper Group, Kestner, Kling, Knoch, Wilson
191	Kämmer & Reinhardt, Porzellanfabrik Rauenstein
192	Kämmer & Reinhardt, Kestner, Knoch
193	Belton type, Knoch
195	Kestner
196	Kestner
199	Heinrich Handwerck, Kestner, Knoch, unidentified
200	Armand Marseille; Catterfelder; Gebrüder Heubach; Hertel, Schwab; Kämmer & Reinhardt; Max Oscar Arnold; Walther & Sohn
A E 200	Belle
P 200	Ideal
201	Arranbee Doll Co., Bähr & Pröschild, Catterfelder, Fritz Dressel, Jumeau, Kämmer & Reinhardt, Kestner, Knoch, Schützmeister & Quendt, unidentified
202	Fritz Dressel, Jumeau, Kling, Simon & Halbig
203	Fritz Dressel, Jumeau, Kestner, Kling, Knoch
204	Bähr & Pröschild, Jumeau, Knoch, Schützmeister & Quendt
205	Armand Marseille, Catterfelder, Jumeau, Knoch
206	Catterfelder, Jumeau, Kestner, Knoch
207	Adolf Greuling, Bähr & Pröschild, Catterfelder, Jumeau

Heinrich Handwerck #99 Dressed in Fur

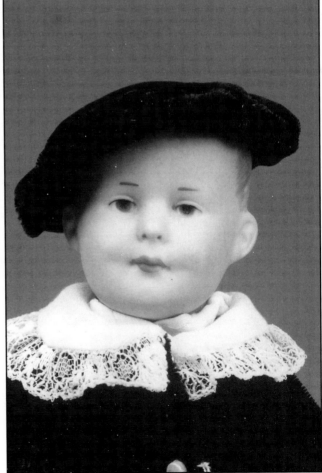

Armand Marseille's Character Boy #600 (Photo Courtesy of Helen Brooke.)

Mold Number	Company Name
208	All Bisque, Adolf Greuling, Catterfelder, Heinrich Graeser, Jumeau, Kestner, Knoch, Walther & Sohn
209	Adolf Greuling, Bähr & Pröschild, Catterfelder, Jumeau
210	Armand Marseille, Arranbee, Fritz Dressel, Jumeau, Kestner, Molly-'es, Richard Scherzer, Roberta, Uneeda Doll Co., Theodor Wendt
211	Fritz Dressel, Jumeau, Kestner
212	Bähr & Pröschild, Fritz Dressel, Jumeau, Kestner
213	Bähr & Pröschild, Hertwig, Jumeau
214	Hertwig, Kämmer & Reinhardt, Jumeau, Kestner, Kling
215	Jumeau, Kestner
216	Jumeau, Kestner, Kling, Knoch
217	Goebel, Jumeau, Kling, Knoch
218	Catterfelder, Jumeau, Kestner
219	Bähr & Pröschild, Catterfelder, Ernst Heubach, Jumeau, Kestner
220	Bähr & Pröschild, Catterfelder, Fritz Dressel, Jumeau, Kestner, Kling
221	Jumeau, Kestner
222	All Bisque, Ernst Heubach, Jumeau, unidentified
223	Armand Marseille, Jumeau, Knoch, Hermann Steiner
224	Bähr & Pröschild, Jumeau, Recknagel
225	All Bisque, Armand Marseille, Bähr & Pröschild, Fritz Dressel, Jumeau, Kämmer & Reinhardt
226	Bähr & Pröschild, G. Geoffroy, Kestner, Recknagel, S. F. B. J.
227	Bähr & Pröschild, Recknagel, S. F. B. J.
229	S. F. B. J.
230	Armand Marseille, Bähr & Pröschild, Fritz Dressel, Jumeau, Knoch, S. F. B. J.
231	Armand Marseille, August Steiner
232	Knoch, Recknagel, Swaine
233	Armand Marseille, S. F. B. J.
234	Kestner
235	Ernst Heubach, Kestner, S. F. B. J.
236	Ernst Heubach, Kestner, S. F. B. J.
237	Ernst Heubach, Kestner, S. F. B. J.
238	Ernst Heubach, S. F. B. J., unidentified
239	Bähr & Pröschild, Kestner, S. F. B. J.
240	Armand Marseille, Baby Phyllis Doll Co., Fritz Dressel, Hermann Steiner, unidentified
241	Amberg, Ernst Heubach, Kestner, Recknagel, Walther & Sohn, unidentified (2)
242	Armand Marseille, Ernst Heubach, Hermann Steiner, Kestner, unidentified, S. F. B. J.
243	Kestner, unidentified
244	Armand Marseille, Bähr & Pröschild
245	Bähr & Pröschild, Hermann Steiner, Kämmer & Reinhardt, Kestner, S. F. B. J.
246	Armand Marseille, Bähr & Pröschild, Hermann Steiner, Kämmer & Reinhardt, Kestner
247	Amberg, Bähr & Pröschild, Hermann Steiner, Kestner, Kling, S. F. B. J., unidentified
248	Bähr & Pröschild, Kämmer & Reinhardt, S. F. B. J.
249	Kestner
250	Armand Marseille, Bähr & Pröschild, Ernst Heubach, Bergmann, Kestner, Walther & Sohn, S. F. B. J.
250 R & B	Arranbee

251	Armand Marseille, Bähr & Pröschild, Borgfeldt, Ernst Heubach, S. F. B. J.
251/A E	Deluxe Reading/Topper Toy Group
251/A E/90	Deluxe Reading/Topper Toy Group
251/A E/100	Eegee
251/A E/Y 29	Deluxe Reading/Topper Toy Group
252	Armand Marseille, Bähr & Pröschild, Ernst Heubach, Schützmeister & Quendt, S. F. B. J.
253	Armand Marseille, Bähr & Pröschild
254	Armand Marseille, Kestner, Kling
255	Armand Marseille, Kämmer & Reinhardt, Kestner, Porzellanfabrik Mengersgereuth
256	Armand Marseille, Kämmer & Reinhardt
257	Armand Marseille, Kestner
259	Armand Marseille, Bähr & Pröschild, Ernst Heubach
260	Bähr & Pröschild, Ernst Heubach, Bergmann, Kestner
261	August Steiner, Bähr & Pröschild, Ernst Heubach
262	Bähr & Pröschild, Catterfelder, Ernst Heubach, Kestner, S. F. B. J.
263	Bähr & Pröschild, Ernst Heubach, Kestner
264	G. Renault & Bon-Dufour, Kestner
265	Bähr & Pröschild, Kämmer & Reinhardt, Rempel & Breitung
266	Armand Marseille, Ernst Heubach
267	Ernst Heubach
268	Ernst Heubach
269	Bähr & Pröschild, Ernst Heubach, Franz Schmidt
270	Armand Marseille, Bähr & Pröschild, Catterfelder
271	Ernst Heubach, unidentified
272	Kestner
273	Armand Marseille, Bähr & Pröschild
274	Ernst Heubach
275	Armand Marseille, Bähr & Pröschild, Ernst Heubach
276	Armand Marseille, Ernst Heubach
277	Bähr & Pröschild
278	Bähr & Pröschild
281	Bähr & Pröschild, Ernst Heubach, Kestner
282	Ernst Heubach, Kestner
283	A. Luge, Bähr & Pröschild, Ernst Heubach, Goebel
284	Ernst Heubach
285	Bähr & Pröschild, Goebel, Kling
286	Goebel
287	Bähr & Pröschild, S. F. B. J.
289	Bähr & Pröschild, Ernst Heubach
290	Kling
291	Ernst Heubach
292	Bähr & Pröschild, Ernst Heubach, Kestner
293	Au Nain Jaune, Carl Knoll, Franz Schmidt
297	Bähr & Pröschild
300	Armand Marseille, Ernst Heubach, Kling, Oskar Bauer, Schützmeister & Quendt
301	Bähr & Pröschild, Ernst Heubach, Schützmeister & Quendt, Unis France, Wiefel, S. F. B. J.
302	Bähr & Pröschild, Ernst Heubach
303	Kling
304	Nicole Döbrich
305	Bähr & Pröschild, Kling, Louis Wolf, Nicole Döbrich
306	Bähr & Pröschild, Jumeau
309	Armand Marseille, Bähr & Pröschild

Mold Number	Company Name
310	Armand Marseille, Vogue
312	Ernst Heubach
313	Bähr & Pröschild, Ernst Heubach
316	E. Bossuat
317	Ernst Heubach, Goebel
318	Armand Marseille, Ernst Heubach, unidentified
319	Ernst Heubach, Goebel, unidentified
320	Armand Marseille, Bähr & Pröschild, Ernst Heubach, Goebel
321	Bähr & Pröschild, Ernst Heubach, Goebel, unidentified
322	Armand Marseille, Bähr & Pröschild, Ernst Heubach, Goebel
323	Armand Marseille, Bähr & Pröschild
324	Armand Marseille, Bähr & Pröschild
325	Armand Marseille, Bähr & Pröschild
326	Armand Marseille, Borgfeldt
327	Armand Marseille, Borgfeldt
328	Armand Marseille
329	Armand Marseille, Borgfeldt
330	Bähr & Pröschild, Goebel
333	Armand Marseille
334	Ernst Heubach, Simon & Halbig, unidentified
335	Simon & Halbig, unidentified
336	Simon & Halbig, unidentified
337	Simon & Halbig, unidentified
338	Simon & Halbig, unidentified
339	Ernst Heubach
341	Arranbee
344	All Bisque
350	Armand Marseille, Bähr & Pröschild, Goebel
351	Arranbee, Kämmer & Reinhardt
351-351K	Armand Marseille
352	Armand Marseille
353	Armand Marseille, Simon & Halbig
356	Armand Marseille, Simon & Halbig
358	Simon & Halbig
359	Adolf Wislizenus, Simon & Halbig
360	Armand Marseille, Simon & Halbig
361	Simon & Halbig
362	Simon & Halbig
363	Armand Marseille, Simon & Halbig
364	Simon & Halbig
365	Simon & Halbig
366	Simon & Halbig
367	Simon & Halbig
368	Simon & Halbig
369	Armand Marseille, Simon & Halbig
370	Armand Marseille, Kling, Max Schelhorn, Simon & Halbig
371	Armand Marseille
372	Armand Marseille, Kling
373	Kling
374	Bähr & Pröschild
375	Armand Marseille, Bähr & Pröschild
376	Armand Marseille, Bähr & Pröschild
377	Armand Marseille, Kling
378	Armand Marseille, Bähr & Pröschild
379	Bähr & Pröschild
380	Bähr & Pröschild
381	Bähr & Pröschild

MOLD NUMBER	COMPANY NAME
382	Armand Marseille
383	Hertwig
384	Armand Marseille, Hertwig
385	Hertwig
386	Hertwig
389	Bähr & Pröschild
390-390n	Armand Marseille, Bähr & Pröschild, unidentified
391	All Bisque
391	Armand Marseille, unidentified
393	Bähr & Pröschild
394	Bähr & Pröschild
395	Armand Marseille, Hermann Steiner
396	Armand Marseille, Ernst Heubach
398	Armand Marseille
399	Armand Marseille, Ernst Heubach
400	Ernst Heubach, Oskar Bauer, Vereinigte Köppelsdorfer Porzellanfabriken
401	Armand Marseille, Berthold Kühn, Hermann Steiner
402	Berthold Kühn, Simon & Halbig
403	Simon & Halbig
405	unidentified
406	Armand Marseille, Ernst Heubach, Kämmer & Reinhardt
407	Carl Bergner, Ernst Heubach
408	Kestner
409	Kestner
410	Armand Marseille
411	Armand Marseille
414	Amberg, Armand Marseille, Ernst Heubach
418	Ernst Heubach
420	Heinrich Handwerck
421	A. Peterhänsel
422	unidentified
427	Ernst Heubach
435	unidentified
437	Ernst Heubach
438	Ernst Heubach
439	Ernst Heubach
445	Ernst Heubach
448	Ernst Heubach
449	Armand Marseille
450	Armand Marseille, Ernst Heubach, Molly-'es, Simon & Halbig
451	Armand Marseille, Ernst Heubach
452	Ernst Heubach
453	Armand Marseille
454	Armand Marseille
457	unidentified
458	Armand Marseille, Ernst Heubach
459	Ernst Heubach
471	Ernst Heubach
478	unidentified
480	Ernst Heubach
482	unidentified
486	Christian Hopf
497	All Bisque
499	unidentified
500	Adolf Greuling, Armand Marseille, Arthur Schoenau, Bruno Schmidt, Simon & Halbig

500K	Hermann von Berg
501	Adolf Greuling, Franz Kiesewetter, Goebel, Guido Knauth
502	Adolf Greuling, Franz Kiesewetter
503	Franz Kiesewetter, unidentified
504	Armand Marseille, Franz Kiesewetter
505	Armand Marseille, Franz Kiesewetter
506	unidentified
507	Franz Kiesewetter
509	Franz Kiesewetter
510	Armand Marseille, Erste Steinbacher, Franz Kiesewetter, unidentified
511	Franz Kiesewetter
513	Armand Marseille, Franz Kiesewetter, unidentified
514	Franz Kiesewetter, Heber
515	Armand Marseille, Franz Kiesewetter
516	Armand Marseille, Franz Kiesewetter
517	Franz Kiesewetter
518	Armand Marseille
519	Armand Marseille
520	Armand Marseilles, Bähr & Pröschild
525	Bähr & Pröschild, Hermann Kiesewetter
526	Bähr & Pröschild
527	Carl Bergner

Cunjo & Otto Dressel, S.F.B.J. Character #237 and Wax Automaton Baby in Buggy (Photo courtesy of Cobb's Doll Auction.)

Frederic Remignard Le Petit Cherubin, Cloth Tag Reads 'Je Marche' (Photo courtesy of Cobb's Doll Auction.)

529	Bähr & Pröschild
530	Simon & Halbig
531	Bähr & Pröschild
535	Bähr & Pröschild
536	Bähr & Pröschild
537	Bähr & Pröschild
539	Bähr & Pröschild
540	Armand Marseille, Simon & Halbig
541	Armand Marseille, Bähr & Pröschild
542	Armand Marseille
546	Bähr & Pröschild
549	Bähr & Pröschild
550	Armand Marseille, Simon & Halbig
550a	Armand Marseille
551-551k	Armand Marseille
554	Bähr & Pröschild
556	Karl Schirmer
560-560a	Armand Marseille
563	Bähr & Pröschild
567	Bähr & Pröschild
568	Bähr & Pröschild
570	Armand Marseille, Simon & Halbig
571	Bähr & Pröschild
573	Ernst Heubach
580	Armand Marseille
581	Bähr & Pröschild
582	Bähr & Pröschild
584	Bähr & Pröschild
585	Bähr & Pröschild
592	Bähr & Pröschild
A E 593	Belle
599	Armand Marseille
600	Armand Marseille, Simon & Halbig, unidentified
602	All Bisque
604	Bähr & Pröschild
606	unidentified
607	Simon & Halbig
608	unidentified
610	Simon & Halbig, unidentified (2)
611	Simon & Halbig
612	Simon & Halbig
616	Fritz Bierschenk, Simon & Halbig
619	Bähr & Pröschild
620	Armand Marseille, unidentified
621	Armand Marseille
624	Bähr & Pröschild
630	Alt, Beck & Gottschalck; Armand Marseille
632	unidentified
639	Alt, Beck & Gottschalck
639	Alt, Beck & Gottschalck
640	Bähr & Pröschild
640a	Armand Marseille
641	Bähr & Pröschild
642	Bähr & Pröschild
643	Bähr & Pröschild
644	Bähr & Pröschild
645	Bähr & Pröschild
646	Bähr & Pröschild

Mold Number	Company Name
650	Alfred Heinz
670	Armand Marseille
678	Bähr & Pröschild
680	Kestner
689	Bähr & Pröschild
693	Alt, Beck & Gottschalck; Simon & Halbig
696	Alt, Beck & Gottschalck; Armand Marseille
698	Alt, Beck & Gottschalck
700	Armand Marseille, Kämmer & Reinhardt, Lucie-Attwell Dolls for Chad Valley, Rheinische Gummi und Celluloid Fabrik Co.
701	Armand Marseille, Carl Knoll, Kämmer & Reinhardt, Lucie-Attwell Dolls for Chad Valley
702	Lucie-Attwell Dolls for Chad Valley
703	Lucie-Attwell Dolls for Chad Valley
704	Lucie-Attwell Dolls for Chad Valley
705	Lucie-Attwell Dolls for Chad Valley
706	Lucie-Attwell Dolls for Chad Valley
707	Bähr & Pröschild
709	Simon & Halbig
710	Armand Marseille
711	Armand Marseille, Lucie-Attwell Dolls for Chad Valley
713	Lucie-Attwell Dolls for Chad Valley
714	Lucie-Attwell Dolls for Chad Valley
715	Kämmer & Reinhardt, Lucie-Attwell Dolls for Chad Valley
716	Kämmer & Reinhardt
717	Kämmer & Reinhardt
718	Kämmer & Reinhardt, Lucie-Attwell Dolls for Chad Valley
719	Kämmer & Reinhardt, Lucie-Attwell Dolls for Chad Valley, Simon & Halbig
720	Kämmer & Reinhardt, Lucie-Attwell Dolls for Chad Valley, Simon & Halbig
721	Kämmer & Reinhardt, Lucie-Attwell Dolls for Chad Valley
722	Lucie-Attwell Dolls for Chad Valley
723	Lucie-Attwell Dolls for Chad Valley
724	Lucie-Attwell Dolls for Chad Valley
725	A. Luge, Carl Bergner, Lucie-Attwell Dolls for Chad Valley
726	Kämmer & Reinhardt
727	Kämmer & Reinhardt
728	Kämmer & Reinhardt, Simon & Halbig
729	Lucie-Attwell Dolls for Chad Valley, Simon & Halbig
730	Kämmer & Reinhardt, Lucie-Attwell Dolls for Chad Valley
731	Lucie-Attwell Dolls for Chad Valley
732	Lucie-Attwell Dolls for Chad Valley
733	Lucie-Attwell Dolls for Chad Valley
734	Lucie-Attwell Dolls for Chad Valley
738	Simon & Halbig
739	Simon & Halbig
740	A. Luge, A. Krauss, Simon & Halbig
748	Simon & Halbig
749	Simon & Halbig, S. F. B. J.
750	Armand Marseille, Simon & Halbig, Sayco
758	Simon & Halbig
759	Simon & Halbig
760	Armand Marseille, Simon & Halbig
767	Bonomi
768	Simon & Halbig
769	Simon & Halbig
770	Simon & Halbig

Mold Number	Company Name
772	Alt, Beck & Gottschalck
773	Kämmer & Reinhardt
776	Kämmer & Reinhardt
777	Kämmer & Reinhardt, Rudolf Leschhorn
778	Simon & Halbig
784	Alt, Beck & Gottschalck
790	All Bisque, Armand Marseille
791	All Bisque
792	All Bisque
800	Armand Marseille, Carl Harmus, Kämmer & Reinhardt, Porzellanfabrik Mengersgereuth, Sonneberger Porzellanfabrik, unidentified
801	unidentified
802	unidentified (also may be marked *W*)
806	unidentified (also may be marked *T R*)
810	Armand Marseille
812	Alt, Beck & Gottschalck
813	unidentified (also may be marked *T R*)
814	unidentified
817	Kämmer & Reinhardt
818	Horsman
820	Armand Marseille
826	Kämmer & Reinhardt
828	Kämmer & Reinhardt, Porzellanfabrik Mengersgereuth
830	All Bisque; Alt, Beck & Gottschalck; Porzellanfabrik Mengersgereuth
831	Kämmer & Reinhardt
837	Simon & Halbig
842	unidentified
845	Simon & Halbig
846	Simon & Halbig
847	Simon & Halbig
848	Simon & Halbig
852	Simon & Halbig
866	Alt, Beck & Gottschalck
868	Alt, Beck & Gottschalck
869	Alt, Beck & Gottschalck
870	Alt, Beck & Gottschalck
871	Heinrich Bätz
873	Kämmer & Reinhardt
878	Simon & Halbig
879	Alt, Beck & Gottschalck
880	Alt, Beck & Gottschalck; Simon & Halbig
881	Simon & Halbig
882	Alt, Beck & Gottschalck; Dornheim, Koch & Fischer
886	All Bisque, Amberg, Recknagel, Simon & Halbig
887	Simon & Halbig
888	Borgfeldt
889	Borgfeldt
890	All Bisque; Alt, Beck & Gottschalck; Ernst Metzler; Simon & Halbig
890a	Otto Jäger
894	Alt, Beck & Gottschalck
896	Simon & Halbig
898	Alt, Beck & Gottschalck; Simon & Halbig
899	Simon & Halbig
900	Armand Marseille, Kämmer & Reinhardt, Porzellanfabrik, unidentified

901	Kämmer & Reinhardt, Simon & Halbig
904	Porzellanfabrik Mengersgereuth
905	Simon & Halbig
908	Simon & Halbig, unidentified
909	Simon & Halbig
911	Alt, Beck & Gottschalck
912	Alt, Beck & Gottschalck
914	Porzellanfabrik Mengersgereuth, Schoenau & Hoffmeister
915	Alt, Beck & Gottschalck
916	Alt, Beck & Gottschalck; Porzellanfabrik Mengersgereuth
917	Kämmer & Reinhardt
918	Simon & Halbig
919	Simon & Halbig
920	Armand Marseille, Simon & Halbig
921	Kämmer & Reinhardt, Simon & Halbig
924	Porzellanfabrik Mengersgereuth
925	unidentified
926	Alt, Beck & Gottschalck; Kämmer & Reinhardt; Porzellanfabrik Mengersgereuth
927	Armand Marseille, Porzellanfabrik Mengersgereuth, Simon & Halbig
928	Porzellanfabrik Mengersgereuth
929	Porzellanfabrik Mengersgereuth, Simon & Halbig
938	Alt, Beck & Gottschalck
939	Simon & Halbig
940	Simon & Halbig
941	Simon & Halbig
949	Simon & Halbig
950	Armand Marseille, Porzellanfabrik Mengersgereuth, Simon & Halbig
951	Armand Marseille
952	Kämmer & Reinhardt
959	Simon & Halbig
966	Armand Marseille, Hugo Wiegand
967	Hugo Wiegand
968	Simon & Halbig
969	Simon & Halbig
970	Armand Marseille, Simon & Halbig
971-971a	Armand Marseille
972	Amberg, Armand Marseille
973	Amberg, Armand Marseille, Kämmer & Reinhardt
974	Alt, Beck & Gottschalck
975	Armand Marseille
977	Kämmer & Reinhardt
978	Alt, Beck & Gottschalck
979	Simon & Halbig
980	Alt, Beck & Gottschalck; Armand Marseille
982	Amberg, Armand Marseille
983	Amberg
984	Armand Marseille
985	Armand Marseille
988	Simon & Halbig
989	Simon & Halbig
990	Alt, Beck & Gottschalck; Armand Marseille; Simon & Halbig
991	Armand Marseille, Vereinigte Köppelsdorfer Porzellanfabriken
992	Armand Marseille
993	Armand Marseille

Mold Number	Company Name
995	Armand Marseille, Hugo Wiegand
996	Alt, Beck & Gottschalck; Armand Marseille
997	Armand Marseille
998	Alt, Beck & Gottschalck
1000	Alt, Beck & Gottschalck; Hermann Steiner; Simon & Halbig; unidentified
1001	Fritz Lutz, Wagner & Zetsche
1002	Alt, Beck & Gottschalck; Fritz Lutz
1003	Fritz Lutz
1004	Fritz Lutz
1005	Borgfeldt
1007	Fritz Lutz
1008	Alt, Beck & Gottschalck; Simon & Halbig
1009	Simon & Halbig
1010	Simon & Halbig
1015	Oskar Schlesinger
1018	Simon & Halbig
1019	Simon & Halbig
1020	Alt, Beck & Gottschalck; Oskar Schlesinger; Simon & Halbig
1024	Alt, Beck & Gottschalck
1025	Oskar Schlesinger
1026	Alt, Beck & Gottschalck
1028	Alt, Beck & Gottschalck
1029	Simon & Halbig
1030	Alt, Beck & Gottschalck; Oskar Schlesinger
1032	Alt Beck & Gottschalck
1035	Oskar Schlesinger
1038	Simon & Halbig
1039	Simon & Halbig
1040	Oskar Schlesinger, Simon & Halbig
1041	Simon & Halbig
1044	Alt, Beck & Gottschalck
1046	Alt, Beck & Gottschalck; Louis Reber
1049	Simon & Halbig
1054	Alt, Beck & Gottschalck
1056	Alt, Beck & Gottschalck
1058	Simon & Halbig
1059	Simon & Halbig
1060	Simon & Halbig
1061	Simon & Halbig
1062	Alt, Beck & Gottschalck
1064	Alt, Beck & Gottschalck
1068	Simon & Halbig
1069	Simon & Halbig
1070	König (also spelled *Koenig*) & Wernicke, Simon & Halbig
1078	Simon & Halbig
1079	Simon & Halbig
1080	Simon & Halbig
1086	Alt, Beck & Gottschalck
1092	Alt, Beck & Gottschalck
1098	Simon & Halbig
1099	Simon & Halbig
1100	Catterfelder
1108	Simon & Halbig
1109	Simon & Halbig
1110	Simon & Halbig
1112	Alt, Beck & Gottschalck

1123	Alt, Beck & Gottschalck
1127	Alt, Beck & Gottschalck
1129	Simon & Halbig
1142	Alt, Beck & Gottschalck
1148	Simon & Halbig
1149	Simon & Halbig
1150	Simon & Halbig
1152	Alt, Beck & Gottschalck
1153	Alt, Beck & Gottschalck
1154	Alt, Beck & Gottschalck
1158	Simon & Halbig
1159	Simon & Halbig
1160	Simon & Halbig
1170	Alt, Beck & Gottschalck; Simon & Halbig
1171	Alt, Beck & Gottschalck
1172	Alt, Beck & Gottschalck
1173	Alt, Beck & Gottschalck
1174	Alt, Beck & Gottschalck
1175	Alt, Beck & Gottschalck
1176	Alt, Beck & Gottschalck
1177	Alt, Beck & Gottschalck
1180	Heinrich Graeser, Simon & Halbig
1199	Simon & Halbig
1200	Catterfelder, unidentified
1210	Alt, Beck & Gottschalck
1214	Alt, Beck & Gottschalck
1218	Alt, Beck & Gottschalck
1222	Alt, Beck & Gottschalck
1226	Alt, Beck & Gottschalck; Bruno Schmidt
1228	Borgfeldt
1234	Alt, Beck & Gottschalck
1235	Alt, Beck & Gottschalck
1236	Alt, Beck & Gottschalck
1237	Alt, Beck & Gottschalck
1246	Simon & Halbig
1248	Simon & Halbig
1249	Simon & Halbig
1250	Alt, Beck & Gottschalck; Franz Schmidt; Simon & Halbig
1253	Franz Schmidt
1254	Alt, Beck & Gottschalck
1259	Franz Schmidt
1260	Alt, Beck & Gottschalck; Simon & Halbig
1261	Alt, Beck & Gottschalck
1262	Franz Schmidt
1263	Franz Schmidt
1266	Franz Schmidt
1267	Franz Schmidt
1268	Alt, Beck & Gottschalck
1269	Alt, Beck & Gottschalck; Simon & Halbig
1270	Alt, Beck & Gottschalck
1271	Alt, Beck & Gottschalck; Franz Schmidt
1272	Franz Schmidt
1274	Franz Schmidt
1278	Alt, Beck & Gottschalck; Simon & Halbig
1279	Alt, Beck & Gottschalck; Simon & Halbig
1280	Simon & Halbig
1288	Alt, Beck & Gottschalck

MOLD NUMBER	COMPANY NAME
1289	Simon & Halbig
1290	Alt, Beck & Gottschalck
1291	Alt, Beck & Gottschalck
1293	Simon & Halbig
1294	Simon & Halbig
1295	Simon & Halbig
1296	Simon & Halbig
1297	Simon & Halbig
1298	Simon & Halbig
1299	Simon & Halbig
1300	Simon & Halbig
1301	Simon & Halbig
1302	Simon & Halbig
1303	Simon & Halbig
1304	Simon & Halbig
1305	Simon & Halbig
1307	Simon & Halbig
1308	Simon & Halbig
1310	Simon & Halbig
1321	Alt, Beck & Gottschalck
1322	Alt, Beck & Gottschalck
1326	Alt, Beck & Gottschalck
1329	Simon & Halbig
1340	Simon & Halbig
1342	Alt, Beck & Gottschalck
1348	Simon & Halbig
1349	Simon & Halbig
1351	Simon & Halbig
1352	Alt, Beck & Gottschalck
1353	Alt, Beck & Gottschalck
1357	Alt, Beck & Gottschalck
1358	Alt, Beck & Gottschalck; Simon & Halbig
1360	Alt, Beck & Gottschalck
1361	Alt, Beck & Gottschalck
1362	Alt, Beck & Gottschalck
1366	Alt, Beck & Gottschalck
1367	Alt, Beck & Gottschalck
1368	Alt, Beck & Gottschalck; Simon & Halbig
1369	Borgfeldt
1370	Simon & Halbig
1373	Alt, Beck & Gottschalck
1376	Alt, Beck & Gottschalck; Schützmeister & Quendt
1377	unidentified
1388	Simon & Halbig
1394	Alt, Beck & Gottschalck
1397	Simon & Halbig
1398	Simon & Halbig
1400	Robert Carl, Schoenau & Hoffmeister
1401	Robert Carl
1402	Alt, Beck & Gottschalck
1406/46	Valentine
1407	Alt, Beck & Gottschalck
1410	Borgfeldt
1426	Simon & Halbig
1428	Simon & Halbig
1429	Simon & Halbig
1431	Alt, Beck & Gottschalck; unidentified

Mold Number	Company Name
1432	Alt, Beck & Gottschalck
1448	Simon & Halbig
1465	Simon & Halbig
1469	Simon & Halbig
1478	Simon & Halbig
1485	Simon & Halbig
1488	Simon & Halbig
1489	Simon & Halbig
1496	Simon & Halbig
1498	Simon & Halbig
1514	Theodor Degenring
1527	Simon & Halbig
1563	Theodor Degenring
1565	Borgfeldt
1566	Theodor Degenring
1571	Theodor Degenring
1571	Theodor Degenring
1601	Heinrich Liebermann
1616	Simon & Halbig
1748	Simon & Halbig
1776	Cuno & Otto Dressel
1800	Schoenau & Hoffmeister
1813	unidentified
1848	Simon & Halbig
1849	Simon & Halbig
1890	Armand Marseille
1892	Armand Marseille
1893	Armand Marseille
1894	Armand Marseille
1895	Armand Marseille, Moritz Resek
1896	Armand Marseille
1897	Armand Marseille
1898	Armand Marseille
1899	Armand Marseille, Peter Scherf, Wenzel Prouza
1900	Armand Marseille, Ernst Heubach, Schoenau & Hoffmeister, unidentified
1901	Armand Marseille, Ernst Heubach, Peter Scherf
1902	Armand Marseille, Ernst Heubach, Peter Scherf, unidentified
1903	Adolf Prouza, Armand Marseille, Pollack & Hoffmann
1904	Anger, Erste Steinbacher, Pollack & Hoffmann, Schoenau & Hoffmeister
1905	Armand Marseille
1906	Ernst Heubach, Schoenau & Hoffmeister
1907	Jumeau, Plass & Roesner, Theodor Pohl, Theodor Recknagel
1909	Armand Marseille, Ernst Heubach, Theodor Recknagel, Schoenau & Hoffmeister
1910	Ernst Winkler, unidentified
1912	Simon & Halbig, unidentified
1913	Heinrich Bätz, Plass & Roesner
1914	Heinrich Bätz, Simon & Halbig, Theodor Recknagel, unidentified
1916	C. M. Bergmann, Simon & Halbig
1920	A. Möller, Simon & Halbig
1921	All Bisque
1922	Ernst Heubach
1923	Maar, Borgfeldt
1924	Hermann Pensky, Theodor Recknagel
1930	Schoenau & Hoffmeister

MOLD NUMBER	COMPANY NAME
2000	Armand Marseille, Nikolaus Oberender
2015	Armand Marseille
2020	Bähr & Pröschild
2023	Bähr & Pröschild
2025	Bähr & Pröschild
2033	Bähr & Pröschild
2042	Bähr & Pröschild
2048	Bähr & Pröschild
2070	Bähr & Pröschild
2072	Bähr & Pröschild
2074	Bähr & Pröschild
2075	Bähr & Pröschild
2081	Bähr & Pröschild
2084	Bähr & Pröschild
2085	Bähr & Pröschild
2092	Bähr & Pröschild
2094	Bähr & Pröschild
2095	Bähr & Pröschild
2096	Bähr & Pröschild
2097	Bähr & Pröschild
2099	Bähr & Pröschild
2112	Allied Grand Doll Manufacturing
2144	Paul Rauschert
2154	Bähr & Pröschild
2500	Schoenau & Hoffmeister
2542	Armand Marseille
2918	Borgfeldt
2966	Sonneberger Porzellanfabriken
3066	Armand Marseille
3091	Armand Marseille
3093	Armand Marseille
3095	Armand Marseille
3200	Armand Marseille
3300	Armand Marseille
3500	Armand Marseille
3600	Armand Marseille
3700	Armand Marseille
4000	Schoenau & Hoffmeister
4001	Schoenau & Hoffmeister
4008	Armand Marseille
4129	Nöckler & Tittel
4274 K	Kaysam Jolly Toy Corp.
4500	Schoenau & Hoffmeister
4536	Paul Schmidt
4595	Citro
4600	Schoenau & Hoffmeister
4700	Schoenau & Hoffmeister
4703	Weiss, Kühnert & Co.
4900	Schoenau & Hoffmeister
5000	All Bisque, Schoenau & Hoffmeister
5300	Schoenau & Hoffmeister
5320	Kaysam Jolly Toy Corp.
5332	Johannes Franz (marking found on doll body)
5430	Porzellanfabrik Rauenstein
5500	Schoenau & Hoffmeister
5625	Gebrüder Heubach
5636	Gebrüder Heubach

5689	Gebrüder Heubach
5700	Schoenau & Hoffmeister
5730	Gebrüder Heubach
5773	Gebrüder Heubach
5777	Gebrüder Heubach
5800	Schoenau & Hoffmeister
5990	Armand Marseille
6211	Horsman & Co.
6399	Borgfeldt
6600	Paul Rauschert
6618	Horsman & Co.
6688	Gebrüder Heubach
6692	Gebrüder Heubach
6736	Gebrüder Heubach
6774	Gebrüder Heubach
6789	Otto Gans, Walther & Sohn
6891	Gebrüder Heubach
6892	Gebrüder Heubach
6894	Gebrüder Heubach
6896	Gebrüder Heubach
6897	Gebrüder Heubach
6969	Gebrüder Heubach
6970	Gebrüder Heubach
6971	Gebrüder Heubach
7027	Gebrüder Heubach
7064	Gebrüder Heubach
7072	Gebrüder Heubach
7077	Gebrüder Heubach
7106	Gebrüder Heubach
7109	Gebrüder Heubach
7124	Gebrüder Heubach
7129	Gebrüder Heubach
7134	Gebrüder Heubach
7138	Gebrüder Heubach
7139	Gebrüder Heubach
7144	Gebrüder Heubach
7211	Gebrüder Heubach
7226	Gebrüder Heubach
7246	Gebrüder Heubach
7247	Gebrüder Heubach
7248	Gebrüder Heubach
7256	Gebrüder Heubach
7307	Gebrüder Heubach
7314	Gebrüder Heubach
7326	Gebrüder Heubach
7345	Gebrüder Heubach
7346	Gebrüder Heubach
7402	Gebrüder Heubach
7407	Gebrüder Heubach
7550	Gebrüder Heubach
7587	Gebrüder Heubach
7602	Gebrüder Heubach
7603	Gebrüder Heubach
7604	Gebrüder Heubach
7614	Gebrüder Heubach
7616	Gebrüder Heubach
7620	Gebrüder Heubach

MOLD NUMBER	COMPANY NAME
7622	Gebrüder Heubach
7623	Gebrüder Heubach
7624	Gebrüder Heubach
7625	Gebrüder Heubach
7631	Gebrüder Heubach
7634	Gebrüder Heubach
7635	Gebrüder Heubach
7636	Gebrüder Heubach
7637	Gebrüder Heubach
7644	Gebrüder Heubach
7647	Gebrüder Heubach
7650	Gebrüder Heubach
7657	Gebrüder Heubach
7658	Gebrüder Heubach
7659	Gebrüder Heubach
7669	Gebrüder Heubach
7670	Gebrüder Heubach
7671	Gebrüder Heubach
7679	Gebrüder Heubach
7686	Gebrüder Heubach
7687	Gebrüder Heubach
7692	Gebrüder Heubach
7701	Gebrüder Heubach
7703	Gebrüder Heubach
7711	Gebrüder Heubach
7714	Gebrüder Heubach
7739	Gebrüder Heubach
7740	Gebrüder Heubach
7743	Gebrüder Heubach
7744	Gebrüder Heubach
7745	Gebrüder Heubach
7759	Gebrüder Heubach
7760	Gebrüder Heubach
7761	Gebrüder Heubach
7763	Gebrüder Heubach
7764	Gebrüder Heubach
7768	Gebrüder Heubach
7779	Gebrüder Heubach
7788	Gebrüder Heubach
7843	Gebrüder Heubach
7850	Gebrüder Heubach
7851	Gebrüder Heubach
7864	Gebrüder Heubach
7867	Gebrüder Heubach
7885	Gebrüder Heubach
7890	Gebrüder Heubach
7911	Gebrüder Heubach
7917	Gebrüder Heubach
7925	Gebrüder Heubach
7926	Gebrüder Heubach
7956	Gebrüder Heubach
7971	Gebrüder Heubach
7975	Gebrüder Heubach
7977	Gebrüder Heubach
8017	Gebrüder Heubach
8050	Gebrüder Heubach
8055	Gebrüder Heubach

Mold Number	Company Name
8173	Kämmer & Reinhardt
8191	Gebrüder Heubach
8192	Gebrüder Heubach
8195	Gebrüder Heubach
8226	Gebrüder Heubach
8232	Gebrüder Heubach
8306	Gebrüder Heubach
8309	Gebrüder Heubach
8316	Gebrüder Heubach
8407	Gebrüder Heubach
8413	Gebrüder Heubach
8420	Gebrüder Heubach
8457	Gebrüder Heubach
8459	Gebrüder Heubach
8473	Gebrüder Heubach
8547	Gebrüder Heubach
8548	Gebrüder Heubach
8552	Limbach
8553	Limbach
8572	Gebrüder Heubach
8588	Gebrüder Heubach
8589	Gebrüder Heubach
8606	Gebrüder Heubach
8682	Limbach
8724	Gebrüder Heubach
8729	Gebrüder Heubach
8759	Gebrüder Heubach
8764	Gebrüder Heubach
8774	Gebrüder Heubach
8778	Gebrüder Heubach
8801	Gebrüder Heubach
8867	Limbach
8887	Gebrüder Heubach
9042	Gebrüder Heubach
9056	Gebrüder Heubach
9072	Gebrüder Heubach
9081	Gebrüder Heubach
9085	Gebrüder Heubach
9141	Gebrüder Heubach
9167	Gebrüder Heubach
9209	Gebrüder Heubach
9219	Gebrüder Heubach
9355	Gebrüder Heubach
9457	Gebrüder Heubach
9500	Rudolph Heinz
9513	Gebrüder Heubach
9572	Gebrüder Heubach
9578	Gebrüder Heubach
9594	Gebrüder Heubach
10050	All Bisque
10532	Gebrüder Heubach
10539	Gebrüder Heubach
10556	Gebrüder Heubach
10557	Gebrüder Heubach
10586	Gebrüder Heubach
10588	Gebrüder Heubach
10617	Gebrüder Heubach

Mold Number	Company Name
10633	Gebrüder Heubach
10727	Gebrüder Heubach
10731	Gebrüder Heubach
10790	Gebrüder Heubach
11010	Gebrüder Heubach
12386	Gebrüder Heubach
13765	Borgfeldt
16647	Hermann Wegner (marking found on doll body)
19251	Ernst Winkler
19252	Ernst Winkler
19555	Franz Schmidt (marking found on doll body)
43594	Richard Fröber (marking found on doll body)
44520	Amberg
46547	Josef Bergmann (marking found on doll body)
56562	Simon & Halbig (marking found on doll body)
56996	Gottlieb Zinner & Son (marking found on doll body)
66543	Hermann Landshut & Co.
70685	Kestner
100279	Heinrich Handwerck
119857	Ferdinand Imhof
132410	E. U. Steiner, Robert Carl (marking found on doll body)
160638	Alfred Heller (marking found on doll body)
193440	Louis Stammberger (marking found on doll body)
201013	Louis Liebermann (marking found on doll body)
214027	Wilson Novelty Company
357529	Hermann Wegner (marking found on doll body)
374830	Armand Marseille (marking found on doll body)
374831	Armand Marseille (marking found on doll body)
421481	Adolf Wislizenus (marking found on doll body)
442910	Rudolf Walch (marking found on doll body)
447828	Rheinische Gummi und Celluloid Fabrik (marking found on doll body)
452711	Wiesenthal, Schindel & Kallenberg (marking found on doll body)
520942	Alt, Beck & Gottschalck (marking found on doll body)
856346	Johann Müller (marking found on doll body)
897388	Louis Reber (marking found on doll body)
945354	Priska Sander (marking found on doll body)
954642	Hermann Steiner (marking found on doll body)
2252077	Ideal
2675644	American Character
2687594	Vogue

CHAPTER FOUR

LETTERS OR INITIALS USED IN MANUFACTURING

Occasionally, a doll manufacturer will choose to use a letter or a series of letters to signify a particular doll, or as a form of identification for their company. This seems perfectly logical, for it is reasonable to see the letters *F & B* used to symbolize Effanbee. Interestingly, Effanbee is itself an acronym for the names Fleischaker and Baum; however, not all letters used for doll identification have such a clear and coherent association.

The letter *A* included in a Kämmer and Reinhardt marking implies the need for a wig on that particular doll head. To understand or analyze the significance of all letter markings would be a formidable assignment. Therefore, no attempt has been made to give an explanation of the markings.

Not all letters and initials that have been given are for the sole purpose of identification. In an effort to provide you with information which may be advantageous to you in your pursuit of dolls, the following charts include letters and initials that are used by organizations connected with dolls in some way.

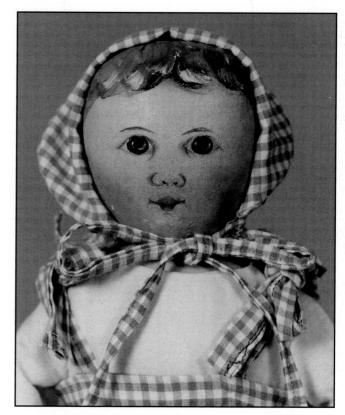

Columbian Doll by the Adams Sisters (Photo courtesy of McMasters Doll Auctions.)

Letters or Initials	Manufacturer
A	Kämmer & Reinhardt
A	Arrow
A	Allied
A	Deluxe Reading/Topper Toy Group
A & M	A & M Doll Co.
A & M	Moehling
A B & C	Althof, Bergmann Co. (accepted as)
A B C	American Bisque Doll Co.
A B C	Butler Brothers
A B G	Alt, Beck & Gottschalck
A C	American Character
A C D	American Character
A D	Mme. A. Dehors
A D	Alexandre Delhaye
A D C	Acorn Doll Co.
A E	Deluxe Reading/Topper Toy Group
A E	Belle
A E	Mary Hoyer
A E	Sayco
A E	Valentine
A H	Adolf Heller
A H A B E	Amber & Hergershausen
A H H	Deluxe Reading/Topper Toy Group
A H H H	Deluxe Reading/Topper Toy Group
A H H K	Deluxe Reading/Topper Toy Group
A H S	Albin Steiner
A H W	Adolf Heller
A H W	Adolf Hülss
A K	A. Kröhl
A L B	Adolf Landsberger
A L S	Anton Link
A M	Armand Marseille
A M	A. Michaelis
A M N	Andreas Müller
A P	Adolf Prouza
A R	Theodor Recknagel
A R	August Riedeler
A R I	A. Riedeler
A S	Arthur Schoenau
A S	August Steiner
A S S	Arthur Schoenau
A V	Porzellanfabrik Neuhaus
A W H	Adolf Hülss
A. B. C.	Althof, Bergmann & Co.
A. C.	American Character
A. F. & C.	mark found on papier-mâché dolls with a Superior label
Aceedeecee	American Character Doll Co.
AeM	A. C. Anger
AHABA	Amberg & Hergershausen
AIAI	Arno Lützelberger
Amer. Char.	American Character
B	Horsman & Co
B	Ideal
B & D	Bawo & Dotter
B & P	Bähr & Pröschild
B & S	manufactured doll shoes
B J & Co.	B. Illfelder & Co.

Letters or Initials	Manufacturer
B K B	Beers, Keeler & Bowman Co.
B N D	British National Doll
B P	Swain & Co.
B P	Bähr & Pröschild
B P	Swaine & Co.
B S	Bruno Schmidt
B S	Ideal
B S W	Bruno Schmidt
B S W	Bähr & Pröschild (Bruno Schmidt)
B. I. & Co.	B. Illfelder
B. K. B.	Beers Keeler Bowman Co.
B. P. D.	Boston Pottery Co. (assumed)
B. S.	initials found on dolls distributed by Alphonse Giroux
BB	Baker & Bennett Co.
Bi, Ba, Bo	Weise & Co
Bi-Ba-Bo	Julius Jeidel
C	Cuno & Otto Dressel
C	Dressel & Koch
C	Terry Lee
C A H O	Canzler & Hofmann
C B	Carl Bergmann
C C	unidentified German doll manufacturer
C D C	Cosmopolitan Doll Corp.
C E & S	Christian Eichhorn & Söhne
C E G D	C. Erich Günther
C E U S	Christian Eichhorn & Söhne
C F & Co.	Carl Feiler & Co.
C H	Carl Hartmann
C H N D	Carl Horn Nachf. (See chapter eight for explanation of German words and phrases.)
C I V	Civil Imperial Volunteer
C K	Carl Knoll
C K F	Carl Krahmer
C L	Charles Laumaunier
C O D	Cuno Otto Dressel
C P	Catterfelder Puppenfabrik
C T	Carl Trautmann
C V	Closter Veilsdorf
C. I. V.	Civil Imperial Volunteer (used on the brim of doll hats)
Caho	Canzler & Hoffmann
CAMA	Armand Marseille
D	Julius Dorst
D	Cuno & Otto Dressel
D & K	Dressel & Koch
D & P C	Dressel & Pietschmann
D A D A	Hermsdorfer Celluloidwarenfabrik
D A L A B A	Arthur Schoenau
D E C O	Otto Denivelle
D E P	initials used on both French and German dolls indicating a claim to registration
D G M Sch	initials used on German doll bodies claiming a registration
D I	Swaine & Co.
D I P	Swaine & Co.
D K F	Dornheim, Koch & Fischer
D O E	Ideal
D P	Dora Petzold
D R G M	initials used on German dolls indicating a registered design or patent

D R M R . . . . initials used by Armand Marseille claiming registration of a doll, protecting it from fraud

D R P . . . . initials used to indicate a patent of the German Government

D R P A . . . . initials used to indicate an application of a patent of the German Government

D V . . . . Swaine & Co.

D. F. B. . . . . De Fuisseaux

D. P. . . . . Hamburger & Co.

D. P. Co. . . . . Doll Pottery Co.

DECO . . . . Effanbee

E & S . . . . Christian Eichhorn & Söhne

E B V R . . . . Emil Bauersachs

E D . . . . E. Dehler

E D . . . . Cuno & Otto Dressel

E D H . . . . E. Dehler

E F Co. . . . . Australian Medal Head Doll Works

E G . . . . Edgard Goldstein & Co.

E G . . . . Ernst Grossmann

E G . . . . Eegee

E H . . . . Ernst Heubach

E H K . . . . Ernst Heubach

E K . . . . Ernst Klötzer

E K . . . . Edmund Knoch

E L . . . . Ernst Liebermann

E M . . . . Ernst Metzler

E M A S O . . . . Ma. E. Maar

E N S . . . . Ens Puppen

E P . . . . Emil Pfeiffer

E S C O . . . . Sommer & Co.

Hard Plastic Mary Hoyer (Photo courtesy of Helen Brooke.)

Georgene Noveltie's Brownie (Photo courtesy of Helen Brooke.)

Letters or Initials	Manufacturer
E S T P	Erste Steinbacher Porzellanfabrik
E U S T	Edmund Ulrich Steiner
E v B	Erich von Berg
E W	Ernst Winkler
E W H	Ernst Winkler
E Z	Emil Zitzmann
E. L. S. F.	East London Toy Factory
E. U. St.	Edmund Ulrich Steiner
E. I. H.	Horsman & Co.
EBASO	Emil Bauersachs
EINCO	Eisenmann & Co., by Gebrüder Heubach
F	Fab Lu (assumed)
F & B	Effanbee Doll Co.
F & B	Fleischmann & Bloedel
F & B F	Fleischmann & Bloedel
F B	Fritz Bierschenk
F C R	Mme. Caroline Ricaillon
F E M A	Beck & Co.
F E W B	Friedrich Edmund Winkler
F N & Co.	Fischer, Naumann & Co.
F N C	Fischer, Naumann & Co.
F N I	Fischer, Naumann & Co.
F P	Friedrichsrodaer Puppenfabrik
F P	Swaine & Co.
F S	Franz Schmidt & Co.
F S & Co.	Franz Schmidt & Co.
F W B	F. Welsch
F. R.	American Doll & Toy Co.
FS & C	Franz Schmidt & Co.
G	Georg Gebert
G	Ideal
G & Co	Greiner & Co.
G & S	Gutmann & Schiffnie
G & S	Gans & Seyfarth
G B	George Borgfeldt
G B N	Bing Art Doll
G D F	unidentified German doll manufacturer
G E	Ideal
G E S U E	Gebrüder Süssenguth
G E T E	Gustav Thiele
G H	Gustav Heubach
G H	Gebrüder Heubach
G K	Gebrüder Kühnlenz
G K N	Gebrüder Knoch
G L	Georg Lutz
G L	unidentified German doll manufacturer
G M	initials used on German dolls to indicate patent protecting such issues as model, performance, and design
G M S	often means that registered mold number includes novelty or combination of special invention on doll
G S	Gans & Seyfarth
G S	Gebrüder Süssenguth
G T	Gerber & Teusch
G W	Gustav Wohlleben
G W	Ideal
Gbr K	Gebrüder Kühnlenz
H	Heinrich Handwerck
H	Horsman & Co.

H & Co	Hamburger & Co.
H C	Heber & Co.
H c H H	Heinrich Handwerck
H C L	Hubert Des Loges
H D D H	Humpty Dumpty Doll Hospital
H H	Hermann Heyde
H H	Heinrich Handwerck
H H D	Hermann Heyde
H H W	Heinrich Handwerck
H J	TrachtenPuppen SpielPuppen
H J L	H. J. Leven
H L	unidentified German doll manufacturer
H P F	Herzpuppen-Fabrik
H S	Hermann Steiner
H S N	Hermann Steiner
H St	Hermann Steiner
H W	Hugo Wiegand
H W	Heinrich Handwerck
H W E N S P F	Hermann Wolf
H W N	Hugo Wiegand
I B	Iris Beaumont
I D M A	International Doll Makers Association
I G E S	J. G, Escher & Sohn
I G O D I	Kohl & Wengenroth
I K W A	L. Bamberger & Co.
I l l c o	Carl Illing & Co.
I We Em	Ines Wetzel
IKWA	L. Bamberger & Co.
J B	Jacques Berner
J B	Jullien Balleroy & Cie
J D E N	Josef Deuerlein
J D K	Kestner
J D S	Julius Dorst
J H & S	Julius Hering & Sohn
J I O	Alt, Beck & Gottschalck
J J	Joseph Joanny
J K	Theodor Recknagel
J M S	Julia Müller-Sarne
J. K.	Horsman & Co.
Jgodi (also spelled *Igodi*)	initials used by Johannes Gotthilf Dietrich (a distributor of Ernst Heubach bisque dolls)
K	Nasco
K	Gilbert
K	Kaysam Jolly
K & Co	Kestner & Co.
K & Co	Kestner
K & H	Kley & Hahn
K & R	Kämmer & Reinhardt
K & W	König (also spelled *Koenig*) & Wernicke
K & W	Koch & Weithase
K B	unidentified German doll manufacturer
K B	Karl Baumann
K H	Karl Hartmann
K K	Käthe Kruse
K P M	Königliche Porzellanmanufaktur
K P M	August Wilhelm Friedolin Kister (A. W. Fr.)
K P N	Karl Pietsch

K R	Kämmer & Reinhardt
K W	Kohl & Wengenroth
K W G	Keramisches Werk
K W W	König (also spelled *Koenig*) & Wernicke
K& R W	Kämmer & Reinhardt
K. T.	Allied
KO-K O	Borgfeldt
L & D	Löffler & Dill
L & D S	Löffler & Dill
L & H	Leibe & Hofmann
L & M	unidentified German doll manufacturer
L A & S	Louis Amberg & Son
L A & S NY	Louis Amberg & Son
L D	Löffler & Dill
L H B	unidentified German doll manufacturer
L L & S	Louis Lindner & Söhne
L P L	Louis Philipp Luthardt
L S	Lambert & Samhammer
L W & C	Louis Wolf & Co.
L W & Co	Louis Wolf & Co.
L. D.	Doléac, L. & Cie
M	unidentified German doll manufacturer
M	Maar
M	Ideal
M E	Ideal
M & S	Müller & Strasburger
M B	Arthur Schoenau

Parian with Molded Ribbon, Curly Hair China, Pair of Flat Top China, and Highland Mary (Photo courtesy of Cobb's Doll Auction.)

Group of Early Ladies: Parian, Spill Curls China, Untinted Bisque with Molded Bodice, Petite Pink Tint China with Bun, and Biedermeier China with Wig (Photo courtesy of Cobb's Doll Auction.)

LETTERS OR INITIALS	MANUFACTURER
M C	Bonomi
M Co	Karl Müller & Co.
M K	Ideal
M K W	Josef Strasser
M L	Emell Toy Manufacturing Co.
M M M	Maar
M O A	Max Oscar Arnold
M R	Moritz Resek
M R W	Max Rudolph
M S S	Mylius Sperschneider
M T F	Averill Manufacturing (Maud Tousey Fangel)
M Ü K A	Müller & Kaltwasser
M. L.	Emell Toy Manufacturing Co.
M. T. C.	Modern Doll Co.
n	Kämmer & Reinhardt denotes a new model
N & T	Nöckler & Tittle
N G	initials indicating newborn with a straight neck used by Theodor Recknagel
N I A D A	National Institute of American Doll Artists
N K	initials indicating newborn with a socket head used by Theodor Recknagel
N O	Nikolaus Oberender
N T	Nöckler & Tittle
N. F.	Uneeda
O-H	Eegee
O B	Oskar Büchner
O C O	Offenbach & Co
O Co	H. Offenbacher & Co.
O D A C A	Original Doll Artists Council of America
O G	Otto Gans
O G A	Otto Gans
O I C	Kestner
O S	Otto Schamberger
O W N	Otto Wohlmann
P	Admiration
P	Arranbee
P	Beehler Arts
P	Belle
P	Sayco
P	Uneeda
P	Princess Ann
P	Ideal
P & H	Pollak & Hoffmann
P & R	Plass & Roesner
P A M A	G. Herold
P E S O	Paul Schmidt
P H	Paul Hunaeus
P I	Ideal
P I G O	Puppenindustrie Gotha
P L	Natural
P M	Porzellanfabrik Mengersgereuth
P N	Porzellanfabrik Neuhaus, S. Bergmann
P R	Paul Rauschert
P R	Hermann Rösel
P S	Paul Schmidt
P S Sth	Paul Schmidt
P Sch	Peter Scherf
P Z	Paul Zierow

Letters or Initials	Manufacturer
P. M. A.	Plastic Molded Arts
R	Räder
R & S S	Rauch & Schelhorn
R A	Theodor Recknagel
R B	Rempel & Breitung
R B W	Richard Beck & Co.
R C	Robert Carl
R D E P	Max Räder
R n	Porzellanfabrik Rauenstein
R&B	Arranbee Doll Co.
R. B. L.	Roth, Baitz & Lipstiz (Baby Gloria Dolls)
S	Theodor Recknagel
S	Eegee
S	Sayco
S & C	Franz Schmidt & Co
S & C	Swaine & Co.
S & H	Simon & Halbig
S & M	Seligmann & Mayer
S & S	Curnen & Steiner
S & W	Strobel & Wilken
S E & S	Erhard & Stephen
S E C O	Strauss Eckardt; Gebrüder Eckardt
S G	Deluxe Reading/Topper Toy Group
S H	Simon & Halbig
S I C O	Edward Schmidt
S I H A	Simon Hahn
S M B	Sigismund Markmann
S P B H	Schoenau & Hoffmeister
S P S	Sonneberger Porzellanfabrik, Carl Müller
S Q	Schützmeister & Quendt
S S	Max Schelhorn
S S N	Sigmund Ullmann
S T	Ideal
S T N	Ideal
S U N	Sigmund Ullmann
S U R	Seyfarth & Reinhardt
S W	Strobel & Wilken
S W C	unknown German doll manufacturer
S Y C O	Sieder & Co.
S. E. S.	Steven Erhard & Son
S. F. B. J.	Société Française de Fabrication de Bébés & Jouets
SP	Sonneberger Porzellanfabrik
T	Ideal
T E	Ideal
T E B U	Theodor Buschbaum
T H	Theodor Hörnlein
T K B	M. Tersch
T P	Theodor Pohl
T P I	Thüringer Puppenindustrie
T P I W	Thüringer Puppenindustrie
T P K	Beck & Glaser
T R	unidentified German doll manufacturer (often includes 806 or 813)
T W	Theodor Wendt
U	Vermont Maid
U	Uneeda
U F D C	United Federation of Doll Clubs
V	Ideal

LETTERS OR INITIALS	MANUFACTURER
V	Valentine
v	Valentine
V H	Deluxe Reading/Topper Toy Group
V M B	Valentine Moritz Bruchlos
V P	Ideal
V T	Ideal
V W	Valentine
W	Bayerische Celluloidwarenfabrik
W	Heubach, Kämpfe & Sontag
W	E. Winkler
W	Ideal
W	Commonwealth
W & Co	Wiefel & Co.
W & S	Walther & Sohn
W D	unidentified German doll manufacturer
W D	Walt Disney Productions
W E E G E M	W. G. Müller
W E P	Wenzel Prouza
W G	F. & W. Goebel
W K	Werner Krauth
W K W	Strasser & Co.
W L	Ideal
W P	Waltershäuser Puppenfabrik
W S K	Wiesenthal, Schindel & Kallenberg
W s T	Weiskirchlitzer Steingutfabrik
W St	Wilhelm Strunz
W u Z I	Wagner & Zetsche
W Z	Wagner & Zetsche
W Z I	Wagner & Zetsche
X	denotes a mid-range in size
Z	Gottlieb Zinner & Söhne
z	denotes measurement in zentimeters used by Franz Schmidt

George and Martha Washington by Emma Clear (Photo courtesy of Billie Nelson Tyrrell.)

CHAPTER FIVE

SIZE CHARTS AND CONVERSIONS

Size numbers that appear on doll heads are among the most important (and yet most likely to be neglected) clues we have in identifying an antique doll. The French manufacturers customarily used only a size number for their descriptive markings. German doll companies were apt to assign a model number. Nevertheless, they did not overlook imprinting most heads with a size number. This marking can frequently do more than just help with an identification. The size number can also determine the age of a doll, and perhaps even more importantly, it can aid in the recognition of a reproduction.

Identifying a doll incorrectly can be a costly mistake. When a legitimate copy of an antique doll is made for the enjoyment or profit of a creditable doll maker, it will be marked with the doll artist's name or initials and the date that it was made. Such is not the custom when a doll is deliberately reproduced as a fraud. In the event of a fraud, no name or initials are offered, and great care is given to repudiate the authentic age of the doll. Experienced, knowledgeable collectors and dealers have been fooled by a well-executed reproduction. One highly publicized incident occurred when a doll was submitted for judging at a U. F. D. C. convention before it was recognized as a fake. Luckily, the party was able to retrieve her $8,000 investment, but such is not always the case.

The first step in making a reproduction doll is to form a mold using an original antique doll head. The reproduction, fabricated from this mold, will show the original size number. Herein lies the rub. In making the mold and firing the bisque for a reproduction doll, the head will shrink and decrease in size by at least seven percent. Accordingly, if a particular doll is significantly smaller than the size number indicates, a further investigation of that doll will be necessary. Considering that antique dolls' bodies settle and joints compress can explain slight variances in length. A 1/2- to 1-inch difference is within the acceptable range.

The charts in this chapter have been listed alphabetically by company. The numeric or alphabetic symbol used to designate height reveals the doll length in inches. Occasionally, a manufacturer preferred to use the head circumference or shoulder head height as the basis for their sizing. These few instances have been specified in the following charts.

For purpose of explanation, the size numbers often represented the measurements in centimeters of a neck opening, a height, or circumference and were not measurement codes. We have included a metric conversion chart for your convenience. If an additional measurement is needed, multiply the centimeter number by .03937 to convert centimeters to inches. To convert inches to centimeters, multiply the inch number by 2.54.

At the end of this chapter, you will notice charts for hard plastic and vinyl. This is included to facilitate the identity of a doll manufactured after 1950. Unfortunately, mold numbers and size numbers are usually not featured on newer dolls. If the box, wrist tag, or other identifying hallmark is not present, many times our first and only clue is the height of the doll. Many popular hard plastic and vinyl dolls are cataloged by size—which, hopefully, can be a starting point if everything else fails.

The size number is a tool to use in identifying a doll. It is an important one, and should not be overlooked.

SIZE CHARTS

A. T. BÉBÉ

Size no.	Height
0	6 inches
1	9 inches
2	11 inches
3	12 inches
4	13-1/2 inches
5	15 inches
6	16 inches
7	16-1/2 inches
8	17 inches
9	18 inches
10	20 inches
12	22-1/2 inches
14	31 inches
15	37 inches

ALL-BISQUE DOLLS

Size no.	Height
1	7 inches
2-1/2	8 inches
3	9 inches
4	9-1/2 inches

Size no.	Height
3/0	2-1/4 inches
2/0	2-3/4 inches
1/0	3 inches
0	3-1/4 inches
1	3-1/2 inches
3	4-1/2 inches
8	7-1/2 inches

ATTWELL, MABEL LUCIE DOLLS FOR CHAD VALLEY

Size no.	Height
0	14-1/2 inches
1	16 inches
2/A or 2/B	18-1/2 inches

BABY MINE

Size no.	Height
2/0	13-1/2 inches
0	15-1/2 inches
1	17-1/2 inches
2	19-1/2 inches
3	21-1/2 inches
4	23 inches

BASS-WOOD DOLLS

Size no.	Height, Better Quality	Height, Lesser Quality
1	11 inches	10 inches
2	12-1/2 inches	11 inches
3	14 inches	14 inches
4	16 inches	–

BÉBÉ BON MARCHÉ

(Note: year/height variations)

Size no	1894	1903-12	1925
1	10 inches	10-1/2 inches	10 inches
2	11 inches	11 inches	11 inches
3	12 inches	12 inches	12 inches
4	14 inches	14 inches	14 inches
5	15 inches	14-1/2 inches	15-1/2 inches
6	16 inches	16 inches	16 inches
7	17-1/2 in	17-1/2 inches	18 inches
8	19-1/2 in	19-1/2 inches	20-1/2 inches
9	21 inches	21 inches	22-1/2 inches
10	23 inches	23 inches	23-1/2 inches
11	25 inches	25 inches	25 inches
12	27 inches	27 inches	27 inches

BÉBÉ BRU

(Note: body type and year/height variations)

Size no. Kid bodies	1907-12 Composition bodies	1952 Composition bodies
0	11 inches	———	———
1	12 inches	———	———
2	13 inches	———	———
3	14 inches	———	———
4	15-1/2 in	13 inches	———
5	17 inches	———	———
6	18 inches	———	———
7	20 inches	———	———
8	21-1/2 in	20-1/2 inches	———
9	22 inches	23 inches	18 inches
10	25 inches	23-1/2 inches	20 inches
11	27 inches	25-1/2 inches	———
12	30-1/2 in	27 inches	———
13	33 inches	30 inches	———
14	35 inches	31-1/2 inches	———
15	36 inches	33-1/2 inches	———

Size letter	Height
A	11 inches
B	12 inches
C	13 inches
D	14 inches
E	16 inches
F	18 inches
G	19 inches
H	20-1/2 inches
I	22 inches
K	25 inches
M	28 inches

SIZE CHARTS

BÉBÉ DE PARIS

Size no.	Height
5/0	11 inches
4/0	12 inches
3/0	13-1/2 inches
2/0	14 inches
1/0	15-1/2 inches
0	17-1/2 inches
1	19-1/2 inches
2	22-1/2 inches
3	25-1/2 inches
4	29 inches
5	31-1/2 inches

BELTON-TYPE DOLLS

Size no.	Height
1	9 inches
3	12 inches
6	14 inches
8	16 inches
12	24 inches
16	30 inches

BÉBÉ JUMEAU

(Note: type and year/height variations.)

size no.	1884-85 Bon Marché	1885-86 Bon Marché	1887-89 Louvre	1887-89 Bon Marché	1890-91 Petite St. Thomas	1894-1913 Various stores	1916-24 Various stores
1	10 inches	9 inches	8-1/2 inches	9 inches	10 inches	10 inches	–
2	10-1/4"	10"	10"	10-1/4"	11"	11"	–
3	10-1/2"	11-1/2"	11"	12"	13"	12"	–
4	12"	12-1/2"	12-1/2"	13-1/2"	13-1/2"	14"	–
5	13-1/2"	14"	14"	14-1/2"	14-1/2"	15"	14"
6	14"	14-1/2"	15"	15-1/2"	15-1/2"	16"	16"
7	15-1/2"	16-1/2"	16-1/2"	17-1/2"	17-1/2"	17-1/2"	17-1/2"
8	17-1/2"	18-1/2"	18-1/2"	19"	19"	19-1/2"	19-1/2"
9	19-1/2"	19-1/2"	19-1/2"	20-1/2"	20-1/2"	21"	21"
10	21-1/2"	22"	21-1/2"	22-1/2"	22-1/2"	23"	22-1/2"
11	23"	23-1/2"	23-1/2"	24-1/2"	24-1/2"	25"	24-1/2"
12	24-1/2"	25-1/2"	25-1/2"	26-1/2"	26-1/2"	27"	26-1/2"
13	–	–	–	–	–	28-1/2"	–
14	–	–	–	–	–	30"	–
15	–	–	–	–	–	32"	–
16	–	–	–	–	–	33-1/2"	–

LONG-FACE

Size no.	Height
9	20 inches
10	22 inches
11	24 inches
12	26 inches
13	28 inches
14	30 inches
15	32 inches

SIZE CHARTS

BÉBÉ LAFAYETTE

Size no.	Height
3	12 inches
4	14 inches
5	15-1/2 inches
6	17 inches
7	18 inches
8	20-1/2 inches
9	22-1/2 inches
10	23-1/2 inches
11	25 inches
12	27 inches
13	29 inches
14	31 inches

BÉBÉ MAGENTA

Size no.	Height
36	14 inches
39	15-1/2 inches
41	16 inches
42	16-1/2 inches
45	17-1/2 inches
50	19-1/2 inches
54	21 inches
55	21-1/2 inches
60	23-1/2 inches
65	25-1/2 inches
66	26 inches
69	27 inches
70	27-1/2 inches
76	30 inches
82	32-1/2 inches

BÉBÉ MONCEY

Size no.	Height
29	11-1/2 inches
32	12-1/2 inches
35	14 inches
40	15-1/2 inches
43	17 inches
47	18-1/2 inches
52	20-1/2 inches
56	22 inches
61	24 inches

BÉBÉ MOTHEREAU

Size no.	Height
4	15 inches
6	17-1/2 inches
8	20 inches

Traditional Japanese Papier-Mâché Doll (Photo courtesy of Helen Brooke.)

SIZE CHARTS

BÉBÉ PRINTEMPS

(Note: year/height variations)

Size no.	1887 Height	1896-1910 Height	1918 Height	1924 Height
1	10-1/2 inches	12 inches	10 inches	–
2	11-1/2 inches	13-1/2 inches	11 inches	–
3	12-1/2 inches	14-1/2 inches	12-1/2 inches	–
4	14 inches	15-1/2 inches	14 inches	–
5	15 inches	17-1/2 inches	15-1/2 inches	–
6	16-1/2 inches	19 inches	17-1/2 inches	17 inches
7	19 inches	21 inches	18-1/2 inches	–
8	21-1/2 inches	23 inches	21 inches	19-1/2 inches
9	23-1/2 inches	24-1/2 inches	22-1/2 inches	22-1/2 inches
10	27-1/2 inches	27-1/2 inches	23-1/2 inches	–
11	–	30 inches	25 inches	25 inches
12	–	34 inches	–	–

BÉBÉ RÉSERVÉ

(Note: type variations)

Non-talker w/o eyelashes	Non-talker with eyelashes, Bébé Baptême	Non-talker with eyelashes	Talker with eyelashes
10-1/2 inches	10 inches	–	–
11 inches	11-1/2 inches	–	–
13 inches	12 inches	12 inches	–
14-1/2 inches	14 inches	15-1/2 inches	14-1/2 inches
16 inches	15-1/2 inches	–	16 inches
16-1/2 inches	17 inches	17 inches	–
17-1/2 inches	18 inches	–	18 inches
18-1/2 inches	–	18-1/2 inches	–
19-1/2 inches	20-1/2 inches	20 inches	–
21-1/2 inches	–	22 inches	–
–	–	25 inches	–
–	–	25-1/2 inches	–
–	–	27-1/2 inches	–

BÉBÉ RIVOLI SIZE RELATIONSHIP

(Note: year/height variations)

1921 Height	1929 Height
10-1/2 inches	–
11-1/2 inches	–
13 inches	13 inches
14 inches	–
15-1/2 inches	15-1/2 inches
17-1/2 inches	–
18-1/2 inches	18-1/2 inches
20-1/2 inches	–
22-1/2 inches	22-1/2 inches
23-1/2 inches	–
25-1/2 inches	25-1/2 inches
27 inches	–
29-1/2 inches	29-1/2 inches
30-1/2 inches	–
32-1/2 inches	–
34-1/2 inches	–

SIZE CHARTS

BÉBÉ SYSTÈME

Size no.	Height
6	16-1/2 inches
7	17-1/2 inches
8	20-1/2 inches
9	22-1/2 inches
10	24 inches

BÉBÉ TOUT BOIS

(Note: different format—dolls are arranged by height)

Year of Manufacture	Height
1914	9-1/2 inches
1905-1914	10-1/2 inches
1902-1911	11 inches
1905	11-1/2 inches
1911-1914	12 inches
1902-1908	12-1/4 inches
1910-1914	12-1/2 inches
1905	13 inches
1902	13-1/2 inches
1905-1914	13-3/4 inches
1908	14-1/2 inches
1905-1914	15 inches
1911-1914	15-1/2 inches
1905-1913	16 inches
1908-1914	16-1/2 inches
1911-1914	17 inches
1905-1914	18 inches
1905-1914	19-1/2 inches
1908-1909	20 inches
1908	23-1/2; 25-1/2; 27 inches

BASS-WOOD DOLLS

Size no.	Height, Better Quality	Height, Lesser Quality
1	11 inches	10 inches
2	12-1/2 inches	11 inches
3	14 inches	14 inches
4	16 inches	–

BÉBÉ VILLE DE ST. DENIS

Size no.	Height
5	15-1/2 inches
6	17 inches
7	18 inches
8	20-1/2 inches
9	23 inches
10	23 inches
11	25-1/2 inches
12	27 inches

C. M. BERGMANN DOLLS

Size no.	Height
4/0	13 inches
1	15 inches
2	16 inches
3	18 inches
4	20 inches
5	22 inches
6	23 inches
6-1/2a	24 inches
7a	25 inches
8	26 inches
9	27 inches
10a	29 inches
12	30 inches
15	34 inches

CHAD VALLEY DOLLS

Caresse Style no.	Height	Carina Size no.	Height
169	11 inches	1	14 inches
170	13 inches	2	17 inches
171	16 inches	3	19 inches
172	18 inches	4	22 inches
173	11 inches	5	24 inches
174	13 inches	6	30 inches
175	16 inches		
176	18 inches		
177	11 inches		
178	13 inches		
179	16 inches		
180	18 inches		
260	11 inches		
261	13 inches		
262	16 inches		
263	18 inches		
264	21 inches		
265	25 inches		
272	11 inches		
273	13 inches		
274	16 inches		
275	18 inches		
276	21 inches		
277	25 inches		
420	11 inches		
421	13 inches		
422	16 inches		
423	18 inches		
426	11-1/2 inches		
427	14-1/2 inches		
428	17-1/2 inches		
429	19 inches		
430	12-1/2 inches		
431	14 inches		
432	16-1/2 inches		
433	18-1/2 inches		

SIZE CHARTS

CHASE DOLLS

Size no.	Height
0	13 inches
1	17 inches
2	20 inches
3	24 inches
5	30 inches

CHINA HEAD DOLLS

(Note: as advertised by L. F. Lauer)

Size no.	Height
0	10-1/2 inches
1	11 inches
1-1/2	12 inches
2	12-1/2 inches
4	17 inches
6	20 inches
8	22 inches
9	25 inches

CUDDLE KEWPIE DOLLS

Size no.	Height
0	11 inches
1	14-1/2 inches
2	17 inches
3	22 inches

DAISEY DOLLS

Size no.	Height
2/0	13-1/2 inches
0	15-1/2 inches
1	17-1/2 inches
2	19-1/2 inches
3	21-1/2 inches
4	23 inches
5	25-1/2 inches

DE FUISSEAUX DOLLS

Size mark	Height of head
F1	6 inches
F2	5 inches
F3	4-1/2 inches
B3	2-1/2 inches
B4	2 inches

DOLLY DIMPLE

Size no.	Height
5	14 inches
6-1/2	15-1/2 inches
7-1/2	19 inches
8	20 inches

EDEN BÉBÉ

Size no.	Height
1	11 inches
2	12 inches
3	14 inches
4	15-1/2 inches
5	16-1/2 inches
6	17-1/2 inches
7	18-1/2 inches
8	19-1/2 inches
9	21-1/2 inches
10	23-1/2 inches
11	25 inches
12	26-1/2 inches
13	27-1/2 inches
14	29-1/2 inches
15	31 inches

ENGLISH RAG DOLLS

Size no.	Height
00	13-1/2 inches
0	15 inches
1	17 inches
2	19 inches

FAIRY MOONBEAM DOLLS

Size no.	Height
0	15-1/2 inches
2	19-1/2 inches
4	23 inches

FAUNALIA DOLLS

Size no.	Height
1	11 inches
2	12 inches
3	13 inches
4	15 inches
5	16 inches
6	18 inches
7	20 inches

SIZE CHARTS

FRENCH POUPÉE DE MODE

Size no.	Height
2/0	11-1/2 inches
0	12 to 12-1/2 inches
1	13-1/2 inches
2	14 to 15-1/2 inches
3	16 inches
4	17 to 17-1/2 inches
5	18-1/2 to 19-1/2 inches
6	21 to 21-1/2 inches

FROZEN CHARLOTTE DOLLS

(Note: year/height variations)

Size no.	1880 Height	1887 Height
5/0	1 inches	–
4/0	1-1/4 inches	–
3/0	1-1/2 inches	–
2/0	2 inches	2-1/2 inches
0	2-1/4 inches	2-3/4 inches
01/0	2-1/2 inches	3
1	3 inches	3-1/4 inches
1-1/2	3-1/2 inches	–
2	3-3/4 inches	3-1/2 inches
3	4 inches	4-1/4 inches
4	4-1/2 inches	–
5	5 inches	–
6	5-3/4 inches	–
7	6 inches	–
8	6-1/4 inches	

GAULTIER (F. G.) FASHION SHOULDER-HEAD DOLLS

Size no.	Height
0/3	10 inches
0/2	11 inches
0	12 inches
1	13-1/2 inches
2	15 inches
3	17 inches
4	18-1/2 inches
5	20-1/2 inches

GOLD MEDAL BABY

Size no.	1912 Height
0	Junior size
1	12 inches
2	14 inches
3	16 inches
5	23 inches

Style no.	Height
85, G/0	10-1/2 inches
171, G c/1	13 inches
2, 239, 240	16 inches
3, 4	18 inches
720, 725	21-1/2 inches
5, 7	23-1/2 inches

GOLLIWOGGS

Size no.	Height
629/1	10-1/2 inches
629/2	12 inches
629/3	15 inches
629/4	17 inches

H-MOLD

Size no.	Height
0	16-1/2 inches
2	19 inches
3	21 inches
4	24 inches

HEINRICH HANDWERCK DOLLS

Size no.	Height
2-1/4	18 inches
2-1/2	20 inches
3	22 inches
4	25 inches
5	26 inches
6	30 inches

Armand Marseille's Character Rockabye Baby #351, and Kestner's Child #171 (Photo courtesy of Cobb's Doll Auction.)

SIZE CHARTS

HOLLYWOOD IMP DOLLS

Style no.	Height
1	23 inches
4	23 inches
11	21 inches
13	21 inches
18	18 inches
22	18 inches
23	22 inches
24	19 inches
25	20 inches

JULLIEN BÉBÉ

Size no.	Height
4	15 inches
5	17 inches
6	19 inches
7	21 inches
8	23 inches
9	25 inches

KÄMMER & REINHARDT DOLLS

Size no.	Height
4/0	3-1/2 inches
3/0	4 inches
2/0	4-1/2 inches
0	5 inches
1	6 inches
1-1/2	8 inches
2	9 inches

KESTNER DOLLS

(Note: Sizes are given for the circumference of the head rather that the height.)

Sizing mark		Circumference of the head
b	Made in Germany 3	6 inches
a	Made in Germany 4	7 inches
A	Made in Germany 5	8 inches
B	Made in Germany 6	8-1/2 inches
C	Made in Germany 7	9 inches
D	Made in Germany 8	9-1/2 inches
E	Made in Germany 9	10 inches
F	Made in Germany 10	10-1/2 inches
G	Made in Germany 11	11 inches
H	Made in Germany 12	11-1/2 inches
I	Made in Germany 13	12 inches
K	Made in Germany 14	12-1/2 inches
L	Made in Germany 15	13 inches
M	Made in Germany 16	13-1/2 inches
N	Made in Germany 17	15 inches
O	Made in Germany 18	16 inches
P	Made in Germany 19	17 inches

KLEY & HAHN DOLLS

Size no.	Height
2/0	9 inches
1	11-1/2 inches
6	15 inches

LAUER FRENCH DOLLS

PARIAN

Size no.	Height
2/0	11 inches
0	12 inches
1	13-1/2 inches
2	14-1/2 inches
3	16-1/2 inches
4	18-1/2 inches
5	21 inches

BISQUE

(Note: body type variations)

Size no.	Height, composition body	Height, Kid body	Height, cloth body
3/0	–	–	8 inches
0	12 inches	–	–
1	14 inches	13 inches	–
2	15 inches	14 inches	13 inches
2-1/2	–	–	14 inches
3	17 inches	–	–
4	20 inches	–	–
5	23 inches	16-1/2 inches	18 inches
6	–	18 inches	–

LENCI DOLLS

Size no.	Height for dolls before 1931
109	23 inches
110	19 inches
149	16-1/2 inches
165	24 inches
169	34 inches
300	17-1/2 inches
500	21-1/2 inches
700	34 inches
950	28-1/2 inches
1500	17-1/2 inches

SIZE CHARTS

LENCI DOLLS

Size letter	Height for dolls after 1931
X	5 inches
XX	7 inches
S	8-1/2 inches
V	8-1/2 inches
F	10-1/2 inches
N	14 inches
P	14 inches
V	14 inches
V	16 inches
Bambino	16 inches
C	16-1/2 inches
E	17-1/2 inches
L	17-1/2 inches
O	17-1/2 inches
B	19 inches
M	19 inches
V	20 inches
OO	21 inches
G	21-1/2 inches
A	23 inches
AA	23 inches
R	24 inches
T	26 inches
T	28 inches
J	28-1/2 inches
HH	29 inches
D	34 inches
H	34 inches
Z	48 inches

L'INTREPIDE BÉBÉ

Size no.	Height
5	14 inches
7	17-1/2 inches
8	18-1/2 inches
9	22-1/2 inches
10	24 inches
12	29-1/2 inches

LOUVRE STORE BÉBÉ

Size no.	Height
0	12 inches
1	14 inches
2	15-1/2 inches
3	17-1/2 inches
4	18 inches
5	19-1/2 inches
6	20-1/2 inches
7	21-1/2 inches

MAMA DOLLS

(Note: As advertised in F. A. O. Schwarz)

Style no.	Height
113	13 inches
212	18 inches
400	18 inches
1300	19 inches

MARSEILLE, ARMAND DOLLS

(shoulder-head dolls)

Size no.	Height
16/0	5 inches
15/0	6 inches
14/0	7 inches
13/0	8 inches
12/0	9 inches
11/0	10 inches
10/0	11 inches
9/0	13 inches
8/0	14 inches
7/0	15 inches
6/0	16 inches
5/0	17 inches
4/0	18 inches
4/0-1/2	18-1/2 inches
3/0	19 inches
3/0-1/2	19-1/2 inches
2/0	20 inches
2/0-1/2	20-1/2 inches
0	19 inches
0-1/2	19-1/2 inches
1	21 inches
1-1/2	21-1/2 inches
2	22 inches
2-1/2	22-1/2 inches
3	23 inches
3-1/2	23-1/2 inches
4	24 inches
4-1/2	24-1/2 inches
5	25 inches
5-1/2	25-1/2 inches
6	26 inches
6-1/2	26-1/2 inches
7	27 inches
7-1/2	27-1/2 inches
8	29 inches
8-1/2	29-1/2 inches
9	30 inches
9-1/2	30-1/2 inches
10	31 inches
12	35 inches
15	38 inches

SIZE CHARTS

MARSEILLE, ARMAND DOLLS

(socket-head dolls)

Size no.	Height
15/0	6 inches
14/0	7 inches
13/0	7-1/2 inches
12/0	8 inches
11/0	8-1/2 inches
10/0	9 inches
9/0	9-1/2 inches
8/0	10 inches
7/0	10-1/2 inches
6/0	11 inches
5/0	11-1/2 inches
4/0	12 inches
3/0	12-1/2 inches
2/0	13 inches
0	16 inches
0-1/2	16-1/2 inches
1	17 inches
1-1/2	17-1/2 inches
2	18 inches
2-1/2	18-1/2 inches
3	19 inches
3-1/2	19-1/2 inches
4	20 inches
4-1/2	20-1/2 inches
5	21 inches
5-1/2	21-1/2 inches
6	22 inches
6-1/2	22-1/2 inches
7	23 inches
7-1/2	23-1/2 inches
8	24 inches
8-1/2	24-1/2 inches
9	25 inches
9-1/2	25-1/2 inches
10	26 inches
10-1/2	26-1/2 inches
11	27 inches
11-1/2	27-1/2 inches
12	28 inches
12-1/2	28-1/2 inches
13	29 inches
13-1/2	29-1/2 inches
14	30 inches
14-1/2	30-1/2 inches
15	31 inches
16	35 inches
17	36 inches
18	38 inches
19	40 inches
20	42 inches
21	48 inches

MIDOLLY

Style no.	Height
400	20 inches
410	22-1/2 inches
415	26 inches
425	29 inches
451	22-1/2 inches
462	25 inches
498	29 inches

MINERVA DOLLS

(Note: type variations)

Size no.	Height for shoulder head only w/ painted hair and eyes	Height for shoulder head only w/ wig and sleep eyes
0	2-3/4 inches	3-3/4 inches
1	3 inches	4 inches
2	3-1/2 inches	4-3/4 inches
3	3-3/4 inches	4-3/4 inches
4	4-1/4 inches	5-1/2 inches

MIRETTE DOLLS

(Note: type variations)

Size no.	Height for Bébé	Height for character baby
7	18 inches	–
11	27 inches	–
12	29 inches	23-1/2 inches

MISS MERRY HEART

Size no.	Height
0	15-1/2 inches
1	17-1/2 inches
2	19-1/2 inches
3	21-1/2 inches
4	23 inches
5	25-1/2 inches
6	28-1/2 inches

MOEHLING DOLLS

Size no.	Height
7/0	10-1/2 inches
5/0	12 inches
1/0	15 inches
0	16 inches
1	17 inches
2	18 inches
3	19 inches
4	20 inches
6	22 inches
7	22-1/2 inches
10	24 inches
12	26 inches

MY DREAM BABY

Size no.	Height
4/0	8-1/2 inches
2/0	9-1/2 inches
1/0	10 inches
2	12 inches
3	14 inches
4	16 inches
5	18 inches
6	20 inches
7	22 inches
8	24 inches

NAIAD DOLL

Size no.	Height
3/0	13 inches
2/0	14-1/2 inches
0	16 inches
1	17 inches
2	19 inches
3	20-1/2 inches
4	22 inches

PERONNE, LAVALLÉE DOLLS

0	12 inches
1	13 inches
2	14 to 15-1/2 inches
3	16-1/2 inches
4	17-1/2 inches
5	19-1/2 inches
6	21-1/2 inches

PHYLLIS DOLLS

1	14-1/2 inches
2	17-1/2 inches
3	21 inches
4	25 inches

PRINTEMPS DOLLS

6/0	11 inches
5/0	12 inches
4/0	13-1/2 inches
3/0	14 inches
2/0	15-1/2 inches
0	17-1/2 inches
1	19 inches
2	22-1/2 inches
3	25 inches
4	29 inches
5	31-1/2 inches
6	35-1/2 inches

ROCK A BYE BABY

(Note: Measurements are in head circumference and type variations)

Size no.	Head circumference for 341 & 351	Head circumference for 341K & 351K
6/0	5-1/2 inches	5-3/4 inches
4/0	6-1/2 inches	6-1/2 inches
3/0	7-1/4 inches	7-1/8 inches
2/0	7-1/2 inches	7-1/4 inches
0	8-1/4 inches	8-1/4 inches
1	8-3/4 inches	8-1/2 inches
2	9 inches	9 inches
2-1/2	9-3/4 inches	9-3/4 inches
3	10-1/2 inches	10-1/4 inches
3-1/2	11-1/4 inches	11-1/4 inches
4	12-1/2 inches	12-1/2 inches
5	13-1/2 inches	13 inches
6	14 inches	14 inches
8	15 inches	14-1/2 inches

Size no.	Head circumference for flange head
11/2	10 inches
11/3	11-1/2 inches
11/4	14 inches
11/6	15-1/2 inches

Size no.	Head circumference for socket head
19/2/0	8 inches
19/0	9 inches
19/1	9-3/4 inches
19/2	10 inches
19/3	11-3/4 inches
19/4	14 inches
19/5	15 inches

SCHMITT & FILS BÉBÉ

Size no.	Height
0	14 inches
1	15-1/2 inches
2	17 inches
3	19 inches
4	20-1/2 inches
5	23 inches
6	25 inches
7	27-1/2 inches
8	30-1/2 inches

SCHOENHUT DOLLS

(Note: Style no. from Schwarz catalog)

Style no.	Height
39	19 inches
46	18 inches
53	19-1/2 inches
62	25 inches
76	29 inches

SCHOENHUT DOLLS

(Note: Style no. issued by Schoenhut)

Style no.	Height	Style no.	Height	Style no.	Height
304	16 inches	310	16 inches	405	19 inches
306	16 inches	310	19 inches	405	21 inches
307	16 inches	310	21 inches	406	16 inches
308	14 inches	311	14 inches	406	19 inches
308	19 inches	311	16 inches	406	21 inches
308	21 inches	311	19 inches	407	14 inches
309	16 inches	312	14 inches	407	16 inches
309	19 inches	314	19 inches	407	19 inches
309	21 inches	315	21 inches	407	21 inches
310	14 inches	405	14 inches	409	14 inches

STEINER, JULES NICHOLAS BÉBÉ

Size no. for A B C D	Height	Size no. exclusively A	Height
4/0	8 inches	4	9 inches
3/0	10 inches	5	10 inches
2/0	11 inches	7	12 inches
0	13 inches	8	13 inches
1	16 inches	9	15 inches
2	18 inches	10	17 inches
3	20 inches	11	18 inches
4	22 inches	13	20 inches
5	24 inches	14	22 inches
6	28 inches	15	24 inches
7	34 inches	17	25 inches
		18	27 inches
		19	28 inches

STRASBURGER, PFEIFFER & CO.

(Note: type variations)

Size no.	Length of sawdust-stuffed dolls with leather hands	Length of hair-stuffed dolls with leather arms, closed fingers	Length of hair-stuffed dolls with leather arms, china hands
2/0	6 inches	–	–
0	7 inches	10 inches	10 inches
1	8 inches	11 inches	11 inches
2	9 inches	11-1/2 inches	12 inches
3	10-1/2 inches	13 inches	14 inches
4	11-1/2 inches	15 inches	15 inches
5	13 inches	16-1/2 inches	17-1/2 inches
6	14 inches	18-1/2 inches	19-1/2 inches
7	16 inches	19-1/2 inches	21 inches
8	17-1/2 inches	20-1/2 inches	22-1/2 inches
9	20 inches	23 inches	24 inches
10	23 inches	–	–
11	24 inches	–	–
12	27-1/2 inches	–	–

TÄUFLING DOLLS

Size no.	Height for black dolls
4/0	4 inches
3/0	4-3/4 inches
2/0	6-1/2 inches
0	8-1/2 inches
1	10-1/2 inches
2	12-3/4 inches

SIZE CHARTS

TÄUFLING DOLLS

Size no.	Height for white dolls
4/0	9 inches
3/0	10 inches
2/0	11-1/2 inches
0	13 inches
1	14-1/2 inches
2	16 inches
3	17-1/2 inches
4	19-1/2 inches

TREBOR DOLLS

Size no.	Height
7/0	10-1/2 inches
5/0	12 inches
2/0	15-1/2 inches

WALKÜRE DOLLS

Size no.	Height
2/0	15 inches
0	17 inches
1	19 inches
2	21 inches
2-1/4	23 inches

WOLF, LOUIS & CO. CHARACTER BABY 152 BY HERTEL, SCHWAB

Size no.	Height
2	12 inches
5	14 inches
10	17 inches
12	21 inches

WOODEN DOLLS

(Note: as advertised by Lauer)

Size no.	Height
6/0	7-1/2 inches
2/0	10-1/2 inches
0	12 inches

HARD PLASTIC AND VINYL SIZE CHARTS

Company	Under 3-1/2 inches	3-3/4 to 4 inches	5 inches	5-1/2 inches	6 inches	7 inches
Alexander Doll Co.						Wendy Ann, Alexander Kin Characters
Common-wealth					Dress-Me Dolls	
Doll Bodies					Dress-Me Dolls	
Hasbro		Dolly Darling				
Hollywood						Little One
Horsman						Jane, Michel
Ideal		Little Princess Girl & Boy		Little Princess Mother	Little Princess Father	
Mark	Doll House Girl & Boy		Doll House Mother	Doll House Father		
Mattel	Sweets Sunshine, Kiddles				Doug Davis, Tiny Cheerful Tearful	Kretor

HARD PLASTIC AND VINYL SIZE CHARTS CONTINUED

Company	7-1/2 inches	8 inches	8-1/2 inches	9 inches	10 inches	10-1/2 inches
A & H						Gigi
Active Teen					High Heel Teen Type	
Admiration						Miss Francie
Alexander Doll Co.	Wendy Ann, Alexander Kin Characters	Little Lady, Wendy Ann, Alexander Kin Characters, Maggie Mixup			Cissette Face Personality, Tinker Bell, Brigetta, Louisa, Lisel	
American Character	Betsy McCall, Sandy, Ben Cartwright	Tiny Tears		Cricket	Cricket	Toni
Arranbee		Little Dear				Miss Coty
Beehler Arts						Teen Doll with High Heels
Belle					Little Margie	
Circle P						High Heel Teen
Commonwealth		Teen with High Heel, Child		Teen with High Heel, Adult Walker	Adult with High Heel	
Cosmopolitan		Cha Cha Heel, Ginger, Little Miss Ginger				Miss Ginger
Deluxe Reading		Penny Brite				
Eegee		Shelly			Little Miss Debutante	
Effanbee			Official Girl Scout Doll		Mickey	Mickey
Hasbro		G.I. Joe		Peace Series	Leggy Jill	
Horsman & Co.		Peggy Petite				Cindy
Ideal		Salty, Pos'n Salty		Pepper, Pos'n Pepper	Black Thumbelina	Little Miss Revlon
Jesco				Kewpie		
Laurie						Teenage High Heel Doll
Lilli Child	Lilli Child					
Mary Hoyer						Vicki
Mattel	Gorgeous Creatures			Skooter, Ricky, Steve & Stephie Sunshine	Baby Go Bye Bye, Buffie	Valerie
Mayfair of Canada						Debbie
Mego		Batman, Dorothy & Toto, Davy Crockett, and various other personality dolls				
Model Toys				High Heel Teen Doll		
Molly-'es				Perky		
Nancy Ann		Muffie	Miss Nancy Ann		Miss Nancy Ann	

SIZE CHARTS

Company	7-1/2 inches	8 inches	8-1/2 inches	9 inches	10 inches	10-1/2 inches
Plastic Molded				Little Miss		High Heel
Arts				Joanie		Teenager
Remco						Libby Littlechap
Rosebud						Softest Vinyl Rose Child
Sayco					Miss America	
Uneeda					Blue Fairy, Pollyanna Star	Tiny Teen, Suzette, Sally
Virga		Ginny				
Vogue						Jill, Jan

Company	11 inches	11-1/2 inches	12 inches	12-1/2 inches	13 inches	13-1/2 inches
A & H		Marcie				
Alexander Doll Co.	Frederich (also spelled Frederick), Lisel, Marta, Lissy Face & Cissette Face Personality		Brenda Starr, Katie, Pamela, Yolanda, Smarty, Janie, Michael, Kelly Face Personality			
American Character		Mary Makeup	Misty, Popi, Tressy		Blue Ribbon Doll, Tiny Tears	
Arranbee	Littlest Angel		Little Dear			
Commonwealth	High Heel Girl					
Debbie Toy		Debbie with High Heel				
Eegee		Babette Suzette	Andy, Growing Hair Doll, Dolly Parton			
Effanbee	Fluffy, Mickey					
Elite		Bonnie, Wendy				
Fab-Lu		Babs, Bill, Randy				
German Lilli		Lilli				
Gilbert				James Bond		
Hasbro		G.I. Joe	G. I. Joe	Jem		
Horsman & Co.		Cinderella, Patty Duke	Mary Poppins			
Ideal	Thumbelina	Dorothy Hamill	Mitzi, Samantha the Witch, Shirley Temple, Tammy, Pos'n Tammy	Mom, James Bond	Dad, Bonnie Braids	
Jesco			Kewpie			
Mattel	Baby Beans, Baby Small Talk, Baby Walk N Play, Bouncy Baby, Small Talk Cinderella	Barbie, Sister Small Talk	Ken, Allan, Guardian Goddesses, Talking Twin Kip		Baby Pattaburp, Cheerful Tearful	
Mego			Kiss, Star Trek, Sonny & Cher and various personality dolls			
Molly-'es			Perky			
Nasco		Hello Dolly				
P & M			Paula May			

Company	11 inches	11-1/2 inches	12 inches	12-1/2 inches	13 inches	13-1/2 inches
Palitoy			Mary Makeup, English Tressy			
Pedigree			Sindy			
Reliable		Teenage High Heel Girl				
Remco						Lisa Littlechap
Ross			Tina Cassini			
Royal			Joy			
Sayco	Miss America					
Unique			Ellie May Clampett			
Valentine					Perfect Patient	
Virga			Schiaparelli			
Vogue	Littlest Angel, Jeff					

Character	14 inches	14-1/2 inches	15 inches	16 inches	16-1/2 inches	17 inches
Active			High Heel Girl			High Heel Girl
Alexander Doll Co.	Little Orphan Annie, Liesl, Louisa, Maria, Brigetta, Wendy, Peter Pan, First Lady Series, Margaret Face Personality		Caroline, Winnie & Binnie Walker, Kelly Face, Maggie Face, Cissy Face Personality	Edith the Lonely Doll, Kelly, Marybel, Sleeping Beauty, Pollyanna, Elise Face Personality	Elise	Elise, Leslie, Maggie Mixup, Mary Ellen Playmate, Maria, Polly, Maggie Mixup, Kelly Face Personality
Allied Grand				Ponytail Girl		
American Character	Betsy McCall, Caroline Kennedy Look a Like, Preteen Tressy, Toni, Sandy, Cricket, Freckles, Ricky Jr.			Eloise, Ricky Jr.		Tiny Tears
Arranbee	Nanette Family, Nancy Lee, Susan			Susan		Angel, Nanette Family
Belle			Bride Doll			
Bonomi			Girl Character			
Cameo	Scootles		Miss Peep	Baby Mine		
Eegee			Gemette			
Effanbee	Little Lady		Patsy, Suzette	Girl Scout		Miss Chips
General Foods			Linda Williams			
Glad Toy				Poor Pitiful Pearl (1 of 2 co.)		
Hasbro			Little Miss No Name			
Horsman & Co.		Tweedie	Betty	Poor Pitiful Pearl (1 of 2 co.), Little Miss Moppet		Pippi Long-stockings

Character	14 inches	14-1/2 inches	15 inches	16 inches	16-1/2 inches	17 inches
Ideal	Miss Revlon, Toni, Betsy McCall, Miss Curity, Mary Hartline, Harriet Hubbard Ayer, Tiffany Taylor		Shirley Temple, Saucy Walker, Cricket, Tara, Mia, Dina, Velvet, Thumbelina	Toni, Sara Ann, Mary Hartline, Harriet Hubbard Ayer, Saucy Walker		Shirley Temple, Soft Stuffed vinyl girl, Plassie, Growing Hair Crissy, Kerry, Brandi, Tressy, Thumbelina, Sara Lee
Jesco	Kewpie			Kewpie		
Juro	Rags to Riches					
Marx			Miss Seventeen			
Mattel	Baby Colleen, Shopping Sheryl		Love n Touch Real Sisters, Shirking Violet	Talking Baby Tender Love, Talking Miss Beasley		Sister Belle
Natural						Miss Ritzy
Remco			Father Littlechap, Mother Littlechap			
Roddy	Beauty Queen					
Sasha				Sasha Series		
Terry Lee				Terry Lee		
Uneeda			Vermont Maid	Coquette		
Vogue		Littlest Angel	Love Me Linda	Little Miss Ginny		

Character	18 inches	19 inches	20 inches	21 inches	22 inches	22-1/2 inches
Active	High Heel Girl					
Admiration			Bride			
Alexander Doll Co.	Elise, Patti, Madeline, Winnie & Binnie Walker, Margaret Face, Maggie Face, Cissy Face Personality		Winnie & Binnie Walker, Cissy Face Personality	Winnie & Binnie Walker, Sheri Lewis, Sleeping Beauty, Coco, Jacqueline, Cissy Face Personality	Edith the Lonely Doll, Kelly, Melinda, Pollyanna, Margaret Face, Kelly Face, Melinda Face Personality	
American Character			Toni, Betsy McCall, Freckles, Eloise, Hedda Get Betta, Whimsies, Tiny Tears	Whimsies, Toodles	Betsy McCall	
Arranbee	My Angel, Nancy Lee		Angel Baby, My Angel	Nanette Family		
Brevete				GeGe		
Cameo		Scootles, Baby Mine		Miss Peep		
Deluxe Reading			Candy	Nancy Nurse		
Doll Bodies			High Heel Girl			
Eegee	Luv-able Skin, Dolly Parton	My Fair Lady		Tandy Talks		Puppetrina

SIZE CHARTS

Character	18 inches	19 inches	20 inches	21 inches	22 inches	22-1/2 inches
Effanbee	Junior Miss, Honey Walker, Suzie Sunshine & Schoolgirl Writing, Tell Bell	Honey Walker, Jr. Miss Bride, Little Lady	Jr. Miss, Honey Walker, Little Lady	Honey Walker		
Eugene	My Little Lady		My Little Lady			
Hasbro	Sweet Cookie			That Kid		
Horsman	Couturier Cindy	Renee Ballerina, Cindy, Squalling Baby				
Ideal	Miss Revlon, Saucy Walker, Sara Lee, Kiss Me, Judy Splinters	Toni, Sara Ann, Harriet Hubbard Ayer, Plassie	Miss Revlon, Saucy Walker, Judy Splinters, Thumbelina	Toni, Sara Ann, Harriet Hubbard Ayer, Kiss Me	Plassie, Miss Revlon, Little Lost Boy	Toni, Sara Ann, Mary Hartline
Jesco	Kewpie		Kewpie		Kewpie	
Juro			Rags to Riches			
Kaysam Jolly				High Heel Girl		
Laurel			Gabby			
M C Doll Co.			High Heel Lady			
Mattel			Chatty Cathy, Cynthia, Living Baby Tenderlove	Scooba Doo	Dr. Doolittle	
Nasco				Hello Dolly		
Natural			Angela Cartwright			
P & M	Paula May					
Petitcollin			Marie Ange			
Plastic Molded Arts			Glamour Doll			
Rite Lee		Miss Lynn				
Royal			Lonely Lisa	Girl in a Velvet Vest, Robin		
Sayco	Miss America	Stuffed vinyl Teenage				
Uneeda		Dollikins, Miss Twist, Soft stuffed Mature Lady				
Valentine			Queen For A Day			
Vogue					Brikette	

Character	23 inches	24 inches	25 inches	26 inches	28 inches	29 inches
Active				High Heel Girl		
Alexander Doll Co.	Sweetie Walker, Winnie & Binnie Walker, Maggie Face, Cissy Face Personality		Winnie & Binnie Walker, Cissy Face Personality			Barbara Jane, Penny
Allied Grand		Bonnie Bride	Bride			
American Character	Toodles		Toni, Toodles			
Arranbee	Nanette Family	My Angel		My Angel		
Arrow		High Heel Girl				

Character	23 inches	24 inches	25 inches	26 inches	28 inches	29 inches
Cameo		Plum			Scootles	
Citro		Polly Pond				
Deluxe Reading		Bride, Princess	Bride		High Heel Girl	Betty the Beautiful Bride
Eegee					Vinyl Girl with Rooted hair	
Effanbee		Alyssa, Bud			Boudoir Doll	
Electrosolids		Ellie Echo				
Horsman			Jackie, Cindy			
Ideal	Miss Revlon	Baby Crissy, Cinnamon				
Jesco		Kewpie			Kewpie	
Juro				Dick Clark		
Laurel			Penny			
Mattel		Dancerina	Charmin Chatty			
Natural		Miss Anniversary				
P & M				Paula Mae		
Royal		Girl				
Sayco	Bride, All Latex Girl					

Character	30 inches	31 inches	32 inches	36 inches	38 inches	42 inches
Alexander Doll Co.	Betty, Mimi	Penny, Mary Ellen	Penny, Barbara Jane	Joanie		Penny, Barbara Jane
American Character	Little Miss Echo, Toodles			Betsy McCall, Linda McCall	Sandy McCall	
Arranbee				My Angel Walking Doll		
Debbie			Debbie Walker			
Disney				Mary Poppins		
Eegee			Susan Stroller			
Effanbee			Mary Jane			
Horsman				Cindy		
Ideal				Daddy's Girl, Patty Playpal, Shirley Temple, Miss Revlon, Judy Splinters	Lori Martin, Peter Playpal	Daddy's Girl
Lorrie				Girl Doll		
Natural	Angela Cartwright					
Uneeda		Pollyanna	Freckles, Princess from Babs in Toyland	Betsy McCall		
Vogue				Ginny		

Exceptional Olive-Colored Bisque Kestner #243, Oriental Character Baby, and Kämmer & Reinhardt #117n Toddler (Photo courtesy of Cobb's Doll Auction.)

A Kämmer & Reinhardt Child, Kestner's Character Child #143 and Gebrüder Heubach's Character Pouty Child #7602 (Photo courtesy of Cobb's Doll Auction)

Kestner Closed-Mouth Shoulder Head; and Alt, Beck & Gottschalck #912 (Photo courtesy of Cobb's Doll Auction.)

Centimeters	Inches
1	.3937
2	.7874
3	1.1811
4	1.55748
10	3.937
15	5.9055
20	7.874
22	8.6614
24	9.4488
26	10.2262
28	11.0236
32	12.5984
35	13.7795
38	14.9606
40	15.748
42	16.5354
45	17.7165
47	18.5039
50	19.685
53	20.8666
55	21.6535
58	22.8346
60	23.622
63	24.8031
65	25.5905
68	26.7716
70	27.559
73	28.7401
75	29.5275
78	30.7086
80	31.496
83	32.2771
85	33.4645
90	35.433
95	37.4015
100	39.37
110	43.307

Inches	Centimeters
1	2.54
3	7.62
4	10.16
5	12.7
8	20.32
10	25.4
12	30.48
14	35.56
15	38.1
16	40.64
17	43.18
18	45.72
19	48.26
20	50.8
21	53.34
22	55.88
23	58.42
24	60.96
25	63.5
27	66.15
28	71.12
29	73.66
30	76.2
32	81.28
34	86.36
36	91.44
38	96.52
40	101.6
42	106.68
45	114.3
48	121.92

CHAPTER SIX

MARKS
& SYMBOLS

By far the most common method used in identifying a doll is to check the back of the head and look for a mold marking. Marks can be found on any part of the doll body. The back of the head was, and is, a favored spot for manufacturers. It is easily observed in the factory or workshop, yet is hidden with a wig once production is completed. Even contemporary artists are fond of using the back of the neck for their hallmarks. Markings or symbols can also be placed on the back, the foot, under the arm, on the side of the body, or on the derrière. In some cases, it is on a wrist tag, label, or sash attached to the doll's clothing—and not on the doll itself.

Over two thousand marks from hundreds of manufacturers are on the following pages. You will find the markings grouped by manufacturers. To locate a marking, it may be necessary to scan through these pages.

Whenever possible, the translation of markings has been taken directly from a doll, tags, or labels. Some, however, are interpretations from observations or descriptions given by others.

The talents of Pat and Bill Tyson, assisted by Trina Miller and Helen Brooke, cannot go unnoticed. Their diligence and artistic abilities helped to ensure the graphic accuracy of these marks.

Also included in this chapter is a rendition of the early German alphabet. Interpretation of a marking can sometimes be obscured because of differences in calligraphy. Having an example of the letter forms that may have been used will be beneficial when interpreting markings. After reviewing the following alphabet, and observing the inconsistencies with our own, it will be apparent to you why many collectors find doll markings somewhat confusing.

A&H	A&M DOLLS	A LA POUPEE NÜRNBERG
I LIKE THE WIDE OPEN SPACES The Doll Of Destiny The Marcie Doll KEN MURRAY TV glamour COWBOY	1904 A & M Made in Austria	A LA POUPÉE de NUREMBER 21 RUE de CHOISEUL LAVALLÉE - PERONNE TROUSSEAUX COMPLETS REPARATIONS PARIS

A.P.B. COMPANY	A. P. D. MANUFACTURING	ABRAHAM & STRAUS	ACME TOY COMPANY
A.P.B. Co. C Made in Boston Mass U.S.A.	A.P.D. MF. Co.	Baby Violet	ACME TOY ACME Standard since 1910 NY

ACORN DOLL COMPANY	ALABAMA INDESTRUCTIBLE DOLL		ALART, EUGENE
A.D.C. AMERICAN MADE	PAT. NOV. 9, 1912 NO. 2 ELLA SMITH DOLL CO.	MRS. S.S. SMITH Manufacturer of and Dealer in The Alabama Indestructible Doll ROANOKE, ALA. PATENTED Sept. 26, 1905	DEPOSÉ

ALDRIS, FREDRIC / ALEXANDER DOLL COMPANY

DOLLS, TOYS & GAMES
F. ALDIS
11, 12 & 19
BELGRAVE MANSIONS S.W.

Created by MADAME ALEXANDER NEW YORK

CHARACTER NAME MADAME ALEXANDER USA ALL RIGHTS RESERVE

CHARACTER NAME MADAME ALEXANDER

JANE WITHERS Alex. Doll Co.

ALEXANDER WALKING ADCo TALKING DOLLS NEW YORK

ALEXANDER 1970

MADAME ALEXANDER DOLLS

ALEXANDER 1962

MADAME ALEXANDER DOLLS

MADAME ALEXANDER PRESENTS TRADE MARK LITTLE COLONEL ALEXANDER DOLL CO. N.Y.

MADAME ALEXANDER NEW YORK

ACADEMY FASHION FA AWARD

MME 1958 ALEX

ALEXANDER
Pat. N. 2171281

TONY SARG
ALEXANDER

ALEX.

Mme Alexander
New York

ALEXANDER

WENDY ANN
Mme ALEXANDER
NEW YORK

Alex Doll Co.

PRINCESS ELIZABETH
ALEXANDER. DOLL Co.

Mme ALEXANDER

+
13

WENDY ANN
Mme. ALEXANDER

Mme.
ALEXANDER

DIONNE
ALEXANDER

BABY JANE
Reg. Mme. Alexander

ALEXANDER
1961

ALEXANDER
1965

ALEXANDER
1973

MADAME ALEXANDER
SONJA HENIE

PR. ELIZABETH
ALEXANDER

AIexANDER
1971

ALEXANDRE, HENRI	ALKID DOLL COMPANY	ALL-BISQUE DOLLS

Alexandre, Henri

★

H&A

ALKID DOLL

TRADE MARK
PAt'd applied for

Baby Rose

497
15
Germany

ED

FG

MB
BABY DARLING

S. F.B.J.

UNIS   JDK   A B G

193 - 19/0

Made
in
Germany

GERMANY

Made
in
Germany
1200
M.S.
∽

HAPPI FAT
GERMANY

497
15
Germany

Alex Doll Co.

DOLLY

JAPAN

MADE IN
JAPAN

NIPPON

O'Neill

ANDY
GUMP
Germany

BABS

235

Made in Germany

Made in Germany

BABS

S & H

ALLIED GRAND DOLL MANUFACTURER

KT

A

AE

MADE by ALLIED DOLL CO.

Allied - Grand Doll Manf.
ALLIED DOLL & TOY CORP.
BROOKLYN, N.Y. ©1967

14 • R

ALMA	ALT, BECK & GOTTSCHALCK

Alma

Création Alma
Made in Italy

639   639 Germany No 6

AB

1064 # 0.

D.R.G.M.
520942
1326
5

AB
1352
6

1222 H 3/0

1123½ 10 Made Germany N.½

"ALBEGO"
10
Made in Germany

A.B.G.

Deponiert

1290 Made in Germany DEP   1268 Germany Dep No 12

J.1.0 © 1920
44

Germany
1360
1910

A.B.&G
1322

J.1.0. © 1919
47

1352

13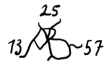
1361
40
Made in Germany

639 Germany N° 6

1064

XX   6

Made in Germany

25
13 57

Germany. N°

1064

Germany #

Germany   #   6

1361
AB&G
Made in Germany

1352
25

Made in
Germany N°

DRGM
(AB&G)

83
150
19

#

XX

Germany N°   DEP.

XO

N°

#

Igodi L.A.S.©
414
1911

L.A.S.

L.A.&S.© 1928

Vanta Baby
LA&S   D.R.G.N.
Germany

LA&S 1921
Germany

LA&S
RA 241/
Germany

©L.A.&S. 1914
#G 44520
Germany

L.A.&S.

GERMANY
A.R.
LA&S 886

BABY PEGGY

©1916 L.A.&S.

L.A.S.
1918

Baby Tufums
LA&S
107
Germany

LA&S
RA 247/
Germany

AMBERG
L.A.&S. © 1928

AMBERG'S
VICTORY
DOLL

S¹²HOPKINS

AMBERG
DOLLS
THE WORLD
STANDARD
MADE IN
USA

19©24
LA&SNY
Germany
98⁴/₃

THE ORIGINAL
NEWBORN BABE
© Jan. 9ᵗʰ 1914 - No.G.45520
AMBERG DOLLS
The world Standard

AMBERG DOLLS
The World Standard

Vanta Baby
Trademark REG.
LOUIS AMBERG + SON N.Y.

Baby Nod
L.A.&S. N.Y.
Germany

Igodi 12309/4DRGM

© L.A.&S.1914
#G 45520
Germany #4

AMBERG
DOLLS
THE WORLD
STANDARD
MADE IN
USA

HEADS COPYRIGHTED BY
LOUIS AMBERG & SON

©
LA&S 1921
Germany

Vanta Baby
LA&S. 3/0 D.R.G.M
Germany

19 ©24
N.Y.
Germany 50
984/2

S¹² HOPKINS

LA&S
RA 241/5/0
Germany

1924
LA&S.N.Y.
Germany 50

AMBERG'S
VICTORY
DOLL

GERMANY
A·R
LA&S 886·2

L.A.&S. ©
414

Baby Tufums
LA&S
107
Germany

Baby Tufums
LA&S
107
Germany

CHARLIE CHAPLIN DOLL
WORLDS GREATEST COMEDIAN
MADE EXCLUSIVELY BY LOUIS AMBERG & SON
BY SPECIAL ARRANGEMENT WITH ESSANAY FILM

Petite
Sally

AMER. CHAR. PETITE

A
PETITE
DOLL

AMER. CHAR. DOLL

PETITE
DOLL

AMERICAN BISQUE DOLL COMPANY

AMERICAN CHARACTER DOLL COMPANY

USA

AB DCo.
USA

PETITE

AMERICAN CHARACTER DOLL

AMERICAN CHARACTER DOLL/PAT.

PÉTITE
AMER. CHAR. DOLL Co

McCALL
1958
CORP

A C

AM CHAR. 63

AMER
CHAR
DOLL

AMERICAN DOLL COMPANY

AM. DOLL. CO.

A.D. Co.

Peters
Weather bird
Shoes

MADE IN USA	BETSEY ROSS DESIGN
	CREATED BY
THE AMERICAN DOLL	
NEW YORK CITY	

AMERICAN MUSLIN-LINED HEAD | ## AMERICAN STUFFED NOVELTY | ## ANCHOR IMPORTER

AMERICAN
MUSLIN LINED HEAD

AMERICAN
MUSLIN LINED HEAD
Nº (#)
warranted fast oil colors

IFE
IKE
INE

ANDEREGG | ## ARENA, FÉLIX | ## ARNAUD, LOUIS HUBERT

Th. ANDEREGG
WOOD
CARVING
EXPORT
MONTREUX
SWITZERLAND

Germany

Mignon

MIGNON

LA

ARNOLD PRINT WORKS | ## ARNOLD, MAX OSCAR

ARNOLD PRINT WORKS
INCORPORATED
1876
NORTH ADAMS, MASS.

SCHUTZ-MARKE

MOA

MOA
150
Made in Germany
Welsch
9/0

MOA
Made in Germany

ARRANBEE DOLL COMPANY

SIMON & HALBIG
ARRANBEE
PATENT
Germany

283
R & B.

MADE IN USA

ARRENBEE

NANCY

R & B

Germany
341 45K
A.M.

R & B

A M
Germany
351   /0

A M
Germany
341 5½ K

R & B

KEWTY

NANCY
ARRENBEE
DOLLS

DEBUTEEN

Germany
ARRANBEE

ARROW DOLL COMPANY	ARROW NOVELTY COMPANY	ART FABRIC MILLS	
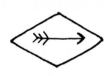		ART FABRIC MILLS NEW YORK Pat. Feb. 13th 1900	PAT. FEB. 13, 1900

ART METAL WORKS	ARTCRAFT TOY PRODUCTS		ARTEL
Fully Patented MAMA DOLL I TALK!! Squeeze me Easy Made in America Corp. 1915 by Louis V. Aronson			ARTELPRAHA ARTELPRAHA

AU BÉBÉ ROSE	ARTCRAFT TOY PRODUCTS		
	Au Nain Bleu E. Chauviere	AU NAIN BLEU 408 Rue St. Honoré PARIS	S.F.B.J. Au Nain Bleu Unis France

AU NAIN BLEU

Au Nain Bleu
E. Chauviere

AU NAIN BLEU
408 Rue St. Honoré
PARIS

S.F.B.J.
Au Nain Bleu
Unis France

AU NAIN JAUNE

293
8/0
S.C.

Au Nain Jaune
Jouets & Jeux
64 AVENUE de Nevilly 64

AU NAIN JAUNE
JOUETS & JEUX
64 AVENUE de NEVILLY 64

AU PARADIS DES ENFANTS

AU PARADIS DES ENFANTS
Au Lavasseur & Quache
Rue de Rivali + Rue de Louvre

AU PARADIS des ENFANTS
PERREAU FILS
156 R. RIVOLI · Rue de LOUVRE

AU PARADIS DES ENFANTS
MON. RÉMOND

AUGUSTA	AUX RÊVES DE L'ENFANCE	AVERILL MANUFAC-TURING COMPANY

U.S.A.
Augusta
Perth Amboy. N.J.
R.

AUX RÊVES de L'ENFANCE
SPÉCIALITÉ de POUPÉES
40 R. DE RICHELIEU PARIS

AUX RÊVES DE L'ENFANCE
JOUETS
POUPEES
ARTICLE UX
JEUX DESOCIETÉ
CARTONNAGES
INSTRUCTIES
40 RUE DE RICHELIEU PARIS

MADAME HENDREN
CHARACTER DOLL
COSTUME PAT. MAY 9th 1916

GENUINE MADAME HENDREN DOLL

copr. by
Georgene Averill
Germany
1005/3652
1386

MADAM HENDRON

GENUINE
"MADAME HENDREN"
DOLL
1717
MADE in U.S.A.

GENUINE
"MADAME HENDREN"
DOLL
617
MADE in U.S.A.

MADAME HENDREN DOLLS
PATENT PENDING

GENUINE
MADAME HENDREN
DOLL
26
MADE in U.S.A.

DOLLY DINGLE
COPYRIGHT BY
G.G. DRAYTON

CHOCOLATE DROP
COPYRIGHT BY
G.G. DRAYTON

99 DRATON

USA

Trade mark Sunny Girl

September Morning Germany

Germany
LITTLE ANNIE ROONEY
REG. U.S. PAT. OFF.
COPR BY JACK COLLINS

HAPPIFAT
Germany

BONNIE BABY
COPR BY
GEORGENE
AVERILL
US PAT
GERMANY

Copr by
Georgene Averill
1005/3652
Germany
1402/45

PRIZE BABY
Reg. US Pat OFF
Made in Germany

GERMANY

BYE LO BABY
© GERMANY
G.S. PUTNAM

© 1923 by
Grace S. Putnam
MADE IN GERMANY

Copr. by
Grace S. Putnam
Germany
1418/25

Floradora
A.M.
Germany

Just ME
Registered
Germany
310/10

MY DEARIE
Germany

Copr. by
Georgene Averill
Germany
1386

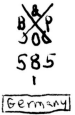
B&P
308
585
Germany

Copr by
J.C. Kallus
Germany
1394/

A 329 M
Germany
G.B.

Phyllis
MADE IN GERMANY

BABY PHYLLIS
Made in Germany
24014

Phyllis
Made in Germany

Für Puppenköpfe
B & P
i. d. M. gest.

5 3 6
6

5 2 9
B & P
2 025

2 7 7
Dep

B P

B & P
5 8 4
Germany

Buporit

2 0 9
4

3 0 9 12
270 dep. 2/0

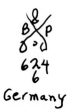
6 2 4
6
Germany

620-5

5 8 5
8
Made in
Germany

2 0 9
German

3 9 4
10

5 8 5
2/0
Germany

2 5 2
d e p

Eden-Bébé

5 8 5
5

6 7 8
10

B P

2 6 1
dep
made in
Germany

B & P
343-6

2 3 9
D e p

B & P
2084-4

6 8 6
3/0
B P
Made in
Germany

B & P
379 14
dep

2 8 3
d e p

B & P
5 8 5
1
Germany

4 2 5
19

&
B P

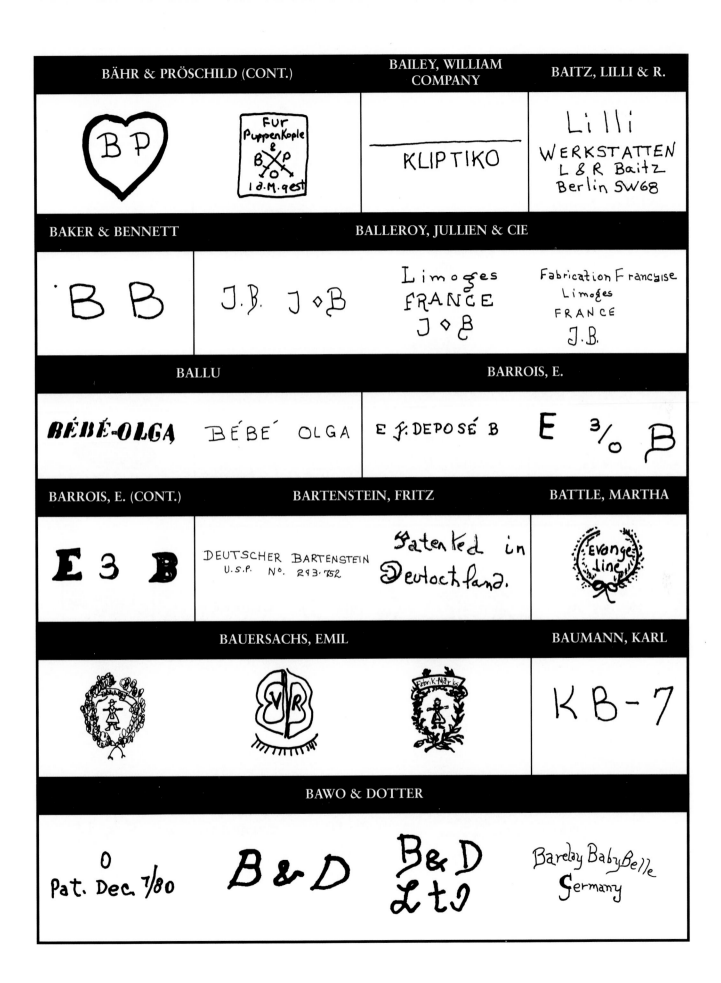

BÄHR & PRÖSCHILD (CONT.)		BAILEY, WILLIAM COMPANY	BAITZ, LILLI & R.

BÄHR & PRÖSCHILD (CONT.)

BP (in heart)

Fur PuppenKople & B X P O i.d.M.gest

BAILEY, WILLIAM COMPANY

KLIPTIKO

BAITZ, LILLI & R.

Lilli WERKSTATTEN L & R Baitz Berlin SW68

BAKER & BENNETT

B B

BALLEROY, JULLIEN & CIE

J.B. J ◊ B

Limoges FRANCE J ◊ B

Fabrication Francaise Limoges FRANCE J.B.

BALLU

BÉBÉ-OLGA

BÉBÉ OLGA

BARROIS, E.

E J. DEPOSÉ B

E ³/₀ B

BARROIS, E. (CONT.)

E 3 B

BARTENSTEIN, FRITZ

DEUTSCHER BARTENSTEIN U.S.P. No. 293.752

Patented in Deutochland.

BATTLE, MARTHA

Evangeline

BAUERSACHS, EMIL

BAUMANN, KARL

KB-7

BAWO & DOTTER

O Pat. Dec. 7/80

B & D

B & D Ltd

Barclay BabyBelle Germany

BAYERISCHE CELLU-LOIDWARENFABRIK	BEAUMONT, IRIS		BEAVER DOLL COMPANY

BÉBÉS DE FRANCE	BECK, RICHARD & COMPANY	BELLET, HENRI	BELLEVILLE & COMPANY
"... et si je tombe, je ne casse PAS"		"POUPARD" ART	MYSTÉRE

BERG VON, ERICH   BERG VON, HERMANN   BERGMANN, C. M.

E v B
Germany
1

Germany
H v B
500/k

H v B
500/k

C.M. BERGMANN
4/0 M
Made in Germany

C.M. BERGMANN
1916
WALTERS HAUSEN

AM
Columbia
C.M. Bergmann

HALBIG
C.M. BERGMANN
S&H

C.M BERGMANN
SIMON & HALBI
12

C M Bergmann
7
Germany

C.M.B.
SIMON & HALBIG
Eleonore

S & H
C.M.B.
3

Cinderella-Baby

G.M. Bergmann
Waltershausen
Germany
1916
6½a

C. M. B
SIMON & HALBIG
Eleonore

C.M.BERGMANN
4/0

S & H
C.M.B

246

BERGMANN, S. JR. & COMPANY	BERGNER, CARL	BERLICH, ROLF	
P 20/0 Germany N	C.B.	ROLF BERLICH PUPPEN CHARLOTTENBURG	

BERNHEIM & KAHN

ETOILE BÉBÉ   BÉBÉ MONDAIN   ⭐ETOILE BEBE⭐   ETOILE BÉBÉ

BERNHOLD, JULIUS	BERTRAND, RENE	BESTER DOLL MANU-FACTURING COMPANY	BIERER, L.
NINI KASPA	GABY	BESTER DOLL C°. BLOOMFIELD	

BIERSCHENK, FRITZ   BING GEBRÜDER BROTHERS

F₃B Germany   FB   BING   BING'S BEAUTY ART DOLLS MADE IN GERMANY   W   BING BEAUTY BABY.

BISQUE NOVELTY MANUFAC-TURING COMPANY		BLOEDEL	BLOSSOM PRODUCTS
Made in USA Reinhardt Pat Sep 19, 14 Sh Bisc Novelty Mfg Co East Liverpool Ohio	H3 Reinhardt East Liverpool Ohio	" BÉBÉ TRIOMPHE "	QUINS

BOHNE, ERNST   BONIN & LEFORT

	NINON MON BABY SELECT
⚓	JOLI BÉBÉ GABY

BÉBÉ LE GLORIEUX   BÉBÉ LE GLORIEUX   BÉBÉ LE PETIT FRANÇAIS

BÉBÉ LE RADIEUX   BEBE LE SPECIAL   BÉBÉ L'UNIQUE

Germany
G. 327 B
D. R. G. M259
A. 12 M.

G. 327 B
Germany
A. 10 M

Alma
4

Pansy.
IV.

G. B. 250
A. 5/0 M
Germany
D.R.G.M. 248

251
G. B
Germany
A 2/0 M
D.R. G.M.
243/1

My Girlie
III.
Germany

© 1923 by
Grace S. Putnam
MADE IN GERMANY

PANSY
IV
Germany

Copr by
J. L. Kallus
Germany
1394

My Girlie
III
Germany

251
G. B
Germany.
A 2/0 M
D.R. G.M
243/1

20-10
Copr by
GRACE S Putnam
Germany

G. 253 ß.
Germany
A11/0M

SCOOTLES

Princess
1
Germany

Just ME.
Registered.
Germany
A 310/7/0. M.

Copr. by
Grace S Putnam
Germany
1415/48

O'Neill

SPLASH ME
MISS YANKEE

Copr. by.
Grace S. Putnam
MADE IN GERMANY

'Jiss-me
ARTISTE

Rose ©
O'Neill

G.B.
O

HOLLIKID

LOTTA-SUN

TUMBLE-BO

WINKIE

JUNO

Babykins
Cop. by Grace S. Putman
made in Germany
1435
50

NOBBIKID
REG US PAT OFF
MADE IN GERMANY

G.B
Germany
A 2/0M
DR. GM

G B.

KEWPIE
GERMANY

NIFTY

Peter Rabbit Acrobat

G 327 ß
Germany
A 12 M

HAPPY HOOLIGAN

HOLLIKID

LOTTA-SUN

KEWPIE

COPY RIGHT
ROSE ONEILL

FLORODORA
GERMANY

KEWPIE
REG U.S.
PAT OFF

BEDTIME

BYE-LO-BABY

FELIX THE CAT

MISS YANKEE

G 327 B
Germany
A 10 M

KEWPIE

MyGirlie
III
Germany

Pansy
IV

Princess
I
Germany

BOSSUAT, ETIENNE	BOUCHET, ADOLPHE HENRI	BRANDL, RESI	BRISTOL, EMMA L.
			BRISTOL'S UNBREAKABLE DOLL 273 HIGH St. PROVIDENCE R.I.

BROGI, AMILCARE	BROWNIES	BRU

CLELIA

Copyrighted 1892
by PALMER COX

B Jne ETCie

B Jne ETC ie

B
R
U

BRU JNE R
II

BRU JNE

BRU JNE R

BRU JNE R
BREVETE SCDG
Y 8 M

BRU JNE R

BRU JNE

B
R
U

BREVETE S.G.D.G.   Y   8 M

BEBE BRU Bte S.G.D.G.
Toot Contre Fd et aor SARA 9 ais Pour
CONFURNEMENT a la Loi

E	1	BÉBÉ Breveté SGDG PARIS	C	BRU Jne N3T

BRÜCKNER, ALBERT	BRUNET, VICTOR	BRUNOT, MARGUERITE	BUCHERER, A. & CIE
PAT'D. JULY 8TH 1901	L'HIRONDELLE	MARGIE DETAIL	MADE IN SWITZERLAND PATENTS APPLIED FOR

BÜCHNER, OSKAR	BÜHL, H. & SÖHNE	BUSCHBAUM, THEODOR	BUSCHOW & BECK
	DEP / H B G S	700 Jebu	MINERVA Schutzmarke

BUSCHOW & BECK (CONT.)		BUSCHOW, WILHELM	BUTLER BROTHERS
MINERVA	METAL HEAD	Mein Liebling Kind	THE 'WIDE-AWAKE' DOLL REGISTERED GERMANY

BUTLER BROTHERS (CONT.)		CAMEO DOLL COMPANY	
PATENTAPPD FOR GERMANY	Ruth	ART QUALITY CAMEO DOLLS	JOY

CAMEO DOLL COMPANY (CONT.)

PETE the PUP	DES REG... 1918 BY. J. L. KALLUS BUN©DIE	ART QUALITY CAMEO DOLLS	"Scootles" DESIGNED AND COPYRIGHT by Rose O'Neill CAMEO DOLL

CAMEO DOLL COMPANY (CONT.)

DES & COPYRIGHT
BY J. L. KALLUS
MADE IN U.S.A.

CANZLER & HOFFMANN	CAPO DE MONTE	CARL, MAX & COMPANY

CARL, ROBERT	CARVAILLO, ADRIEN

  R.C. DEPOSE   Germany. 1400/4   LA VÉNUS

CATTERFELDER PUPPENFABRIK

Catterfelder
Puppenfabrik
264
2

Catterfelder
Puppen-
Fabrik
5

25.
207

S&H
C.T.
7

263
55.

C. P.
208/34 S
Deponiert

C. P.
201.
28

C. P.
209/34 S
Deponiert

7700
Catterfelder Puppenfabrik

C. P.
220
26

7700
Catterfelder Puppenfabrik
2

CAYETTE, MME. E.

BÉBÉ PROPHÈTE
BÉBÉ ORACLE
LA FÉE AU GUI
LA FÉE BONHEUR
LA FÉE AU TRÉFLE
LA FÉE AUX TRÉFLES

AMERICAN

IG ES

FRANCE

MINERVA

TRADEMARK
PARSON JACKSON
CLEVELAND, OHIO

SCHUTZ-MARKE

HOLLYWOOD

FRANCE

MADE IN JAPAN

FRANCE

SICOINE
S.ie A.
FRANCE

MADE IN USA
MARKS BROTHERS CO.
BOSTON

POLAND

30
GERMANY

MADE IN IRWIN USA

A S A D A

BO-PEEP
AMERICAN

CENTURY DOLL COMPANY

Germany
Century
7

CENTURY D°LL CO

CENTURY DOLLS

Germany:
CENTURY DOLL & C°

CERETA OF THE AMERICAN CEREAL COMPANY OF CHICAGO	CHAD VALLEY	
	The Mabel Lucie Attwell Doll (Reg. & Patented) Sole makers Chad Valley Co. Ltd Hygienic Toys Made in England by CHAD VALLEY CO. Ltd.	The Chad Valley Hygienic Textile Toys Made in England Chad Valley BAMBINA (Regr. & Pat)

CHANTILLY CIE	CHARLES, JEAN	CHARRIE, JEAN	CHASE, MARTHA JENKS

CHASE, MARTHA JENKS (CONT.)

	M.J.C. Stockinet Doll Patent Applied For	MJC Stockinet Doll Patent applied for

CHECKENI, DOMINICO	CHAUVIÈRE	CLEAR, EMMA

CLÉMENT, VIE	CLOSTER, VEILSDORF PORZELLANFABRIK	

COCHECO MANUFACTURING COMPANY	COCHRAN, DEWEES			

DC/AA - 52/#24

D/BB -54/#9

1953

Dewees Cochran Dolls c1954

D.C./J.J. 60/2

DC/SS - 58/1

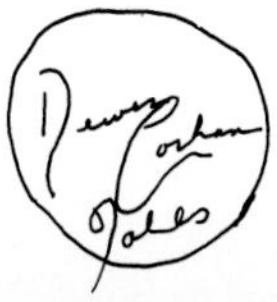

COLECO INDUSTRIES INCORPORATED

COLOMBO, CHARLES

COLONIAL TOY MANU-FACTURING COMPANY

CHUBBY A NATURAL DOLL

RITZIE A NATURAL DOLL

COLONIAL
DOLL
MADE IN
U.S.A.

COLUMBIAN DOLL

COMPOSITION DOLL MARKINGS FROM VARIOUS MANUFACTURERS

COLUMBIAN DOLL
EMMA E. ADAMS
OSWEGO CENTRE
NY

THE COLUMBIAN DOLL
MANUFACTURED BY
MARIETTA ADAMS RUTTAN
OSWEGO, NY

G.L
2020
Superior

M & S
Superior

COMPOSITION DOLL MARKINGS FROM VARIOUS MANUFACTURERS (CONT.)

M & S
50
Germany

W.A.H.
nonpareil
3015

A.F. & C.
Superior
2018

TRADE MARK

CONCENTRA

CONTA AND BOEHME

V
37

IX
36

COQUILLET

CORNET, MARIUS

CORTOT, JEANNE

LA PARISETTE

LA POUPÉE FRANCAISE

BÉBÉ JEANNETTE

MONTREUIL-BÉBÉ

255

CREIDLITZ	CREMER & SON	CROSIER, ALINE	CUNIQUE DES POUPÉES
	CREMER Dolls Toys Games 210 Regent St	PARFAIT – BÉBÉ PARIS MANUFACTURE FRANÇAISE DE POUPEES ET JOUETS	CUNIQUE DES POUPÉES LAUSANNE Place Palud N°1

CURNEN & STEINER	DAMERVAL, FRÈRES & LAFFRANCHY	DANEL & CIE	DARCY, M. ROBERT
	JOLI BÉBÉ	B 8 F	

DARCY, M. ROBERT (CONT.)	DARROW	D'AUTREMONT	DE FUISSEAUX
	R.E. DARROW'S PATENT MAY 1st 1866	D'AUTREMONT PARIS 6 RUE DE DAUPHIN 6	D. F. B.

DE FUISSEAUX (CONT.)	DE LA RAMÉE, MAX-HENRI & MARIE	DE LACOSTE	DE RAPHELIS-SOISSAN, MADEMOISELLE MARGUERITE
D.2,	MA JOLIE	D	JEANNE D'ABC

DE ROUSSY DE SALES		DE WOUILT, MLLE. RENEE	DEAN'S RAG BOOK COMPANY
EXPRESSION IMODESTES ESPIÈGLES			

DEAN'S RAG BOOK COMPANY (CONT.)		DEDIEU, LOUIS	DEGENRING, THEODOR
HYGIENIC AL TOYS (TRADE) MARK MADE IN ENGLAND DEAN'S RAG BOOK CO LTD	HYGIENIC TOYS DEAN'S RAG MADE IN ENGLAND	DE LIAUTY	

DEHLER, E.	DELACHAL, LOUIS	DELCROIX, HENRI	
		PAN	G P PARIS

DELCROIX, HENRI (CONT.)		DELLY PUPPENFABRIK	DEMALCO
	JOLI BÉBÉ		Demalco 5/0 Germany

DEMAREST, MARIE	DEROLLAND, BASILE	DES LOGES, M. HUBERT	DESAUBLIAUX, MLLE.
			GALLIA

DEUERLEIN, JOSEF		DEUTSCHE KOLONIAL KAPOK WERKE	DIAMOND
			◄DIAMOND►

DIAMOND (CONT.)	DIECKMANN, M.	DOMEC TOY COMPANY	
	S. T. F.		

DORNHEIM, KOCH & FISCHER		DORST, JULIUS	

« Colette » Puppel's Mary

| DRAYTON, GRACE GEBBIE | DREIFUSS, ISIDORE | DRESSEL & KOCH | DRESSEL & PIETSCHMANN |

C 'Dep.

D & K N° %

DRESSEL, CUNO & OTTO

C O D 93-S D&P

13/0

Jutta Jutta

1349
Dressel

Jutta
1914

POPPY DOLLS

Jutta Puppen

1469
B. & C Dressel
Germany

Trade mark
POPPY DOLL
GERMANY

Made in Germany
1912-4.
X

Made in Germany
1912 · 5.

4
17 P 67

BAMBINA

Heubach-Köppelsdorf
Jutta-Baby
Dressel
Germany
1922
10

Jutta
1914
5 ½

C & O. D
Germany
2

Germany
13/0

dz.
Indestructible Heads
superior GERMAN

1469
C. & O. Dressel.
Germany
2

EOPATENTDE
HOLZMASSE

A M
COD93-A-DEP
made in Germany

6969
-3-
Germany
17

C.O.D.

C OD
341/3
Germany

Made in Germany
1912·9

C O D 93·5 DEP

A. 1776 M
COD 3/0 DEP
made in Germany

e & o Dressel
Germany

1349
Dressel
S&H
8

S & H
1349
Dressel

Jutta
1914

1896
COD 1 DEP
MADE IN GERMANY

5½ Germany

5

BAMBINA

1348
Jutta
S&H
10

Schutzmarke

Cuno & Otto Dressel
Germany

Germany
78/0

A. M.
C O. D. 93·0· D.E.P.

doz
Indestructible Heads
Superior

1349
Dressel
S&H

1349
Dressel

1469.
& o. Dressel
Germany
2.

C & O
Dressel

Germany
C
2

Made in Germany
1912-3·

1349
Dressel

DRESSEL, KISTER & COMPANY	DUBOIS, PAUL	DUMMIG, CHARLES

ENTRÉE des ALLIÉS
à STRASBOURG

DUNKER, HENRIETTE	DURAN, MME.	DURAND, OCTAVE

" TANAGRETTE "

EATON, T. COMPANY	ECK, BERTHOLD	ECKARDT & COMPANY

Our Pet.
Germany.
3/0

540 - 4
GEO
5

ECKSTEIN, HERMANN	EDELMANN, EDMUND

Melitta
4½

Melitta
A. Germany M.
12

EFFANBEE

EFFANBEE
SUGAR BABY

EFFANBEE
MARILEE
COPY R.
DOLL

EFFANBEE
ROSEMARY
WALK TALK SLEEP

EFFANBEE
PATSY
DOLL

EFFANBEE
DURABLE
DOLLS

EFFANDBEE

EFFANBEE
DOLLS
WALK TALK SLEEP

EFFANBEE
"PATRICIA"

This is
GRUMPYKINS
Trade Mark
A doll so cute you
just want to hug
her
Effan Bee
Dolls

19 © 24
EFFANBEE
DOLLS
WALK TALK SLEEP
MADE IN USA

EFFAN BEE
PATSY ANN ©
PAT. # 283558

260

EFFANBEE BABY GRUMPY COPYR. 1923

EFFANBEE SKIPPY © P. L. Crosly

GUARANTEE EFFANBEE FLEISCHAKER and BAUM NEW YORK

EFFANBEE BABY DAINTY

EFFANBEE BABY GRUMPY COPYRIGHTED

Effanbee

EFFANBEE PATSY PAT.PEND DOLL

DECO 172

Effanbee DOLLS

DECO 174

EFFANBEE SKIPPY © Pd. CROSBY

DECO 176

EFFANBEE BUBBLES CORP. 1924 MADE IN USA

LAMKIN AN EFFANBEE DURABLE DOLL

EFFANBEE ROSEMARY WALK TALK SLEEP MADE IN USA

EFFANBEE BABY DAINTY

THE EFFANBEE BUTTONS MONK

EFFANBEE PATSY COPYR DOLL

EFFANBEE BABY DAINTY

EFFANBEE PATSY

EICHHORN, CHRISTIAN & SÖHNE

EISENMANN & COMPANY

CEUS

Made in Germany E&S

CE&S 79/0

Einco o Germany

SCHUTZMARKE EINCO

EISENMANN & COMPANY (CONT.)

ELEKTRA TOY & NOVELTY COMPANY

Einco 1

Germany Einco

Einco 9 87 HEUBACH 64 Germany

ELEKTRA TOY & NOVELTY CO. NEW YORK

ELEKTRA TOY & N. Co.

E.T.& NCo. N.Y. COPYRIGHT

ELITE DOLL COMPANY

EMASO

ESCHER, J. G. & SOHN

Dep. Elite U.S.1

Emaso

TradeMark

JG ES

EVANS, JOSEPH	FALCK, ADOLPHE & ROUSSEL	FAUCHE, MME.

MANOS.

MARQUE DEPOSEE

FAULTLESS RUBBER COMPANY	FEILER, CARL & COMPANY	FISCHER, ARNO

Fischer

FISCHER, ARNO (CONT.)	FISCHER, NAUMANN & COMPANY

P A F

FISHER PRICE	FLEISCHMANN & BLÖDEL

EDEN-BÉBÉ   *Eden-Bébé*

EDEN-BÉBÉ   BÉBÉ TRIOMPHE

        „Michu"

DEP
10

EDEN BEBE
1

Eden-Bébé

EDEN
PARIS

EDEN BEBE
PARIS
N

EDEN BEBE
PARIS
5

EDEN BEBE
PARIS
7
DEPOSÉ

FLEISCHMANN & CRAEMER

FLEISCHMANN, GEBRÜDER BROTHERS

FLORIG & OTTO

FÖRSTER, ALBERT

FÖRSTER, GUSTAV

FOUCHER, RENE

FOULD, MME. CONSUÉLO POUPÉES

FRANZ, JOHANNES

FRENCH BISQUE DOLL MARKINGS FROM VARIOUS MANUFACTURERS

FRÉRES, BERTOLI

Mark of Bertoli Frères

IDÉAL BÉBÉ

FRÉRES, COSMAN

FRÉRES, MAY, CIE

Splendide Bébé

Bébé Farorl

Bébé le Farori

MASCOTTE
M

FRÉRES, MAY, CIE (CONT.)

MASCOTTE
I

BÉBÉ MASCOTTE
PARIS

BEBE MASCOTTE

BÉBÉ MASCOTTE

FRIEDRICHRODAER PUPPENFABRIK	FULPER POTTERY COMPANY

FURGA, LUIGI & COMPANY	GANS & SEYFARTH

GANS & SEYFARTH (CONT.)

 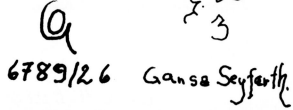

GATUSSE, CLÉMENT	GAULT, J. ROGER

BÉBÉ FAVO

registered by Clément Gatusse

PLASTOLITE   La plastolite paris france

GAULTIER, FRANÇOIS

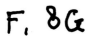    La Poupée de France

GEBAULET	GEBRÜDER SCHOENAU PORZELLANFABRIK

GEBRÜDER SCHOENAU PORZELLANFABRIK (CONT.)	GEM TOY COMPANY	GERBAULET, FRÉRES ÉTABLISSEMENTS (BROTHERS)	GERLING TOY COMPANY
	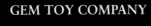	BÉBÉ OLGA	Pat Pending GERLING

GERMAN BISQUE DOLL MARKINGS FROM VARIOUS MANUFACTURERS

The Dolly Princess
62
Special
Made in Germany

Gld Rip
910

806

900

EL 510

700
f 39

727

E 9 S

44 611

B
/10

G.1

GERMANY

LHK

265

GESCHÜTZT, GESETZLICH	GESLAND		

GEYER, CARL & COMPANY

GIEBELER-FALK DOLL CORPORATION	GIMBEL BROTHERS	GIOTTI, ÉTABLISSEMENTS

 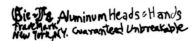 

GIROUX, ALPHONSE & CIE	GODFREYS	GOEBEL, WILLIAM

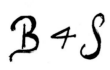   

  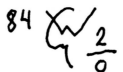 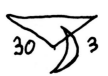

GOEBEL, WILLIAM (CONT.)

GOLD MEDAL	GOLDSTEIN, EDGARD & COMPANY	GOOCH, C.	GOODYEAR TOY COMPANY

GOSS & COMPANY	GOTTHELF, ARTHUR FIRM	GOURDEL, VALES & COMPANY	GRANDJEAN

GRANDJEAN (CONT.) | GRATIEUX, M. FERNAND

GREIF PUPPENKUNST	GREINER & COMPANY	GREINER, LUDWIG

GREINER, LUDWIG (CONT.)		GRE-POIR, INCORPORATED	GROSSMANN, ERNST
GREINER EVERLASTING DOLL HEADS	GREINER'S PATENT HEADS. NO. 0. Pat. March 30th, '58.	Pat. Pending TRADE MARK REG. Balsam Baby Healthful Cuddling Doll Easily Cleaned with Art Gum Gre-Poir Inc.	E.G.

GROSSMANN, ERNST (CONT.)			GUERIN, MLLE. MARTHE	GUILLARD, FRANÇOIS
Gesetzlich Geschnitzt	G		PGU	A.T. GUILLARD JOUETS Rue des Petits Champs

GUILLARD, FRANÇOIS (C0NT.)	GUILLET, LOUIS	GUILLON, SILAS	GÜNTHER, C. ERICH
Le plus grands Magasins DE JOUET de PARIS A LA GALERIE VIVIENE Mr Guillard + Lemaire REMOND suc RUE N= des Petits Chs	AMOUR-BÉBÉ	CAMÉLIA	CEG

GUTTMANN & SCHIFFNIE

"MONA LISA"   G & S   BÉBÉ-COIFFURE

Bébé l'Avenir   Bébé l'Avenir   'Bébé l'Avenir'

"BÉBÈ-COIFFURE"   Bébé l'Avenix   gußchi
G & S   Geimany

HAAG, GEBRÜDER BROTHERS		HACHMEISTER, HERMANN	HAHN & COMPANY

HAMBURGER & COMPANY

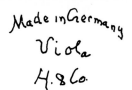

Made in Germany
Viola
H.& Co.

Made in Germany
Viola
H!C.
5

5777
DEP
DOLLY DIMPLE
H
Germany
7

S&H 1249 DEP.
Germany
12
SANTA

Made in Germany 8 Viola

Dep. H&C Registered

Imperial H& Co.

H & Cº

HAMLEY BROTHERS

FUMS UP
THUMBS UP

HAMLEYS
64
REGENT St.
W
DOLL REPAIRED

HANCOCK, S. & SONS

NTI BOY
ENGLISH MAKE

SH&S
ENGLISH MAKE

HANDWERCK, HEINRICH

.79
3½
Germany
HW
2/0

Hah 2/0 H

119 - 13
HANDWERIK
5
Germany

HANDWERCK'S
BEBÉ COSMOPOLITE

79. 3X
HW

BÉBÉ COSMOPOLITE

11½
99
DEP
Germany
HANDWERCK

79
5 n
Germany

W
Heinrich Handwerck
Simon & Halbig
Germany
0 ½

HANDWERCK, MAX

Dep O Elite
T 2/0

Dep.
Elite
D1.

Max Handwerk
Bebe Elite
286/3
Germany

283/28.5
MAX.
HANDWERCK
GERMANY
2¼

Dep.
Elite
E/2

Germany
MAX
HANDWERCK

HANDWERCK, MAX

Dep.
Elite
E ⅔

Germany
MA26
HANDWERGK
0¼

Max
HANDWERCK
Germany

Dep
Elite
U.S.1

Max Handwerk
BebeElite
286/3
Germany

Max
HANDWERCK

Max Handwerk
Bebe ESite
B90/185
4½
germany

Germany

HARMUS, CARL JR.

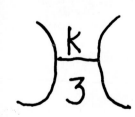

HARMUS
Germany

Harmus
2

PM

PM

Harmus
800.0

Harmus
800.0

Harmus
2

HARTMANN, CARL

GlobeBaby

GlobeBaby
DEP
Germany
C3)f

GlobeBaby
DEP
Germany
C=H

DEP
CH
/o
GERMANY

HARTMANN, KRAL   HASBRO INCORPORATED

}K{
3

G.I. JOE™
COPYRIGHT 1964
by Hasbro®
PATENT PENDING
MADE in USA

G.I. JOE®
COPYRIGHT 1964
by Hasbro®
patent pending
MADE IN U.S.A.

G.I. JOE®
Copyright 1964
BY HASBRO®
Pat. No. 3,277,602
MADE in U.S.A.

HAUSMAN & ZATULOVE	HAUSMEISTER, PAUL & COMPANY	HAWKINS, GEORGE

HAYS, MARGARET G.

HEBER & COMPANY	HECHT, ELSE L.	HEINE & SCHNEIDER
 514 ⊢c⟩ 16/0		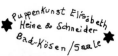

HEININGER, THERESE	HEINZ, RUDOLPH & COMPANY	HELK, BERTHOLD	HELLER, ADOLP
	9500 Neubaus AJ am Rius 2/0x Germany		DIANA 7 D.R.G.M.160638

HELLER, ADOLP (CONT.)	HENDERSON, GLOVE COMPANY	HENZE, L. & STEINHAUSER

HERIN & SOHN	HERING, JULIUS	HERMSDORFER CELLU-LOIDWARENFABRIK
Made in Germany Viktoria J.ФH. 15/0		

HERTEL, SCHWAB & COMPANY

Made
in
Germany
98/10

152
L.W.&Co
12

152
6

2046
151
3

Made
in
Germany
151/0

151
9 1/2

150
2

157
1 1/2

Made
in
Germany
136/4

HERTWIG & COMPANY

BUSTER
BROWN
SHOES

9 Germany K

3
Germany

104

Germany

1 42 7
14/E

HERZ PUPPENFABRIK

HESS, ALBIN

GYMNASTIK
DOLL

HEUBACH, ERNST (KÖPPELSDORFER PORZELLANFABRIK)

271 14/0
EiH·Germany
DRGM

Heubach·Koppelsdorf
321·9/0
Germany

HEUBACH-KÖPPELSDORF
322 -17/0
Germany

D. E. P.

0/0

Heubach-köppssdorf
389 /0
Germany

Germany
275.11/0
Heubach-Köppelsdorf.

1900 4/0w

445-3/0 Germany
Heubach - Köppelsdorf

Heubach-Köppelsdorf
250-15/0
Germony

Heubach-Köppelsdorf
463 - 14/0
Germany

Heubach
250.5
Köppelsdorf
Germany,

Germany
EH289 1/6
D.R.G.M.

275 14/0
E H.Germany
D. R. G.M.

EH 292-4
DRGM

Germany
EH 280/9
D. R. G.M

Heubach
275 4/0
Köppelsdorf

HEUBACH, GEBRÜDER BROTHERS

8192
Germany
Gebrüder Heubach
$\frac{5}{6}$ 1/2
9 $\frac{5}{6}$ 1/2 H

Germany
Gebrüder Heubach

G.7H

Germany

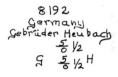
Germany

90 Heu. 95 Germany

7246
Germany

Germany

HEU
BACH

DEP

HEU
BACH

S122
Gebr. Heubach
Germany
$\frac{14}{6}$

8192
Geur. Heubach
Germany
$\frac{16}{6}$

8192
Germany
Gebrüder Heubach

8192
Germany
Gebrüder Heubach

G   H

8192
Germany
Gebrüder Heubach
$\frac{5}{6}$ 1/2
9 $\frac{5}{6}$ 1/2 H

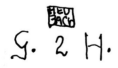
G. 2 H.

8192
Germany
Gebrüder Heubach

HEU
BACH

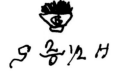
9 $\frac{2}{6}$ 1/2 H

8192
Germany
Gebrüder Heubach
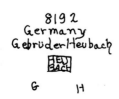
G   H

G. H.
1.

7669
Germany

HEYDE, HERMANN	HIEULLE, EDMOND

Montreuil
S/Bois
France
P.L.

PARFAIT-BÉBÉ
PARIS

HIRSCHLER & HIRSCHLER	HITZ, JACOBS & KASSLER

Kiddiejoy

by Hitz, Jacobs & Kassler

Germany
Kiddiejoy
375/6

HITZ, JACOBS & KASSLER (CONT.)	HORN, CARL

Germany
Kiddiejoy
372
A 1 M

HORSMAN, EDWARD IMESON

170 made in USA

E.I.H. Co. 19©21

E. I. H

CO.

"CAN'T BREAK 'EM"

©

E.I.H. CO. INC.

HORSMAN

Genuine
Baby Bumps
TRADE MARK

©

E.I.H. CO. INC.

E.I.H. © A.D.C°

© 1924
E.I. Horsman Inc.
Made in
Germany

E.I.H © 1910

HGG
1916

MADE IN USA

274

BILLIKEN TRADE MARK

COPYRIGHT 1909 by THE BILLIKEN COMPANY

"Can't Break Em"

GENUINE BABYLAND TRADE MARK

© 1924 E.I. Horsman Inc. Made in Germany

EI © H.Co.
E.I. HORSMAN INC.

© 1924 E.I. HORSMAN CO. INC.

HOYER, MARY DOLL MANUFACTURING COMPANY

ORIGINAL

Mary Hoyer

DOLL

HÜLSS, ADOLPH

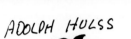

ADOLPH HULSS

SIMON & HALBIG

ABW Made in Germany 156/32

HUNAEUS, DR. PAUL

SIMON & HALBK

AHW Made in Germany 156

HUNAEUS, DR. PAUL (CONT.)

PH
30 GERMANY D.B.P.

156/8

HURET, MAISON

BREVET DEP. SGDG
MAISON HURET N°22 Boulevart Montmarte PARIS.

BREVET D'INV' SGDG
MAISON HURET
Boulevard Montmartre, 22

MEDAILLE D'ARGENT
HURET
22 Boulevd Montmartre PARIS
EXP en UNIVERLLE 1861

HURET
68 RUE DE LA BOETIE

HURET

IDEAL NOVELTY & TOY COMPANY

BABY MINE
½ n V2 92, 102/0 Registered Germany

Moving O sleep Eyes
IDEAL USA DOLL
BABY MINE

ILLFELDER, B. & COMPANY

ROSEBUD
A 3/0 M   101

My SWEETHEART
B.J. & Co.

ILLIG, CARL A. & COMPANY	ILMENAUER PORCELAIN FACTORIES		IMHOF, FERDINAND

SONLIE SERO
JLLCO

1799

D. R. P.
Nº 119857
PATENT c LANDEP

INDESTRUCTIBLE	INDIA RUBBER COMB COMPANY	IRIQUET, MME. VVE	IRWIN & COMPANY

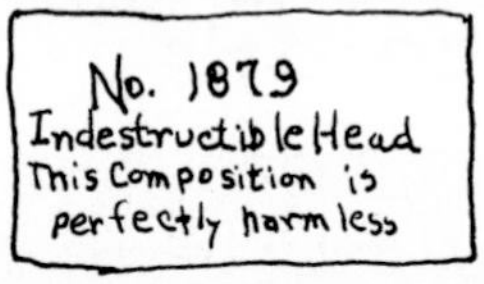

No. 1879
Indestructible Head
This Composition is
perfectly harmless

I.R. COMBCo.

SPÉCIALITÉ
D'ARTICLES POUR POUPÉES
Reparation
Mᵐᵉ Vᵛᵉ IRIQUET
44 Place des Carmes ROUEN

NONFLAM
MADE IN
IRWIN
U.S.A

IRWIN
MADE IN U.S.A.

ISAACS, A. & J.	IZZARD	JEAN, M. ELIE.	JUDGE, EDWARD S.

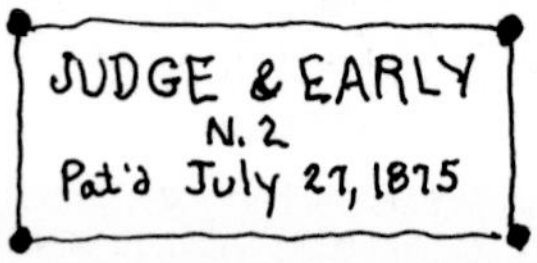

THE CHERUB DOLL

IZZARD
Importerd
MANUFACTURER
136 REGENT Sᵗ 136

CAEN

JUDGE & EARLY
N. 2
Pat'd July 27, 1875

JÜGELT, WALTER	JULLIEN

WALTER JUGELT
NEUSTADT·COBURG·GERMANY

JuLLien

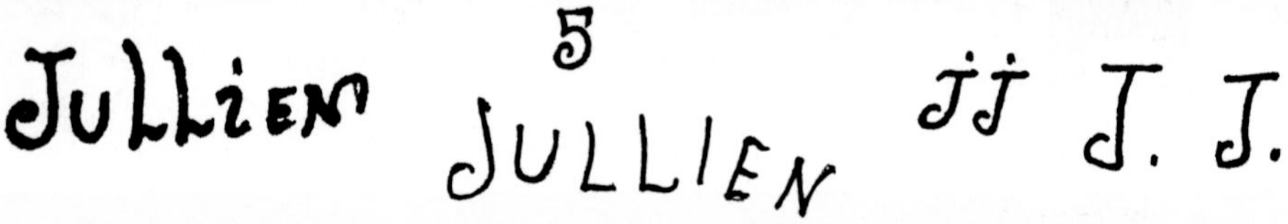

5
JULLIEN

JJ J. J.

JUMEAU

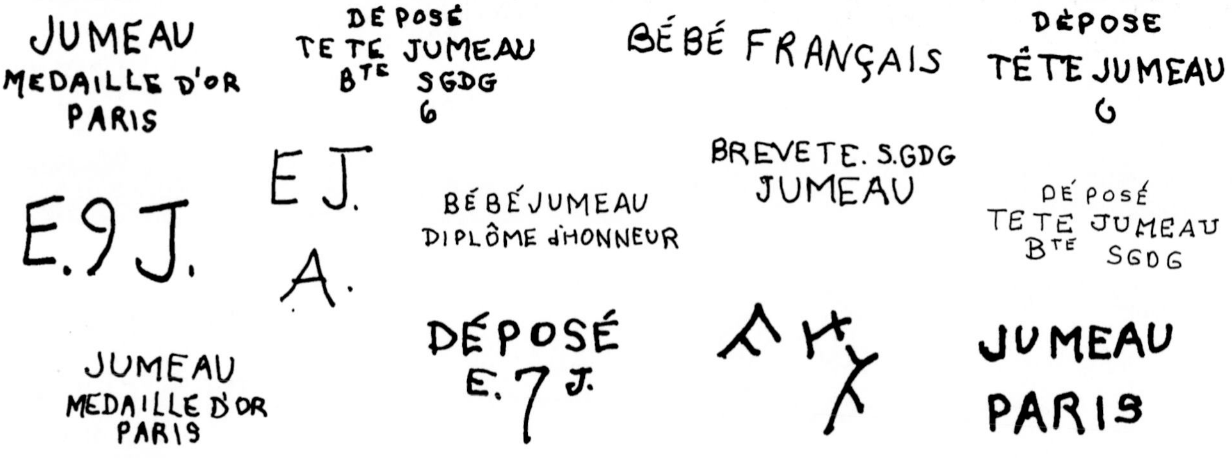

JUMEAU
MEDAILLE D'OR
PARIS

DÉPOSÉ
TETE JUMEAU
Bᵀᴱ SGDG
6

BÉBÉ FRANÇAIS

DÉPOSÉ
TÉTE JUMEAU
6

E.9J.

EJ.
A.

BÉBÉ JUMEAU
DIPLÔME d'HONNEUR

BREVETE. S.GDG
JUMEAU

DÉPOSÉ
TETE JUMEAU
Bᵀᴱ SGDG

JUMEAU
MEDAILLE D'OR
PARIS

DÉPOSÉ
E. 7 J.

JUMEAU
PARIS

BÉBÉ JUMEAU  $^8_{E\,J}$  BÉBÉ JUMEAU
Déposé

DEPOSE
JUMEAU
7

1907

1907
TÊTE JUMEAU

214
DEPOSÉ
TETE JUMEAU
Bᵗᵉ SGDG

UNIS
FRANCE

E. DEPOSE J.

306
JUMEAU
1938
PARIS

PARIS
DEPOSÉ

BÉBÉ
JUMEAU
DEPOSE

JUNG, JACOB | K & K TOY COMPANY

Germany
K & K
45
Thuringia

K & K
56
Made in Germany

Kand K
TRADEMARK

Germany
K & K
60
Thuringia

K & K TOY COMPANY (CONT.) | KAHN, LUCIEN | KALLISTA | KALLUS, JOSEPH L.

K. & K.
58
Made in Germany

MOGLETTE

KALLISTA THEATER FIGUREN
SCHULZ... KE... MARK...

Copr. by
J.L. Kallus
Germany
1394/30

KÄMMER & REINHARDT

K. & R
192
P
9

K ⭐ R
SIMON & HALBIG
126

K ⭐ R
100
50

K ⭐ R
SIMON & HALBIG
126
50
Bébé

K ⭐ R
101
46

K ⭐ R
S & H
118/A
32

K ✡ R
39/717

K R
X
10

K ✡ R
114
79

K ✡ R
127
32

K ✡ R
728/42

192

SH
Germany
126-13

K✡R
S&H
776/A

K✡R
SIMON & HALBIG
119/Baby

G
192

K✡R
926
Germany
11

K✡R
255

K✡R
SIMON & HALBIG
117
76

SIMON & HALBIG
10 K✡R 10

377 ✡(K) 1

K✡R
728/7
GERMANY
43/46

K✡R
SIMON & HALBIG
117/A

S&H
K✡R
13

K✡R
SIMON & HALBIG
126
19
1126-19
Germany

36
K✡R

K✡R
SIMON & HALBIG
117
Germany
70

K✡R
SIMON & HALBIG
403
Germany

K. ✡(&) R.

ROYAL
TRADEMARK
K✡R

HALBIG
K✡R
36

ROYAL
K✡R

191
G
B

K✡R
101 X
39

K (&) R
728/4
GERMANY

⊙
K (&) R
DEP.
Germany

K (&) R
126

K (&) R
SIMON & HALBIG
116/A

K (&) R
SIMON & HALBIG

K (&) R
SIMON & HALBIG
122
32

K (&) R
SIMON & HALBIG
66

KAMPES, LOUISE R. STUDIO	KASPAREK, JEANNE DE MME.	KAULITZ, MARION BERTHA

KAMKINS
A DOLLY MADE TO LOVE
PATENTED
FROM
L.R. KAMPES
ATLANTIC CITY
N.J.

KAMKINS
A DOLLY MADE TO LOVE
PATENTED BY L.R. KAMPES
ATLANTIC CITY, NJ

V 2
K III

K. W. G.

k w
G
$\frac{134}{12/0}$

K. W. G.
$\frac{736}{12}$

K. W. G.
$\frac{1382}{3}$

Hilda
@
J. D. K. Jr. 190
Gesgesch 1070
made in Germany

7½ 154 Dep

made in
Germany
129

B made in 6
Germany
J. D. K
211.

Crown Doll
KESTNER
GERMANY

c made in
Germany
152

b Germany 3

E⅛ made in 9½
Germany.
168

M¾ made in 12¼
Germany
167

made in
Germany.
J. D. K.
260

Made in Germany
D. 168/8

made in
3½ Germany 10½
171

made in
9 Germany 11
171

Made in Germany.

made in 10
F. Germany.
211
J.D.K

made in 14
K. Germany
J. D. K.
215.

Kestner
Made in Germany

Excelsior

A Germany 5

JDK
319

J.D.K.

made in Germany
243
J.D.K.

made in
B Germany 6

made in
M Germany 16
164

J.D.K
260

made in
Germany
26 -81

9.
166
E made in Germany

J.D.K.
made in
Germany

made in
L. Germany 15
141

J.D.K.

Germany
J. D. K.
257
made in
Germany

Excelsior
DRE No 70686
Germany

c made in
Germany   7
152

made in
K. Germany   10
211
J.D.K.

Dep. 195. 6½

154 dep. 7/0
7/0 made in Germany

made in Germany
154.12 dep.
H. made in Germany

made in
D Germany. 8.
162.

L.
made in Germany

made in
O Germany 18.
245
J.D.K.Jr.
1914
©
Hilda

10 P.

CENTURY DOLL 6
kestner Germany
281/5

Hilda
©
J. D. K. Jr.
Gesgesch 1070
made in Germany

G. made in Germany

243·1

217
16

171.

189
4½ 0

E½ made in 9½
Germany
171

H made in
Germany
J.D.K

KIRCHAOFF, CHARLOTTE M.	KISTER, A. W. FR. INCORPORATED	KLETZIN, JOHANN HEINRICH & SONS	KLEY & HAHN

K. P. N.
X

(wreath image)

13
SSCo
61
Germany
Walküre

K&H
Germany

K H
Walküre

K·H
Germany

K&H
Germany
158 6

Germany
K&H
525

Walkure
Germany
56

K&H
549
/
Germany

K&H
546
5
Germany

Walküre
Germany
9

K&H
Germany
169 1

31
Germany.
Walskure

546
5
Germany

292
K. & H
1930
Germany

Special
C5

Special
Made in Germany

The Dollar Princess
G2
Spesal   159
Made in Germany

780
2/0
K&H

Germany
K&H
525

KLING, C. F. & COMPANY

Dep.

K

Germany
189 1

124  72

S/0

767-4

Germany

167 4

190

190

123 2

Germany
190-9

377. ✡ 1

377 🔔

751-6

185

KLÖTZER, ERICH	KNAUTH, EDMOND & KNAUTH GUIDO	KNOCH, EDMUND

501-10

Knauth
3

KNOCH, GEBRÜDER

Made in Germany
Ges No 223 Gesch
6/0

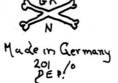
Made in Germany
201
DEP!o

made in Germany
190 11/6
DEP

made in Germany
199
DED

1794/0

185
12/0

Made in Germany
Ges. N. 216 Gesch.
15/0

Made in Germany
Ges. No 216 Gesch
6/0

KOCH, M. J. CESAR	KOENIG & WERNICKE

LUTECIA BABY
Made in Paris

BÉBÉ GLORIA
Made in Paris

K & W
179-7

Germany

K & W
HARTGUMMI
5550
GERMANY

11
Made in Germany

Made
in
Germany
98/12

K & W
23813

10

K & W
1070

K & W No 5/0

282

KOHL & WENGENROTH	KÖHLER & ROSENWALD

KÖNIGLICHE PORZELLAN MANUFAKTUR

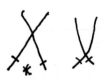

KORN, GUSTAV	KRAHMER, C.	KRATZ-BOUSSAC, HENRI OTHRON	KRAUSS, GEBRÜDER
		LA PARISIENNE	

KRAUSZ, SAMUEL	KRAUTH, WERNER	KRUSE, KÄTHE	

KRUSE, KÄTHE (CONT.)	KUBELKA, JOSEPH	KÜHNLENZ, GEBRÜDER

44-15

44 30

$G \cdot K$ 28.27

Dep.
44-29

$G^{br} 165 K$
Germany

Dep.
44-29

$G^{br} 165 K$
12/0
Germany

$G^{br} 165 K$
9
Germany
9

$G^{br} 44 K$
19
Bavaria

32-29

13-29

Bavaria

32-29

LA FOSSE, MME.	LACMANN, JACOB	LAFITTE & DÉSIRAT	LAMBERT & SAMHAMMER
		**"VITA"**	

LAMBERT, MADEMOISELLE	LANDSBERGER, ADOLPH
BABET **L · B.**	

LANDSHUT	LANGE, ALFRED	LANTERNIER, A & CIE

J.E. Masson
SC
LORRAINE
No
A.L. E.Cie
LIMOGES

LUTIN

FABRICATION FRANCAISE

LIMOGES

PETITE FRANÇAISE
FRANCE
J.V
1D

JE Masson
LORRAINE
No
AL&Cie
LIMOGES

FABRICATION
FRANCAISE
LIMOGES

FABRICATION
FRANCAISE
ALeCie
LIMOGES
CHERIE

DEPOSÉ
TOTO
LIMOGES

DEPOSE
FABRICATION
FRANCAISE
FAVORITE
NO 8
J.E. Masson
SC.
ALiCie
LIMOGES

LAUBSCHER'S PUPPEN FABRIK	LAUFER, ARTHUR	LE MONTRÉER
MISS A. LAUBSCHER GRAAFFREINET		LE TROTTIN LE VICTORIEUX

LEBEL, MME.	LEFEBVRE, ALEXANDRE & CIE	LEIBE & HOFMANN	LEIPOLD, CHARLES
PATRIA		Z & H 4/0	C.W. LEIPOLD 307 8ST NEW YORK

LEJEUNE, LOUIS-AIMÉ	LELIEVRE, YVONNE MADEMOISELLE		LENCI
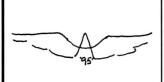'95		Marque deposee P-V FUMSUP	

LENCI (CONT.)	LEPINARY, M. V.		LES ARTS DU PAPIER

LEUTHEUSER, RICHARD	LEVEN, H. JOSEPH		LEVI, EDMOND

LEVY, PIERRE & CIE			L'HEVREUX, LOUIS

LIEBERMANN, ERNST		LIEBERMANN, HEINRICH	LILIENTHAL, MICHEL

LIMBACH PORZELLANFABRIK

Le Joujou Francsis

LA MIGNONNE

LES POUPÉES DE FRANCE

TANAGRA

L'Idéal

MISS DANCING

LINDNER, LOUIS & SÖHNE			LINK, ANTON & COMPANY
Eingetragene Fabrikmarke	S & H L.L. & S 10½	1339 S & H L.Z. & S 11½	
LLACER, E.	**LÖFFLER & DILL**	**LONZ, ANNI**	**LOUDOUZE, MADE-MOISELLE GENEVIEVE**
JUGUETES FINOS E. LLACER ATOCHA, 19 MADRID	L & D 6/0 X		"MINON"
LOUIT, MME.	**LUBECKA, MME. JULIENNE**	**LUGE, A. & COMPANY**	**LUTHARDT, EG. MICH.**
POUPÉES GAULOISES	BICOT	Thuringia Trade mark	Luta Germany
LUTHARDT, LOUIS PHILIPP	**LYONS FRENCH TOY COMPANY**	**LYRO PUPPEN COMPANY**	**MAAR, E. & SOHN**
MAAR, E. & SOHN (CONT.)			**MAASER, ROBERT**
Made in Germany. Armand Marseille 256 A 3/0 M Maar	M 1923 Germany 5		Germany 410. 5/0
MABIT, MADEMOISELLE LOUISE ADRIENNE		**MANN & MANN**	**MANUEL & DE STOECKLIN**
JANUS	LES DEUX GOSSES	MIMOSA	POUPÉES DE PARIS

Les Poupées Parisiennes   LES POUPETTES

Les Poupées Parisiennes

MARIAGE, M. MAURICE	MARKS BROTHERS	MARQUE, ALBERT	MARCOUX, CHARLES

LA POUPÉE LINA

MADE IN
U.S.A.
MARKS
BROTHERS CO
BOSTON
½

a. Marque

MARSEILLE, ARMAND

Germany
310
A ⁰/₀ M

Germany
323
A 6/0 M

A.M.
Germany.
341 /1K.

A M
Germany
341/3K

A.M.
Germany
341/3/0K. K

A.M.
Germong.
347/0

A M
Germang
351 /4K

A.M.
Germang.
353.12/0 K

Armand Morseille
Germany.
370
A 6 M

Armand Marselle
Germany
390
A 11/0 M

Armand Marselle
Germany
390
A 11/0 M

Armand Marseille
Germany
390.
A 12/0X M.

Made in Germany
Armand Marseille
390
DRGM 2½
A. 11/0 M.

Armand Marseille
Germany
401
A 5/0 M

Germang
550
A 3 M
DRGM

590
A. 5 M.
Germany
DR.G.M.

Germany
971
A 5 M
DRGM 267/1

Armand Marseille
A. 975 M
Germany

Armand Marseille
Germany
990
A 3/0 M

1894
A.M. O D.E.P.
Made in germany

3200
AM 8/0 DEP

3700
AM 2/0 D.E.P.
made in Germany

Made in Germany
(horseshoe)
dep. 5/2/0

(anchor) A M

Mode in Germany
A 4M
Z

Germany
G. 329
A. 1. M.
DR.&M. 267/1

Germany
Queen Louise

Germany
Queen Louise

Germany
Mabel

Made in Germany
A Baby o Betty M
DRaM

Made in Germany
Florodora
A. 2. M

Duchess
Germany
AM

Armand Marseille
Germany.
390.
A 12/0x M.

Florodora
A.M. 5½ D.R.P.
made in germany.

Duchess
A.6 M.
Made in Germany

Germany
323
A.6/0.M.

Florodora

Columbia

Florodora
A 2/0XM
Made in Germany
D.R.P.

Florodora
A-4-M
Made in Germany

Baby Gloria
Germany

590
A3M
Germany
D.R.G.M.

231.
D.RMR 248
Fany
A 2/0 M

Germany
985
A 7/0. M

A ELLAR M
Germany
2K

1894.
AM.DEP
Germany

A.M.
Germany
351   2½K

A ELLAR M
Germany
6½

Made in Germany.
Florodora
A.O.M.

M
914.
5

M.H.
A 300 M
12/0x

1897
/0

237
Fany
DRMR 248/4
A 8M

971e
A M
Germany
5

Germany
971 c
A 8M
D.R.G.M 267/1

Armand Marseille
Germany
390 c
A. 4 M.

Made in Germany
Armand Marseille
390 n
DRGM 246
A 0½ M

3200
A.M. 9 DEP

Germany
Mabel

Made in Germany
Florodora
A 5 M.

AM Beauty 6/0
Germany

THIS DOLL IS ONLY
INTENDED TO WALK ON
A SMOOTH SURFACE
Patent JULY 15, 1862
Also in Europe 20, DEC. 1862

The Patent
Autoperipatikos
or
Walking Zouave
Martin + Runyon

MARTIN, M. ALFRED FRANÇOIS XAVIER

MATTEL INCORPORATED

Barbie T.M
PATS. PEND.
©MCMLVIII
by
MATTEL INC

Barbie ®
PAT. PEND.
© MCMLVIII
b
MATTEL INC

Barbie T.M.
Pat. Pend.
©MCMLVIII
by
MATTEL
Inc.

Midge T.M.
©1962
Barbie ®
1958
MATTEL INC
US Patented
US Pat. Pend.

Midge T.M.
©1962
Barbie ®
1958
by
Mattel, Inc.

Midge T.M.
©1962
Barbie ®
1958
by
Mattel, Inc.

Midge T.M
©1962
Barbie ®
1960
MATTEL INC
HAWTHORNE
CALIF, USA

Barbie T.M
Pats. Pend.
©MCMLVIII
by
Mattel
Inc

MATTHES, E. W.

MAUGER & MONTERA

MAUS, WIDOW EDITH

MANOTA
montera Company

MAUS, WIDOW EDITH (CONT.)

MAXINE DOLL COMPANY

MEECH, HERBERT JOHN

Baby Gloria
Germany

Baby Gloria
A Germany M

MEISSEN

MERZ, EMILE

K.P.M.

METAL DOLL COMPANY

METAL HEAD DOLL MARKINGS FROM VARIOUS MANUFACTURERS

PATENTS PENDING
MADE by
METAL DOLL CO,
Pleasantville, N.J.

MÉTAYER, A.	METROPOLITAN TOY & DOLL COMPANY

METROPOLITAN 1929

METTAIS, M. JULES

"BÉBÉ MODÉLE"   BEBE-LIÈGE   BABY
PHÉNIX-BABY

PHÈNIX
★ 95

BÉBÉ-LIÈGE

PHENIX-BABY   POUPÉE MERVEILLEUSE

METZLER	METZLER, GEBRÜDER & ORTLOFF

Made in Germany
·890·
E.M. 0 ½

Made in Germany
Metzler
890
E 8 M

Made in Germany
Metzler
890
E ¾ M

MICHAELIS, AMANDUS & COMPANY	MICHEL, M. SEVERIN	MINERVA

BOUQUET
DE LA
VICTOIRE

MITTELLAND GUMMI-WERKE	MOEHLING, M. J.	MÖLLER & DIPPE	MÖLLER, AUGUST & SOHN

1904
Eduarda Juan
Made in Austria

MÖLLER, AUGUST & SOHN (CONT.)		MOLLY GOLDMAN OF PHILADELPHIA	MONTANARI, MME. AUGUSTA
AMUSO 100 Made in Germany	AMUSO 1920 Made in Germany 46	*Molly ES*	Montanari Manufacturer 251 Regent St. and 180 Soho Bazaar

MONTANARI, MME. AUGUSTA (CONT.)		MORGENROTH & COMPANY	MORIMURA BROTHERS
Montanari 180 Soho Bazaar London	Montanari	Sailzmet M Ciotha	MB Japan 3

MORIMURA BROTHERS (CONT.)	MORITZ, CARL	MORITZ, PAPPE	MORRELL
MB Japan	Taubenbach	★	CHARLES MORRELL 50 BURLINGTON ARCADE LONDON

MORRELL (CONT.)	MOTHER'S CONGRESS DOLL COMPANY	MOTSCHMANN, CHARLES	MÜLLER & FRÖBEL
164 OXFORD STREET MORRELL 50 BURLINGTON ARCADE	BABY STEWART Mothers Congress Doll PHILADELPHIA PA. Pat Nov. 6. 1900	PATENT 29 APRIL 1857 CH. MOTSCHMANN SONNEBERG	TRADE MARK

MÜLLER & STRASSBURGER		MÜLLER, ANDREAS		
	M & S Superior 2015	SCHUTZ MARKE	SPIELMULLER COBURG	

MÜLLER, CARL			MÜLLER, KARL & COMPANY
SPS S 11	Made in Germany S.P. 7	Made in Germany 129 8 S.P.	

MÜLLER, PIERRE	MÜLLER, WILHELM G.	MUNNIER, MAISON	NADAUD, MLLE. A.
Olympia	WGM WEE G EM	Maison Munnier Tarsagon Tarqsoy N° 15717 Paris	JOUETS COTILLON NADAUD 32 Rue du 4 Septembre

NANEAU, M.	NATIONAL JOINT LIMB DOLL COMPANY	NELKE CORPORATION	NEW ERA NOVELTY COMPANY
CENTIL BÉBÉ	NAJO	NELKE	E N N Co

NEWBISC		NIPPON	NÖCKLER & TITTEL
MADE IN USA NEWBISC	NUTOI by New Toy Co.	FY NIPPON	

NÖCKLER TITTEL (CONT.)			NOEL, M. CHARLES
Scierbull's lehrt	N×T 2	N&T₁ 6	MAROLISETTE BSGDG DEPOSE

NORDSCHILD, LEO	NYMPHENBURG		OBERENDER, NIKOLAUS
BELLA PUPPEN		6 3 2 A M 1 DRGM GERMANY 11	Germany DEP 2000 ℭⅹ 8/0 N DEP 2010 Germany 8/0

OBERENDER, NIKO-LAUS (CONT.)	OFFENBACHER, S. & COMPANY	OHLHAVER, GEBRÜDER	
N Germany 125 8/0		Revalo 3 Dep	Revalo

Revalo
Germany

Germany
151 %

11010

Germany
Revalo

Revalo
Germany

Germany

Revalo

Revalo
Dep

Heubach Köppelsdorf
Igodi
Revalo 22.7
Germany

150
Germany

Revalo
10727
Germany

OLIVIER, M. FERNAND PAULIN

ORSINI, JEANNE I.

Copr. By
J.J. Orsini
Germany
1430/4

J.J.O. © 1919
47

ORTYZ, M. JOSEPH (ALSO KNOWN AS ORTIZ)

EXCELSIOR BÉBI

PANNIER

C9P.   Mme Pannier

PARIS BÉBÉ

PARIS-BEBE
Breveté

E.8.D

PARIS BEBE
TETE DÉPOSÉE

PARIS, GEBRÜDER

PARSONS-JACKSON COMPANY

PARSONS-JACKSON CO.
CLEVELAND, OHIO.

PAUL REVERE POTTERY

P.R.P
110.2

PEACOCK

FROM
PEACOCK'S
525 NEW OXFORD ST.
corner of Bloomsbury St.
LONDON, WC!

PECK, MRS. LUCY

FROM
MRS. PECK
THE DOLL'S HOME
131 REGENT STREET
—W—

FROM
MRS PECK
THE DOLL'S HOUSE
131 REGENT STREET
—W—

MRS LUCY PECK
THE DOLL'S HOUSE
131 REGENT ST LONDON
—W—

MRS PECK
THE DOLL HOME
131 Regent Street
LONDON, W

PENSKY, HERMANN	PERIER, M. HENRY

Pehalo
Hannalore
85

La Vraie Parisienne

PERRIN, MME.	PETIT, JACOB	PETRI & BLUM

La Poupée d

PAR BREVET

PETZOLD, DORA	PFEFFER, FRITZ

DORA PETZOLD
REGISTERED
Trade Mark
DOLL
Germany

PFEIFFER, EMIL

PHOENIX GUMMIPUPPEN	PENSKY, HERMANN	PIEROTTI

Pierotti   Pierotti

PINTEL, HENRI & GODCHAUX, ERNEST

P13G
DEPOSE

BÉBÉ CHARMANT
Depose Française

BÉBÉ CHARMANT

A
P2G

G
13
Depose

A

PINTEL, M.	PLASS & ROESNER	POLLAK & HOFFMANN
	Made in Austria P & R 1907	P&H # 1904

PORZELLANFABRIK KLOSTER VEILSDORF

    B.500 II B 503

PORZELLANFABRIK MENGERSGEREUTH

P.M
914
Germany

 P.M
Herzi
Germany
3/

P.M.
Grete
210

950

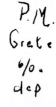

 P.M
Herzi
Germany

M
92.4
Germany

 Germany

 Germany

P.M.
Grete
6/0.
dep

 P.M
Herzi
Germany
3/0

Trebor
Germany.
22
P. 2.M.

P.M
828

PORZELLANFABRIK RAVENSTEIN

Alice)
No 191.
/ A.

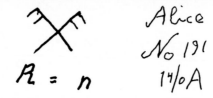 R = n

Alice
No 191
14/0A

Made in Germany
N.2
.A.

No 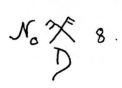 8.
D

296

PORZELLANFABRIK RAVENSTEIN (CONT.)

114   12/0

Alice
No 191
18/0

✗ P 14

Made in Germany
Dora
16/0

POULBOT, M. & MME. FRANCISQUE

Le Petit LARDON
SAC de TERRE
PILEFER
COCO

UN POULBOT
UNE POULBOTTE

COCO
L'Infernal brise-tout

SANSONNET

NINI
NINI
La Princesse

MOUTCHOU
La Moderne
MOUTCHOU

LILI

RINTINTIN
NÉNETTE

BABA   FANFOIS   ZIZINE   MOMO

PRIALYTINE	QUAKER DOLL COMPANY	RABERY & DELPHIEU

LaPrialytine
Paris
0 - B

QUAKER
LITY

BÉBÉRABERY
Sc

BÉBÉ DE PARIS
R.D.

RABERY & DELPHIEU (CONT.)   RADER, MAX

R/D
BÉBÉ RABERY
Sc

R.4.D   R5/0D

40
R.DEP.
10

RADER, MAX (CONT.)   RAGGEDY ANN & ANDY

R.47-1DEP
S
R 47-6 DEP

50 9
Made in
Germany

PATENTED SEPT 7 1915

Raggedy Ann & Andy Dolls
MANUFACTURED by Molly-és
DOLL OUTFITTERS

JOHNNY GRUELLE'S OWN
RAGGEDY ANN AND ANDY DOLLS
Trademark Reg. U.S. Patent Off.
Copyright 1918-1920 by John B. Gruelle

GEORGENE NOVELTIES, INC.
NEW YORK CITY
EXCLUSIVE LICENSED MANUFACTURES
MADE IN U.S.A.

"RAGGEDY
ANN"© DOLL
RAGGEDY ANN DOLL
©KNICKERBOCKER TOY CO. INC.
MIDDLESEX, NJ. 08846 U.S.A.

D. R. G. M.
897388

1046

RECKNAGEL, THEODOR

GERMANY
2
R 127A

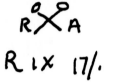

1907
R/A DEP
I72/0

1907
DED
R /. A

R 47A
%

R 3 A
Germany

GERMANY
NK4
A I R

S

R 47A
10/0

22. 1%

1909
DEP
R "/. A

R IX . 11/0

A
131/0

GERMANY
N.G. 2
A I R

GERMANY
2
R 127A

121
R 3 A
Germany

39
5/0

31. 11%

2/0
GERMANy
JK
A5/0 R

GERMANY
NK4
A. I. R

REGAL DOLL MANUFACTURING COMPANY

REHBOCK & LOEWENTHAL

REINECKE, OTTO

"KiddiePalDolly"
REGAL DOLL MFG. Co INC

P M

REINHARDT, CURT F.	REINHARDT, ERNST			
			713 Reinhardt East Liverpool Ohio	Made in U.S.A. E. R. Pat. Sep. 19 14 Reinhardt

RELIABLE TOY COMPANY		REMPEL & BREITUNG	REMPEL, JULIUS
RELIABLE MADE IN CANADA	RELIABLE MADE IN CANADA		

RHEINISCHE GUMMI UND CELLULOID FABRIK COMPANY		RICAILLON, CAROLINE	RIDLEY, E. & SONS
	SCHUTZMARKE 		

RIEDELER, AUGUST (ALSO KNOWN AS RIEDLER, AUGUST)			RIGOT, MADEMOI-SELLE MARIE GEORGETTE
			L'IDÉALE

ROCHARD, ED.	ROCHER, M. MARIUS		ROHMER, MME.
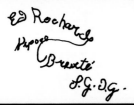	"LE BÉB		

ROLFES & COMPANY	ROOKWOOD POTTERY		RÖSEL, HERMANN

ROSSIGNOL, CHARLES	ROSTAL, HENRI		
C R	TRÉSOR		MON TRÉSOR

ROTH, JOSEPH MANUFACTURING COMPANY (ALSO KNOWN AS ROTH, BAITZ AND LIPSITZ)	ROTKÄPPCHEN	ROUAUD, CHARLES
		MAL'OTO de ma Poupée MAL'AUTO de ma Poupée

ROULLET & DECAMPS		ROYAL COPENHAGEN MANUFACTORY
R. D. L'INTRÉPIDE BÉBÉ 		

ROYAL COPENHAGEN MANUFACTORY (CONT.)	ROYAL TOY MANUFACTURING COMPANY	RUDOLPH, MAX

SAALFIELD PUBLISHING COMPANY	SADIN, M. ARTHUR	SANTY WAX	SAUERTEIG, JOHANNES
MADE IN U.S.A. 167	FAVORI = BÉBÉ	Santy. Inventor 340 fong Room Soho. Bazaar London	Jose Germany 4

SAVARY, M. ANDRE	SCHÄFER & VATER	SCHAMBERGER, OTTO	SCHELHORN, AUGUST (ALSO KNOWN AS SCHELLHORN, AUGUST)
PYGMÉE			

SCHELHORN, MAX FRIEDRICH

SCHERF, PETER

5370

S 370

P Sch.
Germany.
O

Germany
A P. Sch / M

SCHERF, PETER (CONT.)

P. Sch.
Germany
AM

P. Sch.

A M
Germany
P. Sch. 1899 – 10

P.Sch 1899 /
Germany

Germany
P. Sch. 19 01·2

SCHERZER, RICHARD

SCHEYER, O. & COMPANY

SCHILLING

SCHILLING (CONT.)

SCHLAGGENWALD

SCHLAGGENWALD (CONT.)

SCHMIDT, BRUNO

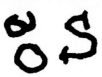

BSW

2096 - 0

B S W

Made in
Germany

B S W

SCHMIDT, BRUNO (CONT.)

28

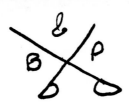

2085-4

4 25

 2025/34 2087

5 x/ 2 2089-4

SCHMIDT, FRANZ & COMPANY

F.S & Cᵒ
1272/40Z
Deponiert

Germany
S & C 1180-13

SIMON & HALBIG
S & C
1340
made in Germany

F. S & Cᵒ
7
Po. 1296

FS & C
1271/32z
DEPONIERT

F.S. & Cₒ

1295
F.S. & Co
Made in
Germany

FJ & Cᵒ
1267

293
⁴/₀
SC

FS & C
1266/23

FS & C
SIMON & HALBIG
1297
Germany

269
S & C

269
S & C

FS & C
1252

FSS Cᵒ
SIMON & HALBIG
1295
Made in
Germany
56

FS
00

Germany
S & C 1180-13

S & C
SIMON & HALBIG

S & C
Germany

FS
00

293
1.
SC

1297/65
F.S. & C.
Made in Germany

Simon
& Halbig

Simon

Simon

S & C
Germany
S & C
SIMON & HALBIG

S2b
11
Grillally

F S & C.
1250/10

FS & C
1266/23

FS & Cᵒ
1271/32Z
Deponiert

SCHMIDT, FRANZ & COMPANY (CONT.)

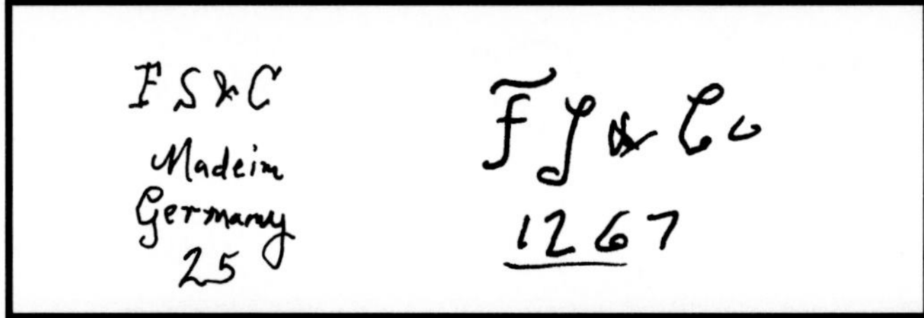

FS&C
Made in
Germany
25

FJ&Co
1267

SCHMIDT, PAUL

Trade Mark
Made in Germany

P*S

Made in
P*S
Germany

SCHMITT, FILS

B^te SGDG
O

SCH

SCHMUCKLER, HEINRICH

Hesli

SCHNEIDER

G

SCHNEIDER, ROBERT

Rosch Co

SCHOENAU & HOFFMEISTER

Porzellanfobrik-Burggrub
769
8/0
Germany

PORZELLAN
FABRIK
BURGGRUB
169
4/0
Germany

S PB H
Hanna

4500 O
S PB H.

Princess
Elizabeth

S PB H
1909

Porzellanfabrik
Burggrub

PB
S H

Germany
S PB H
1906

Princess Elizabeth
Made in Germany

A
S PB H
V

Germany

4000
S PB H

5500
S PB H
dep

S PB H
1900
Germany

DEP
AS
1900

Porzellanfabrik
Burggrub
lastachendeBaby
1930
Made in Germany
D R G M

S PB H
4000-8

PorzellanFabrik
Burggrub
Princess Elizabeth
Made in Germany

Künstlerkopp
S PB H
Germany

S PB H

SCHOENAU, ARTHUR

DEP
AS
1900-9

M.B.
Germany
500

SCHOENHUT, A. AND COMPANY

SCHREYER & COMPANY (ALSO KNOWN AS SCHUCO)

SCHOENHUT DOLL
PAT. JAN. 1911 U.S.A.
¡FOREIGN COUNTRIES

SCHÜTZMEISTER & QUENDT (ALSO KNOWN AS SCHUETZMEISTER & QUENDT)

301

Germany

SG

201

Germany

SCHWÄBISCHE CELLU-LOIDWARENFABRIK	SCHWARZ, C.	SCHWENK, EMIL	SCHWERIN, SIGISMUND

Made   For
G.A. Schwarz
Philadelphia

SCHWERIN, SIGISMUND (CONT.)	SEARS, ROEBUCK & COMPANY	SEDARD, M. EUGENE

BABY RUTH

SELIGMANN & MAYER	SEYFARTH & REINHARDT

Heubach-Koppelsdorf
312 (SuR) 2
Germany

SHINN, LITA & SHINN, BESSIE	SHULMAN & SONS	SIMON & HALBIG
Patented Shinn Sisters	TRADE MARK S N.Y. 1906	S & H S 11 H 949

SIMON & HALBIG (CONT.)

SH 1249 DEP Germany 12 SANTA

S&H

HALBIG K ✡ R Germany 17

S 10 H 941

S&H 1249 DEP. Germany SANTA

1299 SIMON & HALBIG 3½

S H 1039 4 DEP

SIMON & HALBIG

S & H 1160 - 2/0

1849 Jutta S & H

S & H

SIMON & HALBIG G B

1008 SIMON & HALBIG

S&H 1079-6 DEP Germany

A

S & H Germany 3/0

550 Germany G SIMON & HALBIG S & H

S 14 H 949

S 13 H 949

S&H Baby Blanche

S&H. 1079 DEP Germany 8

SH 1069 DEP 2

S 8 H

1079-2 DEP S H Germany

SIMON & HALBIG

1308 S D & H 2

S H 3½ 950

SIMON & HALBIG

S & H
WSK 4/0

SIMON & HALBIG
S & H

S & H.

S & H
DEP
St.

908
S 10 H

S H
908

905
S H

989
12

89
12

979
6

S H 6
920

S & H
887

909
SIMON & HALBIG
6

S & H 739 DEP

S & H
1160-1

1008
SIMON & HALBIG
S & H
Germany

Germany
S H 13 - 1010 DEP.

S 1061 H

S & H
1158
2

1078
S & H
Germany
3/0

S H 1079
DEP.
7½

1079
HALBIG
S & H
Germany

1248
HALBIG
Germany
S & H

S & H
1308
D

S H 1300
3
DEP.

S & H. 1249
DEP
Germany
SANTA

S & H 1249-3
DEP
Germany

S & H
164
Germany
34

1269
Germany
SIMON & HALBIG
S & H
13½

S & H 1269
DEP.
7

1468
S & H
2

1428
9

150
S8H
0

151
S&H
3

HALBIG
S&H
8

SIMON& HALBIG
616
Made
in
Germany

SIMON& HALBIG
made in
Germany
1310-42
1296-36

MON& HALBIG
600
10

1489
Erika
SIMON & HALBIG

DEP
S. H
Germany

SIMON&HALBIG
Germany

S 1041

8½ H

10 SH 9 Germany

SIMON&HALBIG
S₇H
VI

SIMON & HALBIG
made in
Germany
1310-42
1296·36

S 15H
939

908
S,0H

SH
908

7008
SIMON & HALBIG
S&H
Germany

1489
Erika
SIMON & HALBIG

SIMON&HALBIG
600
10

S&H 1269
DEP.
7

SH 1300
3
DEP.

SIMON&HALBIG
S&H
III

K
S&H
K ✡ R
15

S&H
H × IV
Germany

S&H 1009
DEP
St.

S&H
CT
1

S&H 1009
DEP
Germany
3

S&H
W. S. K.

SIMON & JUNGHANS	SIMONNE, F.	SMITH, EDWARD	SMITH, ELLA
Popp Head	PASSAGE DELORME No. 1à/3 SIMONNE AVE DE RIVOLI 188	EDWARD SMITH THE CITY TOY SHOP 8 CHEAP SIDE LONDON. E.C.	PAT. NOV. 9, 1912 NO. 2 ELLA SMITH DOLL CO.

SMITH, ELLA (CONT.)	SOCIÉTÉ ANONYME DE COMPTOIR GENERAL DE LA BIMBELOTGRIE
MRS. S.S. SMITH Manufacturer of and Dealer in The Alabama Indestructible Doll ROANOKE, ALA. PATENTED Sept. 26, 1905	Poupon Parisiana Poupée Parisiana Bébé Parisiana

SOCIÉTÉ BINDER & COMPANY	SOCIÉTÉ FRANÇAISE DE FABRICATION DE BÉBÉ & JOUETS (ALSO KNOWN AS S. F. B. J.)

B J

R
S.F.B.J.
PARIS
10

S.F.B.J.
227
PARIS
6

BÉBÉ MODEA

BÉBÉ PARISIANA

LE SÉDUISANT   BÉBÉ MODERN   BÉBÉ PARFAIT   DÉPOSÉ S.F.B.J.

S.F.B.J.
60
PARIS

"BEBE PARISIANA"   PARIS-BEBE   BÉBÉ PRODIGE

S.F.B.J.
236
PARIS

BÉBÉ FRANCAIS

25
FRANCE
SF.BJ
301
PARIS
8

FRANCE
S.F.B.J.
301

FRANCE
S.F.B.J.
301

BÉBÉ JUMEAU   BÉBÉ PRODIGE

S.F.B.J
249
PARIS

PARIS
2/0

LE PAPILLON   LE SÉDUISANT

SOCIÉTÉ FRANÇAISE DE FABRICATION DE BÉBÉ & JOUETS
(ALSO KNOWN AS S. F. B. J.) (CONT.)

S. F. B. J.
247
PARIS

"BÉBÉ PARISIANA"

BÉBÉ MODERNE

LE SÉDUISANT

EDEN-BÉBÉ

PARIS-BÉBÉ

BÉBÉ PRODIGE

BÉBÉ JUMEAU

BÉBÉ FRANCAIS

BÉBÉ TRIOMPHE

EDEN-BÉBÉ

S. F. B. J.
239
PARIS
Poulbot

SOCIÉTÉ INDUSTRIELLE DE CELLULOID

SOCIÉTÉ LA PARISIENNE DE BÉBÉ ET JOUETS

Sicoïne
SIC A
FRANCE
2/0

Siegfried
made in Germany
9

MAGIC BÉBÉ
BÉBÉ STELLA
BÉBÉ LUX

BÉBÉ EUREKA
BÉBÉ LE RÉVE
PARADIS BÉBÉ

SOCIÉTÉ RAMEL CH. ET CIE

SOCIÉTÉ RENE SCHILLER & COMPANY

J'HABILLE MES SOLDATS

J'HABILLE MES POUPÉES

YERRI et SUZEL

LIBERTY

SOCIÉTÉ SUSSFELD & COMPANY

SOMMERS, E. L. & COMPANY

Sommer & Co.

SPAGGIARI, MME. YVONNE	SPERSCHNEIDER, MYLIUS	SPINDLER, MAX & COMPANY
LES ORIGINAUX DE VOVONNE		

STANDFUSS, KARL	STEIFF

 Karl Standfuss

Bouton dans l'oreille

„Steiff"

STEIFF (CONT.)

   Schutz MARKE

STEINBADER, ERSTE PORZELLANFABRIK

E St P

Germany

3ol
W & Cº
Thuringia

G H
1004

19 G H 04
G E3 H

STEINER, AUGUST	STEINER, EDMUND ULRICH

Steiner-köppelsdorf
A.S
Germany
84
4/o

A . S
Germany
2 61/o

Majestic
2 Regd

Edmund Steiner

STEINER, EDMUND ULRICH (CONT.)

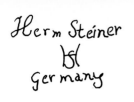

STEINER, HERMANN

Herm Steiner
HS
Germany

15
HSt
Germany
240

HS

HS

DRGM 95464
HS
Germany
247

HS

Herm Steiner
HS
Germany

75
HSt
Germany
240

HS

Herm Steiner
HS

HSt

Made in
Germany
HS

HermSteiner
HS
Germany

S
N

HS
Germany
247

H.401 0 1/2 S
made in Germany

128
Herm. Steiner
22
0.

STEINER, JULES NICHOLAS (ALSO KNOWN AS SOCIÉTÉ STEINER)

Le Petit Parisien
BEBE STEINER

C. & J. Bourgoin

STEINER
S.G.D.G.
PARIS
A11

J STEINER
BTE SGDG
PARIS
FIRE A 8

A 5
LE PARISIEN
BTE SGDG
A 5

STE C
J Steiner Bte S.g.D.g J. Bourgoin

STEINER
S.G.D.G.
PARIS
A11

A3
Le PARISIEN
SGDG.

11
PARIS

STEINER BTE S.G.D.G. STE C 6 BOURGOIN

STE F 3/0

J. STEINER
STE S.G.D.G.
PARIS
FIRE A11

BÉBÉ "LE PARISIEN"
MEDAILLE D'OR
PARIS

MARQUE DEPOSEE
ARTICLE
FRANCAIS

C. STEINER BSGDG
& BOURGOIN

STE A O
J. Steiner Bte SgDg J. Bourgoin

FIGURE B N. 11
J. STEINER BTE S.G.D.G.
PARIS

FIGURE C No 7
STEINER BTE SGDG
PARIS

J Steiner

Bte S.G.D.G. Sie

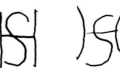

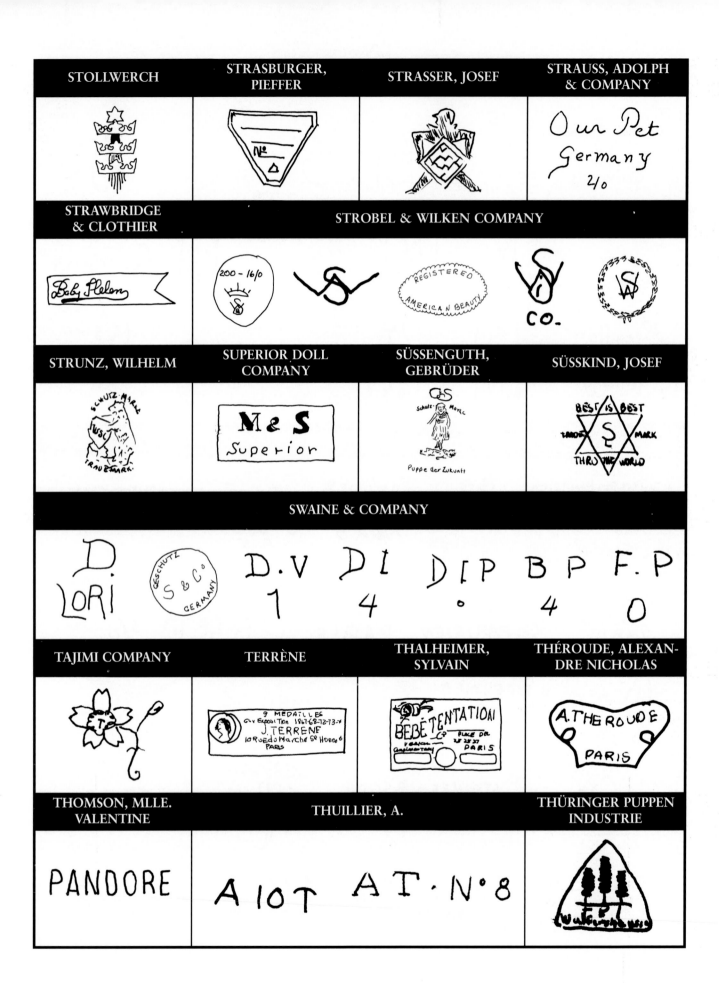

STOLLWERCH	STRASBURGER, PIEFFER	STRASSER, JOSEF	STRAUSS, ADOLPH & COMPANY

STRAWBRIDGE & CLOTHIER	STROBEL & WILKEN COMPANY

STRUNZ, WILHELM	SUPERIOR DOLL COMPANY	SÜSSENGUTH, GEBRÜDER	SÜSSKIND, JOSEF

SWAINE & COMPANY

TAJIMI COMPANY	TERRÈNE	THALHEIMER, SYLVAIN	THÉROUDE, ALEXAN-DRE NICHOLAS

THOMSON, MLLE. VALENTINE	THUILLIER, A.	THÜRINGER PUPPEN INDUSTRIE

THÜRINGER PUPPEN INDUSTRIE (CONT.)

 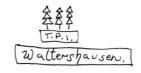  

TIBURÉE, ALEXANDRE CÉLESTIN	TOY SHOP, THE	TRAUTMANN, CARL

TRION TOY COMPANY	ULHENHUTH, HENRY & CIE	ULLMANN, SIGMUN

 6. B.M.

TRION TOY COMPANY	ULHENHUTH, HENRY & CIE	ULLMANN, SIGMUN

UNGER & SCHILDE	UNIS FRANCE	VERDIER & COMPANY

VERDIER & COMPANY (CONT.)	VEREINIGTE KÖPPELSDORFER	VERITA, MLLE. GABRIELLE

VERLINGUE, J.	VERRY, FILS	VOGUE DOLLS

313

VOGUE DOLLS (CONT.)

VOGUE

VOGUE
DOLLS

VOGUE DOLLS 1972
MADE IN HONG KONG

Ginny Doll

Ginny

VOGUE DOLLS INC
PAT.# 2687594
MADE IN USA

VOIGHT, FRIEDRICH	VOIGT, GEBRÜDER	VOIGT, HERMANN	VORMUS, M. ROGER
			KISSMY

WAGNER & ZETZSCHE

Wag Wag

WuZ
HEU:
200 BACH: I
Germany

WuZ
g
Germany

10585
g
W·Z.

1
Harald
W.Z

Hansi
w.z.

Inge
W.Z.

Barbele
W·Z.

WALKER, IZANNAH F.	WALTHER & COMPANY
Patented Nov. 4th 1873 I.F. WALKER'S PATENT NOV. 4TH 1873	 GERMANY 80 11/0 200-16/0 Germany 200 15/0

WALTHER & COMPANY (CONT.)

6789/43

33
6789/38
Made in Germany

210-B 11/0

Germany

208 7/0

Made in Germany

241 12/0
Germany

WEBBER, WILLIAM A. (ALSO KNOWN AS WEBBER COMPANY)		WEISS, KÜHNERT & COMPANY	WELDEMANN COMPANY
		4703 Weiss Kühnert & Co Gräfenthal. 5 Made in Germany	

WELLING, NORAH (ALSO KNOWN AS VICTORIA TOY WORKS)

MADE IN ENGLAND BY NORAH WELLINGS	MADE IN ENGLAND BY NORAH WELLINGS		

WELSCH & COMPANY

200 Welsch Made in Germany		150 Made in Germany Welsch 5/0	SIMON8HALBIG WELSCH

WELSCH, FRIEDERIKE		WENDT, THEODOR	
	F. W. B. GERMANY		210-B-3/0 ⊂T⊃ Made in Germany

WERNICKE, PAUL	WIEFEL & COMPANY		
	301 W&Cº Thuringia	19GH	Gea H I

WIEFEL & COMPANY (CONT.)		WIEGAND, HUGO	
	GH 1904 I	W&Cº Germany	H.W. W 1351 40	Germany 133 H 3 W

WIESENTHAL, SCHINDEL & KALLENBERG

S & H
W.S.K 2/0

Halbig
WSK 1

W.S K
1504.
DRGM
452711

WSK
541
4

WSK
1321

WIMPERN	WINKLER, EDMUND FRIEDRICH	WINKLER, ERNST FIRM

WISLIZENUS, ADOLF

AWs
Germany
II

AW
Special
Germany

101

A.W
W
DRGM
421981

Germany
AW
D

A.W.
MY SWEETHEART
B. J & Cº

A.W. 1
Germany
5

710·7
Germany

AW
W
DRGM
421481

118·4
Germany

AW
Special
Germany

Heubach-Köppelsdorf
A.W.
W
Germany

WITTZAK, EMIL	WOHLLEBEN, GUSTAV	WOHLMANN, OTTO	WOLF, HERMANN

H
W.E.N.S.P.F.

WOLF, LOUIS & COMPANY

78
L. W. & Co.
12

222
22

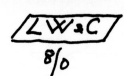
8/0

152
L. W. & Co
12

200
L. W. C°
/0

301
W & C°
Germony

WORDTMANN	WÜRTTEMBERGISCHE SPIELWARENFABRIK	ZEHNER, EDMUND CARL	ZIERL, M. PAUL LUCIEN
			LE JOUJOU PNEU

ZIEROW, PAUL R.		ZINNER & SÖHNE	

CHAPTER SEVEN

BYTES
& BITS

This chapter is separated into two sections. The first part is an alphabetical listing of advertising slogans and sound bytes that a manufacturer or, in a few instances, a store used to sell their dolls. The second part is an assortment of bits of information, not only to assist in recognizing a particular doll, but to help you in a more general way with your doll collecting. For example, just what does *Künstlerpuppe* mean, who is Juanita Quigley, and how can I get in touch with a Cabbage Patch Doll Club?

What good could advertising slogans and sound bytes be in identifying a doll? Maybe more than you think. It is not unusual to remember a jingle from an advertisement. That is exactly what the company had in mind when it promoted its product. The memory of a slogan, such as "The Doll With The Golden Heart," or "You Can't Break 'Em" may not seem like a lot, but it is more than enough to begin your journey.

We usually know more about a doll than we think we do. Learning the manufacturer is the essential, but often concealed, beginning point. You will have no problem finding further information once that is unveiled. What can be difficult is the initial pinpointing of a particular doll. Frequently, the road to disclosure is an arduous one. I hope that the charts in this chapter will guide you in your quest.

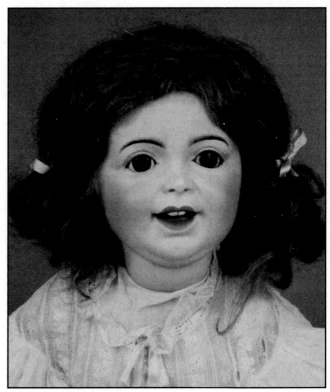

S.F.B.J.'s #236, Laughing Jumeau (Photo courtesy of Helen Brook.)

A Doll Made to Love. . . . . Kamkins
A Doll So Cute, You Just Want to Hug Her . . . . Effanbee
A Faithful Reproduction of the Famous Movie
    Star in Universal Stern Brother Comedies . . . . Averill Manufacturing Co.
A Good Seller for Your Bazaar. . . . . Schoenhut
A Head of Safety, Beyond Harm. . . . . Roth, Baitz & Lipsitz
A Jolly Little Chap with a
    Two-Year-Old Smile that's Catching . . . . Horsman & Co.
A Lovable Petite Doll. . . . . American Character
A New Rag Baby. . . . . *Woman's Home Companion*
A Real Little American Lass about Three Years Old . . . . Horsman & Co.
A Real Standing Doll. . . . . Jacobs & Kassler
A Real True-To-Life Personality
    with a Wonder Wardrobe. American Character
A Real Wild West Youngster . . . . Horsman & Co.
A Spruce Little Fellow in a
    Suit of Snowy Well-Cut White Ducks . . . . Horsman & Co.
A Stocky Little Fellow Just Able to Toddle . . . . Horsman & Co.
A Truly Great Doll . . . . Effanbee
A Wonder of Science . . . . Louis Wolf & Co.
Adtocolite, light, smooth, and tough. . . . . Aetna Doll & Toy Co.
After the Radical Reform of 1908,
    Nothing Remained to Reform . . . . Toys and Novelties, 1909
Alexander Walking Talking Dolls . . . . Alexander Doll Co.
All Babyland Loves the Gimbel Store . . . . Gimbel
All in First Quality. . . . . Franz Schmidt
All Types, All Styles, All Sizes at the Right Prices . . . . . Metropolitan Doll Co.
All Wood Dolls . . . . Schoenhut
All Wood Perfection Art Dolls . . . . A. Schoenhut & Co.
Almost Human . . . . Capo
Alpha Toys . . . . Farnell
Ambisc . . . . Louis Amberg & Son
America's Best Cottons . . . . Collingbourne Mills
America's Wonder Baby Doll . . . . American Character
American Dolls for Americans . . . . Louis Amberg & Son
American Standard . . . . Louis Amberg & Son
America's Most Beautiful Baby Doll . . . . Century Doll Co.
Amfelt Dolls . . . . Louis Amberg & Son
Amkid. . . . . Amberg
Another "Ideal" Achievement. . . . . Ideal
Another Winsome Lassie with Roguish Eyes,
    All Dressed for Daisy Picking in the Fields . . . . Horsman & Co.
Art Dolls. . . . . Many companies used this term—including American
                                                                    Stuffed Novelty; Richard Haueisen; L. Henze &
                                                                    Steinhauser; Horsman & Co.; Paul Hunaeus; Kley &
                                                                    Hahn; Käthe Kruse; Lenci; Maiethau & Wolff; Marga;
                                                                    Karl Müller; Hermann Pensky; Schoenhut; Karl
                                                                    Standfuss; and Heinrich Zwanger
At Last, the Ideal Has Been Reached in
    This Scientific and Artistically Finished Head . . . . Louis Wolf & Co. and B. Illfelder
Aunt Patsy Will Greet You Herself . . . . Effanbee
Babbitt-at-Your-Service Cleaner Boy . . . . B. T. Babbitt Co.
Baby's Clothes Will Now Fit Dollie . . . . Art Fabric Mills
Baby Peggy, The Nation's Darling. . . . . Louis Amberg & Son
Badekinder (bathing children) Come in
    Four Sizes, With or Without a Bath Tub . . . . *Nürnberg Toy Catalog*, 1850

Bass Wood. . . . . Schoenhut (Note: Other dolls claimed to be made of close-grained wood; however, Schoenhut advertised its Bass Wood.)

Basswood Dolls. . . . . Schoenhut

Bauernkinder, the Peasant Children . . . . Horsman & Co.

Be The First in Your Town to Have Snookums . . . . Averill Manufacturing Co.

Beautiful Dolls Have Been Priced Exceedingly Low
  So That They Will Be Quick to Find Little Mothers . . . Siegel Cooper

Beautiful Jubilee Dolls . . . . Strobel & Wilken

Beautifully Dressed Dolls at Moderate Prices . . . . Gimbel

Before The War (World War I) Germany
  Unquestionably Held a Master Key to
  the Doll Industry . . . . *British Trade Journal*, 1917

Best Of All—She Not Only Sleeps or
  Winks Mischievously At You—But Rolls
  Her Eyes From Side to Side and Flirts
  Gaily As She Toddles Along . . . . Ideal

Billy Boy Friend, a Kiddie Play Dolly . . . . Regal

Bisc Finished, undipped—therefore, non-peelable . . . . . . Louis Amberg & Son

Bisque Dolls, Novelty Dolls, Teddy Bears, etc. . . . . Siegel Cooper

Bisquette Heads. . . . . Artcraft Toy Products Co.

Body Twist . . . . Amberg

Bottletot, a Petite Baby. . . . . American Character

Brighten the Heart of Every Child . . . . Reisman, Barron & Co.

Brownies. . . . . Palmer Cox

Bubbling Over With Life and Laughter. . . . . Effanbee

Bully Good Indian . . . . Skookum (Arrow)

Can't Break 'Em . . . . Horsman & Co.

Celebrate. . . . . Borgfeldt

Children Love Them Dearly Because They
  Will Stand or Sit in Practically Any Position . . . . Schoenhut

Children's Cloth Toys. . . . . Art Fabric Mills

China Pot Dolls. . . . . British Ceramic

Cho Cho Sam . . . . Morimura Brothers

Christmas Dolls for the Kiddies . . . . Raleigh's Composition

Christmas is Coming and the Children's
  Pleasure Must Be Provided For. . . . . Cook's Flack Rice cloth advertising doll

Cleanliness Guaranteed by
  National Consumers League. . . . . M. C. W. Foote

Cloth Papier-Mâché. . . . . New England Doll Company

Cocheco Manufacturing. . . . . Arnold Print Works

Cry Baby Doll . . . . Art Fabric Mills

Cute Little Doll With a Bit of a Frown . . . . Effanbee

Daintily Dressed for the Most Critical Clientele . . . . Gem Toy Co.

Dear To Every Little Girl's Heart are
  the Well-Known Nursery Rhymes. . . . . *Ladies Home Journal*

Designed by Portrait Artist. . . . . Artcraft Toy Products Co.

Different from Ordinary Dolls and
  Their Quality is Easily Recognized . . . . Averill Manufacturing Co.

Dolls and Toys for the Younger Children . . . . Gimbel

Dolls Dressed in the Costumes of
  Our Allies for Gifts or Bazaars. . . . . Schoenhut

Dolls for the Entire World are
  Now Made in Germany. *Toys and Novelties*, 1913

Dolls of Distinction . . . . Maxine Doll Co.

Dominion Brand, Made in Canada. . . . . Dominion Manufacturing Co.

Dressed in a Knitted Wool Dress . . . . L'Hotel de Ville

Drinking Baby with Detachable Drinking
   Mechanism Hand to Facilitate Dressing,
   a Flask with Refill Liquid, and a Funnel
   to Replace the Milk . . . . Hermsdorfer Celluloidwarenfabrik
Each Face is Hand Painted, No Stencils Used . . . . Anili Doll Co.
Edma Doll Walks and Talks . . . . European Doll Manufacturing
Electric in Appeal . . . . Effanbee
Every Body Loves Them . . . . Averill Manufacturing Co.
Every Child Knows Kestner Celebrated
   Crown Dolls are the Best . . . . Kestner
Every Doll Has Been Individually Hand
   Painted by a Master Craftsman . . . . Strobel & Wilken
Every Known Kind of Doll and Toy Animal . . . . Amberg
Every Mother Sees Her Own Baby
   in Beautiful Bubbles . . . . Effanbee
Everybody Loves a Pretty Baby—You'll
   Love Her, Too . . . . American Character
Everybody Loves Them . . . . Averill Manufacturing Co.
Exceptional Values in Dolls of Real Beauty . . . . Gem Toy Co.
Expensive Materials and the Most
   Modern Machinery . . . . Effanbee
Exquisite Beauties to Brighten Your Doll Collection . . . . Messina-Vat
Exquisite Parisian Beauties at
   Low Prices That Will Surprise . . . . Louis Eisen
Fairyland, the Perfected Rag Doll . . . . M. C. W. Foote
Fancy Goods and Toys . . . . Horsman & Co.
Fancy Store . . . . Woodford
Featherlight . . . . Hoest & Henderson
Female Toy Making Deport . . . . Elizabeth Horne
Fine Dressed "Favorite" Dolls . . . . F. A. O. Schwarz
Finest and Best . . . . Effanbee
Finest Quality Dolls . . . . Otto Gans
Firmly Jointed With Patented Swivel
   Connection and Steel Spring Hinges
   with a Double Spring Tension . . . . Schoenhut
First Class Models Only . . . . Lona Art Dolls
Flexible Foot . . . . American Character
Flexible, Non-Breakable, Flesh Coloring, Washable . . . . . Rollinson Dolls
For the First Time in History of America,
   the Attempt to Rival European Creations
   of Boudoir Dolls, Art Novelties, Pillows
   Has Been Successful . . . . Etta, Inc.
French Brother, the Blue Devil . . . . Schoenhut
French Felt Dolls . . . . Louis Eisen
Full of Laughter and has One Tiny Tooth . . . . Averill Manufacturing Co.
Gem Dolls In The Quality Group at a Popular Price . . . . Gem Toy Co.
Genuine Madame Hendren Doll . . . . Averill Manufacturing Co.
Geschützt, Germany . . . . Swaine & Co.
Give Her One and She Will Have Wholesome
   Company for a Long Time . . . . The American Doll Co.
Golden Locks and Her Twin Babies Given to You . . . . . . *Woman's World*
Greatest and Most Unique of All the Doll Races . . . . Mary France Woods
Greatest Baby Doll of All Times . . . . Effanbee
Greatest Novelty in Children's Toys Ever Produced . . . . . William A. Webber Co.
Greet a Fine Old Friend in a Brand New Form . . . . Effanbee Dolls
Grown-ups, as Well as Children, Fall in
   Love With It as Soon as They See It . . . . *McCall's* Subscription Doll

Guaranteed This Toy is Made Under
  Sanitary Conditions . . . . Effanbee
Happy Tots . . . . American Character
Have No Equal . . . . Artcraft
He is a Healthy, Husky Youngster . . . . Horsman & Co.
Healthful Cuddling Doll. . . . . Balsam Baby by Gre-Poir
Helga . . . . Wagner & Zetzche
Here are Some of My Novelties . . . . Otto Gans
Here is a Splendid Christmas Present for
  That Little Girl of Yours . . . . *Woman's World*
Here's a Boy Doll They Can Play With . . . . Cameo
Here's Something To Entertain 'em. To Help
  'em In Their Play. Mama Can Make 'em,
  Baby Can't Break 'em, and They Will
  Last for Many a Day. . . . . Art Fabric Mills
High Grade Infant and Mama Dolls . . . . Roth, Baitz & Lipsitz
High Grade Mama Dolls . . . . Fleischer Toy Manufacturing Co.
Holding In Its Chubby Fist An Unbreakable
  Bottle With Milk Fluid and a Real Rubber Nipple . . . . American Character
Hug Me Kiddy Doll. . . . . McCall's Subscription Doll
Hygienic Fabric Toys . . . . Chad Valley
Hygienic Toys . . . . Chad Valley
I am a Bonser Doll. . . . . Bonser Doll Co.
I Can Walk; I Can Talk; I Can Sleep . . . . Ideal
I Come From a Far Off Country Where
  They Make the Finest Dolls . . . . Nugent & Brothers
I Now Live in a Big Beautiful Store, But
  I Want to Belong to Your Little Girl . . . . Nugent & Brothers
I Shut My Eyes When I Lie Down To Sleep. . . . . Nugent & Brothers
I Want a Home and Some One to Love Me . . . . Nugent & Brothers
I Wear Pretty Shoes and Lace Stockings . . . . Nugent & Brothers
I'm Called Little Buttercup, Dear Little Buttercup . . . . . Horsman & Co.
I'm Not a Doll, But a Real Little Girl . . . . Terri Lee
I'm the Doll With the Skin of a Fairy . . . . Louis Amberg & Son and Hergershausen
I'se In Town, Honey. . . . . Aunt Jemima Doll
Importers of French Dolls of All Descriptions . . . . Palais Royal
It Has Become Popular With Art
  Loving Society Ladies . . . . *Toys and Novelties*, 1914
Judy the Girl Friend, a Kiddie Pal Dolly . . . . Regal
Just as Big as a Real Baby . . . . *Woman's World*
Just Like a Real Live Baby . . . . American Character
Just the Sort of Boy Tot Every Little Girl
  Will Want in Her Doll Family, Robbie Reefer . . . . Horsman & Co.
Kiddie Karakters Hendrenize Your Dolls . . . . Averill Manufacturing Co.
Kiddy Pal Dolly. . . . . Regal
King of the Dolls. . . . . Kestner
Know What Modern Quality Means . . . . Modern Doll Co.
Known from Maine to California as
  the Best Line on the Market. . . . . Averill Manufacturing Co.
Largest Maker of Doll Babies in the World . . . . Louis Amberg & Son
Learn American History with the Historical Dolls. . . . . . Effanbee
Lifelike . . . . American Specialty Doll Co.
Lifelike Models . . . . Rollinson Dolls
Life Size Doll Babies Clothes Will Now Fit Dollie . . . . . Art Fabric Mills
Lifelike Reproductions, Soft, Durable, Washable. . . . . . . Käthe Kruse
Looks Like Bisque and Feels Like Bisque . . . . Louis Amberg & Son
Love Always, Ginny Tui, the China Doll. . . . . Jack Built Toys

Lovelier Than Ever	Amberg
Madam Alexander	Alexander Doll Co.
Madame Hendren	Averill Manufacturing Co.
Made by the Famous Humpty Dumpty Circus Toy	Schoenhut
Made Entirely by Hand of Impregnated Nettle Cloth	Käthe Kruse
Made in Clean, Sunny Factories of Fine Materials	M. C. W. Foote
Made Under Clean and Healthful Conditions	M. C. W. Foote
Making a Bigger Hit than the Teddy Bear	*McCall's* Subscription Doll
Manufacturers of Guaranteed Unbreakable and Washable	Lona Art Dolls
Manufacturers of Miniature Dolls and Dolls for Doll Houses	Carl Horn
Marque Déposée Article Français	Chambre Syndicale
Material is the Result of 40 Years' Research	Rhenish Rubber & Celluloid Co.
MEDAILLE D'OR	Jumeau (refers to the gold medal won in 1878)
Medailles D'or 1878	Jumeau
Mercurius	John Wanamaker
Miss 1928	Jacobs & Kassler
Models of Italian dolls	Chad Valley
Most Attractive Little Maiden, All Spic and Span	Horsman & Co.
My Doll's A Patsy—Is Yours?	Effanbee
My Hair is Beautiful Ringlet Curls, Tied With a Pretty Ribbon	Nugent & Brothers
My Head is of the Finest Bisque	Nugent & Brothers
Nanking (nankeen) Doll	Alt, Beck & Gottschalck
Ne Plus Ultra	Butler Brothers
Never Before Has Such A Lovely, Delicate, Fresh Lifelike Expression Been Equaled in a Celluloid Finish Head	Louis Wolf & Co. and B. Illfelder
New and Exclusive Hot Shots	J. Bouton & Co.
New Born Basket Baby	Louis Amberg & Son
New Born Bottle Baby	Louis Amberg & Son
New Glass Eyes That Automatically Keep a Snug Hold in the Socket	Artcraft Toy Products Co.
New Humorous Dolls	Dora Petzold
New York Evening News	Horsman & Co.
No Pins, No Buttons	Amberg
No Two of Them Just Alike	Mary France Woods
None But the Lifelike Eyes Will Satisfy You	Otto Gans
Note These Sensational Features: First: Lifelike, Second: Unbreakable, Third: Washable, Fourth: Light	Rhenish Rubber & Celluloid Co.
Nothing in All Dolldom Can Compare With Them	Missina-Vat
Nothing She'll Hug So Close to Her Heart	Effanbee
O'Neill	Kewpie
Oh, I Want a Girl for Each Month of the Year	Nancy Ann StoryBook Dolls
One of the Many Interesting Items in the Petite Doll Line	American Character
Our Brave Little Sailor Boy	Schoenhut
Outstanding New Lines	Amberg
Painted With Enamel Oil Paint That Won't Come Off	Schoenhut
Parisian Mechanician for Adult Amusement	Swimming Dolls
Peasant Children Artistic, Lovable	Horsman & Co.
Performs When Squeezed	Kat A Korner Kompany
Period Dolls are Exquisite Gifts	*Ladies Home Journal*, for dress patterns
Petite American's Wonder Baby Doll	American Character
Petite Baby Dolls	American Character

Petite Doll Campbell Kid . . . . American Character Doll
Please, I Want A Mother . . . . Nugent & Brothers
Powder and Crinoline . . . . Nancy Ann StoryBook Dolls
Press Me and I Will Play Sweet Lullabies . . . . Phyllis the Musical Doll by J. Bouton & Co.
Reflex Eyes Able To Look In Several Directions . . . . Koenig & Wernicke
Represents Radiant Sunshine . . . . Effanbee
Ribbons and Laces and Pretty Girl Faces . . . . A&H
Rohlinge (Ruffian) Doll, Designed by
   Karl Krausser, That Walks and Turns Head . . . . Kämmer & Reinhardt
Sassy Sue Character Doll . . . . Amberg
Sayco Soft Toys . . . . Schoen & Yondorf
Schoenhut's Unbreakable Wooden Head . . . . Schoenhut
See Our Surprise Doll at the Fair . . . . Roth, Baitz & Lipsitz
See The Largest Line Of Dolls Made by
   Any Doll Manufacturer Anywhere . . . . Reisman, Barron Co.
She Walks, Says "Mama," is Dressed Adorably,
   and is Practically Indestructible . . . . Ideal
Sister Wants a Dolly For Her Birthday . . . . Effanbee
So Comical, Soft, and Cuddly, You Can't Resist It. . . . . . Modern Toy Co.
Sophisticated, the Most Glamorous
   Doll in the World. . . . . American Character
Specializing in Jointed Dolls, Sitting Babies,
   Standing Babies, Sitting and Standing Babies,
   Stiff Jointed Small Dolls, Heads, Wigs,
   Arms, Legs, Bodies . . . . Franz Schmidt
Stockinet Dolls Modeled from Life . . . . Rollinson Dolls
Strictly Sanitary . . . . Bach Brothers
Sweet Sue's Charles of The Ritz Chignon . . . . American Character
Tee Wee Hand Baby, the Living Doll. . . . . American Character
The All American Boy Doll for the All American Boy . . . Cameo
The American Standard . . . . Louis Amberg & Son
The Baby You Can't Resist. . . . . American Character
The Baby's Real Baby Doll. . . . . Hoest & Henderson
The Baden Powell Doll in Formal Uniform . . . . Hamley Doll
The Best is None Too Good for Your Child
   and it Costs No More . . . . The American Doll Co.
The Bully Kiddo, Skookum . . . . Louis Amberg & Son
The Camp Fire Girl a Pretty Companion
   for the Boy Scout. . . . . Horsman & Co.
The Campbell Kids Have Caught the
   Colored Hair Craze . . . . Horsman & Co.
The Character Dolls and Figures, Because of Their
   Distinct Individuality, Their Great Durability, and
   Lasting Qualities, are Winning Their Way Into
   the Hearts of the Doll Loving World . . . . Steiff
The Chinese Boy Is Sure To Bring A
   Smile to Everyone's Face . . . . Schoenhut
The Chubby Little Charmer with a Bow in Her Hair. . . . Century Doll Co.
The Cradle Baby . . . . Jacobs & Kassler
The Crashing Smashing Hit . . . . Amberg
The Cutest Little Baby You Have Ever Loved . . . . American Character
The Doll of the Hour. . . . . Modern Toy Co.
The Dolls That are for Very Little Folks and
   are in High Favor with the Tots, too. . . . . Art Fabric Mills
The Doll That Cries Real Tears . . . . American Character
The Doll That Made the Queen Smile. . . . . Soozie Smiles, as seen in Sears, Roebuck & Co.
The Doll That Teaches Gentle Care and Kindness . . . . . . Effanbee

The Doll With the Beautiful Bright Eyes . . . . Averill Manufacturing Co.
The Doll With the Body Twist All of Its Own . . . . Amberg
The Doll With the Golden Heart . . . . Effanbee
The Doll Your Child Would Choose . . . . Effanbee
The Easily Made Christmas Doll That Fits the Times . . . Schoenhut
The Favorite Story Book Doll . . . . Raggedy Ann and Andy
The French Artistry and Dainty Charm
 of These Exclusive Dolls Will Lend a
 Sparkling Touch to Your Doll Display . . . . Louis Eisen
The French Have A Certain "Esprit" Which
 Prompts Them to Make the Most Beautiful
 Creations in Toys. . . . . *Toys and Novelties*, 1919
The Glad Doll, Pollyanna. . . . . Louis Amberg & Son
The god of things as they ought to be . . . . Billiken doll
The Happiest and Brightest Baby You Ever Saw . . . . Averill Manufacturing Co.
The Ideal Doll . . . . Rhenish Rubber & Celluloid Co.
The Jolliest Dolls of All . . . . Horsman & Co.
The Joy That Goes into Fashioning These Little
 People so That They Will Carry Happiness to
 All the Little Kiddies This Christmas . . . . Raleigh's Composition
The Life Size Doll . . . . Art Fabric Mills
The Line Of Highest Quality. Priced to Keep The
 Sales Force Busy and the Cash Drawer Jingling. . . . . . . Century Doll Co.
The Line Whose Reputation Takes the
 Guesswork From . . . . Acme Toy Co.
The Living Doll . . . . American Character
The Lovable Dimpled Laughing Baby
 That Captures All Hearts. . . . . American Character
The Marvelous Webber Musical Doll . . . . William A. Webber
The Most Beautiful Baby Doll of All Time . . . . Gold Medal Baby
The Most Beautiful of Imported Dolls . . . . Borgfeldt
The Most Popular Character Doll . . . . Amberg
The Next To The Best Thing is Your
 Betty Lee Won't Wear Out . . . . Effanbee
The Original New Born Baby. . . . . Amberg
The Paris Craze For Colored Hair . . . . Horsman & Co.
The Prettiest Dolls in England . . . . Art Toy Manufacturing Co.
The Prettiest Dolls In Toyland . . . . J. C. Penny
The Princess Doll. . . . . American Unbreakable Doll Corp.
The Real Doll House . . . . Elizabeth Horne
The Sheik, Rudolph Valentino . . . . Lenci
The Skin of My Face is Like That of a Fairy . . . . Louis Amberg & Son and Hergershausen
The Standing, Smiling, Dimpled Face Baby . . . . Century Doll Co.
The World Standard. . . . . Louis Amberg & Son
There's Nothing You Can Give A Little Girl
 that She'd Love so Much as Mary Jane. . . . . Effanbee
These Are Not Real Children . . . . Schoenhut all-wood dolls
They Do Not Come Apart . . . . Schoenhut
They Say I'm Beautiful. . . . . Nugent & Brothers
This is a Century Year . . . . Century Doll Co.
This is Bubbles, Bubbling Over With
 Life and Laughter . . . . Effanbee
Treat 'Em Rough Kiddie . . . . Art Metal Works
Tru Flesh. . . . . Ideal
True-To-Life Reproductions of Real Western Indians. . . . Mary France Woods
Tru-To-Life . . . . Dean
Unbreakable Art Dolls. . . . . Horsman & Co.

Unbreakable Dolls Designed and Executed by
  Käte Kruse (note the difference in spelling) . . . . Käthe Kruse
Very carefully guarded secret formula,
  unknown even to the employees . . . . Louis Amberg & Son
Washable, Durable, Colorful, Decorative,
  Featherweight, Undressable . . . . Amberg
We Do Not Compromise Failures . . . . Baltimore Bargain House
We Dolls . . . . Toy Products Manufacturer
Wears the Cute Little Shirt, Tie and Panties,
  and the Well-Known Twist of Hair on Top
  of His Head . . . . Averill Manufacturing Co.
What Is Whispered About In the Message Is
  Shouted Aloud By The Models Themselves . . . . Etta, Inc.
When Lindy Marched Up Fifth Avenue, this
  Lucky Aviation Kid Was There to Greet Him . . . . American Character Doll
Whether it's a Mamma Doll, a Baby Doll,
  or a Novelty Doll it's the Best Made if
  it's a Petite Doll . . . . The American Doll Co.
Which is the Live Baby . . . . Martha Chase Dolls
Who Can Resist the Little Yankee Soldier . . . . Schoenhut
Will Not Crack, Peel, or Chip . . . . American Toy & Manufacturing Co.
Will Walk When Led by the Hand—Not Mechanical . . . F. O. A. Schwarz
Willow England . . . . Hewitt & Leadbeater
Winsome Baby Dolls . . . . Gerling
With Patented Flirting and Solid Eyes
  Having Reflex Action . . . . Otto Gans
Won't You Please Give Me To Some Little
  Girl This Christmas? . . . . Nugent & Brothers
Wooden Art Dolls . . . . Schoenhut
World Famed Soft Dolls . . . . Käthe Kruse
World War I Allies and a Red Cross Nurse . . . . Louvre Store
You Can't Get as Nice a Doll Anywhere
  for the Money They Ask for Me . . . . Nugent & Brothers
You'll Fall In Love With Golden Locks . . . . *Woman's World*
You'll Go Ga-Ga . . . . A&H
Your Trade Deserves the Genuine . . . . Averill Manufacturing Co.
Zulu Lucky Doll . . . . Amberg

A la Poupée de Nürnberg . . . . Paris Toy Shop

Abraham & Straus . . . . American retailer distributing a wide variety of dolls, registering several trade names

Adair-Kertzman, Linda . . . . Doll designer

Adams, Christine . . . . Doll designer

Adams, Emma E. . . . . Doll artist and co-creator of the Columbian Doll

Adams, Marietta . . . . Doll artist and co-creator of the Columbian Doll

Adler & Guth . . . . German doll manufacturing participant

Aktiengesellschaft . . . . German for "joint stock company"

Albert, J. B. . . . . German doll manufacturing participant

Album à photographies pour poupées . . . . French for "photo album for dolls"

Allison, Estell . . . . Doll designer

Alphabet Doll . . . . Doll with china head and limbs on an alphabet-printed cloth body

Aluminum Doll Head Works . . . . Manufactured aluminum doll heads

Amberg, Joshua . . . . Doll designer and son of Louis Amberg

American doll industry . . . . Began around 1910 marking the beginning of the end of the German doll monopoly

American Indian dolls . . . . Made by Alexander; Anderson; Averill Manufacturing Co.; Bouton; Butler; Chad Valley; Cissan; Gustav Föster; Helvetic; Henderson Glove; Horsman & Co.; Jeanette Doll; Lafayette; Lenci; Live Long Toys; Armand Marseille; Marshall Field; Mary McAboy; Nelke; Oakhurst Studios; Mme Paderewski; Saalfield; Sears; Shackman; Gebrüder Schmidt; Steiff; Strauss-Eckhardt; Tambon; Trego; Louis Wolf; Woods; Wyman, among others

American Tissue Mills . . . . A. K. A. New England Doll Co.

Ammer, Louis . . . . German doll manufacturing participant

Anchor Toy Corp. . . . . New York City-based doll importer

Andreas, Albert . . . . German doll manufacturing participant

Angermüller, Franz . . . . German doll manufacturing participant

Anili . . . . Doll designer

Animated platform dolls . . . . Dolls that move by a cranking mechanism

Anschütz, Hugo . . . . German doll manufacturing participant

Apache Doll . . . . The French interpretation of a ruffian

Apfelbaum, Lothar . . . . German doll manufacturing participant

Apfelbaum, M. . . . . German doll manufacturing participant

Applied ears . . . . Molded and affixed to the head rather than being part of the mold

Appropriately dressed . . . . Clothing that fits not only the time period but also the correct doll style

Aprile, Paulette . . . . Doll designer

Arhelger, Liddy . . . . German doll manufacturing participant

Arlt, Otto . . . . German doll manufacturing participant

Arm, Ernst . . . . German doll manufacturing participant

Armature . . . . Framework serves as a support core in a doll's body, usually of metal, wire, or wood

Armstrong-Hand, Martha . . . . Doll designer

Arnaud, Jean Louis Hubert . . . . French doll designer

Arnoldt, Mary (Arnold) . . . . Designed doll clothing under the label "Blue Bird Doll Clothes"

Aronson, Louis V. . . . . Doll designer

Art Doll Designers . . . . Otto Gussmann, Karl Gross, Wilhelm Kreis, William Lossow, Oskar Seyfert, Hugo Spieler, Wilhelm Thiele

Articulated . . . . Term used for a jointed doll with movable limbs

Aschenbach, Eduard . . . . German doll manufacturing participant

Ascher, Adolf. . . . . German doll manufacturing participant
Atlas Doll & Toy Co. . . . . Produced all-metal dolls
Attwood, Florence. . . . . Doll designer
Auction House, Butterfield and Butterfield . . . . 220 San Bruno Ave., San Francisco, CA 94103
Auction House, Christie's . . . . 219 E. 67th St., New York, NY 10021
Auction House, Cobb's Dolls . . . . 1909 Harrison Rd., Johnstown, OH 43031
Auction House, Frasher's . . . . P. O. Box 142, Oak Grove, MO 64075
Auction House, James Julia, Inc. . . . . P. O. Box 830, Fairfield, ME 04937
Auction House, McMasters . . . . P. O. Box 1755, Cambridge, OH 43725
Auction House, Richard A. Bourne. . . . . P. O. Box 141, Hyannisport, MA 02647
Auction House, Skinner Galleries . . . . Route 117, Bolton, MA 01740
Auction House, Sotheby, Inc. . . . . 1332 York Ave., New York, NY 10021
Auction House, Sweetbriar. . . . . P. O. Box 37, Earleville, MD 21919
Auction House, Theriault's . . . . P. O. Box 151, Annapolis, MD 21404
Auction House, Withington, Inc. . . . . P. O. Box 440, Hillsboro, NH 03244
Auer, Wilhelmine . . . . German doll manufacturing participant
Auge & Co.. . . . . German doll manufacturing participant
Aunt Patsy. . . . . Effanbee spokesperson
Aurich, K. W. . . . . German doll manufacturing participant
Auto Dolls (Auto Puppen) . . . . Dolls made to decorate automobiles
Automata . . . . Mechanical dolls
Automaton . . . . Mechanical figure that appears to imitate human-like
                                                            movements
Automobile Dolls. . . . . Dolls dressed in costumes for driving cars. Usually
                                                            consisting of a long overcoat, cap, possibly with a veil
                                                            and goggles
Autoperipatetikos . . . . Small dolls that walk by a clockwork mechanism on feet,
                                                            usually made of pressed metal, and which move back
                                                            and forth
Aux Rêves de L'Enfance. Paris distributor of fine dolls
Averill, Georgene . . . . Owner of Averill Manufacturing and designer of dolls
                                                            including the Bonnie Baby
Averill, Maxine . . . . Doll designer (daughter of Paul & Georgene Averill),
                                                            created "Mignonne"
Axthelm, Ernst . . . . German doll manufacturing participant
Baby Bunting. . . . . General term used for small dolls entirely covered with
                                                            fur made before World War I
Baby Snowball. . . . . Black version of Baby Grumpy
Back (Bock). . . . . May have manufactured doll heads in Vienna
                                                            (1908-1910)
Baden-Powell, General . . . . Founder of Boy Scouts
Baer & Strasburger . . . . A New York City doll importer
Baffert, A. . . . . A Paris doll exporter
Bagley, E. W. . . . . Produced doll parts in London
Bagnaro, G. . . . . A French supplier of knockoff dolls to jobbers and
                                                            trade shows
Bahner, Doscher Co. . . . . A New York City importer of dolls
Bail & Launary . . . . Designed French doll clothing
Bailey & Bailey . . . . U.S. Distributor of Rollinson's dolls
Bailey & Baxter. . . . . Patent holders for process for waxing over of doll parts
Bainbridge & White. . . . . British doll retailer/wholesaler
Baird-North. . . . . Distributed Pudgie Doll
Baker & Bennett . . . . U.S. importer and distributor of dolls and doll clothing
Baker, Charles W. . . . . British wholesale, distributor and exporter of dolls
Ball-jointed body . . . . Wood and composition; jointed at shoulders, hips, knees,
                                                            and most often elbows to allow movement

Ball, Betty . . . . Doll designer
Ball, Margaret . . . . Doll designer
Balleroy, Jullien & Cie . . . . Porcelain factory used to produce doll heads. Used the
 initials J. B.
Ballu, Ernst . . . . Paris doll distributor
Baltimore Bargain House . . . . U.S. Importer and distributor of dolls
Bamba, Ysaekiti. . . . . Japanese doll manufacturing participant
Bamberger, L. & Co. . . . . U.S. distributor of dolls. Registered several trademarks
 including IKWA and Under the China Berry Tree
Bambino . . . . Bleuette's baby brother
Bambolificio Italiano . . . . Italian doll manufacturing participant
The Bandeau Sales Co.. . . . . Distributor of dolls
Bandler, Max. . . . . Manufactured doll stockings
Banigan, Joseph. . . . . U.S. doll manufacturing participant
Banister, John . . . . Imported dolls and toys
Bankograph Co. . . . . U.S. distributor of dolls
Bannawitz, Albert . . . . German doll manufacturing participant
Bapts & Hamet . . . . French doll manufacturing participant
Baraja Bébé. . . . . A French doll
Barbier, George . . . . Doll designer
Barfuss, W. C.. . . . . German doll manufacturing participant
Bark Dolls. . . . . Florida craft dolls made and dressed in tree bark
Barker, A. . . . . English doll manufacturing participant
Barm, Anna. . . . . Crafted knitted and crocheted dolls
Barnard, Frank . . . . Doll designer
Barnett, Isaacs & Co.. . . . . English doll manufacturing participant
Barney, Cecilia. . . . . U.S. designer of rag dolls
Barnicol, Car. . . . . German doll manufacturing participant
Barnicol, George . . . . German doll manufacturing participant
Barnikol, Max A.. . . . . German doll manufacturing participant
Barr . . . . U.S. distributor of dolls
Barreck, Eugene. . . . . U.S. doll manufacturing participant
Barrett, Sara M.. . . . . Owner of The Doll Shoppe in Hollywood, California,
 and manufactured doll costumes
Barrie, Mirren . . . . Doll designer
Barry, Bert B. & Associates . . . . Obtained a U.S. trademark Pinocchio for dolls
Barry, Elizabeth . . . . U.S. doll manufacturing participant
Barthel Brothers & Warren . . . . English doll manufacturing participant
Barthélemy . . . . Made art dolls, including Marquisette
Bartsch, Franz . . . . Czechoslovakian doll manufacturing participant
Barwig, Franz . . . . Carved wooden dolls with painted clothes
Basia. . . . . Name of doll made by, and to support, the Polish
 refugees of World War I
Bass Wood Doll. . . . . Doll made of "close grain wood" with wig and
 jointed limbs
Bathing doll. . . . . Small china or bisque, white or black, beautiful little
 nymphs can be risqué, posed sitting, reclining, or
 standing—usually with graceful arms and legs—art
 deco in appearance, dressed in bathing suits, draped in
 togas, or can be delicately detailed nudes
Battle, Martha . . . . Registered the trademark Evangeline in 1937
Baum, Frank . . . . Doll designer
Baum, Hugo . . . . Doll designer
Bébé . . . . French dolly-faced doll
Beck de, Billy. . . . . Doll designer
Beck, Reinhold . . . . Designer of dolls, including Fine Baby for Amberg
Beckett, Bob . . . . Doll designer

Beckett, June	Doll designer
Behrman, Beatrice Alexander	Doll designer AKA Madame Alexander
Bello, Yolanda	Doll designer
Benjamin Goldenberg	Manufactured dolls for various distributors
Benoliel	Doll designer
Bent limb baby body	Five-piece baby body of composition with curved arms and legs jointed at the shoulders and hips
Benvenuti, Julius	Doll designer
Berndt, Walter	Doll designer
Bierschenk, Fritz	German dealer & exporter
Bildhauer	German for "sculptor"
Bing, John	American and Canadian representative for Gebrüder Bing
Biscaloid	Durable composition used for doll heads
Bisque	Unglazed tinted porcelain with matte finish, used to make doll heads, limbs or entire dolls
Bisquette	Durable composition used for doll heads
Blackeley, Halle	Doll designer
Blown glass eyes	Hollow eyes of blue, gray, or brown
Blue Bird Doll Clothes	Doll clothing designed by Mary Arnoldt and distributed by Borgfeldt
Boite à chapeau	French for "hat box"
Bonnet Doll	Head molded with a hat or bonnet
Boston Store	Doll distributor
Botta	Doll designer
Boudoir Dolls	Known also as Flapper or Sofa dolls. Acquired their name because of the use of decorations on beds and divans—produced by various manufacturers
Boulaye, la De	Doll designer
Brahans, Abigail	Doll designer
Brailtling, Charles	Produced doll parts
Brandon, Elizabeth	Doll designer
Branner, Martin	Cartoonist and inspiration for Periwinkle doll
Bremer, L.	Doll distributor
Breveté	French marking indicating a registered patent
Bringloe, Frances	Doll designer
British Ceramic	The ceramic used in Britain to produce doll and doll parts. Better quality than pottery, but not as fine as porcelain; therefore, required lower firing temperature.
British National Dolls	Made British Ceramic dolls, with *B.N.D.* marking
British Novelty Works, Ltd.	Subsidiary of Dean
Brnoliel, Eileen	Designer of dolls, including Baby Bibs
Brodeur Doll Shop	Made wax dolls and doll repairs
Broken composition fingers	Sawdust and glue mixture to repair, careful not to get on other parts
Brouse, Mary	Doll designer
Brownies	Dolls representing the characters drawn by Palmer Cox
Brüderchen	German for "little brother"
Brüderlein	German for "younger brother"
Brudines, Inc.	Doll distributor
Brummer & Co.	English distributor of wholesale dolls and doll parts
Brundage, Frances	Doll designer, including Dolly Dear
Bruns, Nancy	Doll designer

Brush marks	Small strokes painted around a doll's forehead or temples to suggest hair
Bté	Patent registered
Buckram	Stiff coarse cotton or linen fabric used for heads, faces, and hats
Bull, Rene	Doll designer
Bullard, Helen	Doll designer
Burnell, Patricia	Doll designer
Busch, Wilhelm	Illustrator of Max and Moritz and doll designer
Bush Terminal Sales Co.	Represented several American and British doll manufacturers
Butterick, E & Co.	Published doll body and clothing patterns
Buvard	French for "writing case"
Cacheleux	French doll designer and wholesaler of toys
Cahn, Widow Leon	Designed doll clothing
Callier, Mlle. Isabelle	French doll designer
Cameron, Beth	Doll designer
Campbell, Astry	Doll designer
Caracul	Lamb's skin used to make doll wigs
Caresse	An inexpensive line of cloth dolls by Chad Valley
Carina	A line of velvet jointed dolls by Chad Valley
Caron-Laghez	Designed doll jewelry
Carrier-Belleuse, Albert Ernest	French doll designer and sculptor for Emile Jumeau
Carrier-Belleuse, Albert Ernest	A French doll designer and sculptor for Emile Jumeau
Carter, Art	Doll designer
Cartes de bureau	French for "business cards"
Cartes de Toilette	French for "social cards"
Carton Pâte	French term for a type of papier-mâché body
Carton Moulé	French for "carton"
Cartwright, A. S.	Manufactured doll accessories
Cassini, Oleg	Fashion and doll designer
Cejka	Doll Designer
Celebrity doll	Figure portraying a movie or stage celebrity, such as Shirley Temple or Charlie Chaplin, also known as a "Personality doll"
Celluloid	Highly flammable cellulose nitrate and camphor compound introduced in 1869 and used in doll making. It became illegal in the U.S. during the 1940s
Cerceau	French for "hoop"
Character doll	Lifelike in appearance; may be infants, children, or adults
Check mark	Usually a red mark on back of Jumeau doll heads. Various shapes, sizes. Often no other mark is present.
Cheek, Linda	Doll designer
Chicago Mail Order House	Doll distributor
Chicken feathers of orange or yellow used for hair	Annalee Mobilitee Dolls, 1960-1963
Child doll	Typical dolly face
China	Glazed porcelain
China head style, Adelina Patti	Elaborate mode with center part and rolled curls, painted features
China head style, Alice or Alice in Wonderland	Molded headband with hair back from face, painted features
China head style, Biedermeier	Bold or solid dome head, some with top of head painted, good wig, painted features
China head style, Bun	Braided or rolled bun in back, may be very elaborate or fancy, painted features

China head style, Civil War . . . . Middle part, short curls around head, painted features

China head style, Countess Dagmar . . . . Pierced ears with various elaborate modes with molded bows and fine decoration, painted features

China head style, Covered Wagon . . . . Flat on top, sausage curls around head, painted features

China head style, Curly Top . . . . Ringlet curls over entire head, painted features

China head style, Currier & Ives . . . . Long bangs and molded headband, painted features

China head style, Dolly Madison . . . . Curls over entire head, molded ribbon, painted features

China head style, English . . . . Flesh-tinted china, painted features, solid dome with good wig

China head style, Exposed Ear . . . . Hair pulled back from face in a curly bun exposing ears, painted features

China head style, Flat Top . . . . Middle part, short curls around head, painted features

China head style, French . . . . Glass or beautifully painted eyes, feathered brows, open crown with cork pate and good wig

China head style, Glass Eyed . . . . Painted hair, exposed ears and glass eyes

China head style, highbrow . . . . Very round face, high forehead, center part, flat top, sausage curls around head, painted features

China head style, Highland Mary . . . . Straight top with curls at sides, painted features

China head style, Jenny Lind . . . . Middle part, pulled back into bun, painted features

China head style, Kinderkopf . . . . Child with short neck, round face, and painted features

China head style, lowbrow . . . . Common wavy style—painted blond or black—with painted features

China head style, Man or Boy . . . . Masculine mode, painted features

China head style, Mary Todd Lincoln . . . . Wearing snood, variation includes black hair and snood, blond hair and black snood, or elaborate decoration at crown with flowers and ruffles, painted features

China head style, Pet Name . . . . Common mode, name printed in gold on front of shoulder plate, painted features

China head style, Sophia Smith . . . . Straight hanging sausage curls not curved to the head, painted features

China head style, Spill Curl . . . . Individual curls over forehead and shoulders, painted features

Chiquet F. Le Montréer . . . . French doll manufacturing participant

Claretie, Mlle. Germaine . . . . Created wax dolls

Clark, Albert J. . . . . Traded as Clark's Dollar Store

Clausen & Co. . . . . Imported dolls made by Thüringian cottage industries

Clear, Emma . . . . Doll designer

Climax Rubber Co. . . . . Produced doll clothing

Clockwork mechanism . . . . The working parts found in many nineteenth-century automata similar to the spring machinery works of a clock being operated when wound by a key

Cloth papier-mâché . . . . Name given to the material used by the New England Doll Co.

Club, Annalee Doll . . . . P. O. Box 1137, Meredith, NH 03253

Club, Antique Toy Collectors of America . . . . Route 2 Box 5A, Parkton, MD 21120

Club, Cabbage Patch Kids Collectors . . . . P. O. Box 714, Cleveland, GA 30528

Club, Chatty Cathy Collectors . . . . 2610 Dover St., Piscataway, NJ 08854

Club, Doll Collectors of America . . . . 14 Chestnut Rd., Westford, MD 01886

Club, Effanbee Dolls . . . . 4701 Queensbury Rd., Riverdale, MD 20840

Club, G. I. Joe Collectors . . . . 150 S. Glenoaks Blvd., Burbank, CA 91510

Club, Ginny Doll . . . . 9628 Hidden Oaks Circle, Tampa, FL 33612

Club, Ideal Doll Collector's	P. O. Box 623, Lexington, MA 02173
Club, International Barbie Doll	Box 70, Bronx, NY 10464
Club, Madame Alexander Fan	P. O. Box 330, Mundeline, IL 60060
Club, Newsletter, Nancy Ann StoryBook Dolls	2504 Pioneer Blvd., Grand Island, NE 68801
Club, Rose O'Neill	P. O. Box 668, Branson, MO 65616
Cochran, Dewees	Doll designer
Cohen, Adolph	Doll designer
Cohen, Paul Co.	Bought Amber's import business including Amfelt Art Dolls in 1930
Collins, Jack	Doll designer
Complet costume sur mesure	French for "tailor-made men's suit"
Composition	Wood-based material used to make dolls or doll parts
Concha belt	American Indian belt made with shells or disk-shaped ornaments, often with silver or turquoise; miniatures found on many Indian dolls
Conselman, Bill	Co-creator of the cartoon character "Ella Cinders" which was the inspiration for the doll by the same name
Convert centimeters to inches	Multiply the number by .3937
Corde à sauter	French for "jump rope"
Cornwall Historical Society	Cornwall, CT
Corry, Grace	Designed dolls, including Little Brother and Sister for Averill Manufacturing Co.
Cosson, Mme. Charles	Designed historically accurate doll costumes
Cottage industry	Any industry with the labor force consisting of family members or small groups working at home with their own equipment, such as the manufacturing of wooden dolls in the Appalachian mountains
Courroies pour châles et waterproofs	French for "straps to carry rain covers"
Cowham, Hilda	Doll designer
Cox, Palmer	Doll designer
Craft doll	Produced by a local cottage industry or crafts guild
Cravaches	French for "horse whip"
Crazing	Fine lines that appear over time on a painted or glazed surface as a result of changes in temperature, especially noticeable on composition
Crees, Paul	Doll designer
Crepe paper dolls costumes	Dennison Manufacturing Co.
Cromien, Blanche Rowe	Designed and manufactured doll clothing
Crosby, Persy	Doll designer
Crown	Topmost part of the head, usually cut open
Cry box	Source of sound in a talking or mama doll may be generated by bellows, reeds, or other means (one manufacturer lists wolves' teeth as being the origin of sounds) operated by pulling strings, pressing the body, moving the doll or one of its limbs
Culin, Alice	Doll designer
Cup and saucer	Neck cut, shoulder piece to accommodate flat cutting
Cymbaler, also spelled *Cymbalier*	Dolls that move by a pressure/bellow mechanism
D E P	Initials—which stand for *deponiert*—used both French and German dolls with a mold number indicating a claim to registration
D. E. P.	A claim to registration
D. G. M. Sch.	Initials—which stand for *Deutsche Gebrauchs MusterSchutz*—used to claim registration on German doll bodies.

D. R. G. M.. . . . . German marking indicating a registered design, often this mark—which stands for *Deutsches Reich Gebrauchs Muster*— hints that the registered mold number includes a novelty or a combination of special invention on a doll. Known as a "little patent."

D. R. M. R.. . . . . Initials—which stand for *Deutsche Reich Muster Rolle*—indicate protection of model, performance, and design of an object against fraud. Used on doll heads by Armand Marseille.

D. R. P.. . . . . Initials—which stand for *Deutsches Reichspatent*—used on German dolls to indicate a patent of the German Reich.

D. R. P. A.. . . . . Initials—which stand for *Deutsches Reich Zum Patent Angemeldet*—used on German dolls to indicate that a patent of the German Reich has been applied for.

Damier . . . . French for "Checker Board"

Das Deutsche Kind . . . . German for "the German child"

Das Lachende Baby . . . . German for "the laughing baby"

Das Lebende Baby . . . . German for "the living baby"

Das Süsse Trudelchen. German for "sweet little Gertrude"

Davis Milling Co. . . . . Printed lithograph cloth dolls including Aunt Jemima, Uncle Moses, Wade Davis, and Diana dolls

De Carlégle . . . . Produced dolls

De Carlo. . . . . Doll designer

De Felice, Mlle, Marguerite . . . . Created dolls, some from kid

De Fontenay, Mme. Adam . . . . Awarded honorable mention for her dolls at the 1878 Paris Exposition

De Jaham, G.. . . . . Crafted cloth dolls specializing in black characters

De Kasparek, Mme. Jeanne . . . . Made art dolls

De la Boulaye . . . . French sculptor of clay and wax

De Luxe Manufacturing Co.. . . . . U.S. Manufacturer of doll shoes

De Rochefort. . . . . Produced dolls

De Veriane, Mlle. Renée. . . . . Produced dolls

Decalcomania Decorations. . . . . The practice of applying eyebrows on bisque dolls by way of decals after the first firing

DeFilippo, Vincent. . . . . Doll designer

DeHetre, Terri. . . . . Doll designer

Dehler, Wilhelm. . . . . Produced dolls

Dehors, A. & Mme.. . . . . Produced dolls

Delasson . . . . Produced rubber dolls

Delhaye, Fréres . . . . Produced dolls

Dell & Co. . . . . Produced dolls—the sole agent for Gustav Föster

Deluxe Reading. . . . . A division of Deluxe Toys

Deluxe Topper. . . . . A division of Deluxe Toys

Deluxe Toy Creations . . . . A division of Deluxe Toys

Demalcol. . . . . acronym for Dennis Malley and Company

Démêloirs . . . . French for "large hair comb"

Demische, Anneliese. . . . . Designed doll clothing and trousseaux for dolls

Demische, Anneliese. . . . . Manufactured doll clothes

Dennison Manufacturing Co.. . . . . Manufactured crepe paper doll clothing

DeNunez, Marianne. . . . . Doll designer

Déposé . . . . Indicated a registration, used with regard to a trademark or design, occasionally abbreviated "Dep."

Der Kleine Bösewicht. German for "the little scamp"

Der Neue Mensch . . . . German for "the new man"

Der Unart . . . . German for "the naughty child"

Derdzakian, Eugenie	Made bodies and costumes for character dolls by Marie Marc-Schnür
Des Bas	French for "stockings"
Des Bottines	French for "boots"
Désirat	Designed historically accurate doll costumes
Deval, Brigette	Doll designer
Die Kleine Range	German for "the little tomboy"
Die Kokette	German for "the coquette"
Dirks, Rudolph	Doll designer
Dodge, Katherine	Doll designer
Doll artist	A doll maker, often by hand as one of a kind portraits, or someone who designs dolls for a commercial manufacturer
Doll face	Term used to describe a girl doll with a standardized sweet expression, also known as dolly face
Doll Jobber	The American version of a German Verleger, one who buys dolls from a factory and sells them to retailers, a type of wholesaler
Doll Pottery Co.	Doll distributor
Doll house dolls	Small dolls dressed as family members or domestic helpers
The Doll Shoppe	Sold custom-ordered dolls and doll costumes
Dolls that walk	Autoperipatetikos
Dolly Dimple cut-out dolls	Printed as cut-out dolls on Arkadelphia Milling Co. flour sacks
Dolly face	Typical child doll
Donahey, William	Doll designer
Doremus & Benzer	U.S. distributor of the Muncie Doll
Dorn, Max	U.S. factory agent for imported and domestic dolls also manufactured doll costumes
Doucet, Maison	Dressed historically accurate wax dolls
Drayton, Grace (Wiederseim)	Doll designer including the early Dolly Dingle for Averill Manufacturing Co., and Louis Amberg & Son
Drukker, Hazel	Doll designer including Mibs
Du Pont de Nemours, W. I & Co.	Made materials for doll production
Duborjal, J. & A.	Doll distributor
Dudovich	Doll designer
Dumas, Mme.	Produced French wax shoulder head dolls
Dymaob, A. C. Komcko Go.	Name found on bisque head that is probably Russian
E. I. H.	On a Horsman & Co. doll indicates that it was produced prior to 1922
Eagle Doll and Toy Co.	A member of Doll Parts Manufacturing Association
Eckart, C. F. & Co.	Produced dolls
Eckert	Doll designer
Eckhart, C. F. & Co.	Made dolls
Ed, Carl	Doll designer
Edel, Anton, Jr.	Doll distributor
Edgar & Co.	Imported dolls
Edinburgh Women's Emergency Corp.	A group of philanthropist that produced dolls
Edwardian style	Pertaining to the time period during the reign of Edward VII of England (1901-1910), the clothing is ornate with hourglass shaped dress and long fitted suits
Edwards, John Paul	Designed doll clothing
The Effanbee Lady	Internationally known entertainer who dressed in character costume and told children's stories as a way to promote Effanbee's dolls
The Effanbee Traveling Lady	Fan Fuerst, the Effanbee spokesperson

Effner, Dianna	Doll designer
Ehrendfeld, William	American doll manufacturing participant
Ehrich Bros.	Doll distributor
Eichhorn, Martin	Made and exported dolls
Einenkel, Brunhilde	Made art dolls
Eisen, Louis	An American manufacturer and importer of dolls, particularly from Paris
Eldridge, Charlotte	Doll designer
Ellenbrooke	Doll designer
Ellice, John Co.	Supplied cotton for doll stuffing
Embossed	Raised in relief from the surface, such a design, lettering or numbers in a doll marking
English Rag Dolls	Dolls distributed by Marshall Field
Epinglé à cheveux	French for "hairpins"
Ernst, Charles & Hermann	Sole U.S. distributor of Lenci dolls
Evans, Margaret	American children's artist that also designed cloth dolls
Éventails	French for "fans"
Excelsior	Name used by Kestner and distributed by Butler Brothers
Expert Doll & Toy Co.	Produced stuffed plush or velvet dolls
Eyebrows	Often applied with decals after the first firing of a bisque head on later dolls. Earlier examples have delicately feathered brows. French dolls tend to have heavy brows which almost meet over bridge of nose.
F. & M. Novelty Co.	Made doll eyes
F. A. O. Schwarz	United States toy store
Fabric Products Corp.	Produced dolls
Fabrication Feminine Française	Workshop to produce dolls
Fabrik bon Biskuitköpfe	German for "factory for bisque heads"
Fabrik von Puppenkopfen	German for "doll head factory"
Faded paint on composition	Touch up with face make-up (Max Factor works well)
Fair Trading Co.	Manufactured and distributed dolls
Fairy Moonbeam	Line of wax head dolls distributed by Lauer
Fairy Skin	Horsman & Co. (a synthetic rubber/early vinyl)
Fairy Tale dolls	Made by: Alexander; Amberg; American Wholesales; Arnold Print Works; Asiatic Import; Aston Drake; Averill Manufacturing Co.; Baker & Bennett; Bell & Francis; Bing; Brogfeldt; British Products; Butler Brothers; Buzza Co.; Callot; Chad Valley; Chase; Chessler; Colonial Toy; Davis; Dean; Anna Delay; Deptford Toy Co.; Eaton; Edinburgh Toys; Effanbee; Franklin Studio; Goodyear; Gorham; Grinnel Lithograph; Hanington; Harwin; Hawksley; Heizer; Horsman & Co.; Ideal; Indestructo Specialties; Jeanette Dolls; K & K Toy; Kellogg; Kleinert; Knight & Cooper; Käthe Kruse; Lafayette; Lenci; Marshall Field; Mawaphil; Meakin & Ridgeway; Carl Meyer; Mogridge; Montgomery Ward; Moore & Gibson; Nelke; Peggy Nesbit; New Toy Co.; Oweenee Novelty; Perrault; Printemps; Raleigh; Royal Crown Pottery; Saalfield; Schoenhut; F. A. O. Schwarz; Sears; Selchow & Righter; Shanklin; Siegel Copper; Silber & Fleming; Steiff; Strobel & Wilken; Sun Enamel; Toy Shop; Twinzy Toy; Twinjoy; Charles William; Robin Woods; Louis Wolf, among others
Fan Bush Co.	Manufactured cloth dolls
Fangel, Maud Tousey	Doll designer
Fashion Plate	Illustration depicting a style of clothing or stylish mode
Fashion-type doll	Poupée de Mode, lady doll with bisque head, adult body and dressed in fashionable attire

Term	Explanation
Fate Lade	Fortune telling doll
Feathered brows	Painted with many tiny strokes
Fédération du Jouet Français	Federation of French Toys
Federation of the Doll	English club for girls 10 to 15 years old; each girl given a doll to care for as a sister; meetings to discuss the problems of caregiving
Feiler, Carl & Co.	Manufactured German doll bodies both composition and kid and also doll accessories
Ferny, Alex	Produced art dolls with leather heads
Fiberoid	Term used by K & K for composition dolls
Fiegenbaum & Co.	Imported and distributed dolls
Finburgh, Samuel	Doll designer
Fired	Term used in the production of ceramic, such as bisque or china, meaning to heat in a kiln for the purpose of hardening or binding the pigment or glaze to its surface
First Year Girls	Children that made dolls at the Door of Hope Mission in Shanghai
Fisher, Ruth	Doll designer
Fitzpatrick, James	Made and imported dolls
Five-piece body	Composed of torso, arms and legs
Fixed eyes	Set in a stationary position
Flag printed doll body	Cloth doll bodies made with flags printed on them
Flanders, Harriet	Doll designer
Flange neck	Ridged with holes at the base for sewing onto a cloth doll body
Fleischmann and Blodel	Manufactured French automaton
Fleisher, Max	Doll designer
Flirty eyes	Side to side movement
Flocked hair	Head covered in short fibers glued directly onto head to represent hair
Flora McFlimsey	Generic name used for any doll that comes with a wardrobe of clothing
Florian, Gertrude	Doll designer
Floss	Soft loosely twisted silk or cotton thread used for embroidery, also a fluffy, fibrous thread like material used for doll wigs
Folk art	Objects created by self-taught, usually anonymous craft persons, characterized by its simplicity and charm
Folkmann, (Prof.) H.	Doll sculptor and wood carver
Fork hands	Stick-like fingers found on handcrafted dolls
Formes, tulle pour chapeaux	French for "forms and stands for hats"
Fort Seward Historical Society	Jamestown, ND
Fortune telling doll	Usually small lady dolls with skirts of folded, colored paper onto which a cliché or proverb was written
Frankel, G. & Son	Doll importer and jobber
Frankowska, Mlle.	Produced exceptional cloth dolls
Fraser, Helen	Doll designer
French, Fernel	Doll designer
French, James W.	Patented a hardening process enabling him to make doll heads from egg shells
Friedmann & Ohnstein	Made dollhouse dolls
Friedmann, Miss	Made leather dolls
Friendship Dolls	Name given to the 200,000 dolls sent from the children of America to the children of Japan in 1926-1927
Fritsch, Heinrich	Produced doll shoes and stockings
Frobenius, Lilian	Created dolls with Marion Kaulitz during the Puppen Reform Movement

Frozen Charlottes . . . . Glazed or unglazed bisque, solid one-piece body with distinctive bent arms, straight legs separated to knees, molded and painted hair and facial features, generally undressed and unmarked—occasionally marked "Germany" and with clothing, foot, or head wear

Fuerst, Fan . . . . Spokesperson known as "The Effanbee Lady"

Fürstenberg . . . . An early and important German porcelain factory

G. M. . . . . Initials—which stand for *Geschmacksmuster*—used on German dolls to indicate a patent to protect the intellectual integrity of a doll, including model, performance, and design

G. M. S. . . . . Often this German mark—which stands for *Gebrauchs Muster Schutz*—hints that the registered mold number includes a novelty or a combination of special inventions on a doll

Gaby . . . . Ventriloquist and probable doll designer

Galatoize . . . . Doll distributor

Gallais, P. J. & Cie . . . . Paris book distributor including the works of Poulbot and L'Oncle Hansi

Galluba & Hofmann . . . . German porcelain factory known to produce dolls

Gants peau et fil . . . . French for "leather gloves"

Gardet . . . . French doll sculptor

Gardet, M. . . . . Doll designer and sculptor

Gardin, Laura . . . . Doll designer

Gardner, A. J. . . . . Art doll distributor

Gargier, George . . . . Doll designer

Gaston & Alphonse . . . . French comic characters

Gay Stuffed Toy & Novelty Co. . . . . Made stuffed dolls

Gee, E. M. . . . . Designed doll costumes

Gentille Poupée . . . . French for "pretty doll"

Geradhals . . . . German for "straight neck"

German Export Service Bureau . . . . Obtained orders from American toy buyers

German Manufacturers Association . . . . U.S.-based organization representing more than fifty German toy manufacturers

Gerrard, Lucille . . . . Doll designer

Ges . . . . German marking indicating a registered design

Ginsburg & Wolfe . . . . Produced doll wigs, shoes, and other doll accessories

Giroux, Alphonse & Cie . . . . Member of S. F. B. J. that made dolls

Glaze . . . . Glass-like finish fired onto porcelain and pottery; the glossy surface of china head dolls

Glue spot . . . . The round painted area on top of a doll's head, assumed to indicate the placement of a wig, most often found on china head dolls

Glukin, William & Co. . . . . Produced mask faces for dolls with lithographed features

Gofun . . . . Fine oyster shell composition or paste, applied in thin layers and polished to a high shine, used in the production of Japanese dolls

Goldberg, I. A. & Son . . . . Produced British Ceramic head dolls with cloth bodies

Goldenberg, Benjamin . . . . Bought American Doll & Toy Co. and renamed it Aetna Doll & Toy Co.

Goldfoot & Sayer, LTD . . . . Produced and imported dolls and toys

Goldman, Meyer . . . . Designed and manufactured doll costumes using the trade name Molly-'es

Goldsmith, Philip . . . . Doll designer

Golliwogg	While the British occupied Alexandria, Egypt, during the late 1800s, the natives were known as Ghuls. The Ghuls wore arm bands bearing the letters *W. O. G. S.* ("Working On Government Service"). Thus the nickname Golliwogs was given. When Florence Upton wrote her well-known children's books about the Golliwoggs, she added the second *g*.
Goo Goo	Another term meaning "googly eyes"
Goodnow, June	Doll designer
Googly Eyes	Large round eyes looking to the side
Graefe, Otto	Imported Minerva and Knockabout dolls
Grand Doll Manufacturing Co.	Manufactured dolls
Gray & Dudley Co.	Doll distributor
Gray, Harold	Doll designer
Gray, Jane, Co. (also spelled *Grey*)	Designed and produced cloth body dolls including Kuddles
Graziana, Adolph	Doll designer
Green Ears on some vinyl	Removed with a drop of Tarn-X followed by a cleaning with baking soda
Green, J.	Doll designer
Grillet, Albert	Produced celluloid toys, including dolls such as Poupé Grillet
Gross, Milt	Doll designer
Grows hair by turning button on body	Tressy, by American Character, also a knockoff by Eegee
Gruber, Clemsen	Listed as King of the Dolls in a 1907 Austrian directory, a title often given to Kestner
Guilbert, Pauline	Doll designer
Guild, Doll Artisan	35 Main St., Oneonta NY 13820
Gumery	Doll designer
Gumery, M.	Doll sculptor
Gummi und Celluloidfabrik	German for "rubber and celluloid factory"
Gummipuppen und Spielzeug	German for "dolls and toys of rubber"
Gusset	An insert in the shape of a diamond or a triangle, used for strength and to allow movement, most often used in kid bodies
Gutsell, Ida	Doll designer
Gutta Percha	Literal Malaysian translation is "gum tree," but the term used in doll collecting refers to various materials used to make dolls. In 1878, the Queen suggested that rubber—which could be pressed to squeak—be called Gutta Percha. The term is also used to describe the coating on early wooden dolls.
Hair twist on the top of his head	Signature of Snookums doll by Averill Manufacturing Co.
Half doll	China or bisque figure consisting of upper torso and head molded as one piece; was made to be incorporated onto useful objects, such as table crumb brushes or pincushions.
Hallett, William	Produced composition and leather dolls
Hamac	French for "hammock"
Handler, Elliot	President of Mattel, Inc. during the introduction of Barbie
Handler, Ruth	Doll designer, including Barbie
Hansi	Name of Haralit head portrait doll designed by Herr Kaiser to represent the daughter of Max Zetzsche (do not confuse with Gretel and Yerri designed by L'Oncle Hansi)

Hansi, L'Oncle	Illustrator of the characters Yerri and Gretel that were later made into dolls made of Prialytine
Hard Plastic	Material used after 1948 facilitating fine molding impressions and good color
Harder & Schöler	Manufactured and exported dolls
Harold	Name of Haralit head portrait doll designed by Herr Kaiser to represent the son of Max Zetzsche
Harris Raincoat Co.	Manufactured the doll clothing distributed by Regal
Harvard Toy Works	Manufactured cloth dolls
Harwin	Doll designer
Hassall, John	Doll designer
Heavy Brows	Usually an indication of a French doll
Heizer, Dorothy	Doll designer—also designed historically accurate doll costumes
Hellé, André	Doll designer
Hering, F. & Co.	Made porcelain doll heads
Herman, L.	Produced Mama dolls with Voices, Inc. voice boxes
Herrmann, Carl	Produced dolls and doll parts
Hertzog	German distributor of dolls
Herzkäferchen	German for "heart beetle"
Heyer, Brothers	Imported and distributed dressed dolls
Hilda Cowham Kiddies	Line of dolls designed by Hilda Cowham and produced by Dean
Hiller, Robert	Produced doll bodies
Himstedt, Annette	Doll designer
Hina Matsuri	Girls' Day Festival celebrated on March 3
Hina-Ningyo	Japanese for "festival doll"
Historical Character Dolls of Destiny including: Queen Victoria, Mary Todd Lincoln, Priscilla Alden, Polly Pitcher, Empress Eugenia, Queen Isabella, Empress Josephine, Marie Antoinette, Betsy Ross, Martha Washington, Queen Elizabeth I, Elizabeth Woodville Grey (names listed in advertising are not necessarily registered names of company)	A&H
Historical Society of Pennsylvania	Philadelphia, PA
Historical Society of Tarrytown	Tarrytown, NY
Hitz, Monroe, & Co.	Distributed Goldberger dolls; also, factory agent for the Happi-Kiddie dolls
Höllental	Black Forest
Hopf, Vern	Sales manager for Georgene Novelties
Hopf, A. C.	U.S. representative for Averill Manufacturing Co., Nelke and Knickerbocker
Hopf, Ruby	Arranbee Doll Co.'s head designer and sister of Georgene Hopf Averill
Horsman, E. I.	Founder of Horsman & Co.
Houghton, Elizabeth E.	Doll designer who created Baby Ann
Humpty Dumpty Doll Hospital	Owned and operated by Emma Clear
Hygrade Cut Fabric Co.	Manufactured doll costumes
Ichimatsu	Japanese for "children's play doll"
Illfelder, Leopold	Patented metal dolls
Impersonating Doll Co.	Produced dolls
Incised	Engraved or carved into the surface, such as a trademark, mold number, or name in a doll marking

Industrial Art Schools	European and American schools of vocation that trained designers and craftsmen, many of whom joined the doll profession
Inflation in Germany	In October 1923, two billion marks were valued at 50¢; before 1914, one mark was worth 25¢.
Inge	Haralit head portrait doll designed by Herr Kaiser
Insam & Prinoth	Wooden doll verleger
Intaglio eyes	Sunken, rather than cut, eyes that are then painted
International Doll Makers Association	3364 Pine Creek Dr., San Jose, CA 95132
International Toy Co.	Made wooden dolls
Italian dolls in 1928	To be made with long hair under an edict issued by Mussolini "All dolls made in this country (Italy) are to have long hair"
Jacob, Son & Co.	English agent for Hungarian rubber (Ungarische Gummiwaren-Fabrik) dolls
Japanese Boys' Day Festival	Part of the Japanese cult of chivalry; symbolized bravery and loyalty to country and emperor
Japanese Girls' Day Festival	Part of the Japanese cult of chivalry; symbolized domesticity and loyalty to country and emperor
Jarretières	French for "garters"
Je dors	French for "I sleep"
Je marche	French for "I walk"
Je marche, Je parle, J'envoi des baisers	French for "I walk, I speak I throw kisses"
Je parle	French for "I speak"
Je suis tout en bois	French for "I am all wood"
Jedrek	French doll sculptor
Jeu de loto	French for "loto game"
Jeu de nain-jaune	A miniature card game
Jiggs & Maggie	Cartoon characters illustrated by George McManus
Jobber	The American version of a German Verleger, one who buys dolls from a factory and sells them to retailers, a type of wholesaler
Johnson, G. R.	Imported dolls and doll parts
Jolls, Connie	Doll designer
Jordan, Jeanne	Doll designer
Jordan, Kate	Doll commercial artist and doll designer
Jouets Artistique Français	Workshop in which disabled World War I soldiers made dolls
Joy Doll Corp.	Made composition dolls
Joyland Toy Manufacturing Co.	Made dolls
Judge, Edward	Produced papier-mâché doll heads
Juszko, Jeno	Doll designer
Kachina	Hopi or other Pueblo Indian doll representing a religious spirit, often displayed with elaborate mask
Kahn & Mossbacher	Manufactured doll clothing
Kahn, M. L.	Designed doll clothing, specializing in mama dolls
Kallus, Joseph	Designer of many famous dolls, including Baby Adele, Baby Blossom, Baby Bo Kaye
Kamlish & Cass A K A, Kamlish, J. & Co.	Made British Ceramic dolls
Kämmer, Ernst	Doll designer
Kane, Maggie Head	Doll designer
Kapok	Silky fiber from the seed pod of the ceiba tree used as stuffing in cloth dolls, also known as silk cotton
Kato Kiyomasa	Japanese warrior
Kaufhauskonzern	German for "chain of department stores"
Kaufman, I. & Son	Manufactured doll stockings
Kaufman, Levenson & Co.	Doll distributor

Kaybee Doll & Toy Co. . . . . Made composition dolls including carnival dolls
Keller Toy Manufacturing Co. . . . . Manufactured doll costumes
Kelvedon Village Industry . . . . Cottage industry crafting character dolls
Kerhof. . . . . Doll designer
Kid body. . . . . Doll body made of leather
Kilenyi, Julio . . . . Doll designer
Kindertraum . . . . German for "child's dream"
King Features Syndicate . . . . Cartoon affiliation and doll designer
King of The Dolls . . . . 1907 Austrian directory lists Clemsen Gruber as "King
 of the Dolls"—a title often given to Kestner
King, Frank. . . . . Doll designer
King, Frank O. . . . . Doll designer
Klauppaugen . . . . German for "tip-up eyes"
Kleiner Schlingel . . . . German for "my little rascal"
Kleiner Spatz. . . . . German for "little sparrow"
Kleinpuppenfabrik. . . . . German for "factory for miniature dolls"
Kluge, John Ernst . . . . Wholesale distributor of moderately priced dolls
Knoll, Carl A. K. A., Karlsbaden Porzellanfabrik . . . . . . Manufactured bisque heads and supplied slip to other
 German companies
Koerling, Cyndy . . . . Doll designer
Koliski, W. . . . . Horsman & Co.'s Chief Engineer
Kollin, Mrs. Berry . . . . Doll designer
Könglich Bayerische Porzellan Manufaktur. . . . . German for "Royal Bavarian Porcelain Manufactory"
Königskinder. . . . . German for "the royal children"
Kovar's Inc. . . . . Czechoslovakian hand-carved and painted doll
 distributor
Kramer, Muriel . . . . Doll designer
Krausser, Karl . . . . Doll designer
Kreis, Wilhelm. . . . . Designed art dolls
Kreis, Wilhelm. . . . . Doll designer
Kringle Society Dolls and Kringle Tots . . . . Name used by Marshall Field when advertising dolls
 and toys
Krohn, Alexandre . . . . Designed doll costumes
Kubelka, Joseph. . . . . Proprietor of the Zur Puppendoktorim
Kühn, Ernst. . . . . Manufactured and exported dolls
Kunstgewerbliches Atelier . . . . German for "arts and crafts studio"
Künstlerpuppe . . . . German for "art dolls"
Kunstmaler . . . . German for "artist" and "painter"
Kurbelkopf . . . . German for "socket head"
Küss mich . . . . German for "kiss me"
L'Arlequin. . . . . Produced novelty-type dolls
L'Association de Petits Fabricants. . . . . Organization for master porcelain factories to
 manufacture bisque doll heads
La Bérgére de Trianon . . . . Inscription used by Sévres
La Semaine de Suzette . . . . Weekly publication that included articles about dolls and
 information about Bleuette and Bambino wardrobe.
 Also, introduced Bécassine, and distributed dolls by
 S. F. B. J.—and printed clothing patterns for them.
Labrador Dolls . . . . Handcrafted wooden dolls made by the Alaskan natives
Lacmann, Jacob. . . . . Patented a procedure to produce doll hands and feet
 with a composition base covered in cotton fabric
Lady doll. . . . . Adult face and body proportions
Lafayette Galeries . . . . Large Paris department store
Lafitte, Mme. . . . . Designed historically accurate doll costumes
Lambert . . . . Manufactured French automaton
Lamp Studio . . . . Made cloth dolls

| --- | --- |
Lancelin	Manufactured leather doll shoes, gloves, and accessories from scrap leather
Landolt, Dr.	Carved wooden dolls
Lange, Erben G.	Crafted wooden dolls
Langfelder, Homma & Hayward	New York City import business for Morimura Brothers
Lathe turning.	Method used to shape wood by applying a chisel while it rotates on a lathe
Le Sueur, Sadie P.	Designed doll costumes
Le Vie Femmes	French organization for widows and wounded soldiers to produce doll bodies and clothing
Leinwandgestelle	German for "cloth bodies"
Lejeune Louis-Aimé	Doll designer
Leonhardt, Paul	Produced dolls
Leonia Doll Co.	Produced and distributed dolls
Lepape, M. and Mme George.	Illustrators and doll designers
Lerch, Philip	Produced papier-mâché doll heads
Lesser, Elizabeth	Designed and created dolls
Letitia Penn Doll	A small wooden doll of the Georgian type. The following is the well-loved story of the doll: It began as a gift from William Penn's daughter, Letitia, to Miss Rankin of Philadelphia. Then, from Miss Rankin, the doll traveled to Mrs. Prior. From there, to Anne Massey Brown, and then to the Kirk family—first to Mary, followed by her son, Mahlon. Letitia the doll soon found her way into the possesion of Izole Dorgan before taking a prominent place in the well-known collection of Imogene Anderson, and now resides at the Historical Society of Pennsylvania on Locust Street. (The early history, however, is not accepted as being accurate—the Letitia Penn doll dates from about 1730, rather than the 1699 arrival time in the original tale.)
Libby Doll & Novelty Co.	Manufactured cloth and composition dolls
Ligue de Jouet Français	League formed to produce dolls for children and to give work to women after World War I
Lindner, Johann Simon.	Head of an important German doll Verleger family, accredited with introducing the Täufling to the Sonneberg region
L'Intrepide Bébé	Generic term used for a mechanical walking doll
Lioret, Henri	Invented the phonograph used in the Bébé Phonographe by Jumeau
Lipfert, Bernard	Doll designer—who created Patsy, Shirley Temple, the Dionne Quints, and Baby Dimples
Livre de messe	French for "Book of Mass"
Lloyd & Magnus Co.	Doll distributor
Louisville Doll & Novelty Manufacturing Co.	Produced dolls
Louvre	Exclusive Paris store
Ludlow Guild of Toymakers.	Produced baby and Eskimo dolls
Lunettes, lorgnons, binocles	French for "eyeglasses, lorgnette, opera glasses"
Luster	Delicate pink or metallic color applied to glazed porcelain
Maba	A German doll
Magic skin	Rubbery synthetic material used in the manufacturing of dolls; ages poorly, becoming dark and deteriorating in time
Maler und Gestalter.	German for "painter and designer"
Malles pour poupée	French for "trunk for doll"

Malles pour trousseaux . . . . French for "trunk for trousseau"

Mallet, Beatrice . . . . Doll designer

Mama dolls . . . . Made by: Acme Toy; Alexander; Amberg; American Character; Arcy Toys; Atlas; Atlantic Toy; Averill; Baby Phyllis; Bing; Brückner; Brogfeldt; Butler Brothers; Century; Chessler; Cohen & Son; Davis & Voetsch; Domec; Effanbee; Fleisher Toy; European Doll Manufacture; Gem,Goldberger; Goodyear Toy; Herman; Hermann; Hitz, Jacobs & Kassler; Hoest & Henderson; Horsman & Co.; Ideal; Jeanette Doll Co.; Kämmer & Reinhardt; Kampes; Katagini Brothers; Kletzin; Löffler & Dill; Louisville Doll; Metropolitan Doll; Modern Doll Co.; Modern Toy Co.; Montgomery Ward National Doll Co.; Nibur Novelty Co.; Original Doll Co.; Paramount Doll Co.; Penn Stuffed Toy; Perfect Toy Manufacturing; Pollyanna; Pressner; Primrose; R. B. & L. Manufacturing; Regal Doll Co.; Reisman; S. & S. Doll Co.; Sears; Self Sell Doll Co.; Shaw Doll Co.; Schoenhut; Star Doll & Toy Co.; Supplee-Biddle; Toy Shop; Uneeda Doll Co.; Well Made Doll Co.; Williams; Louis Wolf & Co.

Mammie Wise's baby . . . . Baby Wise (doll produced by Horsman & Co.)

Mangiapani, Julius. . . . . Doll designer

Manhattan Doll Co. . . . . Importer of dolls and a jobber

Manifatture Aritistiche . . . . Produced art dolls

Manikin . . . . Name given to miniature male figures or dolls, such as the Schoenhut wooden male dolls

Manson, Mme. . . . . Doll designer

Marc-Schnür, Marie. . . . . Principal doll designer for Marion Kaulitz dolls

Marion Kaulitz . . . . Instigated the Puppen Reform in 1908 by introducing her character dolls at the toy fair in Munich

Marotte. . . . . Doll on a stick

Marque, Albert . . . . Doll designer

Mask face . . . . Stiff face that covers only the front of the head

Masterller, Janet . . . . Doll designer

Mattel, Inc. . . . . World's largest toy manufacturer

Max and Moritz . . . . Two bad boys drawn by Wilhelm Busch for a book first translated into English in 1870

McAboy, Mary . . . . Doll designer

McCay, Winson. . . . . Doll designer

McClure, Cindy. . . . . Doll designer

McMahan, Valerie. . . . . Doll designer

McManus, George. . . . . Doll designer

Mechano. . . . . Produced metal dolls

Medaille D'or . . . . Indicates French medal won by Jumeau in 1878; therefore, could not appear on a doll made before that date. Similar award won in 1889 by Jules Nicholas Steiner also included in his marking after that date.

Médaillon . . . . French for "locket"

Mein Augenstern. . . . . German for "star of my eye"

Mein Dicker Kleiner Liebling . . . . German for "my fat little darling"

Mein Einzige . . . . German for "my only one"

Mein Glückskind. . . . . German for "my lucky child"

Mein Goldperle . . . . German for "my gold pearl"

Mein Kleiner Schlingel . . . . German for "my little scallywag"

Mein Kleines . . . . German for "my little one"

Mein Liebes Kind . . . . German for "my dear child"

Mein Liebling	German for my darling"
Mein Lieblingsbaby	German for "my darling baby"
Mein Neuer Einziger Liebling	German for "my new unique darling"
Mein Rosiger Liebling	German for "my Rosy darling"
Mein Sonnenschein	German for "my sunshine"
Mein Stern	German for "my star"
Mein Stolz	German for "my pride"
Mein Süsser Liebling	German for "my sweet darling"
Mercié, Antonin	Doll designer
Messick, Dale	Created the Brenda Starr character that inspired the doll of the same name
Metallpuppenkopfen	German for "metal doll heads"
Metropolitan Toy & Doll Co.	Produced dolls and doll clothing
Meyers, Gladys	Designed doll costumes
Michtom, Morris	Founder of Ideal Novelty and Toy Co.
Mignonnettes (also spelled *Mignonettes*)	Name applied to small doll (up to 14 inches) usually associated with French dolls, but occasionally was used elsewhere
Miller Rubber Co.	Manufactured sponge rubber dolls
Mint condition	Term used to describe a doll, cloth, or accessories in a perfect state
Mint in the box	Term used to describe a doll that is retained in its original box, with all the accessories
Miracle Hair	Horsman & Co.
Model Doll Co.	Produced moderately priced dolls
Model Doll Manufacturing Co.	Manufactured cloth-bodied dolls
Model Patent Washable Dolls	Type of doll with early composition head and arms on a cloth body
Modelleur und Fabrikant	German for "sculptor and factory owner"
Modern Doll Co.	Manufactured dolls, including mama and sleeping type
Mohair wig	Made of very fine goat hair
Mold	The hollow form into which porcelain slip, melted wax, composition, or other liquid material is poured; or a paste is pressed into—in order to shape a head or limbs of a doll
Mold number	Impressed or embossed number that indicates a particular design
Molded features	Any feature such as hair, clothes, or facial contours that are formed when material is poured or pressed into a doll mold
Moll, Johann	Appointed Hertwig & Co to manufacture Snow Babies
Monotaro	Japanese warrior
Montres avec chaîne	French for "watch and chain"
Moore, H. A. & Co.	Distributed American Character and Effanbee dolls
Morf, Erika	Patented metal doll heads
Morgenthaler, Sasha	Doll designer
Moroi, Kazue	Doll designer
Moss, Leo	Designed and crafted black portrait dolls of papier-mâché
Motschmann, Charles	Manufactured early voice boxes
Motter, Jennifer Berry	Doll designer
Moufle	French for "mittens"
Multi-faced	A single revolving head having two or more faces that can be changed by rotating a knob
Multi-head	Two or more interchangeable socket-type heads, a screw usually facilitates the change
Museum of Antique Dolls	Savannah, GA

Museum, Playhouse Dolls and Toys . . . . Las Cruces, NM
Museum, Adirondack Center . . . . Elizabethtown, NY
Museum, Aunt Len's Doll House . . . . New York, NY
Museum, Boothbay Railway . . . . Boothbay, ME
Museum, Buccleuch Mansion . . . . New Brunswick, NJ
Museum, Burt County . . . . Tekamah, NE
Museum, Chattanooga . . . . Chattanooga, TN
Museum, Children's . . . . Detroit, MI
Museum, Doll Castle Doll Museum . . . . Washington, NJ
Museum, Eliza Cruce Hall Doll . . . . Ardmore, OK
Museum, Enchanted World Doll . . . . Mitchell, SD
Museum, Eugene Field House & Toy . . . . St. Louis, MO
Museum, Frank's Antique Doll . . . . Marshall, TX
Museum, Gadsden . . . . Mesilla, NM
Museum, Gay Nineties Button and Doll . . . . Eureka Springs, AR
Museum, Geuther Doll . . . . Eureka Springs, AR
Museum, Hobby City Doll and Toy . . . . Anaheim, CA
Museum, House Of A Thousand Dolls . . . . Loma, MT
Museum, Margaret Woodbury Strong . . . . Rochester, NY
Museum, Mary Miller Doll . . . . Brunswick, GA
Museum, McCurdy's Historical Doll . . . . Provo, UT
Museum, National American History . . . . Washington, DC
Museum, Old Brown House Doll . . . . Gothenburg, NE
Museum, Old Fort . . . . Fort Smith, AZ
Museum, Prairie Art & History . . . . Colby, KS
Museum, Raggedy Ann Antique Doll & Toy . . . . Flemington, NY
Museum, Rosalie Whyel of Doll Art . . . . Bellevue, WA
Museum, South Carolina Antique Toy . . . . Pendleton, SC
Museum, The Doll . . . . Newport, RI
Museum, The Mary Merritt Doll . . . . Douglasville, PA
Museum, The Strong . . . . Rochester, NY
Museum, Town of Yorktown . . . . Yorktown Heights, NY
Museum, Toy & Miniature of Kansas City . . . . Kansas City, MO
Museum, Victorian Doll . . . . North Chilli, NY
Museum, Washington Doll's House and Toy . . . . Washington, DC
Museum, Yesteryears . . . . Sandwich, MA
Mutt & Jeff . . . . Cartoon characters
N G . . . . Used by Theodor Recknagel, these initials stand for
                                               Neugeborenes—German for "newborn."
Nachf . . . . Abbreviation for "successor," in German
Nachfolger . . . . German for "successor"
National Doll Co. . . . . Produced mama dolls
National Institute of American Doll Artists . . . . 303 Riley St., Falls Church, VA 22046
National Organization of Miniaturists and Dollers . . . . . 1300 Schroder St., Normal, IL 61761
Nécéssaires de toilette . . . . French for "toiletries"
Nelson, Bill . . . . Doll designer
Neugeborenes . . . . German for "newborn"
New England Doll Co. . . . . A. K. A. American Tissue Mills
New York Historical Society . . . . New York, NY
Nicole, Maryse . . . . Doll designer
Noufflard, Berthe . . . . Doll designer
Novelty Doll Manufacturing Co. . . . . Produced dolls and doll parts
Nürnberger Kunstlerpuppen und
   Stoffspielwarenfabrik . . . . German for the "Nürnberg Art Doll and Cloth Toy
                                              Factory"—which produced art dolls

Bits of Information	Explanation
Nursery Rhyme dolls	Made by: Alexander; Amberg; American Wholesales; Arnold Print Works; Asiatic Import; Aston Drake; Averill; Baker & Bennett; Bell & Francis; Bing; Brogfeldt; British Products; Butler Brothers; Buzza Co.; Callot; Chad Valley; Chase; Chessler; Colonial Toy; Davis; Dean; Anna Delay; Deptford Toy Co.; Eaton; Edinburgh Toys; Effanbee; Franklin Studio; Goodyear; Gorham; Grinnel Lithograph; Hanington; Harwin; Hawksley; Heizer; Horsman & Co.; Ideal; Indestructo Specialties; Jeanette Dolls; K & K Toy; Kellogg; Kleinert; Knight & Cooper; Käthe Kruse; Lafayette; Lenci; Marshall Field; Mawaphil; Meakin & Ridgeway; Carl Meyer; Mogridge; Montgomery Ward; Moore & Gibson; Nelke; Peggy Nesbit; New Toy Co.; Oweenee Novelty; Perrault; Printemps; Raleigh; Royal Crown Pottery; Saalfield; Schoenhut; F. A. O. Schwarz; Sears; Selchow & Righter; Shanklin; Siegel Copper; Silber & Fleming; Steiff; Strobel & Wilken; Sun Enamel; Toy Shop; Twinzy Toy; Twinjoy; Charles William; Robin Woods; Louis Wolf, among others
Nussle, Gottlieb	Doll designer
Odom, Mel	Doll designer
Oil, or not to oil, the eyes	Preferably avoid
Oldenburg, Mary Ann	Doll designer
Ombrelles et parasol	French for "umbrellas and parasols"
Ondine	Name associated with swimming doll
Open mouth	Lips parted with opening cut into the mold or head; teeth usually show
Open/closed mouth	Mouth molded to appear to be open, but no opening cut into the mold or head
Oppenheimer, Maurice F.	Doll designer
Oriental dolls	Made by Alexander; Arnold Print Works; Averill Manufacturing Co.; Bähr & Pröschild; Brogfeldt; Butler Brothers; Cissna; Door of Hope; Eaton; Effanbee; Gamage; Gerzon; Hamley; Hitz; Horsman & Co.; Irwin Smith; Jacobs & Kassler; Jumeau; Kestner; Liberty; Live Long Toys; Armand Marseille; Marshall Field; Montgomery Wards; Morimura Brothers; Oakhurst; Poppy Dolls; Scantlebury; Schoenau & Hoffmeister; Schoenhut; R. Schrott; Schwerdtmann; Shackman; Simon & Halbig; Bruno Schmitt; and Steiff, among others
Original Doll Artists Council of America	21 Hitherbrook Rd., St. James, NY 11780
Orsini, Jeanne	Doll designer
Országos Magyar Háziipari Szövetség	Hungarian for "National Hungarian House Industry League." Produced dolls in Hungarian regional costumes.
Osmond, Marie	Entertainer and doll designer
Otto, Rudolf	Manufactured composition dolls and parts
Outcault, Richard	Doll designer
Owens-Kreiser Co.	Distributor for various American doll manufacturers
Pache & Son	Produced "True to Nature" doll eyes
Painted bisque	Final firing is eliminated, causing the color of the paint to be brighter, but easily rubbed off
Pale bisque	Early (before 1890), either French or German
Paniers de voyage	French for "baskets for travel"
Pantoufles	French for "slippers"

Paperweight eyes	Blown glass eyes with an added crystal to the top resulting in a look with depth and greater realism
Papeterie	French for "stationery"
Papier-mâché	Material made of paper pulp, glue, and perhaps chalk, sand, or other substances that, once molded and dried, becomes a hard substance
Papiermache Fabrik	German for "papier-mâché factory"
Parian	Term used to describe a doll made of untinted bisque
Parisienne	Generic term used for dolls from Paris
Park, Irma	Doll designer
Parker, Ann	Doll designer
Parker, Mary L.	Doll designer
Pate	Covering for the opening at the top of the doll head, may be of cardboard, cork or plaster
Patent	Government grant to an inventor for the exclusive right to make, sell, or use his invention for a specified time
Patent date	Date on which a patent is issued to an inventor for a new or an improved product or process. May be included in a doll marking
Patent Novelty Co.	Manufactured articulated, wooden segmented dolls
Patentpuppen Manufaktur	German for "factory for dolls with patents"
Patina	A desirable mellow and worn finish that a surface acquires after aging
Pauvre Jacques	Paris store
Peddler doll	Popular dolls of the nineteenth century, particularly in England, portrays a vendor or peddler with trays or baskets filled with wares
Peignes à chigons	French for "combs with trim"
Periodical, *Antique Doll Collector*	6 Woodside Ave., Suite 300, Northport, NY
Periodical, *Antique Trader Weekly*	P. O. Box 1050, Dubuque, IA
Periodical, *Baby Boomer Collectibles*	P. O. Box 1050, Dubuque, IA
Periodical, *Barbie Bazaar*	5617 6th Ave., Kenosha, WI
Periodical, *Barbie Fashions*	387 Park Ave. South, New York, NY
Periodical, *Barbie Talks Some More*	19 Jamestown Dr., Cincinnati, OH
Periodical, *Chatter Box News*	22 Ryan St., West Islip, NY
Periodical, *Collectible Toys & Values*	15 Danbury Rd., Ridgefield, CT
Periodical, *Collector Magazine & Price Guide*	P. O. Box 1050, Dubuque, IA
Periodical, *Collector's Corner*	519 Fitztooth Dr., Mianisburg, OH
Periodical, *Contemporary Doll Magazine*	30595 Eight Mile Rd., Livonia, MI
Periodical, *Costume Quarterly for Doll Collectors*	118-01 Sutter Ave., Jamaica, NY
Periodical, *Doll Castle News Doll Directory*	P. O. Box 247, Washington, NJ
Periodical, *Doll Life*	243 Newton Sparta Rd., Newton, NY
Periodical, *Doll Reader*	6405 Flank Dr., Harrisburg, PA
Periodical, *Doll Times*	218 W. Woodin Blvd., Dallas, TX
Periodical, *Doll World*	306 E. Parr Rd., Berne, IN
Periodical, *Dolls, The Collector's Magazine*	170 Fifth Ave. 12th Floor, New York, NY
Periodical, *Fabric of Life*	P. O. Box 1212, Bellevue, WA
Periodical, *National Doll & Teddy Bear Collector*	P. O. Box 4032, Portland, OR
Periodical, *Playthings*	51 Madison Ave., New York, NY
Periodical, *Rags*	P. O. Box 823, Atlanta, GA
Periodical, *The Cloth Doll Magazine*	P. O. Box 1089, Mr. Shasta, CA
Periodical, *The Dollmasters*	P. O. Box 151, Annapolis, MD
Periodical, *Toy Trader*	P. O. Box 1050, Dubuque, IA
Perruque	French for "wig"
Personality dolls	Molded and fashioned to resemble a famous person
Peruggi, Ernesto	Designed and modeled dolls
Pet Names	Agnes, Bertha, Daisy, Dorothy, Edith, Esther, Ethel, Florence, Helen, Mabel, Marion, Pauline, and Ruth

Phalibois	Manufactured French automaton
Phillips, Mary Waterman	Doll designer
Phonograph dolls	Early talking dolls
Pied ou support pour la poupée	French for "vintage doll stand"
Pierced ears	Holes in doll's ear lobes for earrings
Pierced in ears	Holes in doll's ear lobes—and head—for earrings
Pinner, Erna	Doll designer
Plotnick, Frank, Co	Manufactured cloth dolls
Plumb, Charlie	Co-creator of the cartoon character Ella Cinders which was the inspiration for the doll by the same name
Polizer, Morris	Doll costume designer
Pollack & Hoffmann	Produced porcelain dolls
Poppets	Name given to wooden handcrafted dolls from the Kentucky mountains
Porcelain	A hard, nonporous ceramic material, usually translucent
Portrait doll	Modeled after a real or recognizable individual, such as Grace Kelly—or unknown, such as a sculptor's child
Porzellanfabrik	German for "porcelain factory"
Poulbot	Doll designer
Poupée de Mode	French for "doll of fashion"
Poupon	French for "infant doll"
Poured bisque	Later method used in the production of bisque dolls where the slip is a liquid and can be poured into the molds. (Germany after 1870s, France after 1890s)
Poured wax	Head or limbs made from wax that is poured into a mold to produce a doll
Pouty	Closed-mouth doll with a solemn or petulant expression
Pressed Bisque	Early method used in the production of bisque dolls where the slip is rolled into thin sheets and hand-pressed into the molds (Germany until mid-1870s; France until early 1890s)
Pressman, J. & Co.	Produced composition dolls with wooden limbs
Preston, Chloe	Doll designer
Pretz, Florence	Doll designer including the Billiken doll
Printemps	Paris store that distributed dolls
Probik	Doll designer
Provenance	The history of a doll or other art object, including its origin, a record of ownership, and any relevant information
Pug or pugged nose	Small button, slightly turned-up nose
Pull strings	Cords or strings used to operate an apparatus concealed within a doll
Pulliche, Mme	Designed historically accurate doll costumes
Puppen	German for "doll"
Puppen Reform of 1908	Movement which brought character dolls into the marketplace and gave added impetus to the German doll industry.
Puppenbalg Fabrik	German for "factory for doll bodies"
Puppenfabrik	German for "doll factory"
Puppenfabrik Export and Engros	German for "factory for exporting and wholesaling dolls"
Puppengeschäft	German for "doll shop"
Quigley, Juanita	Birth name for childhood star Baby Jane
Rabaut, Louis	Wholesale distributor of dolls
Racker	German for "rogue"
Racone Manufacturing Co.	Manufactured a mechanism to enable a doll to clap its hands

Rainwater, William . . . . Manufactured dolls
Raleigh, Jessie . . . . Doll designer
Ray, Jean. . . . . Doll designer
Red Corset printed on body . . . . Philip Goldsmith doll
Redmond, Kathy . . . . Doll designer
Reflex eyes, able to look in several directions . . . . Patented by Seyfarth & Reinhardt
Regional costume. . . . . Traditional outfit worn in specific region or country
Reinhardt, Ernst . . . . Doll designer
Reismann, Franz . . . . Doll designer
Remove tar . . . . Turpentine followed with a washing in Lux soap
Reproduction. . . . . Doll produced from a mold taken from an existing doll
Resilles . . . . Hair net for a Spanish comb
Rheinboldt et Cie. . . . . Paris doll shop
Riera, Mlle. . . . . Designed historically accurate doll costumes
Riesenbaby . . . . German for "giant baby"
Robinson, Heath . . . . Doll designer
Roche, Lynn . . . . Doll designer
Roche, Michael . . . . Doll designer
Rockwell, Grace Corry . . . . Doll designer
Rohlinge . . . . Doll designer
Rollinson, Gertrude . . . . Doll designer
Rooted hair . . . . Natural or synthetic hair inserted in single strands or
         clusters into a doll's head
Rosebud mouth . . . . Small closed mouth with pursed lips
Ross, Penny. . . . . Doll designer
Rotkäppchen. . . . . Germany's "Little Red Riding Hood"
Roullet and Decamps. . . . . Manufactured French Automaton
Rousselot . . . . Manufactured French Automaton
Roy, Jules . . . . Patented zinc doll heads
Rub. . . . . Spot where the color has worn away
Ruttan, Marietta Adams . . . . Doll designer
S. G. D. G. . . . . Registered, but without government guarantee
S71 . . . . Identifies a Strombecker Kewpie
Sacs à ouvrage. . . . . French for "work bag"
Sag' Schnucki zu Mir . . . . German for "call me darling"
Sakura Ningyo . . . . Traditional lady, cherry Japanese statue doll
Sandreuter, Regina. . . . . Doll designer
Saran. . . . . Thermoplastic resin derived from vinyl, used for doll hair
Sarg, Tony. . . . . Artist and designer of marionettes and dolls
Saving magic skin dolls . . . . Rub cornstarch into the doll every six months. Avoid
         contact with hands—use gloves when touching.
Saxon Novelty Co.. . . . . Manufactured doll parts
Scavini, Elena . . . . Doll designer
Schalk . . . . German for "rascal"
Schlenkerchen . . . . German for "little dangler"
Schlopsnies, Albert. . . . . Doll designer
Schmidt, Minna. . . . . Designed historically accurate doll costumes
Schmiedeknecht Reinhold. . . . . Designed doll costumes
Schneeflöckchen. . . . . German for "little snowflake"
Schneider, Caesar. . . . . Doll designer
Schneider, Johannes George . . . . Produced dolls
Schoenhut, Harry. . . . . Doll designer
Schön, Joseph . . . . Produced dolls from sheet metal
Schönbartmacher . . . . German for "mask and doll maker"
Schrott, Rotraut. . . . . Doll designer
Schusterjunger . . . . German for "little shoemaker"
Schwesterchen . . . . German for "little sister"

Schwesterlein	German for "younger sister"
Scovell Novelty Manufacturing Co.	Produced cloth dolls
Segmented wooden doll	Tinker Toy
Series 200 for Kämmer & Reinhardt	Shoulder heads in bisque or celluloid
Series 200 for Kestner	Character babies
Series 400 for Kämmer & Reinhardt	Socket-head dolls for walker bodies in bisque of celluloid
Series 500 for Kämmer & Reinhardt	May have only been used internally by the company to identify googly dolls
Series 600 for Kämmer & Reinhardt	May have only been used internally by the company to identify black and mulatto dolls
Series 700 for Kämmer & Reinhardt	Celluloid dolls
Series 800 for Kämmer & Reinhardt	Rubber dolls from the mid-1920s on
Series 900 for Kämmer & Reinhardt	Composition dolls from the 1920s on
Sew holes	Holes in the shoulder plate through which string can pass to attach to a body
Shackman, B. & Co.	Imported and distributed dolls, particularly small inexpensive dolls of various material
Shamin	Doll sculptor
Shimizu Katsuzo	Manufactured dolls
Shiny brows	Indicates a later bisque doll (after 1910)
Shoulder head	Head and shoulder made in one piece
Shoulder plate	Shoulder portion molded with a socket for the head
Siedar, Johann	Manufactured walking dolls
Siewert, Helen	Doll designer of the Puppen Reform influence
Siewert, Klara	Doll designer of the Puppen Reform influence
Singer, Jeanne	Doll designer
Slip	Liquid clay and water mixture used in the production of porcelain
Slit head	A cut in top of doll head for purpose of inserting hair
Small bisque dolls, often in cases with extra clothing	Mignonettes, also spelled Mignonnettes
Smith, Celia	Doll designer
Smith, Charity	Doll designer
Smith, Sherman	Doll designer
Smith, Sidney	Doll designer
Société Française de Fabrication de Bébés & Jouets	French Union for the Manufacture of Dolls and Toys
Socket head	Made with neck that fits into a shoulder plate or the opening of the body
Soften old kid	Rubbing with kerosene
Solid dome	Head with no crown opening—may wear wig, or have painted hair
Sommereisen, Karl	Produced aluminum doll heads
Soniat, Mary	Doll designer
Sorensen, Lewis	Doll designer
Souliers	French for "shoes"
Spieler, Hugo	Doll designer
Spielwarenfabrikant	German for "toy factory owner"
Spielzeugmuseum	German for "toy museum"
Spoon hand	Rudimentary hand, usually wood, carved with very little detail, lacking fingers, and in a cupping position
Spring joints in arms	American Character, Sweet Sue
Staninger, Karl	Doll designer
Staring eyes	Glass eyes which do not sleep, also known as stationary eyes
Stationary eyes	Glass eyes which do not sleep, also known as staring eyes
Stearns, R. H. & Co.	Imported and distributed dolls
Steele, Linda	Doll designer

Steiner, Edmund	Doll designer
Steiner, Heinrich	Produced wax dolls
Stern, Helene	Doll designer of the Puppen Reform influence
Stockinette (Stockinet)	Soft jersey fabric used in the manufacturing of dolls
Stoffpuppenfabrik	German for "factory-stuffed cloth dolls"
Stokes, Jane Gary	Doll designer
Stoll & Edwards Co.	Produced cloth bodied dolls
Stringing	Method used to join the elements of a doll body with cord or elastic
Super Flex	Horsman & Co. (a synthetic rubber/early vinyl)
Superior Doll Co.	Manufactured dolls
Sweet, Elizabeth	Doll designer
Swimming Doll	Cork-bodied dolls that simulate swimming
Swinnerton, James	Doll designer
Swivel head	Head with a socket allowing it to turn
Szerelemhegyi, Marga	Doll designer
Szor, Irene	Doll designer, including the Gold Medal Babies, Mary Poppins, and the Princess line
Taeuber, Sophie	Doll designer
Taft, Loredo	Doll designer
Tangled mohair wig	Use plastic fork to carefully remove tangles
Tanono Sekka	Japanese Boys' Day Festival celebrated on May 5.
Täuflinge	Literal translation of this German term is "babies of Christening age." The term is applied to nearly any kind of doll wearing a shift or chemise—most often associated with Sonneberg Täufling (Note: May be spelled with or without the *e*.)
Tenniel	Doll designer
Thanes Valley Toy Co.	Designed and produced a series of Winnie the Pooh and Christopher Robin dolls
Theyer, Martin	Produced and distributed dolls
Thiele, Max	Designed historical and fiction character dolls
Thompson, Martha	Doll designer
Thompson, Pat	Doll designer
Thorp, Ellery	Doll designer
Tinker Toy	Dolls made of wooden beads strung with elastic
Toddler body	Short chubby body of a toddler, often with diagonal joints at the hips
Tódor Kertész	Hungarian store and doll distributor
Tongue and groove joint	Formed by a protruding tongue on one surface that fits into a groove on the other
Topper Corp.	A division of Deluxe Toys
Topper Toys	A division of Deluxe Toys
Topsy turvy	Doll with two heads—joined in the middle, wearing a long skirt that hides one doll at a time
Tout Bois	German for "all wood"
Trademark	Officially registered symbol, word, name, picture, or engraving designed for the exclusive use by a manufacturer to identify its product
Trobe, Carol	Doll designer
Trowbridge, Helen	Doll designer including Baby Blossom and Baby Rosebud
Tuck comb	Carved wooden comb used as a decorative part of a coiffure and inserted into the head of a wooden doll. Made between 1810 and 1840; also known as a yellow tuck comb
Turned head	Shoulder-head type—with the head slightly turned
Tuttle, Eunice	Doll designer

Twelvetrees, Charles	Doll designer
Tyson, Mamie	Doll designer
U.S. Einkaufshaus	German for "U.S. doll importer"
U.S. Einkaufshaus für Puppen und Spielwaren	German for "U.S. store for dolls and toys"
Un chapeau	French for "a hat"
Un corsage blanc	French for "a white waist"
Un costume de fantaisie	French for "a fancy outfit"
Un jupon	French for "a petticoat"
Un pantalon	French for "a pair of drawers"
Une chemise	French for "a chemise"
United Federation of Doll Clubs (U. F. D. C.) Inc.	10920 N. Ambassador Drive, Suite 130, Kansas City, Missouri 64153
United Federation of Doll Clubs (U. F. D. C.) Membership Chairperson	Mary Lu Trowbridge, 1281 Candleridge Drive, Boise, ID 83712
Universal Doll Outfitters	Fashioned knit doll clothing
Universal Fashion Co.	Distributed patterns for doll clothing
Unsere Goldigen Drei	German for "our golden trio"
Unsere Herzige Mami	German for "our cute mammy"
Unsere Süssen Madel	German for "our sweet girls"
Vacchetti, Sandro	Doll designer
Vale, Margaret	Doll designer
Van Briggle, Artus	Painted doll heads for Arnoldt Doll Co. before opening his famous art pottery factory
Van Hollebeke	Produced and distributed dolls, doll parts, and automatons
Van Rozen,	Belgian character doll designer
Vandegriff, Peggy	Effanbee's Aunt Patsy, and author of Dy-dee Doll's Days
Vargas, Antonio	Crafted and repaired wax dolls
Velour strip to hold interchangeable wigs	Pamela by Alexander Doll Co.
Vereinigte Köppelsdorfer Porzellanfabriken	German for "United Köppelsdorf Porcelain Manufacturers" (Armand Marseille and Ernst Heubach)
Vereinigte Puppenfabriken	German for "United Doll Factories"
Vereinigte Spielwarenfabriken	German for "United Toy Factories"
Vereinigung Deutscher Spielwarenhandler	Association of German Toy Merchants
Verleger	A German merchant who buys manufactured goods or places orders
Vichy	Manufactured French automaton
Victorian style	Pertaining to the decorative and ornate mode prevalent during the reign of Queen Victoria (1837-1901)
Vinyl	Material used after 1950—a soft plastic
Vogel, Max	Produced celluloid dolls
Vogelsanger, Paul	Sculptured art doll heads
Vöglein	German for "little bird"
Vogt, Professor, Joseph Wackerle	Designed art dolls
Voice box	Source of sound in a talking or mama doll. May be generated by bellows, reeds, or other means (one manufacturer lists wolves' teeth as being the origin of sounds) operated by pulling strings, pressing the body, or moving the doll or one of its limbs.
Voices, Inc.	Partnership of three principal manufacturers of voice boxes patented in 1926—over fifty doll companies were licensed to use the mama voices and criers
Von Hindenburg	Wooden portrait dolls carved in the trenches during World War I and sold by the Red Cross

Von Uchatius, Fräulein	Crafted dolls by cementing together small pieces of wood
Vorm.	German abbreviation for "formerly"
W on the forehead	Probably stands for "Waltershäuser Puppenfabrik"
Wachspuppenfabrik	German for "factory for wax dolls"
Wagner, Emil	Doll designer
Waite, John	Owner of Quaker Doll Co.
Walker, Izannah	Doll designer
Walters, Beverly	Doll designer
Waltershäuser Puppenfabrik	Name given to the Heinrich Handwerck factory after his death
Wampl, Joseph	Doll distributor
Wanamaker, John	Imported and distributed dressed dolls
Watermelon mouth	Closed smiling—usually a single-line mouth
Wax over	Head or limbs made of composition or plaster of Paris and coated with wax
Webster, Mary Hortence	Doll designer
Weighted eyes	Sleep eyes that operate by means of a weight attached to a wire frame holding the eyes
Weinnëde	German for "crying doll"
White, C. & H.	Produced leather head dolls, often dressed as peddlers
Wick, Faith	Doll designer
Willard, Frank	Doll designer
Wilson, Lita	Doll designer
Wisconsin Deluxe Doll and Dress Co.	Manufactured dolls
Wollpuppenfabrik	German for "factory for wooden dolls"
Wonderland book with character dolls, including Alice in Wonderland, Bride, Senorita, Pinafore Alice, Carmen, Negro Bride, Venetian Lady, Flower Girl, Colonial Girl, Floradora, Dutch Girl, Charmette, Marigold, Annabelle, Spring, Drum Major, Girl Graduate, Fatima, Sweetheart, Colleen, Easter Parade, Stardust, Norwegian Lass, Swedish Maid, Daisy, Florentine Girl, Nurse, Glamour Girl, Gibson Girl, Majorette, Calypso, Ballerina, Canasta Girl, Robin Hood, Maid Marian, Debutante, Miss Jr. Prom, Hadassah, Czech Beauty, Bubbles, China Doll, Cowboy, Cowgirl, Harlequin, Ice Skater, Mardi Gras, Roller Skater, Miss Poland, Casablanca, George Washington, Happy Birthday (names listed are not necessarily registered names from company)	A&H
Woods, Robin	Doll designer
Wright, John	Doll designer
Wright, Phyllis	Doll designer
Wyffels, Berdine	Doll designer
Yamato Ningyo	Japanese for "child doll"
Yoshitsumen	Japanese warrior
Zaiden, David	Doll designer
Zeller, Fawn	Doll designer
Zetzche, Richard	Doll designer
Zitzmann, Mlle.	Doll designer

Zoll.	German measurement equals approximately 1 inch, or 2.5 centimeters
Zur Puppendoktorim	A doll repair shop—German for "at the woman doll doctor's"
Zwanger, Heinrich	President of Nürnberger Kunstlerpuppen und Stoffspielwarenfabrik
Zwerg	German for "dwarf"

Lesley's Ginny

CHAPTER EIGHT

COLLECTION OF CLUES

The following charts and lists are offered to further aid you in identifying particular dolls. I have found that charts are an uncomplicated means of comparing a diverse group of dolls. When charts cannot facilitate a quick and easy result, lists are an efficient means to locate information. My objective in this, as in all other chapters, is to offer a simple, "at-a-glance" method of identification.

The next few pages illustrate a strange inventory of information. Not every company nor doll is represented. Only additional facts about a particular doll or group of dolls that need further clarification are offered. I believe that the streamlined charts and lists give the important and relevant clues needed to enlighten you on your journey of discovery.

Once a doll is identified, you will have an abundance of information available to you for further analysis. I encourage you to read and study as much as you can about dolls. Talk to other collectors, and consider joining a doll club.

The format in this chapter is really quite simple. The clues offered as charts or lists are given alphabetically by company or type of doll.

ALEXANDER'S WENDY/ALEXANDER KINS:

Wendy Ann/Wendy Kins/Alexander Kins, and Bill (the boy) have been made continuously for the past forty-five years. Molded and named for Madame Alexander's grandchildren, William and Wendy Ann. When the real Wendy Ann passed away in 1955, the name Ann was dropped from the doll's name, thus explaining the name change. All the 7- to 8-inch Wendy types have the same chubby round face and pointed chin; single-stroke brows; sleep eyes with molded upper and painted lower lashes; and a small, closed, unsmiling mouth. If marked at all, the doll will have "ALEX" across its back (after 1976, all of these dolls were marked "ALEXANDER"). To distinguish one year from another, refer to the following chart.

DATE	BODY TYPE	BODY COLOR	EYES	MOUTH
1953	Straight legs, non-walker	Tan	Oval	Dark red
1954	Straight legs, walker	Slightly shiny tan	Oval	Dark red
1955	Slightly bent legs, walker	Very good quality bisque look to tan plastic	Oval	Red
1956	Jointed knees, walker, turns head with each step	Pink	Very oval	Dark pink
1974	Straight legs, jointed above knee	Very matte finish	Rounded	Orange lips, blushed cheeks

AUTOMATED DOLLS: There are several types of automated dolls. The following explanations will help you to distinguish between these moving and sometimes musical dolls. "Automata" serves as a blanket term covering all types of mechanical dolls produced in France, Germany, and the United States. Automata dolls reached the peak of their popularity in the latter quarter of the nineteenth century. The visual appeal, charm, and intricacy of movement are all factors to consider when observing automatons, marottes, and the other types.

AUTOMATONS: Musical, mechanical dolls with a revolving cylinder-type music box, and clockwork mechanism. Music box and mechanism hidden in platform base. When the key is wound, the music plays and the doll performs a series of movements. The finest automatons came from France, notably by Roullet and Decamps, Vichy, Rousselot, Phalibois, and Lambert, among others.

ANIMATED PLATFORM DOLLS: Less artistic than automatons, the dolls are activated by a cranking movement, allowing the doll to perform and the music to play only while the crank is being turned. Although visually appealing, the movements seem stiff and awkward. Germany was by far the leading source of animated platform dolls.

AUTOPERIPATETIKOS: A walking doll by means of a clockwork mechanism which caused the feet, usually made of pressed metal, to move back and forth in a walking motion. Originally patented in England in 1862, they were also manufactured in France, Germany, and the United States.

CYMBALERS OR BELLOWS-TYPE: Small, usually under 12-inch dolls that contain a pressure bellow mechanism housed within their bodies. When the body is compressed, the arms come together in a clapping-type motion. The earlier examples were manufactured in Germany; later, Cymbalers were produced in the United States.

MAROTTES: Falling somewhere between a doll and an automaton. By definition, it is "a doll's head on a stick." Most are lavishly dressed bisque dolls sitting atop a music box inside of a drum perched on a stick. When the stick is waved, the doll twirls and the music plays. Most marottes were made in Germany or France.

PULL TOYS: Dolls or other figures mounted on a wheeled wooden platform. The dolls may be stationary, or simple movements may be incorporated into the toy's design. Originating in Germany around the turn of the century, pull toys were the forerunners of the Fisher Price-type toys of today.

PHONOGRAPH DOLLS: In 1887, Thomas Edison invented and patented a "phonographic doll." The earlier phonograph dolls bore little resemblance to the later better-known dolls. The first ones were assembled with a tube-shaped body housing the mechanism. This crude ancestor opened the door for the more sophisticated dolls to follow, such as the Bébé Phonographe Jumeau, Max Oscar Arnold, Dolly Record by Averill, and Mattel's Charmin Chatty.

WALKING, TALKING, KISS-THROWING, FLIRTING DOLLS: Produced during the first quarter of the twentieth century, they performed all of these activities or a combination of any. Operating by a chain-work mechanism, wire arrangements, and pull strings. The talking was achieved with a bellow in the body which was activated by pull strings. Regardless of the type of device used, the best that was produced was a simple "mama, papa" sound. Introduced in Germany, walking and talking dolls were soon copied in France and the United States.

KICKING DOLLS: First patented in 1855 by Jules Steiner, these dolls were modified several times over the next twenty years. A key-wound body housed the fly-wheel regulator and clockwork mechanisms that produced a kicking movement. Jules Steiner of France seems to be the sole manufacturer of kicking dolls.

SWIMMING DOLL: Also known as "Ondine." Advertised as "Parisian Mechanician for Adult Amusement" having a cork body with jointed wooden arms and legs that simulated swimming when wound by a key.

BARBIE: Placing an appropriate age to a Barbie can pose problems. Markings remained the same for several years. A number 6 Barbie can be found with a number 1, 1958, Barbie marking, further complicating matters. Barbie's characteristics are so much more important than a date that may appear within her mark. The following chart is given so that you can categorize a Barbie at a glance. Not only is it beneficial, it may well be practical to do so. A mint number 1 Barbie is valued at several thousands of dollars, a number 6, while quite collectible, has only a fraction of that value.

NAME DATE	BODY	HAIR	EYES	SUIT	MARK	SPECIAL
#1 1959	Heavy solid vinyl; may have odor and a pale pasty look; vinyl fades	Soft silky floss blonde, or brunette ponytail and curly bangs	Very arched brows, black and white eyes, thin line of blue on eyelid	One-Piece, black and white striped; black high-heeled shoes, with holes for stand	"Barbie T.M. Pats. Pend. ©MCMLVIII by Mattel Inc."	Holes in the bottom of feet, with copper tubes up into legs to fit stand; very arched brows; hoop-type earrings; dark red nail and lip color may fade to orange
#2 1959-1960	No change	No change	No change	No change	No change— although some have been found with the ® beside "Barbie"	No holes in the feet, most with pearl stud earrings, dark red nail and lip color may fade to orange
#3 1960	No change	No change	Rounded and tapered brows, blue color added to the eyes, line of dark brown or blue on eyelid.	No change	No change	The eye and brow color is the main difference between #1, #2, & #3. A few #3 Dolls have been found with holes in their feet— some of the many transitional dolls. Dark red nail and lip color may fade to orange.
#4 1960	Heavy solid, vinyl, retains a nice flesh color.	No change	Same as #3, but with blue line over eye	No change	No change	Have a tendency to turn green at the earring holes; dark red nail and lip color may fade to orange

NAME DATE	BODY	HAIR	EYES	SUIT	MARK	SPECIAL
#5 1961	Hollow body and lighter in weight	More sturdy saran, pony-tail and curly bangs, first red hair	Eyebrows extend longer, smaller pupils show more blue color, blue eyeliner	No change	No change	Gold wrist tag with "Barbie" written in script; box shows red hair for first time; nails and lips may be a lighter color
#6 1962—1967	Hollow body	Saran same texture and style, added ash blond or platinum to the blond, brunette and red hair	Early #6 Barbies have dark royal blue eye color, models produced from 1963 on have an aqua blue color	One-Piece, red	Same as #1—#5 or: "MIDGE ©1962 BAR-BIE® 1958 by Mattel, Inc." or: "1958 Mattel Inc. US Patented US Pat. Pend." or: "1960 by Mattel Inc. Hawthorne Calif., USA"	

OTHER POPULAR BARBIE DOLLS:

BUBBLE CUT BARBIE: Short hair style

FASHION QUEEN BARBIE: Three wigs that are inter-changeable

MISS BARBIE: Open and close sleep eyes and inter-changeable wigs

SWIRL PONYTAIL BARBIE: Rooted hair with long sweeping bangs across forehead

DORIS DAY STYLE BARBIE: Very rare, specially root-ed Page Boy hair style

TWIST N TURN BARBIE: Waist-jointed and real rooted eyelashes

LIVING BARBIE: Jointed wrists, bendable elbows and ankles

MALIBU BARBIE: Tanned tone vinyl

LIVE ACTION BARBIE: Battery-operated stage moves Barbie

BUSY HANDS BARBIE: Hands open and close to hold accessories that are included

BRU REPRODUCTION CHART: There is no doubt that the delicately molded, limpid-eyed Bébés produced by the French manufacturer Jne Bru & Cie during the last quarter of the nineteenth century are among the most treasured prizes of the doll world. The beauty and value of a Bru explains why there are more reproductions of Bru Bébé than of any other type of antique doll. Following are a few tips to help distinguish an authentic Jne Bru from a reproduction.

CHARACTERISTIC	REPRODUCTION	AUTHENTIC
Head marking:	Bru Jne	Bru Jne (plus size #)
Body construction:	Hand sewn	Machine sewn
Body stuffing:	Sawdust	Ground cork and grass
Elbows:	Bisque lower arms attached directly to the kid upper arms	Bisque lower arms attached with a hinged joint
Cutting of leather:	Scalloped	Scalloped with pinking
Arms:	Hang straight	Graceful curve
Head:	Poured into the mold with the rim cut off	Pressed into the mold without a rim
Ear piercing:	Into the head	Through the lobe

HASBRO, INC. G. I. JOE: G. I. Joe has developed an almost cult-like following among collectors. The action figure has proven to be more successful than the television program he was named after. Placing a Joe in his proper category can be confusing. To ensure your success, the following profile is given.

1st Series:	1964	11-1/2 inches	The letters TM in mark
2nd Series:	1965	11-1/2 inches	TM replaced by ®, black doll introduced
3rd Series:	1966	11-1/2 inches	Identified by lack of scar
4th Series:	1967	11-1/2 inches	Addition of Pat. No., no scar
5th Series:	1968	11-1/2 inches	Same marking, with scar
6th Series:	1970	11-1/2 inches	Same marking, flock hair introduced
7th Series:	1974	11-3/4 inches	Same marking, Kung Fu Grip hands
8th Series:	1975	11-1/2 inches	Same marking, see-through right arm
9th Series:	1975	11-3/4 inches	Mark adds 1975, molded swim trunks
10th Series:	1976	11-1/2 inches	Same marking
11th Series	1977	8 inches	Introduction of the smaller Joe

(Also, in 1967, Nurse Jane was issued: Female, "Patent Pend. 1967 Hasbro/Hong Kong")

KÄTHE KRUSE: Continued production of these famous cloth art dolls from 1910 until today may explain why they can be so difficult to properly identify. The early Käthe Kruse dolls were made of waterproof treated muslin, cotton, wool, and stockinette. Each doll has a black, red, or purple ink "Kruse" name, and a three- to five-digit number stamped on the bottom of the foot. Reproduction Käthe Kruse dolls are not as troublesome as the Kruse copies; in fact, Ms. Kruse was forced several times to bring litigation of infringement rights against competing manufacturers. Although records indicate that she was always victorious, many copies were produced before a settlement could be reached. To aid you in authenticating a Kruse doll, the following chart is submitted.

SERIES	DATE	TYPE	SIZE	DESCRIPTION
Doll I	1910	All-muslin, toddler body		Identified by three vertical seams on back of head
Doll I		Early	16 inches	Identified by wide hips
Doll I		Later	17 inches	More slender hips
Doll I		1H	17 inches	Wears a wig
Doll I		Bambino	8-1/2 inches	Special doll and only tiny doll ever made (by Käthe Kruse)
Doll II	1922	All-stockinette, arms and legs loose on soft body		Identified by one vertical seam on back of head
Doll II		Schlenkerchen	13 inches	*Schlenkerchen* is German for "the little dangler"
Doll V & VI	1925	All-cloth and weighted with about 5 pounds of sand		Authentic representation of a baby—complete with navel and anus—considered for teaching child care
Doll V		Du Mein	17-1/2 to 19-1/2 inches	Baby with eyes open—*Du Mein* is German for "you're mine."
Doll V		Träumerchen	17-1/2 to 19-1/2 inches	Baby with eyes closed—*Träumerchen* is German for "dreaming baby."
Doll VI		Du Mein	21-1/2 to 23-1/2 inches	Baby with eyes open
Doll VI		Träumerchen	21-1/2 to 23-1/2 inches	Baby with eyes closed
Doll VII	1927	All-cloth, wigs may be added after 1929		Pensive face of Doll I or pouty Du Mein face. Wider hips

SERIES	DATE	TYPE	SIZE	DESCRIPTION
Doll VII		Hemdmatz	14 inches	*Hemdmatz* is German for "small child with a bare bottom."
Doll VIII	1929	All-cloth, swivel head, wigs		Identified by one vertical seam on back of head
Doll VIII		Das Deutsche Kind	21 inches	*Das Deutsche Kind* is German for "the German child."
Doll IX	1929	All-cloth, swivel head, wig		Identified by one vertical seam on back of head
Doll IX		Käthe Kruse's Notstandskind	14 inches	Käthe Kruse's *Notstandskind* is German for "Käthe Kruse's child of distress," resulting from the time of inflation.
Doll X	1935	All-cloth, swivel head		Similar in appearance to Doll I, except smaller
Doll X			14 inches	
Celluloid	1936-1939	All-celluloid	16 inches	Characteristics similar to the earlier cloth dolls
U.S. Zone-Germany	1945-1951	Heavily painted	14 inches	Often with a turtle mark
Hard Plastic	1952	Pink muslin body, human hair wig	14- and 20-inch sizes	Beautiful hand-painted eyes

LENCI VERIFICATION CHART: While ostensibly produced as toys for children, the sophisticated design and high price tag resulted in many Lenci dolls being purchased for adults. This may explain why so many vintage Lenci dolls are found today in near mint condition. It is not unusual for an older Lenci to sell for thousands of dollars. Consequently, frauds are plentiful. Typically, a Lenci is marked with a wrist tag (which is often lost), a clothing label (but not always), or an ink stamp on the bottom of the foot (easily copied). Use the following list to help you identify an authentic Lenci doll.

1. A zigzag stitching on the back of the neck, through tops of arms and legs, and occasionally at the crotch
2. Ears on dolls over 10 inches tall are a double thickness of felt sewn together and then topstitched
3. Human hair or mohair is attached to the head in rows or strips
4. Bodies—occasionally stuffed—are hollow cardboard covered with felt or cloth
5. Well-shaped and proportioned legs and arms, with a very slight bend at the elbows
6. Nicely formed hands with separate thumb, mitt-type stitched fingers, or separate fingers with the third and fourth fingers stitched together
7. Beautifully sculptured face with pleasingly round cheeks; soft expression, with a somewhat surprised expression.
8. Two white dots in each eye: one, upper right-hand corner; the other, lower left-hand corner
9. Artistically applied two-tone lip color
10. White milk glass buttons on magnificent outfits made of felt and/or organdy, three or four holes in shoe buttons
11. Scalloped top socks

NANCY ANN STORYBOOK DOLLS: These popular little dolls were first manufactured in a painted bisque material and later in hard plastic. In the early 1960s, at the peak of production, over eight thousand dolls a day were made. Character identification is obtained only by a wrist tag or a box label. A close inspection of the clothing and accessories can help to classify these tiny treasures. It is important to note that sometimes Story Book is two words and, at other times, one word with a capital *B* in the middle. These are not typographical errors, but an inconsistency that actually is beneficial in dating and identifying Nancy Ann dolls.

DATE	MARK ON CHILD	MARK ON BABY	BOX PATTERN	CLOTHING CLOSURES	IDENTIFI-CATION
1936	No child doll produced	Painted bisque, marked: "Made in Japan"	Pink & blue marbleized pattern—or with starbursts	Silver pin	Gold foil label reads: "Nancy Ann Dressed Dolls"
1937	Painted bisque marked: "Made in Japan"	Painted bisque marked: "Made in Japan"	Colored starbursts	Silver pin	Gold foil label reads: "Nancy Ann Dressed Dolls"
1938	Painted bisque, marked: "AMER-ICAN" or "JUDY ANN USA"	No baby produced	Colored starbursts. Very rare, red book-shaped box with "Judy Ann in Fairyland" printed on it	Silver pin	Gold foil label reads: "Judy Ann"
1938	Painted bisque marked: "STORY-BOOK USA" or "Storybook USA"	Painted bisque marked: "Made in Japan" or "STORYBOOK USA" or "Story-book USA"	Colored starbursts	Silver or brass pin	Gold foil label reads: "Story Book Dolls"
1939	Painted bisque, molded socks, marked: "Story-book doll USA"	Painted bisque, star-shaped hands, marked: "Story-Book Doll USA"	Colored box with small silver dots	Brass pin	Gold foil label reads: "Story Book Dolls"
1940	Painted bisque, molded socks marked: "Story-Book Doll USA"	Painted bisque, star-shaped hands, marked: "StoryBook Doll USA"	Colored box with white dots	Brass pin	Gold foil label reads: "Story Book Dolls"
1941-1942	Painted bisque, transition doll, some with chubby tummies others slim, marked: "StoryBook Doll USA"	Painted bisque, transition doll, some with star-shaped hands, others with fists, marked:"Story-Book Doll USA"	White box with colored dots	Brass pins	Gold wrist tag with character name

DATE	MARK ON CHILD	MARK ON BABY	BOX PATTERN	CLOTHING CLOSURES	IDENTIFI-CATION
1943-1947	Painted bisque, one-piece head, torso and legs, marked: "Story-Book Doll USA"	Painted bisque, fist hands, marked: "Story-Book Doll USA"	White box with colored dots	Dull silver or brass pin or ribbon ties	Gold wrist tag with character name
1947-1949	Plastic painted eyes marked: "Story-Book Doll USA Trade Mark Reg."	Painted bisque body, plastic limbs, marked: "StoryBook Doll USA"	White box, colored dots, Nancy Ann StoryBook Dolls printed between dots	Brass snaps	Gold wrist tag with character name
1949-1953	Plastic, black sleep eyes, marked: "StoryBook Doll USA Trade Mark Reg."	Plastic, black sleep eyes, marked:"Story-Book Doll USA Trade Mark Reg."	No change to box	Brass or painted donut shaped snaps	Gold wrist tag with character name

TERRI LEE: As is often the case with extremely successful and popular dolls, copies are made. These copies can range in quality from the sublime to the ridiculous. Terry Lee dolls were copied by several copycat manufacturers. One in particular is an extremely well-done imitation known as a Mary Jane. Paying close attention to the following statistics should help you to spot a knockoff Terry Lee with little trouble.

	AUTHENTIC TERRY LEE	COPYCAT TERRY LEE
Measurement at waist	9-3/4 inches	9-1/4 inches
Measurement at leg calf	5-1/2 inches	5-1/4 inches
Measurement in height	16 inches	15 inches
Eye	always painted	often sleep

VOGUE DOLLS, INC., GINNY: When dolls are grouped or classified by numbers it is a good indication that no better way to distinguish them could be found. Usually these dolls were, or are, so popular that their production continued over many years with little change. Ginny dolls fall into this category. For well over fifty years little girls have loved Ginny dolls. To make their identification somewhat easier, the following explanations are offered.

NAME	MATERIAL	DATE	MARK	DRESS TAG	DESCRIPTION
Just Me	Bisque	Mid 1930s	"Just Me A.M. 310/11"	Paper tag marked: "Vouge"	Imported and dressed by Jennie Graves and sold to department stores, glass eyes, mohair wigs
Toddles	Composition	1937-1948	On head: "Vouge" on back: "Vogue" or "Doll Co"	Tag marked: "Vogue Dolls"	Jointed at neck, shoulders, and hips; strung; molded hair under mohair wig; painted side glancing eyes
Number 1 Painted Eye Ginny	All hard plastic	1948-1950	On head: "Vogue" on back: "Vogue" or "Vogue Doll"	Tag marked: "Vogue Dolls"	Jointed at neck, shoulders, and hips; strung; molded hair under mohair wig; painted side glancing eyes
Number 2 Non Walker Strung Ginny	All hard plastic	1950-1953	On head: "Vogue" on back: "Vogue"	Tag marked: "Vogue"	Jointed at neck, shoulders, and hips; strung; mohair wig, with gauze strip forming cap; sleep eyes; painted lashes
Number 2 Crib Crowd Baby Ginny	All hard plastic	1950 only	On head: "Vogue" on back: "Vogue"	Tag marked: "Vogue"	Representing a baby complete with a bent-limb baby body
Number 2 Poodle Cut Ginny	All hard plastic	1952 only	On head: "Vogue" on back: "Vogue"	Tag marked: "Vogue"	Identical to the basic number 2 Ginny, except wearing a lamb's wool bubble Poodle-type wig
Number 3 Straight leg Walker with Painted Lashes Ginny	All hard plastic	1954	On head: "Ginny" on back: "Ginny Vogue Dolls Inc./ Pat. # 2687594 Made in USA"	Tag marked: "Vogue Dolls"	Pin-jointed, mohair wig, sleep eyes, with painted lashes
Number 4 Straight leg Walker with Molded Lashes	All hard plastic	1955-1957	On head: "Vogue" on back: "Ginny Vogue Dolls	Tag marked: "Vogue Dolls"	Pin-jointed, mohair wig, sleep eyes, molded upper lashes

NAME	MATERIAL	DATE	MARK	DRESS TAG	DESCRIPTION
Number 5 Jointed Knee Walker Ginny	All hard plastic	1957-1962	On head: "Vogue" on back: "Ginny Vogue Dolls Inc./ Pat. #2687594 Made in USA"	Tag marked: "Vogue Dolls, Inc."	Jointed knee, pin-jointed, mohair wig, sleep eyes, molded upper lashes
Number 6 Rooted hair Ginny	Vinyl head and a hard plastic body	1963	On head: "Ginny" on back: "Ginny Vogue Dolls Inc./ Pat. # 2687594 Made in USA"	Tag marked: "Vogue Dolls Inc."	Synthetic hair rooted in vinyl head, sleep eyes, molded lashes
Modern Ginny	All vinyl	Early 1970s	On head: "GINNY" on back: "Vogue Dolls 1972/ Made in Hong Kong"	Tag marked: "Made in Hong Kong"	All vinyl; jointed at neck, shoulder, and hips
Sassoon Ginny	All vinyl	1978-1979	On head: "GINNY VOGUE DOLL 1977" on back: "1977" or "1978 VOGUE DOLL MOONACHIE N.J. MADE IN HONG KONG	Tag marked: "Hong Kong"	Thin body and limbs

WAX DOLL CHART: There are three types of wax dolls. The wax-over, poured-wax, and the reinforced wax. Wax-over dolls were made by various companies in England, France, and Germany. As the name implies, a head was made usually of composition or papier-mâché and covered with wax. The poured-wax dolls from England produced during the nineteenth century are especially beautiful. Made by casting liquid wax in a mold. Reinforced wax is exactly that, a head that is reinforced from the inside with plaster or with strips of cloth soaked in composition.

Classifying these three types of wax dolls is not difficult if you are armed with useful information. To aid you in determining a particular doll, the following chart should be useful.

CHARACTERISTIC:	POURED WAX	WAX OVER	REINFORCED WAX
Wax color:	Tinted	Clear	Tinted
Hair:	Inserted	Wig or molded	Wig
Eyelids:	Molded	None	Molded
Degree of Realism:	High	Low	Moderate to high
Molded Hair or Hat:	None known	Often found	None known
Hollow Poured Limbs:	Yes	No	No
Composition Limbs:	No	Yes	Yes

WOODEN DOLL CHART: A name is granted to a wooden doll by way of its characteristics. With such noble names as William and Mary or Queen Ann, surely to misname such a historic treasure would be unforgivable. Because they have no markings, a positive identification can be difficult. To avoid using an incorrect title they are often referred to simply as "early wooden dolls." To assist you in properly classifying a particular wooden doll, their notable attributes have been charted. None of the dolls have marks except BeBe Tout en Bois, which has a trademark angle, or "Tout Bois, Holz All Wood"

NAME GIVEN	YEARS	HEAD/ TORSO FEATURES	ARM CONSTRUCTION & ATTACHMENTS	LEG CONSTRUCTION & ATTACHMENTS	HAIR	FACIAL FEATURES
William and Mary	1680-1720	One-piece covered in gesso, painted a flesh color, varnished	Bond linen upper, carved lower with separate fingers and thumbs, may have delicately carved fingernails	All wood, delicately carved detailed toes	Human hair or flax nailed onto head	Unique facial expression, painted almond-shaped eyes, single-stroke brows, well-defined rosy cheeks, closed mouth
Queen Ann	1700-1750	One-piece with egg-shaped head, carved bosom, very narrow waist, covered in gesso, painted very pale flesh color, varnished	Linen upper nailed to shoulders, rounded fingers, carved fingernails	All wood, attached to sides of hips, carved to accommodate pegged tongue and groove joint	Human hair or flax nailed onto head	Bulbous glass or painted oval eyes, series of dots for brows and lashes, well-defined nose and ears, rosy cheeks, closed mouth
Georgian	1750-1800	One-piece with rounded chest, narrow waist, squared hips, flat back, covered in gesso, painted very pale flesh color, varnished	Upper linen stitched through holes drilled in shoulders, hands carved, separate fingers and thumbs, lower arms covered in kid with fingers showing	Carved to fit into hip slots with pegged tongue and groove joints	Human hair or flax nailed onto head	Inserted lozenge-shaped glass eyes, series of dots for brows and lashes, well defined nose and closed mouth
Early nineteenth century	1800-1840	One-piece with base forming a point, upper body, lower limbs covered in gesso, painted flesh color, varnished	Carved and attached with piece of linen	Carved to fit against either side of pointed torso, jointed by single peg going from first leg through torso then into other leg	Sewn human hair or flax glued onto head	Nicely painted features, oversized oval eyes, single-stroke brows, no ears, dark rosy cheeks, closed-mouth

NAME GIVEN	YEARS	HEAD/ TORSO FEATURES	ARM CON- STRUCTION & ATTACH- MENTS	LEG CON- STRUCTION & ATTACH- MENTS	HAIR	FACIAL FEATURES
Transition mid-nine- teenth cen- tury	1810- 1840	One-Piece with high or Empire waist, no gesso, heavily painted only on areas that show	All wood attached by tongue and groove joints at shoulders and elbows	Unrefined but efficient tongue and groove	Carved, may be elabo- rate, paint- ed, styles with curls around face, important addition of a hair comb carved in back of head, known as "Yellow Tuck comb"	Delicate look, nose is wedge inserted in face, heavily painted, usually with ear- rings, closed mouth
Late nineteenth century	1840- 1900	One-Piece with no gesso, heavily painted only on areas that show	All wood, attached by tongue and groove joints at shoulders and elbows	Unrefined but efficient tongue and groove	Common carved, painted style with no tuck comb	The quality of painted features progressively dete- riorated until the end of this time period, resulting in a quite crude, closed mouth
Peg and Dutch Wooden	After 1900	One-Piece crudely shaped, thinly painted, only on areas that show	Stick-type with spoon like hands, jointed with pegs	Stick-type with lower painted white with black feet	Painted very simply, no style	Poorly painted features, closed mouth
BeBe Tout en Bois	1900- 1914	Carved dolly face head, jointed to a wooden or cloth body, nicely paint- ed in flesh color	Fully-jointed ball- type joints	Fully-jointed ball- type joints	Good wig	Glass eyes, nicely painted brows and lashes, open mouth with teeth

SCHOENHUT DOLL CLASSIFICATION

Classifying wooden dolls by A. Schoenhut can be confusing. Names have been assigned and used, but frequently no explanation is given.

NAME	CHARACTERISTICS
Character	All-wood, spring-jointed body; carved hair (possibly with a ribbon or bow) or good wig; intaglio eyes; open/closed or closed mouth.
Bonnet Girl	All-wood, spring-jointed body; carved, molded, and painted hair around face; floral-designed cap molded to head with hair showing in back; intaglio eyes; slightly open/closed mouth.
Schnickel-Fritz	All-wood, spring-jointed body; carved, molded, and painted wavy hair; squinting painted eyes; toothy grin.
Tootsie Wootsie	All-wood, spring-jointed body; lightly carved and molded short hair; small eyes; open/closed mouth.
Manikin	All-wood, spring-jointed matured body; lightly carved men's styled hair; pensive, older look; painted eyes; closed mouth. Costumed in football, baseball, basketball, or circus outfit—complete with accessories.
Schoenhut Baby	All-wood, spring-jointed toddler or bent-limb baby body; painted, but not carved, hair; painted eyes; open or open/closed mouth.
Dolly-Faced Doll	All-wood, spring-jointed body; good wig; painted, round eyes; open/closed mouth with painted teeth.
Walker Doll	All-wood body, jointed at shoulder and hips only; painted features.
Sleep-Eyed Child	All-wood body; good wig; sleep eyes; open mouth with teeth.
Cloth Body	Hollow wooden head; cloth body and limbs; wooden hands; mohair wig; painted features.

INDEX

384

385

386

BIBLIOGRAPHY

BOOKS

- Anderton, Johana Gast, More Twentieth Century Dolls From Bisque To Vinyl Volume I (A-H), Volume II (I-Z) Revised Edition, Wallace Homestead, 1979.
- Anderton, Johana Gast, The Collector's Encyclopedia of Cloth Dolls, Wallace Homestead, 1984.
- Anderton, Johanna Gast, Twentieth Century Dolls From Bisque To Vinyl, Wallace Homestead, 1974.
- Axe, John Collectible Black Dolls, Hobby House Press, 1978.
- Axe, John, Kewpies-Dolls & Art, Hobby House Press, 1987.
- Bech, Jean, Dictionary of Doll Marks, Sterling Publishing Co., Inc. 1990.
- Billy Boy, Barbie: Her Life and Times, Crown Publishers, 1987.
- Bullard, Helen, The American Doll Artist Volume I, The Summit Press, Ltd. 1965.
- Christian, Albert, Spinning Wheel's Complete Book of Dolls, Quest-Eridon Books, 1977.
- Cieslik, Jürgen and Marianne, German Doll Encyclopedia 1800-1939, Hobby House Press, 1985.
- Cieslik, Jürgen and Marianne, German Doll Marks & Identification Book, Hobby House Press, 1990.
- Coleman, Dorothy S., Elizabeth A. Coleman and Evelyn J. Coleman, The Collector's Encyclopedia of Dolls, Crown Publishers, 1968.
- Coleman, Dorothy S., Elizabeth A. Coleman and Evelyn J. Coleman, The Collector's Encyclopedia of Dolls Volume II, Crown Publisher, 1986.
- Corson, Carol, Schoenhut Dolls: A Collector's Encyclopedia, Hobby House Press, 1993.
- Davis, Nina S., The Jumeau Doll Story, Hobby House Press, 1969.
- DeWein, Sibyl and Joan Ashabraner, The Collectors Encyclopedia of Barbie Dolls and Collectibles, Collector Books, 1997.
- Earnshaw, Nora, Collecting Dolls, Pincushion Press, 1992.
- Foulke, Jan, Kestner: King of Dollmakers, Hobby House Press, 1982.
- Fuller, W., Jr., Legend of the Cabbage Patch Kids, Taylor Publishing Co., 1983.
- Garrison, Susan Ann, Raggedy Ann & Andy Family Album, Schiffer Publishing Ltd., 1998.
- Gibbs, Patikii, Horsman Dolls, 1950-1970, Collector Books, 1985.
- Hall, Patricia, Johnny Gruelle: Creator of Raggedy Ann and Andy, Pelican Publishing, 1993.
- Herlocher, Dawn, 200 Years of Dolls, Antique Trader Books, 1996.
- Heyerdahl, Virginia Ann (ed.), The Best of Doll Reader, Volumes I-IV, Hobby House. Press, Inc., 1982, 1986, 1988, 1991.
- Izen, Judith, A Collector's Guide To Ideal Dolls, Collector Books, 1994.
- Jacobs, Laura, Barbie: What A Doll!, Artabras 1994.
- Judd, Polly, Cloth Dolls of the 1920s and 1930s: Identification and Price Guide, Hobby House Press, 1991.
- Judd, Polly and Pam, Composition Doll 1928-1955, Hobby House Press 1994.
- Judd, Polly and Pam, Hard Plastic Dolls: Identification and Price Guide Revised Edition, Hobby House Press, 1994.
- Mandeville, A. Glenn, Alexander Dolls Collector's Price Guide, 2nd Edition, Hobby House Press 1993.
- Mandeville, A. Glenn, Ginny: An American Toddler Doll 2nd Revised Edition, Hobby House Press, 1994.
- Manos, Paris and Susan, The Collectible Male Action Figures, Collector Books, 1990.
- Miller, Marjorie A., Nancy Ann Storybook Dolls, Hobby House Press, 1980.
- Reinelt, Sabine, Magic of Character Dolls, Hobby House Press, 1993.
- Revi, Albert Christian, Spinning Wheel's Complete Book Of Dolls, Galahad Books, 1975.
- Richter, Lydia, China, Parian and Bisque German Doll, Hobby House Press, 1993.
- Smith, Patricia R., Effanbee-Dolls That Tough The Heart, Collector Books, 1983.
- Smith, Patricia R., Collector's Encyclopedia of Madame Alexander Doll 1965-1990, Collector Books.
- Smith, Patricia R., Modern Collector's Dolls I, II, III, IV, V, VI, Collector Books, 1973, 1975, 1976, 1979, 1984, 1991.
- Smith, Patricia R., Modern Collector's Dolls, Seventh Series, Collector Books 1995.
- Smith, Patricia R., Shirley Temple Dolls and Collectibles , Collector Books 1979.
- Theriault, Florence, More Dolls: The Early Years 1780-1910, Gold Horse Publishing, 1992.

VIDEOTAPE

- Dolls of the Golden Age: 1880-1915, Sirocco Productions, 1993.

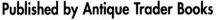